Born in Poland, Professor Dmytryshyn graduated B.A., University of Arkansas, 1950; M.A., University of Arkansas, 1951; and Ph.D., University of California, Berkeley, 1955. He has been a Research Associate at University of California, Berkeley (1955-6), and Columbia University (1956); a Visiting Professor at University of Illinois, Champaign-Urbana (1964-5), and Harvard University (Summer, 1971); and a Fulbright-Hays Research Scholar in West Germany (1967-8). Professor Dmytryshyn, who has been at Portland State University since 1956, is also the author of *Moscow and the Ukraine, 1918-1953* (1956); *Medieval Russia: A Source Book, 900-1700* (1967); and *Imperial Russia: A Source Book, 1700-1917* (1967), and numerous articles that have appeared in various scholarly journals.

SECOND EDITION

USSR
A Concise History

SECOND EDITION

USSR
A Concise History

BASIL DMYTRYSHYN

CHARLES SCRIBNER'S SONS · New York

Printed in the United States of America
Library of Congress Catalog Card Number 77-162787
SBN 684-12540-4   (college paper)
SBN 684-12539-0   (trade cloth)

TO
Sonia and Tania

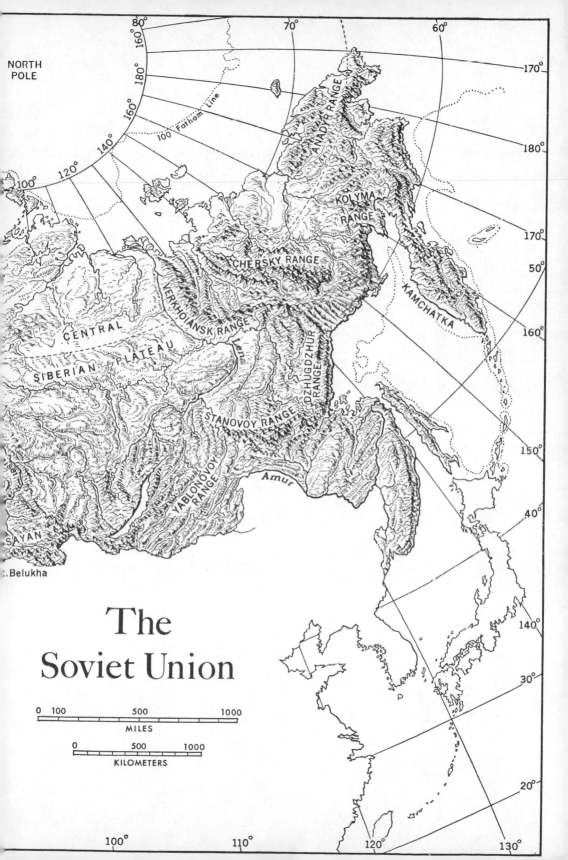

NORTH
POLE

80°
70°
60°

160°
170°

180°

ANADYR RANGE

160°

100 Fathom Line

140°

KOLYMA
RANGE

180°

120°

170°

CHERSKY RANGE

100°

50°

VERKHOIANSK RANGE

KAMCHATKA

CENTRAL

160°

SIBERIAN PLATEAU

Lena

DZHUGDZHUR RANGE

STANOVOY RANGE

150°

YABLONOVOY
RANGE

Amur

40°

SAYAN

.Belukha

The
Soviet Union

0   100   500   1000

MILES

0   500   1000

KILOMETERS

30°

140°

130°

20°

100°
110°
120°

PREFACE

The Union of Soviet Socialist Republics—USSR in brief means different things to different people. To an impartial observer it is the world's first socialist state dominated by a single party, the Communist party. To a Communist or a Communist sympathizer, the USSR represents a "noble experiment" and an example of successful application of Marxist ideas, as elaborated by Lenin, Stalin, and Khrushchev. To most anti-Communists, however, the USSR is at best a failure—a prison of nations, and a country of slave labor camps. Most religious leaders see in it a country of religious persecution. Many intellectuals consider it a utopian ideal marred by inhuman practices. Industrialization enthusiasts think of it as an outstanding example of rapid industrialization. Military men respect it as a great military power. Space devotees see in it a pioneer of space explorations. Political leaders of underdeveloped countries have often used it as a lever against the United States. Critical observers see in the USSR a country capable of solving intricate problems of space travel but incapable of solving its agricultural, housing, and nationality problems—to name only a few. Whatever their validity, these sample illustrations show that the USSR is a protean country; that is, depending on time, place, circumstance, and above all the point of view of the observer, it stirs up passionate partisan feelings and conveys a different meaning to different observers.

Though modest in size this volume seeks to summarize, by way of a concise treatment, the main trends of development of the USSR. By its very nature this book cannot in any way pretend to be either a definitive or an exhaustive treatment. It does not present any startling revelations nor is it novel for the sake of novelty. The primary aim of this work is to provide the student of Soviet affairs with a brief, but accurate, clearly organized and dispassionate, chronological survey of domestic developments and foreign policy of the Soviet Union since 1917. The information contained in this volume is based upon primary sources (some of which are appended), which in turn are supplemented by other pertinent studies of the best scholarship to date.

It is a pleasant custom among scholars to express appreciation to all those who, in any way, have rendered help in the preparation of the work and at the same time to absolve them of all the sins committed by the author. I wish to thank my colleagues at Portland State College for relieving me of some of my teaching duties during the preparation of this work. In particular I wish to express my thanks to Professors Frederick J. Cox, John O. Dart, Jesse L. Gilmore and George C. Hoffmann who directed my attention to some of the inconsistencies in the manuscript.

I am, finally, deeply indebted to my wife, Virginia, whose keen eye, in reading and rereading the manuscript, has contributed to the shaping of every paragraph.

Basil Dmytryshyn

Champaign, Illinois
January 14, 1965

PREFACE TO THE SECOND EDITION

The purpose of this new edition is to trace events since Khrushchev's ouster late in 1964; to include, in accordance with a number of suggestions, additional documentary material; to update the selected bibliography; and, finally, to correct the typographical errors that were overlooked in the first edition.

B. D.

Portland, Oregon
February 1, 1971

CONTENTS

LIST OF CHARTS

LIST OF MAPS

KEY TO ABBREVIATIONS

ASSR	Autonomous Soviet Socialist Republic
CC	Central Committee
CCC	Central Control Commission
CHEKA	Extraordinary Commission for Combating Counter-revolution, Speculation and Delinquency (Secret Police)
CIC	Central Inspection Commission
CM	Council of Ministers
CMEA	Council of Mutual Economic Aid (also known as COMECOM)
COMECON	Council for Mutual Economic Cooperation
Cominform	Communist Information Bureau
Comintern	Communist International
CP(b)U	Communist Party (bolshevik) of the Ukraine
CPC	Communist Party of China
CPR	Chinese People's Republic
CPSU	Communist Party of the Soviet Union
CPY	Communist Party of Yugoslavia
FPRY	Federal People's Republic of Yugoslavia
Gosplan	State Plan
kolkhoz	Collective Farm
komsomol	Communist Youth Organization
LCY	League of Communists of Yugoslavia
MGB	Ministry of State Security
MTS	Machine Tractor Station
MVD	Ministry of Internal Affairs
NEC	National Economic Council
NEP	New Economic Policy
NKVD	People's Commissariat of Internal Affairs
OGPU	Unified State Political Administration
Orgburo	Organizational Bureau
Politburo	Political Bureau
SEC	Supreme Economic Council
sovkhoz	State Farm
sovnarkom	Council of People's Commissars
SSR	Soviet Socialist Republic
VKP(b)	All-Union Communist Party (bolshevik)
YCL	Young Communist League (also known as KOMSOMOL)

✠ I

INTRODUCTION

THE PHYSICAL SETTING

The USSR is a country of many superlatives and extremes. It is, for instance, the largest country in the world. Its area of 8,600,870 square miles represents about one-sixth of the earth's land surface. It is nearly three times the size of the continental United States, is larger than either all Latin America or all North America, and is bigger by far than China and India combined. Occupying a large area of Eastern Europe (about 42 per cent of Europe) and all of Northern Asia (about 43 per cent of Asia), the USSR has some 10,550 miles of land frontier (about twice that of the United States) and about 26,700 miles of coast line. It borders on Norway, Finland, the Baltic Sea, Poland, Czechoslovakia, Hungary, Rumania, the Black and Azov Seas, Turkey, the Caspian Sea, Iran, Afghanistan, China, Mongolia, North Korea, and the Pacific and Arctic Oceans. So vast is the territory of the USSR that it extends through eleven of the world's twenty-four time zones. Needless to say, the size and the location of the USSR are extremely vital economic and military assets in the hands of its present leaders as they also were in the hands of their predecessors.

In terms of relief, the USSR can be divided into three sections: (1) *The Great Plain* that stretches west of the Yenisey River to the country's western borders in the heart of Europe, and that includes the Western Siberian Plain, the Central Asiatic Lowlands, the Ural Mountains, and the Great Russian Plain; (2) *The Uplands of North Eastern Asia* which include the Central Siberian Plateau and such Trans-Baikal mountain ranges as the Yablonovoy, Stanovoy, Dzhugdzhur, Verkhoiansk, Chersky, Kolyma, and Anadyr; and (3) *The Southern Rim of Mountains* such as the Caucasus (Mt. Elbrus, 18,468 feet), the Pamirs (24,590 feet), the Tien-Shan (Mt. Tengri Khan, 22,940 feet), the Altai (Mt. Belukha, 15,157 feet), and the Sayan (Mt. Piramida, 10,801 feet), which give the USSR the appearance of a great amphitheater facing the Arctic Ocean.

Most of the land area of the USSR lies north of the fiftieth parallel. Archangel, for instance, is only 120 miles south of the Arctic Circle. Leningrad, located on the sixtieth parallel, is in the same latitude as Stockholm, Sweden, Cape Farewell, the southern extremity of Greenland, and the northern tip of Labrador. Moscow is in the latitude of Glasgow, Scotland, and Sitka, Alaska. Kiev, the capital of the Ukrainian SSR, is in the latitude of the Aleutian Islands and the northern tip of Newfoundland; while Yalta, a resort town in Crimea on the Black Sea, is in the latitude of Portland, Oregon, Ottawa, Canada, and Milan, Italy. The most southerly point of the USSR is on the thirty-sixth parallel, which is in the latitude of Gibraltar and San Francisco, California.

The northerly location of the USSR, the lack of marine influence, the absence of protective mountains to hold back the cold air from the Arctic, and the massive character and flatness of the territory, exert an important influence on the country's climate. The latter is distinguished by its severity, astonishing uniformity, and continental nature. Because of high pressures and low temperatures, winters in the USSR are cold, long, and windy (in the western and central regions). Areas east of the Ural Mountains have lower temperatures than those of the European part of the USSR. In the Verkhoiansk-Oimiakon area of the Yakut ASSR, for instance, the temperature may drop in the coldest winter to —94° F., in contrast to a "warm" —45° F. in Moscow or —35° F. in Leningrad. The severity of this winter climate, which in some areas lasts from October to May, has a crippling effect on shipping. Many ports of the USSR on the Baltic and Caspian Seas and those on the Pacific and Arctic Oceans are inaccessible to ships from three to six months of the year. The same is true of the rivers of the Soviet Union which are frozen from six to nine months of each year.

Many of the same factors which are responsible for the severity of the winter are also responsible for the extreme conditions of the Soviet summer. Summers throughout most of the USSR are brief, dry, windy, and hot. Verkhoiansk, which, as we noted earlier, has the distinction of being one of the coldest spots in the world during the winter, has recorded a temperature as high as +93° F. in the summer, or the same as that of some regions of the south-western parts of the United States. This extreme annual range in Verkhoiansk is not unusual, for temperatures above +85° F. have been recorded in many places of the Soviet Union north of the Arctic Circle. Yakutsk, on the Lena River in North Eastern Asia, has recorded an extreme maximum of +102° F., Tomsk +95° F., Moscow +99° F., and Leningrad +97° F. The temperature in the desert of Central Asia has reached as high as +125° F. near Tashkent. The severe, frigid cold of the silent winter and the scorching heat, dust, thunder and lightning, hail, and the myriads of mosquitoes of the summer in many parts of the

Tundra and volcano in the Kamchatka region.

USSR, and especially in Siberia, have until recently discouraged colonization as well as exploitation of natural resources.

The extreme continental climate and the northerly location of the USSR have a significant bearing on the country's soil and vegetation zones. The Arctic coast and the regions east of the Yenisey River are characterized by a phenomenon known as *permafrost,* or permanently frozen ground beneath the surface. The depth of the summer thaw of permafrost varies from eighteen inches in peat bogs to six feet, six inches in coniferous forests. The affected area is very large, covering about 3,500,000 square miles or 47 per cent of the territory of the USSR. A sizable portion of the permafrost area along the Arctic coast, (about 15 per cent of the total area of the USSR) several hundred miles in width, is known as *tundra,* an area consisting largely of water-logged bogs and marshes. The tundra is frozen during the winter and is mosquito-infested during the summer, making it thus quite uninhabitable. Because of the severity of the winter, the violence of the winds, the brevity of the summer, the dryness of the climate, the coldness of the soil, and the shallow penetration of the roots, vegetation in the tundra is practically nil. The main growth in the northern parts of the tundra is moss, while the southern part is covered with heather, blackberry, cranberry, black birch, and dwarf willow.

South of this uninhabitable area is the *taiga.* The taiga has been described as "a monotonous, dark, and mournfully silent forest with trees that grow close together, but are rarely fine specimens." Much of the taiga is semimarshy, damp and spongy forest, with spruce, fir, larch, pine, and cedar the predominant species. In its southern regions the taiga has many broad-leafed deciduous trees such as oak, linden, ash, elm, alder, and birch. Approximately one-third of all the USSR is covered by forests (coniferous and deciduous), comprising about 20 per cent of the world's forest area, and which are now, as they have been in the past, a basic resource of the country. In addition to forest, the taiga also contains vast mineral wealth.

South of the taiga is the steppe, or prairie. Covering about 14 per cent of the territory of the USSR, the steppe extends from the Ukraine across the Urals into Siberia. The chief characteristic of the steppe is the absence of trees, which is caused by climatic conditions (limited rainfall, intense evaporation, dryness of the air, and the strength of the winds). Most of the steppe consists of the richest soil in the world—the *chernozem,* or black soil, which crumbles into fine powder when dry and turns into a thick black paste when wet. The richness of the steppe soil and the mineral wealth beneath it have for centuries attracted all kinds of settlers and acted as a lure for countless invaders.

South of the steppe, roughly north and east of the Caspian Sea and extending to the Pamir Mountains, are the three desert and semidesert

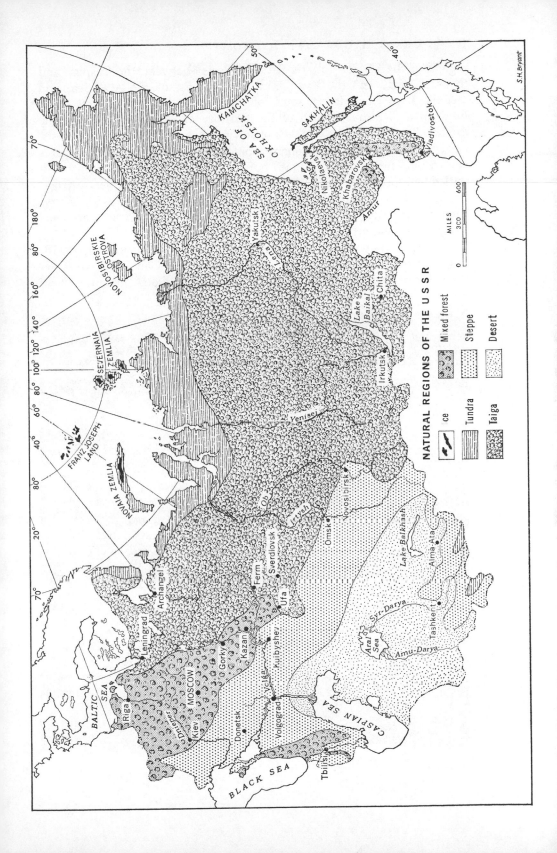

NATURAL REGIONS OF THE USSR

ce
Tundra
Taiga
Mixed forest
Steppe
Desert

MILES

0   300   600

S.H. Bryant

KAMCHATKA
SEA OF OKHOTSK
SAKHALIN
Vladivostok
Nikolaevsk
Khabarovsk
Amur
Chita
Lake Baikal
Irkutsk
Yakutsk
Lena
Yenisei
Ob
Irtysh
Novosibirsk
Omsk
Lake Balkhash
Alma-Ata
Tashkent
Syr-Darya
Aral Sea
Amu-Darya
CASPIAN SEA
Tbilisi
Volgograd
Kuibyshev
Volga
Donetsk
Kiev
Dnieper
MOSCOW
Kazan
Gorky
Ufa
Perm
Sverdlovsk
Archangel
Leningrad
Riga
BALTIC SEA
BLACK SEA
NOVOSIBIRSKIE OSTROVA
SEVERNAIA ZEMLIA
FRANZ JOSEPH LAND
NOVAIA ZEMLIA

70°   180°   80°   160°   140°   120°   100°   80°   60°   40°   20°
50°   40°
70°   80°
70°

regions of the USSR: (1) the Ust Urt desert between the Caspian and the Aral Seas; (2) the Kyzyl Kum desert, east of the Aral Sea; and (3) the Kara Kum desert, south of the Aral Sea. These deserts cover between a fifth and a sixth of the territory of the Soviet Union. The extreme heat in summer, the lack of surface water, the swarms of locusts, and the presence of a poisonous spider called *karakurt* which spares neither man nor beast, have until now prevented these areas from being settled in appreciable numbers, except by nomads. In recent years, irrigation projects have turned fertile parts of the desert (especially the Kyzyl Kum desert) into cotton fields, and orchards of olives, figs, apricots, oranges, and lemons.

Many rivers cut their way across the immense territory of the USSR. Together with many canals (the Baltic-White Sea Canal, the Moscow-Volga Canal, the Volga-Baltic Canal and the Volga-Don Canal) the rivers

The Lenin Volga-Don Canal.

of the USSR serve now, as they have in the past, as major avenues of communication and transportation. Of some 200,000 miles of river in the USSR, about 70,000 are navigable, with Moscow being a "Port of Five Seas." The most important rivers in the European part of the USSR are the Volga, Europe's largest river (2,325 miles and a drainage area of 563,300 square miles) and its tributary, the Kama (1,200 miles); the Dnieper, historically the most important (1,410 miles long and a drainage area of 202,140 square miles); the Don (1,325 miles long); the Ural (1,000 miles long); the Pechora (1,150 miles long); the Northern Dvina (1,100 miles long); and the Western Dvina (640 miles long). In Central Asia the most important rivers are the Amu Darya (1,400 miles long) and the Syr Darya (1,300 miles long). In Northern Asia the most important rivers include the Ob, the second largest river in the USSR (3,200 miles long) and its tributary, the Irtysh (2,700 miles long); the Yenisey, the largest river in the USSR (3,500 miles long) and its tributaries, the Angara (1,200 miles long), the Stony Tunguska (1,000 miles long) and the Lower Tunguska (2,000 miles long); the Lena (3,000 miles long and a drainage area in excess of one million square miles) and its major tributary, the Aldan (1,500 miles long); and the Amur, the chief river of eastern Asia (3,000 miles long).

The usefulness of many of these rivers for transport is limited by the fact that the great majority of them either freeze over during part of each year, or empty into the Arctic Ocean, or into such lakes as the Caspian Sea (the largest lake in the world, 152,500 square miles) and the Aral Sea (26,166 square miles). Since the early 1930's, Soviet engineers have constructed on many of these rivers vast hydroelectric projects which have turned the USSR into one of the world's major producers of electric energy. The largest of these projects are: The Krasnoiarsk Dam of 5,000,000 kw. capacity on the Yenisey River; the Bratsk Dam of 4,500,000 kw. capacity on the Angara River; the Twenty-Second Party Congress Dam of 2,530,000 kw. capacity on the Volga River; the Kuibyshev Dam of 2,300,000 kw. capacity on the Volga River; and the Dnieprostroy Dam of 650,000 kw. capacity on the Dnieper River.

Within the borders of the USSR lie large quantities of fuel and raw material resources. The exact amount of these resources has not been adequately established because only some 75 per cent of the territory has been geologically studied. The USSR is almost self-sufficient with respect to raw materials. Its water resources for hydroelectric power are among the world's largest; while its coal reserves are among the greatest in the world. The most prominent coal centers are those of the Donets Basin (the Donbass), the Kuznetsk Basin (the Kuzbass), the Karaganda area (in the Kazakh SSR), the Cheremkhovo Basin (near Irkutsk), the Bureia Basin (in the Far East), and the Sub-Moscow Basin.

Soviet iron resources match those of water and coal and comprise a

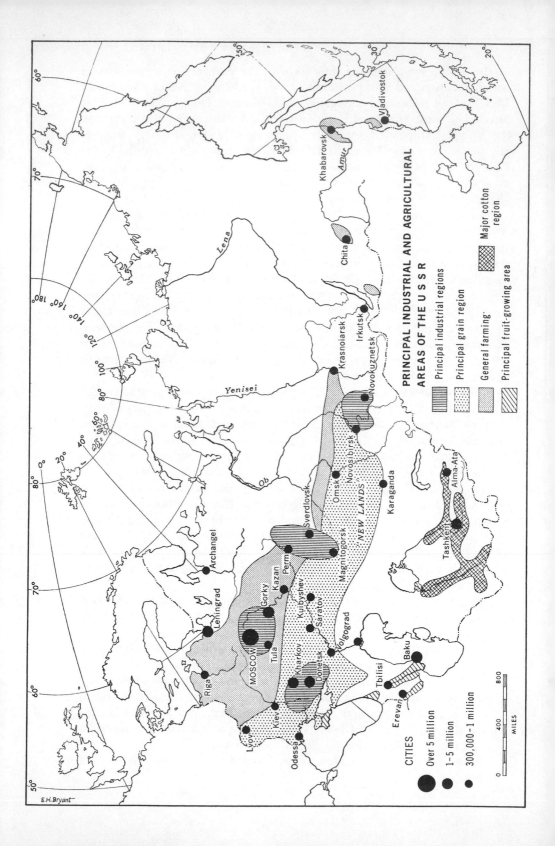

PRINCIPAL INDUSTRIAL AND AGRICULTURAL
AREAS OF THE U S S R

Principal industrial regions

Principal grain region

General farming

Principal fruit-growing area

Major cotton region

CITIES

Over 5 million

1–5 million

300,000–1 million

Vladivostok

Khabarovsk

Amur

Chita

Irkutsk

Krasnoiarsk

Novokuznetsk

Novosibirsk

Omsk

Karaganda

Alma-Ata

Tashkent

Sverdlovsk

Magnitogorsk

NEW LANDS

Lena

Yenisei

Ob

Archangel

Leningrad

Riga

Perm

Kazan

Gorky

MOSCOW

Tula

Kuibyshev

Saratov

Kharkov

Donetsk

Kiev

Lvov

Odessa

Volgograd

Baku

Tbilisi

Erevan

60°

70°

80°

60°

70°

60°

50°

0°

20°

40°

60°

80°

100°

120°

140°

160°

180°

20°

30°

50°

MILES

0   400   800

S.H.Bryant

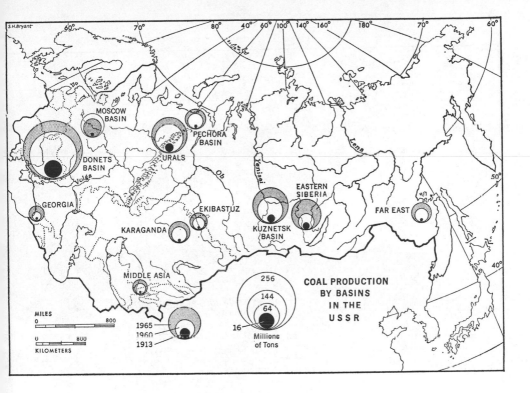

COAL PRODUCTION
BY BASINS
IN THE
USSR

MOSCOW BASIN
PECHORA BASIN
URALS
DONETS BASIN
GEORGIA
EKIBASTUZ
EASTERN SIBERIA
FAR EAST
KARAGANDA
KUZNETSK BASIN
MIDDLE ASIA

256
144
64
16
Millions
of Tons

1965
1960
1913

MILES
0   800

0   800
KILOMETERS

S.H.Bryant

large portion of all the world's iron reserves. Though found at about 600 different locations, only about one hundred Soviet iron deposits have been exploited. The most prominent iron ore deposits of the USSR are those of the Krivoy Rog in the Ukraine, the Urals (Magnitogorsk), the Kerch Peninsula in the Crimea, the Gornaia Shoriia area of Western Siberia (near the Kuznetsk coal basin), the Caucasus (near Lake Sevan), the Kola Peninsula, Nikolaevsk (on the Amur River), and near Moscow (Tula and Kursk). The USSR also has large oil reserves. The latter are located in the Apsheron Peninsula (adjoining the city of Baku), the Emba Basin (Western Kazakh SSR), the Caucasus (Maikop and Grozny), the Pechora Basin, Sakhalin Island, the Turkmen SSR (Krasnozavodsk), the Fergana Valley and the basin of the upper Amu Darya (Uzbek SSR), and the Western Ukraine (Drohobych-Boryslav).

The USSR is a leading source of manganese (Chiatura in the Georgian SSR, Nikopol in the Ukraine, the Kazakh SSR and Eastern Siberia); has abundant copper reserves (the Kazakh SSR, the Bashkir ASSR, the Sverdlovsk and Murmansk Provinces, and the Krasnoiarsk Territory in Eastern Siberia); possesses ample deposits of lead and zinc (the Kazakh SSR, the Kuznetsk Basin, the Chita and Sverdlovsk Provinces, and the Maritime Territory in the Far East); commands vast reserves of

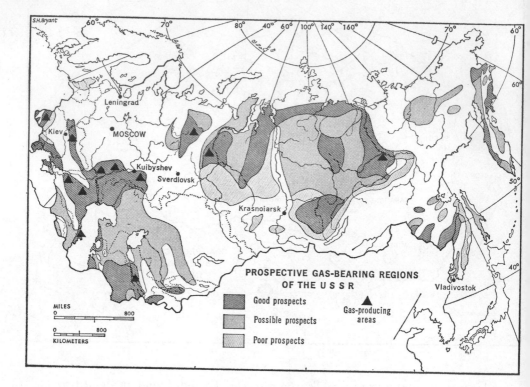

PROSPECTIVE GAS-BEARING REGIONS
OF THE USSR

Good prospects

Possible prospects

Poor prospects

Gas-producing areas

MILES
0   800

0   800
KILOMETERS

bauxite (east of Leningrad, the Bashkir ASSR, Uzbek and Kazakh SSR's, Sverdlovsk, Tula, Novosibirsk, and Kamerovo Provinces and the Altay and Krasnoiarsk Territories); and is one of the largest nickel producing countries in the world (Krasnoiarsk Territory, the Kola Peninsula, Southern and Central Urals, and Northern Caucasus).

The USSR is one of the world's largest producers of gold (the Aldan Plateau in Eastern Siberia, the Maritime Territory in the Far East, the Kazakh SSR, the Buriat-Mongol ASSR, and the Irkutsk and Chita Provinces); has some uranium deposits (the Fergana Valley and the Tannu-Tuva area); has adequate tin resources (the Chita Province, the Maritime Territory in the Far East, the Yakut ASSR, the Kirghiz SSR, the Kazakh SSR, the Caucasus, and the east coast of Lake Ladoga); produces significant amounts of silver; claims priority in the production of platinum; is one of the world's major producers of chromium (the Urals and the Kazakh SSR); and has ample supplies of mercury, antimony, bismuth, cobalt, arsenic, and other rare metals. The USSR, finally, is rich in impor-

Soviet Kazakhstan in the vicinity of Alma-Ata.

tant industrial nonmetalic minerals such as asbestos, potassium, salts, phosphorites, borates, sodium chloride, kaolin, peat, and natural gas.

The population of the USSR matches the diversity of the country's natural resources. According to the census of January 15, 1970, the USSR had 241,748,000 people distributed among more than one hundred different nationalities. Based on their language affiliation, these diverse nationalities of the USSR belong to the following major language groups: *Slavic* (Great Russians, the dominant group, Ukrainians, and Belorussians); *Baltic* (Lithuanians and Latvians); *Romance* (Moldavians); *Finno-Ugric* (Estonians, Karelians, Veps, Komi, Mari, Mordvinians, and Udmurts); *Turkic* (Tartars, Bashkirs, Chuvash, Uzbeks, Kazakhs, Kirghiz, Turkmen, Kara-Kalpaks, and Azerbaidzhans); *Mongol* (Kalmyks and Buriat-Mongols); *Ugric* (Khanty and Mansi); *Kartvelian* (Georgians, Svan, Laz, and Adzhar); *Tungus-Manchu* (Evenki, Eveny, Ulchi, Orochi, and Udege); *Iranian* (Tadzhiks, Ossetians, and Kurds); *Dagestan* (Avars, Darghin, Laks, and Tabasarans); *Nakh* (Chechen and Ingush); and *Abkhaz-Adighe* (Kabardians, Adighe, Cherkess, Abaza, and Abkhaz).[1]

For administrative purposes these diverse nationalities of the USSR are currently grouped into the following fifteen union republics:

[1] For a complete listing of ethnic groups of the USSR, see Appendix 1.

Republic	Area in Square Miles	Population	Capital
Russian Soviet Federated Socialist Republic (RSFSR)	6,593,391	130,090,000	Moscow
Ukrainian Soviet Socialist Republic (UkSSR)	232,046	47,136,000	Kiev
Kazakh Soviet Socialist Republic	1,064,086	12,850,000	Alma Ata
Uzbek Soviet Socialist Republic	159,069	11,963,000	Tashkent
Belorussian Soviet Socialist Republic	80,154	9,003,000	Minsk
Georgian Soviet Socialist Republic	26,911	4,688,000	Tbilisi
Azerbaidzhan Soviet Socialist Republic	33,436	5,111,000	Baku
Lithuanian Soviet Socialist Republic	25,174	3,129,000	Vilnius
Moldavian Soviet Socialist Republic	13,012	3,572,000	Kishinev
Latvian Soviet Socialist Republic	24,595	2,365,000	Riga
Kirghiz Soviet Socialist Republic	76,641	2,933,000	Frunze
Tadzhik Soviet Socialist Republic	55,019	2,900,000	Dushanbe
Armenian Soviet Socialist Republic	11,506	2,493,000	Erevan
Turkmen Soviet Socialist Republic	188,417	2,158,000	Ashkhabad
Estonian Soviet Socialist Republic	17,413	1,357,000	Tallinn
Total	8,600,870	241,748,000	

Other administrative units include nineteen autonomous republics, nine autonomous *oblasts* (regions), 123 *krays* (territories), and ten national *okrugs* (areas). (See page 13.)

The foregoing selected samples reveal that the USSR is an extremely complicated country. It is also a rich, resourceful, and powerful country. Since the late 1920's the power of the USSR has increased appreciably as a result of a policy of forceful industrialization. Whether the peoples of the Soviet Union have been the beneficiaries or the victims of this policy is a highly debatable question among observers of the Soviet scene. This problem as well as the entire development of the USSR since 1917 can best be understood if we first examine briefly the conditions which paved the way for one of the major events in the history of the twentieth century—the Russian Revolution, the course of which made possible the emergence of the USSR.

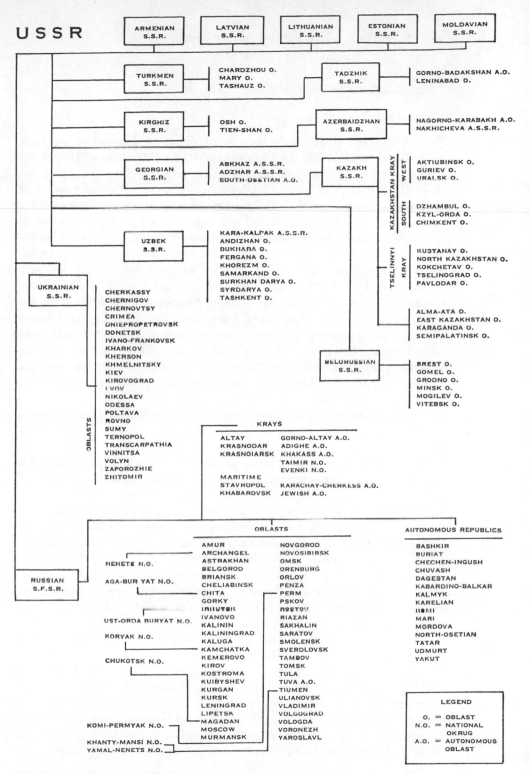

ADMINISTRATIVE DIVISIONS OF THE USSR.

THE HISTORICAL BACKGROUND

Pre-Emancipation Russia

Technically, the USSR made its official debut on December 30, 1922, when the Russian SFSR, the Ukrainian SSR, the Belorussian SSR and the Trans-Caucasian SFSR concluded a treaty creating the union. This formality, however, was preceeded by a whole series of developments of which the Russian Revolutions of 1917 were the most significant. These revolutions—which set Russia and subsequently many parts of the world on a path of far-reaching changes—can be understood only from a knowledge of the political, economic, social, and cultural stimuli, and, above all, the conditions from which they were born. Many of these conditions, such as the autocratic form of the imperial government, the multinational nature of the empire, the relative economic backwardness of the state, the agrarian nature of the society, and the widespread illiteracy and poverty of the people, to name only a few, were products of the totality of Russian history. Some, however, such as the ideals of political liberty, equality, fraternity, and democracy of the French Revolution of 1789, and the promise of economic abundance and opportunity of the Industrial Revolution, were products of West European influences.

Students of Russian history generally agree that the ideals of the French Revolution of 1789 had a profound influence on Russia's development, as they also had on the development of many other countries. The influence of the French Revolution on Russia was neither immediate nor direct, however, but came early in the nineteenth century in two distinct and equally powerful waves. The first came via Germany in the form of an idealistic philosophy; while the second was introduced in Russia by those Russians who acquired first-hand acquaintance with West European conditions during the Napoleonic Wars of 1812–1815. Many Russian officers returned home from their victorious campaigns "with boxes crammed with books, heads full of ideas, and hearts aching over the shortcomings and backwardness of their country." Immediately upon their return these young officers and other aristocrats who shared their new and forbidden European ideas developed an intense interest in Russian history and conditions and a desire to introduce in Russia Europe's most modern institutions, methods, and ideas.

Because Russian conditions prevented open discussion of many of these issues, these aristocrats organized small secret groups of which the most important proved to be the Union of Salvation. Founded in 1816 and consisting of two branches, Northern and Southern, this organization changed its name in 1818 to Union of Welfare. The Northern Branch, with headquarters in St. Petersburg, and led by such wealthy aristocratic guardsmen as Prince Sergei P. Trubetskoi (1790–1860) and Nikita M. Muraviev (1795–1826), advocated: equality of all citizens before the law; freedom of the press; freedom of religion; social justice; advancement of education; expanded social work; promotion of economic welfare by encouraging industry, trade, and agriculture; a representative form of government; abolition of serfdom with adequate safeguards of the interests of landed aristocracy; and a federal arrangement for Russia under a constitutional monarch. The Southern Branch, with its center in the Ukraine, led by representatives of lesser nobility, of whom Colonel Pavel I. Pestel (1793–1826) was the chief spokesman, in the best Jacobin tradition advocated: replacement of the monarchy by a military dictatorship for a period of eight years to be followed by a unified, centralized, egalitarian, and democratic republic; abolition of serfdom; expropriation of landlords; abolition of all privileges based on birth, rank, or wealth; abolition of Finnish autonomy; and ruthless Russification of all territories in the Russian Empire. Such then were the ideals and demands of the first Russian revolutionary movement.

The first Russian revolutionary movement had several distinct characteristics that were to be marks of Russian revolutionaries throughout the nineteenth century. First, it was stronger in its revolutionary zeal than in its effectiveness in organization. Second, its members were drawn almost exclusively from the upper classes and had no contact with the lower strata of the society in whose name they intended to act. Third, they advocated seizure of power by a revolutionary elite to make possible the transition from autocracy to democracy. Fourth, they were Great Russian in their outlook, considered the Russian Empire a political and economic entity, and accordingly in their struggle with Tsarism directed their efforts only towards changing Russia's political, economic, and social system. This stand, in turn, caused them to ignore the struggle of non-Russian peoples against Tsarism or to consider that struggle as being something narrow, limited, and insignificant in comparison with their own "high and noble" ideals. Fifth, the leadership of the first Russian revolutionary movement from its inception demonstrated stubbornness of conviction, unwillingness to compromise, factionalism, and a conspiratorial nature. And finally, the spirit of this movement contained incredible contradictions of nobility and baseness, virtue and criminality, and love and hate.

Notwithstanding the secretiveness of the Northern and Southern Branches, government authorities knew of the existence of these organizations. They failed, however, to act decisively against them because they presented no immediate threat—their membership being pitifully small—and because Tsar Alexander I (1801–1825) was rather kindly disposed towards these young officers. Alexander's death late in 1825 precipitated a crisis known as the Decembrist Revolution. The conspirators were not prepared but moved into action as a result of the dynastic riddle. Under the law of 1797 the next in line in succession to the imperial throne of Russia (Alexander having died childless) was his younger brother Constantine. By a secret agreement with Alexander in 1822, however, Constantine had renounced his right in favor of their younger brother Nicholas. So secret was this arrangement that even Nicholas was unaware of it. Following Alexander's death, accordingly, Nicholas in St. Petersburg took the oath of allegiance to Constantine, while Constantine, who was then in Warsaw, swore allegiance to Nicholas. The confusion in the imperial family, which went on for nearly three weeks, offered the revolutionaries an opportunity to act.

The first Russian Revolution started on December 26, 1825. Irresoluteness, indecision, and lack of a clearly thought-out plan of action by its leaders proved fatal to the success of the plot. Most of the army and civilians of the capital took the oath of allegiance to Nicholas. Only a handful refused, and these marched to the Senate Square, where, joined by a few civilians, they shouted "For Constantine and for the Constitution." Leaderless, cold, and hungry the insurgents failed to act or to surrender to the loyal forces which surrounded them under the personal direction of Nicholas. When persuasion failed, the new Tsar ordered the use of force. In a few minutes the Square was cleared, and the brief defiance of governmental authority in the capital instigated by members of the Northern Branch was over. An insurrection by the Southern Branch a few days later proved no more successful than the action in the capital. Its leaders were seized by loyal troops and the expected popular rising failed to materialize.

Though a dismal failure, the Decembrist Revolution, as this insurrection is commonly known, nevertheless had several significant and far-reaching repercussions. First, it led to a thorough inquiry into the causes of the revolt, and the questioning of suspects as to the plans and the membership of the secret societies. Some 600 persons were investigated, but of this number only 121 were tried. Five of the "leaders" were sentenced to death with the remainder being sentenced to exile and forced labor. The trial of the insurgents revealed in detail the political movement led by the nobility and directed against the Romanov dynasty and autocracy. This revelation forced Nicholas I to push aside the nobles—up to then considered the backbone of Russian autocracy—and to surround himself with a bureaucracy of obedient officials regardless of their social status. The trial of the Decembrists, and their complaints about the wretched conditions of the peasants, the lack of good laws, the corruption of judges, the ignorance of the masses, and the high-handedness of officials, pointed up the evils of Russian life and urgently demonstrated the need for reforms. Some of these demands materialized in such measures as (1) organization of "His Majesty's Own Chancellery"; (2)

publication of the Code of Laws; (3) abolition of paper currency; (4) improvement of public instruction; and (5) improvement of the living conditions of state peasants. Finally, and most importantly, the Decembrist Revolution, its ideals, and the government's treatment of its leaders, served for later generations of Russian revolutionaries as a symbol of self-sacrificing struggle against autocracy.

The Decembrist Revolution was responsible for setting the tenor of the reign of Nicholas I (1825–1855) which was one of autocratic firmness and bureaucratic reaction. Russians were forbidden to travel in Europe, and Europeans were discouraged from travelling in Russia. To make certain that no alien ideas penetrated into the Empire, the government instituted a rigorous, almost absurd censorship of publications, limited educational opportunities in secondary schools to children of trusted officials and nobles, and turned university education into a preparation of upper-class youth for state service. The teaching of history of philosophy, metaphysics, and constitutional law was suspended, and instruction in logic was permitted only by professors of theology. By these and similar actions, which worsened as time went on, the imperial government of Russia further isolated its subjects from the rest of Europe and forced upon them "Autocracy, Orthodoxy, and Nationality."

Ironically this period of the most uncompromising reaction, as the reign of Nicholas I is commonly known, witnessed an exceptional literary creativeness. It was the period of the romantic poetry of Alexander S. Pushkin (1799–1837), Michael Iu. Lermontov (1814–1841), and Alexei V. Koltsov (1809–1842), and of the sultry, exuberant comedies of Nicholas V. Gogol (1809–1852). Leo N. Tolstoy (1828–1910) and Ivan S. Turgeniev (1818–1883) made their literary debuts during the reign of Nicholas I, as did such lesser known Russian writers as playwrights Alexander N. Ostrovsky (1823–1886) and Alexander S. Griboedov (1797–1829), novelist Ivan A. Goncharov (1812–1891), and poet Nikolai A. Nekrasov (1821–1878). The reign of Nicholas I saw the creative work of Vissarion G. Belinsky (1810–1848), considered by some the greatest professional literary critic in Russian history, Michael I. Glinka (1804–1857), the first Russian composer, and Alexander I. Herzen (1812–1870), one of the most important Russian novelists and a revolutionary publicist, whose *Kolokol* (The Bell), published in London, thundered against the abuses of autocracy and, in a different guise, carried on the revolutionary tradition of the Decembrists.

The reign of uncompromising reaction witnessed also a deep philosophical search for answers to Russia's future. This search manifested itself in two divergent currents of thought: Slavophilism and Westernism. The Slavophiles, inspired by the romantic nationalism then in vogue, "extolled the imaginary virtues of the truly Russian national ways," viewed the Orthodox church as a unique source of Russia's strength, were highly critical of the "decadent west," deplored the efforts of Peter the Great in behalf of Russia's modernization, opposed the constitutional form of government, and were enthusiastic about the village commune and "the voice of the people" expressed through a consultative assembly resembling the *Zemsky Sobor* (Landed Assembly) of the seventeenth century. The Slavophiles held in contempt all non-Orthodox Slavs (especially Poles), were great admirers of Great Russian supremacy, and many of them were among the most ruthless and uncompromising agents of the policy of Russification of non-Russian minorities of the Empire. Among the outstanding Slavophile representatives belong Ivan V. Kireevsky (1806–1856) and Peter V. Kireevsky (1808–1856), Ivan S. Aksakov (1823–1886) and Constantine S. Aksakov (1817–1861), Aleksei S. Khomiakov (1804–1860), Yurii F. Samarin (1819–1876), and Prince Vladimir A. Cherkassky (1824–1878).

The Westerners, in the words of a competent observer, "were primarily Russian humanitarians." They admired modern things, believed in scientific progress, favored the constitutional form of government, advocated freedom of thought and of the press, opposed serfdom, deplored the gulf in Russian society that separated the educated few from the illiterate multitude, and, above all, they favored "the education of Russian society in the ideas of a European universal culture in order to lift Russian national development to a super-national level where it would acquire world significance." The Westerners greatly admired the modernization efforts of Peter the Great, and followed with keen interest developments in Europe, be they intellectual, social, economic, artistic, literary, or revolutionary. Among the outstanding representatives of the Westerners belong Herzen, Belinsky, and Timofei N. Granovsky (1813–1855).

Both the Westerners and the Slavophiles—indeed the entire Russian society—were rocked to the foundations by the Crimean War (1853–1856). Russia's defeat in that war at the hands of France, England, Piedmont, and the Ottoman Empire, and above all the rather humiliating restrictions the victors imposed on Russia in the Treaty of Paris, dealt a heavy blow to Russia's prestige in international affairs. The defeat also destroyed the myth of Russia's gigantic strength and of its invincibility and clearly demonstrated its great backwardness. The defeat, finally, exposed the military, administrative, economic, and social ineptness of autocracy, and convinced the Tsar as well as many of his advisors that the long-overdue reforms demanded by the Decembrists and their followers, and opposed by the conservative elements of Russian society, could no longer be postponed. The realization of these reforms fell upon the new tsar, Alexander II (1855–1881). The choice was unfortunate because Alexander was unprepared, by conviction, training, or temperament, to undertake this gigantic task which was to be one of the most significant landmarks in Russian history.

The Impact of the Emancipation on Russia

The "Era of Great Reforms," as the period of Russian history from 1861 to 1874 is commonly known, commenced on March 3, 1861, with the publication of the Emancipation Statute. The most celebrated feature of this history-making document was the abolition of human bondage throughout the Russian Empire. The legal aspect of this action was admirable, but the same cannot be said of the economic side of the Emancipation Statute. The difficulty stemmed from the strong opposition to emancipation on the part of the majority of the nobles, and from the extremely complicated bondage system which had evolved in Russia through the centuries. At the time of the emancipation there were some 60,000,000 inhabitants in the European part of the Empire. Of these, about 50,000,-000 were peasants of one kind or another—about 22,000,000 were serfs of the nobility, some 20,000,000 were classified as state peasants, and the remaining 8,000,000 belonged to other categories of serf and non-serf peasantry. As the conditions of other peasants had been improved during the reign of Nicholas I, the Emancipation Statute affected primarily the serfs of the nobility. Based on their obligations, which varied in different parts of the Empire, these consisted of three basic groups: (1) *barshchina* serfs, or serfs who were tied to the village commune in which they lived and to the estate of the nobleman to whom they belonged and whose land they worked as part of their obligation, often with their own stock and implements; (2) *obrok* serfs, or serfs who were tied to the village commune and the landlord's estate but who paid their dues to their owner in kind or in money; and (3) household serfs, or serfs who had no land and were bound only to their owners.

Because the majority of the nobles disapproved the whole idea of the reform (which actually was carried through by the autocratic Tsar with the assistance of a few enlightened bureaucrats and the liberal section of public opinion), the Emancipation Statute reflected the prevailing conditions in Russia. It freed *all serfs* from their masters but granted land only to the *barshchina* and the *obrok* serfs. The amount of land each ex-serf received varied from area to area (larger portions in less productive and smaller portions in more productive regions), but averaged 6.21 acres per person. This amount equalled roughly the portions of their holdings in the open-field scattered strips they had used as serfs for their own maintenance. This amount, however, was not given to the ex-serfs as individual private owners in the usual sense of the term, but it was transferred to the village communes whose members were to receive equal portions along with the right of periodic redistribution. To complicate the matter even more the state compensated the landlords for the loss of their property and sought to recover its expenses in the form of high annual installments from the peasants known as "redemption payments." These were spread over a period of forty-nine years, with the village commune being made collectively responsible for their payment. This redemption payment system turned emancipation into the purchase of freedom on a costly installment plan.

By making them into "neither land dependents nor free men," this extremely complicated land settlement was a great disappointment to the Russian peasantry, and acted as a major reservoir of discontent and a prime cause of the deterioration of their economic conditions. Other obstacles contributing to the agricultural crisis were the high level of peasant illiteracy; use of antiquated techniques; lack of capital or even stable currency; unrealistically high taxes and redemption payments; the poor quality, low yield, and small, widely dispersed land allotments (which because of the population increase diminished from 6.21 acres in 1861 to 3.5 acres in 1900); rapid growth of rural population without a corresponding increase in opportunities; high rent and high interest rate on loans; low grain prices and thus low purchasing power of the peasantry; poor storage facilities and a costly and poorly organized transport system; and the pressure of foreign competition. All these hindrances made it difficult for the peasants to maintain their low standard of living, to say nothing of improvement. To overcome the relative (though not too critical by West European standards) shortage of land, some peasants were forced to find supplemental work, while others either rented or bought more land from the nobles.

During the first two decades following emancipation, the government did nothing to alleviate the plight of the peasantry. The first step in that direction came in May, 1881, with the establishment of a Peasant Land Bank aimed at granting the peasants credit for buying land, although the activities of the Bank did not acquire real importance until after 1905. Other measures included the reduction of redemption payments by almost 27 per cent in December, 1881; abolition of the poll tax in January, 1887; and, during the 1890's, encouragement of peasant migration from the overpopulated European parts to underpopulated Asiatic parts of the Empire. These measures, their importance notwithstanding, failed to solve the agrarian crisis or even to pacify the peasants who were obsessed with the belief that the land should belong to those who tilled it and were never reconciled to the land settlement of the 1860's.

The end of serfdom also brought the end of the predominant position of the nobility. Though they continued to enjoy preferential treatment in administrative and military appointments, the loss of a considerable part of their land, as well as the free supply of labor, spelled the beginning of a decline for them that could not be halted. There were some nobles who succeeded in turning their estates into prosperous farms. The majority of the nobility, however, being tradition-bound and unable to adjust to the new circumstances, either joined the growing revolutionary force, or went bankrupt, or was forced to sell, rent, or share-rent their holdings. The transfer of land from nobles to non-noble owners was "one of the outstanding phenomena in the economic life of Russia up to the end of the imperial regime."

By abolishing serfdom, the Emancipation Statute destroyed the entire medieval structure of Russian society. The removal of the nobleman from the performance of such duties as judge, policeman, recruiting officer, and tax collector, meant the disappearance of old and the need for the emergence of new institutions. On June 18, 1863, the Tsar approved a new University Charter, which restored university autonomy and removed most of the restrictions introduced during the reign of Nicholas I. A charter affecting the secondary schools went into effect on November 18, 1864. On January 1, 1864, the Tsar approved the *Zemstvo* Statute which created a rural self-governing institution with jurisdiction over schools, public health, food supply, roads, insurance, relief of the poor, maintenance of prisons, and other concerns of local needs. On November 20, 1864, a Judicial Statute went into effect. Considered by some scholars to be a masterpiece of legislation, the Statute separated the judicial branch from the legislative and executive branches and introduced the jury system, the office of justice of the peace, an irremovable judiciary, lawyers, oral pleading in courts, and the concept that henceforth justice was to be "equal for all subjects." A Censorship Decree of April 6, 1865, allowed considerable freedom for publishers of books, periodicals, and newspapers, holding them responsible, however, for printing "pernicious" matters. On June 16, 1870, the Municipal Statute was promulgated, granting the cities of the Empire (except those in Poland and Finland) city government. This action transformed Russian cities from mere administrative headquarters into economic and commercial centers. Finally, on January 1, 1874, the government introduced a new conscription law which replaced the concept of a large standing army with universal military service of trained reserves. The new law reduced the military service from twenty-five to six years of active service followed by fourteen years of active reserve. These and other measures moved the Russian Empire from the medieval to the modern world.

The emancipation of serfs also helped to transfer the Russian Empire from a feudal country into a relatively impressive capitalist-industrial power. A few figures will give an idea of the rate of development and change. In 1861 Russia produced 352,100 tons of pig iron; in 1900 the figure was 3,233,900 tons. In 1861 her coal output was 424,325 tons; in 1900 it was 17,809,125 tons. In 1861 her industry consumed 46,945 tons of cotton; in 1900 it used 288,900 tons. In 1861 she produced no oil; in 1900 oil production was 11,395,450 tons. In 1861 Russia had 2,200 kilometers of railroad; in 1900 there were 53,200 kilometers. In 1861 imports totalled 167,111,000 rubles, and exports 177,180,000. For 1900 the corresponding figures were 626,375,000 and 716,217,000 rubles respectively. In 1861, the free labor force was insignificant. By 1900 it numbered about 3,000,000, and was relatively organized. In 1861 Russia exported 1,354,430 tons of grain; in 1900 grain exports totalled 7,834,700 tons. These changes also affected the population, which between 1861 and 1900 rose from 73,600,000 to 132,900,000. The Emancipation, in other words, created a vast transformation which, although hindered at every step by economic and noneconomic obstacles and pressures, was rapid, productive, and constructive.

The Rebellious Generation

The emancipation of serfs and the subsequent transformation of Russian society and economy early in the 1860's gave rise to a movement known as *nihilism*. Nihilism has been defined as the philosophy and politics of young Russian radicals who sought to build a new and complete philosophy of life upon the foundations that had been laid by their predecessors in the 1840's. The nihilists thought of themselves as democrats and socialists, and accordingly as sworn enemies of aristocracy, political liberalism, and of the bourgeoisie. They were extremely hostile towards all forms of authority and everything abstract or general. They sought to destroy superstition, illusion, and falsehood; campaigned against orthodoxy, monasticism, and Christianity in general; renounced the state, church, and official Russian patriotism of "Orthodoxy, Autocracy, and Nationality," and developed a peculiar, almost sacred, love for Russia and its people. The nihilists idealized natural sciences, desiring earnestly to create a "new man," and towards that end they evolved their own ethical principles. As a haunted minority the nihilists held together and "recognized one another by dress, language, method of criticism, and general views." The most prominent nihilists were Nikolai A. Dobroliubov (1836–1861), Dimitri I. Pisarev (1840–1868), and Nikolai G. Chernyshevsky (1828–1889).

The revolt of young Russian radicals against all forms of authority assumed various forms. The earliest form was that of appeals. In 1861 the angry young men printed a number of illegal leaflets called *Velikorus* (Great Russia), in which they appealed to the educated public to end absolutist rule in Russia, seize power from the incompetent government, convene a constituent assembly to draft a constitution for Russia, and grant gratis to the peasants the land they had worked under serfdom. Another proclamation, entitled *K molodomu pokoleniiu* (To the Younger Generation), printed at the Free Press in London and smuggled into Russia late in 1861, demanded elimination of the Romanov Dynasty; the development of Russia along the principles inherent in the life of the Russian people (especially collective land tenure); the destruction, violent if need be, of all forms of opposition to this drastic transformation of

Russian society; propagation of these ideas among the people; and the formation of secret "circles of like-minded persons" to achieve these goals. Still another proclamation, *Molodaia Rossiia* (Young Russia), composed by a Moscow student in May, 1862, called for seizure of power by "the revolutionary party" which would then transform Russia into a republican and federal state with every nationality having the right to self-determination; introduce a popularly elected judiciary, just taxes, and public education for children; emancipate women; abolish monasteries, inheritance, marriage and the family; extend a welfare program to the aged and invalids; expropriate the land of landlords and distribute it to the peasant communes; socialize factories to be run by elected managers; and replace the standing army by a national guard. In the event "the ruling group" resisted the transformation of Russia from a monarchy to a "socialized republic" the proclamation promised a bloody and pitiless nation-wide revolution.

Aimed at political awakening, these appeals aroused considerable excitement among liberals as well as among the authorities, who arrested several radicals, including Chernyshevsky. Agitation for drastic changes in Russian society continued, however, and manifested itself in the form of further addresses to the public and to the Tsar (i.e., the appeal in 1862 of the Tver nobility), and above all in the organization of clandestine "circles." The earliest of these circles, organized in 1862 by radicals of St. Petersburg, was known as *Zemlia i volia* (Land and Freedom) and sought to persuade the intelligentsia to assume the leadership, join the people, expropriate the landowners, and overthrow autocracy. The society promised to terminate its activity the moment freedom of election to the national assembly had been secured. In 1865 a Moscow student, Nikolai A. Ishutin (1840–1879), organized a secret "circle" whose aim was a purely "economic revolution." The members of the circle differed over tactics. Some favored peaceful propaganda among the masses to arouse them into action, while others advocated creation of an all-powerful secret body to direct fraud, theft, liquidation of "traitors" within the society, and political assassination of high officials in order to frighten the Tsar into "decreeing a social revolution." Early in April, 1866, a member of this group, Dimitri V. Karakozov (1840–1866), attempted to assassinate the Tsar. His failure cost him his life and brought imprisonment for other members of the society.

The question of the use of terror as a political weapon, one of the basic problems of disunity among Russian radicals, assumed new dimensions thanks to the influence of Michael A. Bakunin (1814–1876), Sergei G. Nechaev (1847–1882), and Peter N. Tkachev (1844–1885). A veteran revolutionary, Bakunin formulated his program for Russia in 1868 in the *Narodnoe delo* (The People's Cause), a newspaper he published in Geneva. His program called for abolition of the state, religion, the family, and inheritance. It urged equality for women, advocated free education for children, and insisted that the land be transferred to "those who till it" (i.e., to the village communes), with factories and all the means of production being under control of the workers. Russia, in Bakunin's view, should consist of a free federation of agricultural and manufacturing associations (artels), with national minorities being granted an option of joining or not.

In 1869, Nechaev, the founder of the *Narodnaia rasprava* (The People's Justice), joined Bakunin in Geneva, and together they prepared the *Katekhizis revolutsionera* (The Catechism of the Revolutionary). Echoing some of the ideas of the extreme wing of the Ishutin "circle," this practical advice on conspiracy defined a revolutionary as "a doomed man" without private interests, affairs, sentiments, ties, property, or even a name—an individual who has severed all ties with society and "continues to inhabit it with only one purpose—to destroy it." To secure "perfect freedom and happiness"—the stated basic aim of Bakunin and Nechaev—the *Catechism* advocated absolute secrecy of the membership of the society, sought to turn every member-conspirator into a blind instrument of the leader, propagated subordination of everything to the "Cause," and insisted that everything which "promotes the success of the revolution is moral, everything which hinders it is immoral." In 1870 Bakunin parted company with Nechaev when he caught his young associate attempting to blackmail him. Their credo, however, that the entire political and social structure of Russia must be destroyed before a new and better one could be erected, exercised a profound influence on many Russian revolutionaries.

Some revolutionaries followed the teachings of Tkachev who, as an editor of *Nabad* (The Alarm) in Geneva, tried to outbid the radicalism of Bakunin and Nechaev. Tkachev subscribed to many of the ideals of Bakunin, such as expropriation of all the means of production; elimination of physical, moral, and mental inequality; universal education; transformation of the village commune into a Communist community; and gradual replacement of the centralized state by self-governing communes. Tkachev differed, however, from his contemporaries on the nature of revolutionary organization and tactics. Convinced that the peasant masses were incapable of independent revolutionary action, Tkachev assigned the leadership role to an "intellectually and morally developed" highly centralized conspiratorial minority. "The struggle," he argued, "can be conducted successfully only by combining the following conditions: centralization, severe discipline, swiftness, decisiveness, and unity of action. All concessions, all wavering, all compromises, multileadership, and decentralization of the fighting forces weaken their energy, paralyze their activity, and deprive the struggle of all chances for victory." Tkachev accordingly condemned isolated revolutionary outbreaks by small groups, rejected the federal arrangement for Russia, and placed his trust in utopian ideals of fraternity, equality, and re-education.

The main objective of many young Russian radicals in the early 1870's was not centralized terror but organized education of the masses. The followers of this trend were known as *narodniki* or populists. By birth and psychology the *narodniki* were members of the "repentant nobility," who were strongly influenced by the ideas of Herzen, Nikolai K. Mikhailovsky (1842–1904), and Peter L. Lavrov (1823–1901), the editor of a periodical, *Vpered* (Forward), published in Zurich. The *narodniki* focused their attention on the people—their misery and their grandeur. They idealized the peasant, glorified his virtues, decried his sorrows, and fought for his material welfare. Influenced by the slogan "To the People," in 1874 thousands of young men and women left their jobs and their studies in the cities, and, dressed in peasant clothes, they went to Russian villages to mingle with the people, trying to help them in every way while at the same time trying to deliver to them "the revolutionary message." That message expressed hostility towards centralized political authority; renounced the use of falsehoods as a weapon in the campaign to secure improved social institutions; rejected economic liberalism in favor of a plan to turn Russia into a land of socialism based on village communes; and tried to instill in the people confidence in themselves. The *narodniki* did not advocate the use of terror to achieve a revolution, for, influenced by Lavrov, they believed that revolutions could not be evoked artificially but rather were products of a long series of complicated historical processes and not results of individual wills. In spite of a vigorous effort, the "To the People" movement ended in a total fiasco thanks to the alertness of the police and in particular because of peasant misunderstanding and suspicion of the intention of these young enthusiasts. Hundreds of *narodniki* were arrested and brought to trial, and most of these were banished to Siberia.

The dismal failure of the young intelligentsia to penetrate peacefully the village, in order to bring a vast transformation of Russia through education of the peasant, forced again to the forefront the question of the employment of terror both as a means of self-defense and as a weapon to attain the revolutionary program. On January 24, 1878, a woman revolutionary, Vera I. Zasulich (1851–1919), shot and seriously wounded the Governor of St. Petersburg because of his alleged brutality towards an arrested member of the underground. On April 2, 1879, a terrorist shot at but missed Tsar Alexander II. These and other acts of terror caused again a split among Russian radicals. Those who approved the use of such tactics founded, in June, 1879, a new organization named *Narodnaia volia* (People's Will), while those who opposed the use of terror established a group which called itself *Chernyi peredel* (The Black Partition).

The aim of the *Narodnaia volia* was to terrorize the government and the reactionary elements of Russian society. Its followers considered themselves socialists. They viewed the state as an instrument of oppression and wanted to restore power to the people by way of a political revolution. The program of the *Narodnaia volia* advocated for Russia the establishment of national and local legislative assemblies; independence of the village commune as an economic and administrative unit; ownership of the land by those who tilled it; workers' control of the factories; absolute freedom of thought, speech, press, and assembly; universal suffrage; and replacement of standing armies by a militia. While condemning the blind campaign of destruction advocated by Nechaev and Bakunin, the *Narodnaia volia* approved terror, and favored the establishment of a nationwide network of secret organizations and the infiltration of the administrative apparatus, the army, the intelligentsia, and the young people, in order to prepare a successful rising. The most important victim of the terror of this group was Tsar Alexander II, who was assassinated on March 13, 1881. This action terminated the activity of the *Narodnaia volia* because of police reprisals and public disapproval.

The tactics of the *Narodnaia volia* were also condemned by members of the *Chernyi peredel,* whose aim was agitation among the peasants for an agrarian revolution as the first step towards a complete reconstruction of Russian society on socialist foundations. Organized by Pavel B. Axelrod (1850–1928), George V. Plekhanov (1856–1918), and Vera Zasulich, the program of the *Chernyi peredel* swore allegiance to "the principles of scientific socialism" and expressed skepticism towards political revolutions, holding that the latter had never secured economic freedom for the people nor had even guaranteed political freedom. It urged the peasants to take the land and the workers to seize the factories. Members of the *Chernyi peredel* tried to secure a foothold in Russian villages, sought to influence members of the intelligentsia, and spent considerable time and efforts on winning the attention of the rapidly swelling ranks of Russian workers. Because of the triumph of reaction following the assassination of Alexander II, the efforts of the *Chernyi peredel* were not successful, and in 1883 its leadership fled to Geneva where it founded a new organization, *Osvobozhdenie truda* (Liberation of Labor).

The program of the new group included many demands made earlier by other revolutionary groups—a democratic constitution; salaries for elected officials, the inviolability of the person and home; absolute freedom of conscience, speech, press, assembly, and association; and the replacement of the standing army by a general arming of the people. In contrast, however, to the programs of all earlier revolutionary groups, the *Osvobozhdenie truda* abandoned support for the village commune as a basic element of the future socialist society; advocated capitalism for Russia as a prerequisite for reaching "the highest stage of socialism"; and placed hope in the industrial proletariat and disciplined, closely-knit, class conscious worker's party to achieve a social revolution in Russia. This decisive shift towards Marxist lines enabled the *Osvobozhdenie truda* to establish close ties with Marxist and socialist movements in Western Europe and Germany in particular, and to lay the foundations for the rise of the Russian Social Democratic movement.

The assassination of Alexander II disrupted the activities of many secret groups and inaugurated a period of extreme reaction in Russia. The chief architect and the philosopher of that reaction was Constantine P. Pobedonostsev (1827–1907), the Procurator of the Holy Synod and the tutor of the new Tsar, Alexander III (1881–1894). Though a constitutional lawyer, Pobedonostsev denounced the parliamentary form of government, sovereignty of the people, separation of church and state, the jury system, and even universal education, and castigated everything that represented freedom. To "save" Russia from these modern "evils" Pobedonostsev revived the old reactionary formula of "Orthodoxy, Autocracy, and Nationality." In practice, this revival meant the introduction of religious censorship of sermons, forceful conversion of non-Orthodox subjects of the Empire to Orthodox Christianity, persecution of all other faiths, persecution of all non-Russian minorities through a policy known as Russification, development of extreme anti-Semitism, strict supervision of the *zemstvo* institutions, prohibition of student associations, repeal of university autonomy, exclusion from the curriculum of all classics and West European writers, exclusion from secondary schools of the lower strata of society, and increased reliance on the support of the reactionary nobility.

The Pobedonostsev-directed reaction failed to accomplish its purpose —that of saving Russian autocracy. Some persecuted minorities (Jews and Dukhobors) sought and received asylum abroad, thereby creating bad publicity for the Russian government. Other minorities (Finns, Latvians, Lithuanians, and Ukrainians) reacted to the Russification efforts of the government by developing their own sense of nationalism, which in time evolved into separatism, i.e., a desire to establish their own political independence. Many opponents of reaction joined one or another secret organization or movement. The most prominent of these movements at the turn of the century were the Social Democratic, the Socialist Revolutionary, and the Liberal.

The Russian Social Democratic movement, as we noted earlier, evolved out of the Plekhanov-founded *Osvobozhdenie truda*. Its growth, though hindered by police vigilance and internal dissensions among its spokesmen, was rather rapid thanks mainly to the accelerated industrialization program of Russia master-minded by Sergei J. Witte (1849–1915), the energetic Minister of Finance and Economy. The Social Democratic program, as adopted in 1903 by the party's second congress in London, called for socialist revolution, eradication of capitalism, and the establishment of a dictatorship of the proletariat. To make possible the attainment of these "maximum" objectives the program demanded the overthrow of the tsarist monarchy and the creation of a democratic republic whose constitution would, among other things, guarantee: the sovereignty of the people; universal, equal, and direct suffrage for all citizens irrespective of sex, national or religious affiliation; absolute freedom of conscience, speech, press, assembly, strikes, and unions; the right of self-determination for all nationalities of the Russian Empire; elective judiciary; the separation of church and state, and of school and church; free and compulsory general and professional education in native language; an eight-hour work day; confiscation of all private, church, monastery, and crown estates, and their transfer to the jurisdiction of the local government; the granting to the peasants of land of which they had been deprived by the emancipation of 1861; and replacement of the standing army by a general arming of the people.

The same congress that approved this elaborate program for Russia witnessed also a split within the Russian Social Democratic party over the question of membership. Julius O. Martov (1873–1923) and Axelrod, supported by Leon D. Trotsky (1879–1940), argued that the party should be a broad and therefore somewhat loose organization which would embrace both the working class and some segments of the intelligentsia. Vladimir I. Lenin (1870–1924) (real name Vladimir I. Ulianov) who made his appearance in the political arena in the mid-1890's, supported by Plekhanov, insisted that only individuals who actively participated in underground organizations had the right to influence party policies. In Lenin's view the party was to be an instrument of the revolution, and as such it should consist not of "fellow travellers" but of soldiers dedicated to the party's cause and ready at all times to act on the orders and instructions of the party's central leadership. Since he held that only a select group consisting of the most enlightened and the most courageous workers, under the leadership of a highly centralized body, had a chance of success, Lenin opposed the inclusion of sympathizers and "fellow travellers" within the party's framework. Lenin's views were defeated by twenty-eight to twenty-three votes after unusually heated debates. However, when the congress moved on to the election of its central organs and the editorial staff of the party's paper, *Iskra* (The Spark), Lenin's candidates won by two votes (nineteen against seventeen, with three abstentions). Henceforth (until October, 1952) Lenin's followers in Russia identified themselves as Bolsheviks (from *bolshenstvo*, or majority group), while Martov's group was labelled Mensheviks (from *menshenstvo*, or minority group).

Between 1903 and 1912 the cleavage between the Bolsheviks and the Mensheviks widened. Though he actually commanded the allegiance of only a minority, Lenin insisted that the election of his candidates was

valid and that the central committee of the party was the supreme authority. The Mensheviks, who were numerically strong inside and outside
Russia, refused to acknowledge Lenin's claims and the authority of the
Bolshevik-dominated central committee. To Lenin the Menshevik attitude
represented anarchism. The more he emphasized the idea of unity, discipline, and obedience, the more the Mensheviks insisted on the preservation of their views and accused Lenin of trying to force upon the party his
views of what the party ought to be. The controversy ended in January,
1912, when, at a conference in Prague, Lenin formally established his own
party. Henceforth the Mensheviks continued to adhere to evolutionary
tactics, believing that after the downfall of monarchy Russia must set up a
bourgeois democratic republic as a necessary stage in the establishment of
socialism, and accordingly they were willing to cooperate with the bourgeois parties in the destruction of monarchy as well as in the building of a
democratic republic. The Bolsheviks under Lenin's leadership adopted
revolutionary tactics, refused to cooperate with the bourgeoisie, insisted
that both monarchy and the bourgeoisie were implacable enemies of the
proletariat, and maintained that the monarchy must be immediately succeeded by the dictatorship of the proletariat.

The chief competitor of the Bolsheviks and the Mensheviks for leadership in the Russian revolutionary movement was the Socialist Revolutionaries. Socialist Revolutionaries made their appearance in the early
1890's and represented in some ways the revival of the *narodniki* movement with Marxist overtones. Their program called for universal suffrage;
representative institutions; civil and personal liberties; federal structure
for the Russian Empire with full rights of self-determination for non-
Russian minorities; a progressive tax system; labor legislation; the development in Russia of revolutionary socialism; and socialization of land
without compensation with the state taking control over forests, fisheries,
and all mineral resources. Though they propagated their program among
the factory workers and had many followers among the intelligentsia and
students, the focal point of interest of Socialist Revolutionaries was the
plight of the Russian village. Widespread rural unrests in 1902–1903 inflated the hopes of the Socialist Revolutionaries, spurred their agitation
among the peasants, and produced a sizable amount of literature designed for peasant readers. By being able to capitalize on the deep-rooted
discontent and dissatisfaction of the masses, the Socialist Revolutionaries
gained a considerable following among the peasants and subsequently
emerged as the strongest (numerically) political party in Russia—a position which they retained until they were dislodged by the Bolsheviks in
1918. Like their more radical populist predecessors, the Socialist Revolutionaries approved the use of terror, and among their eminent victims
were two Ministers of Interior, Dimitri S. Sipiagin (1853–1902) and Viacheslav K. Plehve (1846–1904) and the Grand Duke Sergei Alexandro-

vich (1857–1905). The most prominent Socialist Revolutionaries were Mark A. Natanson (1850–1919), Gregory A. Gershuni (1870–1908), Catherine Breshko-Breshkovskaia (1844–1934), Victor M. Chernov (1876–1952), and Yevno F. Azeff (1869–1918).

Occupying the middle position between the revolutionaries (Bolsheviks, Mensheviks, and Socialist Revolutionaries) and the supporters of autocracy were the liberals. By birth the majority of Russian liberals were nobles; by training they were professionals—lawyers, jurists, engineers, teachers, doctors, veterinarians, agronomists, and nurses—many of whom were dedicated *zemstvo* members. Russian liberals, like their European counterparts, longed for social, economic, and political reforms; favored freedom of speech, press, assembly, and conscience; and detested bureaucratic arbitrariness. At the same time, however, Russian liberals rejected revolutionary methods, were suspicious of the masses, both rural and urban, and some even preferred limited suffrage. Beyond a general agreement that autocracy must go, Russian liberals could not agree among themselves on basic issues or a program. Some advocated for Russia the English constitutional system of limited monarchy with a strong bicameral legislature. Others favored a government of responsible ministry, while some wanted only to modify the power of the Tsar. Most Russian liberals insisted that the unity of the Russian state be preserved, opposed a federal arrangement for Russia, and some, like economist Peter B. Struve (1870–1944), supported "enlightened" Russification efforts.

After 1905 Russian liberals split into two parties: Constitutional Democrats, or Cadets; and the Union of October 17, or Octobrists. The Cadets, under the leadership of historian Paul N. Miliukov (1859–1943), stood for a parliamentary constitutional monarchy, with the parliament exercising full powers in drafting the new constitution and other laws; supported many social and economic reforms; and favored the distribution among the peasants of all the land belonging to the State, the Crown, and the monasteries, and compulsory expropriation of large estates with equitable compensation for their owners. The Octobrists, led by Moscow industrialist Alexander I. Guchkov (1862–1936), disapproved of some of the "radical" positions of the Cadets because the Octobrists were satisfied with the promises Nicholas II (1894–1917) made in his October 30, 1905, Manifesto.

The Revolution of 1905 and Its Aftermath

The rise of political parties at the turn of the century and their determined efforts to remake Russia was a major sign of mounting dissatisfaction with autocracy. Other symptoms of popular discontent were: (1) an increasing number of strikes in industry for higher wages, shorter hours, and the elimination of all unfair practices; (2) widespread agrarian disturbances caused by the stagnation of agriculture, the impoverishment of the peasantry, and the general breakdown of the land settlement of the 1860's; (3) clashes between university students and authorities; and (4) a wave of political assassinations of high government officials. The most prominent victims of assassinations were: Minister of Education, N. P. Bogolepov (1847–1901), in February, 1901; Minister of Interior Sipiagin, in April, 1902; Governor of Ufa, N. M. Bogdanovich (1856–1903), in May, 1903; Governor of Finland, N. I. Bobrikov (1839–1904), in June, 1904; and Minister of Interior, Plehve, in July, 1904.

At first, government authorities replied to this increased popular discontent with the customary reprisals, unwarranted brutality, and determination to maintain intact the autocratic powers. Following Russia's involvement with Japan in the Far East in a war which the people neither supported nor understood but which inflicted upon Russia a series of military disasters, government officials relaxed the reign of terror. In November, 1904, the new Minister of Interior, Prince Peter D. Sviatopolk-Mirski (1857–1914), a bureaucrat of liberal inclinations, after some hesitation allowed a *zemstvo* conference in St. Petersburg. The members of the conference unanimously adopted an eleven-point resolution calling for freedom of thought, conscience, speech, assembly, and press; the granting of civil rights irrespective of class, nationality, or religious affiliation; equality of all citizens before the law; political amnesty; agricultural and industrial reforms; democratization and expansion of local self-government; repeal of the "state of emergency" legislation; and summoning of an elective assembly. The last provision did not receive unanimous endorsement because some delegates favored legislative power for the assembly while others were satisfied with only consultative powers.

Private and public organizations throughout the country overwhelmingly endorsed the *zemstvo* resolution; government authorities, however, took a dim view of it. Official rejection of these demands widened the existing gulf between the people and the bureaucracy and contributed heavily to a crisis commonly known as "Bloody Sunday." The latter occurred on January 22, 1905, when a peaceful procession of thousands of striking workers of the capital, headed by a priest, George A. Gapon (1870–1906), bearing a petition to the Tsar listing their grievances and wishes, was fired upon by troops, killing many and wounding hundreds.

The "Bloody Sunday" massacre had an electrifying effect on all the layers of Russian society. Working masses immediately intensified their radicalism and many industrial centers of the Empire (St. Petersburg, Moscow, Warsaw, Riga, Lodz, Odessa, and others) were hit by waves of industrial strikes during the spring and summer months, which greatly affected war production. Liberals increased their agitation for a constitutional assembly, and to coordinate their actions they organized in May, 1905, the Union of Unions. Students, too, intensified their radicalism, clashed with authorities, and forced the closing of schools until the fall of

1905. Incited by revolutionary propaganda and the developing chaos, peasants rose in many parts of the Empire against authorities and burned and looted many estates of the nobility. Encouraged by the developing nation-wide restlessness, nationalities of the Empire (Finns, Latvians, Poles, Ukrainians, Jews, and the peoples of the Caucasus) increasingly agitated for equal rights and autonomy. Revolutionary agitation affected also many members of the armed forces. The most spectacular action was the June, 1905, mutiny of the crew of the battleship *Potemkin*, which sailed without its officers to Rumania. In other words, "Bloody Sunday" opened the 1905 revolution.

Under this mounting nation-wide restlessness, on August 16, 1905, the government issued its first "major concession," an imperial decree which promised Russia an assembly to be elected by those nobles, bourgeoise, and peasants who owned property. The function of the assembly was to be purely an advisory one. This half-hearted "concession" failed to satisfy the liberals and still less the radicals. Early in October, 1905, the country was paralyzed by an effective general strike that engulfed the entire railroad network, telegraph and telephone systems, industrial enterprises, banks, schools, municipal offices, hospitals, newspapers, and many other establishments. So effective was the strike that it brought an almost complete standstill to the whole life of the country. On October 26, the strike caused the emergence of a self-styled workers' "parliament"— the Soviet of Workers' Deputies. Led by the Mensheviks, the Soviet rose in importance and popularity and began to demand a constitutional assembly, a democratic republic, political amnesty, disarming of troops and of the police and arming of workers, an eight-hour working day, civil liberties, and repeal of the "state of emergency" legislation. Since other cities of the Empire followed the example of the capital, there developed a network of Soviets throughout Russia. Under the pressure of all these developments, on October 30, 1905, Nicholas II issued a manifesto drafted by Witte, which (1) granted the people of the Empire "personal inviolability, freedom of conscience, speech, assembly, and association"; (2) promised to allow the disfranchised elements (i.e., property-less strata of society) to participate in the elections to the State *Duma,* or the legislative assembly; and (3) established as "an unbreakable rule" that no law should be promulgated without the sanction of the State Duma, which also was promised "the supervision of the legality of the actions of authorities" appointed by the Crown.

The people received the October Manifesto with mixed emotions. The majority of them greeted it with great excitement followed by noisy demonstrations and celebrations. The ultranationalist groups, however, were shocked by the "concessions" and, led by the uncompromising supporters of autocracy, they organized antiliberal, antistudent, antiminority demonstrations and pogroms in an effort to restore the status quo ante. The

Manifesto failed to satisfy the extreme radicals, who favored the abolition of monarchy, nationalization of land, and introduction of other far-reaching reforms, and who, to realize these goals, insisted on continuation of the strike and opposition to the government. They failed in their efforts because the populace seemed satisfied with the victory and unwilling to press its luck. Popular reaction against revolutionary excesses enabled the authorities to regroup their forces, terminate the activities of the St. Petersburg Soviet (November, 1905) and of the Moscow insurrectionists (December, 1905), and slowly to bring the 1905 revolution to an end by means of further concessions (especially the cancellation of the redemption payments), martial law, punitive expeditions, arrests, and executions. The gradual restoration of order also enabled the authorities to direct Imperial Russia on a period of "constitutional experiment" (1905–1917), which in the words of one observer "modified the whole life of the nation and opened the way to new and significant developments."

One of the most notable developments of the period was the transformation of Russia's absolute, autocratic regime into a constitutional system. The transformation was painful and erratic because the country lacked many needed prerequisites, such as established political parties, a literate population, the experience of self-government, and above all an atmosphere of mutual trust between the representative assembly and the government bureaucracy. Under the Fundamental Laws of April 23, 1906, the Tsar retained his historical title of Autocrat (Article 4); enjoyed the exclusive right of initiating legislation affecting the constitution; controlled the executive branch of the government; appointed all high government officials, who in turn were responsible to him only; proclaimed the state of emergency; enjoyed the exclusive right of directing foreign policy; declared war; concluded peace; negotiated treaties; enjoyed the right to pardon or revise sentences; was the official head of the church; and convoked and dissolved the legislature. No legislation could become a law without his signature. Moreover, under Article 57 of the Fundamental Laws, the Tsar enjoyed the right of promulgating emergency legislation in the intervals between sessions of the parliament by means of imperial decrees, which later had to be submitted for approval by the legislature.

But while he still enjoyed many rights, after 1905 the Tsar was no longer an absolute monarch because the constitution provided for obligatory concurrence of the two legislative chambers, the State Council and the State Duma, in legislation. One should remember, however, that Russia's parliament was not a real parliament in the western sense of the word. For one thing it was highly unrepresentative. Half of the State Council, for instance, was appointed by the Tsar, as was the Council's president; the other half was elected from among the clergy, *zemstvo*, nobility, and representatives of commerce, industry, and institutions of higher learning. Whether appointed or elected, all members of the State Council were well-to-do men and came almost exclusively from the central regions of Russia.

The composition of the State Duma, or the lower chamber, while more representative than the State Council, was far from perfect. The government-prepared electoral law disfranchised the bulk of the urban population (intellectuals and industrial workers), which the officials considered hostile to the government and through an intricate system of indirect voting, insured a large representation of the peasantry, which was believed to be devoted to the Crown. Contrary to the expectations of the officials, once elected the peasants aligned themselves with the left-wing parties, and together they voted for the most radical solutions of the land problem. The government's refusal to accept their radical solutions led to the dissolution of the two Dumas after very brief sessions and to the introduction on June 3, 1907, of a new electoral law. The new law divided the electorate into four groups—landowners (other than peasants), urban population, peasants, and industrial workers—and gave government authorities discretionary powers to subdivide electoral districts into smaller units on the basis of property qualifications, national origin, or residence. By these rules, which in the words of one observer violated "every canon of democratic elections," the government obtained a preponderance of conservative, nationalist, and moderate elements, and with their help introduced a number of far-reaching legislative measures.

The most notable achievement of the "constitutional period" was the agrarian reform commonly known as the Stolypin Land Reform. Set in motion between November, 1906, and May, 1911, by Premier Peter A. Stolypin (1862–1911), the reform sought to solve Russia's agrarian problem in order to place the whole economy on stable foundations. Under the terms of the Stolypin Reform, every member of the village commune was allowed to acquire title to the strips of communal land to which he had a right and to consolidate such strips into a contiguous holding. The aim of this obvious reversal of the previous governmental policy was twofold: to eliminate the village commune as an obstacle to agricultural progress; and to create in Russia an economically healthy class of small farmers—known in Russia as *kulaks*—who would act as a bulwark for the regime against every form of extremism. According to official figures, between 1907 and 1913 about 5,000,000 peasants applied for the consolidation of their holdings, and by 1915 some 7,300,000 peasant households in the European part of the Empire (or more than half of all peasant households) had settled on allotment land.

Behind the success of the Stolypin Land Reform were other vital measures. On January 1, 1907, for instance, the government cancelled all peasant redemption payments. At about the same time authorities granted the State Land Bank for Peasants broad powers in helping the peasants to buy land from the state, crown, and nobility, removed all restrictions imposed in the 1860's on peasant mobility, and inaugurated a program of massive assistance to those peasants who wanted to migrate from the overpopulated European provinces of the Empire to sparsely populated Asiatic possessions. Between 1907 and 1914 some 2,000,000 peasants settled in various parts of Asiatic Russia. Finally, with the help of the *zemstvo* institutions, the government organized a fairly efficient network of agricultural stations staffed by agricultural experts whose task was to help peasants improve their methods of cultivation. Russia's entry into World War I in August, 1914, interrupted this transformation of rural areas and left them pregnant with great explosive potentials.

In addition to the modernization efforts in rural areas, the "constitutional period" witnessed an accelerated industrial growth. Financed by foreign and domestic resources, Russian industry, after a brief interruption by the revolution of 1905, entered upon a period of prosperity and record-breaking gains which lasted until World War I. According to official figures, between 1909 and 1913 Russia's production of pig iron increased by 59 per cent; iron and steel by 50 per cent; coal by 40 per cent; and coke by 60 per cent. The period saw an extraordinary expansion of railroads; rapid growth of industrial combines as well as consumer cooperatives; steady development of mechanization; continued introduction of the latest technological innovations; and an unprecedented growth of urban population. In an effort to calm the growing industrial proletariat the government legalized the organization of labor unions, introduced health and accident insurance for workers, and either imprisoned or forced into exile the leaders of extreme groups. After 1906 the country enjoyed a relative calm and was more prosperous than it had ever been before. The calm was only temporary, for on the eve of World War I labor unrest began to gather dangerous momentum.

The modernization of the economy was accompanied by a concentrated effort to eliminate illiteracy which, according to the census of 1897, was 79 per cent. All responsible leaders recognized the urgency of the problem, and in May, 1908, both legislative chambers approved a government-sponsored education bill which provided for a gradual introduction of free, universal, compulsory education for children between eight and eleven. Because of inadequate funds and facilities (there were less than 100,000 schools in Russia in 1908) and lack of qualified personnel, the education bill envisaged the full attainment of universal education in Russia by 1922. The "constitutional period" saw also a substantial numerical increase of the secondary schools and institutions of higher learning as well as increased educational opportunities for the lower strata of society. On the eve of World War I there were about 1,700 secondary schools, followed by sixty-seven institutions of higher learning.

Finally, the "constitutional period" witnessed in Russia a phenomenal rise in newspapers and periodicals. In 1912 there were being published within the Russian Empire (excluding Finland) 2,167 different periodicals in thirty-three languages, reflecting every shade of opinion from the extreme right to the extreme left. Many of these publications encountered difficulties with the censor; some were even forced to suspend publication for a time. On the whole, however, the Russian press was enjoying the best freedom in its history. The same cannot be said of the publications of national minorities which, while allowed to appear, were subjected to arbitrary abuses by the Great Russian officialdom. In fact, the "constitutional regime" revived the old policy of Russification of border areas (Finland, Poland, and the Ukraine), supported anti-Jewish pogroms, and in innumerable other ways alienated its subject peoples thus inspiring them to work for the dissolution of the Empire.

The outbreak of World War I, and Russia's entry into it on the side of England and France, interrupted the great political, economic, and cultural transformation of Imperial Russia. Initially, the people supported the war, believing that it was one of national defense against unprovoked Austro-German aggression, and were jubilant over the successes of Russian armies against the forces of the Dual Monarchy in Galicia. A series of military disasters on the German front, which inflicted on Russia extremely heavy casualties (Tannenberg, the Masurian Lakes, and Gorlice), caused in part by inept leadership and in part by the superior organization of the enemy, greatly affected the morale of the nation. The inability of the Allies to aid Russia militarily and economically (because of the effectiveness of the German blockade) forced Russia to rely on her own inadequately developed resources and was responsible for further deterioration of morale. Repeated mobilizations of able-bodied men (some 15,000,000 were called into service during the war) produced disastrous effects on industrial and agricultural production, caused the breakdown of the transportation system, and created severe shortages of food and fuel, especially in large industrial centers. Since the authorities were unable to solve these urgent problems and unwilling to listen to constructive criticism or suggestions, early in 1917 Imperial Russia found itself on the brink of revolution.

SUGGESTED READINGS

FISCHER, GEORGE. *Russian Liberalism*. Cambridge: Harvard University Press, 1958.

FLORINSKY, MICHAEL T. *Russia: A History and an Interpretation*. New York: Macmillan, 1955. Vol. 2.

HAIMSON, LEOPOLD H. *The Russian Marxists and the Origins of Bolshevism*. Cambridge: Harvard University Press, 1955.

JORRE, GEORGES. *The Soviet Union. The Land and Its People*. London: Longmans, 1961.

KARPOVICH, MICHAEL. *Imperial Russia, 1801–1917*. New York: Holt, 1932.

KORNILOV, ALEXANDER. *Modern Russian History*. New York: Knopf, 1952.

LEVIN, ALFRED. *The Second Duma*. New Haven: Yale University Press, 1940.

LYDOLPH, PAUL E. *Geography of the USSR*. New York: Wiley, 1964.

MASARYK, THOMAS G. *The Spirit of Russia*. 2nd ed. New York: Macmillan, 1955. Vol. 2.

MAVOR, JAMES. *An Economic History of Russia*. 2nd ed. London: Dent, 1925. Vol. 2.

MEYER, ALFRED G. *Leninism*. Cambridge: Harvard University Press, 1957.

MILLER, M. S. *The Economic Development of Russia, 1905–1914*. London: King, 1926.

MILIUKOV, PAUL. *Russia and Its Crisis*. Chicago: University of Chicago Press, 1906.

OXFORD REGIONAL ECONOMIC ATLAS. *The U.S.S.R. and Eastern Europe*. New York: Oxford University Press, 1956.

PARES, BERNARD. *Russia and Reform*. London: Constable, 1907.

PAVLOVSKY, GEORGE. *Agricultural Russia on the Eve of the Revolution*. London: Routledge, 1930.

PUSHKAREV, SERGEI. *The Emergence of Modern Russia, 1801–1917*. Translated by Robert H. McNeal and Tova Yedlin. New York: Holt, Rinehart and Winston, 1963.

RADKEY, OLIVER H. *Agrarian Foes of Bolshevism: Promise and Default of the Russian Socialist Revolutionaries*. New York: Columbia University Press, 1958.

ROBINSON, GEROLD T. *Rural Russia under the Old Regime*. New York: Longmans, 1949.

SETON-WATSON, HUGH. *The Decline of Imperial Russia, 1855–1914*. New York: Praeger, 1960.

SHABAD, THEODORE. *Geography of the USSR: A Regional Survey*. New York: Columbia University Press, 1951.

TOMPKINS, STUART R. *The Russian Intelligentsia*. Norman, Oklahoma: University of Oklahoma Press, 1957.

TREADGOLD, DONALD W. *Lenin and His Rivals*. New York: Praeger, 1955.

VENTURI, FRANCO. *Roots of Revolution*. New York: Knopf, 1960.

WOLFE, BERTRAM D. *Three Who Made a Revolution*. New York: Dial, 1948.

YARMOLINSKY, AVRAHM. *Road to Revolution*. New York: Collier, 1962.

✂ II

THE MARCH REVOLUTION, 1917

THE COLLAPSE OF THE MONARCHY

The revolutionary storm which had been gathering in Russia for decades exploded in March, 1917. Viewed in retrospect that explosion was one of the most important events in Russian history as well as in the history of modern times. This, however, was not the universal judgment of contemporaries, since the immediate events leading to this great political, economic, and social upheaval were neither spectacular nor extraordinary. War-weary Russia drifted into this calamity thanks to the incompetent military and political leadership which, in return for untold sacrifices and efforts, was capable of producing nothing but inefficiency and corruption at home and military defeats at the front. Rightly or wrongly the Russians believed that a change was necessary and they plunged ahead on a policy of change.

38 ✦

The elimination in December, 1916, of the hated Gregory E. Rasputin (1872–1916), who wielded a demonic influence on the imperial family, was the first sign of the approaching shift. It was followed by increasing rumors of further changes and of trouble, but trouble was neither a novelty nor an exception in Russia. Although the authorities were unable to do anything else constructive, they seem to have been determined to meet the oncoming challenge firmly. With every passing day, however, the situation was deteriorating everywhere, and most of all in Petrograd, the capital. Throughout January and February the dissatisfaction mounted. There were increased strikes in war factories, a situation hardly helpful to the war effort and least of all to soldiers in the trenches. There were also more frequent food demonstrations, some of which turned into riots. The lack of food which affected everyone and angered many, especially women shoppers, was not so much a shortage of food as the result of poor management and inadequate distribution, caused in part by the breakdown of transportation. And since the authorities did nothing to improve it, the situation went from bad to worse.

A major crisis began to develop late in February and early in March. After several postponements the Duma finally reconvened on February 27, amidst a tense atmosphere. Although the Duma consisted basically of loyal supporters of the regime, many of its members expected early ad-

Petrograd, 1917. Soldiers and citizens on their way to the Duma.

journment. There were some members, however, who were determined to remain in session come what may. In anticipation of increased demonstrations during the session of the Duma, the government strengthened the Petrograd garrison. It also intensified censorship, increased house searches, and in trying to apprehend all possible troublemakers, arrested many innocent persons. These measures, however, only heightened the existing tension. On the surface it looked as if the police and troops were in complete control of the situation, but this was only an illusion.

On March 5, the Tsar left the capital for the General Headquarters in Mogilev, leaving behind a signed but undated decree for the dissolution of the Duma. On the same day the Putilov munition factory workers struck, followed by those of other large factories in Petrograd. On March 6, streetcar conductors went on strike, forcing many disgruntled people to walk. On the following day open meetings were held on Nevski Prospekt where soapbox orators spoke of "Bread and Freedom." Although with every passing hour tension increased and the mob swelled, the demonstrations continued to be relatively orderly and the authorities still had full control of the situation.

From General Headquarters, completely unfamiliar with the seriousness of the situation, the Tsar ordered General S. S. Khabalov, commanding officer of the Petrograd garrison, to quell the disorders immediately. Fulfillment of this order became impossible, for on March 8 the unrest spread from the center of the city to the workers' quarters in the suburbs. Now the entire capital was engulfed by the turmoil. There were many street demonstrations and, except for police officials, almost everyone endorsed the manifestants, some of whom even carried banners with the slogan: "Down with Autocracy!" The regular troops still continued to obey orders, but rumors spread that the soldiers—the backbone of Russian autocracy—were favorably inclined towards the demonstrators and would not fire on them. The crowds, growing both in size and in ugly mood, applauded these rumors. This left only the police to deal with the demonstrators, and it became impossible to prevent clashes between the two. A revolution was in the making.

The inability of police authorities to control the crowds only brought more demonstrators and more spectators into the streets. Revolutionary songs and demands for "Bread and Freedom" became more frequent, resulting in more clashes with the police. By March 10 the entire city had been turned into an armed camp of soldiers, police officials, armored cars, and an unruly mob of demonstrators whose shouting was interrupted frequently by rifle and machine gun fire in the main thoroughfares. Since the situation was getting out of hand, the authorities made hasty but all-out preparations for a final showdown with the demonstrators. On the Tsar's orders the Duma was to be dissolved on March 12, and full employment of the troops was to be made to suppress the unruly mob.

The plan was ill-fated. During the night of March 11, soldiers of the Volyn Regiment of the Guard, after their return to the barracks, mutinied and agreed not to fire at crowds in the future. In the morning of March 12 they went even further. Disobeying the orders and attempts at persuasion by their officers, the soldiers poured into the streets and joined the demonstrators. Other regiments followed, and soon the entire Petrograd garrison of the imperial army ceased to exist. Drunk with this success the mob, reinforced by the defiant soldiers, moved through the streets of Petrograd unchallenged, looting, hunting down hated police officials, breaking into arsenals for arms, and into prisons to release the old inmates and to replace them with new ones. The revolution was now in full swing, and before day's end most of the government buildings were under revolutionary control. Paralyzed, the old government apparatus had ceased to function.

Out of the revolutionary turmoil slowly and quite uncertainly a new Russia began to emerge. In the afternoon of March 12 a group of members of the defunct Duma met in the Taurida Palace and elected a thirteen-man committee known as the Temporary Committee. Consisting of members of the Progressive Bloc, which had made its debut in 1915, and of representatives of leftist groups, the Committee invested itself with unlimited powers "to take in hand the reestablishment of state and public order" throughout Russia. On the same day, March 12, and in the same building, there emerged another revolutionary institution—the Petrograd Soviet of Workers' and Soldiers' Deputies. Composed of factory and workshop delegates, leaders of the revolting military units, and "representatives of democratic and socialist parties and groups," the Petrograd Soviet, reviving the goals of its 1905 predecessor, set as its task "the organization of popular forces and the struggle for the final consolidation of the people's government in Russia." To both these revolutionary bodies —the Temporary Committee and the Soviet—revolution-minded Russians began to look for guidance, advice, and leadership capable of restoring order as well as ushering in a new era of liberty and social justice. Inasmuch as the membership, the goals, and the general *Weltanschauung* of the two were vastly different, trouble between the Temporary Committee and the Soviet was unavoidable.

The appearance of these two self-appointed groups as spokesmen for the new Russia created an odd situation, inasmuch as *technically* the old regime was still in existence. Though the central government had ceased to function and one military garrison had disintegrated, the Tsar, the embodiment of the old regime, was with his army in the General Headquarters where the revolutionary developments were not immediately felt. While beneficial in one way, this divorce from the rapidly changing situation was fatal in another way. Far from the scene, Nicholas II and his closest advisers misunderstood the situation as well as underestimated

Petrograd, 1917. In the early days of the Revolution these were the first soldiers to side with the strikers and thus made the Revolution possible in Petrograd.

its seriousness. The Tsar, in particular, remained deaf to all warnings, and failed to see the "handwriting on the wall." When, for instance, at midnight of March 11 Michael V. Rodzianko (1859–1924), President of the Duma, wired the Tsar warning him of the seriousness of affairs in the capital and urging him to institute immediately far-reaching reforms to avert a catastrophe, the Tsar considered it nonsense unworthy of reply. He also remained unimpressed by Rodzianko's second warning of the morning of March 12. By the evening of that day there was no need for warnings, because the old order was dead. Abdication remained the only avenue left and Rodzianko, though a convinced monarchist, suggested it.

Action and resoluteness were not basic characteristics of Nicholas II. It is, however, very doubtful whether swift action on his part could have altered the situation. The revolution had gone too far. General Khabalov learned this when he tried to save the dying order on March 12; his special task force of some six companies simply melted away upon coming into contact with the revolutionaries. The special task force of General N. I. Ivanov dispatched from General Headquarters, also on March 12, met an identical fate. On March 13 the Tsar's train left Mogilev for Petrograd.

It never reached its destination, for it was rerouted to Pskov to the head-quarters of General Nikolai V. Ruzsky (1854–1918), commander of the Northern Front. In this ancient Russian town, all military leaders whom the Tsar consulted, including his uncle the Grand Duke Nicholas (1856–1929), urged him to abdicate in favor of his son, with the Tsar's brother, Grand Duke Michael (1878–1918), acting as regent. It was hoped that such a move would save the dynasty and prevent the spread of anarchy. An identical proposal was made by two convinced monarchists and spokesmen of the Temporary Committee, Guchkov and Vasili V. Shulgin (1878–1945), who had succeeded in reaching Pskov. All this pressure was too much. Repudiated by his people and deserted by his followers, the Tsar agreed and signed the abdication document. On March 16, pleading inability to part with his "beloved son," he changed his mind and abdicated in favor of his brother Michael.

But even this last attempt to save the dynasty failed. Having brought down the old Tsar, Russian revolutionaries were in no mood to accept a new one. Violent protests went up against the arrangement made at Pskov. Sensing strong antimonarchial feelings, Michael hesitated to accept the crown. In this respect he was more realistic than many of his supporters, including Miliukov. On March 16, after consultation with his supporters on the Temporary Committee, the Grand Duke Michael declared that he was resolved "to accept the supreme power only if and when our great people, having elected by universal suffrage a Constituent Assembly to determine the form of government and lay down the fundamental law of the new Russian State, invest me with such a power." The Russian people had no desire to make such an offer. The three hundred-year-old Romanov dynasty, which had been founded by a Michael, technically expired with another Michael. In less than a week the most autocratic country in Europe became the most democratic "republic" in the world. The entire transition was responsible for 169 dead, 1,264 wounded, and an uncertain number of hurt feelings.

THE PROVISIONAL GOVERNMENT VS. THE SOVIET

The remarkable ease with which the monarchy collapsed stunned everyone. Although, outside Petrograd, Russian civilians and soldiers took no direct part in the overthrow of the monarchy, they followed the example set in the capital. Everywhere military units joined the revolutionaries. Everywhere, too, as soon as the news arrived, the old administration, from governors down to the last village official, disappeared without trace or struggle. Throughout Russia—in cities, villages, army units, offices, and factories—there emerged all sorts of self-appointed committees and organizations, generally known as soviets. Some of these tried to maintain order; others engaged in such "extrarevolutionary activity" as raiding and looting. In many respects the downfall of the monarchy meant therefore the beginning of Russia's disintegration and administrative, political, military, and economic chaos.

To deal with this confusion, on March 16 the Temporary Committee of the Duma dissolved itself and established the Provisional Government. It was a conservative body of well-known and respected prerevolutionary public figures. They represented a solid cross section of educated Russians, but they were unfit to lead a revolutionary country in wartime. Prince George E. Lvov (1861–1925), a wealthy landowner, member of an old aristocratic family, and a veteran *zemstvo* leader, became Premier and Minister of Interior; Miliukov, historian, leader of the Cadets, and an outspoken wartime critic of the regime, Foreign Minister; Guchkov, a wealthy Moscow merchant and founder of the Octobrist Party, Minister of War; Michael B. Tereshchenko (1884–1956), a non-party philanthropist and one of the wealthiest men in Russia, Minister of Finance; Andrei I. Shingarov (1860–1918), a Cadet and *zemstvo* member, Minister of Agriculture; A. I. Manuilov, a Cadet and University of Moscow professor, Minister of Education; Alexander I. Konovalov (1875–1948), a Progressive member of the Fourth Duma, Minister of Commerce and Industry; Nikolai V. Nekrasov, (1879–?), leader of the Left Wing Cadet group, Minister of Railways; Alexander F. Kerensky (1881–   ), a lawyer, leader of a non-Marxist Labor group in the Fourth Duma, and a deputy chairman of the Petrograd Soviet, Minister of Justice; and Vladimir N. Lvov, a member of the Conservative Party, Procurator of the Holy Synod.

The task of this first Provisional Government was not enviable. Both its legality and its authority rested on shaky grounds. It had the privilege of issuing orders, but because of the lack of an administrative apparatus, it could not expect compliance. Moreover, as Kerensky rightly noted, from its predecessor the Provisional Government inherited a losing war, an acute food situation, a paralyzed transportation system, an empty treasury, and a population in a state of furious discontent and anarchic disintegration. But this was not all. Peasants demanded land, workers demanded increased benefits and rights, Russia's numerous subject peoples demanded autonomy and self-determination, soldiers demanded the end of hostilities, and Russia's allies pressed for increased war efforts. The chaos was accentuated in that most of these demands were incompatible with the basic philosophy of the new government—that of gradualness, moderation, and respectability.

In tackling these grave problems the Provisional Government would have doubtless been more successful if it had been the only organ of authority in Russia, but such was not the case. In dealing with every major issue the government had to take into account the attitude of the Petrograd Soviet. The latter, representing the victorious revolutionary mob, many professional revolutionaries, and all types of "Johnny-come-latelys," grew into an enormous and unwieldy body which did not know its mind. Like the Provisional Government, the Soviet was a product of the revolution, but unlike the former, whose outlook was liberal-conservative, the latter was politically left-oriented, deliberately "non-bourgeois and class-conscious." The basis of the Soviet was the excited, victorious, armed, and action-ready street mob. With its support, the Soviet, from its very inception on March 12, acted as if it were the governmental authority. It invited the population to rally around it, issued all kinds of proclamations and orders, and even appointed its own officials to establish "peoples' power" in Russia. Yet for many crucial weeks the Soviet had no desire to assume the responsibility inherent in political power. The explanation for this strange behavior of the spokesmen of the Soviet, among whom there was more than a usual number of hotheads, must be sought in Marxist theory. As "orthodox" interpreters of Marxism, these self-appointed spokesmen of the Soviet believed the revolution in Russia was a "bourgeois revolution"; hence, they argued, the political power must be held by bourgeois liberals of the Duma. Members of the Soviet, allegedly representing the working class, could not enter any such government, but neither were they to stand idly by. They were to organize, prepare, and see to it that the revolution was not sidetracked.

Under those odd conditions, genuine and prolonged cooperation between the two revolutionary outgrowths became impossible. This is not to say that no attempts were made in that direction. The Provisional Government itself was the product of a compromise reached between some spokesmen of the Soviet and the representatives of the Temporary Committee of the Duma on March 14. Under that compromise the Provisional Government was to exercise executive authority until a Constituent Assembly elected on the basis of universal, equal and direct suffrage could decide the future form of government in Russia. While such basic issues as war and land problems were side-stepped, under the compromise the Provisional Government obligated itself to issue complete amnesty to all political prisoners; abolish capital punishment; allow freedom of speech, press, and assembly; grant labor the right to organize and to strike; and remove all legal restrictions based on class, nationality, or religion. Since soldiers had played a decisive role in the overthrow of the monarchy and in the revolution, they were to be given political liberties insofar as these were practicable under technical limitations of the service. Under this compromise also, two high ranking spokesmen of the Soviet—Nikolai S. Chkheidze (1864–1926) and Kerensky, respectively Chairman and Vice-Chairman of the Executive Committee of the Petrograd Soviet—were to enter the first government of revolutionary Russia.

Had this agreement been allowed to go into effect unobstructed and for a reasonable period of time, Russia and the rest of the world might have been spared many troubles. But such was not the case. On the morning of March 15, after hearing a report on the compromise, a plenary session of the Soviet not only repudiated it but also passed a resolution prohibiting socialists from serving in a bourgeois cabinet. Chkheidze complied with this decision. Kerensky, however, in one of the passionate appeals for which he was famous, persuaded the assembled members of the Soviet to reverse themselves. This they did through acclamation, and Kerensky entered the government to preserve harmony between it and the Petrograd Soviet.

Ahead, however, were other hurdles and they were not as easy to surmount. In spite of its agreement to let one of its high ranking members join the Provisional Government, the relation between the latter body and the Soviet continued to be ambiguous, contradictory, cool, and even hostile. On March 16, for instance, the Soviet expressed its willingness to support the policies of the Provisional Government insofar as they corresponded to the interests of the proletariat and of the broad democratic masses. At the same time, however, it continued to interfere in governmental affairs and to issue all kinds of appeals and orders in its own right. This created a highly explosive situation which the Russians have labelled *dvoevlastie,* or dual government. Under this arrangement the Provisional Government enjoyed responsibility but had no real authority, while the Soviet had authority but no responsibility. Trouble was inevitable.

The first major crisis between the Provisional Government and the Soviet developed over control of the armed forces. Under the March 14 compromise, all soldiers were to enjoy the same political rights as other citizens. It was understood that while on duty and in war service strict discipline should be maintained, but before this agreement was published, *Izvestiia,* the official mouthpiece of the Soviet, published the now famous Order No. 1. Drawn up on March 14 at the suggestion of some of the soldiers, it was directed to all units of the armed forces. It called for the election of committees from among the lower ranks which, in turn, in all of their "political actions" were to obey the Soviet. Orders of the Temporary Committee of the Duma were to be obeyed only if these did not conflict with those of the Soviet. Moreover, these committees were to have complete control over all weapons, which under no circumstances were to be turned over to officers. While pleading for strict observance of military discipline on duty, Order No. 1 abolished saluting while off duty as well as all elaborate traditional honors to officers. The latter were forbidden to be harsh towards their men.

These instructions, which expressed a fairly accurate picture of the long-standing hostility between officers and their men, greatly accelerated the breakdown of discipline in Russia's armed forces. Attempts to mitigate the effects of Order No. 1 failed completely. Everywhere soldiers talked, debated, voted, and some tried to settle old grievances with their officers. Although there were many who continued to think along traditional lines of their duty to defend the country as well as the achievements of the revolution, there were thousands who left their units and simply went home. The appearance of national military units (Polish, Ukrainian, Georgian, Armenian, and others) responsive to native command but unwilling to listen to orders from Petrograd only deepened the existing chaos. Without discipline and leadership the seven million man Russian army, as an organized fighting unit rapidly disintegrated. Many military commanders who survived the initial storm accommodated themselves to a new situation. There were others, like Minister of War Guchkov, who openly detested the new regime that was introduced in the armed forces, and resigned in disgust because of pressure from the Soviet.

Simultaneously with the Soviet-created army crisis there developed a government-bungled foreign policy dilemma. From its inception the Provisional Government, while taking note of a need for changes in domestic affairs, had acted as if the revolution would have no effect on Russia's foreign policy. The Manifesto to the People of Russia of March 19, for example, spoke of the government's determination "to bring the war to a victorious conclusion" and to observe faithfully all alliances and agreements—both open and secret—which had been concluded between Tsarist Russia and its allies. A government circular to Russia's representatives abroad, intended to assure her allies of the continuity of Russian foreign policy, emphasized the same points. Although these and similar public declarations by Foreign Minister Miliukov were welcomed in London and Paris, they were at variance with the realities of Russian conditions. To gain some of the war objectives—the Straits and the Ukrainian inhabited regions of the Dual Monarchy—it was necessary to have a fighting force. The government had none since so many Russian soldiers had decided to go home. Miliukov's failure to realize this, as well as the fact that the revolution was the result of war weariness and a protest against Tsarist domestic and war mismanagement, was fatal to him and to the Provisional Government.

As for the Soviet, that body for a time had no clear idea about war objectives. Some of its members supported while others objected to the known war aims. It was not until March 27 that the Soviet agreed on a vague but common stand. In an "Appeal to the Peoples of the World" the Petrograd Soviet announced that "it will, by every means, resist the policy of annexations of its ruling classes," and accordingly called upon the peoples of Europe, especially of Austria and Germany, "for concerted, decisive action in favor of peace." It recommended, among other things, the overthrow of their governments and refusal "to serve as an instrument of conquest and violence in the hands of kings, landowners, and bankers —and then by our united efforts, we will stop the horrible butchery, which is disgracing humanity. . . ."

An intensified nation-wide campaign advocating that the new Russia must have a new foreign policy of peace without annexations and indemnities followed. Newspapers, demonstrations, gatherings, and committees everywhere passed resolutions demanding the government's clarification and even change of its war aims. On April 8, under this concentrated pressure the Provisional Government yielded. The aim of free Russia, stated a declaration addressed to the Russian people, was neither the domination of other peoples, nor the forcible annexation of their territories, but "the establishment of a stable peace on the basis of the self-determination of nations." The Russian people did not seek to increase their power at the expense of other peoples, but neither would they tolerate that Russia "should emerge from the great struggle humiliated, undermined in her vital strength."

This government plea for status quo failed because Miliukov made it clear that the new formula did not bind him in administering foreign affairs. The crisis deepened, and new demands were made. The fact that some members of the Provisional Government itself favored the formula of peace "without annexations and indemnities" did not help the situation. On May 1, Miliukov once again was forced to "clarify" the government's stand on foreign policy. In a note sent to various Allied governments in order to calm foreign fears, he denied that Russia was seeking a separate peace. Russia was not only remaining faithful to her obligations but would also "carry the war to decisive victory" in order to gain necessary "guarantees and sanctions."

While assuring Russia's allies, Miliukov's note inspired violent protests and demonstrations and counterdemonstrations in war-weary Russia. The Executive Committee of the Soviet branded it a new "imperialistic" declaration, while Lenin, the leader of the Bolsheviks, who had just returned to Russia from Switzerland via Germany and Sweden, published an infuriating anti-government article in the party's mouthpiece, *Pravda*. To calm the excited public the government issued a new declaration which disavowed Miliukov's interpretation. Miliukov's days as Foreign Minister were over, and he resigned on May 15.

Miliukov's resignation and that of Guchkov two days earlier led to reorganization of the Provisional Government on a coalition basis. Of the fifteen ministers, now nine were liberals and six were moderate socialists from the Soviet. The latter entered the government with full understanding that: (1) the government's policy would be directed towards a general and speedy peace without annexations and indemnities; (2) there would be further democratization of the army; (3) the food, transportation, and financial situations would be improved; (4) a new agrarian policy would be adopted; (5) the Constituent Assembly would be convened as soon as possible; and (6) Soviet ministers would be responsible to the Soviet. These conditions, which became the official policy of the coalition government ended the first phase of dual power in Russia. Once they were members of the government, moderate Soviet spokesmen began to lose ground among the urban as well as the peasant masses. The road was thus cleared for Lenin to adopt the slogan "All Power to the Soviets."

Military and foreign policy crises notwithstanding, the first cabinet of the Provisional Government accumulated an admirable record of achievements. It granted complete amnesty to political and religious prisoners, abolished capital punishment and the exile system, and reformed prisons. It removed all legal restrictions based on class, creed, or national origin. It abolished all special courts and introduced the general system of trial by jury. It guaranteed freedom of speech, press, and assembly. It reorganized food distribution. It widened the base of local administration and reformed the system of peasant administrative machinery. It strengthened the cooperative movement. It instituted the eight-hour working day and granted labor the right to organize and to strike. It reorganized the church adminstration. It inaugurated preparations for an early convocation of the Constituent Assembly whose task, among others, was to be the solution of the agrarian problem. Finally, it restored the autonomy of Finland, reorganized administration in Central Asia and the Caucasus, offered semi-independent status to Poland, and created committees to work out local autonomy for the Ukraine and Latvia.

While many of these achievements simply acknowledged *faits accomplis,* judged according to normal conditions they were nevertheless quite impressive. For revolutionary times, however, they fell short because they ignored basic wants of the masses; i.e., peasant demands for land and workers' demands for better working conditions and wages. Deprived so long by Tsarism of elementary rights, both the Russian and non-Russian peoples knew no limits to their hopes and aspirations when the revolution developed. Rightly or wrongly they demanded more rights and fewer sacrifices, more leisure and less work. The government, consisting of conservative-liberal spokesmen, moved cautiously. With shaky authority, lack of administrative apparatus, a terrible war on hand, finances in disorder, and the economy in chaos, the Provisional Government insisted on the maintenance of status quo and even postponement of some demands until the meeting of the Constituent Assembly. This was a fatal mistake. To the revolution-excited masses this attitude revealed that both at the center and at the periphery as well, government spokesmen were too slow and too conservative and above all distrustful of the masses. This attitude also placed ammunition in the hands of a more radical element which had begun to return from domestic and foreign exile. There was little ahead that was encouraging.

The revolution made possible the return of thousands of veteran revolutionaries—liberals, socialists, peasants, students, and intellectuals.

Out of a Moscow prison came Polish conspirator Felix E. Dzerzhynski (1877–1926), who later was to organize the Soviet secret police. From Siberian exile came such Bolsheviks as Jacob M. Sverdlov (1885–1919), Lev. B. Kamenev (1883–1936), and Joseph V. Stalin (1879–1953). The procession from the West included the anarchist Prince Peter Kropotkin (1842–1921), the novelist Maxim Gorky (1868–1936), and the founder of Russian Marxism, Plekhanov. After brief detention by British authorities, from New York via Canada came the versatile Trotsky and Nikolai I. Bukharin (1888–1938). From Switzerland via Germany and Sweden came a group of thirty-eight exiles, including Gregory E. Zinoviev (1883–1936), Karl B. Radek (1885–?), Anatole V. Lunacharsky (1875–1933), and Lenin, the latter the leader of the Bolshevik faction of the Russian Social Democratic Workers' Party. Lenin's return, though seemingly unimportant at the time, viewed in retrospect inaugurated a new phase of the revolution.

Lenin and his party arrived in Petrograd on April 16. At the Finland Station he was greeted by a relatively large crowd of workers, soldiers and sailors, and representatives of various revolutionary organizations. Chkheidze extended official greetings on behalf of the Petrograd Soviet by inviting Lenin to join in defense of "revolutionary democracy" against external and internal attacks. Lenin, however, had his own ideas on the revolution. After telling the assembled throngs that the Russian revolution marked the beginning of an international revolution by the toiling masses everywhere, he hurried to remold his own party, which, like all the revolutionary groups, was in a sad state. It was small numerically, had played no part in the overthrow of the monarchy, and its spokesmen in Russia were divided on tactics. Immediately after the revolution the Bolshevik mouthpiece, *Pravda*, edited by the youthful Viacheslav M. Molotov (1890–   ), had opposed continuation of the war, assailed the Mensheviks, and demanded all power to the Soviets. When Stalin and Kamenev, upon their return from Siberia, took over the editorship a conciliatory policy towards the Provisional Government was adopted.

Lenin ridiculed the tactics of his followers and on April 20 *Pravda* published his celebrated April Theses. His program consisted of ten points: (1) The war in which Russia was involved was an imperialistic war and any defense of it was inadmissible. Conscientious Socialists could support only a revolutionary war, provided that three conditions were fulfilled: (a) that the state power would pass into the hands of the proletariat and the poorest strata of the peasantry; (b) that all annexations be renounced; and (c) that all ties be severed with capitalist interests. Until these conditions were fulfilled, all-out propaganda must be organized everywhere, and especially in the army, in order to convince everyone that no democratic peace was possible without the overthrow of capitalism. (2) Because of the rapidly changing revolutionary situation in Russia, the party's revolutionary tactics must be flexible and capable of meeting every new situation. (3) The Provisional Government should receive no support. On the contrary its false promises should be exposed. (4) The only possible form of revolutionary government was the Soviet of Workers' Deputies. However, in view of the Bolsheviks' insignificant numbers and inadequate representation in the soviets, the party should for the time being limit its work to criticism of the government and to insistence that all power be transferred to the Soviet. (5) The party must demand not a parliamentary—that would be a step backwards—but a soviet republic without police, army, and bureaucracy. (6) All lands must be nationalized and placed under the control of local soviets, and all landed estates must be confiscated and turned into model farms under soviet supervision. (7) All banks must be merged into one national bank and placed immediately under soviet control. (8) The party's immediate task was not the introduction of socialism but only the bringing of "social production and distribution of products" under control of the soviets. (9) A party congress must be held immediately to amend the party's antiquated program and change its name from Social Democratic to Communist. (10) A new international must be organized.

Lenin's program, as well as his bitter criticism of those party members who were moderate in their demands, met considerable opposition even from his close associates. The Petrograd Party Committee rejected it by a vote of thirteen to two with one abstention. This setback did not deter Lenin from pursuing his goal. Though labelled an anarchist and a man who had long been out of touch with Russian reality, he hammered his points again and again until he won an increasing number of supporters to his way of thinking. This concentrated effort accomplished its purpose. By early May at a special Party Conference in Petrograd he picked up considerable support. Although some of his points were not accepted, the final resolutions were passed by seventy-one votes against thirty-nine, with eight abstentions. Slowly, too, the slogans of Lenin's program—"End of War," "Land to Peasants," and "Take Back the Loot" —began to penetrate down to the war-weary and land-hungry people. Lenin, though opposed to individual ownership of land, sensed their wish and capitalized on it. All-out efforts to gain a military victory, to promote patience, moderation, and postponement of vital issues, as the Provisional Government advocated, had little chance of success.

THE SUMMER CRISIS

The Provisional Government's first colossal failure occurred in its war efforts. In spite of its knowledge of the considerable demoralization of the troops, lack of supplies, and the breakdown of transportation, the govern-

ment ordered preparations for a new military offensive. If victorious—and
the men preparing it did not consider other possibilities—the offensive
was to attain two desperately needed objectives: (1) a demonstration to
the Allies that Russia was capable of military performance, but that because of great domestic problems it desired immediate negotiations for a
general peace; and (2) a buildup of the government's authority and
prestige and the silencing of its bitter critics at home. Intensive preparations for this great undertaking started in May. To check the disintegration of the army and to bolster its fighting spirit, trusted civilian commissars were appointed. Some leaders toyed with the idea of organizing
volunteer "death brigades" and the like. These measures in turn were
supplemented by a barrage of leaflets, pamphlets, resolutions, and appeals by various organizations, including the Soviet, calling upon the
Russian army to defend Russia and such revolutionary gains as freedom
and liberty. Immediately after his appointment as Minister of War, Kerensky toured the front where, through his eloquent persuasion and in
spite of heckling and interruptions, he tried and succeeded in arousing
some fighting enthusiasm.

In spite of warnings and of many technical shortcomings, the offensive
began on July 1, under the supervision of General Aleksei A. Brusilov
(1853–1926). The main thrust of the attack centered in Galicia against
the demoralized forces of the Dual Monarchy. In its initial stages the
offensive was successful. After an unusually heavy bombardment, Russian
infantry broke through the battered and half-destroyed enemy lines.
Casualties were heavy on both sides. The Russians captured several thousand prisoners, some equipment, and a few towns, but failed to break the
enemy's resistance. Hopes placed in the military victory began to evapo-
rate, and on July 19 the Austro-German forces launched their own counteroffensive. Russian forces panicked and fled eastward in the most disor-
derly fashion imaginable, perpetrating many crimes and atrocities on the
defenseless civilian population. Demoralization created by war, defeats,
propaganda, poor equipment, the committee system, and lack of leadership was now complete. Only the units of the Czechoslovak legion, organized in Russia from among war prisoners after the revolution had begun,
showed a degree of orderliness and efficiency. Confident that Russian
forces presented no threat to their security, the Germans, with their attention centered in France, did not press their advance and the front line
stabilized itself east of the prewar frontier.

Simultaneously with these great military reverses at the front there
developed another major political crisis at home, over the issue of self-
determination in general and that of the Ukraine in particular. The collapse of the monarchy had heralded a new era not only for the Russians
but for many non-Russian peoples (Finns, Estonians, Latvians, Lithuanians, Poles, Ukrainians, Georgians, and Armenians). Immediately after the

collapse of the old regime, many of these nationalities organized on their respective territories their own administrations which were reluctant to take orders from Petrograd. Some of these nations demanded only autonomy within the new Russia; others insisted on complete separation. The Provisional Government found itself in a dilemma, as its spokesmen held fast to the theory that it was a successor to and trustee of the powers formerly vested in the Tsar which were to be handed over intact to the Constituent Assembly. To consent to the demands of non-Russian nationalities would have meant the acknowledgment of Russia's territorial disintegration. This the leaders of the Provisional Government, reared in the idea that Russia was indivisible, were unwilling to do, but they had no effective means to prevent this disintegration. The Soviet was of no help inasmuch as many of its members were favorably inclined towards the idea of self-determination. The government was therefore forced to adopt a stumbling middle-of-the-road policy. It agreed to grant independence to some nationalities (Poles and Finns), subject to approval by the Constituent Assembly, but it denied the same right to others. It was a policy that was bound to lead to trouble. The explosion occurred in the area the Russians least expected—the Ukraine.

To most Russians, the Ukraine, which the Tsars had acquired in the course of the seventeenth and eighteenth centuries, was the bread basket of the Empire and a major coal and metallurgical region; hence it was considered an indispensable and inseparable part of Russia. Very few were aware that although the Ukrainian population was Orthodox and spoke a language the Russians could understand, thanks to the Russification policy there had been developing and maturing for some time a national movement. When the monarchy collapsed in March, the Ukrainians, like other subject peoples, were seized with a passion for autonomy. Immediately after the revolution they organized their own revolutionary administration, the Ukrainian Central *Rada* (Council), to deal with regional matters. Initially the *Rada*'s democratically-inclined petty bourgeois members did not demonstrate any serious desire for national independence. They insisted only on broad autonomy within a federated and democratic Russian republic, but the Provisional Government refused to yield to these modest demands. It argued that it lacked authority and that the matter could be disposed of only by the Constituent Assembly. The Ukrainians interpreted this as a dilatory legalistic approach to camouflage Russian imperialism, and on June 23 increased their demands in the First Universal. This document declared that while continuing to maintain their ties with Russia, the Ukrainians were embarking on a policy of exerting the right to organize their own life. A general secretariat was formed to act as a cabinet, and the organization of a Ukrainian army was begun amidst the all-out preparations for the July offensive. In view of the dismal failure of the latter, an understanding with the *Rada* became imperative. On July 12, Kerensky with his two colleagues, Tereshchenko and Irakli G. Tseretelli (1882–   ), arrived in Kiev. Their vague consent to several Ukrainian demands precipitated a crisis within the Provisional Government and four Cadet ministers resigned in protest. In the midst of this governmental crisis came the news of the great military disaster. General fear and government helplessness led to an explosion.

The call to the July uprising, as this crisis is known, was issued on July 16 by the grievance-burdened soldiers. They were immediately joined by the eager and ever-ready sailors from the nearby Kronstadt naval base, and by unemployed and hence restless workers. Although many military units decided to remain "neutral," in a very short time there emerged an angry and leaderless anti-government mob ready to loot and to shoot. On the following day, July 17, the banner-carrying demonstrators, now some 500,000 strong, demanded resignation of the Provisional Government and transfer of all power to the Soviet.

The Menshevik-dominated Central Executive Committee of the Soviet not only declined this call but branded the uprising as premature and treasonable. Tensions increased hour by hour and some government and Soviet officials were roughed up by the angry and ugly-tempered mob. Lenin and his followers watched these developments with interest. They were tempted to lead the infuriated mob but their inadequate strength called for caution. Since there was no one to give the mob positive direction, the force of the uprising subsided as rapidly as it had snowballed in the first place. Leaderless, the crowd lost enthusiasm, dispersed, and went home. The uprising, which resulted in several deaths and in a large number of wounded, was over.

The Provisional Government lost no time in re-establishing its authority. It moved along two levels. Since some Bolsheviks had had a hand in the uprising and in order to undermine their influence, Minister of Justice P. N. Pereverzev disclosed to various "neutral" regiments certain documents which seemed to implicate Lenin as a German spy. Coming as it did on the heels of the Russian defeats, this allegation caused anti-Bolshevik feeling to explode. Several regiments now placed themselves at the government's disposal. On July 19, pro-government forces raided and wrecked the plant and offices of *Pravda,* and without any difficulty occupied Party Headquarters and the Fortress of Peter and Paul. Regiments that had taken part in the uprising were disbanded and sent to the front. Simultaneously with these measures, to Kerensky's annoyance, the government published anti-Lenin allegations in the press and ordered the arrest of Lenin as well as many of his close associates, charging them with incitement to armed insurrection. Some of his associates (Trotsky and Lunacharsky) were apprehended but were later released. Lenin, protesting his innocence, went into hiding first in Petrograd and later in Finland, which was now outside of Russian jurisdiction, where he remained until autumn.

The stern government measures following the July uprising pushed aside the danger from the extreme Left, but at the same time gave encouragement to the forces of the extreme Right which had been silent since March. On July 21, in protest against the government's anticipated labor and particularly agrarian policies, Prince Lvov resigned as Premier. As there was considerable disagreement among various self-appointed leaders and spokesmen over policy and appointments, a new and prolonged government crisis developed. It ended on August 7 when a new coalition government under Kerensky's premiership emerged. It was a moderately left-oriented body. Four of the sixteen ministers were Cadets; the remainder were divided between Socialist Revolutionaries and Mensheviks. All members of the new government were released from responsibility to their party and were approved by the Executive Committee of the Petrograd Soviet. On the surface calm prevailed, but underneath the situation was deteriorating rapidly.

To check this disintegration the government summoned an All-Russian State Conference in Moscow for August 26–28. Its delegates, some 2,500 strong, represented peasants, trade unions, soviets, army committees, liberal, socialist, and bourgeois groups. Neither the extreme Right (Monarchists) nor the extreme Left (Bolsheviks) was invited, with the latter retaliating by calling a strike in Moscow. By means of such a forum the government hoped to feel out "the pulse of the country" and to achieve unity. For three days the assembled delegates made speeches, declarations, demands, and complaints. There were also charges and counter-charges. Instead of unity the conference revealed the existence of a cleavage between the proponents and the opponents of the revolution. The most forceful challenge to the revolution came from General Lavr G. Kornilov (1870–1918), the recently appointed Commander-in-Chief of the Russian armies. To the cheers of non-Socialist members Kornilov denounced the existing anarchy in the army and held the socialists responsible for it. His blunt language made him at once the hero of the Right. His star began to rise rapidly only to fall precipitously.

THE KORNILOV AFFAIR

General Kornilov was of simple Cossack origin, and throughout his life retained that simplicity. He rose to the top not through behind-the-scenes maneuvers but by his own hard work plus several fortuitous incidents. Early in the war, for instance, he was captured by the Austrians but made good his escape, an act which made his name famous. Along with his courage Kornilov was known for his resolution and integrity—attributes not necessarily appropriate for revolutionary and opportunistic times. This had been evident in his inability to handle the revolutionary garrison of Petrograd in the early stages of the revolution. Yet, unable to find anyone suitable, after the failure of the July offensive Kerensky turned to Kornilov to restore order. It was a mistake because the chaos was more political than military, and Kornilov could not handle it. He was neither a statesman nor a politician but a simple soldier who was reputed to have "the heart of a lion and the brain of a lamb."

In Kornilov's view the Soviet represented the source of all Russia's trouble. From the moment he assumed the highest military office, all of his actions were directed towards strengthening his own as well as the authority of the Provisional Government at the expense of the Soviet. He demanded and received a free hand in military operations, in naming his subordinates and in the re-establishment of military courts and the death penalty. Early in September Kornilov saw a golden opportunity to deal directly and more effectively with the Soviet. On September 3, the Germans occupied Riga, and the road to Petrograd—the center of revolutionary activity and Soviet strength—was wide open. In the face of considerable Soviet opposition, Kornilov insisted on evacuation of the capital. The government, afraid of alienating the Soviet, hesitated. To enable it to make up its mind Kornilov dispatched a cavalry corps to the capital, ostensibly to protect the government, but actually to make sure that both the government and the Soviet were ousted. Simultaneously Kerensky was approached clumsily by the former Procurator of the Holy Synod, Lvov, asking him to cooperate with Kornilov. Then followed a tragic comedy of errors.

Lvov succeeded in creating with Kerensky the impression that he was Kornilov's emissary. He urged Kerensky to transfer to Kornilov all power, resign, and place himself under Kornilov's protection. Kerensky interpreted this kind suggestion as a conspiracy, arrested Lvov and dismissed Kornilov. The latter refused to comply and appealed to the people. Using not-too-convincing old cliches, he blasted the Provisional Government for its alleged cooperation with the Germans and for inflicting ruin upon the country, and summoned all God-fearing Russian patriots to action. Convinced that there was a leaderless population and strong anti-Kerensky sentiment in Petrograd, Kornilov ordered additional troop movements to the capital. Meanwhile, sensing approaching danger, the Soviet and all other socialist organizations began to act rapidly. A Committee for Struggle Against Counter-Revolution was organized and the entire Petrograd garrison was alerted, including the ever-eager Kronstadt sailors. Petrograd workers, many of whom were now under effective Bolshevik control, were mobilized and armed. Trenches were dug, barricades were built, barbed wire was strung, some seven thousand possible Kornilov supporters were arrested, and the communication system (rail and wire) was disrupted. Without much effort the Kornilov forces sent to Petrograd were halted, isolated, and subjected to extensive propaganda and fraternization. Upon being convinced that they were helping to restore the ancient regime, even the most trusted of Kornilov's troops refused to fight. The expedition was over and had been an overwhelming failure. General Alexander M. Krymov (1871–1917), one of the main leaders of the expeditionary forces, committed suicide on September 13, and on the following day Generals Kornilov, Anton I. Denikin (1872–1947), and other rebellious officers were arrested. The government appointed a commission to gather evidence, but to the astonishment of all those who had defended the government's action the commission acted very slowly and in a spirit of forgiveness.

The immediate consequence of the Kornilov affair was the complete collapse of the military and of the government, with some ministers being dismissed summarily. The organization of a new government which would represent broad segments of Russian society proved to be a difficult task. While searching for a new government, on September 14 Kerensky organized an inner cabinet of five members. To placate the Left-wing supporters, that body enacted a number of measures close to their hearts. On September 27, against some protest, Russia was formally proclaimed a republic although it had been one in reality since March. Kornilov's army reorganization program was shelved. The State Duma, one of the last remnants of the old order, was formally dissolved. Several moderate Right-wing politicians were arrested, the General Headquarters of the Army was purged, and officers' organizations favorable to the Kornilov movement were disbanded. These measures led to further deterioration at the front. Desertion increased and no one tried to stop it. The Russian army became, in the words of an official report, "a huge crowd of tired, poorly clad, poorly fed, embittered men united by common longing for peace and general disillusionment."

The wholesale elimination of the Right-wing danger and further deterioration of general conditions was accompanied by the rise of the Left. During the crucial hours of the Kornilov crisis, Kerensky in desperation appealed to the Bolsheviks. Trotsky and other leaders, imprisoned since July, were released. Well rested and sensing the absence of leadership among the workers, peasants, soldiers, and in the restless soviets, the Bolsheviks turned their entire attention in the direction of the malcontents. In September they obtained 50 per cent of the seats in the Petrograd Soviet, whereas in July they had held barely 10 per cent. By October, supported by the Left-wing Socialist Revolutionaries, Trotsky had become the Chairman of the Petrograd Soviet. The slogan "All Power to the Soviets" now acquired a new meaning.

THE SOCIAL UPHEAVAL

The Kornilov crisis like all previous crises was a political affair. It was a struggle among a few ambitious self-appointed spokesmen in Petrograd. Although it undermined the already shaky authority of the Provisional Government and thereby helped to shorten its life span, it was not the decisive cause of its downfall. Like all previous petty squabbles, the Kornilov affair was completely overshadowed by the great social upheaval which engulfed all of Russia. In 1917 Russia was predominantly an agricultural country. About four-fifths of her population was peasant. Though strong numerically, the peasants as a group had no direct part in the overthrow of the old regime, with the exception of those who were in the army. As was everyone else, the peasants were surprised by the swift collapse of the old regime. Cautious and reserved at first, they soon became the most radical element in the country, forging far ahead of their spokesmen—the Socialist Revolutionaries.

To the Russian peasants, both in and out of the armed forces, the collapse of the old regime revived their centuries-old aspiration. That aspiration was neither the right to vote, nor a parliamentary government, nor a victorious war, nor territorial gains, but *land*. By land they understood not such schemes neatly devised by intellectuals as nationalization, or socialization, but simple partition of nearby estates. Illiterate, backward, and never reconciled to the land settlement of the 1860's, nor fully satisfied by Stolypin's efforts, the Russian peasants sincerely believed that only through the enlargement of their plots of land would they be able to improve their wretched and, even by Russian standards, miserable condition. Partition of estates thus became in the peasant mind the prime and the only objective, and towards that goal they moved like an avalanche without the slightest detour.

Peasant land hunger affected many vital areas and revealed itself in innumerable ways. In the armed forces, for instance, where the peasants formed an overwhelming majority in numbers and in losses, between March and October over one million men simply "demobilized themselves" and went home to make certain they would get their share of the land. Their departure was devastating to the morale of those who remained. With the thought of land uppermost in their minds, peasant soldiers turned deaf ears to orders, disobeyed commands, listened to propaganda, demoted their superiors, debated, and elected their own representatives. They made all possible excuses to avoid combat duty, traded or threw away their weapons, fraternized with the enemy, and constantly dreamt about land, home, and peace. Peasant soldiers, in other words, lost all stomach for war and all attempts to restore discipline or to revive the fighting spirit were futile. The disastrous July offensive confirmed this fact and the Kornilov affair only accelerated total disintegration. In their desire to get land, peasant armies "voted for peace with their legs."

The behavior of Russian soldiers reflected the prevailing attitude of Russian peasants in villages. In spite of individual instances of "boldness" during the early stages of the revolution, the peasantry as a whole remained restrained for several weeks, but this self-control was short-lived. It ended when the peasants became convinced that the old authority had ceased to exist. Peasant land hunger then became uncontrollable. The removal of local landowners and the division of their property became the cardinal objective of the peasantry, and to attain it they employed numerous devices. In some areas they tried to persuade owners of large estates that it was in their interest to dispose of their land at a nominal price. Those owners who were realists did sell and moved away, but there were many who tried to resist. Against those the peasants used the most ancient of their weapons, the burning of manors. The latter act was accompanied, as a rule, by pillage and murder and followed by partition of the land. In some areas, to gain their objective the peasants forced local landowners to release their managers, supervisors, and other help and in turn demanded prohibitive wages for their own work. Spontaneously and without any centralized guidance, through these and similar devices, by early summer the peasants had brought activity on the large estates to a standstill and thereby prepared the stage for partitioning of the land. Under the pretext that owners were incapable of managing their own affairs, local peasant land committees took over not only arable land, meadows, and forests, but also livestock, agricultural implements, furniture, and other useful articles. The Provisional Government was flooded with owners' requests for help. Its contribution was nil, as the punitive expeditionary forces, composed of peasants, sided with their brethren against the landowners. There was no effective weapon against ancient peasant determination that the land belongs to those who till it.

To a large degree the Provisional Government itself was responsible for the course of the agrarian revolution. On the one hand, the government made it known that it sympathized with peasant aspirations. On the other hand, in the midst of the revolutionary upheaval which brought about its very own existence, the government deplored such revolutionary measures as violence, pillage, force, and other extra-legal activities. Instead it insisted on legal procedures, thorough preparations, and orderly methods in settling the land problem by the Constituent Assembly whose convocation, however, it repeatedly postponed. It was a fatal policy because the peasants grew tired of waiting and, unable to get legal approval of their aspirations, they took the law into their own hands. By late summer and early fall, when the government's authority began to disappear rapidly, peasant attacks on the estates reached epidemic proportions. Chaos reigned supreme and any demagogue willing to approve of their actions—and over a hundred million peasants were interested *only* in approval—was certain of their support.

The Provisional Government was not the only institution that contributed to general agrarian confusion only to find itself out of step with the peasant revolutionary enthusiasm and determination. The Soviets of Peasant Deputies, which had emerged spontaneously in March to take care of peasant problems, like the government soon found themselves trailing behind. Like all revolutionary bodies the peasant soviets lacked cohesion and fragmented into various revolutionary groups. This became clearly evident during and following the meeting of the First All-Russian Congress of the Soviets of Peasants' Deputies held in Petrograd in May, 1917. Many of its 1,115 delegates demanded that large estates and church and state lands be divided among the peasants. The Congress, however, dominated by intellectuals elected by village soviets, went on record as reserving final settlement of the land question to the Constituent Assembly, and in endless debates wasted much time on such non-agrarian issues as "peace without annexation and indemnities," and "coalition government."

Next to the peasantry, the most revolutionary group was industrial labor. Unlike the peasantry, however, the workers—at least those of Petrograd—took an active part in the overthrow of the old regime, and on several occasions demonstrated their readiness to defend the revolutionary gains. This was not because the workers were more revolutionary than were the peasants, but rather because they were centered in industrial areas and were better organized in trade unions, factory committees, and the soviets. These organizations, jointly, from the very beginning of the revolution brought many benefits to the workers. They instituted the eight-hour working day, fought for higher wages, negotiated for improved conditions of work, discussed the problem of unemployment, insisted on factory inspection, and promoted the cultural and economic well-being of the workers. Many of these innovations were long overdue in Russia. Some, like the demand for workers' control over production and distribution, were too extreme. Under revolutionary conditions the net result of both was the furthering of the existing anarchy and chaos. Most of the benefits they gained were wiped out by galloping inflation. To make matters worse, because of increased labor and other costs and the shortage of raw materials, many industries, too many in fact, closed down during the summer. The resulting unemployment was the last thing revolutionary Russia needed. Jobless and hungry workers resorted to violence in many regions. In some places they even seized plants and made a strenuous effort to run them in order to earn their daily bread, which was becoming scarcer and more expensive with every passing day. The government, with its authority constantly declining, deplored the prevailing anarchy but took no firm action to restore industrial stability. Driven into despair many workers in such large industrial centers as Petrograd, Moscow, and the Donets Basin were in as desperate a plight as the peasants and soldiers. They were ready to listen and to follow any demagogue who would promise a change, and Lenin, the realist, did not allow this opportunity to slip away.

SUGGESTED READINGS

BROWDER, ROBERT P., and ALEXANDER F. KERENSKY, eds. *The Russian Provisional Government. Documents.* 3 vols. Stanford: Stanford University Press, 1961.

CARR, EDWARD H. *The Bolshevik Revolution, 1917–1923.* 3 vols. New York: Macmillan, 1951–53.

CHAMBERLIN, WILLIAM H. *The Russian Revolution, 1917–1921.* 2 vols. New York: Macmillan, 1935.

CHERNOV, VICTOR M. *The Great Russian Revolution.* Translated and abridged by Philip E. Moseley. New Haven: Yale University Press, 1936.

CURTISS, JOHN S. *The Russian Revolutions of 1917.* New York: Van Nostrand, 1957.

DENIKIN, A. I. *The Russian Turmoil.* London: Hutchinson, 1922.

FLORINSKY, MICHAEL T. *The End of the Russian Empire.* New Haven: Yale University Press, 1931

GOLDER, FRANK A. *Documents of Russian History, 1914–1917.* New York: Century, 1927.

GOLOVIN, N. N. *The Russian Army in the World War.* New Haven: Yale University Press, 1931.

GRONSKY, P. P., and ASTROV, N. J. *The War and the Russian Government.* New Haven: Yale University Press, 1929.

KERENSKY, ALEXANDER. *The Catastrophe.* New York: Appleton-Century-Crofts, 1927.

KOHN, S., and MEYENDORFF, BARON A. F. *The Cost of the War to Russia.* New Haven: Yale University Press, 1932.

MILIUKOV, PAUL N. *Russia To-day and To-morrow.* New York: Macmillan, 1922.

MOOREHEAD, ALAN. *The Russian Revolution.* New York: Harper, 1958.

PARES, SIR BERNARD. *The Fall of the Russian Monarchy.* New York: Knopf, 1939.

RADKEY, OLIVER H. *The Elections to the Russian Constituent Assembly of 1917.* Cambridge: Harvard University Press, 1950.

RESHETAR, JOHN S. JR. *The Ukrainian Revolution, 1917–1920.* Princeton: Princeton University Press, 1952.

SUKHANOV, N. N. *The Russian Revolution, 1917: A Personal Record.* Edited, abridged and translated by Joel Carmichael. New York: Oxford University Press, 1955.

TROTSKY, LEON. *The History of the Russian Revolution.* 3 vols. Translated by Max Eastman. New York: Simon & Schuster, 1932.

WARTH, ROBERT D. *The Allies and the Russian Revolution.* Durham, North Carolina: Duke University Press, 1954.

☆ III

THE BOLSHEVIK REVOLUTION

BACKGROUND

The Bolshevik triumph in Russia was a product of three fundamental factors: First, the Bolsheviks' ability to capitalize on the mistakes and ridicule the policy of their opponents; second, their readiness to appropriate popular policies of other parties; and third, their determination to translate to the Russian people in simple terms the meaning of "the Bolshevik program" for Russia. That program as exemplified by the April Theses was clear, concise, and easily understood by the war-weary and land-hungry masses. It called, among other things, for immediate Russian withdrawal from the unpopular and losing war; the overthrow of capitalism which it held responsible for the war; the introduction in Russia of a revolutionary government of workers and of poor peasants; and for nationalization of the economy.

Many Russians doubted the success of this radical program. It was ridiculed by the opposition and its wisdom was questioned even by Lenin's own close associates. Convinced, however, that his ideas echoed the feelings of the excited elements among the masses of the Russian people, Lenin remained stubbornly unmoved. His uncompromising stand and untiring reiteration of points soon began to pay dividends. Not only was he able to bring unity to his own party, but he also attracted additional followers, who, like himself, were in the mood for a complete break with the gloomy past, for total desertion of the uncertain present, and for the creation of a promised land of the future. Between March and July, 1917, according to Bolshevik sources, membership increased greatly, but even with the sizable gain in numbers it represented only a small fraction of the 150 million people of Russia.

Most Bolshevik gains resulted from the lack of realism and the disunity among the opposition. The March Revolution made possible the open appearance of many political parties. The Right was represented by the Octobrists, who wanted to preserve Russia on the basis of the 1905 October Manifesto; the Constitutional Democrats, who wished to introduce in Russia a constitutional form of government along British lines; and a group of Public Men who believed in progress to be achieved not through revolutionary methods but gradually and cautiously. The parties of the Center were heterogeneous and picturesque. Non-Marxist Socialists of Kerensky's vintage believed in a strong, orderly, and democratic Russia; the Right Wing Mensheviks adhered to orthodox interpretation of Marxism; the Right Wing Socialist Revolutionary Party, traditional defender of peasant interests, believed in a loose federal arrangement for Russia; the Left Wing Menshevik group, headed by Trotsky, flirted with various parties until July when it joined the Bolsheviks; and the United Social Democratic Internationalists, led by Martov, pursued the same tactics. Parties on the Left included the Left Wing Socialist Revolutionaries, led by Maria A. Spiridonova (1889-?), Boris D. Kamkov, and Natanson; the Bolsheviks; and the Anarchists. Because self-appointed and, in some instances, irresponsible spokesmen of these and other lesser parties sabotaged all constructive proposals and quarreled with each other and the Provisional Government with suicidal energy, they presented Lenin with limitless opportunities.

The first significant chance to exploit the differences of the opposition came to the Bolsheviks early in May. The opportunity was created by Foreign Minister Miliukov. To clarify Russia's position on war aims, as we noted earlier, Miliukov assured her allies that Russia would live up to her obligations. While well received abroad, this assurance created a grave crisis at home. It led to violent demonstrations, protests, to Miliukov's resignation, and ultimately to the formation of a new coalition government of nine liberals and six socialists. Lenin helped much to deepen the crisis by his violent attack on the Provisional Government in the Bolshevik press. On the one hand he criticized the Provisional Government for alleged subservience to British and French capital and for annexationist policies, while on the other hand he assailed the Executive Committee of the Soviet for its confidence in and support of these policies. "No class-conscious worker, no class-conscious soldier will further support the policy of 'confidence' in the Provisional Government. The policy of confidence is bankrupt. . . . We demand that there be only one power—the Soviet of Workers' and Soldiers' Deputies. The Provisional Government, the government of a handful of capitalists must give way to the Soviets."

Lenin's demand that all power be transferred to the Soviets made him and his party the center of opposition to the Provisional Government and the Central Executive Committee of the Soviet. And although the Bolsheviks were still a long way from exercising a decisive influence on national policies, in their new role they nevertheless began to attract idealists and opportunists, the naive and the realists. With their help, the Bolshevik views, ideas, and demands were spread into factories and into the armed forces. The center of Bolshevik attention was not the rank and file but the leadership of factory and military committees. It was an unspectacular but shrewd and dividend-paying policy. By June many factories and regiments in Petrograd had fallen completely under Bolshevik control. At the meeting of the First All-Russian Congress of Soviets opening in Petrograd on June 16, the Bolsheviks, headed by Lenin, presented a solid block of 105 delegates to 248 Mensheviks and 285 Socialist Revolutionaries. Although the Bolsheviks were badly outnumbered, Lenin declared on June 17, to the astonishment and ridicule of the assembled delegates, that his party was ready and willing to take power from the government. But that was not all. He also presented his listeners with a sample of his policy after seizure of power. It was simple: he would arrest and hang some one hundred of the most important capitalists and denounce all lesser ones, regardless of nationality, as enemies of the people.

While many of the delegates listened to Lenin's ingenious proposal in silence, most of the assembled soldier deputies and street mobs applauded it enthusiastically. Since it was clear that Lenin echoed their feelings, control and planned incitement of the two became now one of the prime objectives, and the Bolsheviks lost no time in undertaking it. To test their strength, within a week after Lenin's speech the Bolsheviks announced that they would hold a mass antigovernment demonstration in Petrograd. When informed of this development, the Congress of Soviets, where the Bolsheviks' influence was insignificant, voiced disapproval and forbade it. Although everything was ready, Lenin, while popular with the street mob, was still uncertain of his strength and, afraid to defy the Congress, called off the demonstration. However, not all the preparations were in vain, for on July 1, the Bolsheviks joined the official demonstration sponsored by the Congress of Soviets, whose chief task was the endorsement of the policies of the coalition government. Bolshevik placards, "All Power to the Soviets," "Down With the Ten Capitalist Ministers," and "Peace, Bread, and Freedom," which had been prohibited a week before, now overwhelmed the official banners. To his astonishment Lenin realized that his following in Petrograd was much stronger than he had ever dreamed.

The unexpected show of strength frightened the opposition and greatly inflated the Bolsheviks' own hopes. The next two weeks were filled with all sorts of rumors of additional Bolshevik demonstrations and even of real trouble. Trouble finally came on July 16. The direct cause of the crisis, as we noted earlier, was the news of the complete collapse of the Galician offensive. The sudden news of the disaster, because of the over-enthusiastic reports of earlier successes created panic in Petrograd. In the midst of rising confusion someone spread a rumor that the government intended to send many "revolutionary" regiments to the rapidly disintegrating front. The apprehensive soldiers immediately issued a call to rebellion and were soon joined by the Kronstadt sailors and unemployed workers. On the following day a mob 500,000 strong, consisting of workers, soldiers, civilians, radicals, and ordinary people, Bolshevik-incited and strongly antigovernment, demanded the resignation of the Provisional Government and transfer of all power to the Soviet.

Lenin and his associates, though they directed some of the demonstrations from their headquarters at the Kshesinski Palace hesitated to act. One of the basic reasons for this hesitation was the lack of unity and unanimity among the party chieftains on the course to be adopted. Some members suggested that the party disassociate itself completely from the demonstration and let events run their course. Others advocated caution for fear that any unsuccessful attempt to seize power would bring complete disaster to the party. There were those who wanted to calm the incited mob without dampening its hot revolutionary temper. There were also some who argued that the party of the revolution should neither abandon the revolution nor desert the masses in time of crisis in order not to discredit itself in the eyes of those very people on whose confidence and support Bolshevik victory depended. This hesitation led to confusion and loss of enthusiasm. Since no one issued orders to execute the well-prepared schemes (such as the seizure of power or the arrest of the Central Executive Committee of the Soviet) and no one gave the incited mob positive direction, the momentum of the upheaval subsided as rapidly as it had snowballed in the first place. On July 19 the uprising was over and the Provisional Government lost no time in re-establishing its authority, by curtailing the activities of the Bolsheviks, by arresting some of their leaders, and by putting others to flight.

The failure of the July uprising was a shattering blow to Bolshevik expectations. Suppressed again after a brief period of free activity, the party resorted to conspiracy. To recover from the blow as well as to work out future strategy, the Sixth Party Congress met half secretly in Petrograd early in August. With Lenin and his chief lieutenants absent (in prison or in hiding), the task of reorganizing the greatly weakened forces fell upon relative anonymities. A bright future was in store for Stalin who, although a member of the Central Committee of the party, was relatively unknown either inside or outside party circles. Because his name did not arouse the anger and hatred inspired by others, Stalin was the logical man to organize the party in Lenin's absence, but under Lenin's guidance and influence.

The basic task of the Sixth Congress was the planning of the party's future. Because of the anti-Bolshevik attitude of the Central Executive Committee of the Petrograd Soviet, the delegates, at Lenin's suggestion, agreed to drop the party's famous slogan, "All Power to the Soviets!" in favor of a well-timed and well-prepared armed seizure of power. This change of tactics helped to create a lively debate, which in many ways previewed a more dramatic struggle in the twenties. Bukharin argued that because of her relative industrial backwardness Russia could not establish a successful socialist society unless there were victorious socialist revolutions in Western Europe. On the other hand, Stalin maintained that regardless of whether or not the West European proletariat was victorious, he saw no reason for Russia not to start building socialism. Paradoxically and ironically, Stalin's reasoning, which later evolved into "Socialism in One Country," was at this stage identical with that of Trotsky, whose group had formally joined the Bolsheviks and who in absentia was elected a member of the Central Committee.

A resolution of the Sixth Congress called upon Bolshevik followers to avoid any action that might lead to an open clash. With the leadership either imprisoned or in hiding and the following on the decrease everywhere, this appeal was in many respects meaningless. The events of late August and early September, however, caused unexpected changes. Thanks to the inability of the Provisional Government to deal effectively with the land problem, peasant disturbances began to reach extreme proportions throughout the country. Because of strikes or the lack of necessary material, many factories were forced to close down thus creating increased labor unrest. The July military debacle accelerated military disintegration and added much to the existing chaos. In other words, Russia found herself in a situation that was desperate and deteriorating rapidly. A strong and resolute government might have been capable of salvaging something. Unfortunately for Russia such was not the case. The Provisional Government was weak and vacillating. Because its existence depended on the good will of ambitious, irresponsible, quarreling, and often self-appointed spokesmen of various political groups, the government could neither enforce orders nor inspire confidence. Since no political party had either the sense or courage to step into the political vacuum which suddenly appeared, the Bolsheviks decided to try a comeback.

PREPARATION FOR SEIZURE OF POWER

The first significant step in the Bolshevik seizure of power was the government's decision before the Kornilov crisis to release several of Lenin's imprisoned associates. The Konilov affair brought a whole chain of consequences. Unable to defeat Kornilov alone, Kerensky and the Petrograd Soviet enlisted Bolshevik help. Some 25,000 Bolshevik-organized workers and Kronstadt sailors—the Red Guards—who had been inactive since the July revolt now received arms from the government to defend the revolution. Kornilov's forces, as we have seen, disintegrated before they reached Petrograd. The Bolsheviks, however, lost no time in exploiting to the utmost their "contribution" to the victory over Kornilov. The Provisional Government tried to deflate their strength by demanding surrender of their arms. The "defenders of the revolution," however, refused to comply. Mistrusted and deserted because there had set in throughout Russia a strong "anti-Kornilovism" sentiment, the government could not enforce its demand.

Meanwhile, because they were "in the first ranks" against Kornilov, the Bolsheviks had little difficulty in compiling an impressive record of "victories" and in gaining a following at the expense of their disunited opponents, the Mensheviks and Socialist Revolutionaries. A few days after the downfall of Kornilov, the Bolsheviks were successful in passing through the Petrograd Soviet, by 279 to 115 votes, a resolution which embodied most of their program. It called for the establishment of a Soviet republic in Russia, granting of land to peasant soviets, workers' control of industry, the annulment of all secret treaties, and immediate conclusion of peace. Shortly thereafter the Bolsheviks demanded, and won by 514 to 414, with 67 abstentions, a motion for election of a new Presidium—the all powerful policy-making body of the Central Executive Committee—of the Petrograd Soviet. When it was organized the Presidium consisted of fourteen Bolsheviks, six Socialist Revolutionaries, and three Mensheviks. Trotsky, who replaced Chkheidze as Chairman, lost no time in announcing the withdrawal of Soviet support from the Provisional Government, and demanded immediate convening of the Second All-Russian Congress of Soviets to which all power was to be transferred. Since other parts of the country followed the capital's shift to the Left, the Bolshevik insurrection against the Provisional Government was the next logical step.

Lenin foresaw this development shortly after the Kornilov crisis. From his hideaway in Finland he sensed the emerging political vacuum and urged his followers to move in by first obtaining a majority in the Petrograd and Moscow Soviets and then by seizing power. The Central Committee of the Party rejected this advice as impractical and dangerous. Lenin followed it up with two letters in which he pleaded with his lieutenants that the majority of the Russian people were with the Bolsheviks, that only the Bolsheviks had the policy to satisfy everyone, that even the international climate was favorable and that, because the time was ripe, the party should make *armed insurrection* in Petrograd and Moscow the order of the day. "History," he urged, "will not forgive us if we do not take power now."

Lenin's urgent and impatient pleas, however, failed to persuade many of his more cautious lieutenants in Russia, including Trotsky, Stalin, Kamenev, and Zinoviev. During a debate on September 28 on the armed insurrection, they all were in full agreement with Lenin's emphasis on the urgency for a revolt, but they disagreed on timing and tactics. Zinoviev and Kamenev felt that the time was not ripe. Trotsky, on the other hand, thought that Lenin's military concept of insurrection, to be undertaken by the party alone, was too narrow. He believed that to be successful the insurrection should have a broad base. Such a base he saw in the Soviets. Since the Second Congress of Soviets was scheduled to meet in Petrograd early in November, Trotsky, in his capacity as Chairman of the Presidium of the Petrograd Soviet, did everything in his power to make the rising coincide with the meeting of the Congress.

While both open and secret preparations to overthrow the Provisional Government went on, the country was sinking ever deeper into defeat and chaos. In October someone spread a rumor that, because of the German threat, the government contemplated transferring the capital from Petrograd to Moscow. The Bolshevik leadership was dismayed at such a prospect. If allowed to come about, such a move would upset their plans for the insurrection. They accordingly interpreted it as a "counter revolutionary" measure and called upon all the Leftist parties to "defend the capital of the revolution." The response was almost unanimous. The Petrograd Soviet then assumed full control of troop movements in and around the capital, and on October 26 the Executive Committee of the Petrograd Soviet appointed a Military Revolutionary Committee. Outwardly the purpose of that body was the defense of the capital. In reality, however, it was the General Staff of the Bolshevik Revolution. Trotsky, as President of the Petrograd Soviet, became the chairman of the Military Revolutionary Committee, and in that capacity he soon decreed that in military matters no order was to be executed in or around Petrograd without his or his Bolshevik assistants' countersignatures. As the real master of the garrison, Trotsky thus held in his hands all the vital threads of the insurrection which he manipulated in a masterly manner.

While Trotsky was successfully giving the conspiracy legal and moral

Lenin speaking to a crowd. Trotsky is at the right, facing the camera.

authority and a defensive appearance, Lenin tried to overcome the opposition within the party to the idea of insurrection. It was not an easy task, for his followers, although considered by many as men of action, shared their adversaries' passion for endless, hair-splitting talk. With Lenin in hiding they felt less compelled to follow his impatient suggestions, some of which they even vetoed. And though he raged and even threatened to resign from the party, he could do little. He was in hiding in Finland; they were in Petrograd and free. Early in October, to be closer to the scene of action, Lenin moved from Helsinki to Vyborg. On October 21, he secretly returned to Petrograd and two days later he attended the historic secret meeting of the Central Committee of the Party which decided in favor of insurrection.

During a ten-hour-long debate, two of Lenin's long-time associates, Kamenev and Zinoviev, afraid that an armed uprising would end in total failure, tried to persuade the Central Committee to postpone the coup d'état. They disapproved of immediate armed insurrection on two grounds: (1) they thought that Lenin underestimated the government's forces and overestimated his own; and (2) they believed that the Russian revolution should be timed to coincide with a proletarian revolution in Western Europe which they thought was imminent and indispensable to the success of the Russian revolution. Lenin brushed aside these arguments, which were later proven to be incorrect, and hammered home his own points. The time for an armed uprising was ripe, he argued, because the Bolsheviks had control of the leading soviets, because Bolshevik slogans were popular with the masses, and because the agrarian unrest had developed full momentum. Lenin's arguments won. Of the twelve members present and voting, only Kamenev and Zinoviev cast negative votes on the immediate armed uprising which was proposed for November 2, the day the Second All-Russian Congress of Soviets was to convene. Political direction of the revolution was placed in the hands of the Political Bureau (Politburo). Lenin, Trotsky, Stalin, Gregory Y. Sokolnikov (1888–?), Andrei Bubnov (1883–?), Kamenev, and Zinoviev were selected the first members of this body which subsequently became all-powerful.

The fateful decision in favor of armed insurrection was followed by vacillation as well as by intensive preparation. Since party discipline was loose, many rank-and-file members opposed the decision of the Central Committee, on the same grounds as Kamenev and Zinoviev. On October 29 the Central Committee held another meeting during which the previous decision in favor of the uprising was reaffirmed. Thereupon Kamenev resigned from the Central Committee and two days later, in Maxim Gorky's paper, *Novaia Zhizn* (New Life), he and Zinoviev made public the open secret; i.e., that the Bolsheviks were preparing for an armed uprising on the eve of the opening of the Second All-Russian Congress of Soviets.

The news of the impending Bolshevik insurrection gave rise to all kinds of rumors and speculations, threats and counterthreats, charges and denials. Lenin branded his two longtime but indiscreet lieutenants "traitors to the revolution" and demanded their expulsion from the party. Asked at a meeting of the Petrograd Soviet to comment on rumors of the impending uprising, Trotsky denied the existence of any preparations. To dampen hot tempers that suddenly flared, the non-Bolshevik Executive Committee of the All-Russian Congress of Soviets postponed the meeting of the Congress from November 2 to 7, halted all forms of demonstrations, and demanded that no arms be issued to anyone without its consent. The Bolsheviks, and especially Trotsky, welcomed the postponement as it gave them an additional week to prepare. To make sure that the garrison obeyed his orders, Trotsky appointed trusted commissars to each detachment in and around Petrograd, and officers failing to obey the commissars' orders were either removed or arrested. On November 5, Bolshevik-controlled regiments were ordered to occupy strategic points in the capital. The showdown had come.

The Provisional Government, except for issuing self-assuring statements about its own strength, did nothing to frustrate the impending armed uprising until the evening of November 5, when a cabinet meeting declared a state of emergency. All military units within the city were placed under the command of Colonel Polkovnikov, the military commander of the Petrograd garrison. Trotsky's Military Revolutionary Committee was declared illegal, and an order was issued for his arrest as well as that of other Bolshevik leaders who were free on bail. Bolshevik newspapers were ordered closed, and to enforce these measures loyal troops were ordered in from outside the capital.

The government's showdown with the Bolsheviks came too late. After repeated postponements, vacillation, indecision, and irresolution, the Provisional Government had lost all respect and authority. Only a handful of loyal troops expressed willingness to come to its rescue. The sailors of the cruiser *Aurora*, anchored in the Neva River, refused to obey the order to put out to sea and placed themselves at Trotsky's disposal. Challenged by the government, the Military Revolutionary Committee decided to move fast. It issued arms to its sympathizers throughout the city and ordered its forces to reoccupy the offices of Bolshevik papers which earlier had been taken by government troops. Bolshevik units also seized control of bridges and main thoroughfares in the capital. Railway stations, the State Bank, the central post office and all other key points were occupied without any opposition during the night of November 6–7. Deserted by everyone, Kerensky escaped from the capital to seek in vain for support outside. No attempt was made to stop him as he drove in an open car through the streets of a Petrograd controlled by Bolshevik soldiers. At 10:00 A.M. on November 7, the Revolutionary Military Committee announced the overthrow of the Provisional Government. The people of Russia were assured of "the immediate proposal of a democratic peace, the abolition of landed proprietorship, workers' control over production, and the creation of a Soviet Government." During the night of November 7, after a brief exchange of fire, Bolshevik forces occupied the Winter Palace—the seat of the Provisional Government. Except for two who escaped, all remaining ministers of the Provisional Government were arrested and were sent to the Fortress of Peter and Paul to join their tsarist counterparts. The days of the Provisional Government were over; the Soviet period of Russian history had begun. The transition, all-important not only in Russian but in world history, was responsible for some twenty dead and a few wounded.

THE FIRST PHASE OF THE REMAKING OF RUSSIA

The ease and speed with which the Bolsheviks seized power in Petrograd surprised everyone. Even Lenin admitted that to pass so suddenly from persecution and underground living to a position of power made him slightly dizzy. He lost no time, however, in consolidating his authority. On the same day that the mild and bloodless coup d'état was executed, the postponed meeting of the Second All-Russian Congress of Soviets took place. Out of some 650 delegates, about whose election or even party affiliation no reliable information is available, 390 were registered as Bolsheviks, 80 as Mensheviks, and some 150 as Socialist Revolutionaries. The opening session of the Congress was stormy, and factional strife among the non-Bolshevik delegates prevented them from forming a solid opposition to the Bolshevik armed seizure of power. The Bolsheviks outmaneuvered their disunited and quarreling opponents in the election of the Presidium of the Second All-Russian Congress of Soviets. The new body had fourteen Bolsheviks, seven Left Socialist Revolutionaries, four Mensheviks (who refused however to assume their positions), and one representative from the Ukraine. Some members of the opposition, in protest against Bolshevik machinations and the alleged disrespect for proper procedures, withdrew from the Congress. This was a fatal and foolish move because it left the Bolsheviks, who stood for the "proletariat," and their temporary allies, the Left Socialist Revolutionaries, who posed as the sole representatives of the peasantry, in full control of the Congress, thereby simplifying the Bolshevik task.

The Second Congress of Soviets, under Lenin's guidance, performed three functions. It approved the decree on peace, it adopted a decree on land, and it elected the first Soviet government. Lenin, whose victorious appearance at the Congress stirred much excitement, was the principal speaker on behalf of all three proposals. The decree on peace, which was passed unanimously, called upon all belligerents to start immediate negotiations for a just and democratic peace without annexations and indemnities. On its part, the Congress expressed willingness to consider any other peace proposals, provided they be made speedily and be clear and free of "all ambiguity and secrecy." The decree announced Russian determination to abolish secret diplomacy, publish at once all secret treaties entered into by previous regimes, and annul all agreements which aimed at "securing advantages and privileges for the Russian landlords and capitalists." The Congress appealed at once to all belligerents to conclude immediately an armistice for a period of not less than three months. It also made a particular appeal to "the class conscious workers" of England, France, and Germany to support Soviet Russia's peace move.

The land decree consisted of two parts. The first abolished landed proprietorship without compensation. All landed estates, monastery and church lands, with all their livestock, buildings, and implements, were ordered taken over by local land committees and soviets, pending the meeting of the Constituent Assembly. The instruction on the land, which formed the second part of the decree, abolished forever the right of private property in land. Henceforth land could neither be purchased, sold, leased, mortgaged, nor otherwise alienated. All land was to become the property of the whole people and be used by those who worked on it.

All mineral wealth was to "be reserved for the exclusive use of the state." Lands with highly developed forms of cultivation were not to be divided, but were to be transformed into model farms to be cultivated either by the state or by the communes. The employment of hired labor was prohibited. The land was to be subject to periodic reapportionment "in accordance with the growth of population and the increase in productiveness and efficiency of agriculture."

The Congress entrusted execution of the decrees on land and peace to the Council of People's Commissars, known by its Russian abbreviation SOVNARKOM. Lenin became chairman of the Council. Other members included: Interior, Aleksei I. Rykov (1881–1938); Agriculture, Vladimir P. Miliutin (1884–?); Labor, A. G. Shliapnikov (1884–?); Military and Naval Affairs, Vladimir A. Antonov-Ovseenko (1884–1938), Nikolai V. Krylenko (1885–1938), and Pavel E. Dybenko (1889–1938); Trade and Industry, Viktor P. Nogin (1878–1924); Public Instruction, Lunacharsky; Finance, Ivan I. Skvortsov-Stepanov (1870–1928); Foreign Affairs, Trotsky; Justice, G. I. Lomov-Oppokov; Food Supply, I. A. Teodorovich; Post and Telegraph, N. P. Glebov-Avilov; and Nationalities, Stalin. Before its adjournment on November 10, the Congress elected the All-Russian Central Executive Committee of 101 members (62 Bolsheviks and 39 Left Socialist Revolutionaries) and approved November 25 as the election date for the Constituent Assembly.

Passing of resolutions was one thing; forcing compliance with them was another. The Bolsheviks had won only in Petrograd. Their authority did not extend outside the capital. Since Russia had disintegrated following the March revolution into countless autonomous units, each region, each province, each district, each city, each village, and each local soviet had to be won over separately. This was not an easy task because the Bolsheviks commanded no real popularity. The speed of extension of their control varied, therefore, from area to area. In some places it was bloodless and easy, and in others bloody and difficult. The success or setback depended in large measure on the Bolshevik ability to win over or infiltrate the leadership of the local soviet. Moscow was brought under Bolshevik control by November 15, but only after heavy fighting. Fighting also took place in Kazan, Kharkov, Kiev, Smolensk, Saratov, Voronezh, and in many other cities and towns. In November the Bolsheviks seized control in fifteen main provincial towns. In December an additional thirteen were added, and January, 1918, saw fifteen more towns brought under Bolshevik control.

Next to the cities, the Bolsheviks centered their attention on winning over the army—or whatever remained of it—in order to prevent it from becoming an organized opposition force. This proved a relatively easy task because the Russian army, following the introduction of committees after the March revolution, had ceased to exist as an organized fighting unit. Following the Kornilov affair late in the summer of 1917, the discipline and morale of the army sank even deeper. The bulk of the enlisted personnel, demoralized and sullen, showed no desire to support the hopeless cause of the Provisional Government and simply went home. Those who remained, and especially those around Petrograd, fell under the influence of the Bolsheviks. Under these conditions, various army commanders (those who survived and adjusted themselves to the new circumstances) threw in their lot with the new regime. General Nicholas N. Dukhonin (1876–1917), the Commander-in-Chief, was an exception. At first he cooperated with the Bolsheviks. When on November 20, 1917, he was ordered to inaugurate peace talks with the German High Command, Dukhonin, pressed by the Allies, refused to comply. For his insubordination he was dismissed and replaced by Ensign Krylenko, whose special task force arrived at the army headquarters in Mogilev on December 3. Dukhonin was immediately arrested and, although Krylenko spoke out strongly against lynching, a mob of soldiers, sailors, and peasants, aroused by vengeful orators, dragged Dukhonin out on the railroad platform and beat him to death. One counterrevolution by a general was over. Another was still a thing to come.

The extension of Bolshevik influence over the army and major Russian cities was greatly helped by their control of transportation and communication lines, especially railroads. Russian railroad workers, even before the revolution, were well organized and among the best paid. Following the downfall of the monarchy, railroad workers on several occasions had come to the rescue of the revolution. They developed among themselves very strong soviet institutions as well as a feeling of solidarity with other workers. For that reason, perhaps, the Bolsheviks concentrated their agitation among railroad workers, especially during and after the Kornilov affair. The dividends of this policy were soon evident. By the end of 1917, the Bolsheviks controlled many key railroad lines around Moscow, Kiev, and Petrograd. By 1918, as employees of the Trans-Siberian Railroad, Bolshevik agitators had moved across the great Siberian stretches, even before that area fell under complete Bolshevik control. Their domination of railroad lines during the subsequent Civil War was one of the most decisive factors contributing to the Bolshevik victory.

Meanwhile the new regime of inexperienced and doctrinaire, but lucky, individuals began to introduce far-reaching cultural, social, economic, and political changes in Russia. On November 9, all newspapers which, in the view of the new regime, incited the people to open resistance or disobedience or spread confusion by distortion of facts, were ordered closed. The decree promised that these repressive measures were only temporary and would become inoperative "as soon as the new regime takes firm foot." A decree of November 23 abolished all classes, class distinctions, privileges, organizations, institutions, ranks, and civil grades.

Every Russian became a citizen of the republic. Class institutions also lost all their properties. On November 27 a decree on workers' control conferred upon workers' committees in each factory and shop the right "to supervise production, fix the minimum of output, and determine the cost of production." Business secrecy was declared illegal and the committees were given the right to examine all books and business correspondence. On December 7 all existing legal institutions in Russia (district courts, courts of appeal, the Senate, commercial courts, justices of the peace, magistrates, and the procurator's office) were abolished. Local judges henceforth were to be elected on the basis of direct democratic vote and were to be guided in their decisions by "revolutionary conscience and revolutionary conception of right." On December 11 the members of the Cadet party were declared counterrevolutionaries and made "liable to arrest and trial by revolutionary tribunals." On December 14 the Supreme Economic Council, which for over a decade was to be the central organ for the regulation of the economic life of the Soviet state, was established. On December 27 all banks were declared a state monopoly. All existing private joint stock banks and banking offices, with all their assets and liabilities, were merged into the State Bank. Gold, in coin and in bars, deposited in the bank vaults was ordered confiscated and transferred to the state's general gold fund. On December 20, to suppress any evidence of opposition, the government established "the all-Russian Commission for Suppression of Counter-Revolution, Sabotage, and Speculation," the first secret political police, popularly known as the CHEKA. A decree of December 29 abolished all titles and ranks in the army and annulled all preferences and insignia. The Russian army was to consist of "free and equal-to-one-another citizens." After December 31, church marriage was declared a private affair and only civil marriage was legally binding. Marriage procedures were greatly modified and liberalized, as was divorce. Marriage was annulled by the petition of both parties, or even one of them. Illegitimate children were given the same rights and were held to the same obligations as legitimate. A decree of January 5, 1918, abolished the old institutions of local government. Henceforth local affairs were to be administered by a network of soviets arranged in a hierarchal order. Each soviet was declared to be autonomous, but each lower soviet was to conform with the directions of the soviets on higher levels. The net result of these and other drastic measures was the destruction of many institutions of the old regime and hence further deepening of economic, administrative, cultural, and political chaos in Russia. While many of these measures were eventually amended or discarded, many had come to stay.

These measures generated little enthusiasm for the new regime. With every day the food situation—the spark that had ignited the revolution—deteriorated and the approaching winter promised no relief. By early

December, 1917, bread rations had diminished to one-eighth of a pound per day, forcing the people as well as the government to varied measures of procurement. The countryside was invaded by armed gangs and thousands of individuals to forage or barter goods, jewels, and the like for grain and potatoes. Next to food the fuel crisis became most acute, and there was no relief in sight, as the fuel-producing regions were not under Bolshevik control. In spite of all-out austerity efforts, factories were closed, streetcar service was sharply curtailed, and theaters and restaurants were deprived of light. The new regime helped by some of its actions to create a situation which bred intrigue, conspiracy, extortion, and in general demoralization and dissatisfaction. It was in such an atmosphere that the long-postponed Constituent Assembly met in the middle of January, 1918.

THE THREE DILEMMAS: THE CONSTITUENT ASSEMBLY,
THE NATIONALITY PROBLEM, AND PEACE

The Constituent Assembly was one of the most difficult dilemmas for the new regime. Before they came to power the Bolsheviks, like all the revolutionary and liberal parties, were pledged to support the Constituent Assembly, and in fact one of their chief slogans had been: "Speedy convocation of the Constituent Assembly." Their persistent demand was matched only by the Provisional Government's repeated postponement. The Provisional Government had finally set November 25 as the election date, but it did not live to see it come to pass. The Bolsheviks did not interfere with the elections, which, but for a few districts, were held as scheduled, but they were not pleased with the outcome. Of some 41,700,000 votes, Socialist Revolutionaries (Russian and Ukrainian) polled 17,100,000 votes; Bolsheviks 9,800,000; Cadets 2,000,000; and Mensheviks 1,360,000. When the Constituent Assembly met, out of 703 deputies, 380 were regular Socialist Revolutionaries, 39 Left Socialist Revolutionaries, 168 Bolsheviks, 18 Mensheviks, 17 Cadets, 4 Popular Socialists, and 77 minority representatives. The nation had spoken its mind, but Lenin was determined to hold his power.

Lenin neutralized the Constituent Assembly in several ways. Since the elections had been held under the system of proportional representation (i.e., ballots were cast not for individuals but for party lists drawn prior to the Bolshevik seizure of power) Lenin empowered the soviets to recall the delegates to the Constituent Assembly. When this procedure proved to be not overly effective, many leaders of the opposition were arrested by the government, as were members of the election commission, and the commission itself was ordered disbanded. Though official statements denied rumors of the impending dissolution of the Constituent

Assembly, that action appeared imminent unless of course the Assembly approved "Soviet power, Soviet revolution, and its policies in questions of peace, land, and workers' control."

The Constituent Assembly met in a tense atmosphere on January 18, 1918, in the Taurida Palace. In addition to deputies, some of whom were wanted by Bolshevik authorities, the Palace was packed with armed soldiers and sailors. Because rumors had spread that the Assembly might be besieged, many deputies provided themselves with food and candles. Chernov, a Socialist Revolutionary, was elected the Assembly's president by a vote of 244 to 151. After the customary speeches, the Assembly rejected 237 to 138 the Bolshevik-sponsored "Declaration of the Rights of the Toiling and Exploited People," which was nothing but a summary of legislative changes introduced in Russia up to that time. The setback was only temporary. After a recess, Bolshevik deputies announced their departure from the Assembly. They were followed by Left Socialist Revolutionaries. The remaining deputies were left at the mercy of the pro-Bolshevik Lettish guards and sailors. Though interfered with, this Assembly rejected the Bolshevik dictatorship and approved four important resolutions: it approved an armistice with the Germans; it passed a land decree; it declared Russia a republic; and it called for the convocation of an international socialist conference. At five o'clock on the morning of January 19, 1918, under pressure from the sailors, the assembly adjourned for twelve hours. It never reconvened, for on the same day it was dissolved by the Central Executive Committee on Lenin's orders.

The dissolution of the Constituent Assembly, or as Lenin put it, "a complete and frank liquidation of the idea of democracy by the idea of dictatorship," marked a significant victory for the Bolsheviks for two reasons. First, the resistance-free action pointed out that now, as earlier, personnel changes in Petrograd were made by a handful of self-appointed leaders. The bulk of the population—ignorant of democratic methods and tradition, confused by the multiplicity of political parties and the complicated system of proportional representation, bewildered by promises, charges and countercharges, and above all tired of war—cared little about political strife and was only anxious to be left alone in order to digest the fruits of the revolution. Secondly, the dissolution of the Constituent Assembly removed for the new regime, without undue strain, a serious technical obstacle in the drive to consolidate its power. By the end of January, 1918, it became evident that there was no organized force in Central Russia capable of challenging the Bolshevik power. The new regime, however, had other great problems to settle. One of the most difficult was the nationality problem.

The nationality problem placed the new regime in the most embarrassing dilemma thus far. In theory, Lenin and some of his close associates, to deepen the crisis, had conceded as early as 1903 that minorities of the Russian Empire had the right to self-determination, including separation. Unconditional recognition of the struggle for freedom of self-determination, Lenin argued, however, did not at all obligate the Bolsheviks "to support every demand for national self-determination." As far as they were concerned the fundamental task centered not in the realization of self-determination of nations or peoples, but of the proletariat of every nationality. Accordingly, they agreed to support the creation of a new state only in exceptional cases. "We would be very poor revolutionaries," wrote Lenin in 1913, "if, in a great liberating war of the proletariat for socialism, we were unable to utilize *every* national movement against *separate* negative forms of imperialism in order to sharpen and broaden the crisis." On another occasion he frankly stated that when "we demand freedom of separation for the Mongols, the Persians, the Egyptians, etc., —and for *all* subjugated and unequal nations without exceptions, it is not that *we favor their separation* but *only* that we stand for a *free, willing* unity and merger, and not for a forceful one." Thanks to this dialectic, it became possible to read into Lenin's words at once his support for and opposition to self-determination. The Seventh Party Conference of April, 1917, in spite of some opposition, endorsed this view. Thereafter, to embarrass the Provisional Government in its inability and unwillingness to solve the nationality problem, and in order to attract non-Russians to their ranks, the Bolsheviks posed as the staunchest supporters of the idea of national self-determination. This policy reached a climax on November 15, 1917, i.e., a week after the Bolshevik coup d'état, in "The Declaration of the Rights of the Peoples of Russia." This solemn document proclaimed (1) the equality and sovereignty of the peoples of Russia; (2) the right of the peoples of Russia to free self-determination, even to the point of separation and formation of independent states; (3) the free development of national minorities and ethnic groups inhabiting the territory of Russia; and (4) the abolition of any and all national privileges and disabilities. The Bolshevik advent to power, in other words, formalized Russia's territorial disintegration.

The Ukraine and Finland were the first countries to experience Bolshevik dialectical interpretation of the right of self-determination. On November 19, 1917, or shortly after the Bolshevik seizure of power, the Ukrainian *Rada* proclaimed the establishment of a Ukrainian People's Republic. This change, however, did not imply separation from the Russian republic. It was rather a first step towards making Russia a federation of free and equal peoples. Pending the convocation of the Ukrainian Constituent Assembly set for January 9, 1918, the *Rada* assumed full authority over the territory considered ethnically Ukrainian. In this capacity it abolished without compensation the ownership of landed estates; introduced an eight-hour working day; pledged itself to the speedy conclusion of peace; abolished the death penalty; reaffirmed freedom of speech, press, religion, assembly, unions, strikes, and other liberties gained by the March revolution.

The Bolsheviks answered the *Rada*'s challenge by calling a Congress of Workers', Soldiers', and Peasants' Deputies for December 15, 1917, in Kiev. However, when they were able to control only from sixty to eighty delegates out of more than 2,000, the Bolshevik delegation accused the Congress of misrepresentation of "the will of the masses" and bolted to Kharkov where it declared itself the legitimate and the only power in the Ukraine. On December 24, 1917, the Ukraine was proclaimed a Soviet Socialist Republic (UkSSR). *Pravda* extended greetings to the newly-created republic two days before its formal inception. The Council of Peoples Commissars extended official recognition to the UkSSR on December 29, 1917, and promised the "brotherly republic complete and all possible support in its struggle" with the *Rada*.

One form of this aid was an ultimatum which had been presented to the *Rada* on December 16. This document recognized the Ukrainian right to full separation from Russia unconditionally and without limitations, but charged the *Rada* with perpetrating unprecedented treason to the revolution by its alleged persecution of Ukrainian soviets, by its alleged support of "counterrevolutionary forces" and of various Tsarist generals, and by its refusal to allow Bolshevik troops to cross Ukrainian territory. The *Rada* rejected Bolshevik charges, arguing that it was impossible "to recognize simultaneously the right of the people to self-determination, including separation, and at the same time to infringe roughly on that right by imposing on the people in question a certain type of government." Lenin replied to this argument with Bolshevik invasion of the Ukraine. Ukrainian resistance collapsed and Bolshevik forces occupied a number of Ukrainian cities, including Kiev. On January 22, 1918, a few days before Kiev fell, the *Rada* proclaimed a Ukrainian People's Republic as an independent sovereign state, thereby severing completely the ties with Russia.

Bolshevik practical application of self-determination for Finland resembled the pattern pursued in the Ukraine. Following the Bolshevik coup d'état, the Finnish Diet declared itself vested with the supreme power in Finland. With no objections being raised, the Diet on December 5 went a step further and formally proclaimed Finland an independent state with Per Svinhufvud as Premier. On December 31, 1917, Svinhufvud secured from the Soviet government the first formal recognition of Finland. At the same time, however, to defend "the revolutionary democracy" in Finland there were organized Red Guards as the first step to the dictatorship of the proletariat. Assisted by Russian Bolsheviks these elements began to challenge the non-socialist Finnish government of Svinhufvud. Its overthrow on January 28, 1918, plunged Finland into civil war. With Bolshevik blessing, a Finnish Socialist Workers' Republic was

proclaimed in the south of Finland. This was followed by wholesale introduction of the Bolshevik program and methods, culminating on March 1,
1918, in a treaty of "friendship and brotherhood" with Soviet Russia. The
north of Finland fell under control of Finnish anti-Bolshevik forces led by
General Gustav C. Mannerheim. By the middle of February, 1918, Mannerheim's forces cleared north and central Finland of Bolsheviks. The
clearing process was accelerated after Mannerheim was reinforced by a
German contingent under General von der Goltz. By early May, 1918, all
of Finland was cleared of Red Guards, the Red regime collapsed, its
leaders fled to Soviet Russia, and the Finnish civil war as well as the
Finnish-Russian union of 1809 came to an abrupt end.

Developments in Estonia followed largely the same pattern. On November 28, 1917, the Estonian National Council proclaimed the political
independence of Estonia. In January, 1918, however, the Bolsheviks challenged this act, and plunged the country into a bitter civil war which
ended with German occupation. Events in Latvia and Lithuania differed
slightly. The Latvian National Council assumed authority in Latvia on
November 16, 1917, while Lithuania declared its independence from Russia on December 11, 1917. Because of strong German interests in the
Baltic region, between 1915 and 1917 both states were occupied by German forces. The question of Poland offered the least difficulty (for both
the Provisional Government and the Bolsheviks) since Polish-inhabited
areas were already occupied by the Germans and the Austrians. Because
of this situation, independence of Poland was strongly advocated by the
Bolsheviks. With the Bolshevik seizure of power, centrifugal forces in the
Caucasus increased their demands for separation. At first, on April 22,
1918, a Trans-Caucasion Federal Republic was proclaimed, but age-old
rivalry among the three nations involved (Armenia, Azerbaidzhan, and
Georgia) disrupted the federation. Georgia established its independence
on May 22, 1918; Armenia on May 26, 1918; and Azerbaidzhan on May
28, 1918. Shortly thereafter all three states entered into relations with the
Germans and subsequently were drawn into the whirlpool of bitter civil
war.

The Bolsheviks discovered that next to the nationality problem, peace
was the most difficult issue to resolve. The problem of bringing about the
long promised peace acquired new meaning for the Bolsheviks after their
seizure of power, when it became apparent that without peace they could
not hope to reorganize Russia and the rest of the world according to the
projections of Marx and Lenin. Peace therefore became the prime objective of the new regime, and to achieve it several approaches were ex-
plored. On November 8, 1917, as noted earlier, the Bolshevik-controlled
Second All-Russian Congress of Soviets unanimously approved the Decree on Peace calling for an immediate armistice based on the principle of

self-determination and repudiation of the idea of annexations and indemnities. Class conscious workers everywhere were asked to support these efforts. Because no one expected the Bolsheviks to remain in power any appreciable length of time, these peace efforts generated little enthusiasm. Trotsky, now as People's Commissar for Foreign Affairs, on November 21 notified the Ambassadors of the Allied Powers (and through the ambassadors of neutral countries he also informed the governments of the Central Powers) to regard the Decree on Peace "as a formal offer for an immediate armistice on all fronts and the immediate initiation of peace negotiations." To discredit as well as to force the major powers into negotiations, the Soviet government published secret agreements concluded between the tsarist government and the Western Powers.

Meanwhile, on November 20, 1917, the Soviet government ordered army headquarters to propose to the Central Powers unilaterally and without delay the end of hostilities. Because General Dukhonin, under Allied pressure, refused to carry out this order he was relieved of his command and shortly thereafter was lynched. The new Commander-in-Chief, Krylenko, directed the army units to make their own armistice agreements with the enemy on a local basis. The first such agreement was concluded on November 27. By December 1, 1917, military operations had been halted all along the Eastern Front, and a week later a thirty days' armistice was signed between Germany and Soviet Russia. On December 22, 1917, the first peace congress of World War I was under way at Brest-Litovsk, an ancient town on the Bug River, then the headquarters of the German Eastern Front.

The German delegation was led by Foreign Minister Baron Richard von Kühlman and General Max Hoffmann. Austria-Hungary was represented by its Foreign Minister, Count Ottokar von Czernin. Prime Minister V. Radoslavov of Bulgaria represented his country. The Turkish delegation was led by Grand Vizier Talaat Pasha. The Soviet delegation was at first headed by an old Bolshevik, Adolf A. Joffe (1883-1927), but on January 9, 1918, he was replaced by Trotsky. Other members of the Soviet delegation included a worker, a sailor, and a peasant, who were brought to the conference table to dramatize the change taking place in Russia.

In spite of endless talk the negotiators made no progress in their discussions. The German delegation tried to use the peace talks as a cover for deployment of troops to the Western Front. The Bolshevik delegation on the other hand used peace talks as a means of spreading revolutionary doctrine. The main point of disagreement centered on the question of self-determination. The Bolsheviks understood the principle of self-determination (a means of destroying multinational and colonial powers) as being the right of the proletariat of a given nation, and only that part of the proletariat friendly to the Bolshevik regime, to emerge victorious and represent the people. The Germans on the other hand held that any people, and above all any group of people friendly to Germany, had the right to self-determination. The Ukraine had the unfortunate distinction of being caught between these two extreme interpretations.

The Ukrainians, as noted earlier, were not overly enthusiastic at the Bolshevik triumph and above all at the latter's attempt to speak on behalf of all the peoples of the former tsarist empire. On December 22, 1917, the *Rada* government expressed its willingness to participate in the peace conference at Brest-Litovsk on the basis of no annexations and no indemnities without the direct consent of the peoples concerned. On January 7, 1918, with little preparation, the Ukrainian delegation arrived at Brest-Litovsk. Its presence there from the very beginning was controversial and perplexing. For the Austrians, whose internal and external difficulties demanded immediate peace with a minimum loss of territory, the Ukrainians were an annoyance. Ukrainian demands for Galicia, Bukovina, and the Kholm region outraged the Austrians. Later, however, the Austrians modified their attitude in return for the promise of much-needed Ukrainian grain. Trotsky at first recognized the Ukrainians, but he soon reversed himself upon realizing the danger of a separate treaty between the Ukraine and the Central Powers. He recognized that such a move might not only force him to sign a separate treaty too, but also that it would put the Central Powers in a position to obtain food and other vital necessities and thus to emasculate the danger of the Allied blockade.

Trotsky's fear of a separate treaty between the Ukraine and the Central Powers and his employment of various delaying tactics did not escape the notice of the Germans. From the very beginning, General Hoffmann, who received the Ukrainians "with pleasure," encouraged them to talk about their plans and hopes, gained their confidence and their respect, and entered into negotiations with them. On February 9, 1918, these talks, which Trotsky was unable to control and which seriously menaced his position, culminated in a separate treaty. In return for recognition and support, the Ukrainians pledged to place their surplus of foodstuffs and agricultural products (estimated to be some 1,000,000 tons) at the disposal of the Central Powers.

Since negotiations with the Ukrainians had proceeded smoothly, the Germans felt no need to negotiate with Trotsky. As early as January 18, Hoffmann suggested to Trotsky future boundaries for Soviet Russia. This suggestion evoked a lively debate within the Bolshevik party. Many party members, headed by Bukharin, demanded that the party suspend negotiations with the Central Powers and reply with a revolutionary war. Lenin, aware of the Soviet weakness and therefore desirous of gaining a "breathing spell" for the new regime until victorious revolutions swept all of

Europe, favored acceptance of the German-suggested boundaries. Trotsky advanced his celebrated formula of "No War, No Peace." On January 21, 1918, a party conference in Petrograd considered the matter and voted 32 for Bukharin's idea, 15 for Lenin's, and 16 for Trotsky's. On January 24, however, the party's Central Committee approved Trotsky's proposal by a vote of nine to seven. On February 10, 1918, Trotsky announced his formula to the Germans and dramatically departed from Brest-Litovsk.

The German High Command denounced the armistice on February 16. Two days later, in the name of "humanity" but for the sake of security, conquest, and acquisition of food supplies which the Ukrainians had promised them, the Germans resumed military operations all along the Eastern Front, in order to prevent the Bolsheviks from gaining control there. The Germans encountered no resistance in occupying their sphere of influence, which they then held until the end of the war. The question of acceptance or rejection by the Bolsheviks of German demands now emerged again. On February 18, after considerable maneuvering, Lenin's urge to accept German terms won by seven to four votes (with four abstentions) in the Central Committee. A message to this effect was sent immediately to Berlin. When the German reply arrived on February 23, its content was harsher than their earlier demands. Lenin insisted however that, harsh or not, there was no other alternative and German demands must be accepted. His will prevailed. The final vote in the Central Executive Committee of the Soviet was 116 to 85 with 26 abstentions. On March 3, 1918, Sokolnikov, who had replaced Trotsky as head of the Soviet delegation, signed the treaty at Brest-Litovsk.

The Treaty of Brest-Litovsk—a complicated document—has been viewed by some scholars as one of the most unfortunate peace treaties in history. By its terms Germany and Soviet Russia extended to each other diplomatic recognition, agreed to exchange war prisoners, pledged to discontinue hostile propaganda against each other, and agreed to develop economic relations. The Soviet government also agreed to recognize that Georgia, the Ukraine, and Finland were independent but under German influence. Poland, Lithuania, Latvia, and Estonia fell under more direct German control. The Bolsheviks evacuated the Aaland Islands in the Baltic; the Turks occupied Kars, Ardahan, and Batum; and the Rumanians were allowed to occupy Bessarabia. The total area thus affected consisted of some 1,300,000 sq. miles, and about 62,000,000 people. Before the revolution this area contained some 32 per cent of Russia's arable lands, 26 per cent of her railroads, 33 per cent of her factories, and 75 per cent of her coal and iron mines. Judged by sheer numbers it was a heavy loss. Yet it ought to be remembered that the authority of the Bolshevik regime did not extend over the areas it agreed to acknowledge as being under German influence.

Area of German influence

NORWAY

SWEDEN

Stockholm

Baltic Sea

FINLAND

Murmansk

Archangel

Petrograd

ESTONIA

LATVIA (Livonia)

(Courland)

Riga

LITHUANIA

Volga

MOSCOW

Smolensk

RUSSIA

Danzig

GERMANY

Berlin

Vistula

Warsaw

Brest-Litovsk

POLAND

Cracow

Kiev

Dnieper

Kharkov

Donets

Don

UKRAINE

Prague

Lvov

Vienna

Budapest

AUSTRIA-HUNGARY

Odessa

CRIMEA

Danube

RUMANIA

Belgrade

Bucharest

Black Sea

SERBIA

BULGARIA

Montenegro

Sofia

ITALY

ALBANIA

TURKEY

GREECE

0   100   300
MILES

**TERRITORIAL CHANGES IN
EASTERN EUROPE
MADE BY THE
TREATY OF BREST-LITOVSK, March 1918**

THE SECOND PHASE OF THE REMAKING OF RUSSIA

Signing of the Treaty of Brest-Litovsk, while repulsive to Russian Communists and non-Communists alike, provided Lenin with a territorial base on which to introduce unhindered further revolutionary experiments. One of the first moves was the transfer of the capital from Petrograd to Moscow. To protect the revolutionary experiment from external threats, on January 28, 1918, a Red Army was ordered organized. The new army was open to all "class-conscious" citizens of Russia aged eighteen and over. On April 22 military training became compulsory for all peasants and workers. The bourgeoisie was excluded from this duty, although some 50,000 former tsarist officers were drafted to train the new Red Army. The Bolsheviks immediately restored the death penalty for deserters, terminated election of officers, and greatly curtailed the power of army committees. Each army unit was given a political commissar—usually a high party functionary who was charged with indoctrination and supervision of army personnel. Under the supervision of these commissars, the Red Army was elevated into a significant pillar of the new regime. By August 1, 1919, the Red Army numbered 300,000; by January, 1920, over 5,000,000.

On February 5, the Church was ordered separated from the state, and freedom of worship was officially introduced. The same decree abolished religious and judicial oaths and separated the schools from the Church. The teaching of religious doctrines in schools was prohibited, and all church properties were nationalized. A decree of February 14 introduced in Russia the Gregorian, or West European Calendar. A decree of February 8 confiscated the capital stock of private banks, annulled all bank shares, and discontinued all dividend payments. On February 19 the Land Law, replacing all earlier decrees, was published. The new law abolished all property rights in the land, which was ordered confiscated without compensation and placed at the disposal of those who tilled it by their own labor. All mineral resources became state property. On April 22, all foreign trade was nationalized and all export and import agreements not authorized by the state were forbidden. On April 27, inheritance, whether by law or by will, was abolished and the state became the sole recipient of all property after the death of the owner. On June 11 the government ordered the organization of "Committees of the Village Poor," which were to help with food supplies for the cities and to carry the class warfare into the rural areas. To silence criticism of some of its policies, the government on June 14 ordered the expulsion of Socialist Revolutionaries and Mensheviks from the soviets. On June 28 all large-scale industrial and commercial enterprises (mines, mills, factories, and the like) were nationalized for the purpose of "combating the economic disorganization and the breakdown of the food supply and of establishing more firmly the dictatorship of the working class and the village poor." Finally, on July 10, 1918, these and other legislative measures introduced by the Soviet government thus far were reiterated in the first Soviet constitution.

Adopted by the Fifth All-Russian Congress of Soviets this document proclaimed Russia "a republic of Soviets of Workers', Soldiers', and Peasants' Deputies" and named it the Russian Soviet Federated Socialist Republic, the RSFSR. The constitution declared socialism to be the state program not only in Russia but throughout the world as well. It abolished the exploitation of man by man, social classes, and private ownership of land; declared natural resources to be national property; confirmed the confiscation of all banks; separated the Church from the state and the school from the Church; guaranteed the freedom of religious and antireligious propaganda; proclaimed the duty of all citizens to work on the principle "He who does not work, neither shall he eat"; authorized complete disarming of the wealthy and arming of the workers; and granted only to the workers "the honor of bearing arms in defense of the revolution."

To insure genuine liberty for the workers, the constitution offered workers and poorer peasants "a complete, universal, and free education," transferred to them "all the technical and material resources necessary for the publication of newspapers, pamphlets, books, and other printed matter," and guaranteed their unobstructed circulation throughout the country. The workers, in addition, were granted complete freedom of assembly and the right to organize, and "all premises convenient for public gathering, together with lighting, heating, and furniture" were placed at their disposal. Although it openly favored workers, the constitution declared the equality of all citizens before the law, irrespective of race or nationality, granted "the right of asylum to all foreigners persecuted for political and religious offenses," and extended all rights enjoyed by Russian citizens to foreigners living in Russia provided "they belonged to the working class or to the peasantry working without hired labor."

Under the first Soviet constitution the basic political unit was the village and city soviet. Members of these soviets were elected by show of hands by all men and women over eighteen who earned their living by productive work useful to society. The constitution denied the right of franchise to persons employing hired labor for the sake of profit; to those who lived on income not deriving from their own work; to private businessmen; to monks and priests of all religious denominations; to agents and employees of the former police force; to members of the Romanov family; and to all lunatics and criminals. Above the village and the city, the soviet structure was based on the principle of indirect elections; that is, each local soviet elected deputies to the soviet above it up to the All-

Russian Congress of Soviets. To make certain that the urban proletariat predominated at this "supreme authority," the constitution stipulated that urban areas should have a five to one advantage over rural districts (one city deputy represented 25,000 voters; one rural deputy represented 125,000).

Under the 1918 constitution the supreme authority belonged to the Congress of Soviets which convened twice a year. Between the short sessions of the Congress, the constitution designated the Central Executive Committee as "the supreme legislative, administrative, and controlling body." Elected by and responsible to the Congress, the Central Executive Committee (consisting of some 200 persons, who at the same time were high party functionaries) was responsible for general direction of the government, unified and coordinated all legislative and administrative work, and examined and ratified all drafts and decrees submitted to it by the executive branch of the government, the Council of Peoples' Commissars, commonly known as the *Sovnarkom*. It is imperative to remember that at all of these levels, constitutional rights notwithstanding, the party exercised full control of the state apparatus and thus ruled the country. Before the ink was dry on these and other Bolshevik innovations in their remaking of Russia, they were challenged by foreign intervention and civil war.

SUGGESTED READINGS

ADAMS, ARTHUR E. *Bolsheviks in the Ukraine: The Second Campaign, 1918–1919*. New Haven: Yale University Press, 1963.

BROWDER, ROBERT P., and ALEXANDER F. KERENSKY, eds. *The Russian Provisional Government. Documents*. 3 vols. Stanford: Stanford University Press, 1961.

BUNYAN, JAMES, and H. H. FISHER. *The Bolshevik Revolution, 1917–1918. Documents and Materials*. Stanford: Stanford University Press, 1934.

CARR, EDWARD HALLETT. *A History of Soviet Russia: The Bolshevik Revolution, 1917–1923*. New York: Macmillan, 1952.

CHAMBERLIN, WILLIAM HENRY. *The Russian Revolution, 1917–1921*. 2 vols. New York: Macmillan, 1935.

DEUTSCHER, ISAAC. *The Prophet Armed; Trotsky: 1879–1921*. New York: Oxford University Press, 1954.

KENNAN, GEORGE F. *Russia Leaves the War*. Princeton: Princeton University Press, 1956.

MOOREHEAD, ALAN. *The Russian Revolution*. New York: Harper, 1958.

PIPES, RICHARD. *The Formation of the Soviet Union: Communism and Nationalism, 1917–1923*. Cambridge: Harvard University Press, 1954.

RADKEY, OLIVER HENRY. *The Elections to the Russian Constituent Assembly of 1917*. Cambridge: Harvard University Press, 1950.

REED, JOHN. *Ten Days That Shook the World*. New York: International Publishers, 1919.

RESHETAR, JOHN S. JR. *The Ukrainian Revolution, 1917–1920*. Princeton: Princeton University Press, 1952.

SHUB, DAVID. *Lenin*. Garden City: Doubleday, 1949.

TROTSKY, LEON. *The History of the Russian Revolution*. 3 vols. Translated by Max Eastman. New York: Simon and Schuster, 1932.

TYRKOVA-WILLIAMS, ARIADNA. *From Liberty to Brest-Litovsk. The First Year of the Russian Revolution*. London: Macmillan, 1919.

WARTH, ROBERT D. *The Allies and the Russian Revolution*. Durham, North Carolina: Duke University Press, 1954.

WHEELER-BENNETT, JOHN W. *The Forgotten Peace: Brest-Litovsk, March, 1918*. New York: Macmillan, 1939.

IV

INTERVENTION, CIVIL WAR, AND WAR COMMUNISM

The Bolsheviks' decision to withdraw Russia from the war and their efforts to project her development along the line of Marxist-Leninist teachings were challenged by foreign intervention and civil war. There were several incentives behind foreign intervention, but immediate military considerations were the most significant. Until the Treaty of Brest-Litovsk the Allies (Russia and the Western Powers) had fought the Central Powers on several fronts (France, Italy, the Balkans, the Near East, and Eastern Europe). By this policy of dispersal the Allies were able to lessen the pressure on themselves and thus to weaken their strong adversaries. The sudden ending of hostilities all along the Eastern Front, a move which released many German divisions to be deployed elsewhere, gave the Central Powers an opportunity to improve their military position. Moreover, the Treaty of Brest-Litovsk placed under direct and indirect German control an area of some 1,300,000 square miles, rich in the natural resources and food which the German industry and population badly needed. To prevent the Germans from capitalizing on this success, and in view of the apparent Bolshevik willingness to cooperate with the Germans, the Allies worked tirelessly. When all efforts to persuade the Bolsheviks to reopen the front failed, the Allies decided to intervene.

There was yet another pressing military motive behind the Allied intervention. During the war, because of Russia's military unpreparedness, the Allies had stored vast supplies of arms and ammunition in the Russian ports of Murmansk, Archangel, and Vladivostok (Black and Baltic Sea ports were blockaded by the Germans). German occupation of the Baltic countries and their landing in Finland after the Treaty of Brest-Litovsk threatened these supplies. To prevent them from falling into German or Bolshevik hands, the Allies felt that intervention was essential. Accordingly the British landed their first contingent of troops in Murmansk early in March, 1918. They were joined later by the French and by American marines and a detachment of Czechoslovak and Serbian soldiers. The first Japanese and British units disembarked in Vladivostok on April 5, 1918. Late in June the British reinforced their troops in Murmansk, and on August 5 additional British soldiers arrived in Archangel. By the end of 1918 the Allied powers had some 15,000 troops in northern Russia. In spite of violent Bolshevik objections, between July and September, 1918, Japanese and British units in Vladivostok were reinforced by French, Italian, and American troops. Finally, to prevent unfriendly forces from gaining control of the oil fields of Baku, late in 1918 British troops occupied not only that city but also Tbilisi and Batum in the Caucasus.

Next to military considerations, economic and political considerations acted as powerful stimuli in favor of intervention. The French were eager to intervene in order to protect all or at least a large part of the investment of some 16,000,000,000 francs made by Frenchmen in Russia between 1887 and 1917, which the Soviet government had nationalized. The same consideration, in part at least, motivated the Japanese and British desire to intervene. Japanese intervention in the Far East also had imperial implications. The collapse of Imperial Russia left Japan in a powerful position to build a vast territorial empire in defenseless Eastern Siberia. For that reason the Japanese were the most outspoken advocates of "Allied" intervention and were its "natural leaders" in the Far East. Their troops occupied not only Vladivostok and Northern Sakhalin but most of Eastern Siberia east of Lake Baikal. Because they were overly eager to capitalize on Russia's misfortunes, the Japanese aroused bitter feelings, especially among the Americans, and cast dark suspicion as to their ultimate aims.

Bolshevik reaction to Allied intervention went from the original seeming unconcern to violent opposition. At first, in March, 1918, they had no objection to the presence of Allied troops in northern Russia because they were aware that Allied presence there strengthened their bargaining position with the Germans. They hoped moreover that by non-resistance—in reality they were in no position to oppose the Allies—they might obtain formal recognition of the Soviet government by the Allied powers. However, when these hopes failed to materialize and above all when it became apparent that the German threat was not as dangerous as had been believed, and that some of the Allied powers (particularly Japan) had territorial designs on Russia, the Bolsheviks decided to contest the stay of Allied troops in Russia. Late in July, 1918, Allied ambassadors left Soviet Russia—an action which the Soviets interpreted as a disruption of diplomatic relations—and on July 29, 1918, the Central Executive Committee of the Soviets passed a resolution declaring "the socialist fatherland in danger." Accordingly appeals were sent "To the Toiling Masses of France, England, America, Italy, and Japan" to stop the intervention. Henceforth, as one observer noted, the Bolshevik attitude towards the Allies became "one of active hostility." Arrests of Allied subjects in Russia and of Soviet representatives in Allied countries did not help at all in easing the tension.

Allied intervention in Russia was greatly complicated by the Czechoslovak uprising. During the war the Czech and Slovak residents of Russia, in hope of liberating their country, had organized a brigade. After the revolution the strength of this unit increased to about 45,000—additions coming from among the Czech and Slovak prisoners of war. By the end of 1917 this brigade had become the most stable army unit in Russia, and on December 16, 1917, it was placed under the French Supreme Command with the understanding that it would be transported to France. Although throughout their stay in Russia the Czechoslovaks adopted a neutral view and responded to no appeals, their presence in Soviet Russia as far as the Bolsheviks were concerned was both a danger and an annoyance. Early in March, 1918, the Bolsheviks granted the Czechoslovaks permission to leave Russia for Western Europe via Siberia, since the port of Archangel was icebound.

The long Trans-Siberian odyssey of sixty trains began late in March. On their journey the Czechoslovaks encountered several official barriers, delays, threatened change of orders and the like. It was not until the middle of May, however, that the tension thus built exploded into a real crisis. At Cheliabinsk the Czechoslovaks met a train carrying Hungarian prisoners who were being returned under the provisions of the Treaty of Brest-Litovsk. A brawl between Czechoslovak and Hungarian soldiers left one Hungarian dead and several wounded. Local Soviet investigators tried to detain some of the Czechoslovaks engaged in the affair. This

attempt enraged the others with the result that the detained Czechoslovaks were released and the Soviet investigators disarmed. When informed
on May 25 of this incident, Trotsky, who had become War Commissar,
ordered the immediate disarming of all the Czechoslovaks. The Czechoslovaks responded by occupying Pensa, Samara and all important stations
along the Cheliabinsk-Omsk-Irkutsk railroad line. The Czechoslovak occupation of the Trans-Siberian Railway to the west and the Japanese,
British and American occupation to the east of Lake Baikal cleared the
Trans-Siberian Railway of the Bolsheviks. The successful Czechoslovak
rebellion and occupation of a vast area with no appreciable resistance,
followed by increased Allied landing of reinforcements in the North and
Far East, elevated the hopes of Bolshevik opponents who resented Marxist-Leninist experiments in Russia. Successful intervention in other words
stimulated civil war and civil war in part invited intervention.

THE FIRST PHASE OF THE CIVIL WAR

Civil War or resistance against Bolshevism was a product of many forces
and pressures. It began on a small scale in the winter of 1917–1918 with
the organization in Rostov-on-the-Don of a "Don Republic," by such
former Tsarist generals as Michael V. Alexeev (1857–1918), Kornilov, and
Alexis M. Kaledin (1861–1918). They were joined there by Miliukov,
Rodzianko, and other prominent members of the former Provisional Government. This organization was a short-lived affair. Kaledin committed
suicide on February 13, and Kornilov was killed on April 13. Early in
May, General Peter N. Krasnov (1869–1947), who favored cooperation
with the Germans, succeeded Kaledin, and General Denikin, who favored
cooperation with the Allies, succeeded Kornilov. By their joint efforts
Krasnov and Denikin cleared the Don and Kuban areas of Bolsheviks
early in the summer of 1918. One of Krasnov's main goals was the establishment of contacts with anti-Bolshevik groups beyond the lower Volga.
Another goal was to disrupt Moscow's connections with the food and oil
supplies of the Caucasus. Both objectives called for control of the city of
Tsaritsin. Because Stalin played some role in organizing Bolshevik defenses here, Tsaritsin was later named Stalingrad.[1]

Maintenance of Bolshevik control of other areas proved to be more
troublesome. The Czechoslovak success had electrifying effects on people
dissatisfied with Bolshevik experimentations. Spontaneously throughout
Russia there developed anti-Bolshevik uprisings. The opposition forces
were quite picturesque. They included peasants and workers, monarchists
and conservatives, moderate socialists and socialist revolutionaries, and

[1] Late in 1961, as part of the de-Stalinization process, Stalingrad was renamed
Volgograd.

Russian and non-Russian peoples. Diversified also were their activities and aspirations. In Moscow as early as May, 1918, a party conference of the Right Socialist Revolutionaries expressed its determination to overthrow the Bolshevik regime and to re-enter the war on the Allied side. Many Mensheviks voiced the same sentiment. Left Socialist Revolutionaries went even further. They advocated openly an active anti-German policy and called for annulment of the Treaty of Brest-Litovsk and severance of relations with Germany. On July 6, two members of the Left Socialist Revolutionary Party, posing as members of the CHEKA, assassinated Count Wilhelm von Mirbach, the German Ambassador to Moscow. Fear of German retaliation, which did not materialize, however, and additional acts of terror threw Moscow and Petrograd into chaos. Anti-Bolshevik uprisings occurred in Yaroslav, Nizhni Novgorod, Penza, Saratov, Tambov, Riazan, and some twenty other cities in Central Russia. On August 30, the chief of the Petrograd CHEKA, Michael S. Uritsky (1873–1918), was assassinated. On the same day Lenin was shot and seriously wounded by Dora Kaplan, a member of the Socialist Revolutionary Party.

Anti-Bolshevik opposition was not confined to Central Russia. One center established itself in the North in Archangel, where Tsarist General Eugene Miller (1867–?), with Allied consent, organized a force of some 7,000 to 8,000 volunteers. Another center of opposition began to form in Western Siberia, under a moderate liberal, Peter Vologodsky, who tried to minimize the importance of the soviets. Still another center established itself in Samara on the Volga, under the leadership of Victor Chernov, a Socialist Revolutionary and onetime Minister of Agriculture in the Provisional Government. The aim of this group was re-establishment of the Constituent Assembly which the Bolsheviks had dissolved. This group also established close relations with the Czechoslovaks, and with their aid it was able to secure some gold reserves of the Russian Imperial Bank which had been stored in Kazan. On September 8, to coordinate anti-Bolshevik forces as well as to prevent the developing factional feuds from exploding, under Czechoslovak pressure an All-Russian National Conference convened at Ufa. Its participants agreed to establish at Omsk a new coalition government called the Directory.

The Bolsheviks replied to the opposition's determination to unseat them with their own resolve to stay in power. In Moscow, following the July events, they bombarded Socialist Revolutionary strongholds, arrested many members, and even executed some. Executions were carried out in a number of cities along the middle Volga. Victims included nobles, merchants, former officers, clergymen, both poor and wealthy peasants, and anyone who resisted Bolshevik rule. On July 16, 1918, to prevent liberation by his followers, former Tsar Nicholas II and his entire family were executed near Ekaterinburg, where they had been exiled for safety by the

Provisional Government. To lessen the possible German threat while preparing for the challenge of the opposition, the Bolsheviks concluded three additional agreements with the German government on August 27. In these agreements they promised to supply great quantities of oil to Germany and to pay indemnities totalling six billion gold marks.

With the German danger averted, the Bolsheviks turned their attention towards the Omsk government, whose forces earlier had occupied the strategically located city of Kazan and were then advancing westward. Under Trotsky's command, the Red Army halted this advance and shortly thereafter the Bolsheviks succeeded in improving their position along the lower Volga. Their efforts were greatly aided by the disunity of the opposition. From its formation on October 9, 1918, members of the Directory at Omsk were unable to find any grounds for agreement. They argued, debated, plotted, and conspired against each other. Although the Directory included two Socialist Revolutionaries, on the whole it was nationalist, conservative, and a vigorous opponent of the Socialist Revolutionaries, whom it strongly suspected. When the Socialist Revolutionaries realized that the conservatives had no place for their philosophy, they called upon their members to resist the policy of the Directory. On November 18, the conservatives overthrew the Directory, arrested many Socialist Revolutionary leaders, and offered the post of "Supreme Ruler" to Admiral of the Black Sea Fleet Alexander V. Kolchak (1874–1920). While the execution of the coup was admirable, its timing was deplorable for the conservative cause.

THE COMINTERN

The end of World War I on November 11, 1918, introduced a new phase in Allied intervention and Civil War in Russia. The collapse of the Central Powers had several far-reaching repercussions. First it eliminated the ever-present German threat to the Bolshevik regime. Second, it created a vast power vacuum in war-torn Central and Eastern Europe. The Bolsheviks exploited these advantages to the fullest. On November 13, the Soviet government declared the Treaty of Brest-Litovsk null and void, and ordered the Red Army to occupy areas vacated by German forces. By the end of November, 1918, Red troops had overrun most of Estonia and Latvia. On November 29, an Estonian Soviet Government and, on December 14, a Latvian Soviet Government were set up. At the beginning of February, 1919, Red Army units occupied Vilnius and advanced west as far as the border of East Prussia. Early in March, 1919, the Bolsheviks made a concentrated effort to bring about a revolution in war-torn Europe. In retrospect this effort seems perhaps naive, but it looked different at the time.

When they seized power in Petrograd, many Bolsheviks, including Lenin, anxiously expected the outbreak of revolutions in more industrialized countries. Socialism, in their view, presupposed a high degree of industrial development and a strong working class. Most of them could not visualize enduring success in Russia without a European upheaval. In 1917 and 1918 there were many signs that Europe was on the brink of a great revolution. A disastrous war had inflicted enormous losses, both human and material, on all participants. War-weary troops had mutinied in France, Italy, and Germany. Hungry and overburdened workers had gone on strike. Though wartime censorship and military rule suppressed these signs of uneasiness, everywhere the great political unrest had made itself felt.

Aware of the explosive situation, the Bolsheviks tried to capitalize on it. With the Central Powers the task was easy. During the prolonged negotiations at Brest-Litovsk they ordered wide-scale fraternization with German forces and flooded the German lines with pro-revolutionary propaganda. They were also quite successful in "brainwashing" many German and Austro-Hungarian war prisoners whom they released under the provisions of the Brest-Litovsk Treaty. Following the establishment of normal diplomatic relations with Imperial Germany, Soviet diplomats engaged in various activities traditionally reserved for professional revolutionaries and agitators. These efforts, coupled with the collapse of the Central Powers, were partly responsible for a series of Bolshevik-type upheavals (in Berlin in January, 1919, in Hungary in March, 1919, and in Bavaria in April, 1919). These revolutionary flareups, ill-prepared and inadequately led, collapsed. In view, however, of social and political unrest in the Near and Far East and the slow and uneasy social, economic and political adjustment which followed the end of hostilities in Europe, the Bolsheviks' hopes for an imminent world revolution were kept alive and high.

To promote and coordinate revolutionary efforts abroad and to protect the revolutionary experiment at home, early in March, 1919, Lenin called in Moscow what was to be the First Congress of the Third International or Comintern. It was not a well attended gathering because of poor travelling conditions. The Second Congress of 1920 had somewhat better attendance. The statute of this new organization prepared by the First and adopted by the Second Congress (July 17–August 7, 1920) defined the aim of the Comintern as: "the overthrow of capitalism, the establishment of the dictatorship of the proletariat and of the International Soviet Republic for the complete abolition of classes, and the realization of socialism—the first step to Communist Society."

With their prestige as successful revolutionaries, Russian Communists dominated the Comintern from its very inception, and allowed only those parties and groups which unconditionally subscribed to the famous twenty-one conditions to affiliate themselves with the new organization. These conditions, among others, included: obligation to carry on actively Comintern-approved propaganda; periodic purge of "reformist," "opportunist," and "petty bourgeois" elements; organization of illegal apparatus; proper indoctrination of the armed forces and rural areas; renunciation of "social patriotism," "social pacifism," and "reformism"; denunciation of imperialism and accordingly support of colonial peoples; and rendering of "every possible assistance to Soviet Republics in their struggle against counter-revolutionary forces." The Comintern, in other words, from its very inception was designed to be an international vehicle through which Russian influence could be manifested, not only in the international workers' movement but also as a powerful arm of Soviet foreign policy.[1]

A NEW PHASE IN INTERVENTION AND CIVIL WAR

The defeat of the Central Powers had ended the official Allied justification for intervention in Russia. However, the challenge of the Comintern, the Red Army's rapid occupation of territories evacuated by German forces, and the possibility of Bolshevik-German cooperation, made it necessary to strengthen Allied troops in Russia and to establish closer contacts with anti-Bolshevik forces. As early as November, 1918, the British reinforced their contingents in the Caucasus and northern Russia, and entered Estonia. The French landed in the Ukraine, while the Japanese entrenched themselves more firmly in the Far East. The Supreme Allied Commander, Marshal Ferdinand Foch, British Secretary of War Lord Milner, Winston S. Churchill, and French Premier Georges Clemenceau were strong proponents of this course of action. British Prime Minister Lloyd George and American President Woodrow Wilson advised caution. The policy of moderation won. The Allies recalled some of their units from Russia as early as April, 1919. Others were pulled out because they mutinied, either as a result of Bolshevik agitation, or war-weariness and longing for home. No Western leader dared to overlook this dangerous and widespread attitude.

Following their decision to abandon active military intervention of their own in Russia, the Allies turned to more active military and moral support of the various anti-Bolshevik forces. East of Lake Baikal the Japanese set up Ataman Gregory M. Semenov (1890–1945) in Chita, and Ataman Kalmykov in Khabarovsk as their puppets. The British gave *de facto* recognition to Kolchak, whose authority nominally extended between Lake Baikal and the Ural Mountains. The British also agreed to supply the small force of General Miller in the North; the force of Gen-

---

[1] For the full text of the Constitution and Rules of the Comintern, see Appendix 24.

eral Nikolai N. Yudenich (1862–1933) in Estonia; units of Krasnov and Denikin in the Azov and Don areas; and General Baron Peter N. Wrangel (1878–1928) in the Northern Caucasus. By early 1919 all these generals had acknowledged Kolchak as the supreme ruler of Russia. The French, in accordance with their decision to establish a *cordon sanitaire* consisting of such states as Poland, Rumania, Czechoslovakia, and Yugoslavia, toyed with the idea of supporting Ukrainian aspirations for independence. In other words, the stage was being set for the second phase of the Civil War.

Opposition forces, or as they often were called, the Whites, operated under several handicaps. First, they operated on the periphery of the country, where the population was non-Russian, where the transportation network was very thin, and where the industrial base was quite inadequate. Second, the great distances between various units prevented them from closer and more efficient coordination of operations. Third, personal rivalries and ambitions plagued and hindered the execution of a plan. Fourth, by virtue of their membership, the Whites acquired a conservative, indeed in some instances almost a reactionary, stigma which they were neither able nor willing to dispel. Finally, and most decisively, the opposition had no effective, far-sighted and progressive program, either for the Russian or the non-Russian population, with which to counterchallenge Bolshevik promises. Kolchak, for instance, was negatively inclined towards the independence of the Finns and other peoples. And his land program, as revealed in his declaration of April 8, 1919, insisted on the maintenance of the status quo until convocation of a new Constituent Assembly. It was not a program to generate enthusiasm in revolutionary times.

Early in March, 1919, Kolchak moved his forces, 125,000 strong, westward across the Urals towards Moscow. In this undertaking he was backed by the British and the French, although not overenthusiastically by the latter because of his lack of a sound and realistic program. At first his progress was impressive. By March 13, his troops had occupied Perm and Ufa, and in April they reached within twenty miles of the Volga, threatening Samara and Kazan. Further advances, however, were hindered by the harassment of peasant partisans as well as by the Bolshevik counteroffensive under the direction of Michael V. Frunze (1885–1925). On June 9, Kolchak lost Ufa and fell behind the Urals. Bolsheviks pursued him persistently, and late in July they took Cheliabinsk. On November 14, they occupied Omsk, the seat of Kolchak's government. Kolchak's inability to get along with the Czechoslovaks, who controlled the Trans-Siberian Railway, hindered his advance and his retreat as well. On January 4, 1920, he abdicated his power in favor of Denikin, and sought protection from the French and the Czechoslovaks. The French General Janin turned him over to the revolutionaries. On February 7, 1920, after a summary court martial, Kolchak and his associates were executed. The White cause in Asiatic Russia came to a sudden end. Those who survived proceeded to China and other parts of the world.

After disposing of Kolchak's threat, the Bolsheviks turned their attention to Denikin, whose original base of operation was the area around the Sea of Azov, and to Yudenich, who had his headquarters in Estonia. Both forces received material and technical support from the British. Denikin, hoping to join Kolchak's armies during the height of their victories, opened an all-out offensive against the Bolsheviks along a broad front stretching from Kharkov to the Volga. When Kolchak's forces were hurled back, Denikin changed his plans and divided his force of some 160,000 for a three-frontal attack on Moscow. One army under Wrangel was to move up the Volga; General Sirodin's Don Cossacks were to advance north from Rostov; and General Vladimir Z. Mai-Maievsky (1867–1920) was ordered to clear the Ukraine of Bolsheviks and proceed north. At first Denikin's successes, like those of Kolchak, were astounding. By the end of August his forces had captured Odessa, Kherson, Nikolaev, and Kiev. Kursk fell on September 20, Voronezh on October 6, Chernigov on October 12, and Orel on October 13. White armies reached within 250 miles of Moscow.

At the height of Denikin's victories, Yudenich, with a force of 20,000 men, advanced from Estonia, and on October 11 captured the city of Yamburg on the Luga River, less than one hundred miles from Petrograd. On October 16, his force occupied Gatchina, only thirty miles from Petrograd, and a few days later they reached the outskirts of the former capital. For a moment it appeared that both capitals, Moscow and Petrograd, would fall to the Whites. Within a few days, however, the picture altered drastically. Under Trotsky's leadership, Bolshevik resistance stiffened and Yudenich was forced to retreat. On November 14, Yudenich was at his original starting point, Yamburg, and retreating. His armies crossed to Estonia, where on February 1, 1920, they were demobilized. The White cause in the Baltic area came to a sudden end. Denikin's efforts met the same fate. Outnumbered, overextended, and opposed by enraged peasants and minorities, especially Ukrainians, Denikin lost Orel on October 20, Voronezh on October 24, and Kursk on November 17. During December, 1919, the Bolsheviks occupied most of the Ukraine. Remnants of Denikin's forces retreated to Rostov-on-the-Don. In March, 1920, British ships transferred some 35,000 of Denikin's men to the Crimea, the last stronghold of the Whites. On April 4, Denikin resigned his command in favor of Wrangel and left the country. At about the same time Miller's regime collapsed in Archangel. Wrangel thus remained as the last chance for the Whites.

Wrangel's task was not enviable. From Denikin he inherited an army of depressed fighters but excellent plunderers. Their excesses, coupled

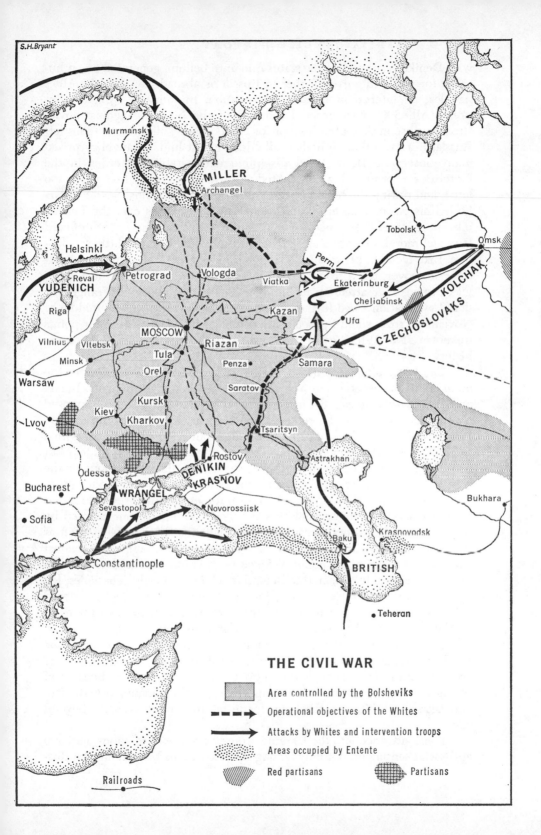

S.H.Bryant

Murmansk

MILLER
Archangel

Tobolsk
Omsk

Helsinki
Reval
YUDENICH
Petrograd   Vologda   Viatka   Perm
Riga   Ekaterinburg   KOLCHAK
Vilnius   Kazan   Cheliabinsk
Vitebsk   MOSCOW   Ufa   CZECHOSLOVAKS
Minsk   Tula   Riazan   Penza   Samara
Warsaw   Orel   Saratov
Kursk
Lvov   Kiev   Kharkov
                                        Tsaritsyn
Odessa   Rostov   Astrakhan
Bucharest   WRANGEL   DENIKIN
                              KRASNOV   Bukhara
Sofia   Sevastopol   Novorossiisk
                                                            Baku   Krasnovodsk
Constantinople   BRITISH

Teheran

THE CIVIL WAR

Area controlled by the Bolsheviks

Operational objectives of the Whites

Attacks by Whites and intervention troops

Areas occupied by Entente

Red partisans   Partisans

Railroads

with Denikin's support of the status quo ante bellum, generated no enthusiasm for the White cause either in Russia or abroad. By 1920 the Allies had lost all interest in Russian intervention. In January, 1920, the Supreme Allied Council ordered the end of the blockade against Soviet Russia and soon thereafter, except for the Japanese, all foreign troops left Russia. But even though he had all odds against him, Wrangel surprised many observers. He restored discipline and established order in the Crimea. He proposed a far-sighted agrarian program (two years too late), and during the height of the Polish campaign against Soviet Russia he led his 70,000-man army north into several victories over the Bolsheviks. Because of these successes, on August 12, 1920, the French offered Wrangel moral, but not material, assistance which brought little satisfaction. Like Denikin before him, Wrangel failed to win the peasant population. Moreover, freed from the Polish front by the armistice, the Bolsheviks turned their attention to him. To escape annihilation, Wrangel ordered evacuation since further resistance was hopeless. In the middle of November, 1920, some 135,000 soldiers and civilians left Russia for points unknown. The White cause was lost, and the Civil War had become history.

The last major crisis of 1920 was the Russo-Polish War. One of the main points of disagreement was the suggested boundary between Russia and Poland—the so-called Curzon Line which had been hastily proposed by the British Foreign Secretary, Lord Curzon. If adopted, the Curzon Line would have reduced Poland to a state along the Vistula Basin, with a predominantly Polish population. The Bolsheviks favored the idea, but the Poles, determined to undo the wrong of the three partitions of the eighteenth century, rejected Curzon's suggestion. In 1919, at the height of the Civil War and White successes, Polish forces occupied several regions inhabited by Lithuanians, Belorussians, and Ukrainians, but claimed by the Russians. The Bolesheviks began to challenge these gains as soon as they were able to free their forces from victorious campaigns against Kolchak, Denikin, and Yudenich. Since negotiation approaches made no headway, each side prepared to defend its claim militarily. The Poles, led by a veteran anti-Russian fighter, Joseph Pilsudski (1867–1935), entered into close political agreement with the Ukrainian anti-Russian forces of Semeon Petliura (1879–1926). In return for some minor territorial adjustments, Pilsudski offered Petliura military aid in his attempt to unseat the Bolshevik regime in the Ukraine. On April 25, 1920, the Polish army advanced into the Ukraine, and by May 6 it had reached Kiev. Because of strong anti-Polish feelings stirred up among the Ukrainians by Russian and Ukrainian agitators, the Poles made no attempt to advance beyond Kiev.

Polish advance into the Ukraine aroused a wave of religious, national and social sentiment, not only among the Ukrainians but among the Russians as well. Bolshevik appeals to all Russians to defend "Mother Russia" fell on responsive ears and pro- and anti-Communists joined hands. In May, 1920, General Mikhail N. Tukhachevsky (1893–1937) launched a counteroffensive in the north while Semeon M. Budenny's (1883–   ) cavalry forces struck at Kiev. Outnumbered, the Poles retreated all along the front back as far as Warsaw. The Bolsheviks were so excited by their victories that they created a Soviet government for Poland and were anxious to extend the benefits of their system not only to Poland but also to Germany and other countries of Western Europe as well. On July 10, Pilsudski appealed to the Allies for aid. Two days later Lord Curzon proposed a truce line along his earlier suggestion, but Moscow, victorious and marching, rejected it. A little later the French sent to Warsaw badly needed materials and a military mission headed by General Maxime Weygand. On August 14, the Poles launched their counteroffensive, outmaneuvered Tukhachevsky's force and soon the Soviet retreat degenerated into a wild rout that halted only outside Minsk. An armistice of October 12, 1920, followed by the Treaty of Riga on March 18, 1921, brought an end to that episode. By the provisions of this treaty Soviet Russia renounced its claim to the territories in question east of the Curzon Line—a situation which lasted until 1939.

Allied withdrawal from Russia, defeat of the White forces, and settlement with Poland gave the Bolsheviks an opportunity to consolidate their position in other uncertain areas. In April, 1920, following the defeat of Denikin and the British departure from the Caucasus, Bolshevik forces occupied Azerbaidzhan. Armenia was brought under Bolshevik domination in December, 1920, and in February, 1921, Georgia was forcibly returned to Moscow's control. The establishment of Bolshevik power in Central Asia resembled that in the Caucasus. Following the defeat of Kolchak and the British withdrawal, Bolshevik forces entered the vast area of Central Asia with no appreciable difficulty. By the end of 1920, Bokhara, Khiva, and Turkestan were occupied, old feudal regimes overthrown, and foundations were laid for slow introduction of the Soviet system. The Bolsheviks had occupied all Siberia west of Lake Baikal by the end of 1919, i.e., following the defeat of Kolchak. The area east of Lake Baikal, which was controlled by the Japanese, was incorporated into Soviet Russia after the Japanese withdrawal in 1922. In other words, except for Finland, Estonia, Latvia, Lithuania, parts of Poland, and Bessarabia, which the Rumanians occupied, by the end of 1921 and early 1922, the old Tsarist Empire from the Black Sea and the Baltic Sea to Kamchatka had new masters.

Bolshevik triumph and White defeat—an event of first magnitude not only in Russian but in world history—poses these two questions: Why did the Whites fail? Why did the Bolsheviks win? The Whites lost because they had neither a constructive program for Russia's future nor a plan that would satisfy the revolutionary aspirations of the masses. From the beginning to the end of the Civil War the Whites demonstrated again and again by their pronouncements and actions that they were opposed to the long-overdue changes in Russia which the revolution had introduced. They opposed, for instance, the division of landed estates among the peasants as permanent. They looked with suspicion on the improvements gained by workers. Their pro-constitutional pronouncements never satisfied the liberals. By their insistence on a Russia "united and undivided" they alienated many non-Russian peoples who aspired to gain national freedom. Finally, distances between various White resistance centers, disunity within each, and half-hearted support by the war-weary Allies contributed much to the White failure in Russia. In other words, the Whites, by their negative policies, attitudes, and mistakes, gave the Bolsheviks excellent propaganda weapons which they used masterfully to their advantage.

WAR COMMUNISM

Bolshevik ability to capitalize on the mistakes of their adversaries (in many instances there was really no need to do so) was only one of two basic factors contributing to their victory. The other was War Communism. War Communism had *four* distinct meanings or characteristics. *First,* it attempted to establish in Russia a Communist society. One form of the Bolshevik remaking of Russia found expression in the program of the Russian Communist Party (bolshevik) adopted by the Eighth Party Congress, March 18–23, 1919. This all-important document—a blueprint for Soviet society—asserted boldly that the Bolshevik revolution "began to lay the foundation of a communist society" in Russia, and as such it ushered in an "era of world-wide proletarian communist revolution." As expected, it approved "the correctness" of basic tenets of the earlier party program (1903), it assailed capitalism and imperialism (holding the latter responsible for wars), and it appealed to workers' solidarity throughout the world in order to realize the inevitable and "the final victory of the proletariat."

The party program held out great hopes for Russia's future. It promised "to liberate woman from all the burdens of antiquated methods of housekeeping, by replacing them by house-communes, public kitchens, central laundries, nurseries, and the like." It resolved to bring the government apparatus into close contact with the people "for the purpose of realizing democracy more fully and strictly in practice, by making government officials responsible to, and placing them under the control of, the masses." It pledged itself to work towards the abolition of all national privileges, extension of the fullest equality of all nationalities, recognition "of the rights of colonies and oppressed nations to political separation" in order to bring closer unity between "proletarians and semi-proletarians of different nationalities for the purpose of carrying on a general revolutionary struggle."

In the field of education the 1919 party program vowed to transform "the school from an instrument of class domination of the bourgeoisie . . into an instrument for a communist regeneration of society." The school was to be at once a conductor of communist principles as well as "of intellectual, organizational, and educational influences of the proletariat" in order to educate a generation capable of establishing communism. Education was to be free and compulsory, general and technical, with instruction in native language, free from religious influence, for both sexes to the age of seventeen. Moreover, the state was to supply all pupils with food, clothing, shoes, and all other school needs. The state was also to assist in adult education and provide libraries, lectures, and movies. The state was to aid financially those students who desired a university education. The party pledged itself in this program to "liberate" the masses from "religious superstition," but cautioned slow procedure towards that objective in order not to offend "the religious susceptibilities of believers."

In the economic sphere the program promised both to increase productive forces and "at all costs to increase the quantity of products required by the population." This goal the party hoped to achieve through a general state plan; concentration of production; and efficient, rational, and economic utilization of all material resources of the country. Trade unions were called upon to help in organizing socialized industry and establishing "a new socialist discipline," in re-educating the masses, and in similar functions. In agriculture the program recognized that "small-scale farming will continue for a considerable time," and accordingly suggested several measures designed to increase agricultural productivity. These included: (1) abolition of scattered fields; (2) supplying the peasantry with improved seeds and artificial fertilizers; (3) improvement of the breed of cattle; (4) distribution of agricultural information; (5) agricultural aid to the peasantry; (6) repair in soviet shops of peasant agricultural implements; (7) establishment of loan agencies and experiment stations; and (8) improvement of peasant lands. Alongside this, the program called for establishment of large soviet farms, aid to agricultural cooperatives, organization of state-operated farms, increase of agricultural activity, support of agricultural communes, all-out struggle against backwardness and rich peasants (*kulaks*), and penetration of rural areas by the party network.

The 1919 program pledged itself "to exert the greatest effort for the improvement of the housing conditions of the toiling masses," and to abolish overcrowded and unsanitary quarters by removing the old and building new ones. It advocated legislation aimed at improving working conditions of the laborer and also resolved "to abolish completely child labor and to decrease further the working hours for young persons," to introduce the premium bonus system to increase labor productivity, and to reduce the working day from an eight to a six hour maximum "without reduction in wages." That promise, however, was conditional on the general increase of productivity of labor and on the workers' pledge to spend two hours overtime without pay studying the theory of trade and industry and in administrative and military training. Finally, the program pledged development of sanitation centers to combat all kinds of infectious diseases, sanitary legislation, and free medical care and drugs to everyone.

The *second* characteristic of War Communism was its heavy contribution to economic chaos, both in industry and in agriculture. The breakdown stemmed basically from two sources. First, the Bolsheviks inherited a faltering economy, in which industrial and agricultural production and real wages were seriously declining while the cost of living and the general price index were rising. Second, immediately after their coup d'état the Bolsheviks introduced many important economic measures. They nationalized, for instance, the banks, foreign trade, and transport; annulled domestic and foreign debts; and placed industry under the workers' control. These and similar measures were not intended to ease the depressed economic situation, but rather to deprive the propertied classes of their influence, to paralyze the opposition, to consolidate Bolshevik political power, and to introduce in Russia a controlled or directed state capitalism.

Lenin called this state capitalism a "gigantic step forward." It was also a step towards accelerated economic disorganization. The leading force behind this disorganization was the system of factory committees, which by a decree of November 27, 1917, were given broad participation in the direction of industry, such as the right to supervise management, the right to determine minimum production levels, and the right to have access to all business correspondence and accounts. Intoxicated by their successes, many of these committees went beyond the legal powers granted them by the decree. They assumed not only the administration of factories but also developed the idea that factories should be run for the benefit of local workers. Since there was no effective authority to defy these syndicalist tendencies, Russian industry, already weakened by war and revolution, faltered further. Many factories were forced to close. Those continuing to operate experienced a sharp decline in workers' discipline as well as in production. Workers talked, debated, elected themselves to various posts, and resisted every attempt of the new government to coordinate and direct the economic life of the country. Their aspirations were warmly supported by Left Socialist Revolutionaries and Left Wing Bolsheviks. The latter group, in fact, favored complete and rapid nationalization of all enterprises, large and small, and firmly opposed the employment of prerevolutionary technicians and industrial experts, unless this was offset by granting greater powers of direct control over production to factory committees.

Another leading cause of accelerated economic disorganization was the territorial amputation of Russia. Between 1917 and 1920, the Soviet Russian economy lost, as a result of either fighting or permanent separation, or German, Allied, and White occupation, such vital economic regions as Finland, the Baltic states, the Ukraine, the Don and Kuban areas, the Caucasus, Central Asia, Siberia, and parts of Northern Russia. These losses reduced the Bolshevik-controlled areas to Central and part of Northern Russia. These losses, too, because of the abundance of natural resources they possessed, created an acute shortage of materials that threatened to paralyze industry. The loss of the Ukraine, for instance, meant, in prewar figures, the loss of some 72 per cent of the coal output, 75 per cent of iron ore, 68 per cent of pig iron, 25 per cent of manganese ore, 35 per cent of locomotive production, 36 per cent of flour mills, and 80 per cent of sugar refineries. Loss of the Urals, which was a fighting front in 1918–1919, meant a loss of an additional 19 per cent of pig iron output. White control of Western Siberia (1918–1919) meant complete cessation of cotton deliveries from Turkestan, while loss of the Caucasus disrupted the flow of oil from Baku and Grozny.

These losses, coupled until early 1920 with the Allied blockade, had far-reaching effects on the economy of Soviet Russia. Shortages of fuel and raw materials sharply reduced the number of operating blast furnaces, rolling mills, and textile mills. Fuel shortage and difficulties in effecting repairs, in particular, augmented the disorganization of railroads. Railroads, in fact, were threatened by a standstill—a situation which, as Lenin put it, created "difficulties for the revolution" and hope for its enemies. The Bolsheviks tried to meet the fuel crisis by converting to wood fuel on the railroads, as well as by intensifying the development of coal resources in the sub-Moscow region. These efforts, however, were only partly successful. While they contributed to military victory they also contributed to further deterioration of the equipment. By early 1920, 69 per cent of Soviet Russia's locomotives were disabled or waiting for repairs, with less than 4,000 in running order as compared with some 14,500 at the end of 1917.

The same territorial losses that paralyzed Russian industry also sharply affected the food situation. Loss of the Ukraine—the breadbasket of Imperial Russia—was felt in particular. Food shortage, the spark which had ignited the revolution, had disastrous effects on industrial productivity. Both in Moscow and in Petrograd, people were divided into various categories based on their occupation as a criterion for food distribution. Although workers were given preference, they did not receive a sufficient amount. The meager diet lowered the general productivity and the efficiency of individual workers. It also encouraged absenteeism, petty theft, speculation, and other devices to supplement the semistarvation diet. By 1920, the average productivity of the worker (as compared with prewar figures) dropped 30 to 35 per cent, and the number of workers employed in industry declined by some 50 per cent. Many industrial cities lost from one-fourth to one-third of their population; Moscow lost one-half. Some of these were drafted into the Red Army. The majority, however, moved to villages in search of food. Their quest was severely hindered by the runaway inflation, which by October, 1920, had reduced the purchasing power of the ruble to no more than 1 per cent of what it had been in October, 1917. War Communism, in other words, reduced Russia to grave economic disorganization.

The *third* distinct characteristic of War Communism was the rapid establishment of direct government control over *all* production and distribution. It might best be described as a policy of total nationalization, centralization, and mobilization. The prime motive for this development was the desire on the part of the government to insure priority for military supplies (and thus meet effectively the challenge of the opposition) and to a lesser extent to prevent sabotage. The first decisive step towards full government control came on June 28, 1918, when an order was issued for wholesale nationalization of large-scale industry. All enterprises with more than one million rubles of capital in mining, metal, textile, glass, leather, cement, timber, and the like, were placed under government control. By the end of 1918 the number of nationalized concerns reached 1,000; by the fall of 1919 some 3,000 to 4,000; and by the end of 1920 some 37,000 enterprises were listed as belonging to the state.

Initially, by a decree of August 8, 1918, the Supreme Economic Council (which had been established on December 14, 1917) and the Commissariat of Agriculture were empowered with regulation and organization of all production and management of "every enterprise of the Republic." The distribution of all commodities was entrusted exclusively to the Commissariat of Food, which had been established on May 27, 1918. On October 30, 1918, the government created a new agency, the Revolutionary War Council, and placed at its disposal "all forces and resources of the people that are needed for the defense of the Republic." A month later, on November 30, there emerged under Lenin's presidency a new institution, the Council of Defense, which in 1920 was transformed into the Council of Labor and Defense. The Council of Defense was given full powers in matters pertaining to mobilization of the forces and resources of the country in the interests of defense, and its decisions were "absolutely binding upon every department and institution, both central and local, and upon every citizen."

Government control of production and distribution and the attempt to mobilize all available resources had three important by-products. First, it led to the introduction of universal labor duty. Already the nationalization decree of June 28 had stipulated that the "entire personnel of every enterprise" was considered to be employed by the state and could not leave the establishment without authorization. Beginning with July 1, any stoppage of work or any strike was officially declared to be a betrayal of "the proletarian cause." Individuals who instigated a strike were branded "enemies of the labor movement," and were "to be handed over to the court of international proletariat." On September 3, 1918, the Commissariat of Labor decreed that in case of a shortage of manual workers, employment agencies had the right to assign the unemployed to any work, and that work connected with the harvesting and delivery of food products was "compulsory for all unemployed," regardless of their training or profession. Persons violating this order were to be reported to local civil authorities. This evolving trend towards universal labor duty received its fullest expression on October 31, 1918. All citizens, except persons under 16 years of age, over 50 years of age, and persons incapacitated by injury or illness, were declared subject to compulsory labor. An earlier decree of October 5 introduced labor books in place of identification cards. Other decrees established penalties for labor deserters, and stern labor discipline of a semimilitary nature.

The second major by-product of centralization and mobilization was an abnormal increase of bureaucracy. As the pace of nationalization quickened, the central administration became swollen with officials concerned with coordination, and the local administration with those concerned with management. This increase was so rapid that by mid-1920 one out of every four adults in Petrograd was said to be an official. The situation in Moscow was about the same. In industry the ratio of administrative personnel to total workers employed doubled in two years. Some administrators, in the early stages of nationalization, were hostile to the new regime; others were merely inefficient. Those who sympathized with the new system were, in the words of one observer, "rich in 'drive' and had genuine organizing capacity but were lacking in experience and in training." The net result was increased confusion. The presence of this vast bureaucracy also set the stage for a struggle between various central administrative bodies whose jurisdictions often overlapped. There were also sharp disagreements between central and local administrative units. Excited by their positions, many new administrators liberally issued orders which often contradicted those already in existence. Attempts to clear up the chaos only worsened the situation.

The third significant by-product of nationalization, centralization, and mobilization was the issuing of a whole series of decrees aimed at drastic transformation of Russia in accordance with communist principles. Thus, for instance, a decree of August 30, 1918, eliminated money as a medium for transactions between state institutions "in order to simplify and regulate the accounts of nationalized enterprises." This decree also abolished all payments in money to and from consumers and soviet organizations and institutions. In the middle of October, 1918, a plan was proposed for "wages in kind" to be introduced in Moscow, Petrograd, and other cities with a population of more than 20,000. Wages in kind were to include "living quarters, the principal manufactured and food products, and certain cultural needs." Under this plan, each factory would have a large farm operated by farm workers and specialists, and each worker's family would obtain food from that farm. Surplus, if any, was to go to the Commissariat of Food to be used elsewhere. On November 21, 1918, the government abolished all private trade. The property of all retail stores was confiscated, and permits to ship goods were revoked. The Commissariat of Food was commissioned to provide the population with articles of personal and household use through a network of state cooperatives to be established by January 1, 1919. The lapse of time between the suspension of all trade and the announced date for opening of state-run cooperatives gave the Black Market impetus to rise into a gigantic enterprise. On November 30, the government denied the right to elect or be elected officials of cooperatives to all persons who used hired labor, lived on unearned income, or had been engaged in trade during the past three years; to monks and nuns; to clergymen of all denominations (except those who supported cooperatives); and to former police officials. An earlier decree of October 30 had imposed also upon wealthier persons of cities and villages a "lump sum tax of ten billion rubles." The burden of tax was to fall on the wealthy part of the population. Wealthy peasants, in addition, were ordered to pay a "tax in kind" on their agricultural products. By these and similar decrees the Bolsheviks hastened Soviet Russia's development down a path to classless society as well as to bitter discontent.

The *fourth*, and in many ways the most distinct, characteristic of War Communism was the development of a violent struggle between the peasantry and the new regime. As Marxists, the Bolsheviks considered agriculture an integral part of socialized national economy. They believed that the state must establish rigid control over agricultural production, introduce large-scale methods of farming, and transform the peasants into agricultural workers. Because this plan generated no enthusiasm among Russian peasants, who were mainly interested in increasing their land allotments and in disposing of their produce as they saw fit, during 1917 the Bolsheviks altered their Marxist doctrines and temporarily approved some wishes of the peasants—above all the partition of landed estates. This approval was popular among the peasantry. Welcomed also was the land decree of November 8, 1917, which on the one hand declared the land state property, while on the other it affirmed the principle of equal distribution. Practical application of this decree, however, forced the peasants to part company with the new regime.

As far as the bulk of the peasantry was concerned, the land law affected the lands of the state and those of the landlord only. Bolshevik attempts to change this view met stubborn opposition. Point Five of the land law, which declared that "the land of ordinary peasants and ordinary Cossacks shall not be confiscated," provided the peasants with strong arguments. Those peasants who could not qualify as "ordinary," divided their land, livestock, and implements among their families in order to save them. Wealthy or poor, with land in their actual possession at last, the peasants showed no disposition to join in the large-scale collective farming which the Bolsheviks advocated. Nor were they willing to part with their produce at a fixed low price as the Bolsheviks began to demand. Because loss of the Ukraine, the Don, the Northern Caucasus, and Siberia reduced the Bolshevik-controlled areas of Northern and Central Russia to a condition of starvation, when all persuasions failed the Bolsheviks attempted to solve the food crisis by forcing the peasants to surrender all grain surpluses.

The first decisive step towards forcible food requisition was a decree of the Central Executive Committee on May 9, 1918. It reaffirmed previous government policy of grain monopoly and fixed prices, recognized the necessity of fighting against speculators, acknowledged the urgency of compelling peasants to surrender their surplus, and appealed to the poor to begin a merciless fight against the *kulaks*. Evaders, branded as "enemies of the people," were liable to arrest, expulsion from the village, and even confiscation of their property. The decree established rewards for information leading to the disclosure of any surplus, and granted broad powers to the Commissariat of Food, including the right to use "armed force in cases of resistance to the requisition of grain and other food products." The Commissariat was also empowered to "dismiss, remove, arrest, and turn over to the Revolutionary Tribunal" all officials who interfered with the execution of its orders.

This "food dictatorship decree," which contributed heavily to the break between the Bolsheviks and their Left Socialist Revolutionary friends, was followed by other vital measures. On May 20, 1918, the Central Executive Committee instructed local soviets to "undertake immediately the task of explaining to the poor that their interests are opposed to those of the kulaks, and of arming the poor with the purpose of establishing their dictatorship in the village." On June 11, 1918, Committees of the Village Poor were ordered created everywhere. Entrepreneurs and all wealthy peasants, who allegedly had grain surplus and other food products, were ineligible for membership in those committees. The latter were charged with distribution of food, needed articles and farming implements, and assistance to local food departments in requisitioning surplus grain from more prosperous farmers. These prerogatives gave the committees complete power in villages, and their armed status gave them added prestige.

To assist the Committees of the Village Poor, on August 6, 1918, the government organized Food Requisition Detachments. Every detachment was to consist of not less than seventy-five workers and poor peasants led by two appointed leaders, and equipped with "two or three machine guns." According to their instructions, food detachments were to obtain grain by either purchase at fixed prices or by requisition. They were also instructed to help the local population to harvest crops, to organize local Committees of the Poor, to distribute part of the requisitioned grain among the needy, and to ship the rest to the nearest government storage depot. They were to demand the surrender of firearms, to inventory all available grain stores, to uncover and confiscate hidden grain, to remain in a village until all grain surplus had been delivered, and they were not to indulge in overzealousness. In practice, however, the food requisitioning process was one of constant excesses. The detachments imposed arbitrary grain quotas upon villages, collected the assessed apportionment of grain by force, subjected whole villages to intensive house-to-house searches, inflicted heavy damage everywhere, and perpetrated all kinds of crimes.

Peasants developed several distinct forms of resistance to the activities of the Committees of the Village Poor, and especially of the Food Requisitioning Detachments, whose numbers by the end of 1918 had risen from 20,000 to 40,000 men. At first the peasants tried to evade the assigned levies by every cunning and resourceful device they could conceive. When these proved ineffective, they resorted to armed defense. Villages in the Volga Region, Western Siberia, Tambov, Saratov, and the Ukraine organized themselves against city intruders, and many officials responsible for the food collection were seized, tortured, and killed. The Bolsheviks replied with punitive expeditions. As a result tensions rose, bitterness grew, and casualties multiplied. In the end, however, the government emerged the victor. When overwhelmed, the peasant resorted to a new device: curtailment of the sown area to that sufficient only to feed his immediate family, leaving the remainder of the land uncultivated. By 1920, consequently, the sown area in Siberia had decreased by some 50 per cent, in the Caucasus by 25 per cent, and in the Ukraine, where in addition the fighting of the Civil War was rather heavy, the decline amounted to some 70 per cent to 80 per cent. This passive resistance, coupled with the continued policy of requisitioning, prepared favorable grounds for the famine which engulfed Russia from 1920 to 1922.

The policy of centralization, nationalization, bureaucratization, and requisition estranged from the government not only the peasants but the workers as well. By 1920 the workers, too, were tired of various regulations, compulsion, military discipline, and calls for additional sacrifices. Some expressed their disapproval of government policies by means of absenteeism from work, others through antigovernment resolutions, and some were brave enough to strike. These signs of disaffection occurred throughout Russia, including such Bolshevik strongholds as Petrograd and Kronstadt.

Everywhere the trend was against "the new Communist slavery" and "the bureaucratic trade unions," and in favor of "Soviets without Communists and Commissars." Because of this growing opposition it became clear that to continue War Communism as a normal system was impossible. A retreat to capitalism in the form of the New Economic Policy (NEP) became the only avenue of escape for the Bolsheviks.

Some Bolsheviks, including Lenin, retreated from War Communism gracefully, acknowledging their mistakes. There were many, however, who had difficulty in reconciling themselves to the inevitable retreat. In their view, War Communism was an attempt to realize an ideal communism. They applauded, for instance, adoption of the state-organized barter system and payments in kind instead of money transactions. They also welcomed the abolition of payment for the use of such services as the post, telegraph, railroad, water and electric supply, and the like. Finally, they approved the bitter "class war" in the villages, viewing it as an essential stage in eliminating bourgeois influence from the countryside. Not all were willing to admit that War Communism with all its excesses was not a system but a temporary expedient—an emergency method of supplying towns and armies with necessities, thus saving them from starvation and perhaps even from defeat in the darkest hours of the Civil War.

SUGGESTED READINGS

BORYS, JURIJ. *The Russian Communist Party and the Sovietization of Ukraine.* Stockholm: Norstedt and Söner, 1960.

BROWDER, ROBERT P. *Origins of Soviet-American Diplomacy.* Princeton: Princeton University Press, 1953.

BUNYAN, JAMES. *Intervention, Civil War, and War Communism in Russia, April-December, 1918. Documents and Materials.* Baltimore: The Johns Hopkins Press, 1936.

CARR, EDWARD HALLET. *A History of Soviet Russia, 1917–1923.* New York: Macmillan, 1952. Vol. 2.

CHAMBERLIN, WILLIAM HENRY. *The Russian Revolution, 1917–1921.* New York: Macmillan, 1935. Vol. 2.

DENIKIN, ANTON. *The White Army.* London: Cape, 1930.

GANKIN, OLGA HESS, and H. H. FISHER. *The Bolsheviks and the World War: The Origin of the Third International.* Stanford: Stanford University Press, 1940.

KAZEMZADEH, FIRUZ. *The Struggle for Transcaucasia, 1917–1921.* New York: Philosophical Library, 1951.

KENNAN, GEORGE F. *Decision to Intervene.* Princeton: Princeton University Press, 1958.

LOCKHART, R. H. BRUCE. *British Agent.* New York: Putnam's Sons, 1933.

MORLEY, JAMES WILLIAM. *The Japanese Thrust into Siberia, 1918.* New York: Columbia University Press, 1957.

PARK, ALEXANDER. *Bolshevism in Turkestan, 1917–1927.* New York: Columbia University Press, 1957.

RESHETAR, JOHN S. JR. *The Ukrainian Revolution, 1917–1920.* Princeton: Princeton University Press, 1952.

SCHAPIRO, LEONARD. *The Origin of the Communist Autocracy; Political Opposition in the Soviet State, 1917–1922.* Cambridge: Harvard University Press, 1955.

ULLMAN, RICHARD H. *Anglo-Soviet Relations, 1917–1921: Intervention and the War.* Princeton: Princeton University Press, 1961. Vol. 1.

UNTERBERGER, BETTY M. *America's Siberian Expedition, 1918–1920.* Durham, North Carolina: Duke University Press, 1956.

VARNECK, ELENA, and H. H. FISHER. *The Testimony of Kolchak and other Siberian Materials.* Stanford: Stanford University Press, 1935.

WHITE, JOHN A. *The Siberian Intervention.* Princeton: Princeton University Press, 1950.

WRANGEL, PIOTR N. *The Memoirs of General Wrangel.* London: Williams and Norgate, 1929.

THE EXPERIMENTAL
TWENTIES

PRELUDES TO KRONSTADT

The Bolshevik military triumph over the Whites at the end of 1920 enabled them to turn their attention to other pressing problems, with which
Russia was amply supplied. Thirty-one months of disastrous participation
in World War I and forty-six months of revolutionary turmoil had produced a catastrophic situation. It has been estimated (the actual figures
can never be ascertained) that between 1914 and 1921, Russia lost some
twenty-six million people. Of that figure, about fifteen million severed
their ties with Russia by establishing independent statehood (Finland,
Estonia, Latvia, Lithuania, Poland). Some two million were actual combat casualties, and about seven million were victims of Red and White
terror, hunger, and disease. The remaining two million—nobles as well as
industrialists, doctors, teachers, scientists, and other professional people,

whose skills the country could hardly afford to lose—fled Russia during the Revolution and the Civil War.

In addition to staggering human losses, war and revolution had inflicted heavy material damage upon Russia. Hundreds of cities and villages had been destroyed. Factories and mines had ceased to produce. Transportation had broken down. Barest needs of life had become unobtainable. The peasantry produced only a fraction of the crops it formerly had. Poor harvests in 1920 and 1921 and seeming indifference of the new regime to the needs of the vast masses of its subject peoples helped to produce famine on a gigantic scale, which affected some thirty-three million and caused the death of some five million people. While Bolshevik leaders blamed much of this great tragedy on war, foreign intervention, subversion at home, and the amateurish experimentation of War Communism, the inescapable fact remained that by the end of the Civil War the Bolshevik "Promised Land" was beginning to resemble hell on earth. Signs of revolt were visible everywhere.

Within the party the restlessness took the form of a vigorous discussion of two closely related issues. The first dealt with the problem of a centralized versus a decentralized decision-making process in determining Russia's future development. The second issue was the attempt to define the precise role trade unions were to play in socialized industry. On the surface these two issues seemed trivial. In reality, however, they touched upon one of the basic elements of Leninism: *centralized leadership*. Under the stress of Civil War, Lenin had succeeded in imposing upon the party a policy of dictatorial ruthlessness and authoritarianism originating in the Politburo, the Orgburo, and the Secretariat. These three new executive organs, each consisting of five members, were approved by the Eighth Party Congress held in March, 1919. Technically these new central bodies were under the supervision of the party's Central Committee. In reality, however, they were transcendent, with full authority over party membership inside and outside Russia. As the leading organs and hence the supreme agencies of power, their decisions were absolutely and unconditionally binding on all parts of the party "regardless of their nationality composition." Strictest centralism and rigorous "outright military discipline" were declared to be essential and the highest organs of power were given complete control over the appointment, transfer, or dismissal of party members, irrespective of the position they might hold inside or outside the party.

The first formidable challenge to these centralizing and disciplinary provisions developed at the Ninth Party Congress, which met from March 29 to April 5, 1920. The challenge evolved out of the controversy over the role trade unions were to play in socialized economy and whether they were independent agents or under strict party control. The critics of Lenin's policy of centralism, who called themselves the Democratic Centralist Opposition, were an offshoot of the Left Communist Movement of early 1918. They were led by Valerian V. Osinsky (1887–?), and included such long time Bolsheviks as Shliapnikov, Timothy V. Sapronov (1886–?), and others. They strongly advocated revolutionary principles of democracy and a collective decision-making process, and violently opposed bureaucracy, expediency, centralization, and hierarchical authority in the party, the government, and industry. In defense of their position they advanced the formula that while the general leadership belonged to the party, political authority belonged to the soviets, and economic authority to the trade unions.

The supporters of centralism rejected this proposition, arguing that it was impossible to separate politics from economics. Trotsky, who was surpassed by none in his advocacy of dictatorial ruthlessness and authoritarianism during the Civil War, insisted that Soviet Russia could attain socialism only through "authoritative regulation of the economic forces and resources of the country, and the centralized distribution of labor power in harmony with the general state plan." Accordingly, he argued that the state should have the right to mobilize civilian labor, and to transfer, assign, and dispatch it in military fashion to perform tasks economically useful for society. Lenin warmly defended Trotsky's views and shortly thereafter wrote an article entitled " 'Left-Wing' Communism: An Infantile Disorder," in which he denounced the opponents of the party's iron discipline and centralization as virtual agents of capitalism.

The defeat of the Whites and the Bolshevik defeat in Poland at the end of 1920 gave the opponents of centralism within the party additional strength for an all-out struggle against Lenin. Sensing an upsurge of anticentralist feeling, the leadership acknowledged at the Ninth Party Conference held in September, 1920, the need for more equality and democracy in the party, pledged itself to fight bureaucratism, and declared the repression of party dissenters "not permissible." The victory of the opposition was partial and short-lived, as it was soon overshadowed by renewal of the controversy over the role of trade unions in future economic development of Russia and their relation to the party and the government. Out of a multitude of suggestions on this problem, there emerged three main platforms. The first, sponsored by Trotsky and Bukharin, held that the unions were agencies of the state and that their main task should center on raising the productivity of labor. At the opposite extreme was the program of the "Workers' Opposition," sponsored by the Left Wing enthusiasts and trade unions themselves. Its spokesman was the fiery and colorful, if somewhat unstable, Madame Alexandra M. Kollontai (1872–1952). This group, citing Point 5 of the 1919 party program on economic issues, demanded that trade unions be given full control over the entire national economy. Between those two extremes was the program supported by Lenin, Zinoviev, Rykov, Kamenev, Stalin, and

Jan E. Rudzutak (1887–?), commonly known as the "platform of the ten." Their platform disapproved both the aforementioned proposals, and favored restoration of internal democracy within the unions. It also assigned to the unions the role of a link with the masses and a defender of workers' interests against bureaucratic tendencies of the state.

Early in March, 1921, the trade union issue, or more properly an acute intraparty struggle over centralism, was overshadowed by the crucial peasant problem. Up to now, except for forcing at gunpoint delivery of the assigned quota of grain, the regime had paid little or no attention to the peasantry. The peasants, as we noted in the previous chapter, resented this new form of exploitation and resorted to various forms of evasion and even armed self-defense. When they had exhausted all other media of resistance, the peasants ceased to produce. By the end of 1920, agricultural production had decreased to about one-half of the total for 1913, and the amount of cultivated land to about three-fourths. Shrinkage of production, unfavorable climatic conditions, and official indifference joined hands to bring about a gigantic tragedy—the famine. To many, Russia seemed ready for a new revolution.

Meanwhile, as the Civil War drew to a close at the end of 1920, deserters and demobilized veterans of many victorious campaigns returned home. Appalled by the unbelievable conditions in the countryside, many of them either instigated or joined rebellions. During the fall of 1920, peasant risings involving bands of tens of thousands erupted spontaneously throughout Russia, especially in agricultural areas, and increased in extent and violence throughout the winter. Now that the White danger had ceased to exist, the peasants saw no reason why they should continue to deliver oppressive exactions. From the countryside the discontent rapidly spread to cities and to the armed forces. Early in March, 1921, the massive discontent culminated in armed defiance of the Bolshevik regime at the naval base of Kronstadt, once a Bolshevik stronghold.

The Kronstadt rebellion, which formally began on March 2, 1921, was a dramatic climax to the anti-Bolshevik rural and urban unrest. The spark igniting it was the development early in 1921 of waves of strikes and demonstrations in Petrograd against food shortages and administrative overcentralization. The authorities put down these unrests forcibly as well as through concessions. The manner in which order was re-established did not please the Kronstadt sailors, who sympathized with the strikers. Inasmuch as anti-Bolshevik unrest had become a nation-wide phenomenon, the sailors, renowned for their revolutionary zeal, expected their own rebellion to succeed. Their platform, as adopted on February 28, 1921, by the crew of the battleship *Petropavlovsk*, was another indicator of envisaged success. It called for immediate re-election of the soviets by free and secret ballot. It demanded freedom of speech, press, and assembly for workers and peasants and for their political parties. It insisted that all political prisoners be released and that the privileged position of the Communist party and its armed detachments be abolished. The platform promised the peasants full rights to do as they liked with their land, and advocated the ending of discrimination in food rationing.

Sensing the danger, the authorities sent to Kronstadt Mikhail I. Kalinin (1875–1946), Chairman of the Central Executive Committee of the Soviet. It was felt that his peasant background might turn the tide. It did not. Kalinin was shouted down, and a throng of some twelve thousand men enthusiastically approved the program adopted earlier. On March 2, 1921, the defiant sailors set up a Provisional Revolutionary Committee, which they selected from among themselves. The government requested the Committee to surrender peacefully. The Committee refused to comply, but at the same time, apparently feeling that justice was on its side, it did very little to strengthen its position. To the sailors' misfortune, the expected revolt on the mainland of Russia failed to materialize. Instead, on March 7, government forces directed by Trotsky and led by Tukhachevsky began vigorous preparation for an assault which took place on March 18. Some 140 delegates to the Tenth Party Congress, which had convened on March 8, joined the soldiers in the final storming of the sailors' stronghold. The fortress fell and some fifteen thousand of its defenders who surrendered were massacred without trial. The Kronstadt rebellion against the Bolshevik regime was over, but the message carried by the revolt was not entirely lost.

KRONSTADT REPERCUSSIONS: PARTY DISCIPLINE AND NEP

Publicly, the Bolsheviks labelled the Kronstadt rebellion and the events which preceded it a work of counterrevolution. Privately, Lenin admitted quite frankly and honestly that the rebels "do not want the White Guards, and they do not want our power either." To prevent any possible future peasant-supported proletarian rebellion against the dictatorship of the proletariat—a situation for which Marxist-Leninist doctrine made no provision—Lenin masterminded, and the Tenth Party Congress approved, two far-reaching policy changes. One dealt with the strengthening of party discipline; the other officially abandoned War Communism in favor of the New Economic Policy (NEP).

The strengthening of party discipline assumed the form of two resolutions: (1) "On Party Unity," and (2) "On the Syndicalist and Anarchist Deviation in Our Party." The first resolution insisted that to maintain its monopoly of power the party must preserve "the unity and solidarity of the ranks" and "unanimity of will." These prerequisites accordingly excluded all signs of factionalism or the formation of dissident groups with separate platforms, whose objective was to "segregate and create their own group discipline." Party factionalism, the resolution went on to suggest, in practice "inevitably leads to the weakening of teamwork" and to the strengthening of the opponents of revolution. While the resolution encouraged criticism of the party's shortcomings, it made clear that "everyone who criticizes must see to it that the form of his criticism takes into account the position of the party, surrounded as it is by a ring of enemies." All factional groups with a platform within the party, such as the Workers' Opposition or Democratic Centralism groups, were ordered to dissolve or face "absolute and immediate expulsion from the Party." The Central Committee was given full disciplinary powers, including that of expulsion from the party.

The second resolution labelled the views of Workers' Opposition on trade unions as "a syndicalist and anarchist deviation," and placed the blame for it on insufficient knowledge of communist theory and on "the influence exercised upon the proletariat and on the Russian Communist party by the petty-bourgeois element." This resolution pledged to "wage an unswerving and systematic ideological struggle against these ideas," stressed that their propagation was incompatible with membership in the party, and instructed the Central Committee to enforce these decisions. Though relatively brief in content, these two resolutions enabled Lenin to gain two fundamental objectives: the strengthening of the party's monopoly on political power before relaxing economic controls in the country at large; and the establishing of a formal procedure for combating factionalism, which, in practice, as one observer aptly put it, meant that "whoever was in a position to pack the Central Committee could dispose of any minority within that body and within the Party at his leisure," by victimization, transfer, expulsion or outright liquidation. This became evident as early as the summer of 1921, when some 200,000 members were expelled from the party. Lenin's centralism, in other words, laid the foundation for Stalin's regimentation.

Far-reaching also in its implication was the Lenin-sponsored resolution on the NEP, which the Tenth Party Congress approved. Intended to appease the starving and restless peasants, this resolution called for replacement of requisitioning by a tax in kind, and abolition of restrictions on peasant trade in surplus products. On March 21, 1921, the government translated this resolution officially into a "tax in kind" decree, which technically began the dismantling of War Communism. Under the new arrangement the tax was to be progressive, was to be less than what the peasant had given through requisitions, and was "to be taken in the form of the percentage or partial deduction from the products raised in the peasant holding, taking into account the harvest, the number of consumers in the holding, and the number of cattle on hand." The new tax law promised the poorest peasants exemption from taxation, while to the industrious it offered certain privileges. It abolished collective responsibility and made each individual peasant responsible only for the tax falling on him. Once he fulfilled his obligation, the peasant could dispose of his surplus, if any, as he wished. He could deliver it to the state in return for industrial products, or he could sell it on the open market.

Because of the harvest failure of 1921, followed by a disastrous famine, the new tax in kind decree benefited neither the peasant nor the government. The chief immediate significance of the decree centered in its creation of a chain reaction effect. Abandonment of requisitioning ended the need for the Food Requisitioning Detachments, which were ordered disbanded. In May, 1922, as a further concession to the impoverished peasantry, the government limited the tax in kind to 10 per cent of production, and prohibited the seizure of livestock as a penalty for nonpayment of taxes. On May 22, 1922, the Central Executive Committee of the Soviet approved a "Fundamental Law on the Exploitation of Land by the Toilers." While preserving in theory the public ownership of land, this law gave the peasant a choice of the form of land tenure— communal, individual, associated, or mixed. It gave him also the right to treat his holding as his own, to lease it, to increase it, and even to use hired labor to cultivate it. The new Agrarian Code, which went into effect on December 1, 1922, embodied all these provisions, and while not recognizing any

Petrograd, 1922. The Red Army on review.

rights in perpetuity, implied that the rights it accorded were of indefinite duration. For the first time since the revolution, the Russian peasant was given a sense of security in existing arrangements. This confidence, in turn, acted as a strong stimulus to increased efforts and intensified production, and launched Soviet Russia on the road to economic recovery. According to official estimates, by 1925, agricultural recovery in the Northern Caucasus reached 77.5 per cent of the year 1916; in Kazakhstan the figure was 71.9 per cent; in Siberia 92.2 per cent; and in the Ukraine 96.1 per cent.

While intended only to appease the peasants, through implication the original NEP decree also exercised a profound influence on other sectors of the economy. In the first place, since the peasant could not legally dispose of his surplus, it was necessary to legalize private trade. The government accomplished this through three key decrees of March 29, of May 24, and of July 19, 1921. The revival of private trade, in turn, necessitated resumption of the use of money as the primary basis of exchange, and the appearance of brokers—commonly called Nepmen—who knew how to find buyers and sellers at the right moment, who could advise on prices, and perform like functions. Between 1921 and 1923, through a series of official decrees, the government introduced stable currency, created a new State Bank of the RSFSR, restored financial and commercial independence of cooperatives, legalized agricultural credit and loan associations, established state saving banks, and a state lottery, and in many other ways returned to the financial methods of the past.

Though not designed to do so, the NEP exerted a powerful influence on industry. This was inevitable, for if the peasant was to be encouraged to increase his production, the surplus of which could be sold on the open market, industry had to manufacture goods for him to buy. It became necessary, therefore, to undo many of the excesses of War Communism. The first step in that direction was government encouragement of industrial cooperatives. This was followed by a promise of release from nationalization or municipalization of small industrial enterprises which employed not more than ten to twenty hired workers. A decree of December 10, 1922, restored to the former owners all those enterprises which had been ordered nationalized, but which had not yet in fact been taken over by the state. A few months earlier the party had approved the idea of leasing small nationalized enterprises. While cooperatives received preferential treatment, private persons were not ruled out. Party members, however, were. By September 1, 1922, out of a total of 7,100 enterprises, some 3,800 employing 68,000 workers had been leased to cooperatives or to former owners. The aim of these and similar measures was to accord to small entrepreneurs of the countryside the same legal security and the same opportunity as had been given to the peasants. "The controlling heights," which employed over 80 per cent of the working force, the government kept firmly under its control. This included all large-scale industry, all transportation, all foreign trade, and all banking and credit facilities. By these concessions, the government gave up little, but gained a great deal of confidence. According to official estimates, industrial production, which had stood at about 18 per cent of the prewar level in 1920–1921, rose to 27 per cent in 1921–1922, and to 35 per cent in 1922–1923. By 1925–1926, the coal industry registered the largest advance, and almost reached prewar output. Iron and manganese trailed somewhat, but were not too far behind coal.

The return to private ownership and management of industrial enterprises and to a free market under the NEP also forced the return to a free labor market. It became necessary to end obligatory state service, which had been introduced during War Communism, and to dismantle much of the machinery of compulsion. Through a series of decrees during 1921 and 1922, the government removed the main restrictions on the movement of workers from one job to another, and reintroduced the wage system. While these measures helped to restore prewar normalcy, they also helped to create unemployment. Depressed conditions of the workers, in turn, provided the trade unions with an opportunity to protect workers' interests in state as well as private enterprises and thus to gain a degree of independence. They could bargain for higher wages, strike against private employers, and in theory even against the state. This independence was illusory rather than real, however, because trade unions remained under absolute control of the Communist party, which, "through its central and local organizations, as before unconditionally directs the whole ideological side of the work of the trade unions."

Though it was inevitable and greatly beneficial to the economic rehabilitation of the country, not all Bolsheviks welcomed the NEP. Opponents of Lenin's "strategic retreat" objected to the NEP on two grounds. First, they argued that the NEP represented the sacrifice of a planned economy, based on heavy industry, to the well-being of the peasants, whom they regarded as the natural enemy of socialism. Second, their Marxist indoctrination told them that a prosperous peasantry and small entrepreneurs sooner or later, by reviving capitalism, would replace socialism, thus changing the entire political superstructure. Lenin tried to assure his skeptical associates that their fears were groundless, inasmuch as the Communist party retained the monopoly of power with which to determine everything. The opposition however was not convinced and continued to regard the NEP as a betrayal of the interests of the workers and of the revolution. Throughout 1921, opponents of the NEP continually voiced their complaints against it and formed factions, notwithstanding the party's ban on such activity. In February, 1922, a group of twenty-two malcontents, former members of the Workers' Opposition, presented their grievances to the Communist International, protesting against mistreatment, persecution, "suppression of the workers' independence and initiative" and other "abnormalities." Another group, led by Alexander A. Bogdanov (1873–1928), Lenin's onetime second-in-command, and calling itself the "Workers' Truth," attacked the party and the NEP for its "state capitalism" which allowed the exploitation of workers for the benefit of "the organizer-intelligentsia." Although authorities suppressed these and similar groups critical of the NEP and "the correctness" of the party line, they continued to reappear under different names and leaders throughout most of the 1920's.

"CONCESSIONS" TO NATIONAL MINORITIES

Concession to the peasants, with all its far-reaching repercussions was only one basic characteristic of the NEP. Another was the "concession" to national minorities. In a previous chapter we noted that before the Bolshevik seizure of power, stubbornly convinced that only centralism was capable of progress and economic strength, Lenin repeatedly rejected the demands of national minorities for political independence. Territorial disintegration of the multi-national tsarist empire and the triumph of local nationalism after the downfall of monarchy, however, forced him, at least outwardly, to reverse his stand. Without abandoning centralism, Lenin and his followers, between March and November, 1917, appeared as strong opponents of the policy of Russification and staunch supporters of the principle of self-determination. By advocating such a policy, the Bolsheviks achieved two basic objectives: they deepened the existing crisis of the Provisional Government, and they won for themselves the support of Russia's subject peoples. The crowning achievement of the Bolshevik "pro-self-determination" policy was the "Declaration of the Rights of the Peoples of Russia" issued on November 15, 1917, which promised Russia's nationalities equality and sovereignty and the right to free self-determination, "even to the point of separation and the formation of an independent state." When national minorities moved to take advantage of these promises, the Bolsheviks reverted in practice to their original stand. In the course of the Civil War, with the help of local Bolshevik organizations and above all with the backing of the Red Army, Lenin offered each nationality a government consisting of his own trusted emissaries and thus reserved for himself the right to determine which nation could separate itself from Russia. Between 1918 and 1920 the Bolsheviks created on the periphery of Russia several "Soviet Socialist Republics" (Belorussian, Ukrainian, Georgian, Armenian and Azerbaidzhan), while within the RSFSR itself they carved out several "autonomous republics" (Bashkir, Volga German, and Kazakh), and a number of "autonomous regions" (Chuvash, Tartar, and Karelian). Each of the "soviet socialist republics" immediately assumed the posture of an independent state and equipped itself with such essential attributes of sovereignty as an "independent government" and a constitution. Similarly as had the government of the RSFSR, the new governments eliminated private ownership of land and all other means of production, assured the political power to the "working class," granted only to the toiling masses freedom of speech, press, and assembly, and introduced the dictatorship of the proletariat as well as all other "benefits" of the soviet system.

But while they posed as independent political entities, each of these republics expressed "complete solidarity with the existing Soviet republics" as well as readiness to enter with them "into closest political union for the common fight, for the triumph of the world communist revolution." On the basis and in pursuance of such statements, early in 1919 all republics unified their military commands, and economic, labor, financial, and railroad administrations. By the end of the Civil War, the unification process affected all major media of communication and transportation. It is essential to remember that local Bolshevik organizations never enjoyed any "autonomy," for, as a resolution on party organization approved by the Eighth Party Congress, March, 1919, stipulated, there was room for only "one unitary centralized Communist Party with a unitary Central Committee directing all the work of the party in all parts of the RSFSR." The resolution further stipulated that "decisions of the Russian Communist Party and its leading institutions" were unconditionally binding on all parts of the party "regardless of their nationality composition," and that the "Central Committees of the Ukrainian, Latvian, and Lithuanian Communists enjoy the rights of regional committees of the party and are wholly subordinated to the Central Committee of the Russian Communist Party."

Stalin, who then was responsible for the implementation of the nationality policy, revealed the Bolshevik duplicity on the self-determination principle, and the reason behind their obsession with centralism, in the following words: "We are," he said in 1920, "in favor of the secession of India, Arabia, Egypt, Morocco, and other colonies from the Entente, because secession in this case would mean the liberation of those oppressed countries from imperialism and strengthening the position of revolutions. We are against the separation of the border regions from Russia since separation would here involve imperialist servitude for the border regions, thus undermining the revolutionary power of Russia and strengthening the position of imperialism."

The natural result of this policy of expedience was the emergence of nationalist sentiment among the non-Russian peoples. The rise of this sentiment was also stimulated by the attitudes of various of Stalin's lieutenants, such as Lazar M. Kaganovich (1893–), Molotov, Sergei M. Kirov (1886–1934), and Gregory K. Ordzhonikidze (1886–1937), who were responsible for the implementation of party directives in various republics. As adherents to the centralist principle, these men strongly despised national minorities and considered everything non-Russian to be either reactionary or bourgeois and hence unworthy of existence. Their overzealousness in imposing centralism and the Russian language and culture on non-Russian peoples surpassed the tsarist Russification policy, lost much good will for the Bolsheviks, caused a great deal of trouble, and on occasion even drew official reprimands. Ruthless centralization of the border areas was continued nevertheless throughout the Civil War, as were all other centralist features of War Communism.

The Tenth Party Congress, which initiated the NEP, also approved a lengthy resolution on the nationality problem. Sponsored by Stalin, the resolution was full of contradicting, ambiguous clichés. On the one hand, apparently to build national ego, it described every Soviet republic as "a deadly menace to imperialism." At the same time it argued that "not a single Soviet Republic, standing alone, can regard itself as insured against economic exhaustion and military defeat by world imperialism," and accordingly called for a close political, economic, and military unity among Soviet republics. Though this new dialectic created little immediate enthusiasm among many party members, all were ordered to assist cautiously the non-Russian peoples to "catch up" with Great Russia. They were directed to help them develop administrative institutions, press, schools, theaters, and other educational and cultural institutions through which communist policy could be disseminated, in order to create a new Soviet culture: "National in form, socialist in content." This was not an easy task, for many minorities of Soviet Russia, especially in Soviet Asia, were at a very low cultural level. For some it was necessary even to devise alphabets, because their languages had never been reduced to written form. In other areas, it meant simply the establishment of schools with instruction in the native language. Determined to pose as liberators and benefactors to these peoples, party leaders quite frequently emphasized the need to accomplish the task at all cost and reminded all party members to carry out their obligations. Although there was some slowdown, the reduction of illiteracy advanced throughout the 1920's and stands as one of the noblest achievements of the NEP period.

While making concessions to minorities in the cultural field, between 1921 and 1924 the Bolsheviks introduced several vital measures which strengthened political centralism. On February 22, 1922, for instance, all Soviet Republics, which were independent in theory, delegated their rights in the sphere of foreign relations to the RSFSR. On May 9, 1922, the RSFSR deprived all republics of their rights in foreign trade. On December 30, 1922, all republics entered into a treaty designed to bring further unity to their policies, by means of a new political federation called the Union of Soviet Socialist Republics (USSR). A new constitution was ready by July 6, 1923, and it was ratified on January 31, 1924.

Like the 1918 constitution, this document was imbued with the militant spirit of the newborn dictatorship of the proletariat. Its preamble announced that since the formation of the Soviet republics the world had been divided into two camps: *the camp of capitalism,* with its alleged "national hate and inequality, colonial slavery and chauvinism, national oppression and massacres, brutalities, and imperialist war," and *the camp of socialism,* with its alleged "reciprocal confidence and peace, national liberty and equality, peaceful co-existence, and fraternal collaboration of peoples." Although in 1924 the USSR consisted of only four states (the RSFSR, the Ukrainian SSR, the Belorussian SSR, and the Transcaucasian SFSR), the constitution expressed a hope that ultimately the socialist system would extend throughout the world. In 1925 the Turkmen and Uzbek, and in 1929 the Tadzhik Autonomous Republics were elevated to full Union status within the USSR. Meanwhile the Transcaucasian SFSR was divided into the Azerbaidzhan, Armenian, and Georgian Republics. As a result of these changes, in 1929 the USSR consisted of nine republics.

In administrative structure the USSR resembled the RSFSR. At the bottom of the state administrative pyramid were the village soviets; then came city and county soviets. Above them were the soviets of territories, provinces, and autonomous and constituent republics. At the apex of the pyramid was the All-Union Congress of Soviets. In theory the Congress of Soviets was the supreme authority of the USSR. In reality it was an unwieldy assembly of some two thousand dignitaries who came to Moscow once a year to listen to the declarations of the leaders, to approve their policies, and to "elect" the All-Union Central Executive Committee to act as the supreme legislative and executive power between the brief sessions of the Congress. Constitutionally, the All-Union Central Executive Committee consisted of two houses: the Soviet of the Union, whose 371 members represented the population of the USSR, and the Soviet of Nationalities, whose members represented territorial-administrative units on the basis of five representatives for each member union republic and one for each autonomous republic. In reality, however, thanks to the policy of biased apportionment, both houses were dominated by the RSFSR. The constitution stipulated that both houses meet three times annually. Between meetings of the Central Executive Committee, the constitution designated a twenty-seven-member Presidium of the Central Executive Committee as "the supreme organ of legislative, executive, and administrative power in the USSR." In essence, though, the administrative and executive functions of the government were handled by the *Sovnarkom* of the USSR.

Under the 1924 constitution the federal government exercised complete control over foreign relations, had the exclusive right to declare war, conclude peace, ratify international treaties, contract foreign loans, and direct foreign and domestic trade. It also had the power to modify the frontiers of the USSR as well as of individual republics, and it controlled the admission of new republics into the union. The federal government established the bases and the general plan of all the national economy; defined the domains of industry; directed transport, post, and telegraphs; and organized and directed the armed forces. It approved the federal and the republics' budgets; set taxes; issued money; established general principles of exploitation and use of natural resources; controlled population movements within the union; supervised courts, education, health, weights and measures, and the rights of foreigners. The federal government likewise had the power to abrogate the acts of union republics if those acts were "contrary to the present constitution." Outside those limits, each member republic was "sovereign," exercised its "public powers independently," and even had the "right to withdraw freely from the union." On the surface this seemed a fair arrangement. In reality, however, from its inception the USSR was a very highly centralized state, led and directed by the Communist party. The latter, while not officially acknowledged in the 1924 constitution, was nevertheless the real source of power and unity.

EXPERIMENTS WITH THE FAMILY, CHURCH, AND EDUCATION

From the moment they seized power, the Bolsheviks felt they could not project Russia's development along Marxist-Leninist lines without introducing drastic changes in family, church, and education. Before the revolution the Russian family was a very conservative social institution. It was dominated by parental authority and governed by ancient customs and traditions. While they varied from place to place, many customs were obsolete and even barbaric. The customs of many non-Russian peoples, especially those in the Asiatic part of the empire, were even worse. Moslem law, for instance, approved polygamy, ignored the dignity of women, and even made possible the purchase as well as the inheritance of a wife. Throughout Imperial Russia, religion exercised a strong influence on family affairs. Church rites were obligatory for all legal marriage. Marriage between people of different faiths was prohibited. Divorce was difficult to obtain.

To weaken religious control over family affairs, as early as December 31, 1917, the Bolsheviks declared that church marriage was a private affair and that only civil marriage was legally binding. They established legal equality of the sexes, greatly liberalized marriage procedures, granted complete freedom of divorce, and gave full equality to children born in or out of wedlock. Later decrees legalized abortions and dropped incest, bigamy, and adultery from the list of criminal offenses. The Family Code of October, 1918, established the independence of all members of the family and deprived fathers of much of the authority they had previously held. To create a further rift between the old and young generation, children were instructed not only to disobey, but to report if their parents tried in any way to influence them against the policies of the new regime.

While these and other early innovations were aimed in part at freeing the individual and the family from religious influences, their fundamental objective was to destroy the patriarchal way of life, the mores of the old order, and the family—the strongholds of tradition and conservatism. Chaos and confusion of the Civil War helped greatly to undermine family life. Many parents had been killed. Families had been torn asunder. Thousands of orphans followed army units through various campaigns. Many more thousands of homeless youngsters joined bands and tramped through the country searching for food, terrorizing the population, stealing and perpetrating all kinds of crimes. In some areas the situation was so bad that authorities were forced to resort to extreme measures. Many of these homeless vagabonds subscribed to Madame Kollontai's ideas of "free love" and similar deviations.

Although the effects of these developments were unfortunate, the government introduced no change in family legislation during the years of the NEP. The new Family Code of 1926 restated the features of earlier legislation on marriage and family, except for two innovations. These were provision for adoption of homeless children, and establishment of guardianship for orphans. When compared with prerevolutionary attitudes, Russian family life showed a drastic change. In 1927, for instance, the divorce-marriage ratio was one to four. In the United States for the same year the ratio was one to six.

Next to the family, the Bolsheviks considered organized religion as the significant obstacle in their attempt to project Russia's development along Marxist-Leninist lines. Their attitude towards religion was influenced in part by Marxist ideology, which held that religion was "the opium of the people," and in part it was influenced by Russian conditions. Before the revolution the Russian Orthodox Church was an inseparable part of the state. It was headed by the tsar, but since the days of Peter the Great it had been administered in his name by the Procurator of the Holy Synod. Under those conditions, Church policy was always in perfect harmony with that of the state—a situation which many Russians resented.

Following the collapse of the monarchy, Church spokesmen tended to be liberal. But as the summer of 1917 progressed, many of them turned to the defense of the old regime in word and deed. This became evident during the meeting of the All-Russian Church Council (*Sobor*) in Moscow late in August, 1917, the first such meeting since 1681. In its composition, the *Sobor* was decidedly conservative. Many of its members, for instance, supported Kornilov's efforts to preserve military discipline—support which boded ill for the Church, inasmuch as Kornilov's efforts collapsed. The *Sobor* also proclaimed Metropolitan Tikhon of Moscow as Patriarch, the first to be installed in Russia since 1700.

One of the first acts of the new Patriarch was the disapproval of the Bolshevik seizure of power and their peace talks with the Germans. The Bolsheviks, still insecure in power and unwilling to antagonize pious Russians, did not retaliate directly against the Church. They struck indirectly, early in December, 1917, by ordering nationalization of all land, including that of the Church and monasteries. Other decrees recognized civil marriages, separated the Church from the state, deprived the Church of state subsidies, made religion a private affair, separated education from the Church, stripped the Church of its jurisdiction over marriage and divorce, and seized Church records of births and deaths. By these decrees, for which they were anathematized, the Bolsheviks dispossessed the Church of its economic power and of its control over individuals, and removed it as a possible barrier to their efforts to remake Russia along Marxist-Leninist lines.

The development of the Civil War intensified considerably the delicate nature of Church-state relations. Although they weakened it greatly, the Bolsheviks continued to view the Church as a hostile organization. All clergy were deprived of voting rights and those who resisted changing conditions were arrested. Those clergymen who actively sided with the Whites—and there were many who did—were executed. In October, 1918, Patriarch Tikhon, because of his renewed indictment of the Bolshevik regime, was placed under house arrest. Shortly thereafter the Bolsheviks ordered further confiscation of Church and monastery property, an action which netted them over seven billion rubles.

While they opposed the clergy and sought to bring an end to religion, the Bolsheviks were unwilling to provoke the devout believers and did not interfere with their worship. They hoped through education to change the people's view. This policy was explicitly outlined in the 1919 party program, which stated that in its religious policy the party was "guided by the conviction that only the realization of conscious and systematic social and economic activity of the masses will lead to the disappearance of religious prejudices." The aim of the party, the program went on to say, was "to destroy the ties between the exploiting classes and the organization of religious propaganda, at the same time helping the toiling masses actually to liberate their minds from religious superstitions, and organizing on a wide scale scientific-educational and antireligious propaganda." Party members were warned to be very careful to avoid "offending the religious susceptibilities of believers, which leads only to the strengthening of religious fanaticism."

At the close of the Civil War, when it became evident that the Bolsheviks were emerging victorious over the Whites, the Patriarch called for submission to the new regime. Shortly thereafter, however, the hostility between the Church and the new regime flared up anew as the result of misunderstanding. During the famine the Church tried to organize its own relief for the starving—an action which the Bolsheviks viewed with suspicion, being afraid that it would be used for propaganda purposes. Soon they relented, but they also asked the Church to give up its gold, jewels, and other treasures. Patriarch Tikhon interpreted this to mean that the state was openly opposing the Church, and refused to surrender the Church treasures. In his opposition he was supported by the émigré Russian church leaders. Their support, however, provided the Bolsheviks with a pretext for Tikhon's arrest in May, 1922, and for a renewed bitter attack against the Church and the clergy. In June, 1923, Tikhon was freed on condition that he disassociate himself from all anti-Communist movements. This he tried to do until his death in April, 1925. His successor, Metropolitan Peter, was arrested in December, 1925, and sent to Siberia. Early in 1926, the government also arrested Peter's successor, Metropolitan Sergei. In view of these arrests it appeared that a reconciliation between the Church and the state had become the only solution. In June, 1926, Sergei appealed to the government for recognition of the Orthodox Church, which was granted in May, 1927. Though branded by many as a surrender to the Bolsheviks, this reconciliation brought one positive result. It ended government support of the "Living Church" which had broken away from the main body in 1922, and which favored liberalization of regulations and practices of the Church as well as curbing the power of its hierarchy.

Although it was now allowed to function, the existence of the Orthodox Church in Russia was precarious. Its activities were limited, its officials suspect, and many of its buildings closed. In 1927, for instance, the authorities closed seventeen churches and thirty-four monasteries, as well as fourteen synagogues, and nine mosques. In 1928, 359 churches, forty-eight monasteries, fifty-nine synagogues, and thirty-eight mosques were closed. Moreover, the Church had to compete with the Communist party-approved antireligious propaganda spread through schools, press, and all other media of communication and education. As early as 1922, the Bolsheviks began to publish a newspaper, *Bezbozhnik* (The Atheist), in which they made a concentrated effort at attacking religion. In 1925, there was organized around *Bezbozhnik* a group which called itself The League of Militant Atheists. Headed by Emilian M. Yaroslavsky (1878–1943), the League sponsored, with the party's blessing, antireligious activities throughout the country; published books, pamphlets, and periodicals; and staged antireligious parades. Though officially its membership was small (in 1928 the League had some 130,000 members), its work among the youth in cities made considerable headway primarily because of official support and the greatly weakened position of the family and of the Church.

From the outset the Bolsheviks realized that however profoundly they weakened the influence of family and church, they could not hope to project Russia's development along Marxist-Leninist lines without introducing drastic changes in education. Three factors seem to have strongly influenced Boshevik determination and efforts. First, they inherited a country whose educational system, while renowned for its academic and scientific excellence (which compared favorably with the best available in Western Europe), was designed for the few. Second, they inherited a country whose population, although forced to remain outside the halls of learning, had a deep respect as well as desire for learning—a condition which in itself was a powerful revolutionary force. And, finally, they inherited a country whose teachers, while approving the revolution, were less than enthusiastic about Bolshevik policies.

The Bolshevik remaking of Russian education had two distinct phases. First, the new regime destroyed the old system of education from elementary through university. On February 5, 1918, the school was ordered separated from the Church, and the teaching of religious doctrines in all state, private, and public educational institutions was prohibited. The Educational Act of October 16, 1918, replaced the Imperial school system by a nine-year unified polytechnical school. Characteristics of the old system, such as examinations, homework, and discipline, were abolished. Coeducation was introduced on all levels. Administration was entrusted to school collectives composed of teachers, students, and school employees. Teaching of classic and modern languages was abandoned, as was that of history. Instead, emphasis was placed on sociologically-oriented social science and practical work. After August 8, 1918, any boy or girl of sixteen or over had the right to enroll in a university, regardless of his or her educational background. A decree of October 8, 1918, abolished all academic degrees. A curriculum reform of 1920 further de-emphasized liberal education in favor of specialization in science, and in the fall of 1922 the government annulled the autonomous status of Russian universities. By these and other decrees the new regime destroyed the old educational system, and critics of these changes were either dismissed or arrested. Some fled abroad, and only a few agreed to cooperate with the new regime.

The second phase of the remaking of Russian education was the introduction of a system which would serve the new regime. One of the essential features of the new system was the promise to bring education to everyone. This promise found its first expression on November 7, 1917, in a statement issued by the People's Commissariat for Education, which called for: (1) an immediate struggle for the elimination of illiteracy through free general obligatory education; (2) training of teachers; (3) high education budget; (4) uniform schools, and (5) a wide network of adult educational institutions. The constitution of July, 1918, promised to provide "the workers and the poorer peasants with a complete, universal, and free education," while the 1919 party program vowed to transform "the school from an instrument of class domination of the bourgeoisie . . . into an instrument for a communist regeneration of society." Education, promised the party program, was to be free and compulsory, general and technical, with instruction in native language, free of religious influence, and for both sexes up to the age of seventeen. The state was to supply all pupils with food, clothing, shoes, and all other school needs. The state was to assist adult education and to aid financially those students who desired a university education.

The implementation of this program was impossible as long as civil war was in progress. With the return of normalcy under the NEP, the Bolsheviks mobilized all agencies to bring not only education but every aspect of culture into the service of the new regime. One vital agency in this effort was the People's Commissariat for Enlightenment, headed by Lunacharsky, a close associate of Lenin. Under the aegis of the Commissariat were all schools from nurseries to universities, theaters, museums, art galleries, films, radio, book publishing, libraries, and adult educational institutions. Other vital agencies through which the party transmitted its indoctrination were the trade unions, the Red Army, the *Komsomol* (Communist Youth Organization), factory schools, night schools, village reading rooms, and village teachers. Though they differed in approach, each agency had the same objective: to transform the thinking process and personal habits of the people from a religious, tradition-bound outlook to a materialistic one, and to strengthen their belief in the economic system of socialism and their faith in the leadership of the Communist party. Despite a great amount of inefficiency, the Bolsheviks made much progress in spreading their propaganda and taught some seven million illiterates the rudiments of reading and writing. It was an effort that had no historical parallel.

EXPERIMENTS IN LITERATURE, THE THEATER,
AND THE CINEMA

The Bolshevik remaking of Russia left a significant imprint not only on the political, economic, and social fabric of the country, but also on every phase of the intellectual life. In literature the impact was initially a negative one, for most of the Russian writers, in common with the majority of the Russian intelligentsia, assumed a hostile attitude towards the new regime, left the country, and joined *émigré* groups in Berlin, Prague, or Paris. Included in this exodus were: Ivan A. Bunin (1870–1953), a leading writer and the first Russian to receive the Nobel Prize for literature; Alexander I. Kuprin (1870–1938), novelist; Michael Artsybashev (1878–1927), novelist; Leonid N. Andreev (1871–1919), short story writer, novelist and playwright; Ilia G. Ehrenburg (1891–), novelist and journalist; Dimitri S. Merezhkovsky (1865–1941), symbolist writer; Viacheslav I. Ivanov (1866–1949), symbolist poet; Aleksei N. Tolstoy (1883–1945), novelist and playwright; Boris V. Savinkov (1879–1925), radical novelist; and Marina I. Tsvetaeva (1892–1941), poetess. Of these, Ehrenburg and Tolstoy returned to Russia in 1923, and Kuprin and Tsvetaeva in the mid-thirties; all the others remained abroad.

Those writers who chose to stay in Russia following the Bolshevik coup were divided into two groups: outspoken opponents of the new regime, and apolitical supporters of the revolution. The first group included Feodor K. Teternikov (1863–1927), a leading symbolist who wrote under the pseudonym of Feodor Sologub; Nikolai S. Guimilov (1886–1921), who was executed in 1921, a poet and a founder of the anti-Symbolist movement known as *Acmeism;* Anna A. Gorenko (1880–), poetess who wrote under the pseudonym of Anna Akhmatova; and poet Osip E. Mandelstram (1892–?). The supporters of the revolution included Maxim Gorky; Alexander A. Blok (1873–1924), symbolist writer; Boris N. Bugaev (1880–1934), a symbolist writer who published under the pseudonym of Andrei Bely; Valery Ia. Briusov (1873–1924), symbolist poet; Sergei A. Esenin (1895–1925), symbolist poet; Vladimir V. Maiakovsky (1893–1930), a leading Russian futurist, and for a few years unofficial poet laureate of the new regime; and Efim A. Pridvorov (1883–1945), a poet who published under the pseudonym of Demian Bedny. Several of the supporters of the new order in Russia became disillusioned with their ideal and committed suicide (Blok, Briusov, and Maiakovsky); while some went into self-imposed exile (Gorky from 1921 to 1928 and Bely from 1922 to 1923). Because of the exodus of leading writers, Russian literature, already in a state of disintegration before the revolution, declined further after the Bolshevik seizure of power.

In addition to the exodus of leading writers, the abnormal conditions of the Civil War and War Communism exercised a negative influence on the cultural life of the country. Between 1918 and 1920 the Bolsheviks succeeded in silencing not only their political opponents but uncooperative writers as well. They achieved the latter through such devices as the suspension of publication of leading literary and academic quarterlies, monthlies, weeklies, and even newspapers; nationalization of publishing houses; granting of a monopoly of publication to the State Publishing Organization, known by its Russian abbreviation as *Gosizdat;* denial to

Maxim Gorky   *Ilia Ehrenburg*

uncooperative writers and journalists of such basic needs of existence as food and fuel; and support of such groups as Futurists, Cosmists, Imaginists, and other bohemians who applauded the goals of the revolution.

Between 1918 and 1920 one of the most celebrated literary groups was centered around the journal *Proletarskaia Kultura* (Proletarian Culture), and was known by its Russian abbreviation as *Proletkult*. *Proletkult* was founded late in 1917. Its basic aim was to develop a new literature by and for the proletariat. In pursuit of that goal, studios were established in Moscow and Petrograd for the training of new writers, and many leading literary personalities, including Briusov and Bely, taught in these studios. In theory membership in the *Proletkult* was reserved exclusively to workers. In reality, however, anyone who accepted Bolshevik ideology and extolled collectivism was welcomed. Lenin and some of his close associates, preoccupied with the more pressing problems of the Civil War, initially supported the aim of the *Proletkult*. However, when its spokesmen (especially Alexander A. Malinovsky, 1873–1928) began to demand independence of party control, the *Proletkult* was placed under the supervision of the People's Commissariat for Enlightenment late in 1920, and disbanded altogether in 1923. Its demise was not tragic because the contribution of its members was significant neither in quality nor quantity.

The fading of the fortunes of the *Proletkult* coincided with the official dismantling of War Communism and the inauguration of the NEP. Though not intended, the NEP had a far reaching impact on literature. The limited restoration of capitalist economy and the resumption of private trade made possible the reappearance of private book printing and selling facilities. The return to normalcy also facilitated the appearance of such new journals as *Literaturnye Zapiski* (Literary Notes), *Krasnaia Nov* (The Red Soil) and *Pechat i Revolutsiia* (Press and Revolution). New conditions favored establishment of cultural contacts with the outside world, and those writers who until then had been deprived of an opportunity to exercise their talents were permitted to return to the literary scene. The NEP, in other words, initiated a new phase in Soviet literature.

The principal themes of Soviet literature after 1921 were the revolution, the Civil War, partisan activities, the famine, and generally the struggle between the old and new ways of life. The most prominent writer of this "revolutionary romanticism" period was Boris A. Wogau (1894–?), who wrote under the pseudonym of Boris Pilniak. His best known works include *Goly God* (The Naked Year), *Mashiny i Volki* (Machines and Wolves) and *Rossiia v Poliote* (Russia in Flight). Another noted writer of this period was Eugene I. Zamiatin (1884–1937), whose satirical fantasy *My* (We) bears a striking resemblance to Aldous Huxley's *Brave New World* and George Orwell's *1984*. Other writers worthy of attention included Isaac E. Babel (1894–?), author of *Konarmiia* (Red Cavalry) and *Evreiskie Raskazy* (Jewish Tales); and Dimitri A. Furmanov (1891–1926), whose novel *Chapaev* emerged as a major classic of Soviet literature on the Civil War.

In addition to these writers, a literary group known as the Serapion Brothers was organized in February, 1921. Among its outstanding members were Constantine A. Fedin (1892–   ), author of the novel *Goroda i Gody* (Cities and Years); Vsevolod V. Ivanov (1895–   ), author of *Bronepoezd No. 14–69* (Armored Train No. 14-69); Veniamin A. Zilberg (1902–   ), who wrote under the pseudonym of Kaverin; Lev N. Lunts (1901–1923), critic and author of an essay *Na Zapad* (To the West), critical of Russian literary isolation from Western Europe; Nikolai N. Nikitin (1895–   ), author of *Poliot* (The Flight), which deals with the Civil War; Nikolai S. Tikhonov (1896–   ), poet and writer who extolled the revolutionary romanticism of the Civil War; Michael M. Zoshchenko (1895–1958), a satirist whose collections *Uvazhaemye Grazhdane* (Esteemed Citizens) and *Nervnye Liudi* (Nervous People) reflect a fading of his optimism for the revolution. The Serapion Brothers had one thing in common: a desire to produce imaginative and nonconformist art, free of political ideology. This demand made the Serapion Brothers unpopular with party officials, and in 1923 Trotsky labelled them "Fellow Travellers"; that is, individuals who were non-Communists.

The Serapion Brothers were also bitterly assailed by such literary groupings that appeared after 1921 as "October," "Workers' Spring," "Young Guard," "Left Front," "On Guard," and the "All-Union Association of Proletarian Writers," known by its Russian abbreviation as *VAPP*, with branches in Moscow, Petrograd, and other cities. Since most members of these groupings belonged to the Communist party, they insisted that proletarian literature should have but one aim: "to serve the cause of world proletarian victory [and] to fight ruthlessly all the enemies of the Revolution."

Preoccupied with more pressing problems of domestic and foreign policy, party leaders stayed away from these literary disagreements until an explosive point was reached. In June, 1925, the Central Committee held a special session devoted to literary matters, and produced a resolution that subsequently came to be known as the "Magna Charta Libertatum" of Soviet writers. Published in all Soviet papers, this document bluntly stated that "in a classless society there is and can be no neutral art," and accordingly pledged the party's moral and material support to proletarian and peasant writers. At the same time, however, the resolution rejected demands that the party commit itself to any particular literary form, and pleaded for understanding, coexistence, and tactfulness towards other literary groups, and especially the "Fellow Travellers."

The principles of the June, 1925, resolution terminated the bitter literary feud between Communist and non-Communist writers, and governed literary life in the USSR until 1929. This period was especially fruitful to such established writers as Fedin, Kaverin, Aleksei Tolstoy, and Ehrenburg. It was also successful for such newcomers as Leonid M. Leonov (1899–), author of *Barsuki* (The Badgers) and *Vor* (The Thief); Iuri K. Olesha (1899–1960), author of a controversial novel *Zavist* (Envy), and Michael A. Sholokhov (1905–), author of a celebrated novel *Tikhy Don* (The Quiet Don). The contributions of these writers, together with those of the Serapion Brothers and other "Fellow Travellers," turned the 1920's into a highly productive period of Soviet literature.

What has been said of Soviet literature during the 1920's is to a certain extent equally true of Soviet theater. Because they recognized the value of the theater as an instrument of mass education, agitation, and propaganda following their seizure of power, the Bolsheviks nationalized all imperial and private theaters throughout the country, and placed them under the supervision of a special department at the People's Commissariat for Enlightenment headed by a veteran director Vsevolod E. Meyerhold (1874–1942). Under his direction the theater was turned into a vast laboratory in search of proletarian art. Curtains, footlights, elaborate costumes, and everything that separated the audience from the actors were banished. The change of scenery took place in full view of the spectators. Actors were trained to be athletes as well as acrobats. Pulleys and ladders —symbols of industrial age—were substituted for the conventional stage background. Mass revolutionary spectacles involving thousands of participants were staged to produce the desired effect. Those who sought new forms applauded Meyerhold's innovations, while those who preferred classic performance were shocked by his violations of old conventions and forms.

During the 1920's Soviet theaters continued to seach for new forms as well as a new repertoire. Many theaters specialized in modern plays based on experiences of the revolution or the Civil War. For a while, the Moscow Art Theater ran successfully Michael A. Bulgakov's (1891–1940) *Dni Turbinykh* (Days of the Turbines), a drama which depicted anti-Bolshevik officers as heroic and gallant defenders of their cause in the Civil War. Another successful play, a realistic presentation of Bolshevik partisans, was adapted from Ivanov's *Armored Train No. 14–69*. The repertoire of Moscow's theaters also included a number of plays based on historical subjects, such as Aleksei Tolstoy's *Tsar Feodor Ivanovich*, Merezhkovsky's *Paul I*, and Andreev's *Seven Who Were Hanged*.

During the 1920's Soviet theaters faced acute competition from the cinema. Like the legitimate theater, Soviet films displayed such features as subordination of the individual to the mass, careful reconstruction of minor details, building of productions not around single actors but ideas, and, of course, sympathy for Communist principles. Technically, Soviet films compared quite favorably with those produced in the United States or Western Europe. This achievement stemmed largely from the efforts of such producers as Sergei M. Eisenstein (1898–1948), whose best known early productions were *Stachka* (The Strike), and *Bronenosets 'Potemkin'* (The Battleship Potemkin); Vsevolod I. Pudovkhin (1893–1953), who directed the documentary *Mekhanika golovnogo mozga* (Mechanics of the Brain), and the pictures *Konets Sankt Peterburga* (The End of St. Petersburg), and *Mat'* (Mother); and Alexander P. Dovzhenko (1894–1959), who directed *Zvenihora, Arsenal,* and *Zemlia* (The Land).

It is essential to remember that the revolution created opportunities not only for the Russians to display their talents but for the non-Russians as well. The Civil War and Bolshevik adherence to centralization and Russification made conditions unfavorable for such a display for several years. The reversal came in April, 1923, when the Twelfth Party Congress ordered party members everywhere to befriend national minorities, to learn their languages, and to help them in every other way to advance. This decision led accordingly to the elevation of many native languages on a par with Russian, establishment of state publishing houses to handle publication of works in native languages, and emergence into prominence of dormant native literary and artistic talents. In Belorussia, for instance, this was a period of creative activity for poet Yanka Kupala (1882–1942) and writer Adam Babareka (1899–1937). Their counterparts in the Ukraine were poets Pavlo Tychyna (1891–) and Maksim Rylsky (1895–), and writers Mykola Kulish (1892–?) and Mykola Khvylovy (1891–1933).

The emergence of Stalin as absolute dictator in the USSR in the late

1920's, and his subsequent determination to plunge the country into a policy of rapid industrialization and collectivization terminated the most productive period of cultural creativeness in the USSR. Between 1929 and 1932, there developed under Stalin's direction a new style known as "Socialist realism." In theory the new trend, in force until Stalin's death in 1953, sought to develop "artistic works worthy of the great age of Socialism." In practice, however, the new style demanded of all writers and artists absolute conformity, and depiction of such of Stalin's favored subjects as sturdy Stakhanovites, contented cows, dedicated milkmaids, devoted pig breeders, vigilant party members, young lovers arguing by the light of the moon about problems of industrial production, enemies of Soviet power, and similar topics. Because party officials adhered strictly to these standards, from 1929 to 1953 "Socialist realism" produced, in the words of one observer, "cultural wilderness" in the USSR.

THE STRUGGLE FOR SUCCESSION

On May 26, 1922, Lenin, the founder and the unchallenged leader of Russian communism, suffered his first major paralytic stroke, lost his speech and the ability to move his right arm and leg, and accordingly was forced to relinquish active leadership of the party and of the Soviet state. Although towards the end of 1922 he partially recovered, his illness precipated among his close associates a bitter struggle for succession to his mantle. Afraid that it might endanger the system he had created, Lenin deplored the developing feud, but at the same time, except for expressing his trust in collective leadership, he did little to stop it. This is clearly evident from a brief memorandum he wrote on December 24, 1922, which has come to be known as his *Testament*. In it he tried to appraise critically all potential candidates—strongly implying that in his judgment none of them alone was capable of being the supreme leader. Trotsky, Lenin thought, was distinguished by exceptional abilities, but "his too far-reaching self-confidence and a disposition to be too much attracted by the purely administrative side of affairs" made him not fully qualified to be leader. Zinoviev and Kamenev, as events before the seizure of power had indicated, were not reliable. Piatakov was "distinguished in will and ability, but too much given over to administration and the administrative side of things to be relied on in a serious political question." Bukharin was the most valuable and favored theoretician of the party "but his theoretical views can only with the very greatest doubt be regarded as fully Marxist, for there is something scholastic in him (he never has learned, and I think never has fully understood the dialectic)." Stalin, Lenin was afraid, though powerful, did not always know "how to use that power with sufficient caution." On January 4, 1923, in a postscript to the *Testament*,

Lenin branded Stalin as "too rude" and capricious, and suggested that a way be found to replace him in the powerful position of General Secretary of the Party, with a man who would have more patience, loyalty, politeness, and attentiveness. Lenin did not live to see his suggestion fulfilled, for he died on January 21, 1924.

Publicly, Lenin's lieutenants exhibited deep sorrow over the illness and death of their leader, ordered the embalmment of his body, and deposited it with unusual pomp in a mausoleum on Red Square in Moscow, which from its inception was elevated into a national shrine. They also elevated his name and his writings to a quasi-religious worship and renamed in his memory his birthplace of Simbirsk on the Volga, Ulianovsk, and Petrograd became Leningrad.[1] Privately, however, during his illness Lenin's lieutenants had begun to maneuver for his succession. Already in 1923 two groups of pretenders could be discerned. In the first was Trotsky, a man of great learning, an inspiring orator, a gifted writer, a sound analyst and strategist, a capable organizer of the Revolution and Civil War, chief of the Red Army, and a member of the Politburo. Next to Lenin, Trotsky was probably the best known Bolshevik, and, although he had joined the party only in 1917, he appeared the strongest candidate for Lenin's post. The other group of pretenders, known as the *troika* or *triumvirate*, included Zinoviev, an able orator, longtime associate of Lenin, leader of the powerful Petrograd party organization, member of the Politburo, and head of the Comintern; Kamenev, another close associate of Lenin, a spokesman of the powerful Moscow party organization and a member of the Politburo; and Stalin, an old-time Bolshevik, the party's general secretary, a member of the Politburo, the Orgburo, and the Commissariat of Workers' and Peasants' Inspection. Though the least known of the triumvirate, Stalin was the most powerful by virtue of his control of the party apparatus, which he used cautiously at first to strengthen his position and to silence the opposition.

Stalin made his first decisive move in April, 1923, when the party approved his reorganization plan. On the surface his scheme was reasonable. It called for subordination of the Politburo to the Central Committee, which was to be enlarged, and for the expansion also of the Central Control Commission, whose members would participate in the plenary sessions of the Central Committee. The approval of these changes, which were in line with Lenin's wishes, gave Stalin an opportunity to pack party and government organs with his trusted men. By these and other schemes Stalin succeeded in isolating not only Trotsky but Zinoviev and Kamenev as well.

Trotsky struck back at Stalin's maneuverings on October 8, 1923, in the form of a memorandum addressed to the Politburo, wherein he as-

---

[1] From 1700 to 1914 the city was known as St. Petersburg; from 1914 to 1924 as Petrograd; and since 1924 as Leningrad.

sailed the dictatorship of the Secretariat and hinted that a change of leadership was desirable. On October 15, a group of forty-six high party members laid before the Central Committee their criticism of Stalin's machinations. They charged that a small political machine had seized control of the party, was imposing its will, was silencing all valid criticisms, and was destroying the initiative of the rank and file. Because his men formed a majority in the Politburo and in the Central Committee, Stalin had no difficulty in branding Trotsky's criticism as a "grave political mistake" and the "Declaration of the Forty Six" as a factional move that threatened the party's unity. On December 5, 1923, to silence all the critics, the Politburo adopted a resolution which, at least on paper, embodied almost all the criticism advanced by the opposition.

On December 11, Trotsky published in *Pravda* an article entitled, "New Course," in which, while endorsing the new policy, he held that as long as the party was dominated by the all-powerful secretaries no democracy within it was ever possible. "The party," he argued, "must subordinate to itself its own apparatus without for a moment ceasing to be a centralized organization." Trotsky's defense of "intra-party democracy," however, was doomed to failure for two reasons. First, he himself was renowned for ruthless dictatorship and thus could expect little sympathy. Second, he levelled his criticism at the party apparatus which controlled the press and voting. A party conference held from January 16 to 18, 1924, overwhelmingly condemned Trotsky's views and oppositions as "petty bourgeois deviations from Leninism" and warned all the critics that neither "factionalism" nor circulation of "forbidden documents" was compatible with party membership. Trotsky thus lost the first round.

The second round he forfeited. Three days before Lenin's death, which was expected momentarily, Trotsky, who had himself been ill for some time, left Moscow to recuperate in the Caucasus. His absence provided Stalin with an excellent opportunity to identify himself as Lenin's rightful successor. On January 26, Stalin delivered a "hieratical oath of loyalty" to Lenin in which he pledged to hold high, to guard, and to strengthen the purity of party membership, the unity of the party, the dictatorship of the proletariat and the worker-peasant alliance. He elaborated on these theoretical points at some length in a series of lectures entitled "Foundations of Leninism," delivered at the Communist University in Moscow in April, 1924. To spread Leninism as interpreted by Stalin, a new journal, *Bolshevik*, was founded, opponents were purged, and some 220,000 new members were admitted into the party to strengthen Stalin's position against the "old guard." By mid-1924, through careful organization and manipulation of party members, appeals for unanimity following Lenin's death, and other devices, Stalin emerged on top. At the Thirteenth Party Congress held in May 1924, Trotsky, by declaring "My party right or wrong," went on record, publicly at least, as approving the new arrangements. In June, 1924, Stalin felt strong and confident enough to criticize the doctrinal "mistakes" of his two triumvirate companions, Zinoviev and Kamenev. To weaken their following, their supporters were assigned to distant places. To all intents and purposes the triumverate was dead.

Late in 1924, however, the struggle for succession took a new turn which again proved to be advantageous to Stalin and disastrous to his opponents. On the eve of the seventh anniversary of the revolution, Trotsky published a volume of essays entitled *Lessons of October*. It embodied two basic themes. The first branded as unrevolutionary the policy of the "Right," and by implication the entire NEP. The second questioned the qualifications of the two members of the triumvirate, Zinoviev and Kamenev, who had opposed the Bolshevik seizure of power in 1917, to head the party. By his charges, Trotsky drove Kamenev and Zinoviev into Stalin's arms, not as his equals but as his subordinates. With their help, Stalin mobilized the entire propaganda machinery of the party against Trotsky; and for weeks, in articles, pamphlets, and speeches, vilified him, exposed his shortcomings, his non-Bolshevik past, his disagreements with Lenin, and his past and present deviations. Before long Stalin, who led the attack, began even to question Trotsky's contribution to victory, and accordingly elevated his own importance. He also identified Trotskyism as "distrust in the leaders of Bolshevism" and a "lack of confidence in the Bolshevik party allegiance, in its monolithic nature." Since Trotskyism had become a major heresy, at the January, 1925, meeting of the Central Committee, Zinoviev and Kamenev demanded that Trotsky be expelled from the party. Stalin overruled the demand and contented himself with Trotsky's abdication from his nominal headship of the Red Army.

Trotsky's *Lessons of October* helped Stalin to emerge not only as undisputed party leader but as its theoretical spokesman as well. Until this time, every Bolshevik from Lenin down believed that the ultimate success of the Russian Revolution and of socialism depended on the help it received from the victorious proletariat of the industrially advanced countries of Western Europe. In spite of many disappointments, they never abandoned belief in the "permanent revolution." In fact, many felt that the more the prospects of a proletarian revolution in Western Europe receded, the more the Russian Bolsheviks had an obligation to help bring about such a revolution. The mismanagement and failure of the Comintern-supported insurrections in Germany and Bulgaria in 1923 dramatically focused Bolshevik attention to their responsibilities abroad. Trotsky, with his power slipping away, was quite critical of Zinoviev's and Stalin's apparent lack of revolutionary fire and their handling of these insurrections. He emphasized, as he had in the past, that for socialism to succeed in Russia it was necessary to make an all out effort, using Russia's resources, to ignite uprisings everywhere. For Trotsky, in other words, Russian revolution was not an end in itself but a stage in the world struggle against capitalism.

Stalin was in full agreement with Trotsky's emphasis—which was also Lenin's view—as late as April, 1924, when he asserted that the Soviet Union was not "an end in itself . . . [but] a link needed to strengthen the chain of the revolutionary movement in the countries of the West and the East." In December, 1924, however, Stalin reversed his position, branded Trotsky's "permanent revolution" as a variety of Menshevism, as "a lack of faith in the strength and capabilities of the Russian revolution, and as a negation and repudiation of Lenin's theory of the proletarian revolution." Instead, he advanced his own theory of "socialism in one country," which was simple but quite persuasive. It argued that seven years of Bolshevik rule had demonstrated that the regime could maintain itself in power without Western European aid. Moreover, Stalin stressed, the USSR possessed all the necessary prerequisites to establish a powerful socialist base by its own efforts. The achievement of this task, in turn, would greatly simplify the world revolutionary struggle, since the Soviet Union could then render any necessary assistance to the workers of other lands. Their triumph would then guarantee "the final victory of socialism in the first victorious country." The difference between Trotsky's and Stalin's positions was consequently not in the end product but in timing and temperament. Stalin's scheme called for the establishment of socialism in Russia first; Trotsky's concept had the order reversed. Stalin's dominance in the party organization, however, decided the issue in his favor.

Following the weakening of Trotsky, Stalin dropped his two former associates, Zinoviev and Kamenev, whose prestige and influence Trotsky had seriously undermined, and turned to Rykov, Michael Tomsky (1880–1936), and Bukharin, staunch backers of the NEP and of Stalin's policies. With their support he embarked on a policy of peasant "appeasement," easing their taxes and removing some restrictions on the hiring of agricultural labor. He also moved cautiously but systematically in further weakening Zinoviev's and Kamenev's positions. The effort required some maneuvering, for both were long-time leading men in the party. Zinoviev, moreover, had a powerful party organization in Leningrad and was in addition the head of the Comintern. The open clash between the former collaborators came at the Fourteenth Party Congress in December, 1925. The challenge to Stalin was doomed to failure because, except for the Leningrad delegation, the membership of the Congress was hand-picked by his supporters, who jeered and insulted all anti-Stalinists, including Lenin's widow, Nadezhda K. Krupskaia (1869–1939). The most courageous speaker was Kamenev, who led a direct attack on the Secretariat, denounced the emergence of a leader (vozhd), and openly stated that he had "reached the conclusion that Comrade Stalin cannot fulfill the role of unifier of the Bolshevik staff." For his courage Kamenev was rewarded by demotion to candidate status on the Politburo and removed from most of his government posts. Molotov, Klementü E. Voroshilov (1881–), Kaganovich, Kirov, Anastas I. Mikoyan (1895–), and others who supported Stalin were elevated to high posts.

The next challenge to Stalin's leadership came from the "United Opposition," a re-grouping which developed late in the spring of 1926. Its leaders were Trotsky, Kamenev, and Zinoviev. Having learned their lessons well, they were careful not to attack the principle of party unity or pose as a faction. They centered their attack on the party bureaucracy, to which they ascribed all the failures and faults of the regime, such as suppression of party democracy, lag in the development of industry, deplorable conditions of industrial workers, and the growing power of the *kulaks*. Stalin replied by replacing Zinoviev in the Politburo with Rudzutak, and by wholesale removal of Opposition followers from party and government positions. He also inaugurated a campaign aimed at discrediting the Opposition's ideas. Thus outmaneuvered by Stalin, but desirous of retaining their influence in the party, the Opposition leaders published in *Pravda* in the middle of October, 1926, a declaration wherein they admitted violation of party discipline, promised to discontinue factional activity, and repudiated many of their left-wing followers. After this capitulation and admission of error, Zinoviev lost his post in the Comintern and Trotsky and Kamenev lost theirs in the Politburo.

Stalin's final reckoning with the "United Opposition" came in 1927, a year that witnessed Communist failure in Britain and in China, and for which the Opposition indicted the current leadership. Early in August, 1927, Trotsky and Zinoviev were expelled from the Central Committee. Thanks to the conciliatory efforts of Ordzhonikidze, however, this order was rescinded in return for their declaration of unconditional submission to the authority of the Central Committee. The truce was short-lived, as both men insisted on the eve of the long-overdue Fifteenth Party Congress that they be allowed to present, or at least to publicize, their views. When both requests were denied, Trotsky resorted to a speech-making tour, and in a stormy meeting of the Central Committee in October, 1927, he publicly revealed the existence of Lenin's *Testament*—a revelation for which he and Zinoviev irretrievably lost their seats on the Central Committee. On November 14, 1927, both were expelled from the party. The Fifteenth Party Congress which met in December, 1927, authorized the expulsion of some seventy-five of their followers. Stalin's victory now was final. In the middle of January, 1928, Trotsky and his family left for Alma Ata in Central Asia, the first stop on his long journey into exile that was to end with his murder in Mexico in 1940.

Following his defeat of Trotsky, Stalin adopted many of the policies of his heretical adversary, including rapid industrialization under central planning, collectivization of agriculture in order to eliminate the influence of the *kulaks*, and generally the abandonment of the NEP. This startling about-face was not endorsed by the so-called "Rightist" group, whose spokesmen were Bukharin, Tomsky, and Rykov. Stalin destroyed this opposition by the tactics he had perfected in his duel with Trotsky; namely, manipulation of elections, call for silence and unanimity in the interests of party unity, demotions, censorship, expulsions, arrests, rowdyism, and demand of unconditional capitulation. On June 2, 1929, Nikolai M. Shvernik (1888–1970) replaced Tomsky as head of Soviet trade unions, and shortly thereafter Molotov replaced Rykov as Chairman of the *Sovnarkom*. On July 3, Bukharin was removed from control of the Comintern, accused of "collaboration with capitalist elements" and Trotskyites, and in November, 1929, was expelled from the Politburo. On November 26, 1929, Bukharin, Tomsky, and Rykov signed a declaration dictated by Stalin admitting that their views were erroneous and those of the Central Committee were correct. Celebrating his fiftieth birthday in December, 1929, Stalin was hailed as undisputed master of the Soviet Union—a *vozhd*—the position he was to hold until his death in March, 1953.

FOREIGN POLICY IN THE 1920'S

Observers of Soviet affairs have offered varied interpretations of Soviet foreign policy. Some have seen in it a mere continuation of traditional tsarist objectives. Others have viewed it as a blueprint for world conquest and the establishment of world communism. Sir Winston Churchill labelled it "a riddle wrapped in a mystery inside an enigma." However defined, from the very first, one of the cardinal objectives of Soviet foreign policy has been to provide security for the territorial base of the revolution.

To defend that base the Bolsheviks enlisted all available resources of conventional and unconventional diplomacy. Immediately after seizing power, they called upon all the belligerents to end the war, went on record as favoring peace without annexations and indemnities, and appealed to class-conscious workers everywhere to come to their aid. They also repudiated all foreign debts of the tsarist regime, condemned tsarist imperialism and its oppressive policy of Russification, and outwardly championed a policy of national self-determination and equality among nations. To expose the "designs of the capitalist states" before world opinion, they published secret treaties, and late in 1917, at Brest-Litovsk, entered into peace negotiations with the Central Powers. These negotiations ended on March 3, 1918, in a treaty whereby in return for security for the territorial base of the revolution, the Bolsheviks formally withdrew a militarily humiliated, economically exhausted, and territorially amputated Russia from World War I.

To protect the revolutionary base, between 1918 and 1920 the Bolsheviks fought against German, Austro-Hungarian, English, French, American, Japanese, Czechoslovak, Polish, White Russian, and other forces led by trained officers and supplied from abroad. In this struggle for survival they saw most of their territory overrun by their opponents at one time or another. Yet, in the end they emerged triumphant. By 1921 they had beaten down all open rebellion, ruthlessly suppressed every conspiracy, and either executed, imprisoned, or forced into exile the opposition leaders. And while the Bolsheviks continued to talk constantly of the danger of foreign intervention, in reality by 1921 the new Soviet state was free from foreign intervention. Except for the rapidly diminishing Japanese threat in the Far East, by 1920 all foreign governments had lifted the blockade of Russia and withdrawn their intervening forces, thanks to lack of common policy, disunity, indecision, and general war-weariness among their own people.

But while in one way the Bolsheviks were victorious, on the other hand they were suffering defeat. In spite of tremendous propaganda efforts, by fair means and foul, and great material and human sacrifices, no other country followed the Russian example. By 1921 the Bolsheviks had been successful in imposing their system only in Russia, Belorussia, the Ukraine, the Caucasus, and the former imperial territories in Asia. They tried, but failed, to gain control in Finland, Estonia, Latvia, Lithuania, and Poland. A series of Communist-led unrests in 1919 in Hungary, Germany, Austria, and Italy also ended in failure. With these setbacks, the prophesies and high hopes for an imminent world-wide revolution began to fade. Sober, realistic thinking brought home the realization that, in spite of the great stress of World War I, the postwar world was beginning to show remarkable stability, that the bourgeois governments were in full control of the situation, that the capitalist states were in no hurry to capitulate as the Bolsheviks had anticipated, and that these states were capable of hurting as well as helping the new Soviet state. As a result of this reorientation, which was strengthened by corresponding changes of attitude abroad, early in 1921 the Bolsheviks decided to abandon aggressive militant communism and formally adopted "co-existence" as the official conventional policy towards the rest of the world.

Though the NEP formally sanctioned the period of peaceful co-existence, the first signs leading to this policy had begun in the midst of the Civil War when the Bolsheviks signed a peace treaty with Estonia on February 2, 1920. On July 12, came a treaty with Finland; on February 26, 1921, with Persia; on February 28, with Afghanistan; on March 16, with Turkey; and on March 18, with Poland. Careful scrutiny of these treaties with bordering states reveals several interesting characteristics. In all, the Bolsheviks underlined the principle of self-determination of nations. In those with Persia, Turkey, and Afghanistan they even spoke of brotherhood of nations, friendship and solidarity in the struggle against Western imperialism, and as a token gesture of their sincerity the Bolsheviks renounced tsarist power policy. To appease the appetite of new nations, in all the treaties the Bolsheviks agreed to minor frontier adjustments, renounced all rights and claims to these territories, relieved all new states from financial responsibilities of the tsarist regime, and to some they even returned national treasures which had been held in Russia. All treaties pledged to refrain from inflammatory propaganda, prohibited the stationing on either's territory of forces hostile to the other, and in the Persian treaty both sides agreed to coordinate their military efforts in suppressing hostile forces.

In signing these treaties the Bolsheviks achieved four objectives: (1) they gained *de jure* recognition from their neighbors; (2) they broke through the Allied *cordon sanitaire;* (3) they isolated or neutralized their adversaries and accordingly forced them into a predetermined line of conduct; and (4) they erected their own legal protective barrier stretching from the Arctic Ocean to the Carpathians, and from the Straits to the Himalayas. Signing of various agreements with Norway, Denmark, Italy, Austria, Hungary, and Germany had the same objective. So it was too with the Anglo-Soviet trade agreement of March 16, 1921, which among other things called for the resumption of trade, prohibited the carrying on of hostile propaganda, and forbade either country to blockade the other. In other words, by all these treaties the Bolsheviks conceded little and gained a great deal. They strengthened their security and gained the minimum safety necessary against unprovoked attacks from abroad, hence security for their institutions, experimentations, and the projection of Russia's development along Marxist-Leninist lines.

There were many leading Bolsheviks who insisted that Russia rely exclusively on her own efforts in building up an industrial base. Reality, however, dictated that the adoption of such a stand would mean a slow and painful process. Quick results in rebuilding industries, in producing needed articles, in making needed repairs, and in tapping new sources of wealth, depended on foreign capital. This could be had through loans or in return for concessions; while foreign goods could come only by trade, hence the signing of a number of trade agreements and the maneuvering to enter into normal diplomatic relations. And while the Bolsheviks realized they would have to pay in one way or another for foreign economic aid, they believed they were in a strong bargaining position. On the one hand they were convinced that postwar prosperity in Europe could not be sustained without Soviet Russia's participation. On the other hand a number of West European businessmen, hoping to reap profits, were pressing their governments to reopen trade with Soviet Russia.

In the effort to attract foreign capital as well as to gain diplomatic recognition, the Bolsheviks encountered one insurmountable obstacle: *the claims of foreign states against Russia.* There were two kinds of claims: first, prewar debts; and second, war debts and claims for reparations for the destruction and confiscation of foreign property. The Bolsheviks tried to disassociate themselves from the first category of claims by arguing that prewar debts had been contracted by a government which had no popular support. To offset the second category of claims, the Bolsheviks made their own counterclaims, far greater than those of the Allies. They argued that the Allied Powers, without formal declaration of war, had invaded Russia, plotted against its government, furnished arms to insurrectionists, and destroyed property, all in violation of the basic principles of international law.

But while the Bolsheviks demurred in theory at recognizing obligations to repay money borrowed by their predecessors, in reality by not doing so they could hardly hope to obtain the new loans needed for reconstruction. On October 29, 1921, Georgi V. Chicherin (1872–1936), People's Commissar for Foreign Affairs, offered a compromise. While refusing to admit either legal or moral liability, he expressed Soviet willingness to meet these debts—the amount to be determined in subsequent negotiations in a conference convened for that purpose. The French, who had the largest investments in Russia—some sixteen billion francs—adopted an uncompromising stand. The English, with fewer investments, although expressing contempt for the Bolsheviks, somewhat naively visualized great opportunities for export, easing unemployment at home, reopening old markets, and outdistancing their French, Italian, and German competitors. The Germans and Norwegians went so far as to send trade delegations to Moscow.

Early in 1922, Bolshevik efforts to gain diplomatic recognition and economic aid from the major powers received strong encouragement when on January 6, the Allied Supreme Council, meeting at Cannes invited Soviet Russia to attend a general European conference at Genoa. The Bolsheviks accepted the offer without hesitation, feeling that they might gain much and could lose little. They were also confident that jealousies among the great powers would pave the way to profitable bargains with individual states. When the Genoa Conference opened on April 10, 1922, it was evident from the outset that both sides were contributing to its failure. The inviting powers—Britain, France, Italy, and Belgium—hoped by means of the conference to force the Bolsheviks to recognize Russia's prerevolutionary debts and to restore private property rights of foreigners within Soviet Russia. In formulating these objectives, the West European representatives were strongly influenced by the widespread belief that Soviet Russia's economic situation was so deplorable that however much her delegates might bluff and bluster at first they would eventually yield and accept almost anything. Soviet delegates, on the other hand, viewed the purpose of the conference in an entirely different light. They hoped to gain loans with which to rebuild the economy of Soviet Russia according to their own designs, and diplomatic recognition from the major powers.

American refusal to participate in the Genoa conference deflated Bolshevik expectations, as they were firmly convinced that not Europe alone but the United States was wealthy enough to lend money on the scale necessary to rebuild Russia. This was not the first American action that had either puzzled or disappointed the Bolsheviks. On March 25, 1921, Secretary of State Charles Evans Hughes, over their protests, had excluded the Bolsheviks from participation in a Washington conference to discuss naval affairs and Pacific and Far Eastern problems. In the summer of 1921, however, in answer to Soviet appeals for aid to the famine victims, the American Relief Administration was organized under the direction of Herbert Hoover. American unwillingness to take part in the Genoa negotiations and in Russian economic recovery left the Bolsheviks too little to gain for them to make concessions to European powers. Instead they decided to use the conference as a propaganda platform from which to call for peace and total disarmament. They also utilized it to exploit differences among various powers in open and secret negotiations, which on April 16, 1922, culminated in the signing of the Soviet-German treaty at Rapallo.

In its terms, which had been in the process of negotiation for many months before the Genoa Conference, and in its many-sided implications, the Rapallo treaty was a triumph for both German and Soviet diplomacy. The two powers, outcasts of European society, re-extended to each other the *de jure* recognition which had been disrupted in November, 1918, renounced all military and civilian war claims against each other, and agreed to enter into closer economic cooperation. Needless to say, for some time thereafter, the Bolsheviks considered the Rapallo treaty a model for other treaties with Western Powers.

But although Rapallo was a great Soviet diplomatic triumph, the Genoa Conference and the subsequent Hague Conference (June 26–July 20, 1922) concerned with the problem of debts and compensations, were basically failures from the Bolshevik point of view. They failed to secure the needed loans and large-scale economic assistance for Russia's reconstruction and further industrialization. Moreover, except for Germany, no major power granted diplomatic recognition to the new Soviet state. The Bolsheviks suffered another setback at a conference on the Straits which met at Lausanne, Switzerland, from November 20, 1922, to July 24, 1923. Although they skillfully used delaying tactics, and insisted that the Straits be closed to keep the British fleet out of the Black Sea, on July 24, 1923, the final document embodied the British position. It provided freedom of navigation through the Straits for war, and merchant vessels both during war and peace. Turkey was given the right to search ships if she herself were at war. No single power could send a larger fleet through the Straits than the largest possessed by a Black Sea power. The Straits and the islands of Lemnos, Tenedos, and Imbros were to be demilitarized, with England, France, Italy, and Japan being responsible for effecting the demilitarization. Late in 1923, the Bolsheviks suffered still another resounding defeat when the Comintern-sponsored revolution in Germany ended in total failure—failure which relegated into the distant future all hopes of extending the Soviet experiment outside Russia.

In spite of these setbacks, as the year 1924 progressed, Soviet diplomacy began to pile triumph on triumph. Convinced that the Bolsheviks were firmly entrenched, amazed at Russian economic recovery under the NEP, hoping to profit from normal diplomatic and commercial relations, and in some cases swayed by pressure groups at home, the Western Powers began to extend diplomatic recognition to the Soviet government. England recognized the USSR on February 1, 1924. Italy followed suit on February 7; Norway on February 15; Austria on February 25; Sweden on March 15; Denmark on June 18; Mexico on August 4; France on October 28, 1924; and Japan on January 20, 1925. Thanks to these recognitions, in less than a year Soviet diplomacy achieved one of the basic goals it had sought desperately since 1918: it became a respectable member of the world community.

This sudden rise of the international status of the Soviet Union acted unfavorably on her relations with bordering states. As noted previously, when the Bolsheviks earlier were fighting for their very existence, Lenin was willing to grant more territory to Russia's neighbors than were "Clemenceau or Curzon," even if in so doing he violated the principle of national self-determination. As long as Bolshevik power was weak there were no controversies with border states along ethnic lines. With the consolidation of their power at home and the growth of their prestige abroad, responsible Bolshevik leaders began to clamor at major party and soviet gatherings for the revision of frontiers, and for protection of their co-nationals—demands which created ill feelings between the USSR and its neighbors.

Alongside the growth of power and international prestige, the Bolsheviks initiated in the mid-1920's an offensive for neutrality and non-aggression pacts to further strengthen the territorial base of the revolution. Officially, this offensive began with the signing of a treaty with Turkey on December 17, 1925, which was followed on April 24, 1926, by one with Germany; with Afghanistan on August 8; on September 28, 1926, with Lithuania; and on October 1, 1927, with Persia. Under Bolshevik guidance there also appeared bilateral treaties between Persia and Afghanistan, and Turkey and Afghanistan. All of these treaties with the

Near and Middle Eastern countries were negotiated and signed under the banner of struggle against British colonial imperialism and freedom for the oppressed Asian people. The treaty with Afghanistan contained, in fact, germs of an anti-British alliance of Asiatic countries under Moscow's sponsorship—an action which was not regarded with favor by the British.

Anglo-Soviet relations deteriorated for other reasons as well. The hopes which both sides had placed in the trade agreement of March 16, 1921, failed to materialize. Bolshevik inability to agree on settlement of old debts, and the Comintern-sponsored bitter anti-British propaganda contributed to the ill feelings. The Labor government's *de jure* recognition of the USSR in no way altered the uneasy truce. In fact, it indirectly contributed to its deterioration. Both Liberals and Conservatives voiced bitter disapproval of the Labor government's attempts to negotiate two treaties with the USSR, and on October 8, 1924, they were able to force its fall. In the midst of the new elections, on October 25, 1924, the British press published the famous Zinoviev Letter to British Communist leaders instructing them on how to prepare for seizure of power in England. While its authenticity has been questioned, the letter nevertheless contributed to an overwhelming Conservative victory at the polls and enabled them to refuse to honor the negotiated treaties.

Throughout the year 1925, Anglo-Soviet relations deteriorated rapidly, thanks to increased Bolshevik activity in Asia. In May, 1926, a real crisis developed when Bolshevik leaders jubilantly greeted the general strike in England as a forerunner of the socialist revolution, and publicly offered financial aid to the strikers. The British rejected Bolshevik contentions that technically the Soviet government did not take part in these and other anti-British actions. Finally, on May 12, 1927, the British government approved a police search of ARCOS, a branch of the Soviet trade delegation—a search which exposed the existence of a Soviet espionage system. This revelation, in spite of Soviet protests of diplomatic immunity of the trade delegation, led on May 26, 1927, to formal termination of the Anglo-Soviet trade agreement of March, 1921, and breaking off of diplomatic relations.

Bolshevik setbacks in relations with England in 1927 coincided with the Bolshevik defeat in China. From the first, in their quest to strengthen the territorial base of the revolution, the Bolsheviks had assigned to China a significant role. They felt that control of China's vast human and natural resources would be a key to their own security as well as to the control of most of the Asian mainland and the islands of the Southwest Pacific. They also believed that their befriending of China would be a potential blow to Western capitalism by depriving it of a source of raw materials and a vast market for finished products.

But to bring China within their sphere of influence, the Bolsheviks had to overcome a number of barriers inherited from the tsarist period.

They took far-reaching steps toward overcoming some of these by support-ing the principle of national self-determination, by various appeals and offers directed to the Asian peoples, and by letters directed to Asian leaders. Of these documents, the Karakhan Declaration of July 25, 1919, addressed to the Peking and Canton governments of China, contributed the most to setting the tone of Sino-Soviet relations. Made at a time when the Bolsheviks controlled only a very small area in Central Russia and were struggling against great odds for their very existence, the Karakhan Declaration was a master stroke of propaganda. To disassociate them-selves in the eyes of the Chinese from the tsarist imperialist pressure and exploitation in China, by the stroke of a pen the Bolsheviks renounced tsarist power politics and all concessions and privileges the old regime had enjoyed in Manchuria and on the Chinese Eastern Railway. They also declared that the new Russia was bringing peace, freedom, and assistance to the enslaved peoples of Asia in general and the Chinese in particular.

These promises succeeded in capturing the imagination of many Chi-nese intellectuals and revolutionary leaders who wished to restore order and unity to their country. Bolshevik influence in China rose to unprece-dented heights and began to climb higher when in the course of 1920 and 1921, in the wake of the departing forces of intervention, Red Armies moved closer to the old frontiers. Now victorious, the Bolsheviks forgot the high-sounding but expedient promises and pledges of the Karakhan Declaration and other documents. Instead they began to exert, together with the Japanese, great pressure on the two Chinese governments, to exploit disagreements and disunity, and to bribe Chinese officials and whole political groups. Soon, too, they forced the return of the Chinese Eastern Railway under virtually the old tsarist conditions. They also helped to organize the Communist party of China, which, as a branch of the Comintern, was an effective tool of Moscow.

And while these developments contributed greatly to reversing pro-Bolshevik sentiment among the Chinese, it was Bolshevik policy towards Mongolia which brought Sino-Soviet relations almost to the breaking point. Early in 1921, under the pretext of driving out General Baron Unger-Sternberg, the Soviets intervened in Mongolia. With their encouragement and help, the Mongolian People's Provisional Government was formed on April 10, 1921, in Kiakhta. Following occupation of Mongolia, the Bolshe-viks signed a treaty of friendship with that government on November 5, 1921. It called for an end to extraterritorial rights and other old privileges, but granted the Bolsheviks the right to operate the postal and telegraph services. Mongolia, the ancient country of nomads, began to march to-wards *Pax Communa* under Moscow's guidance, in spite of the fact that for centuries the Chinese had considered Mongolia a part of China. In December, 1921, the Bolsheviks also helped to found the Tannu-Tuva Republic in the highly strategic and rich basin of the Yenisey River.

These Bolshevik gains at China's expense were possible because of China's utter helplessness and Bolshevik willingness to negotiate and make promises. By far the most important of these promises was an agreement of January 26, 1923, with Chinese statesman Dr. Sun Yat-sen. In return for Dr. Sun's acceptance of Chinese Communists into his Kuomintang party, the Bolsheviks promised military and organizational help, pledged not to advocate communism for China, affirmed that they had no intention of separating Outer Mongolia from China, and agreed that the future of the Chinese Eastern Railway be settled jointly. The last two points also figured prominently in the Bolshevik agreement with the Chinese government in Peking on May 31, 1924.

As realists, the Bolsheviks knew well that they could succeed in China only if the Japanese would not interfere militarily. It was necessary then to pacify Japan—a task that proved quite difficult. Because of Japanese occupation of the Primorsk Province and the island of Sakhalin, Soviet-Japanese relations were anything but cordial. The issue of Japanese fishing rights in Russian-claimed waters contributed to further misunderstanding. Finally, and most decisively, Bolshevik objectives in China, and especially in Manchuria, collided with long-standing Japanese interests there. Only after prolonged negotiations and arguments, Japan and the Soviet Union signed an agreement on January 20, 1925. This provided for the resumption of normal diplomatic as well as broad economic relations. It also stipulated that both parties were "to live in peace and amity with each other," respect each other's territorial rights, and refrain from subversion. While by this agreement Soviet diplomacy forced Japan into predetermined conduct, at the same time the agreement carried the germs of further complications in the future.

With Japan temporarily pacified, the Bolsheviks turned back towards China, where for some time their political and military aides and advisers had been penetrating in great numbers. There were sharp disagreements among top Bolshevik leaders on methods and tactics to be employed in China. Both Stalin and Trotsky wished to turn the Chinese national revolution into a Communist revolution. The death of Sun Yat-sen in March, 1925, which left China temporarily leaderless, appeared as an opportune moment to do it. In the summer of 1925, Chinese Communists attempted to seize the leadership of the Kuomintang. Their efforts, however, were frustrated when Dr. Sun's successor, Chiang Kai-shek, arrested and executed several Communist leaders in Canton in March, 1926. In his further consolidation of power in China, on April 11, 1927, Chiang disarmed the Communists in Shanghai, expelled all Bolshevik advisers, and broke the Kuomintang's ties with Moscow. To add to this disaster of the Soviets' China policy, on April 6, 1927, the Peking government, with whom the Soviets maintained official relations, approved a police raid on Soviet diplomatic establishments in Peking. A number of Embassy personnel were arrested, and documents seized implicated Soviet officials in the anti-government conspiracy. On April 10, 1927, the USSR broke off diplomatic relations with Peking. Chiang's victory over the Peking government brought only further trouble for Soviet officials in Manchuria connected with the operation of the Chinese Eastern Railway.

Soviet diplomatic reverses in England and China in 1927 and increased bitterness of the power struggle between Stalin and Trotsky were the two last major signs of the passing era of the NEP. Stalin's defeat of his rivals, his adoption of the slogan of "socialism in one country," and inauguration of the policy of industrialization and collectivization were also reflected in foreign policy. These gigantic undertakings called for additional security measures. Defense of the USSR became a sacred duty towards which the vast Comintern organization was alerted at its Sixth Congress in 1928.

Simultaneously on the conventional level, though voicing reservations, the Bolsheviks began to participate in the disarmament efforts of the League of Nations, where future Commissar for Foreign Affairs Maxim M. Litvinov (1876–1951) proposed complete and rapid disarmament to be guaranteed by a permanent system of international inspection. In 1928 also, the USSR became the first power to sign and ratify the Kellogg-Briand Pact calling for renunciation of war. On February 9, 1929, the Bolsheviks created under their own supervision an Eastern pact for the renunciation of war—the Litvinov Protocol, which was signed in Moscow by the USSR, Poland, Rumania, Estonia, and Latvia. These efforts were followed by the negotiation and signing of a series of non-aggression pacts in 1932: with Finland on January 24, 1932; with Latvia on February 8, 1932; with Estonia on April 5, 1932; with Poland on July 25, 1932; and with France on November 29, 1932. By these efforts, Soviet diplomacy tied itself to the French security system.

Striking an alliance with France was a victory for Moscow. In the Bolshevik view, France was a first-class European power which constantly threatened the security of the USSR with intervention. Although the two countries had had diplomatic relations since 1924, mutual suspicion prevented them from close cooperation. Bolshevik repudiation of tsarist debts, of which the French held a large share, contributed to further misunderstanding. While both powers had to yield on certain points to overcome these deep-rooted suspicions, the most significant factor that brought them together was the rise of Adolf Hitler in Germany.

The 1920's, in spite of numerous errors and disappointments, were on the whole years of great achievement for the Bolsheviks in their quest for security to the territorial base of the revolution. Both in Europe and in Asia, on the conventional level, they pacified their immediate adversaries. With some they signed various bilateral treaties which forced them into a predetermined line of conduct, while to other states they offered trade and other concessions. At the same time, on the unconventional level, the Bolsheviks succeeded in capturing the imagination of many underprivileged nations, offered them aid and posed as the champions of their freedom and independence. Against great odds, some of their own making and others inherited from their predecessors, and by using fair and foul means, the Bolsheviks elevated their state from obscurity and isolation to international prestige.

SUGGESTED READINGS

ADAMS, ARTHUR E., ed. *Readings in Soviet Foreign Policy. Theory and Practice*. Boston: Heath, 1961.

BABITSKY, PAUL, and JOHN RIMBERG. *The Soviet Film Industry*. New York: Praeger, 1955.

BATSELL, WALTER R. *Soviet Rule in Russia*. New York: Macmillan, 1929.

BAYKOV, ALEXANDER. *The Development of the Soviet Economic System*. Cambridge: Cambridge University Press, 1946.

BORKENAU, FRANZ. *The Communist International*. London: Faber, 1938.

CARR, EDWARD H. *The Interregnum, 1923–1924*. New York: Macmillan, 1954.

———. *Socialism in One Country, 1924–1926*. New York: Macmillan, 1958.

CHAMBERLIN, WILLIAM H. *Soviet Russia. A Living Record and a History*. Boston: Little, Brown, 1930.

CURTISS, JOHN S. *The Russian Church and the Soviet State, 1917–1950*. Boston: Little, Brown, 1953.

DANIELS, ROBERT V. *The Conscience of the Revolution: Communist Opposition in Soviet Russia*. Cambridge: Harvard University Press, 1960.

DEGRAS, JANE. *The Communist International, 1919–1943. Documents*. 2 vols. London: Oxford University Press, 1956–8.

———. *Soviet Documents on Foreign Policy, 1917–1932*. 2 vols. London: Oxford University Press, 1951–2.

DENNIS, A. L. P. *The Foreign Policies of Soviet Russia*. New York: Dutton, 1924.

DEUTSCHER, ISAAC. *The Prophet Unarmed: Trotsky, 1921–1929*. New York: Oxford University Press, 1959.

———. *Stalin: A Political Biography*. New York: Oxford University Press, 1949.

DMYTRYSHYN, BASIL. *Moscow and the Ukraine, 1918–1953*. New York: Bookman Associates, 1956.

DOBB, MAURICE. *Soviet Economic Development Since 1917*. London: Routledge and Kegan, 1948.

EUDIN, XENIA J., and HAROLD H. FISHER. *Soviet Russia and the West, 1920–1927. A Documentary Survey*. Stanford: Stanford University Press, 1957.

———, and ROBERT C. NORTH. *Soviet Russia and the East, 1920–1927. A Documentary Survey*. Stanford: Stanford University Press, 1957.

FISCHER, LOUIS. *The Soviets in World Affairs*. 2nd ed. 2 vols. Princeton: Princeton University Press, 1951.

FISCHER, RUTH. *Stalin and German Communism*. Cambridge: Harvard University Press, 1948.

FISHER, HAROLD H. *The Famine in Soviet Russia, 1919–1923*. New York: Macmillan, 1927.

GORCHAKOV, NIKOLAI A. *The Theater in Soviet Russia*. New York: Columbia University Press, 1957.

KENNAN, GEORGE F. *Russia and the West under Lenin and Stalin.* Boston: Atlantic-Little, Brown, 1961.

———. *Soviet Foreign Policy, 1917–1941.* New York: Van Nostrand, 1960.

LEYDA, J. *Kino: A History of the Russian and Soviet Film.* New York: Macmillan, 1960.

NORTH, ROBERT C. *Moscow and Chinese Communists.* Stanford: Stanford University Press, 1953.

PIPES, RICHARD. *The Formation of the Soviet Union.* Cambridge: Harvard University Press, 1954.

RESHETAR, JOHN S. JR. *A Concise History of the Communist Party of the Soviet Union.* New York: Praeger, 1960.

RUBINSTEIN, ALVIN Z., ed. *The Foreign Policy of the Soviet Union.* New York: Random House, 1960.

SCHAPIRO, LEONARD. *The Communist Party of the Soviet Union.* New York: Random House, 1960.

SHAPIRO, LEONARD., ed. *Soviet Treaty Series.* Washington: The Georgetown University Press, 1950. Vol. 1.

SIMMONS, ERNEST J., ed. *Through the Glass of Soviet Literature.* New York: Columbia University Press, 1953.

SLONIM, MARC. *Modern Russian Literature.* New York: Oxford University Press, 1953.

———. *Russian Theater From the Empire to the Soviets.* New York: World, 1961.

SPINKA, MATTHEW. *The Church in Soviet Russia.* New York: Oxford University Press, 1956.

STRUVE, GLEB. *Soviet Russian Literature, 1917–1950.* Norman, Oklahoma: University of Oklahoma Press, 1951.

TARACOUZIO, T. A. *War and Peace in Soviet Diplomacy.* New York: Macmillan, 1940.

TIMASHEFF, N. S. *Religion in Soviet Russia, 1917–1942.* New York: Sheed & Ward, 1942.

ZAVALISHIN, VYACHESLAV. *Early Soviet Writers.* New York: Praeger, 1958.

※ V I

THE REGIMENTED THIRTIES

THE INDUSTRIAL REVOLUTION

Stalin's triumph first over the "Left" and then the "Right" opposition had two very significant implications. First, it left him the unchallenged master of the Soviet Union—a *vozhd* surrounded by "yes men"—the position he was to hold until his death in March, 1953. Second, it ushered in a new era in Soviet history, an era to which scholars have attached different labels and interpretations. Some have described it as "The Second Revolution." Others have named it "Russia's Iron Age." There are those who labelled it "The Era of the Five Year Plans," while some have simply called it "The Stalin Era." However designated, Stalin's triumph over his rivals was fateful for the USSR and the rest of the world as well.

Stalin inaugurated his absolute one-man rule by launching the First Five Year Plan, aimed at rapid industrialization of the Soviet Union. The surprising element of this action was not the plan itself (the plan had been in preparation for several years), but the decision to launch it. Throughout his struggle with the "Left" opposition, Stalin publicly advocated a policy of prosperity, gradualness, and caution in both domestic and foreign policy. For instance, he dubbed Trotsky, Kamenev, and Zinoviev as "super-industrializers" when they suggested that in view of Russia's economic recovery during the NEP, it was possible to raise the output by slightly less than 20 per cent per year. He also dismissed the opposition-proposed hydroelectric project on the Dnieper River in the Ukraine, the famous Dnieprostroy. He is reported to have remarked that for Russia to build this dam would be similar to a peasant buying a gramophone instead of a cow. Before long, however, the Dnieprostroy became the first major achievement of Soviet planning.

What *really* caused Stalin to change his mind so abruptly is not exactly clear. Most scholars believe, though, that an immediate determinant was the food crisis which began to reach dangerous proportions in 1927 and 1928. We noted in our previous chapter that following the adoption of the NEP, Soviet Russian agriculture recovered to the prewar level as early as 1925. Further progress, however, was hindered by two factors. The first was the existence of the multitude of small farms which were capable of producing only enough to satisfy the needs of their owners. The second was the refusal of the more industrious peasants, the *kulaks,* who produced grain beyond their immediate needs, to deliver it at low prices fixed by the state. In 1927, for instance, thanks to this form of "sabotage," but above all as a result of climatic conditions, state acquisitions of grain from the peasants fell some two million tons short of the minimum required. To remedy this situation, the Central Committee of the party, late in 1927 and early in 1928, instructed all local party members to take energetic measures to extract grain from the peasants, and those members who showed any leniency were purged. As might be expected, the peasants resisted by all the devices known to them the party pressures, which in Stalin's own words included "administrative arbitrariness, violation of revolutionary law, raids on peasant houses [and] illegal searches." In view of these developments, Stalin, while triumphant over his opponents, found himself in a real dilemma. To give in to peasant demands for higher prices might have meant placing additional burdens on the town population. Refusal to yield to the peasantry, on the other hand, as one observer aptly put it, "entailed the threat of famine and unrest in the towns." The dilemma demanded a radical solution. Stalin found the answer in the First Five Year Plan.

Stalin's decision to industrialize stemmed also from his idea of "socialism in one country," and above all from his belief in the ultimate triumph of world revolution, which the successful industrialization was to promote. He made this point quite explicit in January, 1931, in a speech defending his call for increased tempo of industrialization. "Our obligations to the world proletariat," he said, "were more serious and more important" than those to the workers and peasants of the USSR.

We achieved victory not solely through the efforts of the working class of the U.S.S.R., but also thanks to the support of the working class of the world. Without this support we would have been torn to pieces long ago. It is said that our country is the shock brigade of the proletariat of all countries. This is a fitting definition. But this imposes very serious obligations upon us. Why does the international proletariat support us? How did we merit this support? By the fact that we were the first to hurl ourselves into the battle against capitalism, we were the first to establish a working-class state, we were the first to start building socialism. By the fact that we are doing work which, if successful, will change the whole world and free the entire working class. But what is needed for success? The elimination of our backwardness, the development of a high Bolshevik tempo of construction. We must march forward in such a way that the working class of the whole world, looking at us, may say: This is my vanguard, this is my shock brigade, this is my working-class state, this is my fatherland; they are promoting their cause, which is *our* cause, and they are doing this well; let us support them against the capitalists and promote the cause of the world revolution.

The bold and ambitious estimates of the First Five Year Plan rested on four premises. First, it was presupposed that during the next quinquennium there would be no serious harvest failure. Second, a substantial expansion of foreign trade and an increase in long-term credits were envisaged. Third, a sharp increase "in the qualitative indices of national economic construction," such as cost of production and crop yield, was anticipated. And finally, the plan expected "a fall in the proportionate weight of expenditure on national defense in the general economic system." None of these expectations, however, were fulfilled. The harvest of 1930 was good, but those of 1931 and 1932 were grave natural and man-made disasters. Moreover, as a result of the great world depression, prices of grain on the world market declined, and this decline in turn acted quite unfavorably on the Soviet long-term credit position. A hope for increase in the productivity of labor proved also to be a serious miscalculation. Instead of doubling, the actual increase of productivity at the end of 1932 was about 40 per cent. This then affected the estimated cost of the plan, since the expected fall of costs and of industrial wholesale prices was based on the rise of productivity of labor. Finally, the threat of war with Japan, following Japanese occupation of Manchuria in 1931–1932, forced the planners to increase defense expenditures.

These serious miscalculations, however, had little effect on the planners, whose optimism and fanaticism surpassed all limits. Speaking in November, 1929, at a mammoth rally commemorating the twelfth anniversary of the Bolshevik seizure of power, Stalin declared that the Soviet

Union was "advancing full steam ahead along the path of industrialization to Socialism, leaving behind the agelong 'Russian' backwardness," and becoming a country of metal, automobiles, and tractors. To overcome Russia's backwardness faster, and then "to catch up with and to overcome the capitalist world" in industrial and economic development, the Sixteenth Party Congress, held from June 26 to July 13, 1930, adopted the slogan "The Five Year Plan in Four Years." To help realize that goal, appeals as well as orders were issued to all segments of the population at home and sympathizers abroad. To those who argued that the tempo of industrialization was too fast, early in 1931, using Marxist and nationalist arguments and adding a few distortions of his own, Stalin replied in the negative. "The pace must not be reduced," he declared.

On the contrary we must increase it as much as is within our powers and possibilities. This is dictated to us by our obligations to the workers and peasants of the USSR. This is dictated to us by our obligations to the working class of the world.

To reduce the tempo would mean to fall behind. And those who fall behind get beaten. But we do not want to be beaten. No, we refuse to be beaten! One feature of the history of old Russia was the continual beating she suffered because of her backwardness. She was beaten by the Mongol Khans. She was beaten by the Turkish beys. She was beaten by the Swedish feudal lords. She was beaten by the Polish and Lithuanian gentry. She was beaten by the British and French capitalists. She was beaten by the Japanese barons. All beat her— because of her backwardness, military backwardness, cultural backwardness, industrial backwardness, and agricultural backwardness. They beat her because to do so was profitable and could be done with impunity. . . . Such is the law of the exploiters—to beat the backward and the weak. It is the jungle law of capitalism. You are backward, you are weak—therefore you are wrong; hence, you can be beaten and enslaved. You are mighty—therefore you are right; hence we must be wary of you. That is why we must no longer lag behind. . . .

We are fifty or a hundred years behind the advanced countries. We must make good this distance in ten years. Either we do it, or we shall be crushed.

On December 31, 1932, the First Five Year Plan was declared officially completed ahead of schedule, and most of its objectives fulfilled. The reported fulfillment, however, contained many discrepancies. In terms of ruble value (valued at 1926–1927 prices), many items showed a marked increase. For instance, the capital goods industries registered an increase of two and one-half times during the First Five Year Plan. The output of machinery increased four times and that of oil doubled. The output of electric power increased more than two and one-half times. The production of large-scale industry showed an increase of 118 per cent. The output of electrical equipment overfulfilled its quota, as did the collectivization of peasant households. But the First Five Year Plan also lagged at many points. Instead of the projected 10,000,000 tons, iron and steel attained only 6,200,000 and 5,900,000 tons respectively. The output of coal was some 10,000,000 tons short of its 75,000,000 ton target. The production of grain fell some 36,000,000 tons below the 106,000,000 ton estimate. Heavy metallurgy approached its goal by only 67.7 per cent, and consumer goods by 73.5 per cent.

This uneven performance of the First Five Year Plan gave rise to various diametrically opposed interpretations. None of these judgments seem to be valid, for, as one observer rightly noted, "the Soviet economy was planned not for the harmony of its different branches, but for one single purpose, namely the most rapid industrialization and preparation of effective national defense." This the First Five Year Plan achieved. In slightly more than four years the Soviet Union constructed seventeen new blast furnaces and modernized another twenty. It installed forty-five new open-hearth furnaces and modernized another twenty. It built fifteen new rolling mills and reconstructed twelve. It laid the foundation for two new iron and steel centers, those of Magnitogorsk in the Urals and Kuznetsk in Central Siberia. Finally, the period of the First Five Year Plan gave birth to such new industries as synthetic rubber, plastics, and aviation.

In January, 1934, the Seventeenth Party Congress formally adopted the Second Five Year Plan covering the years 1933–1937. The fundamental task of the Second Plan was "the completion of technical construction in the whole of national economy." This, in turn, meant a slight lowering of targets and paying more attention to qualitative improvements. The Second Five Year Plan, like its predecessor, assigned first priority and a high rate of investment to heavy industry. To overcome the lagging of iron and steel, the Second Plan ordered construction of 45 new blast furnaces, 164 open-hearth furnaces and 107 rolling mills. These additions, it was hoped, would allow the production of 16,000,000 tons of pig iron and 17,000,000 tons of steel in 1937. Tied to these goals was a call for considerable extension of machine tool production (milling, grinding, gear-cutting, automatic and semiautomatic machines) and development of the production of non-ferrous metals. Copper was to be developed in the Urals and in Kazakhstan (near Lake Balkash); lead in Kazakhstan, in the Altai region, in the Northern Caucasus and in the Far East; zinc in the Urals and in Siberia; aluminum in Southern Ukraine, east of Leningrad, and in the middle Urals; nickel in the Urals; tin in Kazakhstan and in the Trans-Baikal region; and magnesium in the Ukraine and in the northern Urals.

The Second Plan called also for improvement and double-tracking of the main railroad lines, which were overburdened with passengers, coal, iron, and wheat. This improvement, however, was impossible until the iron industry expanded considerably. To remove some of the pressures on the railroads, the Second Plan provided for construction of the Moscow-

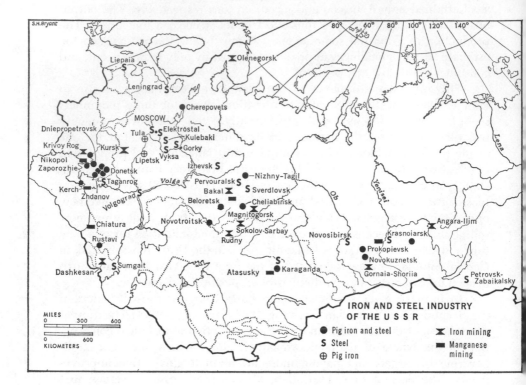

IRON AND STEEL INDUSTRY
OF THE U S S R

- ● Pig iron and steel
- S Steel
- ⊕ Pig iron
- ✕ Iron mining
- ▰ Manganese mining

Volga Canal, widening of the old Marinsky canal system (which links the Baltic with the Volga), improvement of river port facilities and the river fleet, and for construction of highways linking the major cities of European Russia. The Second Five Year Plan, like its predecessor, emphasized the need to develop untapped resources of Soviet Asia, especially the coal and iron of the Ural-Kuznetsk complex. This emphasis had a three-fold goal. First, it aimed at bringing industry into closer proximity to the sources of raw material and power. Second, it sought to overcome the economic and cultural backwardness of various peoples of Soviet Asia. And third, should this goal materialize, it would impress the multitude of Asia's population. Finally, unlike its predecessor, the Second Five Year Plan paid some attention to the development of light industries, housing, bus service, and water and sanitation projects.

The official results of the Second Five Year Plan resembled in many ways those of the First; namely, some items reached the estimated targets while others lagged behind. Thus, for instance, steel production rose from 5,900,000 tons in 1932 to 17,600,000 tons in 1937. Rolled steel trebled in

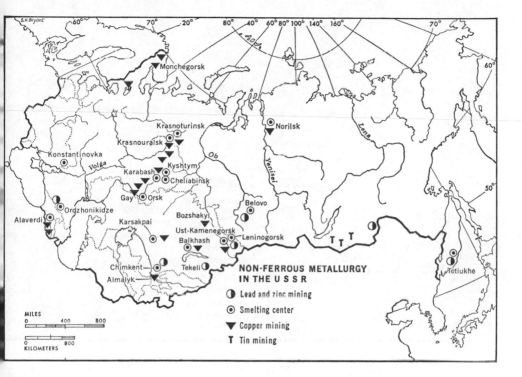

NON-FERROUS METALLURGY IN THE USSR

◐ Lead and zinc mining
◉ Smelting center
▼ Copper mining
T Tin mining

MILES
0 400 800

0 800
KILOMETERS

output. The machine-making industry showed a threefold rise in output, while the automobile industry registered an eightfold increase. But there were many industries and products that did not fare as well. Heavy industry and pig iron, for instance, were slightly behind the assigned goal. Production of oil was 30,500,000 tons instead of the planned 46,800,000. Coal output was 128,000,000 tons instead of the projected 152,000,000. Instead of doubling, the production of cotton goods increased by 40 per cent and that of woolen goods by only 22 per cent. Notwithstanding these shortcomings, by the end of the Second Five Year Plan the Soviet Union was emerging as a a strong industrial country. It possessed an increased capacity to produce iron, steel, coal, and electric power. It also had a whole range of new industries, such as aviation, tractor, locomotive, chemical, aluminum, copper, nickel, and tin. In other words, the Soviet Union at the end of the 1930's had a well-established industrial base capable of further expansion and growth.

Soviet industrialization must be viewed not only through the quantitative growth of its industry and its output capacity, but also through non-

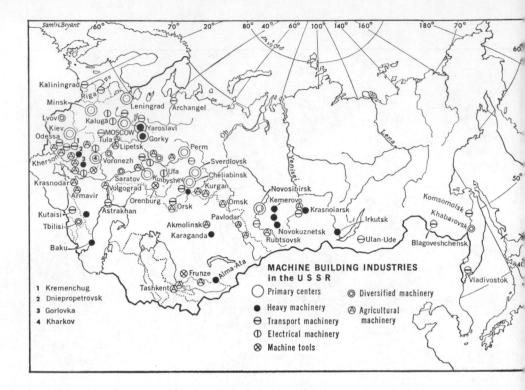

MACHINE BUILDING INDUSTRIES
in the U S S R

1 Kremenchug
2 Dniepropetrovsk
3 Gorlovka
4 Kharkov

○ Primary centers   ◎ Diversified machinery
● Heavy machinery   Ⓐ Agricultural
⊖ Transport machinery   machinery
Ⓘ Electrical machinery
⊗ Machine tools

economic indices, and above all through the methods employed to produce these results. In the absence of machinery and skill and the presence
of abundant manpower, the results were produced by sheer force. Workers were mobilized, directed, and regimented. Since, as we have seen,
Stalin considered the industrialization program a race against time, the
experts who prepared the plans for every sector of the economy and for
every industry were ordered to set the quotas high. Nonfulfillment of
these quotas, which in most instances bore little relation to previous performance, gave Stalin an excuse to blame someone else. Criticism of the
excessive demands was impossible because this implied criticism of the
party line, which was considered infallible. Stalin tolerated only those
suggestions which called for increasing the output and rewarded those
who overfulfilled their assigned quotas, regardless of the methods used.
Those who suggested caution or who failed to exceed the plan were
branded "saboteurs" and automatically invited imprisonment, exile, or
even death. By these policies, Stalin intensified the totalitarian nature of
the system and strengthened his absolute control over it.

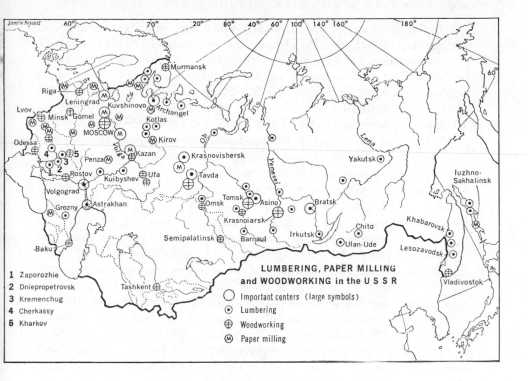

LUMBERING, PAPER MILLING
and WOODWORKING in the U S S R

○ Important centers (large symbols)
⊙ Lumbering
⊕ Woodworking
Ⓜ Paper milling

1 Zaporozhie
2 Dniepropetrovsk
3 Kremenchug
4 Cherkassy
5 Kharkov

Waste of material and great human sacrifices were additional by-products of the fulfillment and nonfulfillment mania. Workers built factories for which no equipment was available, and delivered equipment to plants unable to accommodate it. Many structures were built in the wrong places and had to be abandoned, while, because of poor workmanship, some collapsed before they were finished. The food supply was precarious, housing overcrowded and inadequate, and working conditions in old and new industrial centers were inhuman. Everywhere safety was neglected, barest needs were not provided for, and men and machinery were cruelly overworked. But nothing mattered so long as the plan was either fulfilled or overfulfilled. If fulfillment was really impossible, those "enterprising" officials who wanted to survive either bribed their immediate superiors or manipulated figures and falsified accounts. So long as they succeeded in "covering their tracks" by any device imaginable, no one asked embarrassing questions. When one failed to "fulfill" his part of the plan, the authorities accepted no excuse. Under those conditions, as one observer aptly put it, Soviet "planning bred a new kind of rugged individualism."

In the initial stages, industrializing efforts and propaganda succeeded in capturing the imagination of many Soviet youths. Notwithstanding all sorts of hardships and inadequacies, there appeared throughout the country "shock brigades" and other volunteer groups trying to build factories and vast public projects with bare hands. Because youthful idealism did not last long, authorities were forced to adopt and apply other measures. To stop the heavy turnover of labor and at the same time to increase its productivity, in June, 1931, Stalin proposed a six-point program aimed at remedying the difficulties that handicapped industrialization. It included: (1) organized recruitment of labor, especially from rural areas; (2) abolition of fluctuating labor and of the *uravnilovka* (leveling of wages), which he called a "leftist evil"; (3) strengthening of personal responsibility of managers; (4) training from among the working class of new technical personnel capable of mastering new techniques; (5) maximum utilization of prerevolutionary specialists and technicians; and (6) introduction of businesslike principles of management and cost accounting.

On the basis of this six-point program, in the course of the 1930's the government issued a series of laws and decrees aimed at strengthening labor discipline and the responsibility of workers and managers. A government decree of November 15, 1932, for instance, empowered local authorities to dismiss a worker and to deprive him of his factory food card and housing for one day's absenteeism from work without sufficient reason. Other decrees dealt with punctual arrival at work, producing the standard quota on schedule, striving for overfulfillment of planned goals, improving the quality of production, and taking care of socialist property. The government organized special factory colonies, whose purpose was to

Mikhail Kalinin   *Maxim Litvinov*

inculcate "labor habits" in the inmates and to raise their labor qualifications. Habitual or serious violations of government rules invited imprisonment, exile to Siberia, or even death.

This regimentation of the labor force eliminated unemployment in Soviet Russia. It also deprived the trade unions of the last remnants of their independence. Because he opposed increased exploitation of workers, on June 2, 1929, Tomsky was replaced by Shvernik as head of Soviet Trade Unions. Under his chairmanship, on June 23, 1933, the trade unions assumed many of the functions of the Commissariat of Labor and became a docile instrument of the party in exploiting the workers. To increase the productivity of labor, Stalin abolished wage equalization, recognized the difference between skilled and unskilled workers, and devised and encouraged "socialist competition" and *Stakhanovism*. The *Stakhanov* movement in particular was an enormous propaganda effort. It benefited those few workers who, for one reason or another, were able to attain striking results in their production. It was, however, detrimental to those who were just average, as their norms (not their wages) were increased, because production quotas were based not on the general average but on the average of the best. For the working people of the Soviet Union, the industrial revolution of the 1930's was a bitter experience.

THE AGRICULTURAL REVOLUTION

The industrial revolution which the Soviet Union experienced in the 1930's was accompanied by a great agricultural revolution. In fact, some scholars believe that the agricultural upheaval was more dramatic and sweeping than the industrial. For one thing it affected more people, and it also was fraught with more excesses and real horrors.

Like its industrial counterpart, the agricultural revolution, although it had been discussed during the 1920's, was ordered suddenly and without any real preparation. Most scholars believe that the major cause leading to this great upheaval was the slow rate of expansion of agricultural production during the 1920's—a rate which failed to supply the growing demands of raw materials for industry and foodstuffs for the workers. Or, to put it in another way, ten years after the revolution Russian agriculture was producing less surplus than it had before the revolution. Several factors contributed to this phenomenon. One of these was the breakup of large estates during 1917–1918, which resulted in creation of a small-scale individualistic agriculture. In 1928 there were in the Soviet Union some 25,500,000 peasant households, or an increase of some 7,000,000 in little more than a decade. Furthermore, most of these farms, both new and old, were relatively small (under thirty acres), inadequately equipped, and continued to use primitive methods of cultivation because of rooted conservativism, lack of adequate financial resources and the necessary "know-how." And although during the NEP some progress was made in removing these ills, the net effect on productivity was small and slow—too slow to satisfy the needs of both the growing city population and the growing industry. This became apparent during the harvest of 1925–1926—the year of agricultural recovery—when the marketed surplus of agriculture failed, in the words of one economist, "to recover to the prewar level, despite the recovery both of the cultivated area and of the gross harvest." According to official estimates, only 17 per cent of the total harvest yield was sent to market, and a year later the total dropped to 14 per cent, or about one-half of the prewar period. This sharp reduction of marketed grain during the 1920's affected both the export and import plans of party leaders by demonstrating that under existing conditions the envisaged large-scale industrial expansion, relying on imported machinery in exchange for agricultural surplus, was impossible.

A great deal of agricultural difficulty also stemmed from the fact that under the NEP the Soviet Union had a mixed economy: *the state-owned "socialist sector,"* which included all heavy industry, transport, banking, credit facilities, and foreign trade; and *the private ownership sector,* which predominated in small-scale industry, retail trade, and farming. Though the balance between the two sectors was quite uneven, during the NEP all responsible party leaders sought to preserve the existing cooperation as well as competition between the two. But competition also implied a degree of antagonism. Industry, making a slow recovery from ruin, sought high prices for its products but cheap prices for food and raw materials. By the same token, peasants sought low prices on industrial goods and high prices for their own produce. Moreover, once they recovered from the excesses of the Civil War and War Communism, the peasants began to press for further concessions, such as the reduction of taxes, the abolition of restrictions on hiring of farm workers, and long term leasing of land, and to the dismay of the Bolsheviks they proved to be exceedingly resourceful and productive.

Party and government leaders resisted peasant demands, for to give in would have meant to capitulate to the peasants, whom they hated and despised and whose attitudes and ambitions they considered petty-bourgeois. But so long as the outcome of the struggle for succession was undecided, unwilling to face two formidable opponents—Trotsky and the peasants—Stalin and his "right wing" associates listened to peasant demands. Both he and Bukharin rejected Trotsky's suggestion that additional levies be put on the private sector of economy to help accelerate industrialization. They feared that such a move would discourage peasant initiative, create food shortages, and upset the delicate balance between the two sectors of economy. No sooner, however, was the struggle for succession resolved than Stalin altered his stand quite suddenly.

The first sign of Stalin's changed position towards the peasants came in December, 1927, when, following his triumph over Trotsky, he instructed all local party members to take energetic measures to extract grain from the peasants. Because peasants resisted these measures by all the devices known to them, there was a great deal of "administrative arbitrariness, violation of revolutionary law, raids on peasant houses, [and] illegal searches." These actions continued until July, 1928, and those party members who showed any leniency towards the peasants were purged. The second sign of Stalin's *volte-face* came in April, 1928, at a meeting of the Central Executive Committee of the All-Union Congress of Soviets, where, without any advance warning, Stalin presented the draft of a new land law. This draft sought three objectives: (1) to deprive the peasants of their unrestricted rights to the use of land cultivated by their own labor; (2) to confine those rights to only those peasants who joined collective farms; and (3) to deprive of all rights to any land those peasants who were classified as *kulaks;* i.e., those peasants who were either industrious, or more prosperous than their neighbors, or simply those who were not enthusiastic about the policies of the Communist party. While the draft was tabled and thus failed to become law, it disclosed that Stalin had in mind rapid and forcible collectivization of the peasants in order to help industrialize the country at breakneck speed.

Stalin confirmed this point at the end of May, 1928, when he called upon party members to choose between suicide and rapid collectivization of agriculture and development of heavy industry. He again reiterated this idea at the July, 1928, meeting of the Central Committee when he stressed that while it was an "unpleasant business," since the Soviet Union had neither colonies nor ready capital to industrialize rapidly, it had to resort to exacting a "tribute" from the bulk of its population—the peasants. This frank but blunt statement was the clearest indication thus far that Stalin was parting company both with the peasants and with his former right wing associate, Bukharin.

The peasants received Stalin's decision to collectivize agriculture in order to help industrialize the country with anything but enthusiasm. From the outset therefore the drive towards collectivization turned into a ruthless and bitter war. The outcome of this struggle was never in doubt not only because the party and the government possessed all the coercive means, but also because of the nature of the soviet village itself. On the eve of collectivization there were some 25,500,000 peasant holdings. Out of that number, between 5,000,000 and 7,000,000 were classified as *bedniaks,* or poor peasants, who had neither a horse, nor a cow, nor any appreciable agricultural implements, and so were ready and willing to listen to promises of improvement. Above this destitute group were some 18,000,000 *seredniaks,* or middle peasants, who had most of the necessities of life and who desired no radical change. At the top were some 800,000 *kulaks*—industrious, and, by Soviet standards, the most productive and thus most prosperous peasants, who had the most to lose and who therefore opposed collectivization.

To overcome the *kulak* resistance to collectivization, Stalin carried the class struggle into the village by setting peasant against peasant. First he turned the *bedniaks* against the *kulaks.* The *bedniaks* were offered the *kulaks'* cattle, implements and machinery, and all-out government support in improving their living conditions in collective farms. Thus supported by local party members, the *bedniaks* unleashed a bitter civil war throughout rural areas of the USSR. The success of this upheaval encouraged Stalin to issue a call in December, 1929, to all party members to pass "from the policy of *restricting* the exploiting proclivities of the *kulaks* to the policy of *eliminating* the *kulaks* as a class." Thousands of party and *komsomol* agents, workers, police and army units were ordered to the countryside to perform this task. Their activities brought rural Russia to what one observer aptly called "pandemonium." Villages which resisted this form of "voluntary" association were surrounded by armed units and forced to surrender. Under those conditions the war against the *kulak* turned into a ruthless and chaotic war against *all* peasants. Thousands were killed, many more were arrested and millions were scattered throughout Siberia and the sub-Polar regions. All of their possessions (houses, farms, farm implements, livestock, and the like) were turned over to the collective farms. Other millions, whether they resisted or not, were forced into collective farms. The speed with which this mass collectivization drive was carried out can be best seen from the following official figures. At the end of 1928, only 1.7 per cent of all peasant households was collectivized. In October, 1929, the percentage had risen to 4.1 per cent; in January, 1930, to 21 per cent; and early in March, 1930, it stood at 58 per cent, or more than half of all the households.

The bitterness and chaos which this collectivization drive created seems to have frightened Stalin. On March 2, 1930, *Pravda* printed his now famous article entitled "Dizziness with Success," in which he placed the blame for what had happened on the overzealousness of local party officials who misunderstood party directives, became intoxicated by their initial successes, and lost all sense of proportion and "the faculty of understanding realism." Posing as a defender of peasant interests, Stalin now called his overzealous local party functionaries "opportunists," "blockheads," "lefts," and "distortionists." He admitted that force had been used in the collectivization drive, but warned that "collective farms cannot be set up by force" because to do so "would be stupid and reactionary."

Stalin's call to halt the excesses did not mean the end of collectivization. Many peasants, however, seem to have thought so, for between March and September, 1930, the percentage of collectivized households dropped from 58 per cent to 21 per cent. Following the Sixteenth Party

Congress (June 26–July 13, 1930), which formally echoed Stalin's words on the "voluntary" nature of the collectives, the drive was begun anew. In 1931 the percentage of collectivized households rose to 52.7 per cent and climbed constantly. In 1932 it stood at 61.5 per cent; in 1933 at 65.6 per cent; in 1934 at 71.4 per cent; in 1935 at 83.2 per cent; in 1936 at 90.5 per cent; and in 1938 at 93.5 per cent, with 242,400 collective farms.

The speed and ferocity with which the mass collectivization program was carried out benefited neither the state, nor the collective farms nor the peasants. Before they "joined" collectives, the peasants, in desperation, killed their cattle, pigs, and horses; destroyed their farm implements; and either burned their crops or allowed them to rot in the field. The scope of this form of peasant resistance can be seen from the following figures. Between 1928 and 1934, the number of horses dropped from 36,100,000 to 15,400,000; cattle from 66,800,000 to 33,500,000; hogs from 27,700,000 to 11,500,000; and sheep and goats from 114,600,000 to 36,500,000. Needless to say, the loss of draft animals had negative effects on the agricultural goals of the plan, with the result that agricultural production in 1933 was much lower than in 1928.

Party and government response to peasant resistance was firm and tragic in its final outcome. A joint decree of the Central Committee and of the *Sovnarkom* on January 16, 1930, established the criminal responsibility of all who destroyed their property or killed their cattle and other animals before joining collectives. A decree of February 1, 1930, empowered local authorities, in case of resistance to collectivization or destruction of the property of collective farms, to take all measures "including total confiscation of property of the *kulaks* and their deportation from a given district, territory, or region." Finally, on August 7, 1932, a Draconian law introduced the death penalty without possibility of pardon for any "theft" of property belonging to a collective farm or to the state. Strict enforcement of this decree, coupled with the forcible collection of high levies, produced a man-made famine. The areas most affected were the Ukraine and Northern Caucasus. The government officially denied the existence of famine and refused to accept outside aid. At the same time, however, it kept both regions off limits to foreign correspondents stationed in Moscow until the harvest of 1933 had been brought in. Probably no one will ever know the famine's *exact* toll of lives, but estimates (based on interpretation of the figures of the 1937–1938 census) range from 5 million to 10 million. Whatever figure is accepted, one must agree that for the rural people of the Soviet Union the agricultural revolution, especially this early period, described by one observer as "the period of licenced anarchy," was a bitter experience.

Following "the period of licenced anarchy," agricultural organization in the Soviet Union consisted of four basic institutions: (1) *sovkhozes* or state farms; (2) *kolkhozes*, or collective farms; (3) Machine Tractor

Stations (MTS); and (4) private peasant plots. With only slight modifications these units (excepting MTS's) remain the basic forms of agriculture in the Soviet Union today.

State farms, as their name implies, are entirely properties of the state. They are managed by government-appointed supervisors, who operate them with the help of hired labor and in the same spirit as is any factory in the USSR. Large in size, often exceeding 5,000 acres, these "factories in the field," have been favored by all Soviet leaders (Lenin, Stalin, and Khrushchev) for two basic reasons: first, as state owned and operated enterprises they are thought to be capable of providing the state with a high net production; and second, workers on these farms, like workers in the factories, are under relatively strong party and government control. Because Soviet leaders prefer them, state farms have enjoyed large investments and have been provided more adequately with tractors and other farm machinery. The number of state farms has also increased appreciably from 1,400 in 1927, to 4,337 in 1932, to 5,900 in 1958.

The development of state farms fell into several distinct phases. The first was during the 1920's when the government turned into model specialized farms those large estates which the peasants did not divide among themselves. Because many of these farms operated at a loss, the government later reduced their area. The second phase was roughly during the first two Five Year Plans, when, hoping to obtain a large amount of grain, Stalin ordered an increase in the number of state farms. These hopes, however, failed to materialize because the size of the farms themselves prevented efficient management, while their overspecialization precluded the application of a balanced agricultural technique. In the late 1930's, many unprofitable state farms were liquidated and those that remained were ordered to diversify their operations. During and after World War II the number of state farms rose again as a result of the emergency. The highest increase occurred in Central Asia (Kazakh SSR), in the area of the so-called "virgin lands."

Work on state farms is done by work units called brigades, headed by foremen called brigadiers. Each worker is paid on the basis of straight piece-work wages. The basic unit of cropwork measurement is the *hectare* (or 2.471 acres), and those workers who produce more receive more. State farms have been plagued by a high labor turnover rate, by idleness during the wintertime, and by inefficiency during the remainder of the year. To remedy these difficulties and thus to reduce the high production costs for grain, milk, meat, and other products, the government has tried many policies. Thus far, none seem to have been satisfactory.

Collective farms form the second major agricultural institution in the Soviet Union. In theory, collective farms are "voluntarily" organized farmers' cooperatives, whose members have pooled their land and capital, operate them in common, and share their "net proceeds in proportion to the quantity and quality of work they do." In reality, however, as we noted earlier, party and state officials forcibly imposed the organization of collective farms on the rural population of the USSR. Each collective farm has a charter (based on the Standard Charter of February 17, 1935), which defines the organization of the collective farm and the responsibilities of its members and officers. Economically, collective farms operate under certain handicaps. The land they use belongs to the state, and may neither be sold, leased, bought, nor given to a member who withdraws. The use of this land is determined by the national plan, which determines what, where, and in what quantity anything is to be produced. Each collective farm owns cattle, horses, simple implements, buildings, seed, fodder, and the like, but it may not dispose of this property for two reasons. First, through such disposal it would deprive itself of its means of existence; and second, without these implements, it could not fulfill the task which the plan has imposed on it. Until 1958, no collective farm owned any heavy machinery. That was supplied by the government-operated MTS's.

In theory, collective farms are democratic organizations. Under the Charter, the highest authority on a collective farm is the general meeting which elects the officers, decides on the admission of new or expulsion of old members, confirms the budget, the building program, and annual production, approves the reports of its officers, and determines the remuneration for its members. In practice, however, many of the "elected" officials, especially chairmen, have been party appointees, as have also been the members of the management board. Work on collective farms, like that on state farms, is done by work units of fifty to one hundred individuals called brigades, and by smaller units called *zvena* (links).

The state has always had first claim on all products of collective farms, and has always been able to take the lion's share of the production. The state collects its share in four ways. First, it receives some in the form of a tax-in-kind levy. The amount of this tax, which differs from area to area, is determined not by the actual harvest, or the area actually sown, but by a theoretical estimate of what should have been obtained from all the arable land at the disposal of a given collective farm. Another share the government receives in the form of repayment of debts, which practically all collective farms owe. The third way the state obtains much of the collective farms' production is in payment for services performed by the government-owned MTS's, although this source has declined since 1958. Finally, the state receives a substantial share from special "voluntary" commitments made by local party officials.

After all deliveries to the state have been made, each collective farm must reserve certain quantities for seed, fodder, and other needs. The remainder is then divided among the members of the collective farms as payment in kind. The share of individual members depends on the number of "labor days" credited to each. A "labor day" is a conditional unit. It may mean one, two, three, or a fraction of a calendar day, depending on the type of work done and the results achieved. A watchman may get as little as one half a "labor day" for one calendar day's work, while the chairman of the farm may collect three "labor days" for one calendar day. The obligatory minimum of "labor days"—a basic condition for remaining a member of a collective farm—was originally set at from 60 to 100 per year. During World War II that minimum was increased from 100 to 150. Should there be any surplus left after each member is paid his share, that surplus is either sold to the government or on the open market, and the money divided among the members of the collective farm.

Since the mid-1930's, the Soviet government has invested heavily in collective farms. According to official figures, in 1958 there were 78,200 collective farms. At their disposal were 1,700,000 tractors, 483,000 harvester combines, 660,000 trucks, and 277,000 skilled specialists. From the technical point of view, this heavy mechanization makes collective farms a progressive form of agricultural economy. Persistent attention of Soviet leaders to the collective farms shows, however, that mechanization alone will not produce grain, milk, meat, or vegetables, and that collectives are not as profitable as they were intended to be. Scholars have listed many reasons for the failure of the collective farm system. These include: peculiarities of the centralized system of economy; political and administrative over-supervision; vast bureaucracy; and peasant indifference. It must be remembered, however, that there are some collective farms that are prosperous.

Machine tractor stations, established on June 5, 1929, were, until 1958, the third major agricultural institution. Owned and operated by the state, the MTS's functions were manifold. They operated tractors, combines, and other complex agricultural machinery, and performed all the heavy work on collective farms from plowing, to seeding, to cultivating, to harvesting. In return for this work, the MTS's, or more properly the state, received a share of the crop. In the 1930's and the 1940's, the share was from 10 per cent to 20 per cent of the farm's grain crop. In 1953, fixed rates were introduced for different areas. The MTS's served also as a major instrument for controlling collective farms, a function which they performed in innumerable ways. Led by party members, the MTS's served finally as disseminators of party propaganda among the peasant population. In 1930, there were only 158 MTS's in the USSR; in 1935 the figure was 4,375; in 1940 the figure stood at 7,069; and in 1958 it was 7,900. In 1958, most of the MTS's were ordered to disband gradually, and to sell their assets to the collective farms.

Private peasant plots form the last major agricultural institution in the USSR. Granted to each household by the collective farm statute of 1935, these plots vary in size, depending on the nature of local economy, but legally they are not less than 0.62 and not more than 1.24 acres. Local conditions, law, and size place limits on the number of animals each plot may have. Throughout most of the European part of the USSR, each private peasant plot is allowed one cow, two calves, one sow, ten sheep or goats, an unlimited number of fowl and rabbits, and not more than twenty beehives. Though small in size, from the very beginning these plots have played a vital role in peasant lives, because peasant industriousness has turned them into a significant supplementary source of livelihood. They provide food, vegetables, eggs, and other necessities, some of which they even sell on the open market. Peasants have always treated these plots as their own, and by all devious means have tried to enlarge them. The party and the government, on the other hand, have as persistently sought a formula or a policy which would enable them to abolish these plots altogether.

CULTURAL AND SOCIAL UNIFORMITY

Stalin accompanied his vast industrial and agricultural transformation of the USSR by an excessive cultural and social regimentation. Authorities differ on the nature of this uniformity, as they do on most aspects of Soviet history, but most of them believe that these changes were an integral part of the economic planning with but one difference. Whereas, by economic planning Stalin sought to exploit the abundance of natural resources, to develop heavy industry, to strengthen the military might of the USSR, and to mechanize agriculture in order to increase its productivity, by cultural and social regimentation he aspired to exploit and control all the movements, thoughts, and ideas of every individual, in order to create a uniform, monolithic, and obedient modern totalitarian society, ruled by an "infallible" supreme leader whose word would be the ultimate law of the land. Stalin achieved these aims by "coercion" as well as by "persuasion," or the "stick and carrot" approach.

The remaking of Soviet culture and society started late in 1929, or shortly after Stalin's triumph over his opponents, and following his elevation on his fiftieth birthday to *vozhd*, "beloved leader" and "great genius" of the USSR. In 1930 he brought Soviet philosophers to submission, and Marxism-Leninism-Stalinism emerged as the only accepted philosophy in the Soviet Union. Stalin's own most notable "contribution" to this philosophy dealt with the problem of the "withering away of the state." Until Stalin changed it, the official view on this crucial theoretical issue of Marxism was that the state, which was considered by the Marxists to be a product of class struggle and an instrument of coercion, would disappear progressively with the triumph of the revolution and with the disappearance of class antagonisms. Following the revolution many demands were made to dissolve the state, and considerable literature was written on that problem. Stalin ended the controversy by announcing in 1930, in 1934, and in 1939, that the state would "wither away," not through its weakening but through development of its economic, political, and military strength to the uttermost capability in order to enable it to eliminate its external as well as internal opponents.

Next after philosophy, Stalin ordered a vast change in the writing and teaching of history. The first sign of the impending shift occurred at the end of 1931, in the form of a letter to the editors of the *Proletarskaia Revolutsiia* (Proletarian Revolution) in which Stalin made it clear that he would not tolerate any questioning of Lenin's views by any historian. This warning officially approved the sanctity of Lenin's works, and served as the first step to sanctifying Stalin's pronouncements. A more concrete measure affecting history was a decree of May 16, 1934, issued jointly by the Central Committee and the *Sovnarkom*, which declared the teaching of history in Soviet schools to be unsatisfactory, and ordered that all texts based on "abstract schematic character," "abstract definitions of social and economic formations," and "abstract sociological schemes," be replaced by a more conventional presentation with emphasis on individuals and nations. Historian Michael N. Pokrovsky (1868–1932), the chief architect of the old Marxist school, was posthumously branded a "traitor," and his works and his followers were subjected to bitter denunciation and criticism.

It is important to remember that Stalin's "new concept" of history aimed at restoring not all but a few *selected* glories and achievements of Russia's imperial past to suit the present. He ordered, for instance, the acceptance of Christianity to be viewed as an act of progress in the history of the Russian people, and many of the early princes to be presented as progressive leaders and true sons of the Russian people. Ivan the Terrible and Peter the Great were turned from despots into reformers, tireless fighters for national unity and national might, and bitter opponents of all traitors. Alexander Nevsky's victory over the Livonian knights in 1242, and Napoleon's defeat in 1812 were ordered viewed as national efforts against foreign invasion in defense of freedom. Before long Stalin elevated Generals Michael Kutuzov (1745–1813), Alexander Suvorov (1730–1800), and other heroes of the Russian past to prominence and interpreted Russian past territorial conquest in Europe and Asia not as acts of imperialism but as circumstances dictated by historical forces.

Stalin's rediscovery of the Russian past differed from prerevolutionary treatments in one significant respect: It included histories of non-Russian peoples of the USSR. But while this action was commendable in one way (histories of some peoples were written for the first time), it was distortive in another way. Russian heroes were always portrayed as superior, and non-Russians, though equally great, were *ipso facto* inferior. The same was true of all Russian literary figures and of the Russian language, which was lauded as the language of the revolutionary teachings of Marx and Engels as elaborated by Lenin and Stalin. The study of Russian became obligatory for all non-Russian minorities, and any avoidance of usage of it at home or in schools was considered a renouncement of the revolutionary method. Those who objected were branded traitors and dealt with accordingly. This form of "Soviet patriotism" was applied broadly during and after World War II.

Aware that no nation can hope to become a leading industrial and military power without a loyal, literate, and technically well-trained citizenry, Stalin paid much attention to the schools in his efforts to impose new uniformity on the Soviet people. In July, 1930, universal primary education was introduced, and in September, 1931, the Central Committee repudiated the experiment in progressive education in favor of academic education of the traditional disciplinarian type tailored to the totalitarian objectives of the Communist state. Report cards, grades, student discipline, and authority of teachers—discarded during the 1920's because of their "bourgeois origin"—were reintroduced early in the 1930's. Alongside physics, chemistry, mathematics, and biology, Soviet schools were now ordered to emphasize such "Communist virtues" as devotion to work, labor discipline, conformity, sobriety, love of country, and hatred of its enemies, and belief in the infallibility of its leaders. The new curriculum placed a twofold responsibility on the schools. First, they were to serve as the chief supplier of trustworthy and efficient functionaries to manage the new factories, to administer government agencies, to enforce party and government directives, and to develop the state's technological resources. The schools' second task was to serve as a conveyor of political indoctrination of the state's "most treasured possession, the children." The same dual responsibility was entrusted to the teachers. Each teacher was to be a fountain of knowledge as well as an effective propaganda emissary of the regime, to advertise its achievements, to promote its beliefs, to indoctrinate the young, and to disseminate the official information. Teachers who failed to qualify for those tasks were dismissed, and those who remained were upgraded both socially and financially.

Next to schools, Stalin made great efforts to bring new uniformity to the family. "Free love," "free divorce," and legalized abortions—the pride of the experimental twenties—were officially condemned as "bourgeois inventions," and the seriousness of marriage and of family stability were stressed. Two pressures operated behind the new emphasis. First was an alarming decrease of the birthrate, which, if allowed to continue unchecked, threatened to undermine both the labor supply and the national defenses. According to some estimates, between 1926 and 1937, the increase in the birthrate in the USSR was about 13,000,000 below that which had been projected by demographers. Second was the increasing

problem of juvenile delinquency which resulted from the wholesale dissolution of family ties during the early stages of industrialization. Many of
the delinquents were children of parents sent to forced labor camps. No
one dared to show any kindness to these orphans in order not to share the
fate of their parents. Most of the delinquents roved in gangs perpetrating
crimes and vandalism. Some were placed in state-operated orphanages,
but in many of these establishments, as one observer noted, "the authorities had lost all control and the toughest of the children reigned supreme
amid dirt and violence."

To curb the nationwide lawlessness, on April 7, 1935, the government
decreed that any minor over twelve years of age found guilty of "hooli-
ganism" was "to be liable to all grades of criminal penalty," including
death. Those guilty of contributing to the delinquency of minors became
liable to not less than five years' imprisonment. On May 31, 1935, the
government increased parental responsibility for the misdemeanors of
their children. A decree of June 7, 1936, prohibited abortion except when
medically authorized, made divorce more difficult, and reinstated the family as the basic unit of the social organism. The decree also provided state
subsidies to large families and soon thereafter the title of "Mother Hero-
ine" was given to women who gave birth to and reared ten children.
Those mothers who bore seven children received the medal of "Mother's
Glory," and those who had five or six children were awarded the medal
of "Motherhood." By strengthening family ties, Stalin also strengthened
the principle of collective responsibility of the family for its members, a
factor which in part accounts for the heavy toll of victims during the
purges.

By the end of the 1930's, the imposed changes in family and school,
together with the industrial and agricultural transformations, produced an
interesting shift both in thinking and in actual structure of Soviet society.
Officially, the new society in 1937 was said to have consisted of workers,
who comprised 36.2 per cent; peasants, who comprised 63.8 per cent; and a
stratum called intelligentsia which had been recruited from both—all
living in friendship among themselves. This "harmony," it was explained,
stemmed from the abolition in the USSR of all classes and of private
ownership of the instruments and means of production, liquidation of the
capitalist system, elimination of the exploitation of man by man, and the
removal of all vestiges of discrimination.

Official claims that the Soviet Union produced during the 1930's a
society free of class divisions and class antagonisms did not correspond
with reality, however, because the same period that witnessed the liquidation of the old classes experienced also the emergence of new social strata.
Industrialization, collectivization, and Stalinization produced all kinds of
party and government functionaries, technical specialists, factory man-

Mikhail Tukhachevsky   Nikolai Yezhov

agers, artists, writers, collective farm managers, Stakhanovites, and countless bureaucrats who received high salaries, prizes, bonuses, honoraria,
and even royalties. Many of these "distinguished people" enjoyed com-
fortable residences, had cars, country houses (*dachas*), and substantial
bank accounts. Below this new group of Soviet "aristocrats" were ordinary
workers whose membership increased greatly during the 1930's, peasants
whose membership was reduced drastically, and millions of inmates of
various correctional institutions and labor camps. Between the new "aristocracy" and the rest of the population there was a vast cleavage, which
manifested itself in power and influence, as well as in the way of living.

The great cleavage between the "haves" and the "have nots" in the
USSR, which the 1930's put into focus, gave rise to various interpretations. Those scholars who subscribe to the Marxist definition of social
classes—the exploiters and the exploited—deny the existence of class divisions in the USSR. In their view, everyone has an opportunity to rise on
the social ladder and no group in the Soviet Union has either a class
psychology or a definite status in production. Other scholars believe, however, that like any other country the USSR has its own classes which differ
as to their place in the national economy, their relation to the means of
production, and the size of their share in the national income. There are
also many scholars who maintain that during the 1930's the Soviet Union
produced two main classes: First, the *obeying* class—the class that has no
power over the means of production; no voice as to what should be
produced, where, and in what amount; and no voice about conditions of
either work or pay. The second is the *commanding* class, the class that

controls the means of production, decides what is to be produced, where and how, and determines not only the distribution of the products but prices, wages, rewards and penalties as well.

Two factors seem to have been instrumental in the rise of social inequality in a "classless society." One was Stalin's replacement in 1931 of wage equalization with wages that differentiated between skilled and unskilled workers. The second, and most important cause for this inequality, was the nature of the Soviet planned and regimented economy, which, from its inception, in the absence of a market mechanism, demanded not only planned distribution of raw materials but of manpower as well. To fulfill the task assigned by each successive plan it was necessary not only to mobilize but to "freeze" a certain part of the population in industry, a certain part in agriculture, some in public service, and some in managerial work. The peasants were "frozen" on the collective farm as early as March 17, 1933, while workers could not legally find any employment without "labor booklets" after January 15, 1939. These measures enabled Stalin to distribute manpower, penalties, and rewards more easily. These measures also served effectively in recruiting a reliable bureaucracy for the regime.

To produce the new cultural and social uniformity, Stalin relied on coercion as well as persuasion. He executed thousands of people and sent millions more into oblivion. Those who remained were subjected to intensive propaganda indoctrination. All media of public communication (newspapers, radio, publishing houses, periodicals, bulletins, posters, and the like) were mobilized to publicize Stalin's goals. They recruited support for his policies, checked on the enforcement of party and government decisions, agitated for the realization of production quotas, called for liquidation of the "enemies" of the Soviet regime, publicized the achievements of the Stakhanovites and other "socialist competitors," and exposed the unsatisfactory performance of the laggards. The aim of this all-out and unprecedented propaganda effort, as one observer rightly noted, was "neither to convince nor even to persuade, but to produce a uniform pattern of public utterance in which the first trace of unorthodox thought immediately reveals itself as a jarring dissonance."

PURGES

Stalin accompanied the great industrial, agricultural, cultural, and social transformation of the Soviet Union during the 1930's by a vast purge. Scholars have sought in vain reasonable explanations of the causes which led to this odious spectacle. Some have argued that Stalin needed scapegoats to cover up his economic failures. Others have advanced the view that he sought to eliminate all possible challengers to his power, domestically based but foreign inspired. There are those who have submitted that the purge is an inherent element of the system itself, designed to terrorize every individual in order to incapacitate him of independent action. Finally, there are many who believe that Stalin's own madness was the chief cause of this abhorrent bloodbath.

Purge (the Russian word for it is *chistka,* which literally means "cleansing") was not a new phenomenon for the Soviet monolithic system. During the 1920's the party conducted four major "cleansings" of its ranks to remove the weak and the unfit. The purges of the 1930's, however, differed from previous purifications in four respects: in the number of party victims; in the number of nonparty casualties; in the spectacular "show" trials; and in the "confessions of guilt" by most of the victims.

Before the climax was reached in the late 1930's, this abominable spectacle had several "rehearsals." The first preview of things to come was early in 1928 in the Shakhty district in the Donets Basin, where the secret police (OGPU) arrested and brought to trial several non-Communist engineers. They were accused of counter-revolutionary plots, sabotage, and cooperation with Germany in order to prevent the successful execution of the First Five Year Plan. The second preview came early in 1930 in Kharkov with a "show trial" of forty-five prominent Ukrainians. They were accused of maintaining contact with Ukrainian political emigration and foreign powers (Poland and Germany), of preparing plans to organize Ukrainian peasants to resist collectivization, of planning to assassinate Stalin and his lieutenants, and of trying to separate the Ukraine from the USSR in order to restore the capitalist system of economy. The third preview trial took place in Moscow. The victim was an "Industrialists' Party" allegedly headed by Professor Leonid K. Ramzin. The defendants were accused of holding Menshevik views, of sabotaging industrial expansion, and of conspiring with France. The fourth trumped-up preview "trial" took place in 1931. Like their predecessors, the defendants, former Mensheviks headed by Professor V. Groman, an economist of the State Planning Commission, and historian N. N. Sukhanov, were accused of sabotage and conspiracy with émigré groups and foreign powers. The final preview, the "trial" of a group of engineers of the British Metropolitan-Vickers Company, took place in the Ukraine in April, 1933, at which alleged British sabotage was blamed for some of the inadequacies of the First Five Year Plan. In all of these "trials," most of the defendants received long prison terms or exile.

Simultaneously with these burlesques, Stalin ordered the "purification" of the party. Many local party members, especially those who showed any leniency towards the peasants, lost their jobs in an extensive purge, early in 1928, while others were expelled during 1929. Some were sacrificed as scapegoats following the publication of Stalin's article "Dizziness with Success," in March, 1930. Many more party members lost their jobs, and some even their lives, as the result of a purge ordered by the Central Committee on April 28, 1933. Officially the aim of this purge was "to achieve a higher ideological standard of party members, to strengthen the party organization politically, and to secure further confidence in the party on the part of millions of non-party men and women." This purge was to be conducted publicly and was to seek out "alien and hostile elements," open and secret violators of party discipline, those who had doubts of the wisdom of party decisions, opportunists, and all those who had allegedly succumbed to capitalist influence, and who did not want to fight "class enemies" and *kulaks*.

The purge officially began June 1, and ended in November, 1933. It affected the following cities and areas: Moscow, Leningrad, the Urals, Donets, Odessa, Kiev, Vinnitsia, Eastern Siberia, the Far East and Belorussia. The toll of victims was considerable. In the Ukraine alone, some 27,000 party members and candidates were expelled as "class enemies and undesirable and demoralized elements." They were replaced by new and, apparently in Stalin's view, more devoted individuals. Many of those who were purged in the Ukraine and other border regions were accused of harboring "bourgeois nationalist views"—a charge which paved the way for a turn in Stalin's nationality policy. Until this time the party officially viewed Russian great power chauvinism as the main danger to the Soviet system. Thereafter, non-Russian national deviations acquired that distinction. The road was paved for mass persecution of minorities.

The real holocaust started late in 1934 following the assassination on December 1, 1934, of Kirov, a member of the Politburo, and Stalin's chief lieutenant in Leningrad, by a young disillusioned Communist named Leonid V. Nikolaev. Officially, Stalin blamed Kirov's murder interchangeably on foreign powers, on Trotsky, on Zinoviev, and on the Right Opposition. In his famed speech before the Twentieth Party Congress in 1956, however, Khrushchev hinted that Stalin himself was the chief architect of Kirov's death. Being close to Stalin and having access to information not available to others, Khrushchev may speak with authority. Whatever the final judgment on the cause of Kirov's death, Stalin used it as an excuse for mass executions and repressions. To eliminate even the slightest legal opposition to his actions, the Central Executive Committee, on December 1, 1934, issued a decree which almost completely deprived all those accused of "terroristic acts" of any right of defense. This, in turn, paved the way for mass arrests, confessions extracted by force, and deportations or executions of thousands of persons.

The first victims of these executions were Nikolaev and his thirteen alleged accomplices who were executed on December 30, 1934. Because they implicated many of Stalin's former critics and opponents, thousands of party members were screened during the early months of 1935. Many were arrested, including Zinoviev and Kamenev, some were shot, and some were deported to Siberia. This "purification" of the party and of its auxiliaries continued throughout 1935 as did the search for new men to replace those who disappeared. Thus, Andrei A. Zhdanov (1896–1948) took over Kirov's place in Leningrad; Nikita S. Khrushchev (1894–) rose to prominence in the Moscow party organization; Georgi M. Malenkov (1902–) emerged as a star in the Secretariat; Andrei Ia. Vyshinsky (1883–1954) became the Chief Procurator of the USSR; and Lavrentii P. Beria (1899–1953) became a high-ranking official of the secret police (NKVD).

Stalin started a new wave of "purifications" on January 14, 1936, when the Central Committee decreed that all party members must exchange their old party cards for new identification—a process which again eliminated many "passive people." Of those members who remained in the party, Stalin demanded increased vigilance in exposing hidden enemies. A new wave of denunciations, arrests, and expulsions followed, laying the groundwork for the first major spectacle which took place on August 19, 1936. Sixteen "Old Bolsheviks," including Zinoviev and Kamenev, who had been imprisoned in 1935, were arraigned for a public trial. The defendants were accused of organizing, under Trotsky's guidance, a "terrorist centre" whose aim was to carry out terrorist acts against Stalin and company. They were also blamed for Kirov's death. Some of the accused admitted, while others denied, their guilt. All sixteen were sentenced to death and were immediately executed.

Because "testimonies" of the August, 1936, trial implicated many other "founding fathers" of Russian communism, late in January, 1937, Stalin arranged the second spectacle which was better organized and more subtle than was the first. It was conducted by the new head of the NKVD, Nikolai I. Yezhov (1895–?), who replaced prisonbound Henry G. Yagoda (1891–1938). The seventeen defendants, headed by Piatakov, Radek, and Sokolnikov, were now accused of connivance with Nazi Germany and Japan to dismember the USSR, of sabotage, and of wrecking socialist construction. All seventeen defendants "confessed" their guilt. Thirteen were sentenced to death and executed. Four received long-term sentences, but their ultimate fate has never been made public.

By implicating new "conspirators," the second spectacle paved the way for further arrests and trials. This time the victims came from the Red Army. On June 11, 1937, several army commanders, including Marshal Tukhachevsky of Civil War fame, were arrested, tried, and executed.[1] Like their predecessors, they were accused of espionage on behalf of Germany and Japan, anti-party conspiracy, cooperation with Trotsky, and plotting territorial dismemberment of the USSR. Arrest of other high-ranking officers followed. According to some estimates, the Red Army lost

[1] Tukhachevsky and many of his codefendants were "rehabilitated" between 1956 and 1958.

35,000 men, or about half its officer corps. Of the purged officers, 30,000 were below the rank of colonel. Among the victims were 3 marshals, 13 army commanders, 57 corps commanders, 110 division commanders, 220 brigade commanders, all 11 deputy commissars of war, 75 members of the Supreme Military Council, all military district commanders, all air force, and all but one navy fleet commander. Needless to say, this wholesale elimination of the military leadership created doubts as to Soviet military capabilities.

The last major spectacle took place in March, 1938. The defendants were twenty-one former members of the Right Opposition, headed by Bukharin, Rykov, and Christian G. Rakovsky (1873-?). Also among the defendants was former head of the NKVD, Yagoda, who was accused of poisoning the writer Maxim Gorky in June, 1936, and Valerian V. Kuibyshev (1888-1935) in January, 1935. Like all their predecessors, these defendants were charged with sabotage, espionage on behalf of Germany and Japan, attempted dismemberment of the USSR, and conspiracy to kill all leaders of the USSR. Bukharin was accused, in addition, of conspiracy to kill Lenin and Stalin as early as 1918—an accusation he denied to the end. To the other charges, Bukharin and his associates "confessed," and all but three were sentenced to death and executed.[1] The three who were spared received long prison terms and their ultimate fate has never been made known.

In terms of victims, the purges of the 1930's were very costly. At the Eighteenth Party Congress in March, 1939, Stalin admitted that between 1934 and 1939 party membership dropped from 1,874,488 to 1,588,852. Not all of these, of course, were executed. Many were, however, and only some of those who perished had the benefit of public "trial." A few succeeded in committing suicide: Mykola O. Skrypnyk (1872-1933), Tomsky, and General Jan B. Gamarnik (1894-1937). The overwhelming majority were executed without due process of law. Among them were many foreign Communists who had sought political asylum in the USSR. Those top members who remained—Khrushchev, Malenkov, Molotov, Beria, Voroshilov, Mikoyan and others—were trusted, faithful, and dedicated Stalinists, his "comrades-in-arms." There is no reliable estimate of the victims of the purge who were not party members. According to some observers, they numbered in the hundreds of thousands.

Stalin accompanied the wholesale elimination of his real and imaginary opponents with the elevation of his own stature. This he accomplished by a very skillful manipulation of propaganda and a technique that may be characterized as the retroactive lie. Through all media of modern mass communication he induced everyone to attribute to him

---

[1] The *New York Times*, October 19, 1962, reported Bukharin's rehabilitation. No formal announcement, however, has yet been made.

wisdom and genius in everything from politics, economics, and history, to military leadership, science, art, music, and linguistics. He had his pictures constantly displayed in all public buildings and erected his statues in all prominent public places. Many cities were named for him, as were streets, mountains, collective farms, canals, and even the constitution of 1936. As an "all-knowing" and "faultless" leader, Stalin could not make mistakes or have any shortcomings. These were *ipso facto* attributed to his opponents, who were described as "wreckers," "spies," "saboteurs," and "enemies of the people." Turning of heroes of yesterday into traitors of today called for "doctoring" of pictures and complete rewriting of Russian history of the twentieth century. Stalin completed the latter task in 1938 in the form of a *Short Course on the History of the All-Union Communist Party* (*bolshevik*), which until his death was the main subject of study for all Communists.

THE CONSTITUTIONAL STRUCTURE

The great industrial, agricultural and social transformation of the USSR in the 1930's, by destroying the legal order introduced during the NEP, made necessary the sanction of a new one. The latter came in the form of a new constitution (known as the "Stalin Constitution" until de-Stalinization in the 1950's) which, after highly publicized nation-wide discussion, was officially adopted on December 6, 1936. On the surface the new constitution (still in force in 1964) [1] is a reasonable document. It defines the USSR as a socialist state of workers and peasants who possess all the political power. It declares that the USSR has liquidated capitalism, abolished the exploitation of man by man, and instead established "the socialist system of economy and the socialist ownership of the instruments and means of production." All land, natural resources, waters, forests, industrial enterprises, means of transportation, and "the bulk of the dwelling houses in the cities and industrial localities, are state property, that is, belong to the whole people." The constitution recognizes private property but keeps it within narrow limits, inasmuch as the economic life of the USSR is determined and directed by a state plan of national economy. The latter, as we noted earlier, seeks an increase in public wealth, steady improvement in the material and cultural standards of the working people, and above all the strengthening of the independence of the USSR and its capacity for defense. Accordingly, "Work in the USSR is a duty and a matter of honor for every able-bodied citizen, in accordance with

[1] Early in 1962, Khrushchev proposed that a new constitution be prepared to reflect changes which have taken place since 1936. No target date was set for its completion. For full text of the present constitution, see Appendix 26.

the principle: 'He who does not work, neither shall he eat.' The principle applied in the USSR is that of socialism: 'From each according to his ability, to each according to his work.' "

In addition to the right to work, the present constitution grants Soviet citizens "the right to rest and leisure," "the right to maintenance in old age and also in case of sickness or disability," "the right to education," free medical service, and paid vacations. The constitution accords equal rights to men and women in all spheres of activity; insures freedom of religious worship and antireligious propaganda; guarantees freedom of speech, press, assembly, and demonstration; freedom from arrest "except by decision of a court or with the sanction of the procurator"; and "inviolability of the homes of citizens and privacy of correspondence." Finally, Soviet citizens are guaranteed the right to unite in public organizations, such as trade unions; cooperatives; youth, sport, and defense organizations; and cultural, technical, and scientific societies. The most active and politically conscious citizens "unite in the Communist Party of the Soviet Union, which is the vanguard of the working people in their struggle to build a Communist society and is the leading core of all organizations of the working people, both public and state."

The constitution makes it abundantly clear that all these rights and freedoms are conditional and are guaranteed only in "conformity with the interests of the working people, and in order to develop the organizational initiative and political activity of the masses of the people." What conforms is decided not by the recipient, but by the benefactor of these rights and freedoms. Since the Communist party enjoys a complete monopoly of power, controls everything, and acts as the guardian of the working people in the USSR, the party determines what the interests, needs, desires, and aspirations of the people are. Soviet citizens are free to agitate for party-sponsored candidates and policies. They are free to write about the party's achievements, to take part in party-sponsored public gatherings, to speak at public party-controlled meetings, to approve the party's policies, and to acclaim the party's leaders. If they should use their rights to any other purpose they could be accused of counter-revolutionary propaganda. In other words, Soviet citizens are free to say "yes" to everything the party does, but they are not allowed to say "no."

The highest organ of state power under the present constitution, and the only legislative body within the USSR, is the Supreme Soviet. The Supreme Soviet is a bicameral legislature with co-equal houses: a *Soviet of the Union,* elected on the basis of population (one deputy per 300,000 people), and a *Soviet of Nationalities,* elected on a territorial basis by nationality unit (twenty-five deputies from a union republic, eleven from an autonomous republic, five from an autonomous region, and one from a national area). The deputies to the Supreme Soviet are "elected" every four years. In reality, however, they are selected by the party leadership on the basis of their loyalty to the party or efficiency in their place of work. Since no opposition parties are allowed in the USSR, the electorate, with no other choice on election day, traditionally votes over 99 per cent for the single party-selected candidate in each electoral district. Needless to say, party members form the overwhelming majority of every Supreme Soviet. There are, however, a few deputies who are non-party members, but who are considered by the party to be reliable adherents of its program. Their presence in this honorable body is designed to maintain the fiction that the Soviet system is based on popular support and that the Supreme Soviet is truly a representative assembly.

The constitution specifies that the Supreme Soviet must meet at least twice a year. It can also be convened in extraordinary sessions. The infrequency of its meetings, the enormous size of its membership (close to 1400 members), and the restricted length of its sessions (from one to seven days), are clear indications of the limited role of the Supreme Soviet. The procedure of the body has also become standard. As a rule both houses meet separately for the first meeting, during which each selects its chairman, approves the procedure and the agenda for the session, and elects various standing commissions for preliminary preparation of legislation, such as Legislative Proposals, Budget, Foreign Affairs, and Economic. The second meeting is a joint session of the two houses, attended by the all-important dignitaries, at which the government presents a report on the annual budget for the coming year or any other major current problem. Following this presentation, each house again meets separately, listens to speeches of praise or criticism, and gives unanimous approval of the government's policy. Before its adjournment the Supreme Soviet automatically, unanimously, and without any discussion, approves the decrees of the Presidium of the Supreme Soviet as well as the work of the Council of Ministers.[1]

Fifty-one out of fifty-two weeks, formal legislative power is constitutionally vested in the Presidium of the Supreme Soviet. "Elected" every four years by both houses at a joint session, this thirty-three man body—all top party members—serves as collegial president and officially represents the Soviet state. The constitution grants this body broad powers. It convenes and dissolves the Supreme Soviet. It issues decrees and interprets the laws of the USSR. It appoints and dismisses military commanders and Foreign Office personnel and receives foreign dignitaries. It has the power to conclude and to break off international agreements, order mobilization, and declare a state of war or martial law. But although powerful constitutionally, the Presidium of the Supreme Soviet is little more than a formal instrument for promulgating some of the decisions of the party.

[1] In 1946 the *Sovnarkom* was renamed the Council of Ministers.

POSITION OF THE USSR SUPREME SOVIET

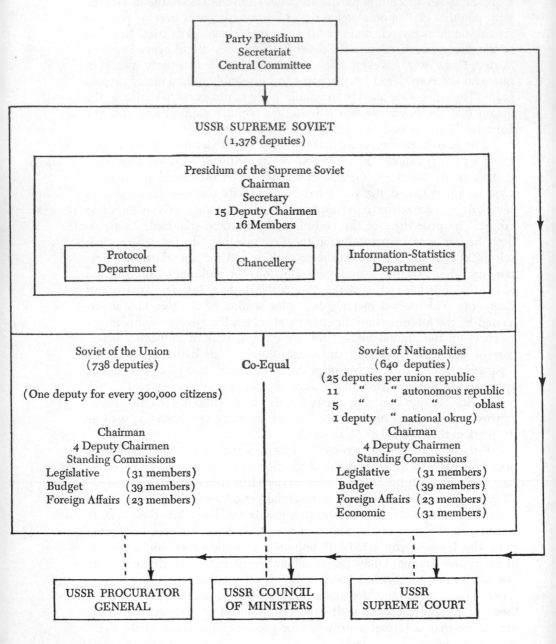

Party Presidium
Secretariat
Central Committee

USSR SUPREME SOVIET
(1,378 deputies)

Presidium of the Supreme Soviet
Chairman
Secretary
15 Deputy Chairmen
16 Members

| Protocol Department | Chancellery | Information-Statistics Department |

Soviet of the Union
(738 deputies)

(One deputy for every 300,000 citizens)

Chairman
4 Deputy Chairmen
Standing Commissions
Legislative   (31 members)
Budget   (39 members)
Foreign Affairs (23 members)

Co-Equal

Soviet of Nationalities
(640 deputies)
(25 deputies per union republic
11   "   " autonomous republic
5   "   "   " oblast
1 deputy   " national okrug)

Chairman
4 Deputy Chairmen
Standing Commissions
Legislative   (31 members)
Budget   (39 members)
Foreign Affairs (23 members)
Economic   (31 members)

| USSR PROCURATOR GENERAL | USSR COUNCIL OF MINISTERS | USSR SUPREME COURT |

- - - - Formal Constitutional Control
➤ Actual Control

SOURCE: U.S. Senate Subcommittee on National Policy Machinery.
Organizing for National Security (Washington: G.P.O., 1961), II, 369.

Another such instrument is the Council of Ministers. The Council of Ministers is the highest executive and administrative organ of state power in the USSR. It is the most important agency in the governmental structure for highlighting problems and planning policy, and it is the body primarily responsible for implementation of the law. Decisions and orders of the Council of Ministers are binding throughout the entire USSR. It is "elected" by the Supreme Soviet to which it is also accountable. Between sessions of the latter, the Council is accountable to the Presidium of the Supreme Soviet. As the highest administrative body, the Council of Ministers coordinates and directs the work of all the ministries and other agencies under its jurisdiction. It executes the national economic plan and the state budget, strengthens the credit and monetary system, conducts foreign affairs, is responsible for the maintenance of public order, supervises the general structure of the armed forces, and has the right to suspend decisions and orders of the Council of Ministers of every union republic. From its very inception, the Council of Ministers (or its predecessor, the *Sovnarkom*) has also acted as a legislative agency, issuing resolutions on many problems that constitutionally belong within the exclusive jurisdiction of the legislative branch of the government.

The Council of Ministers is currently composed of a Chairman (Premier), two First Deputy Chairmen, several Deputy Chairmen, heads of various ministries, state committees, and other agencies—individuals important because of their positions or their responsibilities. While the membership of the Council of Ministers has varied, (it has increased or decreased as necessity demanded), all members of the Council have always been the highest party functionaries. The post of Premier has been held by such party leaders as Lenin, Stalin, and Khrushchev (and temporarily by their personal selections—Molotov, Malenkov, Bulganin). The posts of Deputy Chairmen and ministers have, as a rule, been reserved to members of the party's Politburo, Presidium, Orgburo, the Secretariat, or the Central Committee.

The functional units of the Council of Ministers are ministries, state committees, and specialized agencies whose heads are members of the Council of Ministers. There are three types of ministries within the USSR: (1) *All Union Ministries,* which direct the branch of state administration entrusted to them throughout the territory of the USSR, either directly or through bodies appointed by them. The All-Union Ministries include railroad, transport, machine-building, foreign trade, electric power, and certain other key branches of the economy. (2) *Union Republic Ministries,* which, as a rule, direct the state administration entrusted to them through corresponding ministries of the union republics, and are subordinate both to the Republic Council of Ministers and to the parent ministry in Moscow. Union Republic Ministries include agriculture, communication, internal affairs, health, conservation, and similar problems. (3) The *Re-*

public Ministers which, though technically not a part of the Council of Ministers of the USSR, direct activities peculiar to the republic in which they exist. Republic Ministries include local industry, municipal services, social maintenance, irrigation, and like problems.

Among other high agencies of the central government are state committees and various specialized agencies. Structurally, they are similar to ministries, but they are not administrative bodies. Their function is to supervise and coordinate activities of ministries, make preliminary examination of various problems and the like. The most vital of these agencies is the State Planning Committee (*Gosplan*)—the central authority supervising the USSR's planned economy. *Gosplan* is the economic staff of the Council of Ministers. It formulates the specific plans for implementing the broad economic objectives laid down by the party. It is a powerful bureaucratic agency that has direct operational control not only over its counterparts in the republics but also over the planning departments in individual ministries and state committees. However powerful, *Gosplan* is, like all other specialized agencies and ministries, an auxiliary of the party, called upon "to guard and defend the interest of the working class." Soviet courts perform the same function.

The judicial system of the USSR consists of four tiers of courts. At the base of the system are People's Courts. The members of these courts are elected by the voters by direct, secret ballot for a period of three years. There are no special qualifications, and any citizen of the USSR entitled to vote may be elected, provided he or she is nominated by the Communist party or one of its auxiliaries as a candidate. Above the People's Courts are the territorial, provincial, and regional courts, and the courts of autonomous regions. The judges of these courts are elected by the respective soviets for a term of five years. The autonomous republics and union republics have their own Supreme Courts, whose members are elected by their respective Supreme Soviets for five-year terms. The highest tribunal of the land is the Supreme Court of the USSR, whose members, too, are elected for a term of five years by the Supreme Soviet of the USSR.

Although it is the highest tribunal, the power of the Supreme Court is limited. It does not possess any powers of judicial review over legislation. It cannot declare any laws of the Supreme Soviet or of its Presidium to be unconstitutional. The chief aim of the Supreme Court and that of other Soviet courts is "to educate the citizens of the U.S.S.R. in a spirit of devotion to the fatherland and to the cause of socialism, in the spirit of an exact and unfaltering performance of Soviet laws, careful attitude towards socialist property, labor discipline, honest fulfillment of state and public duties, [and] respect towards the rules of the socialist commonwealth." In other words, the Soviet judiciary is an organ of state power under the command and guidance of the Communist party.

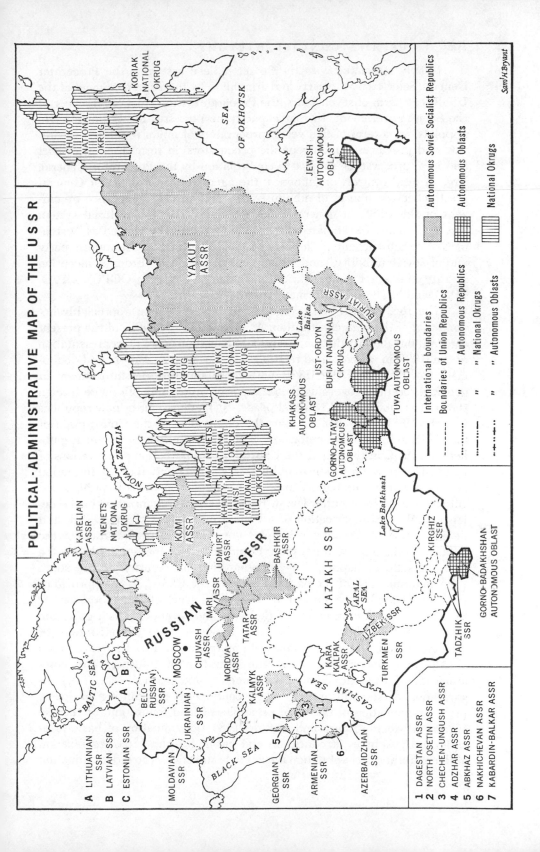

POLITICAL-ADMINISTRATIVE MAP OF THE USSR

Sam/H.Bryant

	Autonomous Soviet Socialist Republics	
	Autonomous Oblasts	
	National Okrugs	

——————	International boundaries	
— — — —	Boundaries of Union Republics	
· · · · · ·	" " Autonomous Republics	
· · · · · ·	" " National Okrugs	
—·—·—·—	" " Autonomous Oblasts	

A LITHUANIAN SSR
B LATVIAN SSR
C ESTONIAN SSR

1 DAGESTAN ASSR
2 NORTH OSETIN ASSR
3 CHECHEN-INGUSH ASSR
4 ADZHAR ASSR
5 ABKHAZ ASSR
6 NAKHICHEVAN ASSR
7 KABARDIN-BALKAR ASSR

KORIAK NATIONAL OKRUG
CHUKOT NATIONAL OKRUG
SEA OF OKHOTSK
JEWISH AUTONOMOUS OBLAST
YAKUT ASSR
BURIAT ASSR
Lake Baikal
UST-ORDYN BURIAT NATIONAL CKRUG
TUVA AUTONOMOUS OBLAST
TAIMYR NATIONAL OKRUG
EVENKI NATIONAL OKRUG
KHAKASS AUTONOMOUS OBLAST
GORNO-ALTAY AUTONOMCUS OBLAST
NOVAIA ZEMLIA
NENETS NATIONAL OKRUG
YAMAL NENETS NATIONAL OKRUG
KHANTY MANSI NATIONAL OKRUG
KOMI ASSR
UDMURT ASSR
BASHKIR ASSR
KARELIAN ASSR
RUSSIAN SFSR
MARI ASSR
TATAR ASSR
CHUVASH ASSR
MORDVA ASSR
MOSCOW
KAZAKH SSR
ARAL SEA
KIRGHIZ SSR
UZBEK SSR
GORNO-BADAKHSHAN AUTONOMOUS OBLAST
TADZHIK SSR
KARA KALPAK ASSR
TURKMEN SSR
Lake Balkhash
BALTIC SEA
BELO-RUSSIAN SSR
UKRAINIAN SSR
MOLDAVIAN SSR
KALMYK ASSR
CASPIAN SEA
GEORGIAN SSR
BLACK SEA
ARMENIAN SSR
AZERBAIDZHAN SSR
LITHUANIAN SSR
LATVIAN SSR
ESTONIAN SSR

Closely associated with the Soviet judicial system is the Procurator General. Selected by the party and appointed by the Supreme Soviet of the USSR for a term of seven years, the Procurator is the chief legal officer of the Soviet government. In that capacity he possesses broad powers. He appoints, for a term of five years, procurators of union republics, territories, and provinces. Union republic procurators, in turn, appoint district and local procurators, subject to confirmation by the Procurator General. Free of local controls or influence, the agents of the Procurator General are to check on abuses of administrators and on law observance by citizens of the USSR in general. Like the court, the procuratorial system serves as an arm of the party. Procurators are officially viewed as "watchmen of socialist legality," "leaders of the policy of the Communist party and of Soviet authority," and "champions of socialism." From its inception in 1917, the secret police, variously known as CHEKA, OGPU, NKVD, MVD, and MGB, has performed the same function.

The 1936 constitution extended federal jurisdiction appreciably beyond that of the 1924 constitution. As outlined in Article 14 of the present constitution, the jurisdiction of the USSR embraces: (1) representation of the USSR in international relations, conclusion, ratification, and denunciation of treaties of the USSR with other states; and establishment of general procedure governing the relations of Union Republics with foreign states; (2) questions of war and peace; (3) admissions of new republics into the USSR; (4) control over the observance of the Constitution of the USSR and insuring conformity of the Constitutions of Union Republics with the Constitution of the USSR; (5) confirmation of alterations of boundaries between Union Republics; (6) confirmation of the formation of new territories and regions and also of new Autonomous Republics and autonomous regions within Union Republics; (7) organization of the defense of the USSR, direction of all the armed forces of the USSR, and determination of directing principles governing the organization of the military formations of the Union Republics; (8) foreign trade on the basis of state monopoly; (9) safeguarding the security of the state; (10) determination of the national plans of the USSR; (11) approval of the consolidated state budget of the USSR, and of the report on its fulfillment, and determination of the taxes and revenues which go to the Union, the Republican, and the local budgets; (12) administration of the banks, industrial and agricultural enterprises, and trading enterprises of All-Union importance; (13) administration of transport and communications; (14) direction of the monetary and credit system; (15) organization of state insurance; (16) contracting or granting of loans; (17) determination of the basic principles of land tenure and of the use of mineral wealth, forest, and waters; (18) determination of basic principles in the spheres of education and public health; (19) organization of the uniform system of national economic statistics; (20) determination of the principles of labor legislation; (21) legislation concerning the judicial system and judicial procedure and criminal and civil codes; (22) legislation concerning union citizenship and the rights of aliens; (23) determination of the principles of legislation concerning marriage and the family; and (24) issuing of All-Union acts of amnesty. As the above cited items indicate, the jurisdiction of the USSR is so comprehensive that it virtually excludes the possibility of independent legislation by the Union Republics. This factor, however, has not prevented every republic's constitution from proclaiming "sovereign status," and the right "freely to secede from the USSR."

THE PARTY AND ITS AUXILIARIES

The source of all power in the USSR, constitutional provisions notwithstanding, is neither the government nor the people but the Communist party of the Soviet Union (CPSU). This power, although a living reality since 1917, was not formally acknowledged by the Soviet constitution until that of 1936. No critical observer of Soviet affairs was ever misled by this "omission," because party leaders have repeatedly stressed the supreme position of the party, and have defined it as "the vanguard of the working class and the highest form of its political organization"; "the instrument of the absolute dictatorship of the proletariat and the embodiment of its unity of will"; "the directing kernel of all organizations of the working people, both public and state"; "the personification of the unity of proletarian principles, of proletarian will and of proletarian unity"; and "the chief leader in the system of proletarian dictatorship." As the only party in the USSR, the Communist party has directed, controlled, and guided every political, economic, scientific, cultural, intellectual, sport, and social institution, and all other developments, either directly or through its members. In fact, not one important decision within the Soviet Union has been taken without the guidance of party directives.

In its organizational structure the CPSU is like a pyramid rising from a broad base of primary organizations (296,440 in 1961) to the single directing body at the top. In theory the party is governed by the principle of "democratic centralism," which the current party statute (1961) [1] defines as "(a) election of all leading party bodies from the lowest to the highest; (b) periodic reports of party bodies to their party organizations and to higher bodies; (c) strict party discipline and subordination of the minority to the majority; [and] (d) the unconditionally binding nature of the decisions of the higher bodies upon lower ones." The claim that final authority rests with the party members is, however, a myth. All life in the

[1] For full text of the 1961 party statute, see Appendix 38.

Soviet Union is ruled from the apex of the pyramid—the leadership of the party—and the membership of each lower body is approved by and directly responsible to its immediate superior. This cardinal rule, originally adopted by the Eighth Party Congress in 1919, has never been altered in the party statute, although the statute itself has been amended several times (Twelfth Party Conference in 1922, Fourteenth Party Congress in 1925, Seventeenth Party Congress in 1934, Eighteenth Party Congress in 1939, Nineteenth Party Congress in 1952, Twentieth Party Congress in 1956, and Twenty-second Party Congress in 1961). Since the CPSU is the guiding force in the USSR, this structural organization applies equally to soviet, trade union, cooperative, and all organizations.

The apex of all power in the USSR is the Political Bureau, or Politburo, of the Central Committee of the CPSU, which between 1952 and 1966 was known as the Presidium. Charged by the party statute with directing "the work of the Central Committee between plenary meetings," the Politburo is the supreme and the *only* policy-making body in the Soviet Union. Headed by the leader of the party, the Politburo is responsible for initiation, formulation, coordination, and execution of domestic and foreign policies. To all intents and purposes it is a law unto itself. Nominally, the members of the Politburo (full members and candidates) are elected by the party's Central Committee (CC). Actually, however, they are selected by the leader of the party on the basis of their loyalty, administrative ability, and political prowess. The Politburo is a highly secret organization, and apart from the identity of its members [1] very little is known about its formal organization or its working procedure. There are many strong indications that although all important policy questions are discussed at the Politburo's plenary sessions, they are in essence decided by the leader of the party. Since the leader's "line" is the party line, leaders of the CPSU have been elevated beyond criticism. Their views have never been questioned (or any attempts were silenced), and their statements, however crude and simple, have been treated as revelation. Until his death in January, 1924, Lenin was the undisputed party spokesman. Thereafter, Stalin dominated the party until his death in March, 1953, and subsequently, until his sudden removal on October 15, 1964, all party policies were determined by Khrushchev.

The second most important policy-making body in the Soviet system is the Secretariat of the CC of the CPSU. It is headed by the First Secretary, whose position, since 1924, has been synonymous with leadership of the party. The First Secretary is currently assisted by several secretaries,[2] whose duties and responsibilities are divided along both

---

[1] For membership see Appendices 2 and 3.

[2] The Twenty-Fourth Party Congress (March 30–April 8, 1971) selected the following secretaries: L. I. Brezhnev, P. N. Demichev, I. V. Kapitonov, K. F. Katushev, A. P. Kirilenko, F. D. Kulakov, B. N. Ponomarev, M. S. Solomentsev, M. A. Suslov, and D. F. Ustinov.

TOP ECHELONS OF THE COMMUNIST PARTY OF THE USSR

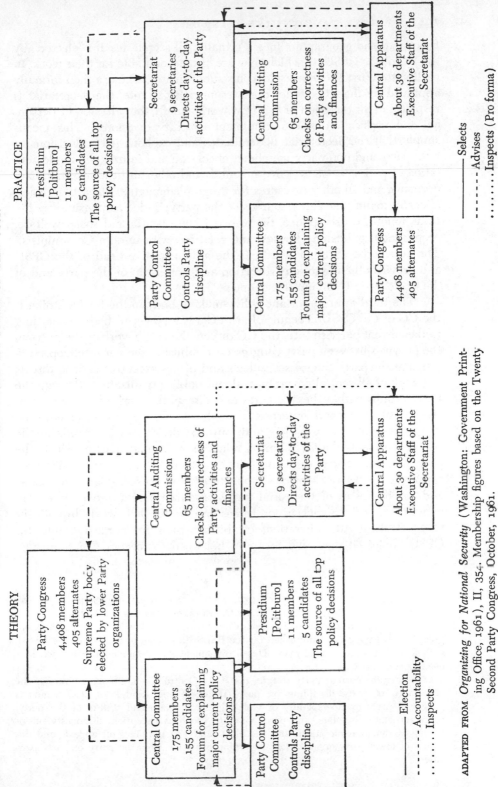

ADAPTED FROM *Organizing for National Security* (Washington: Government Printing Office, 1961), II, 354. Membership figures based on the Twenty Second Party Congress, October, 1961.

functional and geographic lines. Formally, all secretaries are "elected" by the CC of the CPSU, to which they are also accountable for their work. In reality, the First Secretary selects his subordinates, who are then formally approved by the CC. Under the present party statute, the Secretariat is responsible for direction of "current work, chiefly the selection of personnel and verification of the fulfillment of party decisions." This means simply that the Secretariat disseminates and explains party decisions to both party and non-party members; checks on and insures the implementation of policy by party, governmental, and other institutions; mobilizes economic and all other pressures for the implementation of party policies; allocates manpower and resources of the party; and is responsible for the trade unions, courts, police, the armed forces, health and social welfare, propaganda, publishing houses, and relations with foreign Communists.[1] The Secretariat, in other words, is the administrative head of the CPSU and provides the day-to-day direction and leadership of the party and of the world-wide Communist movement.

The third most important policy-making body in the Soviet Union is the CC of the CPSU. Technically the CC is a powerful body. According to the current party statute, the CC directs the entire work of the party in the intervals between party congresses; establishes the norms of representation at the party congresses; selects and places executive cadres; directs the work of all central governmental and public organizations through the party groups within them; creates and directs the work of various agencies, institutions, and enterprises of the party; appoints the editorial boards of central newspapers and journals; distributes the funds of the party; represents the CPSU in its relations with other parties; elects the party Politburo, Secretariat, and (since 1956) the Bureau for the RSFSR;[2] organizes the Party Control Committee;[3] convenes regular conferences and/or congresses of territorial party organizations; approves party organizations in the Soviet armed forces and guides their work through the Chief Political Administration; establishes rules for admitting into the CPSU Soviet citizens who formerly belonged to foreign Communist or

---

[1] Until its abolition in October, 1952, many of the current functions of the Secretariat were within the jurisdiction of the Organizational Bureau, or Orgburo.

[2] The RSFSR has never had its own Communist party. The Twentieth Party Congress in February, 1956, established for the RSFSR a Bureau of the CC of the CPSU, with Khrushchev as its chairman. This arrangement was approved by the two succeeding congresses.

[3] Under the current party statute, the Party Control Committee: (1) verifies the observance of party discipline by party members and candidates; (2) conducts purges of party members guilty of violating the program and statute of the party, party and state discipline, and party morality (such as deception, dishonesty, insincerity, slander, bureaucratism, and the like); and (3) examines all appeals and decisions of lower party organizations regarding expulsion from the party or party penalties.

workers' parties; issues instructions to lower party bodies on the admission of new members or candidates, or their transfer to other party organizations; keeps other party organizations informed about its work; holds plenary sessions every six months; and expels its own members or candidates from membership should they sully their honor or dignity.

In theory the CC of the CPSU is a powerful body, and its decisions and resolutions have always had the force of law. In reality, however, the CC is dominated by the leader of the party, and its chief function is the approval of his policies. The leader controls the CC through its individual members, who, while technically "elected" at each regular party congress, are in essence personally selected by him on the basis of their loyalty, administrative ability, and political prowess. The members of the CC represent the most influential element of the party, the government, trade unions, armed forces, and cultural, scientific, and other organizations.[1] Apparently to make their loyalty absolute, the current party statute calls for a compulsory turnover of "not less than one-quarter" of the membership of the CC every four years. Only the future will tell whether this new rule will be used to insure the "continuity of leadership" or to serve as a permanent purge of undesirables.

The last member of the policy-making bodies is the Party Congress. Theoretically it is the most important body of the CPSU, to which every party organ is accountable. According to the current party statute, the Congress convenes every four years to review, amend and approve the program and statute of the party; to determine the line of the party in domestic and foreign affairs; to elect members and candidates of the CC and of the Central Inspection Commission;[2] to hear and approve reports of the CC and other central bodies; and to decide, if need be, the question of expulsion from the party of a member or candidate member of the CC. Made up of delegates from all corners of the Soviet Union and from all walks of party life, the Congress is supposed to embody the wisdom and the will of the whole party. For the first few years of Communist rule in Russia, party congresses were held annually and they participated rather actively in policy determination. Since about 1927 they have degenerated into rubber stamp organs, and have been held irregularly for the purpose of granting automatic and unanimous approval of the principles and current policies of the self-perpetuating party leadership. The leadership controls the Congress through the members who, while technically elected at the meetings of lower party bodies, are in reality carefully selected by the central party leadership in Moscow.

[1] The Twenty-fourth Party Congress in April, 1971, "elected" 239 full members and 155 candidates of the CC. This is the highest membership in the history of the party.

[2] Presently the CIC has 84 members, and according to the party statute it "supervises the expeditious and proper handling of business by the central bodies of the party, and audits the accounts of the treasury and the enterprises of the CC CPSU."

Technically each union republic, except, as noted earlier, the RSFSR, has its own Communist party, presidium, secretariat, central committee, and party congress. It is to be remembered, however, that union republic Communist parties are not independent organizations, but integral parts of the CPSU which determines absolutely everything for all the republics. Each union republic Communist party acts as an instrument of the Kremlin's policies, carries out its directives, controls life in the union republic, and receives praise for successes and/or condemnation for failures. As intimate parts of the CPSU, union republic Communist parties are important reflectors of policy changes within the Soviet Union. The importance of the union republic Communist parties depends on the relative position a given republic occupies in the life of the USSR.

Below the union republic Communist parties are territorial, regional, area, and district party organizations. Within their respective jurisdictions, each of these organizations is charged with the execution of orders and policies of the central bodies of the party. At each level, too, the administrative-executive organs of the party play the decisive role. At the lowest level of party structure are primary party organizations, formerly known as cells. The primary party organizations are organized on a functional basis at the place of work—in factories, schools, collective farms, military units, offices, and such places. Three party members are required to form a primary party organization. Although it is at the lowest tier of the structural hierarchy, the primary party organization performs many vital functions. It accepts into the CPSU new members whom it is required to guide in the spirit of devotion to the party. It is required to oppose any attempts at introducing "revisionist distortions into Marxism-Leninism and its dogmatic interpretation"; to organize the masses to carry out "the current tasks of communist construction," and promote competition among them for the fulfillment of production quotas; to strengthen labor discipline; to struggle against disorganization and waste; to participate actively in the economic and political life of the country; to criticize all the defects of lesser officials; and to "see to it that every communist observes in his own life" and inculcates in others the elaborate code of "moral principles" of the party. The primary party organization is also used as a scapegoat for all the failures and/or mistakes of the party leadership.

The current party statute defines the CPSU as "the tried and tested militant vanguard of the Soviet people, which unites on a voluntary basis the more advanced, the politically more conscious section of the working class, collective-farm peasantry, and intelligentsia of the USSR." The statute also acknowledges that the CPSU is "an integral part of the international communist and working-class movement," and as such it subscribes to Marxist-Leninist principles of proletarian internationalism and "actively promotes the unity of the entire international communist and workers' movement and of the fraternal ties with the great army of communists of all countries." Any soviet citizen may become a member of the CPSU if he or she accepts the party program and statutes, takes an active part in Communist construction, works in one of the party's organizations, and blindly fulfills all the decisions of the party leadership. Such was not the case in earlier times. Until 1939 applicants for party membership were divided into four groups: industrial workers of five years' standing; industrial workers of less than five years' standing, agricultural laborers, Red Army men who were formerly workers or collective farmers, and "technicians"; collective farmers, teachers in elementary schools, and members of peasant handicraft cooperatives; and other employees. In reality, however, from the inception of the party, the dominant group within it, both in numbers and in influence, has always been the intelligentsia.

Party membership has always carried with it rights and privileges as well as duties and obligations. As a member of the ruling class a party member enjoys all available material benefits, and has all existing avenues open to his advancement. He also has the right "to elect and be elected to party bodies"; to discuss questions of the party's policies at party gatherings; to introduce motions; to criticize lesser party officials; to be present at a party meeting when his "activity or conduct is discussed", and to address questions or suggestions to higher party bodies, including the CC of the CPSU, and demand an answer. In return for these "rights" a party member is obligated to fight for communism; to set an example of the Communist attitude toward work; to raise labor productivity; to take the initiative in all that is new and progressive, and support and propagate advanced methods; to master technology and to improve his qualifications; to safeguard and increase public property; to carry out party decisions firmly and undeviatingly; to explain the policy of the party to the masses; to help strengthen the party's ties with the people; and to take an active part in the political, economic and cultural life of the country. Party members are further obligated to set an example in the fulfillment of public duty; to master Marxism-Leninism; to combat "all manifestations of bourgeois ideology"; to observe rules of "communist morality"; to be an active proponent of the ideas of socialist internationalism and Soviet patriotism among the masses; to combat survivals of "nationalism and chauvinism"; to strengthen the friendship of the peoples of the USSR; to observe party and state discipline; to be ready to denounce his own as well as the shortcomings of others; and to be sincere towards the party, hide nothing from it, be vigilant at all times and be blindly obedient. Any deviation by a party member from these prerequisites or any manifestation of factionalism or cliquishness is incompatible with retaining party membership.

Although admission requirements have altered considerably, they are still complicated because the party wants to remain an organization of the elite. To be eligible for party membership one must be conscientious, active, and devoted to the cause of communism, be at least eighteen years old, and be recommended by at least three party members. After an application for membership has been examined by a general meeting of the primary party organization, if it is recommended and then approved by a district or city committee of the party, the applicant becomes a candidate for one year. The probationary period is designed to provide candidates with an opportunity "to familiarize themselves with the Program and Statute of the CPSU . . . and [to] test their personal qualities." At the end of the probationary period a successful candidate again goes through the same procedure and screening, and only then does he become a full party member.

The party acquires many of its members from among the ranks of the All-Union Leninist Communist League of Youth, popularly known as the *Komsomol*. Founded in 1918, and organizationally patterned after the party, the *Komsomol* conducts all of its activities under the leadership of the party. It is comprised of young people between the ages of 14 and 26 and, while it does not include the whole of Soviet youth, between 1918 and 1962 the membership of the *Komsomol* has grown from 22,000 to 19,400,000. In addition to providing the party with new members, ever since its establishment the *Komsomol* has served as the party's most active assistant in every phase of activity. With its members scattered throughout the Soviet system, trade unions, industry, collective and state farms, armed forces, and such institutions the *Komsomol* has been called upon by the party to perform many urgent tasks. In the 1920's it assisted the party in the liquidation of illiteracy. During the 1930's it actively participated in industrialization and collectivization while in the 1940's it helped to defend the USSR against Nazi invasion. The *Komsomol* has always assisted the party in the training of technicians, in political indoctrination, in propagation of the party's current policies among Soviet youth, and in the struggle against juvenile delinquency. The *Komsomol* has been called upon to foster such qualities of individual character as "loyalty to the party chiefs, iron discipline, self-sacrificing bravery, ideological purity, unshakable conviction, incessant vigilance, uncompromising militancy, and hatred toward enemies." Finally, it has also been directly responsible for the guidance of the still younger party auxiliaries, the Young Pioneers (children from nine to fifteen) and the Little Octobrists (children from eight to twelve). In other words, the *Komsomol* has been the right arm of the party among Soviet youth.

In addition to normal procedure, the party has been able to acquire new members through mass recruitments. It accepted many members during the Civil War period when it was in need of wider support. Following Lenin's death in 1924 (and Stalin's rise to power), over 200,000 new members were accepted into the party ranks. Many thousands were permitted to join the party during the early stages of industrialization and collectivization as rewards for skills and accomplishments. Thousands of heroes of World War II were brought into the party ranks. The party also registered a sizeable increase in membership during the early stages of Khrushchev's rise to power. By normal and abnormal processes, heavy obligations and strict requirements notwithstanding, between 1905 and 1961 party membership has demonstrated the following growth:

GROWTH OF THE MEMBERSHIP OF THE CPSU

	Members	Candidates	Total
1905	8,500	——	8,500
1917	23,600	——	23,600
1918	115,000	——	115,000
1921	576,000	——	576,000
1922	410,430	117,924	528,354
1924	350,000	122,000	472,000
1926	639,652	440,162	1,079,814
1933	2,203,951	1,351,387	3,555,338
1934	1,826,756	874,252	2,701,008
1938	1,405,879	514,123	1,920,002
1940	1,982,743	1,417,232	3,399,975
1941	2,515,481	1,361,404	3,876,885
1945	3,965,530	1,794,839	5,760,369
1952	6,013,259	868,886	6,882,145
1956	6,795,896	419,609	7,215,505
1959	7,622,356	616,775	8,239,131
1961	8,872,516	843,489	9,716,005
1963	9,581,149	806,047	10,387,196
1965	10,811,443	946,726	11,758,169
1968	12,484,836	659,389	13,180,225
1971	13,810,089	645,232	14,455,321

The numerical growth of the party has enabled it to strengthen and improve its supreme and absolute power over all aspects of life in the USSR from the highest councils of state to the lowliest private dwelling.

During the period of unprecedented growth of its membership, the party has also undergone a permanent purge. On several occasions the membership of the party has been submitted to a thorough examination from the point of view of the prevailing ideological orthodoxy, devotion to the cause of communism, and personal character and behavior. Major purges took place in 1921, 1926, 1927, 1929, 1933, 1934–1938, 1946, 1953, and 1957. Of these, as noted earlier, the most spectacular and the one with the most victims was the purge of 1934–1938. The main objective of this purge was not so much the cleansing of the party of undeserving members, but extermination of a vast majority of old Bolshevik leaders. The list of accused read like a "Who's Who" of the Russian Revolution, and included Lenin's close associates, old party members, leaders of the government, army commanders, ambassadors, and other "founding fathers" of Russian communism. They were accused of, and "confessed" their part in, murder, attempted murder, high treason, plotting with foreign powers, and "wrecking." The purge extended to every sphere of Soviet life and was carried out with ruthless thoroughness, even in the remotest corners of the land, in the armed forces, in factories, and on collective farms. Following Stalin's death, some of the more important victims were "rehabilitated." Countless thousands were less fortunate, but from their graves they cannot protest.

FOREIGN POLICY IN THE 1930's

The basic challenge facing Soviet foreign policy during the 1930's was: how to provide security for the militarily weak but rapidly industrializing territorial base of the revolution, in the face of Hitler's decision to plunge into a vast territorial conquest in Europe and the renewed Japanese efforts to build an empire at China's expense. Stalin faced this enormous challenge by ordering total mobilization of all the available resources of both conventional and unconventional diplomacy. His efforts were facilitated by the determination of many victims of aggression to resist Japanese and Nazi conquests.

The tone for unconventional diplomacy was set during the Sixth World Congress of the Communist International held in Moscow from July 17 to September 1, 1928. It was embodied in the speeches of Communist leaders who came to Moscow for the occasion, and above all in *The Programme of the Communist International* which the Congress adopted. This verbose and complex document defined itself as "the program of struggle for World Communism"—a definition which caused some observers to label it a "blueprint for world conquest." It was the most important Communist document since the publication of the *Communist Manifesto* in 1848. Perhaps for this reason it has never been withdrawn or criticized, and the principles it enunciated, with only slight modifications in details and emphasis, remain in effect to this day.

The Programme dealt at considerable length with revolutionary objectives, Communist strategy and tactics, the kind of revolutions to be fought for, and the place of the proletariat, of the anti-colonial movements, and of the Soviet Union in this struggle. *The Programme* defined the Soviet Union as "the one and only fatherland of the international proletariat," and declared that the revolutionary role of the USSR was "exceptionally great" for three reasons: (1) because the USSR was "the international driving force of revolution that impels the proletariat of all countries to seize power"; (2) because it was "The living example proving that the working class is not only capable of destroying capitalism, but of building up socialism as well"; and (3) because it was "the prototype of the fraternity of nationalities in all lands united in the World Union of Socialist Republics and of the economic unity of the toilers of all countries in a single world Socialist economic system that the world proletariat must establish when it has captured political power."

As the leader of "the citadel of world revolution," the Communist party of the USSR demanded that the international proletariat pledge its exclusive allegiance to the USSR; subordinate its local interests to those of the USSR; render assistance to make the First Five Year Plan a success; come to the defense of the USSR "by all means in its power" in case of an attack; promote proletarian revolutions everywhere and colonial revolutions in areas dominated by Western Powers; and consider Communist right wing reformists and social democrats "the most dangerous enemies of communism and of the dictatorship of the proletariat." On its part the Communist party of the Soviet Union pledged that it would not shrink "from fulfilling its international obligations and from rendering support to all the oppressed, to the labor movements in capitalist countries, to colonial movements against imperialism and to the struggle against national oppression."

Military weakness of the USSR, and its planned plunge into vast economic experimentation in the late 1920's and early 1930's, prevented Stalin from active adherence to these pledges. There was nevertheless a great deal of noisy propaganda during this period. Some of the noise was directed against armaments and alleged military preparations of the major world powers. Some of it was directed in behalf of independence of colonial peoples and the strengthening efforts of the USSR. Much energy, however, was wasted on fighting social democrats for their alleged willingness to betray the revolution. This struggle was bitter everywhere, but was fatal only in Germany where Communist obstructionist tactics teamed with those of the extreme nationalists, thereby helping to destroy the Social Democratic-led Weimar Republic—a cooperation that enabled Hitler to come to power.

Stalin greatly underestimated the significance of Hitler's rise to power. Three assumptions seem to have been responsible for his miscalculation: (1) Hitler's violent opposition to the Versailles settlement which envisaged a Franco-German war and hence improvement of the security of the USSR; (2) firm belief in the strength of the German Communist party, which polled over six million votes in the election of 1932; and (3) Soviet need for uninterrupted flow of German machinery during the initial phases of industrialization. Throughout 1933, Stalin and his associates stressed publicly their desire to continue friendly relations with Germany based on the Rapallo spirit. As late as January, 1934, during the meeting of the Seventeenth Party Congress, Stalin pleaded for friendly relations with Hitler, arguing that the existence of different political and economic systems should not serve as an obstacle to good relations between the Soviet Union and Germany. Hitler, however, ignored all of Stalin's overtures. The only "friendly" gesture was his decision to ratify, in

May, 1933, a renewal of the 1926 neutrality treaty with the USSR which had been pending since 1931. Instead of cooperation, throughout 1933, Gestapo agents carried out mass exterminations of German Communists, and the Nazi press intensified its anti-Soviet campaign. Hitler's intransigence forced Stalin to turn to different tactics and emphasis.

The new tactics—commonly referred to as the period of the "Popular Front"—sought to establish friendly relations with all countries threatened by, and all movements opposed to, the rise of new German chauvinism, which was publicly proclaiming its determination to seek *Lebensraum* at the expense of its neighbors. On the surface, the new communist tactics represented a considerable departure from those set forth by the Sixth Congress of the Comintern in 1928. In reality, however, the departure was not so radical, because alongside the ultrarevolutionary methods of the unconventional diplomacy pursued by the Comintern, Stalin followed a cautious policy on the conventional level. This policy, as we noted in an earlier chapter, was responsible for such actions as Soviet entry into the disarmament negotiations sponsored by the League of Nations in 1928, signing and ratification of the Kellogg-Briand Pact in 1929, and conclusion of a series of non-aggression pacts with the Baltic states, Poland, and France in 1932, and with Italy in 1933.

The "new course" in Soviet foreign policy was nevertheless responsible for several significant developments. The first was the establishment of diplomatic relations with the United States on November 16, 1933. One of the most important factors that brought the two countries together was Japan's conquest of Manchuria in 1931–1932, and its determination to build a vast empire in the Far East. Hitler's triumph in Germany served as another motive that pressed for the need to establish the normal diplomatic contacts interrupted since the revolution. Before normal relations could be resumed, however, both governments felt a need to remove certain barriers that stood between them. Prominent among these was the question of debts, which had already been discussed but on which no agreement had been reached. In its eagerness to establish normal relations with the United States, the Soviet government promised neither to sponsor nor to permit within its jurisdiction propaganda or other activity aimed at the overthrow of the United States government. It likewise agreed to allow religious freedom and legal protection to American nationals residing in the USSR. None of these promises, however, materialized, and the relations established between the two countries continued to be, in the words of one competent observer, "troubled, distant, and devoid of real political content."

The entry of the Soviet Union into the League of Nations on September 18, 1934, was the second significant manifestation of the "new course." It was a major departure, because hitherto, or at least until 1928, Soviet leaders had repeatedly expressed their contempt for the League. The situation in 1934 was different. With Japan, Germany, and Italy "on the warpath," the League seemed to offer Stalin an effective instrument for fighting the aggressive policies of his adversaries, as well as a forum from which to dispel a widespread impression that the USSR sought to conquer the rest of the world. These two goals were pursued with considerable vigor and determination by Litvinov, Commissar for Foreign Affairs. As a permanent member of the Council, the Soviet Union became a strong supporter of the League, a firm advocate of an effective collective security system in order to avert war, and a bitter critic of the League's inability and apparent unwillingness to check Axis expansion.

The third significant manifestation of the "new course" was Soviet adherence to the French Security System in 1935. As in post-Bismarckian days, both countries were attracted to each other by the presence of the German danger. The road for the Franco-Soviet understanding was paved by the Non-Aggression Pact of November 29, 1932, by a commercial treaty of January 11, 1934, and by a close relationship between Litvinov and French Foreign Minister Louis Barthou. The Franco-Soviet rapprochement of 1935 consisted of two parts. The first was a Treaty of Mutual Assistance of May 2, 1935, by whose terms the two governments obligated themselves to assist one another in case either of them was subjected to an unprovoked attack. The second part came on May 16, 1935, in the form of a treaty signed by the Soviet Union, France, and Czechoslovakia. In its provisions, this tripartite act was identical with those of the Franco-Soviet treaty in all but one respect: it provided that the Soviet Union was obligated to come to the aid of Czechoslovakia only if France also fulfilled its obligation to Czechoslovakia. Whether or not this condition was a reflection of the growing Soviet suspicion of the West, during the subsequent Munich crisis of September, 1938, this escape clause helped the USSR to pose as the only defender of Czechoslovakia's sovereignty, and to place most of the blame on France in view of the latter's inability or unwillingess to act.

The entry of the Soviet Union into the League of Nations, but above all its joining of the French Security System, forced Stalin to alter the tactics, but not the ultimate aim of the Comintern. This formality was officially taken care of at the Seventh and last Congress of the Comintern, held in July–August, 1935, with the sanctioning of "the Popular Front." The Popular Front had two aspects. On the one hand, Communists everywhere were ordered to join hands with the *leadership* of those labor unions, social democratic, bourgeois, peasant, and even right wing parties which opposed Nazi, Fascist, or Japanese aggression. At the same time, while "united at the top," the Communists were to pursue a policy of "the united front from below"; i.e., they were to try to win the rank-and-file away from its leaders.

This all-out effort to subvert, while posing as defender and champion of the interests and achievements of all people regardless of their political affiliations, was responsible for considerable increase in Communist membership and in political influence, both in Europe and in Asia. In Europe classic manifestations of this policy appeared in France—where the Popular Front was first tried out—and in the Spanish Civil War. In France, as early as 1934, the Communists joined hands with socialist-led trade unions against the French extreme right, dropped their opposition to French armaments in 1935, and were instrumental in the selection of Leon Blum as Premier of the Popular Ministry in 1936. Blum's reluctance to introduce the Communist program, however, brought an end to this cooperation period, led to Communist-organized strikes, and to his downfall in June, 1937.

The manifestation of the Popular Front in Spain was somewhat more complicated. Late in August, 1936, in answer to previous Italian and German armed intervention on behalf of General Francisco Franco, the Soviet Union intervened on behalf of Spanish republicans. Before the end of the year the USSR sent to Spain large quantities of military supplies and hundreds of military and political experts who, together with thousands of non-Soviet "volunteers" were able to gain control not only of military operations but of secret police, intelligence, censorship, propaganda, and other activities. The problem of logistics, along with French and British reluctance to help in the face of increased German and Italian support of Franco, forced the Soviet Union to abandon its operations. Throughout most of 1937, Soviet efforts in Spain were directed towards two main goals: to prolong the struggle as long as possible in order to divert German interest away from the Soviet Union; and to liquidate all the "Trotskyites" and other "anti-Stalinists" in Spain—an effort that was pursued with determined ruthlessness.

In Asia the policy of the Popular Front received classic expression in China, where it centered around the exploitation of strong anti-Japanese feelings among Chinese intellectuals. The Communists joined patriotic cries to make a vigorous effort to end the bitter civil war between Chinese Nationalists and Communists, and pleaded for a United Front against the Japanese invaders. Chiang's reluctance to listen to these "patriotic appeals" until he had disposed of the Communists, forced many of his admirers and followers into the Communist camp. Following the signing of the Anti-Comintern Pact on November 17, 1936, by Germany, Italy, and Japan, the demand for a united anti-Japanese action increased. To break his uncompromising attitude towards Communists, Chiang was kidnapped on December 12, 1936, but was released unharmed on condition that he form a United Front with the Communists against Japan. An agreement to this effect was concluded on September 22, 1937, and continued to operate fairly well until the end of 1938. As a sign of improved relations with the Communists, in August, 1937, Chiang signed a non-aggression pact with the USSR and replaced his German advisers with Soviet experts. Improved Sino-Soviet relations did not escape Japanese attention, and between 1937 and 1939 the Soviet Union and Japan, in several armed clashes, tested their military preparedness as well as their determination to resist. Both were found to exist in sufficient quantity on both sides.

The situation in Europe, however, presented a different picture. On October 3, 1935, Italian forces invaded Ethiopia, and the League, although called upon to resist, failed to cope with the aggression. On March 7, 1936, in violation of the Locarno Treaty of 1925, Hitler marched into and occupied the Rhineland. Neither England nor France nor the League made any move to stop Hitler's great gamble. These and other signs of Western irresoluteness and appeasement enabled the Nazis to execute a whole series of *faits accompli,* which greatly strengthened Germany's position and which endangered the position of other powers, including the USSR. In 1936, and again in 1937, Stalin sought to reach an agreement with Hitler, and renewed his efforts with even greater determination following German annexation of Austria on March 12, 1938. The first outward manifestation of "friendliness" was the replacement in May, 1938, of Soviet Ambassador to Berlin Jacob Surits, who was Jewish, by Alexei T. Merekalov, a Great Russian, who was instructed to improve German-Soviet relations. The second step came in July, 1938, when both governments agreed to refrain from hostile and abusive propaganda against their respective heads of state. This was later broadened to include other aspects.

The dismemberment of Czechoslovakia in September, 1938, at Munich, was a major turning point, not only for Europe but for Soviet foreign policy as well. Encouraged by Western weakness and retreat, during the summer of 1938 Hitler increased his invective against Czechoslovakia. Alarmed by the mounting crisis and manufactured war psychosis, on September 30, 1938, Britain lost her prestige, France her honor, and Czechoslovakia much of her territory. The exclusion of the Soviet Union, however, from this classic appeasement played into Stalin's hands. Throughout the entire crisis, the Soviet government repeatedly asserted its willingness and readiness to fulfill its obligations both as a member of the League of Nations and under the provisions of the Franco-Soviet-Czechoslovak Treaty of 1935. This readiness was, however, conditional on French willingness to honor their pledge and/or on Polish or Rumanian willingness to allow Soviet troops to move across their respective territories. Since Stalin was aware that neither of these conditions was likely to materialize, scholars have questioned the sincerity of his offer. Genuine or not, Soviet pledges made a deep impression on many Czechoslovaks.

By dismembering Czechoslovakia, the Nazis lowered the resistance of Czechoslovakia's neighbors, opened the whole Danube region to German expansion, and indirectly endangered the security of the USSR. These developments made an early understanding with Germany not only urgent but imperative. Fortunately for Stalin, Hitler's actions greatly facilitated the realization of this goal. Shortly after he disposed of Czechoslovakia, Hitler directed his attention to Poland. Negotiations to resolve some of the problems between Germany and Poland started on October 24, 1938, but from the outset a deadlock developed on account of German demands, which among others included formal return of Danzig to Germany, Polish acquiescence to an extraterritorial highway and railway across the Polish Corridor, cooperation in colonial questions, and a common policy towards the Soviet Union within the framework of the Anti-Comintern Pact.

Because the Poles rejected outright the German offers to turn Poland into a German satellite, Hitler now became receptive to Stalin's feelers and made many "friendly" gestures of his own. At the end of October, 1938, he initiated talks with the Soviet Union for the conclusion of a trade agreement and further eased anti-Soviet propaganda. At the New Year's reception, Hitler broke his old precedent by cordially greeting and chatting with the Soviet Ambassador. He also departed from his usual blistering references to communism in his address to the Reichstag on January 30, 1939, and instead was bitterly critical of the Western Powers for their "hysterical, unscrupulous, tactless, and extremely malicious" press and propaganda. Stalin echoed Hitler's words on March 10, 1939, in his address to the Eighteenth Party Congress, where he too did not spare words in attacking the West and its press for spreading "vociferous lies" about "the weakness of the Red Army," "the demoralization of the Red Air Force," and "riots" in the Soviet Union. He declared that the aim of this and other suspicious uproar was "to incense the Soviet Union against Germany, to poison the atmosphere, and to provoke a conflict with Germany without any visible grounds." Stalin's concurrence with Hitler's contention that London and Paris were the *Weltlügenzentralen* (world centers of lies) paved half the way to a Soviet-German understanding.

The other half was prepared by the belated Franco-British firmness and unwillingness to make further concessions to Hitler in his efforts to remake the political map of Europe. On March 31, 1939, convinced belatedly that Hitler's appetite could not be satiated, the British unexpectedly extended to Poland a military guarantee and began to put out feelers to Rumania, Hungary, and the USSR for joint action against Hitler's aggression. Hitler reacted to these moves by abrogating the 1934 German-Polish treaty and the 1935 Anglo-German Naval treaty, by ordering all-out military preparations for a general attack on Poland to be launched at the end of August, 1939, and by concentrating on reaching a Nazi-Soviet understanding at all costs. Aware of Hiter's anxiety, Stalin put a high price on his friendship with the Nazis, as likewise he did on his friendship with the

After signing the Non-Aggression Pact in Moscow, 1939 (left to right), Von Ribbentrop, Secretary Gaus (Germany), Stalin and Molotov.

Western Powers. Hitler's willingness and Western unwillingness to agree to far-reaching territorial changes in Eastern Europe led to the famed Nazi-Soviet Pact of August, 1939.[1]

The Pact consisted of three parts. The first was a trade agreement signed on August 19, by which Germany granted the Soviet Union a two-year credit of 180 million German marks for the purchase of German goods. The second part was a ten year Non-Aggression Pact, signed on August 23, which obligated each partner to absolute neutrality should one of them "become the object of belligerent action by a third power." The third part consisted of a secret protocol which divided Poland along the San-Vistula-Narev Rivers, and which assigned Lithuania to the German, and Estonia, Latvia, Finland, and Bessarabia to the Soviet sphere of influence. Assured of Stalin's "friendship," on September 1, 1939, Hitler ordered his armies into Poland, and World War II became a reality.

SUGGESTED READINGS

ADAMS, ARTHUR E., ed. *Readings in Soviet Foreign Policy*. Boston: Heath, 1961.
ARMSTRONG, JOHN A. *The Politics of Totalitarianism*. New York: Random House, 1961.
BAUER, RAYMOND A., ALEX INKELESS, and CLYDE KLUCKHOHN. *How the Soviet System Works*. Cambridge: Harvard University Press, 1956.
BECK, F., and W. GODIN. *Russian Purge and the Extraction of Confession*. New York: Viking, 1951.

[1] For the full text of the Pact, see Appendix 28.

BELOFF, MAX. *The Foreign Policy of Soviet Russia, 1929–1941.* 2 vols. New York: Oxford University Press, 1947–1949.

BORKENAU, FRANZ. *World Communism: A History of the Communist International.* New York: Norton, 1939.

BRZEZINSKI, ZBIGNIEW K. *The Permanent Purge: Politics of Soviet Totalitarianism.* Cambridge: Harvard University Press, 1956.

CATTELL, DAVID T. *Communism and the Spanish Civil War.* Berkeley: University of California Press, 1956.

CHAMBERLIN, WILLIAM H. *Russia's Iron Age.* London: Duckworth, 1935.

DALLIN, DAVID J. *The Real Soviet Russia.* London: Hollis and Carter, 1947.

———, and BORIS NIKOLAEVSKY. *Forced Labor in Soviet Russia.* New Haven: Yale University Press, 1947.

DEUTSCHER, ISAAC. *Stalin: A Political Biography.* New York: Oxford University Press, 1949.

DJILAS, MILOVAN. *The New Class.* New York: Praeger, 1957.

DOBB, MAURICE. *Soviet Economic Development Since 1917.* London: Routledge and Kegan, 1948.

FAINSOD, MERLE. *How Russia is Ruled.* Cambridge: Harvard University Press, 1953.

———. *Smolensk Under Soviet Rule.* Cambridge: Harvard University Press, 1958.

GSOVSKY, VLADIMIR. *Soviet Civil Law.* 2 vols. Ann Arbor, Michigan: University of Michigan Press, 1948.

GUINS, GEORGE C. *The Soviet Law and Soviet Society.* The Hague: Nijhoff, 1954.

HAZARD, JOHN N. *The Soviet System of Government.* Chicago: University of Chicago Press, 1957.

HUNT, R. N. CAREW. *The Theory and Practice of Communism.* New York: Macmillan, 1957.

JASNY, NAUM. *The Socialized Agriculture of the U.S.S.R.* Stanford: Stanford University Press, 1949.

KENNAN, GEORGE F. *Russia and the West Under Lenin and Stalin.* Boston: Atlantic-Little, Brown, 1961.

KULSKI, W. W. *The Soviet Regime: Communism in Practice.* Syracuse: Syracuse University Press, 1956.

MC CLOSKY, HERBERT, and JOHN E. TURNER. *The Soviet Dictatorship.* New York: McGraw-Hill, 1960.

MEISEL, JAMES H., and EDWARD S. KOZERA. *Materials for the Study of the Soviet System.* Ann Arbor, Michigan: George Wahr, 1953.

MOORE, BARRINGTON JR. *Soviet Politics: The Dilemma of Power.* Cambridge: Harvard University Press, 1951.

NORTH, ROBERT C. *Moscow and Chinese Communists.* Stanford: Stanford University Press, 1953.

ORLOV, ALEXANDER. *The Secret History of Stalin's Crimes.* New York: Random House, 1953.

RESHETAR, JOHN S., JR. *A Concise History of the Communist Party of the Soviet Union.* New York: Praeger, 1960.

RUBINSTEIN, ALVIN Z., ed. *The Foreign Policy of the Soviet Union.* New York: Random House, 1960.

SCHAPIRO, LEONARD. *The Communist Party of the Soviet Union.* New York: Random House, 1960.

SCHWARTZ, HARRY. *Russia's Soviet Economy.* 2nd ed. New York: Prentice-Hall, 1954.

SCOTT, DEREK J. R. *Russian Political Institutions.* New York: Praeger, 1961.

STEINBERG, JULIEN, ed. *Verdict of Three Decades.* New York: Duell, Sloan and Pearce, 1950.

TARACOUZIO, T. A. *War and Peace in Soviet Diplomacy.* New York: Macmillan, 1940.

TIMASHEFF, NICHOLAS S. *The Great Retreat.* New York: Dutton, 1946.

TOWSTER, JULIAN. *Political Power in the U.S.S.R., 1917–1947.* New York: Oxford University Press, 1948.

VYSHINSKY, A. Y. *The Law of the Soviet State.* New York: Macmillan, 1948.

WEISSBERG, ALEXANDER. *The Accused.* New York: Simon & Schuster, 1951.

❧ V I I

THE PATRIOTIC
FORTIES

THE "UNHOLY ALLIANCE," AUGUST 23, 1939—JUNE 22, 1941

The Nazi-Soviet Pact of August, 1939, has been variously interpreted. Hitler is reported to have considered it an essential step towards "a new distribution of the world." His critics, however, have called it "the greatest blunder of his life." In retrospect, Stalin viewed the pact as providing an opportunity to prepare his forces against German invasion. Stalin's critics, however, maintain that his prime objective in signing the pact was to bring about a war between Germany and the Western Powers that would deplete the resources of both and leave the Soviet Union in an unchallengeable position in Europe.

Whatever the motives, the "Unholy Alliance," as the pact is often called, was a turning point in the history of the world for several reasons. First, it was a revelation of the methods and possibilities of totalitarian diplomacy based on secrecy, freedom of action, rapidity of decision, and disregard for public opinion. Second, for the Communists and the Nazis alike, the pact was a supreme test of discipline which they passed with flying colors. Third, the pact disclosed Stalin's open approval and even encouragement of Hitler's immediate aggressive plans in Europe. Fourth, the pact enabled Stalin to extend the territorial base of the revolution into the heart of Europe. And, finally, the pact was *the* prelude to World War II.

The war began on September 1, 1939, when, assured of Soviet "friendship" and confident that the West would not honor its pledge, Hitler ordered his armies into Poland. On September 3, England and France formally declared war on Germany. This formality had no immediate effect on Hitler, as his war machine, brought to a high pitch of efficiency and possessing the most modern weapons, rolled victoriously over Poland. The Polish organized armed forces, though fighting heroically, could not withstand the German onslaught. They were stunned, then demoralized, and then annihilated. In less than three weeks the Polish state had ceased to exist. Its government fled, eventually to London, where it was recognized by the Allies as legitimate. These developments, in turn, brought into operation the arrangements of the Nazi-Soviet Pact.

Soviet forces entered Poland on September 17, and proceeded to occupy their assigned sphere of influence with no appreciable resistance, since the fate of the Polish army had already been decided. According to one estimate, the operation cost the Soviet Union 737 dead and 1,862 wounded, against a Polish loss of 300,000 men, most of whom were taken prisoners. The Soviets attempted to justify their aggression by pointing to the expiration of the Polish state with resultant chaos, and professing a "sacred duty" to liberate and take under Soviet protection Ukrainians and Belorussians living in Eastern Poland. The last point, which ultimately became the official version, forced Stalin to yield some territory which had been assigned to the Soviet Union by the secret protocol of the pact, but which was ethnically Polish. The new arrangement, as worked out between Stalin and German Foreign Minister von Ribbentrop late in September, 1939, assigned Lithuania to the Soviet sphere of influence and set the German-Soviet frontier along the San-Bug-Narev Rivers. Both powers also agreed to cooperate against Polish "agitation," and promised to place "no obstacles" before their respective nationals should they desire to migrate to their "fatherlands." Between 1939 and 1941, some 437,000 Germans were repatriated from Soviet Russia and about 55,000 persons went to the USSR.

The fourth partition of Poland, as this arrangement is often called, netted the Soviet Union some 76,500 square miles, and 13,000,000 inhabitants. From the outset, the Soviets treated these territories as their own. Hasty, but elaborate preparations were made for election of national assemblies, which took place on October 22, 1939. In Western Ukraine, 4,433,997, or 92.83 per cent of the eligible voters approved the selected list of candidates, while in Western Belorussia 2,672,000, or 96.7 per cent of voters participated in the election, and overwhelmingly approved the official candidates. On October 27, the newly elected national assembly of Western Ukraine formally proclaimed Soviet rule, passed a resolution requesting the Soviet government to incorporate the Western Ukraine into the USSR, confiscated without payment all movable and immovable property of the Polish nobility, the Church, and state officials, and nationalized all banks and industrial enterprises. The national assembly of Western Belorussia passed a similar resolution and took identical actions on October 29. On November 1, 1939, with pomp, fanfare, and publicity, the Supreme Soviet of the USSR granted these "requests," and Western Ukraine and Western Belorussia in less than a month and a half became integral parts of the USSR.

Following the formalities of incorporation, the new areas were given the Soviet administrative system, party, *Komsomol* and Pioneer organizations, secret police, and other "benefits" of the Soviet system. To accelerate the integration process, numerous old institutions, such as schools and cooperatives, were liquidated, as were many of their spokesmen, and new ones were introduced. The reorganization of life in the new areas was guided by trusted officials who were brought for that purpose from Soviet Russia. The peasantry was left alone throughout most of 1939, but early in 1940 a decided effort was made to introduce collective farms, state farms, and MTS's.

Soviet incorporation of the Baltic states assigned to it by the Nazi-Soviet Pact was accomplished in two stages. First was the treaty stage. On September 28, 1939, the Soviet Union forced Estonia to sign a pact of mutual assistance, which granted the USSR the right to maintain naval bases and airfields and limited garrisons on Estonian territory. On October 5, 1939, the USSR forced Latvia to make identical arrangements, and on October 10 came Lithuania's turn. With each country the Soviet Union also concluded trade agreements and promised to respect their sovereignty and their social and economic system. Lithuania, in addition, was given the city of Vilnius and vicinity, which until 1939 had been part of Poland. In June, 1940, during Hitler's vast conquest of Western Europe, Stalin introduced the second stage of the incorporation of the Baltic states —that of ultimatums. Lithuania received a Soviet ultimatum on June 12, and Latvia and Estonia on June 16, 1940. The ultimatums accused each government of anti-Soviet actions, demanded the admission of additional Soviet troops, and formation of governments "friendly" to the USSR. Without waiting for replies, Soviet forces moved in, arrested all "suspected" officials, dissolved parliaments, set up new governments, and announced new elections to be held on July 14, 1940. Under those conditions the Soviet-sponsored Working People's League received an over-whelming majority of votes. On July 21, the new parliaments "requested" that their territories be incorporated into the USSR. The Supreme Soviet of the USSR granted their requests early in August, 1940, and Lithuania, Latvia, and Estonia became Soviet Socialist Republics. These additions increased the territorial base of the revolution by 65,237 square miles and a population of 5,400,000.

Soviet attempts to bring Finland under control were not successful. Early in October, 1939, the Soviets requested that Finland sign a pact of mutual assistance, allow the establishment of military and naval bases, and agree to far-reaching territorial changes. The Finns considered these requests unreasonable and refused to surrender any part of their territory. In reply, the Soviet Union, on November 28, 1939, unilaterally renounced its 1934 non-aggression pact with Finland, severed diplomatic ties on November 29, ordered full-scale military operations on November 30, and on December 1, in anticipation of a quick victory, set up a "democratic government" for Finland in the USSR under Otto Willi Kuusinen, an old veteran of the Comintern. For three months the Finns fought an unequal duel, but fought it amazingly well, and earned the sympathy and applause of the whole world. The Soviet Union for its action was expelled from the League of Nations on December 14, 1939. Hostilities were ended by the peace treaty of March 12, 1940, through which the USSR acquired some 16,173 square miles of Finnish territory with a population of 450,000.

Hitler's preoccupation in Western Europe during May and June, 1940, enabled Stalin to strengthen the Soviet position not only in the Baltic but in the Black Sea area as well. On June 26, 1940, Molotov delivered a note to the Rumanian ambassador in Moscow, demanding the return of Bessarabia and the surrender of Northern Bukovina to the USSR. On June 27, the note was followed by an ultimatum, and on June 28, without waiting for a reply, Soviet armed forces began the occupation of both territories. The occupation of this area, which netted 21,178 square miles and 3,717,000 people, was undertaken in the name of "national liberation." New territorial gains made possible the creation of a Moldavian Soviet Socialist Republic, which "joined" the USSR.

Soviet interest in Rumania and in the Balkans sharpened German suspicion, while extension of German "protection" over the Rumanian oil fields in October, 1940, aroused Soviet anxiety. It was the first major clash between the "incompatible allies." Early in November, 1940, both sides tried to find a compromise, but from the outset it became apparent that the German and Soviet positions were far apart. Fresh from his victorious campaigns in Western Europe, except against England, Hitler hoped that the Soviet Union would join his "new order." To avoid future misunderstanding, and at the same time hoping to involve the USSR in a war with

England, Hitler suggested that the USSR expand towards India, the Persian Gulf, and the Arabian Sea. Molotov agreed in principle to these suggestions, but he also insisted that Germany recognize Soviet interests elsewhere. These included: (1) German recognition that Finland belonged to the Soviet sphere of influence; (2) German recognition that Bulgaria was within the Soviet sphere; (3) German guarantee of a Soviet air and naval base in the Straits; (4) German recognition of Soviet interest in the fate of Turkey, Greece, Yugoslavia, Rumania, Hungary, and Poland; (5) German recognition that the area south of Batum and Baku in the general direction of the Persian Gulf was "the center of the aspirations of the Soviet Union"; and (6) Japanese renunciation of rights to concessions for coal and oil in Northern Sakhalin. Hitler's reaction to these Soviet ambitions was an order to his military to prepare for a *blitz* campaign to "crush Soviet Russia." Preparations for "Operation Barbarossa" were ordered completed by May 15, 1941. The incompatible allies parted company.

German military preparations started at once with a vast buildup of forces along the German-Soviet frontier in Poland, and strengthening of German positions elsewhere. By mid-February, 1941, the Germans had an army of 680,000 men in Rumania. Bulgaria was occupied early in March, and Yugoslavia and Greece were conquered in April, 1941. Soviet reaction to these provocative moves was two-fold. On the surface, Soviet leaders displayed considerable naïveté, sent conciliatory protests and inquiries about German moves, displayed a "friendly" attitude towards Berlin, and went out of their way to deliver punctually the German orders for food, petroleum, manganese ore, non-ferrous and other metals necessary to the success of the Barbarossa Operation. At the same time, however, the Soviets made every effort to improve their position vis-à-vis Germany. In response to the German military buildup, the Soviets strengthened their garrisons all along the German frontier, and to avoid a conflict on two fronts, on April 13, 1941, in Moscow, the USSR and Japan signed a mutual non-aggression pact. The Nazi-Soviet honeymoon came to a sudden end at dawn on June 22, 1941, when Hitler's armies rolled into the USSR.

CONVENTIONAL WARFARE, JUNE 22, 1941—MAY 7, 1945

"Operation Barbarossa" was actually a quite simple plan. Its three fundamental objectives were: the destruction of Soviet armed forces; the capture of political and industrial centers of the USSR (Moscow and Leningrad); and the occupation of coal, iron, and grain centers of the Ukraine and the Caucasus. The Germans hoped to achieve these objectives in three phases. During the first phase of the operation, both ground and air forces were to thrust deep into Soviet territory, create chaos, disrupt

On the Eastern front, 1941. Russian prisoners captured behind the German lines.

supply lines, encircle and destroy Soviet forces west of the Dvina-Dnieper line, and prevent the organization of new defenses. During the second phase, the Germans were to capture Leningrad, Moscow, and the Ukraine, in order to deprive the Soviet forces of political direction and economic strength. In the final phase the Germans were to advance to and hold firm the Volga-Archangel line.

To execute this plan, the Germans divided their forces into three groups. The first was Army Group North in East Prussia, under Field Marshal von Leeb, consisting of three panzer, three motorized, and twenty-four infantry divisions, the First Air Fleet, and Finnish forces, directed against Leningrad. The second was Army Group Centre in northern Poland, under Field Marshal von Bock, consisting of nine panzer, seven motorized, and thirty-four infantry divisions, and the Second Air Fleet. The third was Army Group South, in southern Poland and Rumania, under Field Marshal von Rundstedt, consisting of five panzer, three motorized, and thirty-five infantry divisions, the Fourth Air Fleet, three Italian divisions, two Rumanian armies, and Hungarian and Slovak units. Overall command of these forces was by Field Marshal von Brauchitsch.

Opposing this force were some 150 Soviet divisions grouped into three fronts. The Northwestern Front, under Marshal Voroshilov was responsible for the defense of Leningrad, Karelia, and the newly acquired Baltic states. Marshal Semeon K. Timoshenko's (1895–   ) forces of the Western Front guarded the approaches to Smolensk and Moscow. The Ukrainian Front was defended by Marshal Budenny. Little is known about Soviet orders, as the Soviet government has at the time of this writing neither published any authoritative study nor released any pertinent documents.

Whatever the nature of Soviet plans, they were upset by the German "surprise attack." At dawn on June 22, 1941, the *Luftwaffe* bombed and destroyed that part of the Soviet Air Force within its reach, and in one day's operation achieved complete air supremacy. Supported by the *Luftwaffe*, German panzers and infantry broke through Soviet defenses, and by evening were deep inside Soviet territory. Army Group North took Kaunas on June 22, reached the Dvina on June 26, occupied Riga on June 29, and by July 8 reached a new line of Soviet defensive positions south of Pskov, where the Germans encountered the first stiff resistance. Though not as spectacular as the German thrust, the Finnish offensive made remarkable progress in recovering territories Finland had been forced to yield to the Soviet Union in March, 1940.

The most spectacular of the German thrusts was that of Army Group Centre. Spearheaded by panzers and supported by the *Luftwaffe*, one German column advanced rapidly towards Vilnius, which fell on June 24, and headed for Minsk, while another column approached Minsk from Brest-Litovsk. The two columns joined on June 27, encircling large Soviet forces around Bialystok and Grodno. After fierce fighting, Soviet forces consisting of some 320,000 men, 3,000 tanks, and 2,000 heavy guns, surrendered to the Germans. By July 6, German panzers reached the Dnieper River and here, similarly as in the north, encountered signs of increased Soviet resistance. The resistance, however, was not strong enough to prevent the Germans from crossing the river on July 9, taking Smolensk on July 16, and capturing an additional 300,000 prisoners. The road to Moscow was wide open.

The progress of Army Group South was slow because the front was wide and natural barriers more numerous. These factors enabled Soviet forces to withdraw in a more orderly fashion, to counterattack at times, and to prevent the Germans from breaking through and encircling them in pincer movements. Army Group South advanced along three lines. One column advanced along the Lublin-Kovel-Lutsk-Zhitomir-Kiev line. Another moved along the Przemysl-Lvov-Vinnitsia-Dnieper River line. The third column advanced from Rumania towards Odessa and Dnieprope-trovsk. Distances enabled Soviet forces to escape all German encirclement attempts, except one at Uman, where early in August Soviet forces lost 103,000 men, 300 tanks, and 800 heavy guns. This loss cleared the road to

ARCTIC
OCEAN

Petsamo

Murmansk

WHITE SEA

Archangel

U N I O N

FINLAND

Petrozavodsk

O F   S O V I E T

Oslo

NORWAY

SWEDEN

Helsinki

Stockholm

Tallinn

LENINGRAD

Tikhvin

Novgorod

Volga

Gorky

Kazan

ESTONIA

Pskov

Kalinin

S O C I A L I S T

Riga

LATVIA

MOSCOW

Libau

BALTIC SEA

LITHUANIA

Vitebsk

Tula

Kuibyshev

Vilnius

EAST
PRUSSIA

Smolensk

R E P U B L I C S

Saratov

BERLIN

Minsk

Orel

Voronezh

WARSAW

Gomel

Stalingrad

GERMANY

P O L A N D

Kursk

Prague

Kiev

Kharkov

Lvov

CASPIAN SEA

Danube

Krivoy Rog

Rostov

VIENNA

Budapest

Kishinev

HUNGARY

Odessa

Sea of Azov

RUMANIA

Sevastopol

Novorossiisk

CAUCASUS MTS.

Mozdok

Bucharest

YUGOSLAVIA

ADRIATIC SEA

BLACK SEA

Batum

Belgrade

BULGARIA

Sofia

ITALY

ALBANIA

Istambul

T U R K E Y

Ankara

GREECE

Athens

MEDITERRANEAN
SEA

The GERMAN INVASION OF RUSSIA
1941 - 1942

— — — — Line of deepest German penetration, 1941-1942

Borders of
U.S.S.R.
June, 1941

MILES

0   100   500

Sam'l H. Bryant

Kiev and the Dnieper, and thus led to the successful conclusion of the first phase of the "Barbarossa Operation."

Execution of the second phase encountered considerable difficulty. On the one hand, Soviet land forces recovered from the initial shock and paralysis and began to offer increased resistance all along the front. Also, the Soviet Air Force recovered enough to cause harassment to the German advance. But far more important was the German inability to fix the priority of the next strategic objective of the campaign. For some five weeks, Hitler and his generals were unable to agree on what to do next. At first Hitler insisted that Leningrad should be the next primary objective in order to link up with the Finns, establish a new line of communication by sea, and clear the Baltic of the Soviet fleet. His generals, von Bock and Guderian among others, insisted that Moscow should be made the primary objective because it was the capital of the USSR, a vital communication center, and an important industrial base. They felt that the German attack on Moscow would draw most of the Soviet forces to its defense, and hence to their doom. In mid-August, however, Hitler changed his mind, relegated both Leningrad and Moscow to secondary importance, and gave priority to conquest of the Ukraine, in order to place the resources of that region at Germany's disposal.

The second phase of the "Barbarossa Operation" started accordingly with the assault on Kiev, which fell on September 19. Though many Soviet units succeeded in escaping the German pincer movement and retreated towards Kharkov, the Kiev battle netted the Germans 650,000 prisoners. Rain and mud, however, slowed the German advance, and the desired objective was not attained. An advance towards Leningrad, which started early in September, also ground to a halt at the end of the month, partly as a result of stiff Soviet defense and partly on orders from Hitler, who meanwhile developed a "new plan" of attack. The "new plan" called for reduction of Leningrad through siege and starvation, encirclement and capture of Moscow, conquest of the Crimea, and above all of the Donbass and the Caucasus in order to gain the coal and oil resources of these regions for Germany. This fantastic plan, however, failed to take into account two vital factors. The first was that both men and machines needed rest and maintenance, which they had not received since June 22. The second was that the freezing rains and snow, which had already begun affecting the morale of the men, sharply reduced the mobility of the machines and hence the superiority of the German forces and accordingly increased the importance of the superiority of Soviet manpower.

Under the new plan, the assault on Moscow was given high priority, and full scale operations started on September 30. On October 3, Orel fell to the Germans, and by October 20, around Viazma and Briansk the Germans captured some 665,000 Soviet prisoners. Thereafter, however,

German progress slowed considerably. The first contributing factor was mud, which increased fuel consumption but not territorial gains. The second was the sudden drop of the temperature to 40° below zero. The third was the stubborn resistance on the part of fresh reserves from Siberia, who were provided with good equipment and winter clothing. These factors forced the Germans to give up their goal of capturing Moscow and to break off the attack with heavy losses. The failure to take Moscow was offset, in part, by gains in the Ukraine, where late in September, 1941, in the battle of the Sea of Azov, the Germans captured some 100,000 prisoners, occupied Odessa on October 16, Kharkov on October 24, Rostov-on-the-Don on November 21, and the Crimea. These gains, however, were to be only temporary, for early in December, 1941, when rains and mud halted the exhausted Germans, the Russians opened their first major counter offensive along the entire front.

The aim of the Russian winter offensive was to drive the exhausted, overextended, and nature-immobilized German forces as far back as possible and to keep them constantly off balance. Fighting was fierce and casualties were extremely heavy on both sides, not only from combat but from the severe weather as well. The least change in battle position came around Leningrad. The heaviest fighting took place around Moscow, where as early as the end of December, 1941, the Germans lost some of their advanced positions under Soviet pressure. From others they retreated voluntarily. Voluntary or under pressure, the German withdrawal cost them some 250,000 men, 1,000 tanks, and 1,500 heavy guns. For the moment it appeared that Soviet forces might even recapture Smolensk, but fierce German defense spoiled that effort. The Soviet counter offensive in the Ukraine was the most costly in terms of Soviet casualties. In the Kerch peninsula the Germans took 170,000 prisoners, Sevastopol yielded them an additional 90,000 men, and early in June, 1942, in the Donets area 240,000 Soviet soldiers surrendered. The winter offensive was extremely costly for the USSR, but it achieved an important goal. It inflicted very heavy casualties on the Germans as well, and prevented them from resting, reorganizing, and reequipping their land and air forces to launch a new offensive in 1942.

In the summer of 1942, against the advice of some of his generals, Hitler ordered a new offensive in the Ukraine. Its aim was to destroy Soviet forces in the Don area and Stalingrad and to capture the oil-rich Caucasus. For the exhausted German forces, this was a superhuman task, although initially they made considerable progress. They retook Rostov on July 23, occupied Maikop on August 8, Mozdok on the Terek River on August 25, and reached Stalingrad early in September. Lack of fuel, waning of energy, and the approach of winter, coupled with effective Russian resistance, made further German advance impossible. A disaster of first magnitude for the Germans was in the making, and it struck on November 19, 1942, in the form of a second Soviet winter offensive, which was as complete a surprise as any achieved before by the Germans.

The aim of the second Soviet offensive was simple. It sought to break through the overextended German lines along the Don River in order to cut off the retreat of German forces from Stalingrad. Soviet efforts were simplified by the panic of Hungarian, Rumanian, and Italian formations. Four days after the offensive started, the German Sixth Army of 285,000 men, commanded by General von Paulus, was encircled in Stalingrad. An immediate breakthrough might have saved this force, but Hitler refused to listen to suggestions for withdrawal. Instead he ordered a relief attack, which after an initial success was halted by December 25, 1942, and then turned into a full-scale retreat. The Sixth Army was doomed, and its survivors, consisting of 91,000 men, including twenty-four generals, capitulated on January 30, 1943. It was "the greatest defeat that a German army had ever undergone," and according to some observers was a turning point of World War II.

The Soviet offensive was stalled late in February, 1943, by a combination of two factors. The first was the effective German resistance which culminated in a tank battle at Pavlovgrad, where the Soviets lost 650 tanks, 1,000 guns, and the city of Kharkov. The second was the mud which hampered all operations. The lull in fighting enabled both sides to prepare for new blows. The Soviets brought up reinforcements along the entire front, and were able to strengthen their forces with modern American tanks, guns, and trucks received under the Lend-Lease Program. When the Germans launched their last offensive in July, 1943, the Soviet steam roller was ready to inflict heavy losses on the Germans which they could not replace. Early in August, Soviet forces retook Orel, occupied Kharkov on August 23, Novorossiisk in mid-September, Poltava and Smolensk by the end of September, Kiev in early November, and by the end of 1943 they established several bridgeheads across the Dnieper. These advances were very costly in lives, as the Germans, though greatly outnumbered and retreating, offered cunning and savage defense. These advances, however, cleared the way for a massive frontal attack all the way from Lapland to the Black Sea which took place in 1944 in the form of ten major thrusts.

The first Soviet blow was struck in January, 1944, against Army Group North, forcing the Germans to abandon their encirclement of Leningrad. The second blow came in February and March in the Ukraine and forced the Germans to retreat to the old Polish and Rumanian frontiers. The third blow came in April and May against the Crimea, while the fourth struck in the Karelian Isthmus, forcing the Finns out of the war. The fifth Soviet blow, dealt by 146 infantry divisions and 43 armored brigades, struck Army Group Centre late in June, 1944. Soviet forces

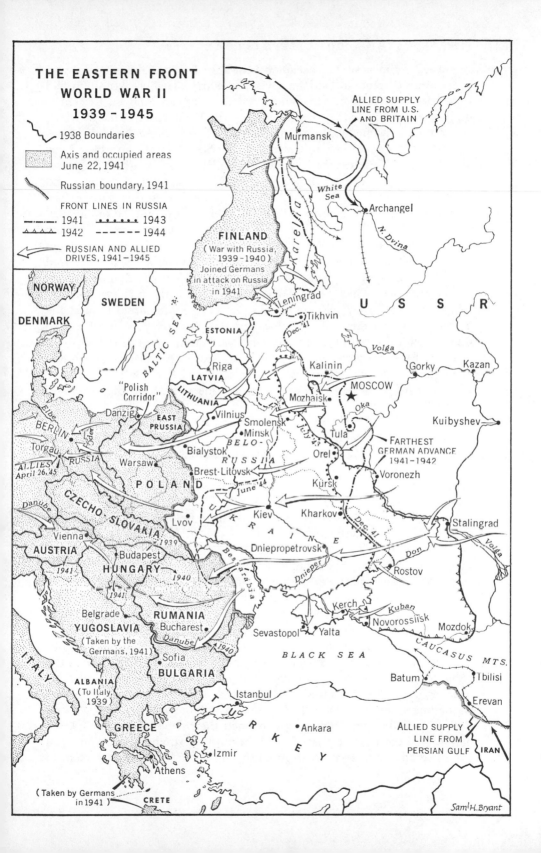

THE EASTERN FRONT
WORLD WAR II
1939 – 1945

- 1938 Boundaries
- Axis and occupied areas June 22, 1941
- Russian boundary, 1941

FRONT LINES IN RUSSIA

- –·–·– 1941   ••••••• 1943
- △△△△ 1942   – – – – 1944
- RUSSIAN AND ALLIED DRIVES, 1941–1945

ALLIED SUPPLY LINE FROM U.S. AND BRITAIN

Murmansk

White Sea

Archangel

N. Dvina

Karelia

NORWAY

SWEDEN

DENMARK

FINLAND
(War with Russia, 1939 – 1940)
Joined Germans in attack on Russia in 1941

Leningrad

Tikhvin

Dec. 41

U   S   S   R

BALTIC SEA

ESTONIA

Riga

LATVIA

Kalinin

Volga

Gorky

Kazan

"Polish Corridor"

LITHUANIA

Vilnius

MOSCOW

Mozhaisk

Oka

Kuibyshev

Danzig

EAST PRUSSIA

Smolensk

Minsk

BELO-

RUSSIA

Tula

BERLIN

Elbe

Torgau

Warsaw

Bialystok

Brest-Litovsk

FARTHEST GERMAN ADVANCE 1941–1942

Orel

ALLIES April 26, 45

POLAND

Danube

CZECHO-SLOVAKIA

Lvov

June 44

Kiev

Kursk

Voronezh

July 43

Dec. 41

Vienna

1939

Dniepropetrovsk

Kharkov

Stalingrad

Volga

AUSTRIA

1941

Budapest

HUNGARY

1940

Bessarabia

U   K   R   A   I   N   E

Dnieper

Don

Rostov

Belgrade

YUGOSLAVIA
(Taken by the Germans, 1941)

RUMANIA

Bucharest

Danube

1940

Sofia

BULGARIA

Sevastopol

Yalta

Kerch

Kuban

Novorossiisk

Mozdok

BLACK   SEA

CAUCASUS   MTS.

ITALY

ALBANIA
(To Italy, 1939)

T   U   R   K   E   Y

Istanbul

Batum

Tbilisi

Erevan

GREECE

Ankara

ALLIED SUPPLY LINE FROM PERSIAN GULF

IRAN

Izmir

Athens

(Taken by Germans in 1941)

CRETE

Sam'l H. Bryant

overran German positions, occupied Minsk on July 3, Vilnius on July 13, and captured some 30 German divisions. This Soviet breakthrough had significant repercussions. It endangered the German hold on the entire Baltic area, and it also opened the road to the Vistula and Warsaw, which Soviet forces reached early in August, 1944. The sixth Soviet blow struck against German positions in Galicia, where Soviet forces occupied Lvov on July 25, and reached the San and Vistula Rivers and Carpathian passes early in August. The seventh Soviet blow was against Rumanian and German forces along the Dniester River. The Rumanians surrendered unconditionally on August 23, and shortly thereafter joined the war against Germany. The collapse of German positions in Rumania opened for the Soviets the road to the Balkans and Hungary. Late in August, Soviet forces occupied Bucharest and Ploesti, and on September 16, they entered Sofia, the capital of Bulgaria. The eighth Soviet blow struck in the direction of Budapest, which Soviet forces approached early in November, and Belgrade, which they took on October 19. The ninth thrust cleared the Baltic states of German forces that had been cut off previously by the summer offensive, and the final blow hit the Petsamo region and northern Norway. By these gains and maneuvers, Soviet forces placed themselves in an advantageous position for a final assault of Germany from the East, while the Allied forces were preparing for the same from the West and the South.

The final Soviet assault against Germany began in mid-January, 1945, along a front stretching from the Baltic to the Carpathians. The attack was led by four army "fronts," the First Ukrainian Front, under Marshal Ivan S. Konev (1897–), north of the Carpathians; the First Belorussian Front, under Marshal Georgi K. Zhukov (1896–), in central Poland; the Second Belorussian Front, under Marshal Konstantine K. Rokossovsky (1896–), north of Warsaw; and the Third Belorussian Front, under General Ivan D. Cherniakovsky, (1906–1945), in East Prussia. The combined force of the four fronts consisted of 275 infantry divisions, twenty-two armored corps, twenty-nine armored brigades, and three cavalry corps. As German defenses were now negligible, the Soviet advance was rapid. Warsaw, or what remained of it, fell on January 17, Cracow and Lodz on January 19, and Elbing in East Prussia on January 26. German resistance in East Prussia was fierce, and it was not until March 30 that Danzig was taken by storm, and Königsberg did not surrender until April 9. Early in March, Soviet forces established bridgeheads across the Oder River for the final push against Berlin, which they surrounded by April 25, and occupied on May 2. Meanwhile, Soviet forces south of the Carpathians, under Marshals Rodion Ia. Malinovsky (1899–) and Feodor I. Tolbukhin (1894–1949), opened their drive and occupied Budapest on February 13, 1945, Bratislava on April 3, and Vienna on April 13. Allied advances from the west, south, and north forced the Germans to accept unconditional surrender on May 7, 1945. The war in Europe was over, but peace was not in sight.

UNCONVENTIONAL WARFARE, JUNE 22, 1941—MAY 7, 1945

The fundamental aim of the Germans' eastern campaign in June, 1941, as of their other campaigns, was to conquer, to rule, and to exploit. Like their previous campaigns too, this undertaking neglected positive political planning, and as one authority justly noted, had neither a plan for enlisting the Soviet population on the German side, nor a blueprint of political conduct except the extermination of all "undesirables." Three erroneous assumptions seem to have contributed to the German failure to prepare for the use of political warfare. First was the belief that the eastern campaign, like the previous *blitzkriegs,* would be a very brief affair and would end before the close of 1941. Second was the gross underestimation of Soviet military capabilities and willingness to resist. Third was the Nazi aim of making themselves permanent masters of the East, thus gaining space for settlement and expansion. These three factors, and especially the last one, from the outset precluded humane treatment of the conquered peoples and negated any possibility of the remaking of Eastern Europe along national lines.

Unaware at first of the real Nazi intentions, the Soviet population in most instances viewed the rapidly advancing German forces as liberators. While the welcome was more enthusiastic in the recently acquired areas of the Soviet Union (Bessarabia, Eastern Poland, and the Baltic States), everywhere the Germans came anti-Soviet sentiment burst into the open, manifesting itself in innumerable ways. At the front, it was expressed in mass surrender of Soviet soldiers. Among the peasants, anti-Soviet grievances revealed themselves in the breakup of collective farms and MTS's, and in the division of their properties. Among nationalities of the USSR, the German advance raised hopes that at last their national aspirations could be realized. Everywhere the retreat of Soviet forces was accompanied by the destruction of Stalin's statues, the abolition of Soviet institutions, emptying of prisons, and reopening of churches. The hopes of these peoples stemmed from rumors based on German propaganda, some official, but mostly unofficial, which invited Soviet soldiers to surrender, depicted Germany as a liberator, and promised self-government and private ownership of land. These hopes vanished one by one, as the Germans, intoxicated by their initial successes, began to implement their real policies.

The first to be disappointed with German promises and treatment were prisoners of war, whose numbers rose by late December, 1941, to 3,355,000, and increased by 1,653,000 in 1942. Many of these surrendered voluntarily, while others had no choice. So staggering was the number of prisoners that the Germans were not prepared to accommodate them, nor were they willing to treat them humanely. Initially, they released some, especially non-Russians, to work on farms or to clear war-damaged enterprises. Fearing, however, that freed men would join the partisans, the Germans soon abandoned this practice, and herded the prisoners into hurriedly-constructed camps. Left under the open sky without food or shelter, thousands of men perished in various epidemics. Many others died from beatings and abuse by their guards. Some were shot, others were poisoned, and some fell prey to their comrades who, in desperation to survive, turned to cannibalism. According to German figures, between 1941 and 1944, some 1,981,000 Soviet prisoners died, and 1,308,000 simply disappeared. Rumors of these abuses and cruelties cancelled the effect of surrender leaflets, stiffened Soviet military resistance, embittered the civilian population, and provided the Soviet regime with an excellent propaganda weapon. A labor shortage forced the Germans to change their policy in 1942 and bring many prisoners to Germany to work in agriculture and in industry. This, however, did not change their *Untermensch* status or exploitation and abuse. The Soviet government could not and did not attempt in any way to help, for its official attitude was that any soldier who fell into enemy hands was *ipso facto* a traitor and hence not deserving of protection from his government. Understandably, therefore, German prisoners in the Soviet Union received little or no consideration.

The second group disappointed with German occupation policies was the peasantry. Their disappointment stemmed from the widespread belief that with the coming of the Germans the *kolkhoz* system, against which they had so many grievances, would be abolished. Initially, German army units made no efforts to stop peasant division of the property of collective farms or of the MTS's. Some German officials, in fact, supported such a course of action in order to capitalize on peasant opposition to the Soviet regime. Those in authority, however, opposed peasant aspirations, for they felt that the division of land, cattle, and machinery among individual peasants was contrary to the long-range Nazi plan for colonization of Eastern Europe. They were also afraid that to sanction peasant demands would jeopardize the grain supply for the German army, which provisioned itself as it fought in the East. Mounting peasant disappointment and dissatisfaction, however, forced the Nazis to make two "concessions." The first, made in August, 1941, included abolition of the term *kolkhoz*, enlargement of private peasant plots at the expense of *kolkhoz* land, and the promise of unlimited private cattle breeding. The second "concession" came on February 15, 1942, in the form of a new agrarian law abolishing all Soviet decrees and regulations concerning collective farms, which were now designated communal economies. The change was in name only, for, as before, the peasants were forced to work under the direction of their masters, to deliver the assigned quotas of grain, and to be compensated according to a system of "labor days." German propaganda hailed the new agricultural arrangement as the dawn of a new era. Soviet peasants viewed it as a new form of exploitation. For those peasants who had dreamt so long of farming their own land, the German agricultural policy was a bitter disappointment, and many cast their lot with the partisans. Neither was the policy beneficial to the Germans. Immediately they procured most of the food required for the armies in the East, but the methods by which they did it contributed heavily to their loss of the war.

Next to mistreatment of prisoners of war and peasant exploitation, the most revolting aspect of German policy was the so-called *Ostarbeiter* program. Between 1942 and 1945, the Germans removed from the occupied areas of the USSR some 2,800,000 civilians to slave in German agriculture, mining, and industry. Except for the few volunteers in the initial stage of the program, all those sent to Germany went against their will. The Germans assigned every district a quota and rounded up their captives arbitrarily in villages, market places, and even churches. The captives were then packed into freight cars without food or sanitary facilities and shipped off to Germany. The treatment in Germany of the *Ostarbeiters* was no better. Considered *Untermenschen*, they were punished, exploited, and humiliated. Those who became ill or incapacitated, the Germans returned home to face starvation. The methods used by the Germans in procuring a labor force, which included forcible abortion of pregnant women, separation of mothers from babies, of children from families, and often burning of whole villages, spread bitterness and fear among the population. To escape this kind of treatment, many able-bodied men and women joined the partisan movement, which grew in force and intensity in proportion to German brutality. In 1944, when the collapse of the Third Reich was in sight, the Germans improved somewhat their treatment of the *Ostarbeiters*, but this "understanding" was too little and came too late.

Another German "change of heart" that came too late was Nazi support of the celebrated Vlasov movement. The founder of the movement was a well-known Soviet general, Andrei A. Vlasov (1900–1946), whom the Germans captured on July 12, 1942, and who later agreed to fight against Stalin on condition that the Germans drastically alter their policy towards Soviet peoples. From its inception the Vlasov movement encountered many difficulties. It was opposed by old Russian émigré groups, by the minorities of the Soviet Union, and by many Nazis as well. It was enthusiastically supported by some officers of the German army, mainly because Vlasov's appeals increased the desertion of Soviet soldiers. With the blessing of these officers, late in 1942 there was organized a Russian committee and an army of liberation from among Soviet pris-

Marshal G. K. Zhukov   *K. E. Voroshilov*

oners of war. But just as the movement was about to move into high gear, Hitler, in June, 1943, vetoed its activity, for he felt that the aims of the Vlasov movement were contrary to German goals. Discouraged by the Nazi blindness, many of Vlasov's followers joined the partisans. Thousands who could not or did not, the Germans transferred to the West, to the Balkans, and to other theaters of operation to fight as mercenaries.

Soviet and Allied advances during 1943 and 1944, coupled with the increasing German shortage of manpower, forced some Nazi fanatics to change their views not only about the Vlasov movement, but other national movements as well. The "sponsor" of this new outlook was Heinrich Himmler, the Gestapo chief, who in 1943 and 1944 launched Latvian, Estonian, Ukrainian, Belorussian, Moslem, Turkic, and Caucasian military formations. In September, 1944, Himmler also consented to the formation of a Committee for the Liberation of the Peoples of Russia under Vlasov's leadership. In 1942, these and other later innovations would have been far-reaching. In 1944 it was an empty and hollow gesture. Vlasov and many of his close associates were captured after the war, and on August 2, 1946, the Soviets announced that they had been executed.

The last group disappointed with the Germans was composed of the Soviet minorities—Estonians, Latvians, Lithuanians, Belorussians, Ukrainians, and others—who thirsted for relief and who hoped to re-establish their independent existence with German help. Their demands were modest, but they ran contrary to German plans, which called for the division of conquered areas of the USSR into four Reich Commissariats, the East, Ukraine, Muscovy, and Caucasus. Each Commissariat was administered by low caliber officials and presided over by true autocrats, of whom

Erich Koch in the Ukraine was doubtless the most brutally bestial. It was also in the Ukraine that the clash between national aspirations and German designs burst wide open. This was inevitable, for in the preinvasion propaganda the Nazis cleverly played on Ukrainian hatred of the Kremlin, posed as defenders of the Ukraine, offered comfort and support to many nationalist spokesmen, and skillfully exploited the strong separatist tendencies of the Ukrainians. At the same time the Nazis assigned to the Ukraine a highly important role in their search for *Lebensraum*. They viewed the abundance of Ukrainian raw materials as a valuable source of supply for German industry, considered the Ukraine's fertile soil not only as a significant food base for the Third Reich, but also as an indispensable area for future German agricultural settlement, and envisaged the Ukraine's strategic location as an excellent starting point for further German economic and political penetration into Central Asia, the Near and the Middle East. Needless to say, these elaborate schemes precluded the establishment of a Ukrainian state that in any way could endanger German domination.

Between June and September, 1941, the Nazis took four steps which revealed that they had no intention of creating a Ukrainian state. First they arrested the Ukrainian nationalists who, in Lvov on June 30, 1941, proclaimed an independent Ukrainian state. Second, on August 1, 1941, they gave to Rumania some 10,000 square miles of Ukrainian territory along the Dniester River, including the city of Odessa. Third, on August 1, 1941, they transferred Galicia, or Western Ukraine, to the Government-General of Poland and banned Ukrainian political activities there. Finally, in September, 1941, Hitler appointed Koch, the most outspoken proponent of the *Herrenvolk* idea and the most violent anti-Ukrainian Nazi spokesman, to be the autocrat of the Ukraine, where for the next two years he inaugurated a real reign of terror. His abuses and atrocities disillusioned many Ukrainians, some of whom joined either nationalist-led or Communist-led partisans. Caught between the hammer and the anvil was the bulk of the terrorized and exploited population, which, as one authority rightly noted, "called down a plague on both their houses."

Of the many devices with which Soviet and non-Soviet peoples fought the Germans, once their intentions became known, the most fascinating was the partisan movement. The partisan struggle was a spontaneous development, and grew as a reaction to the German policies and above all as an answer to the behavior of German personnel. Initially, partisan groups consisted mainly of isolated Soviet army stragglers, many of whom were far from enthusiastic in their attitude towards Soviet authority. Some of these early partisan units dispersed, others surrendered, and those that were pro-Soviet inclined or inspired received little support from the bulk of the population bewildered by the far-reaching changes taking place.

The partisan movement shifted into high gear late in 1941 and early in 1942. Of the factors contributing to the increased partisan membership and activity, the following seem to have been the most significant: (1) German treatment of prisoners of war, which forced many stragglers to join the partisans; (2) German treatment of the civilian population, and especially their recruiting methods for *Ostarbeiters;* (3) German exploitation of the peasantry; (4) German "double crossing" of native nationalists; (5) the stiffening of Soviet resistance along the entire front; (6) Soviet material assistance to the partisans; and (7) German inability to liquidate partisan pockets of resistance and their liberal application of brute force and terror in the attempt to do so.

While a full study of the partisan movement still remains to be written, it presented the Germans with a "front behind the front." From their hideouts in the forests, the partisans prevented cooperation between civilian population and the occupying authorities, attacked German outposts, weakened German morale, and repeatedly disrupted German communications. Because the last activity was felt by every single unit at the front, the Germans moved to protect their overextended lines by every device possible, including commitment of regular combat forces to mopping-up operations in partisan-infested areas. This effort, however, was often more fierce and resulted in a proportionately larger number of casualties than combat at the front because of the hit and run nature of partisan tactics, and the great speed with which they operated. They appeared on the scene, completed their mission, and withdrew into their forest hideouts where it was next to impossible to ferret them out. In the spring of 1943 the Germans used front line divisions—some 100,000 strong—to clear the Briansk forest, but the results achieved did not justify the cost. The same was true of two other mass operations—the summer, 1943, offensive against Soviet partisans led by Sidor A. Kovpak (1887–   ), who crossed the Ukraine into the Carpathians, and the perpetual German offensive against the non-Soviet Ukrainian Insurgent Army organized by "Taras Bulba," whose original base of operations was in Volyn. The Germans lost against the partisans because, imbued with fantasies and intoxicated with their earlier victories, they failed to understand the aspirations of other men.

In contrast to the German policy of brutality, exploitation, and extermination, Soviet policy during the war was one of concessions, promises, and above all attempts to arouse national patriotism. These innovations were necessary in order to offset heavy losses, rumor, confusion, and panic, created by the lightning German thrust deep inside Soviet territory. The thrust was deep indeed and the losses staggering. By November, 1941, the Germans controlled an area embracing about 40 per cent of the whole Soviet population, and supplying 68 per cent of Soviet pig iron output, 58 per cent of steel, 60 per cent of aluminum, 38 per cent of the grain, 84 per cent of sugar, and 41 per cent of railroad lines. The Germans also held some 3,355,000 prisoners of war. German advances in 1942 increased considerably Soviet losses, both material and human.

It is imperative, however, to remember that Soviet losses were not *ipso facto* German gains. As they retreated the Soviets tried to evacuate all movable property (plants, machinery, tools, raw material, cattle, and even people) to new locations in the Urals and Central Asia, where everything was put back into production. Those establishments that could not be removed (houses, buildings, bridges, the Dnieprostroy Dam, and the like) the Soviets destroyed.

Just as important as the "scorched earth policy" was the upsurge of national patriotism. In part this upsurge was spontaneous. It represented an outburst of national pride and anger at the sadistic Nazi mistreatment of prisoners and peasants, their relegation of Slavs to an inferior racial status, and their unfolding of far-reaching colonization designs. In part, however, the upsurge of national patriotism was Stalin-sponsored. He gave the first signal for its rise in his first speech of the war on July 3, 1941, when he compared Hitler's early successes to those of Napoleon in "the great patriotic war of 1812." Stalin's second signal came on November 7, 1941, in his address to the troops he reviewed at Red Square, when he intoned, "Let the manly images of our great ancestors—Alexander Nevsky, Dimitri Donskoi, Kuzma Minin, Dimitri Pozharsky, Alexander Suvorov, and Mikhail Kutuzov—inspire you in this war."

Stalin's invocation of saints and warriors of Imperial Russia was immediately followed by what one observer called a "grotesquely immoderate glorification of Russia's imperial past," and in effect a large-scale rehabilitation of many prerevolutionary traditions and institutions. This rehabilitation was most immediately noticeable in the armed forces. Its first manifestation came in the form of a series of medals established by the Presidium of the Supreme Soviet, such as the Medal of the Patriotic War (May 20, 1943), Medals of Suvorov, Kutuzov, and Nevsky (July 29, 1942), and Medals of Ushakov, and Nakhimov (March 3, 1944). To revive the old imperial glamour, guard regiments and guard divisions were created in May, 1942; Cossack formations were restored later in the year; and in January, 1943, epaulettes, once scorned as symbols of a reactionary caste system in the army, were reintroduced as part of the military uniform. Saluting became obligatory and was strictly enforced, and officers were given exclusive clubs with separate messes.

Next to the armed forces, most affected by the rehabilitation of imperial tradition was the Church—the institution which had held a central place in that tradition. Following the outbreak of war, Church leaders came to the defense of their country, as had their predecessors on so many occasions. They sent messages to the faithful, reminding them of their duties, warned against cooperation with the enemy (and excom-

Berlin, 1945. Russian tanks enter the city.

municated those who cooperated), praised the "patriotic" work of the partisans, hailed Stalin as "the divinely appointed [sic] leader" of the nation, and collected and donated some 150 million rubles in addition to many valuables for the purchase of tanks, planes, and other equipment. On its part, the government toned down anti-religious propaganda, disbanded the League of Militant Atheists, reopened many of the closed churches, and invited Metropolitan Nikolai of Kiev to become a member of the Extraordinary State Committee for investigating crimes committed by the Nazis. The climax of this cooperation between the Orthodox Church and the Soviet state came on September 4, 1943, when Stalin received church leaders in the Kremlin and consented to the convocation of the *Sobor* and the formal election of a patriarch and a synod to assist him. The patriarch, installed in office on September 7, 1943, immediately appealed to Christians everywhere to fight Hitlerism, and through the *Journal of the Patriarchate of Moscow*, as in the imperial period, seconded many government policies. In October, 1943, the goverment created a Council for Affairs of the Orthodox Church as an adjunct to the *Sovnarkom*, allowed the restoration of organized theological instruction, relaxed rules on the religious instruction of children, and decorated many clergy for their war efforts.

To win the war it was necessary not only to rehabilitate the old traditions but to make peace with the more recent past as well. In the face of Hitler's all too real conspiracy, all bogus conspiracies of the 1930's, such as Trotskyism, Bukharinism, and the like, were discreetly dropped. Many of those who had survived the great purges were released from concentration camps and drafted into the armed forces, or assigned to other important jobs. Among the rehabilitated were scientists, writers, and many of Tukhachevsky's disciples, including Generals Rokossovsky and Tolbukhin, who soon became heroes of the victory at Stalingrad. Because the bulk of the Soviet population had little enthusiasm for the Communist party, its role was de-emphasized and the proletarian slogans replaced by such patriotic utterances as "Down with the Fascist Invader." In line with the new trend, in 1943 the *Internationale* was replaced by a new national anthem, whose first line was: "Unbreakable union of free-born republics, Great Russia has welded forever to stand."

The return to Great Russian tradition did not overlook the minorities, especially those whose efforts and sacrifices were needed in the war. On October 10, 1943, the Presidium of the Supreme Soviet established a high military decoration for Ukrainians, the Medal of Khmelnytsky. At the end of the year, the Southern Front was designated the Ukrainian Front, and the armies which operated there were renamed Ukrainian Armies. Identical changes were introduced in the central sector of the front, where Belorussian names were adopted. In February, 1944, the constitution was amended to give each Union Republic the "paper right" to have its own commissariat of armed forces and of foreign affairs. In 1944, a poem expressing love for the Ukraine even won the Stalin Prize. Outwardly these and other concessions represented a vast change and were so interpreted both at home and abroad. In reality, however, the change was negligible because Stalin neither retreated from centralism nor did he reject the total regimentation of life.

POSTWAR RECONSTRUCTION AND REHABILITATION

Four years of active Soviet participation in the greatest of all wars inflicted staggering human and material losses on the USSR. It has been estimated that the war cost the Soviet Union some 7.5 million military casualties. Of that figure, about 3 million perished in German prisoner-of-war camps; the remainder were combat casualties. No exact figures are available on the number of civilians killed, or on those who were either seriously wounded or maimed for life, or on those who chose not to return to the Soviet Union at the end of the war. Their number, however, exceeded the military casualties, and in all probability the war cost the USSR some 20 million people.

The material losses were just as staggering. According to official Soviet figures, war operations destroyed 1,710 cities, 70,000 villages, 32,000 industrial enterprises, 98,000 collective farms, 1,876 state farms, 2,890 MTS's, 7 million horses, 17 million head of cattle, 20 million hogs, 40,000 miles of railroad track, 84,000 schools, and most of the bridges, hospitals, and libraries. Officially these losses, set at 679 billion rubles (in prewar prices), were attributed to the Germans, but the Soviets' own "scorched earth policy" accounted for a good deal of the immense loss. At any rate, the close of World War II left the Soviet regime a colossal task of economic reconstruction of its land and cultural and psychological rehabilitation of its people.

Economic reconstruction became the special assignment of the Fourth Five Year Plan (1946–1950). Its announced aims were: to rebuild the war-ravaged areas of the country; to restore heavy industry and agriculture to their prewar levels, and then to surpass this level considerably; to raise the cultural and material level of the population; to overtake and surpass the scientific advances outside the USSR; and to maintain a large standing army. These ambitious goals were based on Stalin's determination (announced on February 9, 1946) to triple Soviet industrial production in order to make the USSR "ready for every eventuality." To attain that state of preparedness, Stalin proposed that by 1960 Soviet industry should produce annually up to 50 million tons of pig iron, up to 60 million tons of steel, up to 500 million tons of coal, and up to 60 million tons of oil.

To achieve this ambition, the Fourth Five Year Plan (adopted in March, 1946) allocated 250 billion rubles for capital investment, and planned to produce 19.5 million tons of pig iron, 35.4 million tons of crude oil, 250 million tons of coal, and 25.4 million tons of steel by 1950. The plan also gave high priority to the production of other strategic minerals (copper, aluminum, and nickel), as well as heavy machinery, transportation equipment, atomic energy, conventional arms, and the now famous MIG jet fighters. The plan envisaged an increase of 36 per cent in the productivity of labor, "to be achieved by making the utmost of the eight-hour working day," automation, a reduction of 17 per cent in the cost of production, a vast improvement in the quality of industrial production, a 17 per cent increase in food and consumer goods, and a 7 per cent higher harvest in 1950 than in 1940. In 1948 the planners added to these optimistic targets the construction of several huge projects for the improvement of electrical output, the communication network, and the irrigation system. These projects included: a dam on the Volga near Kuibyshev; a dam on the Volga at Stalingrad; a dam at Kakhovka on the Dnieper; an irrigation canal in Central Asia to fertilize the desert of Kara-Kum; the Volga-Don Canal; and planting of gigantic forest belts in the Ukraine and in the southern steppes to aid in drought control.

On April 17, 1951, the Soviet government announced that the Fourth Five Year Plan "has been successfully fulfilled and the most important plan goals have been considerably exceeded." Western scholars seriously questioned the validity of this claim, because the official report did not contain a single figure on actual physical output of industrial goods, but, in the words of one observer, was reduced "to long series of percentages related to some mysterious quantities which have never been publicized." Through painstaking research, however, Western scholars have concluded that at the end of 1950, Soviet production of many key raw industrial materials had exceeded their assigned quota, while the production of low priority goods lagged behind. Thus, it is believed that in 1950 the Soviet Union produced about 27.3 million tons of raw steel, 20.8 million tons of rolled steel, 264 million tons of coal, and 37.6 million tons of oil. Production of shoes, textiles, and household appliances was below the set target, as was the production of grain. The Fourth Five Year Plan, in other words, experienced the same uneven performance as its predecessors.

The recovery and progress in agriculture did not keep pace with industry. As in the past, the productivity and yield were low, while the number of people employed and production costs were high. There were good reasons for this discrepancy and lag. The war had devastated agriculture, destroying its implements, and reducing drastically the number of animals as well as people. In 1946 the Soviet Union had only 10.5 million horses, 47 million cattle, 10.4 million hogs, and 69.4 million sheep and goats. Corresponding figures for the year 1916 were 38.2 million, 58.4 million, 23 million, and 96.3 million respectively. These shortages resulted in low supplies of meat and dairy products, and they also affected power, since Soviet agriculture still depended heavily on draft animals. Moreover, as a nonpriority sector, agriculture received inadequate consideration in 1946 from the planners, who allocated only 12.3 billion rubles in contrast to 68.8 billion rubles for industry and 10 billion rubles for transport. Finally, in 1946 nature played havoc with the bold planning schemes in the form of a devastating drought, the worst since 1891–1892, which affected the Ukraine, the Volga, and other grain-producing areas of the Soviet Union. As in the past, the drought was followed by a terrible famine, the third of the Soviet period, causing thousands of casualties.[1]

Party and government authorities devised three different policies for dealing with the postwar agricultural crisis. The first was introduced on September 19, 1946, in the form of a joint resolution of the Central Committee and of the Council of Ministers, which attempted to restore some order in the rather chaotic postwar situation. The basic aim of the resolution was to recover for the collective farms the land and equipment which the peasants had appropriated for themselves during and after the war. On October 8, 1946, a special Council on Collective Farms was organized to deal with this situation, and a year later *Pravda* claimed that

[1] In December, 1963, Khrushchev publicly confirmed the occurrence of this famine, for which he held Stalin responsible.

some 14 million acres of misappropriated land had been recovered. The Council also dealt with other abuses hindering agricultural recovery, such as misuse and pilfering of the property of collective farms by local officials for personal advantage, inflated administrative staffs, and violation of numerous "democratic principles" of management of collective farms. The Council relieved many functionaries of their jobs and antagonized those peasants who were forced to give up all land in excess of the legal allotment. No information is available on whether these changes increased agricultural productivity.

The second postwar policy designed to increase agricultural productivity came in 1947 in the form of a Three Year Plan for the development of stock breeding. This new plan called for an increase by at least 50 per cent in the production of meat, lard, milk, butter, eggs, wool, and like products; a 20 per cent increase in the number of cattle, hogs, sheep, and goats; and an increase in the area sown with fodder crops. Apparently, the goals were not attained, because in April, 1949, the government reiterated these aims, and ordered that energetic measures be taken to end these discrepancies. Repeated Soviet attention to this problem in the 1950's and in the early 1960's indicates, however, that the problem is far from being solved.

The third major postwar policy in agriculture was the celebrated amalgamation of collective farms; i.e., a merging of several collectives into one gigantic farm. The aim of this policy, which was devised by Khrushchev, was threefold. First, it sought to increase agricultural productivity by a more thorough utilization of machinery; second, it sought to strengthen party control over the countryside; and, third, it sought to deprive peasants entirely of their private plots. The amalgamation experiment was first put to use in the Ukraine in 1947 on a trial basis. Because of its "success" there it became a nationwide policy in April, 1950. Officially, the Soviet press hailed the new policy as a "peaceful" and "voluntary" undertaking. In ruthlessness, however, the amalgamation almost equalled the original collectivization. Between April 5, 1950, and October, 1952, the number of collective farms was reduced from 254,000 to 97,000. There were indications that in many places these changes led to open revolts which the authorities suppressed with brutal force. This restlessness forced the party to abandon further amalgamation, at least for the time being, and, as in the past, the authorities placed the blame for the excesses on local party officials.

Peasant opposition to the amalgamation stemmed from official insistence that amalgamation be accompanied by the formation of *agrogoroda*, or farm cities of about 5,000 people. Each farm city was to provide peasants with the "luxuries" of city living, such as theaters, parks, and apartment houses. It was also hoped that the farm cities would make for greater efficiency and flexibility as well as tighter administrative control.

Under the new arrangement, peasants were to give up their private plots and be compensated by a plot in a common area, which would make peasant evasion of collective work more easily detectable by local authorities. It was this scheme of eliminating private plots that created the widespread peasant opposition and forced postponement of the whole experiment. The bitterness which this experiment generated hindered rather than improved grain production, which by 1950 was below a good prewar year in spite of the fact that the area of the USSR meanwhile had increased considerably.

On December 14, 1947, the peasants, and with them the rest of the population, were hard hit by the government's complex currency "reform." This reform sought to decrease the money in circulation, which war needs and occupation had increased. It also endeavored to curb the inflationary trend which had increased prices ten to fifteen times over the prewar level. It also aimed at eliminating from business the "speculative elements" which scarcity of goods and the abundance of money caused. To achieve these goals, the government abolished rationing, set up a state-fixed level of prices and ordered that all cash be exchanged for new currency at a rate of ten old rubles for one new ruble. By this low exchange rate, which reflected the real depreciation of the ruble, the government penalized all those who had hoarded cash as well as those who had saved their money in banks. The reform, however, had no effect on taxes, wages, and the innumerable fixed obligations to the state, which were to be paid at the same rates in the new currency.

Postwar economic recovery of the USSR was accompanied by a vast cultural and ideological "rehabilitation" of the people. The need for "rehabilitation" was obvious. To gain support of the people during the war, the regime appealed to patriotism, appeased the Church, de-emphasized Communist themes, and through innumerable other actions had instilled the hope that there was a more relaxed and more prosperous life in store for them. During the war, too, millions of Soviet civilians not only welcomed the Germans as liberators but were willing to cooperate with them. Millions of soldiers surrendered to the enemy, and additional millions moved across "foreign" territories, talked to "foreigners," and observed "foreign" ways of life. Regardless of circumstances or duration, the war exposed the Soviet people to "foreign" influences, and, in the words of the *Bolshevik*, the official journal of the party, deprived many of them "of the true Soviet information." The influences of the war, in other words, called for a postwar "brainwashing."

Postwar "rehabilitation" assumed different forms, the earliest of which was the development of the "elder brother" idea. The aim of this concept (inaugurated by Stalin in his celebrated victory speech of May 24, 1945, in which he singled out the Russian people as "the most outstanding nation of all the nations forming the Soviet Union," and subsequently developed further by Zhdanov) was threefold. First, it sought to depict the Great Russians as teachers, inspirers, helpers, great benefactors of freedom, cultural promoters and pioneers, and leaders of "socialist construction." Second, it sought to minimize the existence of influences other than Russian on the non-Russian minorities, such as Polish influence on the history of the Ukraine, or Islamic influence on the Turkic peoples of Central Asia. Finally, the "elder brother" concept sought to stress non-Russian solidarity with or servility to Russia and to emphasize similarities that united them rather than differences that divided them. Those who were skeptical of these aims and claims—and there were many—were *ipso facto* branded "bourgeois nationalists" and traitors. Immediately after the war, Stalin punished collectively several minorities for their cooperation with the Germans. Among those were Crimean Tartars, Kalmyks, Chechens, Estonians, Latvians, and Lithuanians, who were uprooted from their homes and scattered throughout Siberia. According to Khrushchev the Ukrainians were spared the same fate only because of their numbers.

The "elder brother" concept, of necessity, also affected the interpretation of Russian history. Russian contributions to all branches of knowledge and human endeavor were highly exaggerated. Russians were given credit for developing the steam engine, for producing the electric light, for inventing the radio, for pioneering aviation and aerodynamics, for discovering penicillin, and for priorities in innumerable other discoveries. Alongside this self-exaltation, Soviet propaganda depicted Russian history as one of constant foreign invasions (Mongol, Turkish, Tartar, Polish, Swedish, French, English, Japanese, American, and German), in which the Russians unilaterally and selflessly acted as liberators of peoples from alien yokes and as saviors of European civilization. This virtuous presentation of the Russian past (which made no mention of Russia's own vast conquests in Europe and Asia) was followed by denial of Western war efforts in World War II, and portrayal of the USSR as an innocent victim of Nazi aggression, which was allegedly encouraged by British and American "imperialists."

Another aim of such claims, many of which challenged basic and universally accepted historical facts, was to serve as a prelude to a concentrated anti-Western campaign, which moved into high gear during the summer of 1946. Through a series of decrees and official pronouncements, most of the Western authors were labelled corrupt. Western literature and art were declared decadent, antihuman, and sinister, and their reproduction was prohibited in the USSR. Those Soviet works of the past which, even through the slightest implication, pointed to Western influence on Russian development were severely criticized for alleged "servility," and their authors were branded traitors and "homeless cosmopolitans."

Viacheslav Molotov   *Andrei Gromyko*

The abnormal inflation of the superiority of the Soviet system was another major aspect of postwar rehabilitation. Stalin gave the official sanction for its development on February 9, 1946, in his analysis of victory in World War II, which, he said, meant that the Soviet social system had won, that the Soviet political system had won, that the Soviet armies had won, and that all their economic planning had won. Stalin's depiction of the victory over Germany as "the best proof" of the superiority of the Soviet system over all others meant the end of criticism in any form whatsoever of the Soviet system. Those who questioned the wisdom of this decision or who failed to demonstrate their patriotism to the satisfaction of their superiors were branded as traitors and *agent provocateurs,* as were those who disclosed "state secrets." Little or no effort was necessary to achieve the latter distinction because a decision of the Council of Ministers of the USSR of June 8, 1947, defined as state secrets all information of a military, political, and economic nature, and all information on scientific discoveries, inventions, and improvements of all kinds. By all these actions the Soviet government isolated itself and its people from the rest of the world, discouraged all social and cultural contacts with the West, including marriage of Soviet citizens with foreigners, which was prohibited on February 15, 1947, and drew around its territory an "iron curtain." The self-imposed isolation increased in intensity as time went on and was not modified until after Stalin's death, and then only on a limited scale. For Soviet minorities, for millions of former prisoners of war, and for all those who had been exposed to foreign influence during the war, the postwar "rehabilitation" was a bitter experience.

About one million Soviet citizens escaped the "rehabilitation" treatment. These were the "displaced persons" (DP's). At the end of the war there were some five million such individuals, consisting of former prisoners of war, *Ostarbeiters,* and those who had fled from the Soviet Union. Of these, about three million were in areas under Western military control, and some two million found themselves in areas under Soviet military control. At the Yalta Conference in February, 1945, Stalin, Roosevelt, and Churchill had agreed that all citizens of Allied countries should be repatriated at the end of the war. In accordance with this decision, the Soviet government established a number of repatriation missions throughout Western Europe to "assist" Soviet citizens, assembled in various DP camps managed by the United Nations Relief and Rehabilitation Administration (UNRRA), to return home. Some returned voluntarily, but hundreds of thousands refused repatriation. Ignorant of the reasons behind their unwillingness to return home, Western authorities, especially American, used force to help Soviet repatriation missions fulfill their task. Hundreds of people chose suicide rather than return home. Early in 1947, United States authorities halted forcible repatriation, but by that time some two million people had been returned to the USSR. Most of the remaining DP's, with UNRRA aid, eventually succeeded in making their homes in Australia, Canada, the United States, Latin America, and other countries of the Western world.

THE EAST EUROPEAN SATELLITE SYSTEM

The Soviet Union, as we have seen, suffered huge losses in World War II, but it also made tremendous gains. The first of these was the emergence of the USSR as one of the two great powers. This rise stemmed from the collapse of German power in Europe and that of the Japanese in Asia, and from the great weakening of English and French influence in world affairs. The second Soviet gain was territorial. The USSR acquired Southern Sakhalin and the Kurile Islands in the Far East, annexed the Tannu-Tuva Republic in Central Asia, secured from Czechoslovakia the Carpatho-Ukraine, took from Germany Königsberg and vicinity, gained from Finland the Petsamo region and Karelia, and retained all territories acquired during the period of the Nazi-Soviet Pact, namely Estonia, Latvia, Lithuania, Eastern Poland, Bessarabia, and Bukovina. The final major Soviet gain in World War II was the extension of the Russian Communist system into Poland, East Germany, Czechoslovakia, Rumania, Albania, Hungary, Bulgaria, and until 1948, Yugoslavia.

The extension of Soviet influence throughout Eastern Europe, commonly known as the creation of the satellite system, was a well-planned undertaking. It consisted of three decisive steps during the war and sev-

SOVIET TERRITORIAL GAINS IN EUROPE

1939 - 1949

U.S.S.R. in 1938

Soviet satellite states

Acquired by the U.S.S.R.
1939 - 1945

Communist
but not Soviet satellites

Sam H. Bryant

eral vital postwar moves. The first decisive step was taken early in the war in the form of organization in the USSR of National Liberation Committees for every East European country. Each committee was headed by high-ranking native Communists who had sought sanctuary in the USSR. Thus, the German National Liberation Committee was headed by Walter Ulbricht, the Czechoslovak by Klement Gottwald, the Polish by Jakub Berman and Wanda Wasilewska, the Hungarian by Matyas Rakosi, the Rumanian by Ana Pauker, and the Bulgarian by George Dimitrov. While a full study of the activity of these committees remains to be written, their aim seems to have been fourfold: they were to serve as nuclei for postwar governments "friendly" to the USSR; they were to act as recruiting agencies for military formations of East European nationals residing in the USSR; they were to be rallying points of resistance against Nazi occupation; and some were to compete with "bourgeois" governments-in-exile in London.

The second decisive Soviet step towards acquisition of a postwar sphere of influence in Eastern Europe was a concentrated diplomatic offensive. At first this offensive was directed towards the British. It started in December, 1941, during the Eden-Stalin conversations, when Stalin demanded British recognition of Soviet frontiers as of June, 1941; i.e., recognition of Soviet annexation of parts of Finland, Estonia, Latvia, Lithuania, Eastern Poland, Bessarabia, and Bukovina. Eden rejected these demands, as did Churchill during his visit to Moscow in August, 1942. The British were supported in their resistance by American officials, who felt that all boundary settlements should be postponed until the end of the war. In 1943, however, the Americans altered their position. The change came at the Teheran Conference in December, 1943, where Roosevelt sided with Stalin against Churchill's plan for invasion of the Balkans. The rejection of Churchill's scheme, which aimed at forestalling Soviet occupation of Eastern Europe, meant the division of Europe into two camps—the Western, controlled by England and the United States, and the Eastern, controlled by the USSR.

An immediate sign of postwar political realignment was Allied recognition of Soviet frontiers, based on the Curzon Line, with Poland being compensated by territories taken from East Prussia and those east of the Oder River. The Allies also tacitly recognized Estonia, Latvia, and Lithuania as parts of the USSR, and consented to the Soviet demand for Königsberg (which was renamed Kaliningrad) to be Russia's port in the Baltic. In May, 1944, the Soviets gained a further foothold in Eastern Europe when the British offered to recognize Soviet influence in Rumania in return for Soviet recognition of a similar British position in Greece. In October, 1944, the British went further and recognized the dominant Soviet influence in Rumania, Hungary, and Bulgaria, in return for a reciprocal arrangement in Yugoslavia. These diplomatic gains were greatly strengthened by armistice terms with Rumania (on September 13, 1944), Bulgaria (on October 28, 1944), and Hungary (on January 20, 1945), which granted Soviet authorities almost unrestricted political and economic rights in those countries, pending the signing of peace treaties. The Yalta Conference of February, 1945, acknowledged not only these rights but all other earlier decisions as well. To dispel growing Allied fears over the fate of Eastern Europe, however, Soviet leaders consented to allow Polish and Yugoslav representatives of the governments-in-exile to join the Communist-led governments, agreed to assist all the other liberated peoples of Eastern Europe to form broadly representative provisional governments, and pledged to establish, through free elections, governments "responsive to the will of the people." Events were soon to reveal, however, that when under Soviet influence people had strange and unusual wills.

The third decisive Soviet move towards gaining control over Eastern Europe took the form of direct negotiations with the Polish and Czechoslovak governments-in-exile. With the Czechoslovaks the task proved to be an easy one as the two countries had no outstanding differences. On the contrary, because of the German danger the Czechoslovaks had traditionally entertained strong Pan-Slavic and Russophile views. These views were further strengthened by memory of the Soviet offer of aid during the dismemberment of Czechoslovakia at Munich in September, 1938. On July 18, 1941, the two governments renewed diplomatic relations which had been interrupted since 1939, exchanged ministers, and pledged to aid and support each other in every way in the struggle against Nazi Germany. The Soviet government, in addition, "consented" to the formation of Czechoslovak military units on Soviet territory. By a special military agreement of September 27, 1941, the Soviet government recognized these units as part of the Czechoslovak armed forces, but retained for itself the right to approve appointment of the Supreme Military Commander and supervise operative and technical matters.

Meanwhile the Soviet government made additional moves aimed at attracting the Czechoslovak government to its side. In May, 1942, though not a party to it, the Soviets repudiated the Munich settlement and all policies that led to it, an action that forced the British and the French to do likewise. On December 12, 1943, the Soviet government signed with Czechoslovakia a twenty-year Treaty of Friendship, Mutual Assistance, and Post-War Collaboration. For the duration of the war, both governments promised to render each other military assistance against Nazi Germany and pledged not to enter into any negotiations or conclude any armistice or peace treaty without mutual consent. For the postwar period, both parties pledged that in the event one of them should find itself involved in a war with Germany or with any other state directly or indirectly united with Germany, the other would come to its support.

Both governments also promised not to conclude any alliance or take part in any coalition directed against the other, and agreed to maintain close and friendly relations, to develop economic cooperation on the widest possible scale, and to render each other every possible economic assistance after the war.

Following the conclusion of this treaty, which was hailed by the Soviet press as "an example of the strengthening of friendly relations of the Soviet Union with the European states," there began a gradual infiltration into the Czechoslovak government-in-exile by members of the Czechoslovak National Liberation Committee. At first, several assumed posts of unofficial observers in the Czechoslovak National Council in London. Later some were accepted into the government as Ministers-without-Portfolio or as advisors, in which capacity they served as the "eyes and ears" of Moscow. Early in 1945 when the Czechoslovak government began to prepare for its return to the homeland, several members of the National Liberation Committee obtained ministerial posts which they considered vital to their subsequent seizure of power; namely Interior, Information, and Agriculture. The stage was set for the extension of Soviet influence into Czechoslovakia.

Soviet transformation of Poland into a satellite encountered several difficulties, the foremost of which was the territorial problem. While in alliance with Nazi Germany, the Soviet Union, as we have noted, acquired some 76,500 square miles of Poland's eastern territories which were immediately incorporated into the USSR. In June, 1941, German forces occupied these territories. Polish leaders in London insisted that the Soviet government repudiate its part of the Nazi-Soviet alliance and restore the eastern territories to Poland. On July 30, 1941, the Soviet government, in an agreement which normalized Soviet-Polish relations, declared that the "Soviet-German treaties of 1939 concerning territorial changes in Poland have lost validity," but remained noncommittal as to the ultimate future of these territories. Their attitude remained unchanged until it became apparent that Germany would be defeated. Then the Soviets came forth with ethnic, cultural, linguistic, and religious claims to these territories. Polish rejection of these claims made genuine Soviet-Polish cooperation impossible.

The second problem hindering Soviet-Polish wartime cooperation was the military. In 1939, the Soviets captured some 300,000 Polish prisoners whom they scattered throughout Siberia. Following the Nazi invasion of the USSR, the Soviet government "consented" to the formation on Soviet territories of a Polish army. By a special agreement of August 14, 1941, the Soviet government recognized these forces as part of Polish armed forces subject to Polish laws and decrees, and retained for itself only the right to approve the appointment of the military commander and to supervise operative and technical matters. Early in December, 1941,

Stalin and the Polish Prime Minister, General Wladyslaw Sikorski, worked out additional details on this problem.

Trouble soon developed, however. Instead of the promised 96,000, Soviet authorities recruited only 44,000 Poles. For the remainder, they claimed lack of supplies and equipment. This was one major stumbling block. The other was Polish inquiry as to the whereabouts of several thousand missing Polish officers. Unable to satisfy the Poles, in 1942 Soviet authorities halted all further recruitment and ordered an immediate transfer of all Polish forces from the USSR to the Middle East. Relations further deteriorated because of Soviet charges that Polish diplomats were spying on behalf of Western powers. Meanwhile, the Soviet government organized new Polish army units within the framework of the Red Army, and publicly announced on March 1, 1943 the organization of a Union of Polish Patriots in Moscow to act as the "true" spokesman of Poland. In the midst of these vital developments, on April 13, 1943, the Germans announced discovery of mass graves of the missing Polish officers in the Katyn Forest near Smolensk. Polish willingness and Soviet unwillingness to submit the matter to an investigation by the International Red Cross led to the rupture of diplomatic relations between the Polish government in London and the USSR. On May 8, 1943, the Soviet government announced the formation of "Kosciuszko," a Polish division, and early in June, 1943, the Polish "Patriots" in Moscow adopted a program for Poland which called for far-reaching social and economic reforms, and which insisted that the Polish Eastern frontiers be a bridge and not an obstacle to an understanding with the USSR.

Because the Union of Polish Patriots was willing to cooperate with the Soviet Union and agree to all their demands, the Soviet government ignored the Polish government in London, and rejected its offers to restore diplomatic relations. On July 21, 1944, following the liberation of most of Eastern Poland, the "Patriots" from Moscow were joined in the city of Lublin by other Poles, and established the Polish Committee of National Liberation, which on December 31, 1944, declared itself the Provisional Government of Poland. Moscow extended recognition to the new body on January 5, 1945, and concluded with it in April, 1945, a twenty-year Treaty of Friendship. On July 6, 1945, the Western powers recognized the new coalition regime in Poland. It was a one-sided coalition because key posts—14 out of 21—were controlled by men who had received their political training in the USSR and who, in addition, could always rely on the support of the Soviet Armed Forces.

The extension of Soviet influence throughout Eastern Europe after 1945 was greatly simplified by the presence of the overwhelming Soviet military power. The Soviet army was not only the "liberator" but the absolute master of every country as well. In Poland it governed directly, and in all others its influence was indirect. But everywhere the Soviet army placed its full power behind the demands of members of the National Liberation Committees, and any opposition to these demands was called Fascist-inspired. Under these conditions no country of Eastern Europe was able to organize any effective opposition or resistance to these machinations. Those who made an attempt to do so were arrested, "tried," and executed. Soviet mastery over Eastern Europe was made easier, too, by the absence of Western military forces and the seeming indifference of Western statesmen over the fate of that area.

Next to the power of the Red Army, the extension of Soviet influence throughout Eastern Europe after 1945 was greatly aided by the skillful Communist political tactics. In every country the Communists created coalition governments which gave the appearance of representation, but which were incapable of competing for power. In Yugoslavia and Albania the coalition governments were known as the National Liberation Front; in Bulgaria it was the Fatherland Front; in Rumania the National Democratic Front; in Hungary the National Independence Front; in Poland the National Unity; and in Czechoslovakia the National Front. In each of these coalition governments, the Communist party was usually the best organized, had the complete backing of the Soviet army, and succeeded at the beginning in seizing key ministries, such as Interior, Information, Defense, Justice, and Agriculture. Control of these ministries enabled the Communists to muzzle some opposition groups, appease others, and eliminate all the rest. In Czechoslovakia the final elimination of opposition took the form of the dramatic death of Jan Masaryk, son of the founder of the Czechoslovak republic; in Poland it was the flight of Stanislaw Mikolajczyk, head of the Polish Peasant Party; and in Bulgaria the execution of Nikola Petkov, leader of the Agrarian Union.

The Soviets also extended their influence throughout Eastern Europe by control of the economies of these countries. They achieved this by such means as reciprocal trade agreements, the joint stock company system (such as the Soviet-Rumanian Oil Company, or the Soviet-Hungarian Danubian Navigation Company), investments, financial loans, and similar schemes. These measures were further strengthened by the appointment of Soviet citizens to key posts in satellite countries as managers, directors, and "experts." In Moscow in January, 1949, the USSR, Bulgaria, Czechoslovakia, Hungary, Rumania, and Poland (later joined by Albania) set up a Council of Mutual Economic Aid, commonly known as COMECON, or the Molotov Plan. The Plan had four major objectives: to see that the satellites aided in reconstruction of the USSR; to industrialize the East European countries; to create a Soviet-East European economic bloc; and to coordinate the economies of the satellites, who were forced to reject the Marshall Plan. This coordination placed the Soviet Union in a position where it could eliminate all other countries from trading directly

BILATERAL POLITICAL AND CULTURAL TREATIES BETWEEN THE USSR AND ITS SATELLITES

	USSR	Poland	Czecho-slovakia	Hungary	Rumania	Bulgaria	East Germany
USSR		FMA 4/21/1945	FMA 12/12/1943	FMA 2/18/1948	FMA 2/4/1948	FMA 3/18/1948	F 7/6/1950 CC 1/8/1952
Poland	FMA 4/21/1945		FMA 3/10/1947 CC 7/4/1947	FMA 6/18/1948 CC 1/31/1948	FMA 1/26/1949 CC 2/27/1948	FMA 5/29/1948 CC 6/28/1947	F 7/6/1950 CC 1/8/1952
Czechoslovakia	FMA 12/12/1943	FMA 3/10/1947 CC 7/4/1947		FMA 4/16/1949	FMA 7/21/1948 CC 10/14/1947	FMA 4/23/1948 CC 6/20/1947	F 6/23/1950
Hungary	FMA 2/18/1948	FMA 6/18/1948 CC 1/31/1948	FMA 4/16/1949		FMA 1/24/1948 CC 11/25/1947	FMA 7/16/1948 CC 10/29/1947	F 6/26/1950
Rumania	FMA 2/4/1948	FMA 1/26/1949 CC 2/27/1948	FMA 7/21/1948 CC 10/14/1947	FMA 1/24/1948 CC 11/25/1947		FMA 1/16/1948 CC 6/20/1947	F 8/22/1950 CC 9/20/1950
Bulgaria	FMA 3/18/1948	FMA 5/29/1948 CC 6/28/1947	FMA 4/23/1948 CC 6/20/1947	FMA 7/16/1948 CC 10/29/1947	FMA 1/16/1948 CC 6/20/1947		F 8/25/1950 CC 5/5/1952
East Germany		F 6/6/1950 CC 1/8/1952	F 6/23/1950	F 6/26/1950	F 8/22/1950 CC 9/20/1950	F 8/25/1950 CC 5/5/1952	

FMA = Friendship and Mutual Aid   CC = Cultural Cooperation   F = Friendship

SOURCE: Zbigniew K. Brzezinski, *The Soviet Bloc: Unity and Conflict.* Rev. ed. (New York: Praeger, 1961), p. 109.

with the satellites, and could restrict all foreign trade of these countries to the USSR.

Soviet economic influence and control of Eastern Europe manifested itself in many other ways. The most immediately noticeable was the nationalization of large industry followed by that of all lesser enterprises. Complete nationalization of industry in Bulgaria took place in December, 1947; in Rumania in June, 1948; and in Hungary in December, 1949. These nationalization laws were accompanied by planned industrial expansions. Yugoslavia, in 1947, was the first of these countries to announce a Five Year Plan. Czechoslovakia announced its own in October, 1948, and Poland, Bulgaria, Hungary, and Rumania followed soon after. In each country, heavy and war industries were given preference, while light and consumer industries were given lip service.

Alongside industrial expansion, each satellite country experienced a vast agricultural revolution. At first the new regimes decreed the division among peasants of all large estates of nobles, and lands belonging to the state and to the Church. Beginning with Poland on September 6, 1944, and ending with Bulgaria on March 12, 1946, expropriation decrees were issued in each of the East European countries. The purpose of this reform was fourfold: it eliminated the landlord class, which was considered "dangerous" to the new regime; it helped to reward the "faithful"; it helped to win the support of those who were economically insecure; and it paved the way for collectivization. Everywhere the agricultural reform in Eastern Europe was accompanied by excesses and deliberate stimulation of class hatred.

Between 1946 and 1948 all East European satellites adopted new constitutions patterned on the Soviet constitution. The aims of these constitutions were clear. First, they legalized the liquidation of political forces opposed to Soviet domination. In Bulgaria, Albania, Yugoslavia, and Rumania, this meant formalizing the abolition of monarchies; in Hungary, that of the Regency; and in Poland and Czechoslovakia that of the nationalist republican regimes. Second, the new constitutions provided "the peoples' democracies" with a legal framework for implementation of the Communist economic, political, and social program. Each constitution empowered its government with the right to eliminate private property, to monopolize trade, to nationalize industry, and to collectivize agriculture. Each constitution vested legislative power in popularly "elected" legislative assemblies which met twice a year for a short period, and delegated their rights to steering committees known as presidiums.

After 1945 all satellite states were subjected to a strong Russification policy. The main instrument of this policy was the local Communist party and its auxiliaries, which in the last analysis were nothing but subservient branches of the Communist party of the USSR. Unconditional and blind devotion to the Soviet Union was the first prerequisite for party membership, and each new member accepted was further indoctrinated with pro-Russian attitudes. Outside the party, the Russification process was carried on through schools, theaters, newspapers, radio, and various societies organized for that purpose. Glorification of Russian achievement was emphasized everywhere, and Russian language, history, and literature were among the leading subjects in schools on all levels.

The Soviets encountered considerable opposition to the extension of their influence in every East European country, but only in Yugoslavia was this opposition successful. Commonly known as "Titoism," the Yugoslav opposition to Soviet domination developed gradually. It stemmed, among other things, from the Soviets' exaggeration of their efforts and belittling of Yugoslav military achievements; from Soviet opposition to Tito's ambitions to establish control over the Balkans; from Yugoslav resistance to Soviet attempts to establish joint companies to exploit Yugoslav resources and to plant Soviet intelligence agents in the Yugoslav army, the Yugoslav Communist party, secret police, and all other sensitive organs of the system. Soviet-Yugoslav tension remained a "family affair" for some three years. It came into the open early in 1948, when Stalin rejected the Yugoslav bid to conclude a trade treaty, ordered withdrawal of the Soviet military mission from Yugoslavia, and accused the Yugoslav Communist party of an undemocratic and unfriendly attitude. The climax came on June 28, 1948—the anniversary of Kossovo and Sarajevo—when to the astonishment of the entire world Stalin expelled Yugoslavia from the Cominform.[1] This was followed by all-out political and economic warfare, and even actual armed skirmishes. Tito resisted all Soviet and Soviet-inspired satellite pressures. His successful defiance of Stalin encouraged other satellite Communists to attempt to do likewise. Their efforts, however, were not successful, and many "Titoists" in various East European countries were executed. Titoism, or other-than-Moscow-directed movement towards communism, continued to develop, and with considerable Western help has outlived Stalin.

FOREIGN POLICY IN THE 1940's

During the 1940's, the Soviet quest for security for the territorial base of the revolution passed through three distinct phases: an "Unholy Alliance" with Hitler against the Western Powers; a "Grand," or "Strange" Alliance with the Western Powers against the Axis; and a "Monolithic" Alliance with the satellites against the Western Powers. These alliances greatly

[1] For the full text of this document, see Appendix 31.

increased the territory as well as the military and economic might of the USSR because, in every case, the Soviets succeeded in retaining all the gains of preceding alliances.

The Nazi-Soviet Pact of August, 1939, as we noted earlier, was a quite lucrative bargain for the USSR. In less than two years the Soviets added to their territorial base parts of Finland, Estonia, Latvia, Lithuania, Eastern Poland, Bukovina, and Bessarabia, or a net gain of 179,088 square miles and some 22,567,000 people. These gains had an immense strategic value. They strengthened the Soviet position around Leningrad and in the Baltic, placed Soviet armies within striking distance of Central Europe and the Danube Basin, and improved the Soviet position in the Black Sea area. So advantageous were the new additions that the Soviets wasted no time in incorporating these areas into the USSR. Neither did they conceal their appetite for further gains. The latter factor heightened German suspicion and contributed eventually to the Nazi invasion of the USSR.

Immediately, the spectacular progress of the Nazi invasion of the USSR annulled all the Soviet gains. This same invasion, however, drew the Soviets to the side of all those opposed to the Nazi "new order" in Europe and laid the foundations for the "Grand Alliance." Churchill was the first to cast aside politics and personal feelings in the face of the Nazi menace. The day after the Nazi invasion, he offered the Soviets friendship, alliance, and "whatever help we can." On July 12, this offer was formalized in a Protocol signed by the British and Soviet governments, wherein both agreed neither "to negotiate nor conclude an armistice or treaty of peace except by mutual agreement" and "to render each other assistance and support of all kinds in the present war against Hitlerite Germany." Shortly after Churchill's commitment, convinced that the Soviet Union had the capacity to resist the Nazis, President Roosevelt extended American Lend-Lease aid to the USSR. Shipments of needed supplies began immediately and were increased considerably following the conclusion in Moscow on October 1, 1941 of an interim agreement. By the middle of 1942, the United States had sent 2,000 light and medium tanks, and 1,300 planes. During the same period, British shipments to the USSR included 2,400 tanks and 1,800 planes. Under a new Master Lend-Lease Agreement of June 11, 1942, the Soviet Union obtained tanks, planes, ships, trucks, jeeps, telephone equipment, machine tools, shoes, textiles, electric furnaces, aluminum, copper, steel, food, seeds, oil, and large quantities of other war supplies worth some thirteen billion dollars in all. Struggling for their very existence, the Soviets welcomed these supplies and pressed for more. The bulk of the shipments reached the USSR through Vladivostok, Murmansk, and Iran. Because the Iranian supply route was the safest, late in August, 1941, Soviet and British forces occupied Iran for the duration of the war.

The "Grand Alliance" was indeed a "strange alliance." From its inception it was plagued by fear, mistrust, and suspicion. Many factors contributed to this unusual atmosphere. In the early stages of the war the foremost cause of suspicion was the problem of the "Second Front." Hard-pressed by the Germans, the Soviets were extremely anxious to have opened large-scale military operations in Western Europe to relieve some of the pressure on themselves. The British and Americans sympathized with the Soviet problem, but were in no position to offer immediate relief. A full-scale invasion across the English Channel required, as events in June, 1944, were to confirm, a mammoth effort for which neither Britain nor the United States was adequately prepared. Both countries were being drained by supplies shipped to the Soviet Union under the Lend-Lease program, and both were fighting powerful enemy forces in the Pacific, China, Southeast Asia, and Africa. The Soviets seem never to have been able to understand or appreciate these other Allied engagements, and Western attempts to reach a compromise proved largely futile because the Soviets "invariably interpreted such Allied efforts in the worst possible light."

In the long run, however, Western inability to open the second front early in the war proved beneficial to the Soviets, as they were able to profit from the weakness of their Allies by extracting far-reaching political concessions. These included: Allied recognition of Soviet incorporation of parts of Finland, Estonia, Latvia, Lithuania, Eastern Poland, Bukovina, and Bessarabia; and Allied recognition of Soviet interests in Central Europe, the Balkans, the Middle and Far East. In return for these gains, the Soviets made two conciliatory gestures. On January 1, 1942, the Soviet Union joined twenty-five other states in signing the so-called Declaration of the United Nations—a broad statement of principles similar to the Atlantic Charter, and on May 22, 1943, Stalin dissolved the Comintern.

The anti-Axis coalition tried to solve the complex problems of wartime and postwar cooperation through various agreements, meetings, and conferences. Of these, the following were the most influential: The Harriman-Beaverbrook-Stalin talk in September, 1941; the Eden-Stalin talk of December, 1941; the Sikorski-Stalin talk of December, 1941; the Anglo-Soviet treaty of May 26, 1942; the Master Lend-Lease Agreement of June 11, 1942; the Churchill-Stalin talks of August, 1942; the Casablanca Conference (Churchill-Roosevelt-DeGaulle) of January, 1943; the Moscow Conference of Foreign Ministers (Molotov-Eden-Hull) of October, 1943; the Teheran Conference (Stalin-Churchill-Roosevelt) of November, 1943; the Cairo Conference (Roosevelt-Churchill-Chiang Kai-shek) of December, 1943; the Czechoslovak-Soviet Treaty of December 12, 1943; the Breton Woods Conference of July, 1944; the Dumbarton Oaks Conference of August–September, 1944; the Stalin-Churchill talk of October, 1944; the Franco-Soviet Treaty of December 10, 1944; the Yalta Conference (Stalin-Churchill-Roosevelt) of February, 1945; the San Francisco Conference of April, 1945; and the Potsdam Conference (Stalin-Truman-Churchill-Atlee) of July–August, 1945. As far as Soviet security was concerned, the most momentous of these gatherings were the Teheran, Yalta, and Potsdam Conferences.

The Teheran Conference (November 28–December 1, 1943) was the first summit meeting of the Big Three and proved to be a major triumph of Soviet diplomacy. A great share of that triumph resulted from Western, especially American, overzealousness in attempting to remove all possible obstacles responsible for Soviet suspicion of Allied action. It also stemmed from Soviet victories over the Nazis in the face of slow Western progress towards opening the Second Front. In return for Soviet agreement to join the United Nations (on condition that the executive organ of the new international body would have no power to make binding decisions), and to enter the war against Japan after the defeat of Germany, the Western Powers at Teheran passively agreed to Soviet annexation of the Baltic states; formally acknowledged Soviet incorporation of Eastern Poland, Bessarabia, and Bukovina into the USSR; compensated Poland for its losses with Silesia, Pomerania, and East Prussia (except Königsberg); abandoned Churchill's plan for invasion of the Balkans and North Italy as well as his scheme to create a Danube Federation; and by these commitments confined their interest to Western Europe. None of these commitments was definite. Each, however, laid the ground for the Yalta and Potsdam Conferences and for the postwar division of Europe into two parts—Western, under British and American influence, and Eastern, under Soviet control, with Germany a potential battleground of the future.

Problems which the Teheran Conference had failed to solve, and those which had arisen subsequently, were the subject of the second summit meeting of the war at Yalta in the Crimea, in February, 1945. At Yalta, more than at Teheran, Soviet military victories were the lever for Soviet gains. Allied forces were in control of France, the Low Countries, most of Italy, and had yet to subdue Japan, while Soviet armies were in complete control of the Baltic states, Poland, most of Slovakia, Hungary, Rumania, Bulgaria, Yugoslavia, and were massing for the final assault on Vienna and Berlin. Three problems figured prominently on the agenda of the Yalta Conference: the German, the Polish, and the Far Eastern. On the German problem, the Big Three resolved that Germany be totally disarmed; that Nazism and German militarism be totally destroyed; that those responsible for war crimes be tried and punished; that all German industry capable of military production be eliminated or controlled; that Germany make compensation in kind for the damage she had caused; that German frontiers, both eastern and western, be altered; and that Germany be divided into four zones of occupation—Soviet, British, American, and French. The same arrangement was worked out for the occupation of Austria.

The Yalta Agreement also provided a special status for Vienna and Berlin—that of joint occupation and rule by all four powers as a symbol of the Grand Alliance that won the war. The Western Powers held as self-evident that the joint occupation of Berlin by all four powers, of and by itself assumed free access to the city located in the heart of the Soviet zone. They asked no specific provisions for such free access in order not to offend the Soviets, and they also abandoned Berlin "as the most desirable objective for the forces of the Western Allies." The absence of Western forces in Berlin and of free access to the city at the time of the German collapse placed the Soviet Union in an advantageous position. To reach their respective sectors of Berlin, the Western Powers had to pass through the Soviet zone. From the start, the Soviet authorities prescribed limited air, rail, and road connections with Berlin for the Allies, and forbade any communication except by means of these routes. These restrictions prepared the ground for trouble of the first magnitude.

On the Polish problem the Big Three agreed that the Curzon Line, or Molotov-Ribbentrop Line, be the basis for the new Polish frontier in the East; that Poland be compensated at German territorial expense; that the Moscow-sponsored government for Poland be "reorganized on a broader democratic basis with the inclusion of democratic leaders from Poland itself and from Poles abroad"; and that after reorganization the government should hold "free and unfettered elections," on the basis of universal suffrage and secret ballot, as soon as possible.

The Far Eastern problem was the third major issue discussed at Yalta. The Soviets agreed to enter the war against Japan "in two or three months" after the German surrender, on three conditions: that the status quo in Outer Mongolia be preserved; that the Kurile Islands be handed over to the Soviet Union; and that Russian rights "violated" by the Russo-Japanese War of 1904–1905 be restored. These included: (1) the return of Southern Sakhalin to the USSR; (2) internationalization of Dairen; (3) lease of Port Arthur as a Soviet naval base; (4) joint Soviet-Chinese operation of the Chinese Eastern and South Manchurian Railroads; and (5) recognition of Soviet pre-eminent interests in Dairen and Manchuria. While Soviet rights in Outer Mongolia and Manchuria were conditional on Chiang Kai-shek's approval, which Roosevelt was to obtain, the Big Three agreed that Soviet claims "shall be unquestionably fulfilled after Japan has been defeated." The decisions at Yalta have been variously interpreted. However interpreted, these decisions—based in large measure on an erroneous Western estimate of the situation and on a mistaken appraisal of Soviet intentions—were a major triumph of Soviet diplomacy of World War II.

The "Big Three" at Yalta, February, 1945.

Two months after Yalta, Roosevelt met sudden death from a cerebral hemorrhage, leaving Vice-President Harry S. Truman in his vacated post. The change in American leadership had no effect on the military course of the war as Allied forces rolled victoriously over Germany, and on May 8, 1945, at Rheims, forced the Nazis to accept unconditional surrender. The change of American leadership had an important bearing on diplomatic relations, however. This became evident during the Potsdam Conference (July 17–August 2, 1945), which convened to deal with the complex problems created by the German collapse. The Potsdam Conference differed in several respects from the Teheran and Yalta meetings. First, at Potsdam the three leaders did not draw together "in the same warm, personal association in a common cause as at the two wartime meetings." Second, at Potsdam they could neither submerge nor postpone the issues that might estrange them. Third, the conferees at Potsdam met under the cloud of the first successful explosion of an atomic bomb in the proving grounds at Los Alamos, New Mexico. Finally, the chief figures met in an atmosphere of increased charges and countercharges of "bad faith" and of violations of wartime pledges. These signs indicated that while the Potsdam Conference would reach agreement on some, it would end in failure on other problems.

The Big Three addressed themselves at Potsdam to two main problems: the postwar settlement in Europe; and the achievement of military victory over Japan. In view of the Nazi collapse, the future of Germany was the main item on the agenda. The victors reaffirmed the decisions of Yalta, recognized the Four Power Zones of occupation and agreed that the aims of the Allied occupation policy in Germany were: disarmament; demilitarization; de-Nazification; trial of war criminals; democratization of German political, educational, and judicial systems; decentralization of German political institutions; and de-industrialization of German war and heavy industries. As far as it was practicable the Germans were to receive uniform treatment in all four occupation zones, and, during the period of occupation, Germany was to be treated as a single economic unit, administered by the Allied Control Council with headquarters in Berlin. The victors approved the mass transfer of German population from Poland, Czechoslovakia, Rumania, Hungary, and Yugoslavia into the four zones of occupation. They also agreed to take jointly all necessary measures "to assure that Germany never again will threaten her neighbors or the peace of the world," but stated that it was not their intent "to destroy or enslave the German people."

Several problems plagued the victors at Potsdam. These were: (1) Soviet demand that Germany pay twenty billion dollars in reparations, ten of which would go to the USSR; (2) Soviet unilateral disposition of German territories east of the Oder-Neisse Rivers; (3) Soviet high-handed rule in Rumania and Bulgaria; (4) composition of the Soviet-sponsored government in Poland; (5) Soviet bid to gain the trusteeship over Libya; and (6) Soviet insistence on a voice in the Straits. The Western Powers interpreted the Soviet *faits accompli* and demands for further expansion of Soviet influence as a threat to their safety. The Soviets, on the other hand, saw in Western reluctance to yield to their demands an anti-Soviet sign. To solve these problems, and to deal with those that might develop in the future, the Big Three agreed at Potsdam to establish the Council of Foreign Ministers consisting of the USSR, United States, Britain, and France. Their attempts to find solutions to these postwar problems form a record of failure and frustration.

The Potsdam conferees displayed considerable unanimity on the prosecution of the war against Japan. The military chiefs formulated a common course of action, while political leaders prepared the wording of an ultimatum to Japan known as the Potsdam Declaration. The latter called for immediate and unconditional Japanese surrender; restoration of Manchuria, Formosa, and the Pescadores to China; relinquishment of all Pacific Islands acquired since 1914, and all other territories "taken by violence and greed"; granting of independence to Korea; destruction of war industries; trial of war criminals; and reorganization of Japan, with Allied help, along democratic lines. Japanese rejection of those conditions led to the atomic bombing of Hiroshima on August 6, and Nagasaki on

August 9. On the latter date Soviet forces under Marshals Malinovsky and
Kiril A. Meretskov (1897–   ) invaded and commenced the occupation of
Southern Sakhalin, North Korea, and Manchuria. On August 14, the Japanese accepted the terms of the Potsdam Declaration, and on September 2,
1945, aboard the USS *Missouri* in Tokyo Bay, they signed the surrender
papers. At last World War II was over, but peace was far from restored.

There were many signs before, during, and after the Potsdam Conference which suggested that, in spite of the terrible losses by victor and
vanquished alike, genuine peace was beyond the reach of man. The end
of war saw the eclipse of Nazi power in Europe and of Japanese imperialism in Asia. These eclipses created a vast power vacuum. The defeated
Germans and Japanese were in no position to fill it; neither were the
British, nor the French, nor the Chinese, who, although victorious,
emerged from the war greatly weakened in terms of power. The task of
filling this vast power vacuum fell accordingly on the United States and
the Soviet Union—the two colossi—who emerged from the war as super
powers in a category by themselves. Peace of the world depended on
their cooperation, but events soon revealed that the two giants could not
find grounds for genuine cooperation.

Literature on the development, manifestations, and objectives of the
"cold war," as the period after 1945 is commonly known, is voluminous
and controversial. The following constants are generally accepted as the
"causes" responsible for the deterioration of East-West relations: (1) the
enduring legacy of Soviet-Western suspicion; (2) the impatient Soviet
quest for security which, while understandable, endangered the security
of the Western Powers; (3) Soviet tendency to view the West as an
enemy, once the common foe had been defeated; (4) Soviet fear of
United States atomic power; (5) Soviet attempt to compensate this
imbalance of power through control of large territories in Eastern Europe; (6) the rapid American dismantlement of its war machine, and
withdrawal from Europe and Asia; (7) the sudden American decision in
August, 1945 to end all Lend-Lease aid; (8) Soviet envy of the unprecedented American economic growth and expansion during the war, in
contrast to their own vast destruction; (9) Soviet use of the chaos of war
and the misery of its immediate aftermath to propagate political unrest
wherever possible; (10) Soviet utilization of Italian, French, and other
Communist parties to extend Soviet influence beyond their "legitimate"
sphere; (11) Stalin's own xenophobia, imperial ambitions, and sense of
insecurity; and (12) Soviet belief, based on Marxist-Leninist tradition,
that all of Europe, indeed the whole world, must eventually fall under the
sway of Moscow's spell.

After 1945 the aim of Soviet foreign policy was quite simple. It
sought to retain and consolidate Soviet influence in areas the USSR had
gained during World War II, and, using all possible means, to expand

that influence into the regions the Western Powers considered to be theirs. In the Far East, realization of these goals proved to be relatively easy, thanks to the collapse of the Japanese empire with the resulting power vacuum, the far-reaching Anglo-American concessions at Yalta, and the weakness of Nationalist Chinese forces. Under the Yalta arrangement, as mentioned earlier, the USSR recovered everything Imperial Russia had lost to Japan in the war of 1904–1905: namely, Southern Sakhalin, control of the Chinese Eastern and South Manchurian Railroads, and the ports of Dairen and Port Arthur. Nominally, these Soviet gains were at the expense of Japan. Actually, however, they were at the expense of China, since, as one authority noted, "had Soviet Russia not claimed the fruits of Czarist imperialism, China would have recovered the position in Manchuria which she had lost fifty years ago to Russia and Japan." These Soviet gains, plus the severance of Outer Mongolia, were formally acknowledged by China in a Sino-Soviet treaty of August 15, 1945, ironically called a "Treaty of Friendship and Alliance," in return for the Soviet pledge "to render to China moral support and aid in military supplies and other material resources." This support, however, failed to materialize. Instead, Soviet forces seized and removed plants, equipment, and materiel in Manchuria as "war booty," and refused the Nationalists the right to use Dairen as a port of entry for their troops. These actions contributed greatly to the dramatic deterioration of Nationalist forces in 1947–1948, and to the remarkable Chinese Communist advances to the banks of the Yangtze and beyond. Throughout this period, the Soviet government maintained a façade of "neutrality" and "non-interference" in Chinese affairs. However, on October 2, 1949, the day following the proclamation of the Chinese People's Republic, the USSR granted diplomatic recognition to the new regime in China, and in December, 1949, Mao Tse-tung went to Moscow to negotiate a new Sino-Soviet alliance.

In the Near and Middle East after 1945, Soviet interests were most intense in Iran, Turkey, and Greece. The objective was to gain access to the Persian Gulf and control of the Straits. In Iran, Soviet interests seem to have been in a relatively strong position, guaranteed by the presence of Soviet forces in Northern Iran which had been dispatched there in 1941 to safeguard the flow of Lend-Lease supplies to the Soviet Union. Under a treaty of January 29, 1942, among Iran, the USSR and Britain, all Allied troops were to respect the territorial integrity, sovereignty, and independence of Iran and were to withdraw within six months after the end of the war. The Soviets did not observe strictly these provisions. They denied the Iranian authorities access, for instance, to Soviet-controlled areas, supported the local Communist (Tudeh) party, and refused to evacuate at the end of the war. In September, 1945, with Soviet backing, the Tudeh party requested autonomy for Persian Azerbaidzhan, and when the request was denied, an Autonomous Azerbaidzhan Republic was proclaimed under veteran Communist Ja'far Pishevari. On January 19, 1946, Iran appealed to the United Nations, charging the USSR with interference in its domestic affairs, and combined United Nations-United States pressure early in March, 1946, forced the Soviets reluctantly to evacuate their forces from northern Iran.

Soviet interest in Turkey met the same fate. As early as May 20, 1945, the Soviet government unilaterally denounced the Soviet-Turkish Treaty of Friendship and Neutrality (signed on December 17, 1925 and renewed on March 24, 1941), and demanded the cession of Kars and Ardahan, joint Russo-Turkish control of the Straits, and a new alliance of friendship along the lines of those signed with the East European countries. The Turks rejected these demands. Early in 1946, the Soviets rejected the United States' mediation proposal for a revision of the Montreaux Convention of 1936, and on August 7, 1946, announced new demands. These were: (1) that the Straits be open at all times to merchant ships of all countries; (2) that the Straits be open at all times to warships of the Black Sea powers; (3) that the warships of non-Black Sea powers be denied passage through the Straits, "except in cases specially provided for"; (4) that the Straits be operated by the Black Sea powers; and (5) that the Straits be defended jointly by the USSR and Turkey. Since neither Britain, Turkey, nor the United States favored the Soviet arrangement, the Soviets shelved the entire matter.

In Greece, Soviet interest manifested itself in the support, both direct and indirect, of the Communist-led Greek Liberation Front (EAM), and the Greek People's Liberation Army (ELAS). This support was contrary to the wartime Soviet-British understanding which made the British responsible for the liberation of Greece and for the restoration of order. A Communist regime in Greece, however, offered the Soviets a prospect of realizing complete control of the Balkans, seizing the Straits, and establishing Soviet influence in the Eastern Mediterranean. The monarchist victory at the polls resulted in a bitter civil war in December, 1946, veiled Yugoslav and Bulgarian intervention, and a United Nations investigation. Determined British resistance, American aid in the form of the Truman Doctrine, and development of the Yugoslav-Soviet dispute in June, 1948, however, spoiled Soviet efforts to turn Greece into a satellite as the first step towards seizure of the Straits.

In Eastern Europe, as we noted earlier, the Soviets were able to realize their goals with no appreciable difficulty because Soviet armed forces were in actual control of the area. In every country of Eastern Europe the Soviets installed governments in which native, but Moscow-trained, Communists were assured strategic posts. With these governments the USSR then signed long-term bilateral mutual assistance treaties and alliances (Czechoslovakia, December, 1943; Yugoslavia and Poland, April, 1945; Rumania and Hungary, February, 1948; and Bulgaria, March,

1948). These alliances were further interlocked by a dozen or more bilateral agreements among the states of Eastern Europe. All of these treaties emphasized the pledge of mutual assistance in case of direct renewed German aggression, or aggression of "any other state which would unite with Germany directly or in any other form in such a war." The Soviets also strengthened their military and political influence in Eastern Europe through various barter agreements, reparations, formation of binational stock companies, investments, direct loans, control of key industries, and wholesale export of cultural, social, economic, administrative and legal institutions. By these actions the Soviets turned the East European countries into satellites, and curbed all of their contacts with the non-Communist world. These actions, however, aroused Western suspicion and led to vigorous counter measures.

The Soviets did not accept Western opposition to their plans in Iran, Turkey, and Greece, nor Western criticism of Soviet machinations in Eastern Europe. On February 9, 1946, Stalin delivered his now-famous pre-election speech, wherein he "dropped the front of agreeable and co-operative meeting of minds," reaffirmed the basic Communist teachings on the causes and nature of capitalist wars, blamed the West for World War II, dropped the pretense that the defeat of Germany eliminated the danger of war, lauded the superiority of the Soviet system, and called for a "new mighty upsurge in the national economy" that would treble pre-war production. This gloomy outlook on relations with the non-Communist world—made a month before Churchill's famous "Iron Curtain" speech on March 5, 1946, at Fulton, Missouri—set the pattern for Soviet behavior. Thereafter, the Soviets automatically branded as a "warmonger" anyone opposed to their actions, and denounced all attempts to bring stability to the postwar world as "smoke screen for capitalist expansion." Under those conditions it was impossible to find grounds for a *modus vivendi*.

The "cold war" entered a new phase in 1947 following the announcement of the Truman Doctrine, on March 12, 1947. The aim of the Doctrine was simple. It sought to render immediate assistance to Greece and Turkey, then under Soviet pressure, in order to prevent a repetition of what had happened to various states of Eastern Europe. It was official notice that the United States would do everything possible to "contain" Soviet expansion. Soviet reaction was prompt. The Truman Doctrine was denounced as "a fresh intrusion of the USA into the affairs of other states," a violation of the United Nations Charter, and an example of the United States postwar policy of imperialism.

Soviet reaction to the Marshall Plan was even more violent. Proposed on June 5, 1947, the Marshall Plan was a coordinated, long-range program of massive assistance aimed at bolstering the economic recovery of Europe. All European countries ruined by war, including the USSR, were invited to prepare a list of their needs, and a conference was convened in

Paris late in June, 1947, to work out details. On June 29, the Soviets refused to participate in the program, withdrew from the Conference, and denounced the Marshall Plan as "The American Plan for the enthrallment of Europe"; American interference in the affairs of other countries; a "glaring example" of violation of the United Nations Charter; "an attempt to split Europe into two camps"; and a striving of American monopolies "to avert the approaching depression." Because they interpreted the Marshall Plan as an anti-Soviet act, the Soviets forced Poland and Czechoslovakia to withdraw their acceptance of American aid.

The Soviets' formal answer to the Marshall Plan was the partial resurrection, in September, 1947, of the Comintern under the label of Cominform (Communist Information Bureau, with headquarters in Belgrade, and, after the Yugoslav-Soviet dispute, in Bucharest), and organization in January, 1949, of the COMECON, with headquarters in Moscow. The aim of these organizations was manifold. They were to coordinate policies of the Communist parties; to oppose actively the Marshall Plan (in France and Italy, Communist opposition led to general strikes and considerable labor violence); to serve as instruments to enforce unquestioning adherence to the Moscow line; to promote the consolidation of Communist power in Eastern Europe; to act as avenues of intra-East European planning and integration; to serve as a vehicle for Moscow's struggle with Tito; and to be a symbol of Communist unity and cooperation, and a symbol of a permanent cold war against the West.

Of all the postwar problems, none contributed more to East-West antagonism than the German dilemma. The dilemma stemmed from what one observer rightly called "a schizophrenic attitude" of all powers towards Germany; that is, their fear of Germany's resurrection, their willingness to punish the Germans, and their eagerness to win the Germans over in view of Germany's geographic, demographic, and industrial situation. This attitude was clearest in the postwar German policy of the Soviets. At first, the Soviets favored an exploitative policy, insisted on heavy reparations, dismantled German industrial plants, sought to have a voice in the Ruhr, and did everything possible to weaken Germany industrially and to aid Soviet postwar reconstruction. Afraid, however, that a mere policy of revenge might align the Germans against the USSR, the Soviets shifted their stand. The shift came on July 10, 1946, at the Paris meeting of the Council of Foreign Ministers. The new Soviet policy on Germany, as outlined by Molotov, consisted of the following points: (1) the "spirit of revenge" ought not to be a guide in the framing of a treaty with Germany; (2) it would not be "in the interests of the world's economy and tranquility in Europe" to destroy Germany as a state, or to destroy her main industrial centers and turn her into an agricultural nation; (3) Germany ought not to be destroyed, but transformed "into a democratic and peace-loving state which, alongside of agriculture, would have its own industry and foreign trade, but which would be deprived of the economic and military potentiality to rise again as an aggressive force"; (4) Germany ought neither to be dismembered into several autonomous states nor federalized but unified along "democratic lines"; (5) the USSR was "in principle in favor of the conclusion of a peace treaty with Germany"; and (6) before concluding such a treaty, Germany must establish a single, responsible, democratic government "capable of extirpating the last vestiges of fascism," and able to fulfill all its obligations towards the Allies, especially reparations. The American answer to this Soviet bid for German support came in a speech by Secretary of State James F. Byrnes, on September 6, 1946, at Stuttgart, in which he made similar comments concerning the German economy and announced that the United States did not consider the German eastern frontiers as final. These two speeches, in the opinion of many observers, are regarded as "the unofficial funeral of the Potsdam agreement and the overt beginning of a race for Germany between the Western Powers and the USSR."

The race for Germany prevented the working out of a common policy for Germany by the Council of Foreign Ministers. Meetings of the Foreign Ministers were held in Paris (April–July, 1946), New York (November–December, 1946), Moscow (March, 1947), and London (November–December, 1947); but the sessions of all these conferences were devoted almost entirely to endless recriminations and propaganda speeches; and the meetings ended in utter failure. The sessions of the Allied Control Council in Berlin fared no better. They became more bitter, less frequent, and more fruitless. On March 20, 1948, the Soviet delegation walked out of the meeting of the Control Council, and the administrative machinery for four-power rule of Germany was at an end. On June 24, 1948, the Soviets halted all traffic to and from Berlin and put the Western Powers to the first endurance test. The West countered the Berlin blockade with the almost miraculous airlift. So effective was this countermove that the Soviets gave up after 324 days. Arrangements were worked out for the lifting of the blockade and for reconvening the Council of Foreign Ministers in Paris in May, 1949. But this meeting was no more successful than any of the preceding conferences.

Unable to find an agreement with the Soviets, the Western Powers adjusted their own differences, some of which were quite serious, and embarked on a policy which ultimately resulted in creation of a West German Federal Republic at Bonn. The Soviets, too, took steps which transferred their zone—about one-third of Germany with much of the original agricultural and industrial potential—into a satellite. As early as April, 1946, they abolished all political parties and approved only the Socialist Unity Party led by Moscow-trained men and supported by Soviet armies; nationalized coal, electric power, metallurgical, machine tool, chemical, textile, and other industries which they did not seize outright and transfer to Soviet ownership; cut up the large estates; and initiated a policy of collectivization. On October 7, 1949, the zone was ready for an "advanced status"—that of a People's Republic. These actions confirmed that the division of Germany was there to stay until such time as one side should decide to capitulate to the other.

SUGGESTED READINGS

ANDERS, WLADYSLAW. *Hitler's Defeat in Russia.* Chicago: Regnery, 1953.

ARMSTRONG, JOHN A. *Ukrainian Nationalism, 1939–1945.* New York: Columbia University Press, 1956.

BELOFF, MAX. *Soviet Policy in the Far East, 1944–1951.* New York: Oxford University Press, 1953.

BYRNES, JAMES J. *Speaking Frankly.* New York: Harper, 1947.

CHURCHILL, SIR WINSTON S. *The Second World War.* 6 vols. Boston: Houghton Mifflin, 1948–1953.

CIECHANOWSKI, JAN. *Defeat in Victory.* New York: Doubleday, 1947.

CLAY, LUCIUS D. *Decision in Germany.* New York: Doubleday, 1950.

CONQUEST, ROBERT. *Soviet Deportation of Nationalities.* New York: St. Martin's, 1960.

DALLIN, ALEXANDER. *German Rule in Russia, 1941–1945.* London: Macmillan, 1957.

DALLIN, DAVID J. *The New Soviet Empire.* New Haven: Yale University Press, 1951.

DEANE, JOHN R. *The Strange Alliance.* New York: Viking, 1947.

DIXON, BRIGADIER C. AUBREY, and OTTO HEILBRUNN. *Communist Guerilla Warfare.* New York: Praeger, 1955.

DJILAS, MILOVAN. *Conversations with Stalin,* New York: Harcourt, Brace and World, 1962.

EISENHOWER, DWIGHT D. *Crusade in Europe.* New York: Doubleday, 1948.

FEIS, HERBERT. *Between War and Peace: The Potsdam Conference.* Princeton: Princeton University Press, 1960.

———. *Churchill-Roosevelt-Stalin.* Princeton: Princeton University Press, 1957.

FISCHER, GEORGE. *Soviet Opposition to Stalin.* Cambridge: Harvard University Press, 1952.

HART, B. H. LIDDELL, ed. *The Red Army.* New York: Harcourt-Brace, 1956.

JACKSON, W. G. F. *Seven Roads to Moscow.* New York: Philosophical Library, 1958.

KERN, ERICH. *Dance of Death.* New York: Scribners, 1951.

KERTESZ, STEPHAN. *The Fate of East Central Europe.* Notre Dame: University of Notre Dame Press, 1956.

LANE, ARTHUR BLISS. *I Saw Poland Betrayed.* Indianapolis: Bobbs-Merrill, 1948.

MAC VICKER, CHARLES P. *Titoism: Pattern for International Communism.* New York: St. Martin's, 1957.

MIKOLAJCZYK, STANISLAW. *The Rape of Poland.* New York: Whittlesey House, 1948.

NAGY, FERENC. *The Struggle Behind the Iron Curtain.* New York: Macmillan, 1948.

NETTL, JOHN P. *The Eastern Zone and Soviet Policy in Germany.* New York: Oxford University Press, 1951.

NORTH, ROBERT C. *Moscow and the Chinese Communists.* Stanford: Stanford University Press, 1953.

RIPKA, HUBERT. *Czechoslovakia Enslaved.* London: Golancz, 1950.

ROSSI, ANGELO. *The Russo-German Alliance.* Boston: Beacon Press, 1951.

ROZEK, EDWARD J. *Allied Wartime Diplomacy: A Pattern in Poland.* New York: Wiley, 1951.

RUBINSTEIN, ALVIN Z., ed. *The Foreign Policy of the Soviet Union*. New York: Random House, 1960.

SCHWARTZ, HARRY. *The Red Phoenix. Russia Since World War II*. New York: Praeger, 1961.

SETON-WATSON, HUGH. *The East European Revolution*. New York: Praeger, 1956.

SHERWOOD, ROBERT E. *Roosevelt and Hopkins*. New York: Harper, 1948.

SHIRER, WILLIAM L. *The Rise and Fall of the Third Reich*. New York: Simon and Schuster, 1960.

SHULMAN, MARSHALL D. *Stalin's Foreign Policy Reappraised*. Cambridge: Harvard University Press, 1963.

SLUSSER, ROBERT, ed. *Soviet Economic Policy in Postwar Germany*. New York: Praeger, 1953.

SNELL, JOHN L., ed. *The Meaning of Yalta*. Baton Rouge: Louisiana State University Press, 1956.

———. *Wartime Origins of the East-West Dilemma over Germany*. New Orleans: Hauser Press, 1959.

SONTAG, RAYMOND J., and JAMES S. BEDDIE, eds. *Nazi-Soviet Relations, 1939–1941*. Washington, D.C.: State Department, 1948.

STETTINIUS, EDWARD R. JR. *Lend-Lease. Weapon for Victory*. New York: Macmillan, 1944.

———. *Roosevelt and the Russians: The Yalta Conference*. New York: Doubleday, 1949.

TANNER, VAINO. *The Winter War: Finland Against Russia, 1939–1940*. Stanford: Stanford University Press, 1950.

TRUMAN, HARRY S. *Memoirs*. 2 vols. New York: Doubleday, 1955.

ULAM, ADAM B. *Titoism and the Cominform*. Cambridge: Harvard University Press, 1952.

VOZNESENSKY, NICHOLAS. *Economy of the U.S.S.R. During World War II*. Washington: Public Affairs Press, 1948.

WEI, HENRY. *China and Soviet Russia*. Princeton: Princeton University Press, 1956.

WOLFF, ROBERT L. *The Balkans in Our Times*. Cambridge: Harvard University Press, 1956.

ZAWODNY, J. K. *Death in the Forest: The Story of the Katyn Forest Massacres*. Notre Dame, Indiana: University of Notre Dame Press, 1962.

$\mathcal{K}$ V I I I

THE DE-STALINIZED
FIFTIES

THE STRUGGLE FOR SUCCESSION

On the night of March 1–2, 1953, Stalin is reported to have suffered a massive brain hemorrhage, losing consciousness and the power of speech. "The best medical personnel" was called to treat him ("under the continuous supervision of the Central Committee and the Soviet Government"), but his condition continued to deteriorate. He was officially declared dead on March 5, 1953, and was entombed with great honors on March 9, 1953, next to Lenin in the mausoleum on Red Square. At present it is not clear whether his death was "timely or well timed." Whatever the final judgment on the exact time and circumstance of his death, Stalin's demise threw the struggle for succession wide open.

This struggle had begun in earnest with the official disclosure on January 13, 1953, that nine distinguished physicians (some of whom were

Jewish) had been arrested and had allegedly confessed to the murder of Zhdanov, who died under mysterious circumstances on August 31, 1948, and Alexander S. Shcherbakov (1901–1945), who had been Chief of the Main Political Administration of the Soviet Army. The announcement further alleged that some of the accused physicians were agents of American intelligence (recruited by the American Joint Distribution Committee, a Jewish charitable organization), whose mission was to liquidate Marshals Alexander M. Vasilevsky (1895–), Leonid A. Govorov (1897–1955), and Konev, Admiral G. I. Levchenko, and General S. M. Shtemenko, and certain other public figures, thus undermining Soviet defenses.

There is some evidence indicating that the faked "doctors' plot" and the intended "trial" were to serve as a prelude to further accusations, arrests, and a massive purge similar to that of the late 1930's. It is not known who was the *real* instigator of the purge nor who were its intended victims. In his secret speech at the Twentieth Party Congress in February, 1956, Khrushchev claimed that the new bloodbath was "aimed at the removal of the old Politburo members and the bringing in of less experienced persons so that these would extoll him [Stalin] in all sorts of ways." A similar view was advanced by many Western observers as early as October, 1952; i.e., immediately after the Nineteenth Party Congress announced changes in the structure and membership of the leading party organs. These changes included doubling of the membership of the Central Committee, abolishment of the Politburo and the Orgburo, and division of the latter bodies' functions between the greatly enlarged Presidium (of twenty-five members and eleven candidates) and the Secretariat (of ten secretaries). While it is inconceivable that such vital changes would have been made without Stalin's approval, the architect of these innovations and the spokesman on their behalf before the Congress was Khrushchev.

Whatever the final judgment on the *real* intentions behind the "doctors' plot" and changes in the party, the present evidence suggests that they were early manifestations of the struggle for succession. The struggle centered among four principal rivals: Malenkov, a member of the Secretariat and the Presidium, whom Stalin had selected as the main speaker at the Nineteenth Party Congress, thus unofficially designating him as the heir apparent; Molotov, a member of the Presidium and an "Old Bolshevik" of long party standing; Beria, a member of the Presidium and head of the security forces of the USSR; and Khrushchev, a "rising star" in the Secretariat, with a wealth of practical experience with the problems of nationality and agriculture acquired as First Secretary of the Communist party of the Ukraine. Outwardly, Malenkov's and Beria's positions seemed to be the strongest. The future, however, was to reveal that this assumption was incorrect.

Stalin's passing opened a new chapter in the struggle for succession. Even before they revealed to the public the news of Stalin's death, his old lieutenants made an attempt to divide among themselves authority in the government and in the party. In the government the new distribution of power was as follows: Malenkov became the Chairman of the Council of Ministers of the USSR, the position Stalin had held since 1941. Beria, Molotov, Nikolai A. Bulganin (1895–), and Kaganovich became First Deputy Chairmen. Voroshilov replaced Shvernik as Chairman of the Presidium of the Supreme Soviet, with Shvernik taking charge of trade unions. Vital changes were also introduced in the party. The recently enlarged Presidium was reduced to ten members (Malenkov, Beria, Molotov, Voroshilov, Khrushchev, Bulganin, Kaganovich, Mikoyan, Maxim Z. Saburov (1900–), and Michael G. Pervukhin (1904–) and four alternates (Shvernik, Panteleimon K. Ponomarenko (1902–), Leonid G. Melnikov (1906–), and Mir D. Bagirov (1896–). The Secretariat was decreased to four persons (Malenkov, Semeon D. Ignatiev, Peter N. Pospelov (1898–), and Nikolai N. Shatalin). Khrushchev was released from his duties of First Secretary of the Moscow Party Committee in order to arrange the funeral of Stalin and "to concentrate on work in the Central Committee of the CPSU." These changes introduced the era of "collective leadership" in the USSR.

The "collective leadership" accomplished three things "collectively." It belatedly issued the announcement of Stalin's death, in which it paid loveless and griefless tribute to the "wise leader," and made an appeal for "steel-like and monolithic unity of the party," "high political vigilance," "stalwartness in the struggle against external and internal foes," and "the prevention of any kind of disorder and panic." The second action of "the collective leadership" was the staging of Stalin's funeral with orations by Malenkov, Beria, and Molotov. Malenkov promised "peace" and a "happy life," pledged that the party and the people would continue "high political vigilance, irreconcilability and firmness in the struggle against internal and foreign enemies," and declared that the USSR had "everything needed for the construction of a complete Communist society." Beria repeated the warning against "confusion and panic," and stressed the need to "intensify and sharpen the vigilance of the party and of the people against the intrigues and machinations of the enemies of the Soviet state." Molotov warned the rest of the world not to "rock the boat" because Soviet military might was formidable. The three funeral addresses, as one observer justly noted, "were more of a political platform than a cry of grief." The final act of the "collective leadership" was a wholesale removal of men who had been close to Stalin in the final hours of his life; namely, Minister of Health Tretiakov, who had treated Stalin; Alexander N. Poskrebyshev (1891–), Chief of Stalin's personal secretariat; Stalin's

Moscow, March, 1953. Pallbearers (right to left) Beria, Malenkov, Vasily Stalin, Molotov, Bulganin, Kaganovich and Shvernik carry Stalin's coffin.

son, Vasily;[1] the Commandant of the Kremlin, Lieutenant General Spiridonov; the Commander of the Kremlin Guards, Major General Kosynkin; the Commandant of the City of Moscow, Lieutenant General Sinilov; and the Commander of the Moscow Military District, Colonel General Artemev.

"Collective leadership" suffered its first setback on March 10, 1953, when Malenkov, apparently overeager to pose as Stalin's rightful heir, reproduced an altered photograph in *Pravda*. The picture was originally taken on February 14, 1950, on the occasion of the conclusion of the Sino-Soviet Treaty. It included many Soviet and Chinese dignitaries, but now only Stalin, Mao Tse-tung, and Malenkov appeared in it. Apparently the new "collective leaders" did not appreciate Malenkov's high-handed elimination of their images from the photograph. On March 14, 1953, at a

[1] It was reported in 1962 that Stalin's son Vasily had died of alcoholism.

plenary session of the Central Committee, Malenkov "requested" that he be freed "from duties as secretary of the CC of the CPSU." The request was granted and the post went to Khrushchev, who thus became *de facto* boss of the party machine. On the following day, a vast reorganization of the government was announced, with mergers of some ministries and abolition of others. Under this reorganization, Malenkov remained Premier, Beria took charge of all internal affairs, Bulganin of defense (with Marshals Zhukov and Vasilevsky as his first deputies); Mikoyan of domestic and foreign trade, and Molotov of foreign affairs. The new reorganization of party and government positions revealed that within the "collective leadership" a new *troika* had emerged, consisting of Malenkov, as the head of government bureaucracy, Beria, as the head of the secret police, and Khrushchev as spokesman for the "infallible" party.

Immediately, as the head of the huge internal army and of the security organs, Beria appeared to be in the strongest position. His advantage, however, was short-lived. On April 4, 1953, came the official announcement that all the charges against the physicians involved in the "doctors' plot" were invented, that confessions were obtained by torture, that the officials responsible for fabricating these falsehoods would be punished, and that of the nine doctors, seven who survived had been released and exonerated. This news caused the dismissal and arrest of several of Beria's subordinates. His own turn came on June 26, 1953, when he was arrested and denounced as an "adventurer," "hireling of foreign imperialist forces," a British agent since 1919, and an "enemy of the people," who had "wormed his way into a position of confidence." He was charged with "criminal anti-Party and anti-state work," machinations to seize power and to eliminate the "collective leadership," interference in every way with solution of the "urgent problems in agriculture," attempting to undermine the collective farms, sowing "discord among the peoples of the USSR," and with intensifying "the activity of bourgeois nationalist elements." Beria was "tried" on December 17, 1953, under the "Kirov Law" of December 1, 1934; i.e., without being present or represented by counsel. He "confessed" to all the charges and within twenty-four hours of the "trial" was shot. Subscribers to the *Bolshaia Sovetskaia Entsiklopediia* (Great Soviet Encyclopedia) were asked to remove with a razor blade Beria's photograph and the account of his life and to paste in that space an article on the Bering Sea. With Beria perished also six of his close associates—V. N. Merkulov, V. G. Dekanozov, B. Z. Kobulov, S. A. Goglidze, P. Ia. Metshik, and L. A. Vlodzimirsky—who were labelled as terrorists, counterrevolutionaries, and long-time anti-Soviet conspirators. These charges against top Soviet security officials were no more credible than similar charges Beria and his officers had often fabricated for use against others. They did help, however, to undermine the position of the

Lavrentii Beria   *Anastas Mikoyan*

security organs as a "state within a state"—the position they had acquired under Stalin.

The decline of Malenkov's and Beria's fortunes increased those of Khrushchev. Following his "appointment" to the Secretariat, Khrushchev turned his attention to a thorough overhaul of the party machine throughout the country, replacing "doubtful" or "unreliable" party secretaries with his own trusted men from the Ukrainian and Moscow party organizations he once had headed. The most notable changes occurred in the Leningrad, Armenian, Georgian, Azerbaidzhan, Uzbek, Kazakh, Moldavian, and key RSFSR party organizations. Khrushchev also reorganized local party committees and increased the number of district party secretaries, thereby strengthening the position of the party everywhere. These changes, in turn, strengthened his own position in the Central Committee. With the help of his appointees, on September 13, 1953, Khrushchev became the First Secretary of the Central Committee, the position Stalin had used to emerge as absolute dictator. To all intents and purposes, this appointment eliminated the "collective leadership."

As First Secretary, and hence the leader of the party, Khrushchev soon began systematically to build up his image. In April, 1954, on his sixtieth birthday, he was proclaimed a Hero of Socialist Labor, and was awarded the Order of Lenin. Before long, the party press, which he controlled, began to hail him as an "Old Bolshevik," an aide to Lenin and Stalin, and an organizer of victories during the Civil War and World War II. During 1953, and more so in 1954, Khrushchev emerged as the chief spokesman on basic domestic and foreign policies and a chief critic of all other high-ranking Soviet officials. His views were repeatedly cited by others, and eventually his word became the law of the land. He travelled extensively throughout the country, discussed all kinds of problems, and made himself known to local party officials. Khrushchev, while paying lip service to "collective leadership," everywhere tried to create an image of himself as the effective, colorful, powerful, and rightful successor to Stalin.

Early in 1955, the "collective leadership," or what remained of it, received a further setback. This setback came about over the issue of the direction of economic development of the USSR. To appease the population following Stalin's death, his uneasy heirs agreed to pay long overdue attention to agriculture and to the production of consumer goods. Malenkov outlined the new course before the Supreme Soviet on August 8, 1953. It called for improvement in agriculture; consolidation of collective farms, "organizationally and economically"; accumulation of abundant food supply; accumulation of raw materials for light industry; devising of greater economic incentive for collective farms; correcting and revising the peasant attitude towards personal plots; tax reform; and substantial reduction of peasant "obligatory delivery quotas." Because these promises, some of which were fulfilled during 1953, sharply departed from communist orthodoxy, they were attacked by more militant party functionaries.

The issue of consumer *versus* heavy industry came to a head on December 21, 1954, when *Izvestiia*, the government's—or Malenkov's— mouthpiece, urged editorially a build-up in consumer goods, while *Pravda*, the party's—or Khrushchev's—mouthpiece, advocated the development of heavy industry. On January 24, 1955, *Pravda's* editorial went further. It branded the emphasis on consumer goods as "utterly alien to Marxist-Leninist political economy and to the general line of the Communist Party," and stressed that "heavy industry was, is, and will be the granite foundation of all branches of the socialist economy, the cornerstone of the might of the Soviet country and of its people's well-being." Khrushchev repeated these warnings more bluntly on January 25, 1955, at the Central Committee Plenum, where he declared that to claim priority for light industry was a "slander of the Party" and a new form of anti-Leninist "right deviation." It became obvious that there was room for only one spokesman in the USSR.

The decision came on February 8, 1955, when, in Malenkov's presence, a clerk read Malenkov's letter of resignation to the hastily convened Supreme Soviet. In this obviously artificial document, Malenkov "requested" that he be relieved from the post of Chairman of the Council of Ministers in order "to strengthen the leadership" of that body. Although for over twenty years he had been a high-ranking party functionary, and as a member of the Committee of State Defense had been responsible for increasing Soviet aircraft production during World War II, he now pleaded insufficient experience in state and "local work and the fact that I did not have occasion, in a ministry or some economic organ, to effect direct guidance of individual branches of national economy." As if these falsehoods were insufficient, he acknowledged his "guilt and responsibility for the unsatisfactory state of affairs which has arisen in agriculture" (which Khrushchev had managed since 1949), conceded that renewed emphasis on heavy industry was the only "correct foundation" for a sound agricultural and consumer industry program and promised to "perform in the most conscientious manner my duty and the functions which will be entrusted to me" in the future. The Supreme Soviet granted Malenkov's "request" and, at Khrushchev's suggestion, appointed Bulganin as Chairman of the Council of Ministers.

Malenkov's "resignation" signalled the end to collective leadership and the emergence of Khrushchev as undisputed and supreme dictator in the USSR. In that capacity Khrushchev further reshuffled party and state functionaries on all levels, doubled the membership of the Secretariat in July, 1955, and elevated some of his closest supporters (Alexei I. Kirichenko (1908–   ) and Michael A. Suslov (1902–   ) to the Party Presidium without benefit of Congress action. These moves, in turn, strengthened his position in the Central Committee and in the party. At the Twentieth Party Congress in February, 1956, Khrushchev was the most conspicuous spokesman. He delivered the opening address, gave the report on behalf of the Central Committee, rudely interrupted other speakers, and, at a secret session, delivered a devastating attack on Stalin. The Congress approved Khrushchev's selection of, and considerable increase in, the membership of the Presidium, the Secretariat, and the Central Committee. Since most of the new men were his own loyal supporters, Khrushchev's influence in the policy-making bodies increased appreciably. Confident of their support, he relaxed some of the stringent rules of labor discipline, made concessions to the peasants, and introduced far-reaching administrative decentralization of economic enterprises.

In June, 1957, "Old Bolsheviks" Malenkov, Molotov, Kaganovich, and Saburov made an attempt to strip Khrushchev of his powers. Taking advantage of Khrushchev's official visit to Finland, they convened a meeting of the Party Presidium and demanded his resignation. Khrushchev fought back their demands and, supposedly with the help of Marshal Zhukov, succeeded in transferring the question of his resignation to the Central Committee where he had many allies and where, after a week of bitter struggle (June 22–29), he won. Malenkov, Molotov, Kaganovich, and Saburov were dismissed from their party and government posts, and accused of violating the 1921 party ban on factions, obstructing policies designed to ease international tension, resisting economic reorganization, opposing material incentives in agriculture, and conspiring to seize power in the party and the government. The purge of the "anti-Party" group enabled Khrushchev to consolidate his position in the Presidium whose membership was now "pro-Khrushchev" (Khrushchev, Bulganin, Voroshilov,[1] Mikoyan, Suslov, Kirichenko, Leonid I. Brezhnev (1906–), Marshal Zhukov, Ekaterina A. Furtseva (1910–), Shvernik, Averky B. Aristov (1903–), Nikolai I. Beliaev, Nikolai G. Ignatov (1901–), Frol R. Kozlov, and Kuusinen). Late in October, 1957, Khrushchev abruptly stripped Zhukov of his authority and on March 27, 1958, as an anticlimax to the victory over all of his rivals, he relieved Bulganin of his duties and assumed the post of Chairman of the Council of Ministers. Subsequently, Bulganin also publicly "confessed" his membership in the "anti-Party conspiracy" and was relegated into obscurity. From March, 1958, until October 15, 1964, no one doubted that Khrushchev, as party secretary, foremost member of the Presidium, and Premier, was the supreme dictator in the USSR, and had proven to be one of Stalin's most perceptive students.

DE-STALINIZATION

The struggle for succession was accompanied by a development known as "de-Stalinization," or downgrading of Stalin. The *real* reasons for "operation cutdown" are unknown. The available evidence suggests, however, that like all things in a regimented state, the downgrading of Stalin was a well-planned undertaking, carefully timed, masterfully controlled, and doled out in tolerable, properly spaced, and gradually habituating doses. Four distinct phases may be discerned in the process: the early, or moderate phase (March, 1953–January, 1956); the dethronement phase (February, 1956–January, 1957); the reappraisal phase (January, 1957–October, 1961); and the phase of liquidation of his memory (October, 1961–present).

One of the basic characteristics of the early phase of de-Stalinization was the heavy emphasis by his heirs on the principle of "collective leadership," and criticism of one-man rule. The classic formulation of the new trend is contained in an article entitled "Collectivity is the Highest Principle of Party Leadership." Published in *Pravda* on April 16, 1953, the article stressed that the solution of all important problems of party work must be "the fruit of collective discussion"; that regardless of their experience, wisdom, and ability, individual leaders do not possess and "cannot replace the initiative and experience of a whole collective"; and that party leaders must be able to accept criticism of themselves and must show "readiness to bend their will to the will of the collective." The article did not mention Stalin's name, but the implication was obvious.

[1] At the Twenty-second Party Congress in Oct., 1961, Voroshilov was identified with the "anti-party" group, and "confessed" his guilt.

Accompanying the attack on what became known as "the cult of individual" was the campaign designed to inflate the fame of Lenin and deflate the name, stature, and reputation of Stalin. The most striking revelation in this connection was the official chronicle of the fifty years of the Communist party, published in the summer of 1953. This curious document repeated time and again that it was Lenin who founded the party, led it to victory, provided the inspiration for its success (even after his death), and authored the "collective leadership principle." Stalin, in contrast, was credited only with development of "the Marxist-Leninist theory in conformity with the new historical conditions." By omitting Stalin's name from the account of the Bolshevik revolution and the Civil War, the new "history" exploded the Stalin-created legend that he was Lenin's right-hand man before, during and after the revolution. This was indeed a radical departure, for while he was alive Stalin was credited with almost every known achievement, thanks to his "unerring foresight," "wisdom," "genius," and "infallibility." His writings, in the words of one observer, "had the force of sacred writ and were considered the irrefutable source of all judgments on any matter he ever discussed." The most ironic part of this rewriting of history was the fact that it was done by the very men Stalin had selected and elevated to the highest positions in the Soviet system.

The undermining of Stalin's reputation manifested itself in innumerable other ways. Following his funeral, references to his name declined sharply in the press as did quotations from his works. His pictures disappeared from publications and public displays, except on great ceremonial occasions. An article in the first volume of the *Bolshaia Sovetskaia Entsiklopediia*, published after his death, deprived Stalin of the exclusive authorship of the *Short History of the Communist Party*. His revolutionary activities in the Caucasus, which had been glorified by Beria in a book that went through nine editions (the last one in 1952), were officially condemned—not only because of Beria's "treachery" but also because of historical inaccuracies and falsehoods. The "collective leadership" suspended in 1953 the annual award of Stalin Prizes, issued amnesties to some victims of Stalin's mistreatment, reduced the population of concentration camps, posthumously rehabilitated some of the purge victims, promised to improve living standards, allowed relative freedom of movement, decreased police power, and abandoned many other harsh aspects of Stalin's rule. These carefully prepared preliminaries paved the way for the second phase of the de-Stalinization process—the dethronement of Stalin at the Twentieth Party Congress in February, 1956.

The dethronement assault was led by Mikoyan on February 16. He was followed by Khrushchev with the now famous "secret speech" on the night of February 24–25, 1956.[1] Labelled by some observers as "perhaps

[1] For the full text of the speech, see Appendix 37.

the most important document ever to have come from the Communist movement," Khrushchev's de-Stalinization speech (from which foreign Communists were excluded) is remarkable for its half truths, its false-hoods, and its revelations. The list of Khrushchev's charges against Stalin is sweeping. He accused his former chief: (1) of violating collegiality in leadership and in work; (2) of practicing "brutal violence not only towards everything which opposed him, but also towards that which seemed to his capricious and despotic character, contrary to his concepts"; (3) of imposing "his concepts and demanding absolute submission to his opinion"; (4) of originating the concept "enemy of the people"; (5) of inaugurating a reign "of the most cruel repression"; (6) of violating "all norms of revolutionary legality" and ignoring all norms of party life; (7) of acting in the name of the party, its Central Committee, and its Politburo; (8) of using "extreme methods and mass repression" against anyone who dared to disagree with him; (9) of branding and liquidating many honest communists as "enemies," spies, and wreckers; (10) of ar-resting and shooting (between 1934 and 1938) 70 per cent of the mem-bers of the party's Central Committee; (11) of elevating "himself above the Party and above the nation"; (12) of deviating from all precepts of Leninism; (13) of gaining confessions "with the help of cruel and inhu-man torture"; (14) of ignoring all pleas of innocent victims; (15) of causing "tremendous harm to our country and to the cause of Socialist advancement" by mass arrests of party, soviet, economic, and military personnel; (16) of creating uncertainty, suspicion, and distrust in the country; (17) of not preparing the country against the German invasion, in spite of repeated warnings by Soviet and foreign observers; (18) of interfering with actual military operations, of which he knew nothing, thereby causing "our army serious damage"; (19) of taking all credit for military victories of World War II, and thus belittling the heroic efforts of the Soviet peoples; (20) of ordering mass deportation of Soviet minor-ities accused of collaborating with the Germans; (21) of growing "more capricious, irritable, and brutal" after World War II; (22) of causing the conflict with Yugoslavia; (23) of being ignorant of conditions in the country at large; (24) of believing himself to be "the greatest leader" and the "sublime strategist of all times and nations"; and (25) of self-glorifi-cation, erecting statues of himself and naming cities, collective farms, canals, and prizes for himself.

Khrushchev's charges contained little that was new; however, coming from one of Stalin's "closest comrades-in-arms," they carried considerable authority. At the same time, the indictment of Stalin was in many ways distortive and one-sided. Khrushchev, for instance, attributed the purges to Stalin, yet it was Lenin, not Stalin, who invented purges. Stalin's con-tribution was to make them "more bloody and capricious." Khrushchev deplored Stalin's intolerance, domination, and absolutism. Yet it is doubt-

Nikolai Bulganin and Nikita Khrushchev with India's President Rajendra Prasad, in India, 1955.

ful whether Stalin could have acquired these traits so easily had it not been for the Leninist organizational principles of the party, with the "lack of respect for minority views within its membership and for majority opinion outside it." Khrushchev ridiculed Stalin's infallibility, yet failed to acknowledge that this claim was and is an inherent part of the system and of the doctrine that claims to be "scientific." Finally, Khrushchev deplored Stalin's self-glorification, yet was silent on the fact that it was he and the other "masters of the art of serving and surviving" who glorified Stalin's name, blindly executed his will, helped to destroy all others in advancing his and their own fortunes, and thus created "the cult of individual."

Khrushchev's carefully selected audience of 1,436 high party functionaries is reported to have responded to his indictment of Stalin with "animation," "movement in the hall," "applause," and occasional "laughter." Western observers have labelled the speech "the anatomy of terror," and "the most damning indictment of Communism to come from the lips of a Communist ruler." Whatever the ultimate judgment of this strange and awful document, perhaps without parallel in history, the indictment fully confirmed Lord Acton's immortal truism that: "Power tends to corrupt and absolute power corrupts absolutely." Khrushchev asked his listeners not to allow "this matter to get out of the Party, especially not to the press," in order not to "give ammunition to the enemy." Needless to say, Khrushchev's address has not been published in the USSR. A special resolution of February 25, by the Twentieth Party Congress entitled "On the Cult of Individual and Its Consequences," confirmed, however, that a closed session was held, and called upon the Central Committee to liquidate the "cult" in all of its manifestations everywhere.

The secret, however, did leak out abroad and made a deep impression on Communists and non-Communists alike. The complete text of Khrushchev's speech was published on June 4, 1956, by the U.S. State Department. Moscow took notice of this publication on June 30, 1956, in a resolution of the Central Committee of the CPSU entitled "On Overcoming the Cult of Individual and Its Consequences." The resolution paraphrased many key passages of Khrushchev's secret speech (with no specific charges); acknowledged that the "cult of individual" had harmed Soviet society; argued that Stalin's "cult of individual" was not a natural outgrowth of the Soviet system or of Leninist norms of party life, but a result of foreign intervention, capitalist encirclement, World War II, and Stalin's own character; reasoned that any opposition to Stalin had been impossible because, as the leader of the party, Stalin fought for socialism, acquired authority and popularity, and anyone who spoke out against him "would not have received the support of the people"; and pretended that "many of the facts and incorrect actions of Stalin, particularly in the area of violations of socialist legality, became known only recently, only after the death of Stalin, principally in connection with the unmasking of the Beria gang and the establishment of Party control over the organs of state security." This "revelation," as one observer justly noted, could be credible only "if it were assumed that Khrushchev and his lieutenants, as well as the persons whom he ousted from the Central Committee, had been asleep for the two decades preceding 1953."

On January 17, 1957, Khrushchev made an attempt to "rehabilitate" Stalin. Speaking at the Chinese Embassy in Moscow, he declared that

It is, of course, a bad thing that Stalin launched into deviations and mistakes which harmed our cause. But even when he committed mistakes and allowed the law to be broken, he did that with the full conviction that he was defending the gains of the Revolution, the cause of socialism. That was Stalin's tragedy. But in the fundamental, in the main thing—and for Marxist-Leninists the fundamental and main thing is the defense of . . . the cause of socialism and the struggle against the enemies of Marxism-Leninism—in this fundamental and main thing, I . . . would to goodness every Communist could fight as Stalin fought. The enemies of Communism have deliberately invented the word "Stalinist" and are trying to make it sound abusive. For all of us, Marxist-Leninists . . . Stalin's name is inseparable from Marixsm-Leninism. Therefore, each one of us, members of the Communist Party of the Soviet Union, strives to be as faithful to the cause of Marxism-Leninism . . . as Stalin was faithful to this cause.

This reappraisal remained in force until October, 1961, when the phase of liquidation of Stalin's memory was introduced.

DOMESTIC DEVELOPMENTS IN THE 1950's

Stalin's death opened the way for the rise of new leaders, and also made possible the introduction of many interesting innovations. The first of these was "the legal reform." This reform consisted of four amnesty decrees (March 27, 1953; September 17, 1955; September 20, 1956; and November 1, 1957) by the Presidium of the Supreme Soviet and a revision of the criminal codes. Under the 1953 and 1957 amnesty decrees, all persons serving short-term sentences (up to five years) for lesser offenses were freed, as were all pregnant women, women with small children, juveniles, men over sixty, women over fifty-five, and all those who were incurably ill. The 1955 and 1956 amnesty decrees freed all those who had been sentenced in person or in absentia to ten-year imprisonment for collaboration with the enemy during World War II or for surrender to the enemy. Persons serving terms for "counterrevolutionary activity, major theft of socialist property, banditry, and premeditated murder"—and these formed a major portion of the prison population—were not affected by the decrees. Thus, while freeing many persons, these amnesties were only limited concessions.

Revision of the criminal codes was also a limited concession. Officially, its aim was to "provide on the one hand for an increased struggle against such crimes dangerous to society as treason against homeland, espionage, sabotage, banditry, murder, and robbery; and on the other hand for reducing penalties for minor civil, economic, and administrative violations or replacing them with administrative or public pressure." In accordance with this objective, in April, 1954, the Supreme Soviet extended the death penalty to persons committing premeditated murder under "iniquitous" circumstances, and a decree early in 1955 imposed strict penalties for damage to crops on collective and state farms. At the same time, Stalin's heirs placed limits on the power of the police to arrest without a warrant or to imprison without a trial, permitted the marriage of Soviet citizens to foreigners, abolished crimes by analogy, reduced the maximum term of imprisonment, and annulled some of the most objectionable procedures instituted during the Stalin era. They rejected, however, as "alien," demands that the accused be presumed innocent until proven guilty, that confessions not be accepted as evidence without independent corroboration, and that defendants be represented by counsel from the beginning of the investigation.

In addition to the "legal reforms," Stalin's heirs offered limited concessions to Soviet minorities. The most notable of these concessions was curtailment of the Russification policy introduced on a large scale after World War II, and dismissal of some of the officials responsible for its execution. Of those dismissed, the most prominent was Melnikov, the First Secretary of the Communist party of the Ukraine, who, in June, 1953, was replaced by Kirichenko, the first Ukrainian ever to be so selected. On February 19, 1954, the Ukraine—Khrushchev's former domain —with fanfare and publicity received the Crimea from the RSFSR. The aim of this administrative transfer seems to have been twofold. It sought to meet the Ukrainians half way and thus to reduce their gravitation towards independence from Moscow. It also sought to pose as a gift of the "elder brother" to the "younger brother" on the much publicized occasion of the tricentennial of the unification of Russia and the Ukraine. Another "concession" to minorities was the elevation of several non-Russians to the Presidium of the CPSU. This distinction went to Kirichenko, Kuusinen, and Nuritdin A. Mukhitdinov (1917–   ). Still another "concession" came early in 1957, when the Chechens, Ingush, Balkars, and certain other minority groups punished by Stalin for their cooperation with the Germans during World War II, were "rehabilitated." While some of these "concessions" modified some aspects of the Soviet nationality policy, they did not change the policy itself.

Although significant, the "legal reforms" and "concessions" to minorities were overshadowed by an acute crisis in agriculture and a dilemma in industry. The crisis in agriculture, or failure of agriculture to keep food production abreast of the rapidly growing population, stemmed from many natural causes but above all from such factors as official repression; peasant hostility; extremely overcentralized, authoritarian and often inept and perverse planning; inadequate supply of draft power; poor allocation and employment of capital; lack of initiative on the collective farm itself; widespread deceit; inadequate compensation of the collective farm members for their efforts; pilferage and neglect of property; low labor incentives; inflated clerical staff; wasteful methods; and material and human losses during World War II. To raise agricultural production, as was mentioned in the previous chapter, late in the 1940's Soviet authorities experimented with crop rotation, merged collective farms, and devised a shelter-belt program, irrigation schemes, and an ambitious but unsuccessful three-year plan to increase livestock numbers. In spite of the gloomy outlook, the Fifth Five Year Plan (1951–1955) called for about a 50 per cent rise in agricultural output during the five years. This increase was to be attained by raising sharply the yields per acre and productivity per animal. It is not known whether the planners really believed this goal to be attainable. At the Nineteenth Party Congress in October, 1952, Malenkov boasted, however, that the "grain problem, formerly considered the most

A modern collective farm showing the little fields (back of the houses) which belong to the farmers.

acute and serious problem, has been solved definitely and finally." Events soon revealed that this boast was an empty one.

Five months after Stalin's death, his successors admitted publicly (August–September, 1953) that all was not well with Soviet agriculture. It is difficult to say whether this admission was intentional, to spur the "campaign," or exaggerated in the official records as a result of concealment of produce and income by the peasants. The condition of Soviet agriculture, as painted by Malenkov in his speech before the Supreme Soviet on August 8, and Khrushchev's report before the Central Committee of the party on September 3, was not bright. Both men attributed its sad condition to the historical need to develop heavy industry first, to war, to misplanning, to improper incentives, and to government failure to encourage the peasant to cultivate his private plot. Both promised to turn concentrated attention to agriculture in order to produce an "abundance of food for the population and of raw materials for light industry in two to three years." As a first step in that direction of "abundance," the government revised the tax structure, reduced by about one-half the levies of private holdings, cancelled tax arrears, granted tax deductions to peasants who purchased livestock and reduced quotas for compulsory deliveries of animal products and vegetables. The government nullified these "concessions," however, by tightening party control of the collectives and by raising the number of "labor days" required of collective farm members.

To relieve the acute food shortage, in February, 1954, Khrushchev laid before the Central Committee a plan that sought to bring under cultivation vast areas of "virgin and idle lands" in the Urals, Siberia, and Central Asia. This plan called for the ploughing of some 32 million acres of "virgin land" in 1954, to be increased to some 74 million acres in 1956. The newly sown areas were to be organized into state farms devoted largely to grain production. To make this plan a success, machinery and people were moved to the new regions (some voluntarily, some under pressure). The plan achieved some success in 1954, failed because of drought in 1955, scored a major triumph in 1956, and has experienced difficulties in subsequent years. Whether this ambitious attempt to create a new granary in an area of fertile soil but little precipitation will be a success or a failure, only the future will tell.

In his quest to increase the food supply, in January, 1955, Khrushchev launched a "corn program"—which called for the cultivation of some 69 million acres of corn, potatoes, and root crops for fodder, in order to increase livestock production. A few months later he sent an agricultural delegation to the United States in order to learn the "secret" of corn growing, and invited American agricultural experts to visit and comment on Soviet collective farms. The observations of these groups brought further concessions to the peasant in the form of various material incentives, followed by a radical reform of the collective farm system. In March, 1956, for instance, the government made available liberal cash payments to farm workers; granted tax exemptions to farms in April, 1957; abolished the collective farms' compulsory delivery quota to the state, in July, 1957; granted the collective farms a nominal voice in the planning of their production; and in June, 1958, allowed the collective farms to purchase the equipment of the MTS's. These "concessions," however, failed to produce the desired goal—the expansion of production of foodstuffs. Three factors seem to have contributed to this failure: the tightening of party controls over the collective farms; official efforts to curtail peasants' use of private plots; and penalizing of those who spent too much time cultivating their plots. At a December, 1958, meeting of the Central Committee, it was publicly revealed that all was not well with collectivized Soviet agriculture. The Committee approved, however, a plan for a vast increase of grain, meat, milk, and other products by 1965. Dismissal in 1960 and 1961 of many officials responsible for the failure to carry out the program suggests that these ambitious goals might be difficult to attain.

The "collective leaders" also faced a serious dilemma in industry. This dilemma revolved around the question of the relative importance to be attached to the production of heavy industry and the production of consumer goods. Under the Fifth Five Year Plan (1951–1955) adopted in August, 1952, the production of pig iron was to climb from 22.0 to 33.9 million tons; steel from 31.4 to 44.2 million tons; coal from 281.9 to 377.5 million tons; oil from 42.3 to 69.5 million tons; and electricity from 104.0 to 163.0 billion kilowatt hours. If realized, as planned, by 1955 these targets would have given the USSR "a level of military-economic potential more than twice as great as at the beginning of World War II." But these targets also called for great sacrifices. Uncertain of the loyalty and support of the Soviet people and fearing "disorder and panic," Stalin's heirs shifted the emphasis somewhat from heavy to consumer industry and excited the Soviet peoples' hopes with a number of vague promises.

Malenkov launched the "new course" on August 8, 1953, in his speech before the Supreme Soviet. It was not a radical shift. He stressed that armaments and heavy industry, which he called "the basis of the foundation" of the Soviet economy, must be developed "in every way." At the same time he promised that the government would give attention to consumers' needs; make available more resources for the people's satisfaction; press for more production as well as better quality; see that at least a minimum of essential goods was available everywhere; spend more on housing, hospitals, and schools; and try to supply cities with plentiful quantities of potatoes and other vegetables. In October, 1953, Mikoyan further excited the hopes of Soviet consumers with the promise that by 1955 or 1956 Soviet industry would produce annually about 330,000 refrigerators, 500,000 vacuum cleaners, and 1,000,000 television sets. A large department store, the famous GUM, was opened on Red Square opposite the Kremlin, and another store specializing in children's toys across from the headquarters of the secret police. Soviet sales executives were urged to study and learn from "capitalist" methods of attracting, serving, and satisfying consumers.

The new course was short-lived. Late in 1954 and early in 1955, as noted earlier, a serious division developed within the "collective leader-

The Dnieprostroy Dam and power station in the Ukraine.

ship" on the issue of consumer versus heavy industry. Khrushchev repudiated Malenkov and his consumer goods program and adopted a Stalinist policy of heavy industry. During the Sixth Five Year Plan (1956–1960), approved by the Twentieth Party Congress in February, 1956, production of pig iron was to increase from 33.3 to 53.0 million tons; steel from 45.2 to 68.3 million tons; coal from 390.1 to 593.0 million tons; oil from 70.6 to 135.0 million tons; and electricity from 166.8 to 320.0 billion kilowatt hours. Late in 1956, however, party leaders confessed that the planners had overestimated the country's material and human resources, that the targets could not be fulfilled under existing conditions, and that the original drafts would have to be completely revised. The revised version took the form of a Seven Year Plan (1959–1965). Its declared aim was "a further mighty upsurge of all branches of the economy on the basis of priority for the expansion of heavy industry and a substantial rise in the country's economic potential so as to insure a continuous improvement in the living standards of the people." In accordance with this objective, the plan listed the following order of priorities: (1) iron and steel industry; (2) non-ferrous metal industry; (3) chemical industry; (4) fuel industry; (5) electrification; (6) machine building; (7) lumber industry; (8) light industry; (9) food industry; and (10) consumer industry. By 1965, the Seven Year Plan expected the USSR to produce 65 to 70 million tons of pig iron; 86 to 91 million tons of steel; 230 to 240 million tons of oil; 500 to 520 billion kilowatt hours of electric power; and 596 to 609 million tons of coal. To expedite the achievement of these goals, Khrushchev divided the USSR into 105 economic regions. Of these, seventy were in the RSFSR; eleven in the UkSSR; four in Uzbek SSR; nine in Kazakh SSR; and the remaining eleven republics constituted one economic region each.

Late in 1958, Khrushchev announced a drastic educational reform. Its aim was to give young people experience in factories and farms at an earlier age, to narrow the gap in the severe shortage of skilled manpower, and to control the white collar jobs. Under the new system, "unanimously acclaimed" by the Soviet press, Soviet education begins with an eight-year school, instead of the previous ten-year system. The first four years are devoted to general academic training. In the fifth through the eighth years, students, in addition to traditional subjects, are introduced to technical studies and practical work. Further secondary education consists of "full-time employment in production, supplemented by correspondence study or by attendance at evening or shift classes." Entrance to the higher educational institutions is now dependent on proof of having spent two or three years at work, and on the recommendation of a *Komsomol*, party, or trade union organization. Those who qualify obtain their education tuition-free.

The 1950's witnessed many other innovations and concessions. The new regime, for instance, adopted a more liberal tourist visa policy, opened many cities to foreign tourists, allowed some of its selected citizens to travel abroad, decreased terror and censorship, relaxed labor discipline, and increased the supply of goods in the shops. By Western standards these "concessions" were small. By Soviet standards they were large, and for the moment at least they made the life of the average Soviet citizen a little easier and more hopeful. None of the concessions, however, diminished the power of the dictatorship of the party. On October 4, 1957, these and innumerable other novelties were overshadowed by the first successful Soviet launching of a man-made satellite, the *Sputnik*. That action paved the way for later Soviet feats in space, and inaugurated the decade which could be labelled the Cosmic Sixties.

THE INTELLECTUAL FERMENT

Stalin's death, the ensuing struggle for succession, and de-Stalinization produced in the USSR an interesting intellectual ferment popularly known as "the thaw." The most pronounced ebullition occurred in literature. The agitation among writers, already present at the end of 1953, became a full-fledged movement early in 1954. The literary ferment, which was centered around the journal *Novyi Mir* (New World), took a threefold course. It sought to dismantle Stalin's literary orthodoxy; it tried to escape the party's tutelage and "its constant preachment of propaganda"; and it attempted to reassert the right of writers to produce "sincerity" and "immediacy of expression." An outstanding example of the new course was Ehrenburg's novel *Ottepel* (The Thaw), which complained that it was difficult, if not impossible, for real art to triumph under Soviet conditions. Other works of the "thaw period" included *Seasons of the Year*, by Vera F. Panova; *The Fall of Pompeev*, by Nikolai E. Virta; and *The Daughter of a Public Prosecutor*, by Iuri Ianovsky. While these works voiced criticism of party and government bureaucrats corrupted by power, none departed significantly from the precepts of "socialist realism." Their publication nevertheless roused hopes, both in the USSR and abroad, that Soviet literature was at last to be freed from its shackles.

Criticism of the upper strata of Soviet society and, indirectly, of some aspects of Communist faith itself, while favored by the repressed writers, encountered stiff opposition from party hacks and scribblers. The clash between the two groups, mild at first, grew progressively bitter, and in April, 1954, led to expulsion from the Union of Soviet Writers—"the intellectual fountainhead of the USSR"—of several of its members, including the novelist-playwright Virta. Later, writer and playwright Feodor I. Panferov (1896–1960) was dismissed from the editorial board of the journal *Oktiabr* (October); and in August, 1954, poet Alexander T. Tvardovsky (1910–   ), editor of *Novyi Mir*, was replaced by poet Konstantin M. Simonov (1915–   ).

By these dismissals the party achieved several objectives. It ostracized the most vocal critics of "socialist realism"; it denied them the right to attend the Second All-Union Congress of Soviet Writers, held in Moscow between December 14 and 26, 1954, to discuss literary problems created by new developments; it prevented the outbreak of open hostility at the Congress between the proponents and the opponents of liberalization in literature; it "demonstrated" to the world the existence of complete harmony among Soviet writers; it reasserted that "socialist realism" was "the only creative trend in literature of socialist society"; and it re-emphasized that, because of its subordination to politics, Soviet literature must continue to serve as the party's "active assistant in Communist education of the masses."

Early in 1956 the literary restlessness, dormant since December, 1954, was reactivated. The new agitation was sparked by Khrushchev's bitter denunciation of Stalin's criminal deeds at the Twenty-second Party Congress in February, 1956. The ensuing campaign against "the cult of individual" provided writers with a "legal" framework to renew their criticism of the party's tutelage in literature. Khrushchev's speech also led to the posthumous rehabilitation of many victims of Stalin's terror and to the return of those who survived it. During the height of the assault on Stalin, an attempt was made by a group of Soviet writers associated with the almanac *Literaturnaia Moskva* (Literary Moscow), to organize a semi-autonomous organization of Moscow writers outside the party-controlled Union of Soviet Writers, with the aim of demolishing the foundations of "socialist realism." Other examples of the renewed effort included a novel

Boris Pasternak   *Evgeni Evtushenko*

by Daniel A. Granin, *A Personal Opinion*, serialized in *Novyi Mir*, which
portrayed a "repentant" party member who had come to the realization
that party bureaucrats represent the main obstacle to progress; and a
novel by Vladimir D. Dudintsev (1918–), entitled *Not by Bread Alone*.
Dudintsev's work created a real uproar among party officials because of
its realistic portrayal of unscrupulous party members who use their positions to satisfy and expand their own ruthless ego and ambition, and
because of its blunt assertion by a main character that "Someone who has
learned to think can never be deprived of freedom." Still another example
of the literary tumult in 1956 was the rise to prominence of poet Evgeni
A. Evtushenko (1933–), whose depiction of the hard life of the people
made him the *bête noire* of the die-hard champions of "socialist realism."

The real literary sensation of 1956 was *Dr. Zhivago*, a complex novel
critical, sharply but indirectly, of the Soviet regime, by poet and novelist
Boris L. Pasternak (1890–1960). The furor caused by *Dr. Zhivago*
stemmed to a large extent from: (1) the stern and serious, although
politely worded, refusal by the editors of *Novyi Mir* to publish the novel
in the USSR; (2) Pasternak's granting of permission to an Italian pro-
Communist publisher to produce it abroad; (3) the highly publicized
official Soviet efforts to dissuade the Italian publisher from bringing out
the novel, and (4) the selection of Pasternak as the recipient of the 1958
Nobel Prize for literature. Although Pasternak declined the latter honor,
his presentation of the negative aspects of Soviet life made him the target
of savage criticism by party leaders, including Khrushchev, and by many
members of the Union of Soviet Writers. Critics abroad, however, have
classed *Dr. Zhivago* with the important works of modern times.

Writers' criticism of the negative aspects of Soviet life alarmed party bureaucrats, with the result that there developed a partial curb on literary deviations from "socialist realism." In 1957 Khrushchev summoned the leading Soviet authors to his *dacha* (villa), bluntly told them that he would not tolerate their insubordination, and warned that if they rebelled against the party he would repress them with all force. Khrushchev made no attempt to return to Stalin's restrictions, but his ominous warning induced many recalcitrant writers to admit their "errors." To uphold the principles of absolute conformity, there was also established in 1958 a Union of Writers of the RSFSR, headed by a literary die-hard, Leonid Sobolev. The aim of the new group was to halt the spread of the disturbing new trend in Soviet literature, and whenever possible to emphasize positive rather than negative characteristics of Soviet life.

The latter goal in fact became the central theme of the Third Congress of the Union of Soviet Writers held in Moscow in May, 1959. In a special message to that body, the CC of the CPSU reminded the members that they must inspire people for communism, must educate them according to Communist principles, must develop in them high moral virtues, must become passionate propagandists of the Seven Year Plan, must bring cheerfulness, vigor, and energy into the heart of man, and accordingly must reject "bourgeois ideology and morals." Khrushchev, who addressed the gathering, repeated most of these same clichés.

In contrast to his ominous warning of 1957, however, he insisted on tolerance among writers, hinted of his willingness to relinquish some aspects of party control of literature and leave literary matters to the collective judgment of writers themselves to be solved in "a comradely fashion," and guaranteed that there would be no return to the intolerable phenomena associated with "the cult of individual." To implement these unusual grants of autonomy, the most far reaching since the mid-1920's, the Presidium of the Union of Soviet Writers replaced Aleksei A. Surkov (1899–   ) as its secretary with Constantin A. Fedin (1892–   ), and reinstated Tvardovsky and Panferov to their editorial posts (with *Novyi Mir* and *Oktiabr* respectively) from which they had been dismissed in 1954. These changes greatly enlivened Soviet literary and cultural life and turned the second half of the 1950's into a highly productive period in Soviet literature.

What has been said of Soviet literature during the 1950's is equally true of Soviet theater and the cinema; i.e., they too rebelled against standardization of style. In theater the first sign of deviation occurred in 1954 with the staging of Leonid Zorin's *Gosti* (The Guests), a satire critical of party bureaucracy and careerism, which was condemned by the Ministry of Culture after only two Moscow performances. Khrushchev's de-Stalinization speech in February, 1956, though not concerned directly with the theater, brought new life to it, as de-Stalinization meant rehabilitation of many playwrights, decline of the popularity of the prerevolutionary Russian plays, in official vogue from 1947 to 1953, and appearance in the repertoire of foreign plays and of Soviet comedies and dramas. Among foreign plays, the most popular were *My Family* by Eduardo de Filippo, *Dangerous Corner* by John B. Priestley, and *Dial M for Murder* by Agatha Christie and Fredrick Knott. The most popular Soviet plays from 1956 to 1960 were *Alone* by Sergei Aleshin, *Eternally Alive* by Victor Rozov, and *The Factory Girl* by Volodin. The popularity of Soviet plays stemmed from their treatment of such "contemporary themes" as marriage, divorce, unrequited love, and lonely women whose husbands had sought and found new passions. Because these themes were "alien to socialist realism," they were criticized by many die-hard party scribblers, such as V. Kochetov.

Soviet cinema in the 1950's experienced an even greater rejuvenation than the legitimate theater. In fact, according to some observers, the period after 1954 was "the second greatest phase in the history of Russian cinema." This glowing praise stems largely from the release by Soviet producers of such films as *Three Men on a Raft* (1954); *Othello* (1955); *The Forty-First* (1956); *Don Quixote* (1957); *The Cranes Are Flying* (1957), the winner of the Grand Prix de Cannes; *A Man Is Born* (1957); *The House I Live In* (1957); *A Man's Destiny* (1959); and *Ballad of a Soldier* (1960). All of these films were worthy of the name of art, were free from schematism, were "no longer dedicated to the party, or its offshoots, but to humanity," and treated such problems as human conflict, the fate of mankind, the chaos of war, dissolution, demoralization, corruption, adultery, and other class-free elements of human life.

The 1950's also significantly affected Soviet music. The impact, however, was a negative one. A few days after Stalin's death came the death of composer and conductor Sergei S. Prokofiev (1891–1953), whose best known works include the opera *War and Peace,* the ballets *Romeo and Juliet* and *The Stone Flower,* the symphonic tale *Peter and the Wolf,* the ballet suite *The Scythian Suite,* and numerous concertos, scores for motion pictures, and other compositions. Because of Prokofiev's universal fame, Stalin never officially disgraced him. He reprimanded him, however, on several occasions for "formalism" and suppressed some of his works in the USSR. Composer Dimitri D. Shostakovich (1906–   ) was subjected to similar harassment for his failure to comply with Stalin's musical tastes, and it was not until 1954 that his heirs reversed Stalin's policy and, in recognition of the composer's achievement, awarded Shostakovich the title of "People's Artist." But shortly after he received that award Shostakovich was assailed by the party press for deviations in his *Tenth Symphony.* The composer apologized, acknowledged the "shortcomings" in his remarkable work, and since then has remained in relative silence. Another gifted composer of symphonies and ballet scores,

Aram I. Khachaturian (1903–   ), apparently adopted the same attitude following the party's rejection of his plea in November, 1953, that it abandon the tutelage over music and allow "the composer and the librettist [to] work exactingly on their own responsibility," producing works that would be "beautiful in form" and "provocative and bold in approach."

It is essential to remember that the intellectual ferment in the 1950's also affected many non-Russian peoples of the USSR. The ebullition among the intellectuals of Soviet minorities began in 1956; i.e., after Khrushchev's dramatic exposure of Stalin's crimes. Many writers were cleared of suspicion, others were rehabilitated posthumously, and the few of them who had survived Stalin's terror were allowed to return from exile. To pacify the growing excitement, Stalin's heirs permitted non-Russian minorities to receive foreign cultural delegations, allowed many selected groups to travel abroad to establish cultural and scientific contacts with "capitalist countries," and granted greater freedom to use native languages in the publication of literary works. In view of Stalin's bitter repression of minorities, these changes were more than a "thaw"; they represented a real spring.

In the mid-1950's, to calm the intellectual storm at home and at the same time to sell Soviet achievement abroad, Stalin's heirs launched a program of "cultural competition" with the non-Communist world. Under the program, selected groups of Soviet performers were allowed to thrill

Moscow University.

foreign audiences, while foreign entertainers were permitted to thrill Soviet audiences. The most outstanding example of the "cultural competition" in 1956 was the tour of the United States and Western Europe by violinist David F. Oistrakh (1908–   ); the performance of the Boston and London Philharmonic Orchestras in Leningrad and Moscow in September and October, 1956; and the triumphal visit to London of the Bolshoi Ballet in October, 1956. Because of the apparent success of these exchanges, Soviet leaders decided to expand the program of cultural competition, and since 1957 the Ministry of Culture has dispatched thousands of Soviet performers to "capitalist countries" of South East Asia, the Near East, Western Europe and the Western Hemisphere, and has received thousands of foreign artists from "capitalist countries." Since the mid-1950's Soviet leaders have also sent educators, scientists, scholars, and other groups to various international conferences, and on many occasions have hosted international scientific and scholarly gatherings.

Last but not least, the 1950's witnessed also a great change in the official attitude toward sports. Sports, especially soccer football, ice skating, and gymnastics, have always been popular in the USSR. The excellence of Soviet athletes, however, had been questioned because during Stalin's regime they were not allowed to compete with athletes from the "capitalist countries." Limited contacts with athletes from satellite countries were "staged" in the Soviet favor. Stalin's heirs reversed the isolation policy in sports. In 1956 Soviet athletes participated in great numbers in the Olympic Games in Melbourne, Australia, where they won thirty-seven gold, twenty-nine silver, and thirty-two bronze medals. In April, 1959, in an effort to coordinate sports activities and to increase interest in sports, the Union of Sport Societies and Organizations was organized. Increased interest in sports led to impressive results at the 1960 Olympic Games, where Soviet athletes won fifty gold, thirty-four silver, and forty bronze medals, and where they set many Olympic records. Competition with foreign athletes has led to the development of such events as swimming, wrestling, boxing, tennis, skiing, rowing, basketball, and various track and field events. In all of these, Soviet athletes, who are basically professionals, have shown promise and excellence. Party leaders have used the achievements of their athletes as weapons in the ideological struggle with the West, and have elevated their performers to an exalted position in Soviet society similar to that of artists.

As depicted in the preceding pages, the intellectual ferment of the 1950's produced far-reaching changes in Soviet society. On the whole, these changes, despite occasional alarming setbacks, were beneficial to literature, the performing arts, and sports. Judged by a normal yardstick of measurement, these changes were not spectacular. Viewed, however, from the perspective of Soviet reality, they were revolutionary.

FERMENT IN EASTERN EUROPE

Stalin's death and the ensuing struggle for succession led to many vital developments not only in the USSR but in the East European satellites as well. Of the many developments in the satellite countries, the most prominent were the East Berlin uprising of June, 1953; the Polish upheaval of June–October, 1956; the Hungarian revolution of October, 1956; and the Soviet-Yugoslav rapprochement between 1953 and 1956. None of these events led to disintegration of the Stalinist system, but they shook the system to its foundations and forced Stalin's heirs to evolve a more flexible arrangement of control.

The first concussion struck in East Germany, the satellite whose regime was probably the most Soviet-dependent. As early as April, 1953, East German leaders pleaded with Moscow for urgent assistance, and requested that the USSR reconsider its capital development policy in East Germany. Early in June, 1953, East German authorities openly admitted "aberrations in the past," reduced delivery quotas and taxes for the farmers, made available state loans to private business, and promised improvement in living standards for everyone. Events soon revealed that these concessions were insufficient. On June 16, 1953, encouraged by the lack of self-assurance on the part of the authorities, construction workers in East Berlin protested against a 10 per cent increase in compulsory work quotas, and demanded "butter, not a people's army." Within hours the nonviolent protest spread to other parts of Berlin as well as to other parts of East Germany. The demonstrators were in an ugly mood, shouted down the Communist leaders who attempted to pacify them, and defied the efforts of the East German security forces called to disperse them. Unable to restore order with its own efforts, the East German regime asked Soviet authorities for protection and help. Both were granted immediately. The Soviet army intervened, quelled the uprising, and restored the East German regime to power. By June 18, the unrest in East Berlin was over, but the message it carried was not entirely lost.

The East Berlin uprising was significant for two reasons. First, it revealed the unpopularity of the East German regime with the people, and its utter dependence on Soviet military support for its existence. Second, it demonstrated an urgent need for further concessions not only in East Germany, but throughout the Soviet Empire. In East Germany the immediate concessions included dismissal of high officials who had wavered in the face of the crisis; formal acceptance of the principle of "collective leadership" of Ulbricht and Grotewohl; public acknowledgment by East German officials of error in formulating past policies; reduction of investment in heavy industry; reduction of income taxes and prices; granting of partial amnesty to minor offenders; return to East German control of enterprises managed by the USSR; and termination of reparations to the USSR. None of these concessions weakened Communist control. They did, however, promise an improvement in standards of living, and thus relieved some of the political tensions in the country.

Many East Germans did not wait for this improvement to materialize. During 1953, some 305,737 sought asylum in West Germany. By October 1, 1955, that figure rose to 2,664,000, and by the end of the 1950's it reached 4,000,000. Most of those who fled were young and skilled. No country can afford to lose the services of the best element of its population, and least of all a country whose entire life is almost totally regimented. The mass exodus of population also became bad propaganda for communism, which pictures itself as "the way of life of tomorrow." Because the bulk of the escapees fled to West Germany via Berlin, by the end of the 1950's Berlin had become the most explosive spot in international relations.

The East Berlin uprising left a deep imprint on Soviet leaders. Between July 4, and October 29, 1953, they forced the "new course" of concessions on Hungary, Rumania, Bulgaria, Czechoslovakia, and Poland, in that order. Each satellite regime adopted the principle of "collective leadership," and promised (alongside continued industrialization) to improve the standard of living; to abandon the policy of economic autarky; to increase wages and to decrease prices; to give increased attention to agriculture; to slow the tempo of collectivization; to encourage private initiative in small production and trade; to curb the activity of the police; and to release those who had been imprisoned unjustly. Viewed by the normal yardstick of measurement these concessions were minor. Measured, however, by the standards of Eastern Europe these promises heralded a new era, and any attempt to alter this "liberalizing" development, as events in 1956 in Hungary and Poland demonstrated, was bound to meet with stiff resistance.

The "new course" in Eastern Europe was short-lived, however. It came to an end early in 1955, or shortly after Khrushchev forced Malenkov's resignation and advanced "the Khrushchev formula" for future Communist development and relations. That formula, designated by some writers as neo-Stalinism, called for an increased development of heavy industry; improved agricultural productivity; improvement of the standard of living; closer economic integration of the USSR and its satellites; greater emphasis on common ideological unity and uniformity; closer military ties with the USSR; and a continued common approach in the realm of foreign policy.

A major manifestation of Khrushchev's formula was the Warsaw Pact, entitled "On Friendship, Cooperation and Mutual Aid." It was signed on May 14, 1955, by Albania, Bulgaria, Czechoslovakia, East Germany, Hungary, Rumania, Poland, and the USSR. Ostensibly a belated answer to the North Atlantic Treaty Organization, the Warsaw Pact, concluded for the duration of twenty years, was a political and military agreement. The members pledged to settle international disputes by peaceful means; to cooperate in all international actions aimed at insuring peace and security; to hold mutual consultations in event of a threat of war; to afford immediate assistance in case of armed aggression against one or several members of the pact; to establish a joint command of their armed forces (Marshal Konev was designated first Supreme Commandant); to establish a political consultative committee; not to enter into any coalitions or agreements contrary to the terms of the treaty; to strengthen economic and cultural ties among themselves without interfering in each other's internal affairs; and to invite other states to join the pact on condition they adhere to the terms and principles of the treaty. Communist China had an observer in Warsaw who announced his government's full support of the efforts of the Warsaw Pact members. On the surface, the Pact offered East European satellites a greater independence of action than they had under Stalin. In reality, however, it formalized Moscow's control over the East European countries and tied their destinies more closely to that of the USSR.

The Soviets reinforced military and political ties with their East European satellites through increased economic integration. One of the major forms of this integration was specialization of industrial production. Under this scheme, devised late in 1954, East Germany was to specialize in the production of electrical equipment and precision instruments; Poland in ship building, mining equipment, and rolling stock; Czechoslovakia in engines, automobiles, and machine building; Hungary in diesel engines, buses, and motor trains; and Rumania in oil pipes and drilling equipment. The role of the USSR was that of principal supplier of iron ore, manganese, cotton, food, and other raw materials, as well as the active source of credit and technical know-how, for satellite countries. Plans were also worked out for the integration of foreign trade, investment, transportation, labor allocation, financial and clearing systems, and of many other fields. These arrangements made the development of each satellite economy dependent on the development of the economy of the other satellites, and above all on that of the USSR. These arrangements, too, paved the way in 1956 for synchronization of East European Five Year Plans with the Sixth Five Year Plan of the USSR. As a climax to this grand achievement of economic integration, in Moscow in March, 1956, members of the Warsaw Pact set up a Joint Nuclear Research Institute, headed by Professor Alexander V. Topchiev (1907–   ), of the Soviet Academy of Sciences. Shortly thereafter the stress and strain of the neo-Stalinist arrangements, which appeared to end the hope for further reforms, led to violent explosion in Poland and in Hungary.

The upheaval in Poland took two distinct, but inseparable forms: a mass strike in Poznań in June, 1956; and a "revolution" in October, 1956. The immediate cause of the Poznań strike was the official ignoring of a demand by workers of the ZISPO enterprises, producers of railroad cars, for improved working conditions. This bold demand, however, was preceded by a whole series of developments, of which the following were the most significant: (1) a gradual weakening between 1953 and 1956 of the power of the secret police; (2) growing criticism within the party of the methods used by the party leadership; (3) creation in the spring of 1955 of various party discussion clubs to debate issues, develop ideas, and crystallize attitudes; (4) open criticism of Stalin after Khrushchev's de-Stalinization speech, and questioning of the wisdom of Polish blind imitation of the USSR; (5) an amnesty in April, 1956, which freed some 30,000 persons; (6) public ridicule of the Polish parliament for voting unanimously on all issues; (7) public criticism by the Congress of Polish Economists early in June, 1956, of the primacy of heavy industry, and a demand that the government follow reform and not the neo-Stalinist line; and (8) official admission that the standard of living had declined between 1955 and 1956.

Encouraged by these signs of change, on June 22, 1956, a freely elected delegation of ZISPO workers left for Warsaw to demand satisfaction of their grievances. A few days later a rumor spread that the delegation had been arrested. This rumor instigated a walkout of the ZISPO workers, who were joined by others, and in a few hours the city of Poznań was turned into a seething antigovernment camp. The strikers carried placards with such slogans as: "We Want Freedom!" "We Demand Lower Prices and Higher Wages!" "Down with Phony Communism!" "Down with Dictatorship!" and "Down with the Soviet Occupation!" The strikers broke into police stations and prisons and freed many persons. Order was restored only after Polish Regular Army units arrived on the scene. According to official estimates, the Poznań strike was responsible for 38 dead and 270 wounded. Because Poznań was at the time host to an international trade fair, news of the strike leaked out immediately and became a worldwide sensation. Moscow took note of the anti-Soviet slogans, labelled the development in Poznań "foreign imperialist inspired," and warned that it would not tolerate a break in Soviet-Polish unity. At the same time, however, it offered to provide Poland with 25,000,000 dollars' worth of consumer goods to alleviate the most acute shortages.

The Poznań strike created a deep rift within the Polish Communist leadership. Some members wanted to pursue "the essentials of Stalinism, but without Stalinist methods." Others stressed the need for continued changes, for liberalization of the system, and for more personal freedom. The question was resolved on October 9, 1956, with the resignation of Hilary Minc, architect of the Stalinist economy in Poland, and the reentry of Wladyslaw Gomulka, whom Stalin had purged in 1949. Because of mounting criticism of Soviet methods in Poland, the Kremlin viewed this change with grave concern and invited the Poles to Moscow for consultation. When the Poles declined this invitation, Khrushchev, Kaganovich, Mikoyan, and Molotov arrived, uninvited, in Warsaw on October 19, 1956, and alerted Soviet troops for possible action. This move increased the already tense atmosphere of Soviet-Polish negotiations, the purpose of which was to convince the Soviet delegates that the changes in personnel were designed to improve Soviet-Polish relations, and that the contemplated reform aimed at strengthening the building of socialism in Poland. The negotiations were very stormy, but the Poles succeeded in convincing the Soviets that their apprehensions were unfounded. Apparently satisfied, the Soviet delegates left Warsaw on October 20, ordered the return of Soviet troops to their bases, and left Poland to march along "the Polish road to socialism." On November 18, 1956, Gomulka and his associates went to Moscow to work out an agreement to regularize their relations on the basis of "mutual respect, non-interference, and sovereignty." The Soviet government cancelled the Polish debt to the USSR in the amount of 2.4 billion rubles, and agreed to recall Marshal Rokossovsky from Poland. On their part, the Poles promised to support undeviatingly the foreign policy of the USSR and agreed to continue to allow the stationing of Soviet troops in Poland, retaining for themselves the right, however, to control their disposition and movements.

The partial success of this relatively mild revolution in Poland ignited a violent revolt in Hungary—a satellite whose regime was renowned for its brutality. Like its Polish counterpart, the upheaval in Hungary was preceded by a whole series of developments, of which the following were the most significant: (1) the bitter feud between Imre Nagy, the proponent of the "new course," and Rakosi, who considered the "new course" an anti-party, un-Marxist, and un-Leninist development; (2) the triumph of Rakosi early in 1955, following the downfall of Malenkov; (3) the resumption by Rakosi of Stalinist economic policies, collectivization, purges, and reign of terror; (4) disapproval of Rakosi's neo-Stalinist policies by many Hungarian communists, who felt that his actions were an impediment not only to communism in Hungary but to proper relations with the USSR; (5) Khrushchev's de-Stalinization speech and the posthumous "rehabilitation" of many Hungarian victims of the Stalinist reign of terror; (6) organization early in 1956 of the Petofi Clubs to discuss issues, the growing ferment among the youth and intellectuals, and an open call by some party members for "an end . . . to this present regime of gendarmes and bureaucrats"; (7) Soviet removal of Rakosi on July 18, 1956, or shortly after Rakosi publicly announced his decision to liquidate "all troublemakers"; (8) public pledge by the new party leader, Erno Gero, for improvement, his acknowledgment of inadequacies and promise to "rehabilitate" all those who had been unjustly treated; (9) mounting pressure for further changes, and Moscow's decision to reinstate Nagy to power early in October, 1956; and (10) partial success of the Polish revolution, which the Hungarians interpreted as signaling the end to Stalinism and to Stalinists.

The Hungarian upheaval started on October 23, 1956, as a peaceful demonstration on behalf of a less brutal regime for Hungary. It assumed a warlike character after the security forces provoked the demonstrators into violence. On October 24, Soviet tanks and armored cars joined the battle and restored order. Meanwhile, Mikoyan and Suslov arrived from Moscow, removed the unpopular Gero from party leadership, authorized Nagy and Janos Kadar to initiate a series of reforms and promised to withdraw Soviet forces in the near future. On October 30, in a major policy declaration, the Soviet government further promised to re-examine its economic relations with all the satellites, to recall economic and military advisers, and to build its future relations "on the principle of full equality, respect for territorial integrity, state independence and sovereignty, and noninterference in the domestic affairs of one another." Em-

Budapest, 1956. The Russian Army occupies revolt-torn Hungary. These Russian soldiers were objecting to this picture's being taken.

boldened by these concessions and determined to prevent the return of a Rakosi-type dictatorship, the Hungarians immediately produced a coalition government, allowed freedom of the press, disbanded the security police, appealed to the United Nations to pressure Soviet forces out of Hungary, repudiated their association in the Warsaw Pact, and officially declared neutrality for Hungary.

Hungary's defection from the Moscow-led "socialist camp" was a severe blow to Stalin's heirs. On November 2, the Soviets decided to intervene with force to prevent Hungary from assuming a neutral development. The Soviet decision was greatly facilitated by the absorption of the American public in the Presidential election, by the Anglo-French-Israeli attack on Egypt, and by the partial disunity among the Hungarians. The intervention was swift and well-planned. On November 3, the Soviets set up a new government for Hungary under Kadar, who had broken with Nagy, to rival the Nagy government. They responded immediately to Kadar's "request" for Soviet military aid to "smash the sinister forces of reaction" and "to restore order and calm" throughout Hungary, and ordered tanks and armored cars against Budapest. For several days the Hungarians fought an unequal duel, but fought it amazingly well, and earned the sympathy and applause of the whole world. Soviet restoration of order destroyed some 4,000 buildings, killed about 2,900 Hungarians and wounded some 13,000. The number of Soviet casualties is not known. The restoration of order was accompanied by mass arrests, deportations to the Soviet Union, and the flight of some 200,000 Hungarians to the West. Nagy and his officials sought political asylum in the Yugoslav Embassy. On November 22, they left the embassy on a safe conduct pass given by the Kadar government, but were arrested by Soviet authorities, "tried," found guilty, and executed. Soviet methods of keeping the unwilling satellite within its system shocked world public opinion and jolted the system to its foundations.

The course of events in both Hungary and Poland was greatly influenced by the decision of Stalin's heirs to reach an understanding with Tito of Yugoslavia. What really prompted them to take this action is not exactly clear. No one denies, however, that it was a major Soviet *volte face*, as well as a major step in the de-Stalinization process. The rapprochement with Tito was a carefully calculated undertaking, because the Soviets were uncertain of Tito's reaction and were unwilling to acknowledge their own mistake or to approve the idea of "national communism" which Titoism represented. Following his challenge of Soviet imperial unity, the Soviets had equated Tito's regime with the most despised "capitalist imperialists" and considered treasonous any sign of laxness towards him. Until Stalin's death, in the Soviet vocabulary Tito was a "lackey of the capitalists," a "bloody maniac," a "traitor," and a "fascist gangster." Meanwhile, with United States' economic and military aid, Tito strengthened his position, established contact with many neutral states, and emerged as a major spokesman of the "neutral bloc."

The Soviet rapprochement with Tito, like de-Stalinization, came piecemeal, and was doled out in tolerable, properly spaced, and gradually habituating doses. A few weeks after Stalin's death, the Soviets dropped most of the anti-Tito slogans; proposed early in June, 1953, the resumption of normal diplomatic relations; forced the other satellites to follow suit; ordered the easing of satellite pressure against Yugoslav frontiers; made concessions in December, 1953, to Yugoslavia on the matter of navigation on the Danube; agreed to resume railroad traffic; and set free Yugoslav prisoners in the Soviet bloc. Early in 1954, the Soviet press broke a precedent by quoting lengthy passages from a Tito speech opposing the European Defense Community. In September, 1954, the USSR and Yugoslavia signed a barter agreement ending the Cominform blockade of Yugoslavia. This action was followed by increased cultural contacts, by warm recollection in Moscow of the tenth anniversary of the liberation of Belgrade, by Soviet admission to the Yugoslavs in private that "in 1948 Yugoslavia was unjustly treated and condemned," and by Soviet pleas to "let bygones be bygones" and develop a new understanding.

Stalin's heirs were divided over the issue of excessive fraternization with Tito. Some anti-Titoists, led by Molotov, opposed concessions, fearing that they would lead to the disintegration of Soviet influence in Eastern Europe. Khrushchev, Mikoyan, Bulganin, and Kaganovich favored further concessions, hoping that these would bring the defector back and thus contribute to the strengthening of communism. The proponents of the rapprochement idea won, and on May 26, 1955, a Soviet delegation headed by Khrushchev arrived in Belgrade. In his airport speech, Khrushchev blamed the break in Soviet-Yugoslav relations on Beria and other dead police officials, and pleaded for resumption of friendly relations "on the basis of the teachings of Marxism-Leninism." Tito remained silent to these overtures, although in subsequent discussions he expressed willingness to cooperate but not to follow. In return, he obtained from Khrushchev a promise to dissolve the Cominform (the announcement was made on April 17, 1956), and an agreement that there exist "national roads to communism."

Following the Belgrade talks, Soviet-Yugoslav relations improved further. On September 1, 1955, the two countries signed a new trade agreement; in January, 1956, the USSR agreed to build several industrial projects in Yugoslavia; and on February 2, 1956, the USSR granted a loan of 84 million dollars (54 million in goods, and 30 million in gold). In his de-Stalinization speech, Khrushchev blamed Stalin for the break with Tito, and early in June Tito repaid Khrushchev's visit. His reception in Moscow was friendly, but his demands unacceptable. In return for his support of Soviet foreign policy, Tito insisted that the Soviets remove all anti-Titoists in the satellites, give him a greater voice in Balkan affairs, and acknowledge national communism and independence of the satellites. Khrushchev politely rejected these demands, and unrest in Poland shortly after Tito's visit to Moscow put the first chill to the new Soviet-Yugoslav friendship.

Early in September, 1956, Khrushchev, until now Tito's chief "appeaser," warned satellite leaders against Tito's independence, and informed them that the Yugoslav League of Communists was not a pure Marxist-Leninist organization. Later that month, however, he spent a week in Yugoslavia, and early in October invited Tito to the Crimea, trying to persuade him to oppose national Communist movements. His efforts were futile, as were Tito's efforts to gain from Khrushchev a promise for increased liberalization of East European regimes. The October, 1956, revolutions in Poland and Hungary proved both men right: Khrushchev, that any liberalization would lead to revolt and weakening of Soviet control; and Tito, that failure to liberalize would result in revolt. Following the removal of Molotov and Malenkov from power in June, 1957, Tito sought to establish closer understanding with Khrushchev, but his unwillingness to submit to Soviet leadership brought an end to the brief Soviet-Yugoslav honeymoon of the 1950's.

Moscow, November 7, 1959. Garrison troops parade in celebration of the forty-second anniversary of the socialist revolution.

FOREIGN POLICY IN THE 1950's

During the 1950's the Soviet quest for security to the territorial base of
the revolution assumed many aspects. Of these, the following were the
most important: the Korean conflict; accommodation with Communist
China; penetration of underdeveloped areas; "relaxation of tensions" in
Europe; and pressure against the West in Germany. Not all of these
aspects brought the desired results, but they did, however, improve the
international position of the USSR, and enable the Soviets to maintain the
diplomatic initiative throughout most of the decade.

Like many issues of the Cold War, the Korean conflict was an unre-
solved dilemma left over from World War II. Under the terms of the
Potsdam Declaration, Korea (an integral part of Japan since 1910) was to
emerge as a "free and independent" state. At the time of the Japanese
surrender, however, Korea was divided into two parts along the 38th
parallel—the northern under control of Soviet forces, and the southern
under control of American forces. Soviet-American inability to find a
solution for Korea brought the Korean issue before the United Nations. In
November, 1947, the United Nations General Assembly approved a resolution calling for free election of an all-Korean government, and set up a
Temporary Commission to supervise such an election. Because the Soviets
would not allow it to enter North Korea, the Commission performed its
task only in South Korea, where a republic was set up with Syngman
Rhee as President. In October, 1948, the Soviets announced formation of
a government of their own in North Korea.

On June 25, 1950, encouraged by signs of widespread discontent with
the Rhee regime, the almost total unpreparedness of South Korean
military forces, and an official American declaration that South Korea
was outside the United States' defense perimeter, North Korean forces,
trained and equipped by the Soviets, attacked South Korea under the
absurd pretext that South Korea had attacked first. Well equipped, and
having the advantage of surprise, the North Korean forces advanced rapidly southwards. Alarmed by this aggression, the United States called an
emergency session of the United Nations Security Council, which the
USSR decided to boycott. The Security Council appealed to North Korean forces to halt their aggression immediately and withdraw behind the
thirty-eighth parallel, and asked all United Nations' members to "furnish
such assistance to the Republic of Korea as may be necessary to repel the
armed attack and restore the international peace and security in the area."
Because the North Koreans failed to heed the United Nations' request,
President Truman committed American land, air, and naval forces against
the North Korean invasion, and, as other United Nations members followed suit, the Korean conflict assumed global significance.

For the first three months of the struggle, the North Korean forces, well equipped and having had the advantage of surprise, pressed the United Nations forces very hard and came perilously close to victory. Fortunes turned in September, 1950, however, when United Nations forces under General Douglas MacArthur launched a seaborne invasion near Seoul and counterattacked at Pusan. This action panicked the North Korean forces, who either retreated or surrendered in great numbers. By October, all of South Korea was cleared of the invader. With the implicit sanction of the General Assembly, United Nations forces advanced across the 38th parallel to the Yalu River in an effort to unify all of Korea. Many scholars have questioned the wisdom of this decision because it gave Communist China a pretext for entering the Korean conflict with "volunteers," thereby adding new dimensions to the struggle. United Nations forces were overwhelmed by Chinese manpower and were forced to retreat to the south of the thirty-eighth parallel. After much bitter fighting, a stalemate developed roughly along the thirty-eighth parallel, and in April, 1951, MacArthur was replaced as Commanding Officer of the United Nations forces by General Matthew Ridgway. Convinced that victory was impossible, as well as alarmed by the general Western rearmament effort, the Soviets "pressured" the North Koreans and the Chinese to enter into truce negotiations. These negotiations began at Panmunjom in July, 1951, and dragged on until July, 1953. The delay was caused by Communist charges that the United States had used "bacteriological warfare" in Korea, and by unprecedented anti-American propaganda, which in its viciousness outdid all Nazi efforts. Negotiations were also delayed by the problem of prisoners of war, thousands of whom decided to resist all efforts of repatriation to North Korea or China. An agreement was finally reached, but to the present day an uneasy truce prevails in Korea.

The Korean conflict was closely tied with the second major problem of Soviet foreign policy in the 1950's, the Sino-Soviet relationship. In the previous chapter, it was pointed out that Communist victory in China resulted from Soviet aid, dramatic disintegration of Chiang's authority, and all-out efforts of Mao's forces. In the long run the Communist victory in China was of great importance in the balance of international forces. Immediately, however, it was a hollow triumph. After some twenty-five years of civil war, accompanied by Japanese occupation, China was a barren land. Its economy was devastated; its communications disrupted; its administration disorganized; its millions hungry and technically backward. To make these conditions even more deplorable, before they allowed Mao's forces to take over Manchuria, the Soviets stripped that region of its modern industry valued at an estimated 858 million dollars, set up various joint Sino-Soviet companies, kept Chinese Communist influence out of North Korea and Outer Mongolia, retained the bases of Port Arthur and Dairen, and in innumerable other ways made it clear that they considered Communist China another satellite to be exploited for Soviet interests.

Because they regarded their victory as primarily their own accomplishment, Mao and his associates did not appreciate Soviet treatment of Communist China. Early in 1950, after some two months of negotiations, Mao succeeded in working out a more satisfactory arrangement with the USSR. By a treaty signed on February 14, 1950, both countries pledged to take joint action against renewed aggression by Japan "or any other state which should unite with Japan directly or indirectly," and promised "in the spirit of friendship and cooperation and in conformity with the principles of equality, mutual interests, and also mutual respect for the State sovereignty and territorial integrity and noninterference in internal affairs of the other High Contracting Party—to develop and consolidate economic and cultural ties between the Soviet Union and China, to render each other every possible economic assistance, and to carry out the necessary economic cooperation." In accordance with these high sounding principles, the USSR agreed to transfer gratis to China by the end of 1952 "all its rights in the joint administration of the Chinese Changchun Railway, with all the property belonging to the railway"; to withdraw Soviet forces from the naval base of Port Arthur not later than the end of 1952; to transfer the administration in Dalny to Chinese control; and to grant China $300,000,000 in credits, at 1 per cent annual interest, to pay for Soviet deliveries of industrial equipment. Although the Korean conflict postponed the execution of these pledges, viewed in retrospect the Sino-Soviet treaty of February 14, 1950, was the first major retreat of Soviet influence in the Far East.

Following the signing of the Sino-Soviet treaty, relations between the two Communist colossi, on the surface at least, appeared satisfactory, as both regimes shared a common ideology as well as hatred for the United States. The USSR, for instance, spearheaded the campaign for Peking's admission to the United Nations, provided arms and materiel for Chinese "volunteers" fighting in Korea, supported the Chinese in their "bacteriological warfare" charges against the United States, sent thousands of technicians to assist Chinese reconstruction, and admitted thousands of Chinese to Soviet schools and factories for technical training. Underneath the façade of cooperation, however, the Moscow-Peking axis experienced considerable difficulty. The difficulty stemmed from resentment by the proud men of Peking of their secondary status in the Communist movement; Soviet exclusion of Chinese influence in Korea and Mongolia; and the fact that Soviet aid was a pittance compared with Peking's need.

Sino-Soviet relations, though strained, appeared normal as long as Stalin was alive. His death in March, 1953, however, brought changes. The first concrete sign of change in Sino-Soviet relations came in October, 1954, when Khrushchev, Mikoyan, and Bulganin journeyed to Peking to negotiate a new series of political and economic agreements. What exactly transpired during these negotiations is not known, but the Soviets agreed: (1) to evacuate by May 31, 1955, all of their military units from Port Arthur, and to transfer all the naval base's installations to the Chinese without compensation; (2) to transfer entirely to the Chinese, by January 1, 1955, the Soviet share of four mixed Sino-Soviet companies, which had been set up earlier in Sinkiang Province and in Dairen; (3) to acknowledge Chinese hegemony in Manchuria; and (4) to assist on a much greater scale than hitherto the Chinese industrialization efforts. Mao and his associates also succeeded in extracting from the Soviet visitors a pledge that henceforth Peking's voice would receive more consideration in matters of international Communist strategy in general, and in Asian affairs in particular.

After 1955, signs of the existing tension between Moscow and Peking over the issue of ultimate leadership of the Communist world became more numerous. To weaken Soviet overlordship of the Communist bloc, the Chinese adopted a more liberal policy in 1956, and launched the slogan "Let a hundred flowers bloom, let a hundred schools of thought contend!" They encouraged the Poles to resist Soviet pressures, called upon the Soviet Union to refrain from interfering in the affairs of other Communist countries, criticized Stalin's "tendency toward great-power chauvinism" and his lack of "the spirit of equality," and, following the upheaval in Hungary and Poland in 1956, Chou En-lai even journeyed to

China, 1959. Khrushchev, Mao Tse-tung, and Liu Shao-chi.

Eastern Europe to act as mediator between Moscow and its East European satellites. But while competing with Moscow for leadership in the Communist world, Mao and his associates emphasized that they acknowledged Moscow as "the center of the international Communist movement," sided with the Kremlin against Tito, and against the West, and constantly sought increased economic aid from the USSR. The Soviets gave the aid (April, 1956, and February, 1959) but gave it reluctantly and in small amounts, aware apparently that any increase of the military and economic position of China would *ipso facto* endanger the position of the USSR in the Far East.

Whether by coincidence or by design, at the time when they were losing influence in the Far East to the Chinese, the Soviets tried to strengthen their position among the key peoples of many underdeveloped areas of Southeast Asia, the Near East, Africa, and Latin America. These areas had long occupied an important place in Soviet ideological pronouncements and long-range political strategy. It was, however, not until after Stalin's death that the Soviets made a concentrated effort to penetrate these regions. The immediate Soviet objective and tactics varied considerably from country to country. The long-range aim of this penetration, still in full swing at present, is obvious and manifold. It seeks: (1) to exploit dissatisfactions of the less developed countries of the world with their present political and economic conditions; (2) to foster the belief among the leaders of the underdeveloped countries that their past poverty and present weakness stem from previous political status; (3) to establish a measure of good will, especially among politically articulate groups, by supporting their political and economic objectives; (4) to portray all Western programs for these countries as merely a disguise for old "imperialism" intended to maintain the nonindustrial countries in a state of economic subjugation; (5) to present the USSR as a benevolently disinterested "brother" and champion of underdeveloped countries in their struggle for economic independence; (6) to identify itself with national aspirations of new countries and to create the impression that only the USSR is interested in their industrialization; and (7) to emphasize the superiority of the Soviet type of economy for rapid industrial development.

One of the unique features of Soviet penetration of underdeveloped areas has been its concentration on key strategic and economically and politically vulnerable countries. In Southeast Asia, Burma, Indonesia, and India seem to have been singled out for a concentrated Soviet effort at penetration. In Burma, Soviet penetration started late in 1956 and early in 1957, following the much-publicized visit to that country of Khrushchev and Bulganin in November, 1956, and that of Mikoyan in April, 1957. The Soviet government agreed to build as a "gift" to the Burmese people a series of projects to be completed by 1963. These included a technological institute, hotel, hospital, cultural and sports arena, permanent agricultural and industrial exhibition, theater and conference hall. The Burmese government, in turn, agreed to match the value of this "gift" with surplus rice. In Indonesia, the Soviets were attracted by its resources (rubber, tin, petroleum), its size, and its critical internal problems. The penetration there began late in 1957, when the Soviet government offered to Indonesia a $100,000,000 credit to help its deteriorating economic conditions. The Soviets agreed to survey Indonesian resources and transport facilities, plan industries, train technicians, and supply needed machinery and equipment. They also offered a generous supply of military equipment, and have constantly sided with Indonesian nationalists against the Dutch over the issue of Dutch New Guinea. With India the Soviets established closer ties in February, 1955, when they took the initiative and agreed, under terms very favorable to India, to build and equip a steel plant at Bhilai in Madhya Pradesh. Late that year Khrushchev and Bulganin made a triumphant and unprecedented tour through India; and in November, 1956, the USSR offered India a $126,000,000 low interest loan, agreed to train Indian technicians; and, while careful not to mix political propaganda with mechanical assistance and training, the Soviet government has flooded India with Soviet books, periodicals, newspapers, and films.

In the Near East, the main targets of Soviet penetration during the 1950's were Egypt, Syria (after February, 1958, the United Arab Republic), and Iraq. The Soviets started their offensive towards Egypt in 1955, as a consequence of Egypt's difficulty in marketing its cotton in the West, Egypt's desire for arms, and Egyptian President Gamal Abdel Nasser's "positive neutralism" and his defiance of the Western Powers. The arms deal was made in September, 1955. It was followed by Soviet promises to help Egypt build the High Aswan Dam, the visit of Soviet foreign Minister Dimitri Shepilov to Cairo, and Soviet diplomatic support of Egypt following the French-British-Israeli invasion of Egypt in October of 1956. Before it joined Egypt for a brief period to form the United Arab Republic, Syria was another Near Eastern country where Soviet influence sought to establish a base. Between 1955 and 1957, the USSR and its satellites offered a $300,000,000 credit to Syria, signed military and economic agreements, and promised large-scale economic and technical assistance. After 1958, as a result of Nasser's firm stand against local Communists, Soviet interest shifted from the United Arab Republic to Iraq, where a revolution brought Abdel Karim Kassem to power. Kassem's withdrawal from the Baghdad Pact delighted the Soviets, but his refusal to accept wholeheartedly Soviet plans for Iraq was a disappointment.

In Africa, Soviet interest in the 1950's seems to have been geared not to any one country but to all new emerging countries. The aim of this drive was to gain in Africa acceptance of the USSR as powerful, respectable, and a sympathetic friend. Soviet efforts in Africa were greatly aided by their example of rapid economic development and by their freedom, in African eyes, of the stigma of colonialism. The Soviets, during the 1950's, did not seek actively to establish a political base in Africa. Instead, they concentrated on developing an exchange-of-persons program and enlisting the support of students, representatives of labor and commerce, and politicians. Thus, the Soviets offered scholarships and awards to African students, sent delegations and missions to independent African countries to promote trade, develop favorable publicity, and further Soviet interests, and increased the African Studies Program in Soviet universities.

During the 1950's the Soviets also intensified their interest in Latin American countries. Until 1956, Argentina was the main center of Soviet attention. In 1953, the two countries signed a trade agreement under which Argentina sent to the Soviet Union its surplus of hides, grain, wool, and other raw materials, and received in return petroleum products, coal, sheet iron, steel bars, rails, cement, aluminum ingots, and other industrial materials. In mid-1955 the USSR held a trade exhibition in Buenos Aires featuring a wide variety of industrial equipment—its first such exhibit in Latin America. After 1957, the Soviets sought to expand their influence to Brazil, and other Latin American, Central American, and Caribbean countries, everywhere insisting on peaceful coexistence and friendship. Following Fidel Castro's seizure of power in Cuba in 1959, their interest increased appreciably, and it remains to the present day.

Stress on "peaceful coexistence" and "friendship," or what is also known as a policy of "relaxation of tensions," was after Stalin's death, on the surface at least, one of the guiding principles of Soviet relations with other key countries. The aim of this policy was simple. It sought in return for Soviet adherence to normal behavior in international relations to gain a great deal of good will and thereby to weaken the effectiveness of various anti-Soviet defensive alliances that had emerged after 1948. Among the most notable manifestations of the "relaxation of tensions" policy were: (1) Soviet renunciation on May 30, 1953, in a note to Turkey, of Stalin's program of territorial claims against Turkey along the Georgian and Armenian frontiers, on condition that Turkey be willing to work out in the Straits "conditions equally acceptable both for the USSR and for Turkey," and that Turkey withdraw from the NATO, the Balkan, and the Baghdad Pacts; (2) the Soviet decision, after ten years of delaying tactics, to sign on May 15, 1955, a treaty with Austria, which terminated the Four Power occupation of that country, in return for Austria's pledge to follow a neutralist policy and its agreement to pay, over a six-year period, $150,000,000 for the return of enterprises the Soviets had seized at the close of World War II, and Austrian agreement to enter into close economic ties with the USSR; (3) Soviet agreement to participate in the Geneva Summit Meeting (July 18–23, 1955), to discuss disarmament, the existence of two Germanies, prohibition of atomic weapons, foreign bases, "competitive coexistence" with the West in the underdeveloped areas, and increased trade (but not to discuss the question of East European satellites, unification of Germany, the activities of international communism, or President Eisenhower's "open skies" proposal); (4) the Soviet decision in September, 1955, to return to Finland the Porkkala Naval Base with all of its equipment and without compensation, in return for a renewed Finnish pledge to maintain with the USSR the close economic ties which stemmed from the April 6, 1948, Treaty of Friendship, Cooperation, and Mutual Assistance; and (5) the Soviet leaders' (Khrushchev and Bulganin, preceded by Malenkov) visit to England in April, 1956, where they mixed their pronouncements on coexistence and increased Soviet-British trade possibilities, with criticism of British postwar policies, warnings against British military action in the Near East, threats to make a deal with the West Germans, and brandishment of the hydrogen bomb.

Late in 1956 (following the upheavals in Poland and Hungary), apparently disappointed by its results, the Soviets abandoned the policy of "relaxation of tensions" in favor of "increased vigilance" and "military preparedness." Viewed in retrospect, the "relaxation of tensions" policy had little chance of success. Its main weakness was Soviet unwillingness or inability to see that their concessions or promises were minor, while their demands or expectations were enormous. Soviet unwillingness to negotiate seriously any of the major questions of the Cold War was another weakness of the "relaxation of tensions" policy. But while the policy failed to achieve the desired objective (weakening of the anti-Soviet alliance system) it did succeed in nurturing the image of Soviet "reasonableness" and enabled the Soviets, in spite of great stresses at home, to maintain the diplomatic offensive everywhere.

The 1950's witnessed some change in Soviet "manners" but not in Soviet objectives. The clearest testimony of this truism was contained in the Soviet position on Germany, where they continued to adhere to a policy set by Stalin—a policy which sought to bring all of Germany under Soviet control. Until mid-1953, the Soviets hoped to achieve this goal by posing East Germany as an example for West Germans to follow; by concentrated appeals "to all the peace-loving peoples of Europe" to protest against West German participation in European recovery and in the European Defense Community; and by veto power, stemming from their control of East Germany, over any program for all of Germany which they might find unacceptable.

Soviet efforts to win over the West Germans received severe setbacks in June, 1953, as a consequence of the East Berlin uprising. That upheaval, followed by a mass exodus of East Germans to West Germany, destroyed the Soviet belief that East Germany exerted a "magnetic influence" upon West Germany. It also revealed the unpopularity of the East German regime with the people, and its utter dependence on the Soviet military for its very existence. Soviet efforts to prevent West Germany from joining Western Europe fared no better. In spite of Soviet protests, West Germany experienced extraordinary economic reconstruction and recovery under the Marshall and Schuman Plans, rose rapidly into a respectable "free and equal member of the community of nations," and emerged as a vital link in NATO defenses. The failure to attract West Germans to East Germany, as well as inability to prevent West Germany from joining Western Europe, left the Soviets with their last but most powerful alternative: veto power over any program for Germany which they considered unacceptable.

Since 1954, the All-German program most unacceptable to the Soviets has been the manner of German unification. It was suggested at the Berlin Conference of Foreign Ministers (January 25–February 18, 1954) by the West that the four victorious powers promulgate and supervise free elections throughout Germany for an All-German national assembly. That assembly then would draft a constitution, negotiate a peace treaty, and form an All-German government which would have the right to decide the future development and international ties of Germany. The Soviets countered this proposal with their own plan, under which representatives of East and West Germany would join as equal partners to form a government and a parliament consisting of "democratic parties and organizations." That parliament then would draft an electoral law, prepare "free and equal elections" for a new national assembly, and negotiate a peace treaty. The new Germany, under this Soviet proposal, would be neutralized and demilitarized of all German and foreign troops and bases. The West rejected the Soviet position, the essence of which was government-controlled elections, while the Soviets rejected the Western proposal, the essence of which was free elections. The Berlin meeting of Foreign Ministers on Germany, like all the previous meetings, ended in failure.

The problem of German unification was one of the main topics on the agenda at the July, 1955, Summit Meeting in Geneva. The four heads of state agreed that as victors in World War II it was their common responsibility to settle the German question and the problem of German reunification, "by means of free elections . . . [to be] carried out in conformity with the national interests of the German people and the interests of European security." The Foreign Ministers were to work out arrangements for this. Late in October, 1955, the Foreign Ministers met in Geneva, but from the outset it was clear that their views were far apart. The controversy centered over the meaning of "the national interests of the German people." The West understood national interests as reunification in accordance with the rights of peoples and liberty of individuals, and proposed that Germany be reunified by a free election to be carried out in 1956. To dispel Soviet fears, the West also offered a treaty of assurance, which would give the USSR far-reaching safeguards against German aggression. The Soviets refused this offer. They took the position that they too favored German unification, but only under the condition that this unification would extend the "benefits" of the Soviet system to all of Germany. These diametrically opposed positions made a deadlock in negotiations inevitable. This deadlock prevails to the present day, and unless one side yields, it will continue into the future and be as permanent as the division of Germany itself.

Following evaporation of the so-called "Geneva Spirit," the development of Germany along two vastly different economic, political, social, and cultural lines remained relatively undisturbed until November 27, 1958, when the Soviet Union introduced a new element. In a note to the United States, Britain, France, and West Germany, Khrushchev proposed that the Western Powers negotiate to end the occupation status of Berlin. These negotiations were to be completed within six months, after which Berlin would be turned into a free city. The note stated that the Soviet Union was willing to assume full responsibility for the employment of West Berliners, and that it would not interfere in the internal affairs of Berlin. Khrushchev also stated that he was even willing to have this document "recorded in a resolution of the United Nations." On January 10, 1959, the Soviet government followed up its six-month time limit with a proposal to convene a twenty-eight nation peace conference to draw up a German peace treaty. The Soviet proposal called, among other things, for withdrawal of all foreign troops from Germany; denial to Germany of the right to join any political or military bloc that did not include all signatory nations; German renunciation of all claims to territories east of the Oder-Neisse Rivers; and assumption by the two German states of the main burden of negotiating German unification.

The West interpreted the Soviets' six-months' time limit to negotiate the question of Berlin as an ultimatum and responded firmly. It also rejected the Soviet proposal on a German peace treaty, which in essence was that which had been offered by Molotov at the Berlin Conference in 1954. Western firmness made the Berlin situation a major international crisis. A new meeting of Foreign Ministers was arranged for Geneva in June, 1959, to solve the problem, but despite some Western concessions the problem remained. The desperate situation began to look brighter following the announcement that Khrushchev would visit the United States, and that President Eisenhower would later go to the USSR. Khrushchev arrived in the United States in September, 1959, shortly after Soviet technicians landed a rocket on the moon. Following a cross-country tour, Khrushchev joined the President at the presidential retreat, Camp David, where the two leaders, behind closed doors, impressed each other with the need to pursue a calm and not a reckless policy. Events soon proved that the "Spirit of Camp David" was to be a short-lived affair.

SUGGESTED READINGS

The Anti-Stalin Campaign and International Communism. New York: Columbia University Press, 1956.

BARGHOORN, FREDERICK C. *Soviet Russian Nationalism.* New York: Oxford University Press, 1956.

BASS, ROBERT H., and ELIZABETH MARBURY, eds. *The Soviet-Yugoslav Controversy: A Documentary Record, 1948–1958.* New York: Prospect Books, 1958.

BOORMAN, HOWARD L., *et al. Moscow-Peking Axis.* New York: Harper, 1957.

BRANT, STEFAN. *The East German Rising.* New York: Praeger, 1957.

BRZEZINSKI, ZBIGNIEW K. *The Soviet Bloc: Unity and Conflict.* Cambridge: Harvard University Press, 1960.

CONQUEST, ROBERT. *Power and Policy in the USSR.* New York: St. Martin's, 1961.

DALLIN, DAVID J. *Soviet Foreign Policy After Stalin.* Philadelphia: Lippincott, 1961.

EMBREE, G. D. *The Soviet Union Between the 19th and 20th Party Congresses, 1952–1956.* The Hague: Nijhoff, 1959.

FISCHER, LOUIS. *Russia Revisited.* Garden City, N.Y.: Doubleday, 1957.

HALASZ, NICHOLAS. *In the Shadow of Russia.* New York: Ronald, 1959.

HALLOWELL, JOHN N., ed. *Soviet Satellite Nations.* Gainesville, Florida: University of Florida Press, 1958.

KHRUSHCHEV, NIKITA S. *For Victory in Peaceful Competition with Capitalism.* New York: Dutton, 1960.

KULSKI, W. W. *Peaceful Co-Existence.* Chicago: Regnery, 1959.

LAQUEUR, WALTER Z. *The Soviet Union and the Middle East.* New York: Praeger, 1959.

LASKY, MELVIN J., ed. *The Hungarian Revolution: A White Book.* New York: Praeger, 1957.

LEVINE, IRVING R. *Main Street, U.S.S.R.* Garden City, New York: Doubleday, 1959.

LEWIS, FLORA. *A Case History of Hope.* Garden City, New York: Doubleday, 1958.

LIPPMANN, WALTER. *The Communist World and Ours.* Boston: Little, Brown & Co., 1959.

MACKINTOSH, J. M. *Strategy and Tactics of Soviet Foreign Policy.* London: Oxford University Press, 1962.

MOSELY, PHILIP E., ed. "Russia Since Stalin," *The Annals of the American Academy of Political and Social Science,* vol. 303 (January, 1956).

NEAL, F. W. *Titoism in Action.* Berkeley: University of California Press, 1958.

NORTON, HOWARD. *Only in Russia.* New York: Van Nostrand, 1961.

RUBINSTEIN, ALVIN Z., ed. *The Foreign Policy of the Soviet Union.* New York: Random House, 1960.

RUSH, MYRON. *The Rise of Khrushchev.* Washington: The Public Affairs Press, 1957.

SCHWARZ, HARRY. *The Red Phoenix. Russia Since World War II.* New York: Praeger, 1961.

SLONIM, MARC. *Russian Theater From the Empire to the Soviets.* New York: World, 1961.

SWEARER, HOWARD R. *The Politics of Succession in the U.S.S.R.* Boston: Little, Brown and Co., 1964.

SYROP, KONRAD. *Spring in October: The Polish Revolution of 1956.* New York: Praeger, 1958.

ULAM, ADAM B. *The New Face of Soviet Totalitarianism.* Cambridge: Harvard University Press, 1963.

U.S. Department of State. *The Sino-Soviet Economic Offensive*. Washington: Department of State, 1958.

———. *The Geneva Meeting of Foreign Ministers October 27–November 16, 1955*. Washington: Department of State, 1955.

WEI, HENRY. *China and Soviet Russia*. Princeton: Princeton University Press, 1956.

WOLFE, BERTRAM D. *Khrushchev and Stalin's Ghost*. New York: Praeger, 1957.

ZINNER, PAUL E., ed. *National Communism and Popular Revolt in Eastern Europe*. New York: Columbia University Press, 1956.

IX

THE COSMIC SIXTIES

On April 12, 1961, Yuri A. Gagarin, a Major of the Soviet Air Force, successfully completed the first manned orbital flight around the earth aboard the space ship *Vostok I*. Four months later, on August 6, Herman S. Titov, another Soviet Air Force Major, completed seventeen orbits in the space ship *Vostok II*. In mid-August, 1962, Major Andrian G. Nikolaev in *Vostok III*, dubbed "The Falcon," completed sixty-four orbits, while his "travelling companion" Colonel Pavel R. Popovich in *Vostok IV*, dubbed "The Golden Eagle," made forty-eight orbits; and in mid-June, 1963, Lieutenant Colonel Valeri F. Bykovsky completed eighty-two orbits in "The Hawk," while his female "travelling companion" Lieutenant Valentina V. Tereshkova completed forty-eight orbits in "The Seagull." On October 12, 1964, the Soviets launched a three-man space ship, the

309

Yuri Gagarin   *Marshal Rodion Malinovsky*

Voskhod, which with Colonel Vladimir Komarov, scientist Konstantin Feoktistov, and physician Boris Yegorov aboard, completed sixteen orbits. As technical achievements and as pure human adventure, these flights were both breath-taking and history-making. They inaugurated the "cosmic age," pointed up the growing Soviet space flight capability, underscored the very great challenge the West faces in this field, exerted pressure on the United States to duplicate Soviet achievements, and intensified the rocket armament race. Above all, the flights presented the Soviets with an excellent opportunity to emphasize, both at home and abroad, that these achievements were "a fresh triumph of Lenin's ideas," an embodiment of "the genius of the Soviet people," and a manifestation of "the might of socialism."

Gagarin's, Titov's, Nikolaev's, Popovich's, Bykovsky's and Teresh-kova's flights were preceded by a whole series of experiments. Of the major reported successes, the following were the most important: the launching on October 4, 1957, of the first *Sputnik;* the launching on November 3, 1957, of the second *Sputnik* with a dog aboard; the direct hit on the moon, on September 12, 1959, of a space rocket; the launching on October 4, 1959, of a space rocket which circled the moon and photo-graphed its hidden side; the launching on May 15, 1960, and recovery of a space ship weighing about 9,000 lbs., with two dogs aboard; the launch-ing on February 12, 1961, of a *Sputnik* weighing close to 13,000 lbs., a prototype for the launching of a man into space, equipped with an auto-matic interplanetary station discharged by subsidiary rocket in the direc-tion of Venus; and the launching on March 9, 1961, and again on March

25, 1961, of a space ship, each weighing 9,000 lbs., carrying experimental animals and biological specimens. In addition to these impressive experiments, Soviet scientists carried out a number of less spectacular feats. During 1960, for instance, they tried out four heavy rockets in the Pacific, 167 experimental rockets in the upper atmosphere, and 160 meteorological rockets; in 1961, they launched 115 research rockets with telemetering devices for the study of space and the upper layers of the atmosphere; while in 1963 they orbited seventeen earth satellites to study space. One of those satellites, dubbed *Poliot I* (Flight I), launched on November 1, 1963, was a maneuverable space station, a prototype of vehicles needed to start interplanetary explorations. It was equipped with special guiding instruments and a system of rocket engines to make possible repeated maneuvers in various directions while orbiting the earth. On April 12, 1964, the third anniversary of Gagarin's trail-blazing flight, the Soviets launched another maneuverable space station, *Poliot II*.

It is too early and the information is yet too fragmentary to make a sound appraisal of the factors behind Soviet space achievements. Competent observers, however, have offered the following explanations: Soviet recognition at an early date of the importance of rocket development for the future; mobilization of all available forces and resources to attain that goal; the rich scientific tradition inherited from Imperial Russia; the systematic training of qualified scientists; creation of a favorable social climate for scientists, and assurance of a high position for them in society; development of science and technology in the USSR with the same speed in peacetime as in war; and obtaining help from abroad through both normal and abnormal channels.

While in the early 1960's Soviet science and technology were making history in space (the Soviets have not publicized any of their failures), Soviet agriculture was "setting records" on earth. The latter record, however, was not one of progress but of dismal failure. The dry fall of 1959 and the bitter, snowless winter that followed ruined about one-fourth of the winter grain crops. Early in the spring of 1960, the two main grain-producing areas, Northern Caucasus and Southern Ukraine, were badly hit by black dust storms, while most of the Soviet Union experienced late cold and rain. Rains also slowed down much of the harvest in the Ukraine, while a cold summer delayed the ripening of crops in Kazakhstan and Siberia. An unusual press silence about the 1960 harvest, absence of criticism of the districts that lagged behind, and an all-out effort by the government, especially in the "virgin land" areas, to harvest as much as possible, pointed dramatically to an agricultural crisis. During 1960 the government dispatched to the "virgin lands" some 64,000 skilled men from the Ukraine and about 150,000 young people from all over the USSR to help in gathering the harvest. Special brigades of propagandists were brought in to arouse enthusiasm. Continuous rain and wind, how-

Boris Shaklin of the Russian Olympic Team, 1960.

ever, prevented men and machinery from working to full capacity, with the result that in mid-October, 1960, millions of acres of grain were lying unthreshed in Siberia and Kazakhstan, while in the Ukraine the harvesting of corn was behind schedule. These developments severely affected the Plan, and the projected harvest target of 152,400,000 tons for 1960 remained a planner's dream.

To deal with this crisis, Khrushchev called a meeting of the Central Committee in January, 1961. It was an unusual gathering, since, in addition to some 240 members and candidates of the Central Committee, the meeting was attended by some 2,000 carefully selected representatives of the party, the government, the economy, science, technology, and journalism, who, under party rules, had no business there. Khrushchev and the First Secretaries of all union republics admitted in their reports that there were serious shortages and shortcomings in agriculture; that grain production in 1960 was 20,000,000 tons less than planned; that the livestock

Ballet in Moscow, 1964. A scene from Stravinsky's The Soldier.

situation was no better; that the country was suffering from shortages of meat, milk, and butter; that in 1960 some 9,334,000 head of sheep had starved in the USSR; that privately owned livestock had increased at a far greater rate than that of collective or state farms; and that in view of these factors the USSR would have to postpone overtaking the United States in per capita production of dairy and meat products (originally set for 1961) by at least five years.

Khrushchev put the prime blame for the 1960 failure of the agricultural plan not on climatic conditions but on poor organization of agriculture by party and economic organs; the obsolete structure of agricultural administration; backwardness in agricultural science and machine construction; low standards of agricultural engineering; large-scale pilfering of grain before and during the harvest; and juggling of figures by officials. He cast grave doubts on the accuracy of Soviet statistics by revealing that many party officials, to gain favor in higher quarters, assumed high obligations they could not fulfill or could fulfill on paper only. Some, Khrushchev revealed, bought produce in the stores, which was then counted "by a collective farm toward fulfillment of its production" and delivered to the state. He labelled this practice a distortion, a form of speculation, and even a serious crime, and affirmed that anyone found guilty "should be expelled by the party and brought to trial for their violations of party and government resolutions." [1] Khrushchev pledged to "divert a part of capital investment" to agriculture, and insisted that people should actually get milk, meat, and other products instead of simply a promise. Later in the spring of 1961, Khrushchev embarked on a tour of the country's most vital agricultural regions, where he obtained many pledges from local party officials for increased agricultural production. These pledges were extremely high and probably unattainable even if the harvest were to be perfect. Apparently all did not go well, because in November, 1961, Khrushchev again toured the agricultural regions of Central Asia, dismissing officials responsible for the agricultural program.

Agricultural shortages notwithstanding, in October, 1961, the Twenty-second Party Congress unanimously approved the Khrushchev-sponsored party program. The new program—the party's third (the first was adopted at the Second Congress in London in 1903, and called for the overthrow of Tsarism and the establishment of the dictatorship of the proletariat in Russia; the second was adopted at the Eighth Party Congress in March, 1919, and called for the building of socialism in Russia)— calls for the building of the foundations of communism in the USSR to be completed by 1980, at which time the principle "From each according to

---

[1] Between May, 1961, and May, 1964, thousands of persons were reprimanded and jailed for "economic crimes," and about 200 were sentenced to death by shooting.

his abilities, to each according to his needs" is to be in operation. Compared with its two predecessors, the present program is more voluminous as well as more ambitious, and it bears the strong imprint of Khrushchev. The program consists of two parts dealing with ideology and problems of foreign policy, and with the building of a Communist society in the USSR. The latter goal is to be achieved in two stages: 1961–1970, when the USSR is to create a material and technical base of communism, surpass the United States in per capita production, and improve the living standards of the people; and 1971–1980, when the USSR is to reach the principle of distribution according to needs and "a gradual transition to a single form of public ownership."

The new party program envisages for the USSR by 1980 an increase of the volume of industrial output "by not less than 500 per cent," and a raise of the productivity of labor "by 300 per cent to 350 per cent." It also hopes to achieve an annual output of three trillion kilowatt hours of electricity, 250,000,000 tons of steel, substantial increases of aluminum and oil, great expansion of the chemical industry, large-scale integrated automation of production, modernized construction, modernized and expanded transport and communication system, and a "rapid rise in the output of consumer goods." The bulk of this expansion is to take place east of the Urals in order to create there a new and powerful metallurgical base.

For agriculture the Twenty Year Plan sets a two-fold aim: to produce an abundant supply of food and to eliminate in the main "the distinction between town and country." To attain these goals, Soviet agriculture is expected to achieve a high degree of mechanization. By 1980 its total volume of production is to increase by 250 per cent; grain output is to double, milk to triple, meat to quadruple, and the productivity of agricultural labor is to rise by 400 per cent to 500 per cent. The Plan envisages extensive irrigation projects, wide application of chemicals, an extensive network of research institutions and experimental stations, and a "scientific system of land cultivation and animal husbandry." State farms, and above all collective farms, are to remain the basic units of production, but their functions are to undergo many changes. They are to continue to supply the state with needed food and are in addition to provide peasants with a guaranteed monthly income, public catering, kindergartens, nurseries, boarding schools, clubs, hospitals, and the like. When that is achieved, collective farms are expected to turn into "amalgamated urban type communities with modern housing, communal utilities, services, and cultural and medical institutions." The Plan hopes that the extension of "the luxury of city living" to the countryside will make peasant plots economically "obsolete" and unprofitable and that the peasants "will give them up of their own accord."

A kindergarten on a collective farm.

By 1980 the Plan expects living standards in the USSR to be "higher than in any capitalist country." The national income is to increase by about 400 per cent; per capita real income is to rise 250 per cent; wages of industrial workers are to increase by 250 per cent; while those of collective farmers are to quadruple. There is to be for everyone plenty of meat, fats, dairy products, fruits, vegetables, attractive clothing, footwear, and automobiles. By 1980 every Soviet family is to have "a well appointed apartment meeting the requirement of health and cultural living," and all public transport facilities are to be free, as is to be water, gas, and heating. The Plan promises a 30 to 36 hour working week (provided the productivity of labor rises as anticipated), increase of paid vacation to one month, an end to night shift work, and introduction of modern labor safety devices and hygienic measures at all enterprises. The Plan also promises to meet the medical needs of all the people, build hospitals, sanitoria, rest homes, provide longer maternity leaves, free food, catering service at all public enterprises, and many labor-saving devices for the home. By 1980, according to the Plan, the state is expected to provide free nurseries, kindergartens, free hot lunches, free books and clothing, free education at all educational institutions, and increased old age and disability pensions. All of these promises are conditional on a peaceful international situation, increased productivity, and increased sacrifices. Should all this be achieved, some Westerners have observed, Soviet leaders may well be forced to erect a high wall to prevent the entry of envious outsiders.

To realize the economic goals of the Twenty Year Program on time, Khrushchev introduced two significant measures in 1962. The first was substantial price increases for food (31 per cent for beef; 34 per cent for mutton; 19 per cent for pork; 25 per cent for butter, and 31 per cent for sausage products) beginning June 1, 1962, in order to transfer to the urban population some of the cost of increasing agricultural output. Khrushchev's second measure was a radical reorganization of the party and government structures. The new reorganization, approved by the CC at its November, 1962 meeting, put an end to the decentralization measures of 1957 and concentrated all economic planning in the USSR in the Supreme Economic Council (SEC), headed by First Deputy Premier and former Minister of Armaments, Dimitri F. Ustinov. Directly below the SEC are three pivotal agencies: the *Gosplan*, responsible for long-range planning, National Economic Council (NEC) responsible for the current plan, and the National Building Agency. The new reform reduced sharply the number of economic regions which had been set up in 1957, and approved formation within the party structure of two bureaus, one for agriculture and one for industry and construction. The aim of all these changes was threefold: to strengthen party control over the economy; to increase agricultural and industrial production; and to eliminate waste, inefficiency and corruption.

As the year 1963 progressed it became evident that these goals were very elusive. Contributing to this elusiveness were such factors as the delegation of powers, uneconomic prices, rapid industrial growth without checks and balances, the shortage of capital, badly and costly organized repair of equipment, "sluggish response" and even opposition to demands for a faster rise of labor productivity, dissipation of funds, lack of equipment, uneconomic location of industrial plants, and extremely high labor turnover in industrial enterprises. On June 4, 1963, all of these factors culminated in an official announcement that the much vaunted Seven Year Plan (1959–1965) had been scrapped.

Simultaneously with these developments, in an effort to solve the perennial grain problem, during the summer of 1963 the Soviet government successfully negotiated two large grain purchases. One was from Canada, involving 6.5 million tons; the other was from Australia, involving 1.6 million tons. Soviet officials also sought to purchase some 5 million tons of grain in the United States. American unwillingness to offer the Soviets long-term credits without some genuine easing of international tensions and insistence that at least half of the American grain be trans-

Moscow, 1964. Sales hall of a market.

ported in United States ships (whose owners charge $10.00 more per ton), brought Soviet-American negotiations to an impasse which was not resolved until the end of the year. The volume of Soviet purchases of grain abroad in 1963 (together with those of all Soviet East European satellites) reflected the magnitude of the failure of Soviet collectivized agriculture to achieve "the mighty upsurge in output," which Khrushchev had predicted on numerous occasions. This magnitude was even more intensified by the fact that in 1963 the USSR had the largest sown area in its history—some 350,000,000 acres.

The agricultural crisis was the basic preoccupation of the December, 1963, and the February, 1964, plenary meetings of the CC of the CPSU. To dramatize the importance of these meetings, Khrushchev invited some 5,000 to 6,000 "guests" from all walks of Soviet life who listened and approved his "new economic plan." The latter is a "crash" program involving expenditure of 42 billion dollars over seven years (1964–1970) to triple the chemical industry, which Khrushchev labelled "a mint from which gold flows." The bulk of the investment is to be diverted into production of agricultural chemicals in order to turn from the present grain shortage to an abundance of flour, milk, meat, and eggs. Some is to go for the production of all sorts of synthetic consumer items. Since the program is silent on any attempt at removal of the built-in inefficiency of the system itself, it is impossible to determine whether this unprecedented diversion of money and manpower from heavy industry into a hitherto neglected sector of the economy will bring the promised improvement of living standards.

The same Twenty-second Party Congress that approved a Communist utopia for the USSR, to be realized by 1980, levelled bitter denunciations against Molotov, Voroshilov, Malenkov, Kaganovich, Bulganin, and company (men who had unsuccessfully sought to unseat Khrushchev from his party post in 1957), for their continuous adherence to the "personality cult," "anti-party activity," "factionalism," and their active participation in Stalin's crimes.[1] The Congress also administered the coup de grâce to the dead dictator. For the first time publicly, Khrushchev labelled Stalin a murderer, instigator of mass repression against Communists and army leaders, a man who seriously violated Lenin's principles and who abused power. Many handpicked delegates to "the monolith congress" seconded Khrushchev's charges against Stalin as they also did his denunciation of Molotov and company. On October 30, 1961, the cheering delegates voted unanimously to remove Stalin's remains from the hallowed place beside Lenin in the mausoleum on Red Square for reburial alongside the Kremlin Wall, and to erase Stalin's name from the tomb. The proposal for the removal was made by I. V. Spirodonov, leader of the Leningrad party organization, and was promptly endorsed by the Moscow, Georgian, and Ukrainian delegations. Shortly after this action, the city of Stalingrad was renamed, as were other cities, streets, collective farms, mountains, canals, factories, and the like throughout the USSR and its European satellites, save Albania. These actions cleared for free and open discussion in the Soviet Union the reign of terror during the Stalin regime. Khrushchev even suggested that a monument be erected in Moscow to the victims of Stalin's purges—a proposal which was quickly endorsed by the Moscow City Soviet.

It is impossible to forsee the ultimate direction the removal of Stalin's name and memory may assume.[2] Immediately the obliteration of his name has brought on two visible repercussions: a new wave of rehabilitation of Communist, but not of non-Communist, victims of Stalin's terror; and relaxation of rigid controls over intellectuals. The most notable members of the new wave of rehabilitation were Bukharin, cleared posthumously in October, 1962; Chicherin, restored to good repute in December, 1962; and Nikolai A. Voznesensky (1903–1950), cleared in December, 1963. The vindications of the early 1960's, like those of the late 1950's, had one thing in common: they did not tell the truth, the whole truth, and

---

[1] Late in March, 1964, *Pravda* disclosed that Molotov, Malenkov and Kaganovich had been expelled from the party.

[2] Early in 1964 Soviet film studios released two anti-Stalin films: *Silence* and *The Living and the Dead*. The former is a story of a young veteran's trials during the postwar years of Stalin's terror; the latter depicts defeats of Soviet armies by the Germans as a result of Stalin's inept military leadership.

nothing but the truth. Neither did they restore "the right to draw conclusions from the moral wrong done the victims by the state." They were, in the words of one observer, "a pragmatic affair in which truth is a matter of convenience and innocence or guilt a utilitarian consideration."

The obliteration of Stalin's name, as decreed by the Twenty-second Party Congress in October, 1961, resulted also in a partial relaxation of controls over intellectuals. The most outstanding proof of this was the publication in the November, 1962, issue of *Novyi Mir* of a novel *One Day in the Life of Ivan Denisovich*, by Alexander Solzhenitsyn. The novel has been described as a literary masterpiece and "the most startling work ever to have been published in the Soviet Union." Its chief significance, however, is that it is a revolutionary document. It is a tale of forced labor camps under Stalin, a stark account of the systematic attempt to degrade and brutalize a whole nation in the name of "socialism," and an indictment of Soviet society. Why Soviet officials authorized the publication of this major assault on tyranny and totalitarianism remains a mystery. The entire edition of *Novyi Mir* (95,000 copies) sold out immediately, and the issue has already become a collector's item.[1]

The appearance of Solzhenitsyn's shattering work increased the demands by Soviet intellectuals for additional relaxation and forced party leaders to clarify the party's position on "ideological matters." The clarification took place at a series of conferences between party leaders and intellectuals during the first half of 1963. The most important of these conferences was the March, 1963, meeting between party spokesmen and writers and artists, and the June, 1963, session of the CC. The principal speaker on both occasions was Khrushchev, who reminded Soviet writers, artists, composers, cinematographers, and theatrical "workers," that the task of Soviet literature and art was "to produce in vivid artistic imagery the great and heroic epoch of Communist construction [and] to depict truthfully the assertion and victory of new Communist relations in our life." He cautioned the intellectuals not to spend their energies on "one sided" presentations of such aspects of Soviet reality as "lawlessness, arbitrary reprisals and abuse of power" during "the years of the personality cult," and reprimanded Ehrenburg for presenting in his memoirs, *People, Years, Life*, "everything in gloomy colors"; film producer Sergei Gerasimov for his "misrepresentation of Soviet youth"; Evtushenko for his defense of abstractionism; and Shostakovich for his admiration of "music without melody." He warned the intellectuals, whom he termed "the smiths of human psychology," that unless they presented positive aspects of the Soviet life that the workers and peasants had achieved they could not expect the party's support. Khrushchev did not remain in power

[1] Solzhenitsyn's novel was mentioned for a Lenin Prize, highest award a Soviet artist or scientist achieves in the USSR, but in April, 1964, *Pravda* stated definitely that the novel was not art.

long enough to implement fully this advice to Soviet intellectuals. On October 15, 1964, without any advance indication, the CC of the CPSU removed him from the Presidium of the CC, from his post as First Secretary (a position that went to his long-time protégé, Leonid I. Brezhnev), and from the Chairmanship of the Council of Ministers (the latter position went to Aleksei N. Kosygin [1904–]).

The news of Khrushchev's downfall was welcomed in Peking, whose leaders blamed him personally for aggravating the Sino-Soviet dispute. Elsewhere, even among foreign Communist parties, Khrushchev's fall created bewilderment and disbelief. The apprehension was perhaps more widespread abroad than within the USSR, for, during his tenure in office (in spite of such decisions as the suppression of the Hungarian Revolution in 1956, approval of the building of the Berlin Wall in 1961, and placement of Soviet missiles in Cuba in 1962), Khrushchev had emerged as a symbol of "reasonableness," "peaceful coexistence," and "common sense." It was perhaps for that reason that his successors sought immediately to assure the world and the Soviet people that the change in leadership did not imply a change in policy.

In addition to apprehension, Khrushchev's sudden eclipse gave rise to much speculation. Some observers attributed his fall to his handling of the dispute with the Chinese Communists, which had inspired less than unanimous support among leaders of the Communist parties throughout the world. Other observers, however, have emphasized the failures of his domestic policies, such as his inability to resolve the agricultural dilemma and to satisfy the increasing desires of the Soviet people for a better material life. Both of these theories found support in official statements on the reasons for Khrushchev's removal. These ranged from the initial statement that he had retired voluntarily because of advanced age and failing health, to later charges of nepotism, personality cult, errors in judgment, phrasemongering, undignified conduct, and mismanagement of the economy, to name only a few. Only the future can tell how successful will be his former lieutenants and "comrades-in-arms" in resolving the dilemmas which they collectively helped to create.

KHRUSHCHEV'S FOREIGN POLICY

In the early 1960's the Soviet quest for security to the territorial base of the revolution assumed five distinct aspects. These were: increasingly aggressive economic, military, and political penetration of key countries of Southeast Asia, Latin America, and Africa; reckless defiance of the authority of, and contempt for, the United Nations; deterioration of relations with the Western Powers coupled with challenge of the Western position in Germany, up to October, 1962; search for improved relations with the United States throughout 1963 and 1964; and growing tension with Peking over the question of leadership of international communism.

The increased Soviet aggressiveness in underdeveloped areas, as in the past, has manifested itself in innumerable ways. One of the clearest expressions of the new trend came on December 6, 1960, in the form of an 18,000 word "Declaration of Representatives of the Communist and Workers' Parties," signed in Moscow by spokesmen of eighty-one Communist parties throughout the world. Labelled by some observers as a new Communist manifesto, this "declaration" may be viewed as a program of action for future Communist policy. Close examination of this policy reveals that it is pregnant with dangers. The danger stems from the "Declaration's" formal announcement that the Communist world aims to step up its defenses "by all means"; that it intends to follow a more active and more militant policy in underdeveloped countries in order "to eradicate all Western influence, political, military and economic, in these areas"; that it plans to support politically, economically, and even militarily, all pro-Communist front organizations in underdeveloped countries, and that it will "prevent or decisively rebuff interference by the imperialists in the affairs of the people of any country which has risen in revolution." All of these points were incorporated into the new party program adopted by the Twenty-second Party Congress in October, 1961.

While varying from country to country, the new Soviet aggressiveness in the early 1960's has sought to establish a firm political base—not in every country, but in one key or troubled country of an area. In Southeast Asia this distinction seems to have gone to Indonesia. The two countries began to expand their contacts (established late in 1957) following Khrushchev's extended tour of the island nation in February, 1960. Following that trip, the USSR granted to Indonesia $250 million in credits; agreed to supply Indonesia with heavy cruisers, long-range jet bombers, jet fighters, ground-to-air missiles, and other sophisticated weapons; assumed responsibility for training of Indonesian economic and military specialists; and contracted to build 410 miles of road and a metallurgical plant in Borneo, an iron and steel plant in West Java, a hydroelectric power station and an aluminum plant in North Sumatra, and an atomic reactor. How deep or how permanent is Soviet influence in Indonesia is difficult to determine at this point. Many Western observers, however, have noted that Soviet penetration has coincided with a marked hardening of Indonesian official feeling against all Western and Indonesian institutions, parties, and newspapers critical of communism.

In the Americas the new Soviet "aggressiveness" centered its attention on Cuba. The Soviets were attracted to Cuba as a result of the deterioration of United States–Cuban relations, the assumption by the Castro regime of a radical trend, and a hope that the Cuban revolution would set off popular anti-American upheavals throughout Latin and

Leonid Brezhnev   *Aleksei Kosygin*

Central America. Soviet penetration of Cuba began in earnest following Mikoyan's visit to the island country in February, 1960, at which time he signed a trade agreement and granted a loan of $100 million. Since then Moscow has fully endorsed all of Castro's nationalization decrees; concluded (in June, 1960) a new trade agreement providing for the delivery of Soviet oil to Cuba and the sale of Cuban sugar to the USSR; agreed to equip the Cuban army with Soviet weapons; promised Cuba all possible help, including rockets, "if the aggressive forces of the Pentagon should dare to start an intervention against Cuba"; and dismissed the Monroe Doctrine as something having no vitality. Following the rupture of diplomatic relations with the United States late in 1960, and especially after the unsuccessful United States–backed attempt early in 1961 to unseat Castro, the Cuban regime decided to throw its lot with Moscow.

Closer ties between Cuba and the USSR began to develop in the second half of 1962, following the arrival in Moscow (in July) of Raul Castro, the Cuban Minister of Armed Forces, to negotiate a military agreement, and the August visit of Che Guevara, Cuban Minister of Industries. Both visits resulted in an agreement to send Soviet personnel and materiel, including ICBM's, to Cuba. This military build-up in turn led directly to the October–November, 1962, United States–Soviet military confrontation, which for a moment threatened mankind with thermonuclear annihilation. Pressed by the United States, Khrushchev withdrew offensive missiles from Cuba. Whether this withdrawal was complete is not known, for Castro has not allowed international inspection to verify it. He has continued to maintain close ties with Moscow and has made two highly publicized tours of the USSR, one in May, 1963, and one in January, 1964. During the latter journey Castro negotiated a five-year economic agreement, under which the Soviet government consented to purchase 24.1 million tons of Cuban sugar, and pledged to assist Castro militarily if Cuba were either attacked or invaded by the United States. In return for these gains Castro promised to side with Khrushchev in his ideological quarrel with the Chinese, and cautiously endorsed, but did not become a signatory to, the limited nuclear test ban treaty. Because of Castro's personal ambitions no one can foresee how permanent is the present Soviet-Cuban tie.

In Africa, the continent whose people were rapidly gaining independence from the West, the center of Soviet attention in the early 1960's was the Congo. The Soviets were attracted to the Congo by its strategic location; its resources; its political instability; its military weakness; the continued Western economic influence; and the amenability of one of the Congo spokesmen, Premier Patrice Lumumba, to Soviet suggestions. Soviet overzealousness in the summer of 1960 in an attempt to turn the Congo into a Soviet base in Africa backfired. In September, 1960, anti-Lumumba forces expelled the Soviet ambassador from the Congo, forced Lumumba out of office, and the ensuing chaos brought United Nations intervention. In mid-February, 1961, Soviet interests suffered a further setback with the murder of Lumumba. The Soviet government blamed U.N. Secretary-General Dag Hammarskjöld for Lumumba's death, demanded the withdrawal of United Nations Forces from the Congo, refused to pay its share for the U.N. Congo expedition, recognized the pro-Lumumba regime of Antoine Gizenga in Stanleyville as the legal Congo government, and threatened to intervene on his behalf. Thus far, the Soviets have not carried out their threat after a United States warning that any unilateral intervention would mean an all-out global war.

Aware that the best agents for Soviet communism are the Africans themselves, the Soviets have, in the early 1960's, stepped up their ideological penetration of African intelligentsia. In February, 1960, they established in Moscow a "University for the Friendship of Peoples," later renamed Patrice Lumumba University, and began to woo African students with free tuition, medical care, inexpensive housing, and up to $2,500 a year in spending money. The aim of the University is twofold. It seeks to train from 3,000 to 4,000 students from Africa, as well as Asia and Latin America,[1] to be good propagandists in their areas for Soviet achievement and power, and it hopes to create a link between Soviet-trained intelligentsia of Africa, Asia, and Latin America to oppose Western influence in

[1] According to some reports, in 1963 there were about 1,000 African students in the countries of the Soviet bloc (China excepted) studying in academic institutions, and about 2,500 studying propaganda and revolutionary tactics. No figures are available on the number of Asian and Latin American students in the Soviet bloc.

Red Square at night with Lenin's Tomb in the foreground.

all of these regions. In October, 1960, the Soviets created an "Afro-Asian Solidarity Committee," and they have also organized machinery for setting up an "All-African Journalists" organization. Meanwhile, too, they sponsored in the USSR an "African Week" and an "Algerian Week," and in innumerable other ways have sought to influence the young intelligentsia of the Dark Continent.

Soviet efforts to woo the potential leaders of the new African nations have received three serious setbacks. Two of these occurred in satellite countries (Bulgaria and Czechoslovakia), where many African students publicly protested against alleged racial discrimination, political indoctrination, and inadequate housing conditions. One setback occurred in Moscow, where on December 18, 1963, in Red Square some five hundred African students staged the biggest antigovernment protest in forty years. Technically this unprecedented demonstration was triggered by the death under mysterious circumstances of a Ghanian student. The display by the students of such signs as "Moscow, a Second Alabama!" indicated that racial discrimination was also a serious, if not the prime, issue. The demonstrators surged through Red Square, battled police, and were pacified only after their representatives were received by the Minister of Higher Education, Viacheslav P. Eliutin, who promised to investigate their complaints. What impact this incident will have on Soviet influence in Africa, only the future can tell. Immediately, those students who were financially able left the Soviet Union and either returned home or enrolled in Western universities.

Apparently because the United Nations upset Soviet designs for the Congo (as it earlier did for Korea), late in 1960, the Soviets started an intensive effort to weaken the world body. Speaking as the head of the Soviet delegation to the Sixteenth General Assembly of the United Nations in October, 1960, Khrushchev revealed that he was not content with the present arrangement of the U.N. In formal speeches, and through such antics as removing his shoe to pound his desk in full view of millions of television viewers, he argued that the world organization must reflect the present distribution of world power, which he believes to consist of the Communist, the Western, and the uncommitted blocs. He demanded that the office of Secretary-General be replaced by a three-man directorate, a *troika,* which would have a built-in Soviet veto to prevent the world organization from ever acting against Soviet plans. Should the United Nations fail to agree to this suggestion, Khrushchev warned, the USSR would either leave the organization or act outside it. This proposal, coupled with Khrushchev's unruly behavior and his personal attack on Dag Hammarskjöld, created a bad impression and evoked firm opposition. The sudden tragic death of Hammarskjöld in Africa, while on a mission in the Congo in September, 1961, gave the Soviets an opportunity to revive the *troika* scheme. After lengthy behind-the-scenes negotiations, however, the Soviets agreed on a compromise candidate, U Thant of Burma, to fill out Hammarskjöld's term. In November, 1962, U Thant was unanimously elected to a five-year term as Secretary General of the United Nations. Early in 1963, in an apparent effort to strengthen their bargaining position in the U.N., the Soviets announced that they would stop payment to the U.N. on some budget items towards which the USSR had hitherto paid its share. This challenge to the U.N., which found itself in

Moscow, 1961. The Twenty-second Congress of the Communist party in Congress Hall.

acute financial difficulties, apparently was intended to serve as a reminder that unless it behaved in a manner acceptable to the Soviets, the USSR had the power to destroy it.

The first two years of the 1960's also witnessed a marked deterioration of Soviet relations with the Western Powers, and especially with the United States. In part this deterioration stemmed from Soviet challenge of the Western position in underdeveloped areas. In part, it stemmed from the Soviets' extreme anti-American propaganda, which pictured the United States as a country of unemployment, starvation, racial injustice, warmongers, and imperialist designs. Largely, however, it resulted from increased Soviet efforts to dislodge the Western position in Germany. The tension between Washington and Moscow increased late in April, 1960, following Khrushchev's angry speech in Baku, in which he warned the Soviet people not to expect too much from the forthcoming summit meeting designed to work out an agreement on Berlin and disarmament. Then on May 1, 1960, came the ill-fated flight of an American U-2 reconnaissance plane, which the Soviets brought down over Sverdlovsk deep inside the USSR. The United States government maneuvered itself into a trap by first claiming that the U-2 was an unarmed weather plane. To the amazement of the entire world, Khrushchev forced United States admission that the U-2 was not a weather plane but a high-flying craft on a photographic espionage mission, by producing the captured pilot, Francis G. Powers. This incident doomed the May, 1960, summit meeting in Paris.[1]

The suspension of the summit meeting created an unprecedented uproar. Almost overnight, there poured forth a vast stream of literature on the subject, full of contradictory statements, charges, and counter-charges, each side trying to find a scapegoat. As expected, the Communists unanimously accused President Eisenhower for the failure of the summit, in view of his admission of his knowledge of air reconnaissance over the USSR and his unwillingness to apologize for it as Khrushchev had insisted. As expected, too, Western observers held Khrushchev fully responsible for wrecking the summit meeting, in view of his ill-tempered outbursts and his unrealistic demands that the President publicly acknowledge that the United States had committed an aggression against the USSR, apologize for it, and punish all those responsible.

The U-2 incident, the failure of the summit, and the Soviet shooting down in June, 1960, of an American RB-47 plane in the Arctic Ocean, brought about a frigid atmosphere in Soviet-United States relations. This atmosphere continued until the outcome of the Presidential election became known. Following the Democratic victory, Khrushchev sent President-Elect John F. Kennedy a congratulatory message, and in January, 1961, as a gesture of "friendship," the Soviets released the imprisoned flyers of the RB-47 plane. Early in June, 1961, the two leaders met in Vienna to feel out each other's position on world problems. During the meeting Khrushchev handed to Kennedy an eight-point *aide mémoire*, outlining the Soviet view of the German situation. On June 17, the Western Powers handed Moscow a detailed outline of their position. As neither side made any concessions, the stalemate over Germany continued.

On August 13, 1961, the Berlin situation, and with it the international situation, took a turn for the worse. To prevent further East German escapes to the West, East German authorities, with Soviet approval, erected a concrete wall across Berlin and began to tamper with Allied traffic within the city. This challenge, plus frequent petty provocations along the border, made Berlin the most explosive spot in the world. The danger was increased by lack among the Western Powers of a unified approach on Berlin. Early in September, 1961, Khrushchev, in violation of his own self-imposed moratorium, ordered resumption of Soviet thermonuclear test explosions in the atmosphere. This action, designed, in Khrushchev's own words, to act as the "Sword of Damocles," both shocked and unified world public opinion. Many questioned Khrushchev's sanity, and

---

[1] On February 11, 1962, the Soviet Government released Francis G. Powers in exchange for Soviet agent Colonel Rudolf Abel who had been imprisoned in the United States.

some began to make hasty preparations for what looked like the approaching holocaust.

Relations between the United States and the USSR continued to deteriorate throughout 1962, and reached the critical point in the thermonuclear confrontation of October, 1962. Kennedy's skillful, daring, and decisive handling of the Cuban crisis was a major turning point in the relations between the two colossi. The importance of the crisis centered not so much in the dismantlement of Soviet missile bases, as in exploding the myth, which had been the basis of Soviet atomic blackmail, that the USSR was prepared to run greater risks than was the United States. The removal of this blackmail, which Soviet leaders had skillfully exploited in the past, led to an improved atmosphere in Soviet-American relations. On June 20, 1963, the two powers, aware of the slowness of diplomatic channels of communication in time of crisis, agreed to establish a direct communication link between the White House and the Kremlin; and on July 25, 1963, the USSR, the United States and the United Kingdom negotiated successfully a treaty on a partial nuclear test ban.

The latter agreement consists of a preamble and five articles. In it the three powers solemnly pledged to stop test explosions of nuclear weapons in the atmosphere, in outer space and under water (but not underground), in order "to put an end to the contamination of man's substances." They invited all other powers to join the ban (many states immediately expressed their readiness to be a party to the treaty). They each reserved the right to propose amendments to the treaty, as well as the right to withdraw from its obligations should any one of them feel that its national interests had been jeopardized. A power which withdraws from the treaty is required to give three months' notice of its intended action. While this agreement did not solve all the issues of the troubled world, it was nevertheless a major breakthrough in the Cold War, or mutual suspicion to which the world has been subjected since 1945.

Following the signing of the partial test ban treaty, Soviet-United States relations (and, in fact, Soviet relations with other Western Powers) continued to improve. Soviet leaders, for instance, officially expressed grief at President Kennedy's assassination, dispatched Mikoyan to Washington to attend the funeral, and offered information to United States authorities on the accused Presidential assassin, Lee H. Oswald, a self-proclaimed Marxist who had spent two years in the Soviet Union. Early in 1964 American and Soviet officials began negotiations aimed at establishing consular relations, and on April 21, 1964, in an attempt to break the stalemate in the disarmament negotiations, President Lyndon B. Johnson and Khrushchev simultaneously announced a "substantial reduction" in the production of enriched uranium. The United States' overall cutback is to amount to about 40 per cent. The Soviet action promised discontinuation of construction of two large new atomic reactors for the production of plutonium, "substantial reduction over the next several years" of production of uranium for nuclear weapons, and allocation of more fissionable material for peaceful uses. These cutbacks are not formal agreements and provide neither inspection nor policing, but they do, however, represent bold moves by both powers toward controlling armaments by mutual example in the atmosphere engendered by the partial test ban treaty of 1963.

The last major aspect of Soviet foreign policy in the early 1960's was the growing tension between Moscow and Peking. The exact nature of this strain is difficult to ascertain because the available information is very inconclusive. The evidence indicates, however, that the two Communist colossi, while in complete agreement on the final strategic aim—spreading of communism throughout the world—seem to be unable to agree on whether the present epoch is one of imperialism or revolution; whether world wars are inevitable or avoidable; whether transition from capitalism to socialism must be peaceful or violent; whether peaceful co-existence with the non-Communist world is possible or desirable; whether "revisionism" or "dogmatism" forms the main danger to international communism; and whether bloc leadership should be centered in Moscow under control of *white* men, or in Peking under control of *nonwhites*.

Until June, 1960, the bulk of the Sino-Soviet disagreement was in the main impersonal; that is, on the Soviet side it was directed against unnamed "dogmatists," and on the Chinese side against unnamed "revisionists." This polite form of dispute ended abruptly late in June, 1960, at a conference of Communist leaders in Bucharest. Before the assembled, but selected, delegates, Khrushchev levelled bitter criticism of Chinese policies and attitudes. He accused Mao Tse-tung (the Chinese delegation was headed by P'eng Chen) of Stalinist behavior, called him an "ultra-leftist, an ultra-dogmatist, [and] a left revisionist," upbraided him for his selfishness, reproached him for his ignorance of modern warfare, and indicted him for his subscription to and mechanical repetition of Leninist theories that were detached from realities of the modern world. The Chinese hit back by accusing Khrushchev of smear tactics, of underhanded dealings aimed at undermining Chinese prestige, and of underestimating the true nature of imperialism. Bitter feelings notwithstanding, for the sake of unity both sides agreed on a joint communiqué and on a full-scale debate of their charges at a meeting of all Communist parties to be held in Moscow in November, 1960.

Between June and November, 1960, Sino-Soviet relations deteriorated further. In part the deterioration resulted from the Soviet decision in August, 1960, to recall many technicians from China and from Soviet suppression of Chinese-Russian journals in the USSR. In part, however, it stemmed from a Chinese circular, sent to all Communist parties, which blamed Khrushchev for the revolts in Poland and Hungary, criticized him for the de-Stalinization policy, questioned his ability to lead an international revolutionary movement, assailed him for alleged unwillingness to support revolutionary struggles all over the world, and reprimanded him for his eagerness to seek an accommodation with the West.

At the November, 1960, meeting, held in secret for over three weeks, the Chinese (led by Liu Shao-chi and Teng Hsiao-ping) renewed their criticism of Khrushchev. They accused him of "opportunism" and "revisionism," reproached him for his lack of knowledge of Marxism, criticized him for his propagation of absurd disarmament ideas, upbraided him for his fear of nuclear war, and denounced him for his support of neutralist leaders. Khrushchev replied to the Chinese charges by accusing them of fractionalism—"the sort of accusation made only in the last resort," and, when it is made, in the words of one observer, all Communists "hold their breaths and the world, for a moment, stands still." The end product of the conference was the previously mentioned "Declaration of Representatives of the Communist and Workers' Parties," a temporary compromise between the Soviet and Chinese positions—which the Chinese signed under protest and only on the strict understanding that another meeting would be held within two years to resolve the outstanding Sino-Soviet differences.

Late in 1961, the Sino-Soviet tension erupted anew at the Twenty-second Party Congress. The disagreement developed over Khrushchev's bitter denunciation and Chou En-lai's firm defense of Albania's "Stalinist" policies. Apparently the clash between the two men was very bitter, for on October 23, in the midst of the party congress, Chou left Moscow for Peking where he was greeted at the airport by Mao. No reason was given for his sudden departure. Its meaning, however, was obvious. Whether by coincidence or design, a few days after Chou's departure the Soviets set off the world's greatest man-made explosion. Early in December, 1961, the USSR severed its diplomatic ties with Albania. This decision made "the monolithic unity of the socialist camp" a myth.

The outbreak of hostilities in the Sino-Indian border dispute in September, 1962 (in which the Soviet Union assumed a "neutral" position) and Soviet withdrawal of offensive weapons from Cuba in October, 1962 (under pressure from the United States), complicated greatly the precarious nature of relations between Moscow and Peking. During and especially after these crises the two Communist colossi hurled increasingly bitter denunciations of each other's policies, and their differences occupied the spotlight at the meetings of Rumanian, Bulgarian, Hungarian, Czechoslovak, Italian, Mongolian, and East German Communist party congresses from November, 1962 to January, 1963.

During the first half of 1963, Sino-Soviet relations went from bad to worse. On March 8, 1963, the Chinese introduced the territorial element into the dispute by reminding the Soviets that the Amur Basin and the Primorsk Province in the Far East had once belonged to China and that their future would have to be "negotiated." At the same time, in a series of long letters, the Chinese began to press for a meeting with Soviet officials to resolve their "ideological" differences. After some maneuvering both sides agreed to a confrontation which took place in July, 1963. Both sides, however, took steps that led to the failure of the meeting. The Chinese, for instance, on June 14, issued a twenty-five point statement as an agenda for discussion, which the Soviets labelled as being "slanderous" and refused to publish. Before the Sino-Soviet meeting Khrushchev improved his relations with Yugoslavia (China's bitter adversary), and was successful in timing the Chinese-Soviet talks to coincide with the talks with the Western Powers on a partial nuclear test ban. The success of the latter and the failure of the former brought Sino-Soviet relations to their lowest point. In fact, the Chinese labelled the test ban agreement "a capitulation to United States imperialism," and a "dirty fraud" designed "to prevent all the threatened peace-loving countries, including China, from increasing their defense capabilities."

Following the failure of the July, 1963 Sino-Soviet ideological confrontation, relations between Moscow and Peking continued to deteriorate dramatically. In a series of editorials in *Jen-min jih-pao, Hung-chi,* and the *Peking Review,* the Chinese hurled venomous insults at Soviet leaders in general and at Khrushchev in particular. They referred to him as "a Bible-reading and psalm-singing buffoon" and "the greatest capitulationist and splitter of our times." They accused him of supporting Mao's enemies inside China; stigmatized him for his alleged opposition to Mao's ambitious program of communes and rapid industrialization, the renowned "great leap forward" which resulted in a colossal disaster in 1958–1959; and denounced him as a more dangerous enemy of communism than Tito or even Trotsky. The Chinese accompanied their verbal challenge of Soviet leadership by a series of direct actions. In December, 1963, for instance, they dispatched Chou En-lai on a two-month's journey through African countries to compete with the Soviets for the allegiance of key African leaders. Early in 1964, they successfully negotiated diplomatic relations with the government of President Charles de Gaulle of France. And, about the same time, they were also trying to seize control of the African-Asian Solidarity Conference held in Algiers.

For several months Soviet leaders took no official note of Chinese insults, apparently hoping that their silence would induce the Chinese to silence. When this approach proved ineffective, Khrushchev altered his tactics. He referred to Mao on different occasions as "a subversive splitter," "a racist," "a mixture of petty bourgeois adventurist and a great-power chauvinist" and a "worn-out galosh" that should be discarded. He made the Sino-Soviet split a central issue of the February plenary meeting of the CC of the CPSU, and officially disclosed the Soviet position on the nature as well as the development of the conflict. Simultaneously with these disclosures Khrushchev and his associates were busily engaged in retaining the allegiance of as many leaders of Communist parties throughout the world as possible. Late in 1964, the Soviet position was supported by Communist parties of the following countries: Algeria, Argentina, Austria, Britain, Bulgaria, Ceylon, Chile, Cyprus, Czechoslovakia, Denmark, East Germany, Finland, Holland, Hungary, India, Mongolia, Poland, United States, and Yugoslavia. The Chinese position was endorsed by the parties of Albania, Cambodia, Indonesia, Japan, Malaya, New Zealand, North Korea, North Vietnam, and Thailand. Still maneuvering were the parties of Australia, Belgium, Brazil, Burma, Cuba, France, Italy, Norway, Peru, Rumania, and Switzerland. On October 16, 1964, just one day after Khrushchev's sudden removal, the Chinese Communists added a new element to the dispute with their successful detonation of an atomic device. The Sino-Soviet rift—perhaps the most significant political event of the present-day world—has dramatically revealed two fundamental things: that the monolithic unity of the Communist world is a myth—not a reality; and that present and future are pregnant with both opportunities and dangers for all mankind.

DOMESTIC DEVELOPMENTS UNDER BREZHNEV AND KOSYGIN

Compared with Khrushchev's domestic program, that of Brezhnev-Kosygin has to date exhibited continuity in certain areas and change and retreat in others. The continuity feature is perhaps best illustrated in the performance of Soviet space, defense, and defense-related industries. Between January 1, 1965, and January 1, 1971, Soviet scientists and technicians launched over 320 artificial earth satellites in the "Cosmos" series; placed into earth orbit and later recovered seven space stations (three in the "Proton" and four in the "Zond" series); orbited fifteen communication and weather satellites in the "Molniia" series; sent nine space ships in the "Soiuz" and "Voskhod" series (five manned and four unmanned) into earth orbit; and launched four probes to the planet Venus (in the "Ventura" series, one of which soft-landed on the distant planet early in 1971) and thirteen to the Moon (in the "Luna" series). From the technological point of view the most spectacular of these efforts was the successful September, 1970, soft-landing and return of a robot craft that brought back three and one-half ounces of dust from the moon, followed by the November, 1970, soft-landing of an eight-wheeled moonrover "Lunakhod," the first self-propelled vehicle to maneuver on the lunar surface.

What has been the *real* scientific achievement of these and many other Soviet space probes is most difficult to determine because the Soviets have continued to be very secretive about their space work. This much is certain, however. Because it is defense-related, the Soviet space program has been given all the necessary financial support. This support in turn has enabled Soviet scientists to test the latest equipment and techniques such as manual space-ship control, stabilization systems, the welding of metals in vacuum and weightlessness, space rendezvous, and remote-controlled soft-landing. One of the experiments ended in tragedy on April 24, 1967, with the flaming crash of a space ship, "Soiuz 1," that killed its pilot V. M. Komarov. To a casual, uninformed observer, Soviet space efforts, however extensive they may have been, have failed to capture the imagination and the enthusiasm of mankind in the same way as the historic July, 1969, landing, walk about, and the safe return from the moon's surface by United States' astronauts Neil A. Armstrong and Edwin E. Aldrin. Careful scrutiny of Soviet space efforts to date, however, indicates that they have very sophisticated hardware with an extensive, second-to-none, back-up system and that they have achieved the same knowledge and success as the Americans.

The Brezhnev-Kosygin leadership has tried to keep up not only with United States space accomplishments but with U.S. defense capabilities as well. That this would be the case was made clear early in December, 1965, with the official announcement that the 1966 budget would include a 600 million ruble increase in defense spending. The increase for 1967 was 1.1 billion rubles; for 1968 it was 2.2 billion; for 1969 it was 1 billion; and for 1970 it was 200 million. These figures are inconclusive since historically the published defense expenditures have reflected only a portion of the total Soviet investment in defense. It has been estimated that in 1969 the Soviets actually allocated to defense, space and nuclear energy programs about 13 per cent of the country's GNP. With this allocation they have increased their stockpiles of intercontinental missiles and have built up their land, air, and naval forces to unprecedented heights. This effort has seen the Soviet Union transformed into a mighty sea power with fleets in all the oceans and major seas of the world.

The heavy investment in space and defense-related industry has forced sacrifices in other sectors of the economy. The most adversely affected was agriculture, which, as in the past, received much official attention, promises, and administrative changes but very little in actual rubles. Immediately after assuming power the new leaders introduced a series of stop-gap measures aimed at appeasing the rural population and at halting the deterioration of the national diet. They restored private plots of collective farmers to their former size. They reinstated the norms for privately owned livestock, which since 1955 had been greatly reduced. They repealed the tax on cattle owned by city dwellers, which had been in force since 1956. They pledged assistance to collective farmers in acquiring livestock, feed, and pasture. And they decreed that in all state farms, which had been converted from collective farms, the former members who had passed retirement age were to keep or be given back their original private plots, unaltered in size.

The ills of Soviet agriculture came under close scrutiny of the March, 1965, Plenum of the CC of the CPSU. In accordance with Brezhnev's recommendations, the Plenum: (1) approved a doubling of state investments in agriculture from about 20 billion rubles in 1961–65 to 41 billion in 1966–70; (2) decreed that state purchases and delivery quotas (which in the past had changed from year to year) remain stable throughout the 1965–70 period; and (3) ordered a sizable increase (ranging between 12 and 53 per cent) in prices for state purchases from collective farms. In addition, to ease the burden of the rural population, in April, 1965, the new leaders removed the rural surcharge from many items of clothing, footwear, and other necessities, and a year later they offered collective farmers a guaranteed monthly wage (similar to that of state-farm workers) to replace the old exploitative system of deferring payment until crop deliveries had been made to the state. Though given little publicity, the most important innovation of the new leadership was its decision to table the Khrushchev-initiated campaign to transform all collective farms into state farms—a scheme that between 1961 and 1964 had generated a great deal of popular discontent and indirectly contributed to Khrushchev's downfall.

In an apparent effort to demonstrate that collective farms would remain intact, the government announced early in 1966 that the Third All-Union Congress of Collective Farms would convene later that year to draw up a new Model Collective Farm Charter to replace Stalin's Charter, which had been in existence since 1935. While that meeting was delayed for unexplained reasons until November, 1969, the ills of Soviet agriculture were given lengthy attention at the Twenty-Third Party Congress in April, 1966, and the Plenum of the CC of the CPSU in May, 1966. None of these meetings produced any revolutionary decisions. The new Charter, which was adopted in 1969, contained two insignificant innovations. It extended to the collective farmers a unified social security scheme, and it set up a system of collective farm councils at all levels. All other changes in the Charter are either nebulous or devoid of any real safeguards for the collective farmers. Thus, every member of the collective farm is now guaranteed a wage, but the amount of that wage is not indicated. Similarly, the collective farm is adjured to assist its members in tending their private plots and livestock, but it leaves that assistance to the whim of local bureaucrats. The result is that in spite of a number of changes Soviet agriculture remains, as it has been in the past, the Achilles heel of Soviet economy.

But while the Brezhnev-Kosygin leadership has been unwilling to make any meaningful or constructive changes in agriculture, it has introduced a number of changes in other vital areas of Soviet life. Immediately the most significant departure from Khrushchev's policies was the termination, in November, 1964, of Khrushchev's Party reforms that had in 1962 divided Party bureaucracy into industrial and agricultural components. In the long run, however, the most significant innovation of Khrushchev's successors was the departure from de-Stalinization—the cornerstone of Khrushchev's domestic program. In an apparent effort to halt "the erosion of discipline," the men who wrested power from Khrushchev have denounced his abuse of the term "period of the personality cult," have sought to silence all criticism of the late dictator, and have expelled from the Party many of Stalin's vocal critics, including Khrushchev.

Though the trend toward neo-Stalinism since Khrushchev's ouster has been only partial, it nevertheless has encountered strong criticism from the Soviet scientific and literary community, and two oppositions seem to have emerged: the Scientific Opposition and the Literary Opposition. The chief spokesmen for the Scientific Opposition, which has been able to attract followers from the academic world, the technological intelligentsia, and even a number of the scientists in the Armed Forces of the USSR, have included: Lev Landau, who until his death in 1968 was regarded as the most gifted Soviet theoretical physicist; Piotr Kapitsa, the dean of Soviet physicists; Andrei D. Sakharov, the father of Soviet controlled thermonuclear reaction; and Zhores A. Medvedev, a geneticist and author of a major work in the sociology of science. As formulated in Sakharov's famed document entitled "Thoughts on Progress, Peaceful Coexistence and Intellectual Freedom," the aim of the Scientific Opposition is fivefold. It advocates the establishment of a genuine freedom of thought and discussion in the Soviet Union to solve the pressing problems facing Soviet society. It pleads for an end to bureaucratic despotism and censorship. It favors a liberal-democratic reform of the Soviet system, based on a multi-party political order. It criticizes the monopoly of the Communist Party, dominated and staffed by "hypocrites and demagogues." And it opposes the continued preaching by the Party of class struggle and hatred, and considers as "madness and a crime" the Marxist-Leninist premise that world ideologies and nations must remain incompatible. The relative isolation of the members of the Scientific Opposition from the citizenry at large and the lack of a free press and an open political forum in which to propagate and disseminate their ideas has to date prevented the Scientific Opposition from emerging into a meaningful "anti-establishment" force in the USSR. An exception to this was the organization late in 1970 of the Human Rights Committee, headed by Sakharov, whose declared aim is "to give consultative aid to the organs of power in applying guarantees of the rights of man."

The Literary Opposition to the revival of neo-Stalinism has centered around Alexander Solzhenitsyn, author of three great literary works, *One Day in the Life of Ivan Denisovich, Cancer Ward,* and *The First Circle,* and recipient of the 1970 Nobel Prize for literature. Other prominent members of the Literary Opposition include: Andrei Seniavsky, Yuli Daniel, Yuri Galanskov, Alexander Ginzburg, Pavel Litvinov, Vladimir Bukovsky, Viktor Khaustov, Valentin Moroz, Andrei Amalrik, Ivan Dziuba, and Viacheslav Chornovil. The principal aim of the Literary Opposition, which has attracted into its midst many artists, writers, teachers, doctors, translators, students, and even ordinary workers, seems to be threefold: it seeks to expose all the inequities in and contradictions of the Soviet system; it calls for an end to the officially sponsored reign of terror against all forms of dissent and persecution of ethnic and religious minorities; and it pleads for the establishment in the USSR of a philosophy and system based on a universal moral law that would be binding on everyone and that would express the eternally valid human qualities and truths.

The Literary Opposition has tried to diffuse its ideas in a variety of ways, ranging from protest demonstrations and clandestine publications to smuggling of literary works abroad and defections of its members and/or of its sympathizers. The earliest of demonstrations occurred in April, 1965, in front of the Moscow Writers' Club by a group of students who demanded the end of "socialist realism." Another demonstration protesting the arrest and trial of Daniel and Seniavsky took place in Pushkin Square on December 5, 1965. Since then every arrest and trial of a dissenter has attracted silent demonstrators. Among the clandestine publications by the Literary Opposition the most remarkable is the *Chronicle of Current Events* that made its debut in the spring of 1968. The bi-monthly *Chronicle* carries information on the latest arrests, interrogations, trials, and imprisonment of anti-Soviet dissenters, and prints texts of vital documents and letters of protest about official persecution of ethnic and religious minorities (Jews, Ukrainians, Crimean Tatars, Estonians, Baptists). Until his confinement to an insane asylum in February, 1969, the most prominent contributor to the *Chronicle* was former Major General Piotr Grigorenko, who once taught cybernetics at Frunze Military Academy. Several members of the Literary Opposition, after official censors rejected their works for publication in the USSR, have managed to have these works published abroad under their own names or under pseudonyms. The most outstanding of these works are *Cancer Ward* and *The First Circle* by Solzhenitsyn and *Will the Soviet Union Survive Until 1984?* by Amalrik. Late in 1970 a book entitled *Khrushchev Remembers,* whose promoters claim it to be an authentic memoir secretly smuggled out, was published in the United States. While Khrushchev obviously does not belong to the Literary Opposition, the unusual interest that this memoir has generated throughout the world makes it imperative that it be included among the latest works critical of Stalinism and its recent revival.

Since Khrushchev's downfall in October, 1964, a number of prominent Soviet citizens have defected from the Soviet Union and have sought political asylum in the West. Doubtless the most celebrated defector has been Svetlana Alliluyeva, Stalin's only daughter, who after settling in the United States published several critically revealing accounts of her life and times in the USSR. Other prominent defectors include Anatoly V. Kuznetsov, a young writer who defected in July, 1969, and was granted political asylum in Great Britain, and Natalia Makarova, the prima ballerina of the Leningrad Kirov Ballet, who also was granted asylum in Great Britain in September, 1970, and has since come to the United States.

Officials have dealt severely with members of the Literary Opposition, much more severely than with members of the Scientific Opposition, since they doubtless feel that the work of scientists is more indispensable to the survival of the system than that of writers and/or artists. Many members of the Literary Opposition have been sentenced to long prison terms for their beliefs, while others, as in Tsarist times, have been confined to insane asylums. There is considerable evidence that seems to suggest that Soviet officials, as did their Tsarist counterparts, have singled out Jewish and Ukrainian dissenters for unusually harsh treatment. The anti-dissenting repression reached a milestone late in December, 1970, with the sentencing of eleven Soviet citizens (nine of whom were Jews) for the alleged plot to hijack a Soviet plane in order to emigrate to Israel. The initial death sentence for two Jewish defendants, which was subsequently reduced to long prison terms, produced adverse reaction throughout the civilized world, but only the future will tell what ultimate, positive results may be produced. It is not the historian's task, however, to speculate about future developments, for generally speaking he is a "prophet" of the past—not of the future.

FOREIGN POLICY OF BREZHNEV AND KOSYGIN

In contrast to the somewhat zigg-zagging shifts in domestic politics, the foreign policy of Brezhnev and Kosygin has been to a remarkable degree a continuity of that of Khrushchev. In the Far East, China has continued to command the attention of Soviet leaders. Three basic factors seem responsible for holding that attention: (1) the unparalleled intensity of Chinese distaste for Soviet officials and their policies; (2) the size and nature of China's potential military threat to the USSR; and (3) Soviet insistence that their military might be the final arbiter of the destinies of all communist states.

Shortly after Khrushchev was ousted from power, Chou En-lai visited Moscow for "frank" and "comradely" talks. Since neither side has revealed the content of their conversations it is impossible to know what was discussed. Subsequent developments seem to indicate that both sides retained their earlier views of each other—a situation that has precluded the establishment of any meaningful dialogue between the two great communist powers. In fact, since 1965 relations between the two giants have deteriorated nearly to a breaking point.

Sino-Soviet relations became very strained early in 1965 by two outside factors: the increased military involvement of the United States in South Vietnam, and President Johnson's decision to bomb selected targets in North Vietnam. In April, 1965, in an apparent effort to make their military assistance to North Vietnam effective, the Soviets asked the Chinese for the use of two airfields in southwestern China (and the right to station five hundred men on them); for an air corridor, or air transit rights; for permission to send four thousand men through China; and for the right to use harbor facilities in southern China. Though the Soviet request was "reasonable," it did imply the establishment of a more or less permanent Soviet military presence in China, and as such it created a split within the Chinese leadership. Liu Shao-chi, China's Chief of State, and several of his associates supported the Soviet request; Mao Tse-tung and Minister of Defense Lin Piao opposed it. The split over the Soviet request set the stage for Mao to purge his opponents and critics, and it also unleashed Mao's celebrated "Cultural Revolution."

As might be expected, Sino-Soviet relations deteriorated sharply during the period of "Cultural Revolution." One sign of this deterioration came in the form of border incidents, accompanied by charges and countercharges that each side was massing military forces along the frontiers to launch an armed attack. Another sign of the deterioration of relations between China and the USSR was Chinese rejection of the Soviet invitation to attend the Twenty-Third Congress of the CPSU (March 29–April 8, 1966). Still other indications were the decision to limit their reciprocal diplomatic representation to the level of chargé d'affaires and the resumption of vicious verbal attacks that surpassed in intensity all earlier attacks. So bitter in fact became the polemic that late in 1966, *Pravda* announced in a long editorial that Soviet leaders were prepared to do everything necessary to overcome Mao's policies.

Mao responded to this challenge with a three-week massive siege, early in 1967, of the Soviet Embassy in Peking by his young Red Guards, who subjected Soviet personnel to abusive treatment.

Following this incident the Soviets launched an aggressive radio campaign in an apparent effort to foment unrest inside China. Using various Chinese dialects they attempted to incite Chinese peasants and workers to sabotage and armed resistance, and they also encouraged the non-Chinese minorities, especially the Uighurs in Sinkiang, to rebel against Mao's rule. Until early 1969 this campaign was accompanied by serious border clashes, each more severe than the last. In March, 1969, this escalation erupted in a violent clash between Soviet and Chinese armed forces along the Ussuri River and later at various points along the protracted Sino-Soviet frontier. Both sides suffered heavy casualties and, as in the past, each held the other responsible for starting the conflict. To control this dangerous roulette game, early in 1970 both sides appointed top diplomats to work out a satisfactory arrangement for quieting the border dispute. Lengthy negotiations took place in Peking, but produced no concrete results except the decision to exchange ambassadors and to tone down the volume of their propaganda.

In the Near East the focal point of Soviet intentions, as in the past, has been Egypt. Strategic considerations have been the motivating force behind their interests in Egypt. From Egypt the Soviets could move south to Sudan, or west to Libya, or east to Aden. Throughout this period Soviet commitment to Egypt has been economic and military. On the economic side they have completed the construction of the High Aswan Dam—the showpiece of the Nile; they have revamped the Helwan steel and iron complex near Cairo; they have helped in the discovery of high-grade iron ore in the Bahariya Oasis in the Western Desert, north of Aswan; and they have offered technical assistance in drilling for oil in the Western Desert, near the Siwa Oasis. To protect their investment, the Soviets (and their East European satellites) generously supplied Egypt with all kinds of conventional weapons (tanks, planes, armored cars), and after the large-scale destruction of these weapons during the Arab-Israeli war of June, 1967, they not only have resupplied them, but have installed many sophisticated surface-to-air missiles and radar stations and provided Soviet crews to operate them. According to foreign intelligence, over twenty thousand Soviet technicians and military men were in Egypt late in 1970. The sudden death of President Nasser in 1970 did not alter the Soviet position in Egypt. On the contrary, judged by official and semi-official pronouncements, the Soviets have committed themselves to defend Egypt in the same manner and perhaps to the same degree that the United States has committed itself to defend Israel. Only the future will tell whether these commitments will bring peace to the troubled region or whether they will lead to dangerous confrontations between the two super-powers.

The Brezhnev-Kosygin leadership has also pursued Khrushchev's aim in Europe. That aim was and remains clear and simple: the removal of United States' influence in Europe in general and the dismantling of NATO in particular. In pursuit of that goal Khrushchev's successors have renewed the call for a European security conference to be followed by a European security pact. They have expressed interest in becoming a major participant in West European trade. They have concluded several agreements for marketing Soviet oil. They have participated in every trade fair and commercial promotion. They have joined several conferences aimed at fixing shipping rates. They have signed an agreement with the Italian Fiat Company for a plant that would triple Soviet output of passenger cars. And they have even expressed interest in joining the American-sponsored Intelsat consortium. Taking advantage of the Franco-American chill, in June, 1966, Soviet leaders extended a royal welcome to Charles de Gaulle, and in January, 1969, they concluded with the French government a five-year agreement aimed at increasing trade between the two countries and at bringing closer cooperation in space research, atomic energy, civil aviation, and other vital areas. To weaken the influence of the United States in Europe, Soviet leaders also agreed in mid-1970 to sign a Treaty of Friendship with the government of West Germany.

But while Khrushchev's successors have sought by every conceivable means to undermine the position of the United States in Europe, they also took every necessary step to strengthen Soviet control in Eastern Europe. One form of that control has been the establishment within the framework of the COMECON of several supra-national corporations to integrate East European economy with that of the USSR. The most prominent of these are a ball-bearing corporation with headquarters in Warsaw, Poland; a steel corporation with headquarters in Budapest, Hungary; and a chemical corporation with headquarters in Halle, East Germany. Other Soviet moves aimed at making Eastern Europe dependent on the USSR include construction of the "Friendship Oil Pipe Line"; the International Bank for Economic Co-operation; and the recent proposal to establish a joint research center. Soviet pressures to integrate East European economies with that of the USSR have encountered a number of problems. The foremost of these has been their inability to resolve satisfactorily the problem of joint investment, prices, currency, and convertibility.

The other form of the Brezhnev-Kosygin new colonialism in Eastern Europe has been the integrating of Soviet military forces with those of East European countries. Using the framework of the Warsaw Pact, the Soviets have re-equipped the Pact's forces with modern weapons (tanks and anti-aircraft missiles), have motorized all infantry divisions, and have supplied them with the latest planes (MIG-21 and SU-7 fighter bombers) and helicopters. To coordinate their tactical operational efficiency, as well as to test the mobility of men and materiel, the Soviets introduced massive annual joint staff maneuvers of ground, air, and naval forces. While this cooperation has been somewhat one-sided (the Soviets have refused to share nuclear weapons with their partners and have kept their own officers at all important posts), nevertheless this coordination has demonstrated that the Warsaw Pact forces, in the words of General Lyman Lemnitzer, Supreme Commander of NATO forces, "can do a lot with only a short, or even no warning time at all."

Soviet efforts to integrate East European countries into the Soviet system have not been entirely smooth. Opposition has come from Rumanian leaders, who have refused to participate in several meetings of the COMECON and in all military maneuvers of the Warsaw Pact powers. Opposition has come also from reform-minded leaders of Czechoslovakia, who sought to establish a "Czechoslovak way of socialism." Soviet response to these two challenges has differed. Doubtless because they felt that Rumanian recalcitrance was the lesser of the two evils, the Soviets apparently decided to swallow their pride and have allowed the Rumanians to experiment with their brand of socialism, including flirtation with a number of Western countries, such as West Germany, France, and the United States. They dealt very harshly, however, with Czechoslovakia's challenge.

It is not known how Soviet leaders arrived at the decision to intervene and occupy Czechoslovakia on August, 21, 1968. It must be noted, however, that there were at least two basic signs that forewarned of that decision. One clear sign was the enormous Soviet displeasure with the replacement, in January, 1968, of staunch Stalinist Antonin Novotny by reform-minded Alexander Dubček, as Secretary General of the Czechoslovak Communist Party. The other sign was grave Soviet concern over the Czechoslovak decision to alter the direction of Czechoslovakia's domestic development, including the removal of censorship, the casting aside of all forms of conformity, the questioning of the tenets of Leninism, the insistence on democratic election and freedom of association, and the dismantling of all the remnants of Stalinism and of repression.

Soviet response to Czechoslovak liberalization steps progressed through a series of warnings to the brutal repression. At first the Soviets tried to persuade Czechoslovak leaders to alter their direction of the long-overdue reforms. When that failed they issued strong public warnings and sought, in a series of top-level meetings, to persuade Dubček and his associates to change their course. Then, on August 21, 1968, just as indications seemed to be that the differences between the two countries were resolved, the Soviets struck without warning. With exceptional speed and efficiency, Soviet, East German, Polish, Hungarian, and Bulgarian forces—some 250,000 strong—invaded and occupied Czechoslovakia in order to stop the reform. The population was shocked and bewildered and the occupation forces encountered no organized resistance. Dubček and his immediate associates and supporters were arrested and secretly brought to Moscow where they were branded as traitors to international communism. Thanks to the universal condemnation of Soviet action the Soviets reinstated their Czechoslovak prisoners to their former posts on condition that they alter their reforms to Soviet satisfaction, and a few weeks later they forced upon the Czechoslovak government a "Treaty of Friendship" that gave the occupying forces the right of indefinite presence as well as freedom to enter and leave Czechoslovakia at Soviet discretion. Within a year Dubček and his associates were removed from power, his supporters were purged, and Czechoslovakia was brought back to the bosom of neo-Stalinist brotherhood.

In its relations with the United States the Brezhnev-Kosygin leadership has followed very closely Khrushchev's approach; that is, it has sought to find an accommodation with the United States without sacrificing Soviet interests. The Soviet search for that goal has taken many forms. In July, 1967, during his brief trip to the United States for an appearance before the United Nations to condemn Israel, Kosygin met with President Johnson at Glassboro, New Jersey, to exchange views on a variety of problems facing the two super-powers. The meeting produced no major breakthrough, but the talks between the two leaders were cordial and dignified. In August, 1967, after years of negotiations, the two governments signed a treaty to check the spread of nuclear weapons, and in July, 1968, the Soviets endorsed a long-standing American proposal to restrict the missile race. The Soviet-led invasion and occupation of Czechoslovakia put a temporary chill on American-Soviet relations, but concrete signs of improvement became again visible early in 1969, when the Soviets greeted President Richard M. Nixon's inauguration with a call to ratify the nuclear non-proliferation treaty and a proposal that the two super-powers commence talks on strategic arms limitation control (SALT). These discussions, which have alternated between Helsinki and Vienna, have to date produced no concrete results. They have, however, provided an opportunity for each side to present its case and to understand the other's position. The Soviets have also proposed the opening of some consulates in cities other than the capitals of their respective countries, have continued their friendly cooperation in Antarctica, have hailed the landing of the United States' astronauts on the Moon, have extended a cordial welcome to some of the astronauts in the Soviet Union, and, following the explosion aboard Apollo XIII deep in space, they offered all possible assistance to the endangered crew.

These and many other friendly contacts and cooperation seem to demonstrate that, though the two powers are governed by different ideologies, they nevertheless have many common interests.

Cooperation between the two would doubtless have been better had it not been for the involvement of the United States in a war in Vietnam and its support of the position of Israel vis-à-vis the Arabs. The Soviets have interpreted American decisions and actions in these two areas as challenges to their leadership in the socialist camp. And since leadership implies not only the ability to lead but also to protect, Khrushchev's successors have greatly increased the flow of Soviet arms to the two areas of conflict for use against the forces of the United States and its allies. The Soviets also have been very reluctant to exert their influence to find a solution in either Southeast Asia or the Middle East that would be satisfactory to all concerned. However deplorable, Soviet reluctance is not to be viewed as failure, for as long as it serves Soviet interests it is gain, albeit unspectacular, for the Brezhnev-Kosygin leadership.

SUGGESTED READINGS

BOFFA, GIUSEPPE. *Inside the Khrushchev Era*. New York: Marzani & Munsell, 1963.

BROMKE, ADAM, ed. *The Communist States at the Crossroads Between Moscow and Peking*. New York: Praeger, 1965.

BROWN, J. F. *The New Eastern Europe: The Khrushchev Era and After*. New York: Praeger, 1966.

BRZEZINSKI, ZBIGNIEW, ed. *Africa and the Communist World*. Stanford: Stanford University Press, 1963.

————, ed. *Dilemmas of Change in Soviet Politics*. New York: Columbia University Press, 1969.

CHORNOVIL, VYACHESLAV. *The Chornovil Papers*. New York: McGraw-Hill, 1968.

CLEMENS, WALTER C., JR. *The Arms Race and Sino-Soviet Relations*. Stanford: Hoover Institution, 1968.

CONQUEST, ROBERT, ed. *Agricultural Workers in the USSR*. New York: Praeger, 1969.

————. *Russia After Khrushchev*. New York: Praeger, 1965.

CRANKSHAW, EDWARD. *Khrushchev: A Career*. New York: Viking, 1966.

————. *The New Cold War, Moscow v. Peking*. Baltimore, Md.: Penguin, 1963.

DALLIN, ALEXANDER, ed. *Diversity in International Communism. A Documentary Record, 1961–1963*. New York: Columbia University Press, 1963.

————, and THOMAS B. LARSEN, eds. *Soviet Politics Since Khrushchev*. Englewood Cliffs, N.J.: Prentice-Hall, 1968.

DJILAS, MILOVAN. *The Unperfect Society: Beyond the New Class*. New York: Harcourt, Brace and World, 1969.

DZIUBA, IVAN. *Internationalism or Russification?* London: Weidenfeld and Nicolson, 1968.

FEIFER, GEORGE. *Justice in Moscow*. New York: Simon & Schuster, 1964.

FISCHER-GALATI, STEPHEN. *Eastern Europe in the Sixties*. New York: Praeger, 1963.

————. *The New Rumania: From People's Democracy to Socialist Republic*. Cambridge, Mass.: MIT Press, 1967.

FLOYD, DAVID. *Mao Against Khrushchev: A Short History of the Sino-Soviet Conflict.* New York: Praeger, 1964.

GRIFFITH, WILLIAM E., ed. *Communism in Europe: Continuity, Change and the Sino-Soviet Dispute.* Cambridge, Mass.: MIT Press, 1966.

HAYWARD, MAX, ed. *On Trial: The Soviet State versus "Abram Tertz" and "Nikolai Arzhak."* New York: Harper & Row, 1966.

HYLAND, WILLIAM, and RICHARD W. SHRYLOCK. *The Fall of Khrushchev.* New York: Funk & Wagnalls, 1969.

JASNY, NAUM. *Khrushchev's Crop Policy.* Glasgow: Outram & Co., 1965.

JOHNSON, PRISCILLA, and LEOPOLD LABEDZ, eds. *Khrushchev and the Arts: The Politics of Soviet Culture, 1962–1964.* Cambridge, Mass.: MIT Press, 1965.

KARCZ, JERZY F., ed. *Soviet and East European Agriculture.* Berkeley: University of California Press, 1967.

KASER, MICHAEL. *Comecon: Integration Problems of the Planned Economy.* London: Oxford University Press, 1965.

KASSOF, ALLEN, ed. *Prospects for Soviet Society.* New York: Praeger, 1968.

KENNEDY, ROBERT F. *Thirteen Days: A Memoir of the Cuban Missile Crisis.* New York: Norton, 1969.

KHRUSHCHEV, NIKITA S. *Khrushchev Remembers.* Boston: Little, Brown and Co., 1970.

LABEDZ, LEOPOLD, ed. *International Communism After Khrushchev.* Cambridge, Mass.: MIT Press, 1965.

LARSON, THOMAS B. *Disarmament and Soviet Policy, 1964–1968.* Englewood Cliffs, N.J.: Prentice-Hall, 1969.

LINDEN, CARL A. *Khrushchev and the Soviet Leadership, 1957–1964.* Baltimore, Md.: Johns Hopkins University Press, 1966.

MARCHENKO, ANATOLI. *My Testimony.* New York: Dutton, 1969.

MORISON, DAVID. *The USSR and Africa.* London: Oxford University Press, 1964.

PENKOVSKY, OLEG. *The Penkovsky Papers.* New York: Doubleday, 1965.

PLOSS, SIDNEY. *Conflict and Decision-Making Process in Soviet Russia: A Case Study of Agricultural Policy, 1953–1963.* Princeton: Princeton University Press, 1965.

ROBERTS, HENRY L. *Eastern Europe: Politics, Revolution and Diplomacy.* New York: Knopf, 1970.

RUSH, MYRON. *Political Succession in the USSR.* New York: Columbia University Press, 1965.

SAKHAROV, ANDREI A. *Progress, Coexistence and Intellectual Freedom.* New York: Norton, 1968.

SALISBURY, HARRISON E. *War Between Russia and China.* New York: Norton, 1969.

SOLZHENITSYN, ALEXANDER I. *The First Circle.* New York: Harper & Row, 1968.

TATU, MICHEL. *Power in the Kremlin: From Khrushchev to Kosygin.* New York: Viking, 1969.

TERTZ, ABRAM [pseud.]. *The Makepeace Experiment.* New York: Vintage, 1966.

TOMA, PETER A., ed. *The Changing Face of Communism in Eastern Europe.* Tucson, Ariz.: University of Arizona Press, 1970.

UNITED STATES. DEPARTMENT OF STATE. *World Strength of the Communist Party Organizations.* 21st Annual Report. Washington, D.C.: Government Printing Office, 1969.

ZAGORIA, DONALD S. *Vietnam Triangle: Moscow, Peking, Hanoi.* New York: Pegasus, 1967.

APPENDICES

APPENDICES

ETHNIC COMPOSITION OF THE POPULATION
OF THE USSR, ACCORDING TO THE CENSUS
OF JANUARY 15, 1959 [1]

Russians	114,114,000
Ukrainians	37,253,000
Belorussians	7,913,000
Uzbeks	6,015,000
Tartars	4,968,000
Kazakhs	3,622,000
Azerbaidzhans	2,940,000
Armenians	2,787,000
Georgians	2,692,000
Lithuanians	2,326,000
Jews	2,268,000
Moldavians	2,214,000
Germans	1,620,000
Chuvash	1,470,000
Latvians	1,400,000
Tadzhiks	1,397,000
Poles	1,380,000
Mordvinians	1,285,000
Turkmenians	1,002,000
Bashkirs	989,000
Estonians	989,000
Kirghiz	969,000

Peoples of Dagestan including:		947,000
Avars	270,000	
Lezghians	223,000	
Darghin	158,000	
Kumyks	135,000	
Laks	64,000	
Nogais	41,000	
Tabasarans	35,000	
Aguls	7,000	
Rutuls	7,000	
Tsakhurs	7,000	

Udmurts	625,000
Mari	504,000
Komi and Komi-Permiaks	431,000
Chechen	419,000
Ossetians	410,000
Bulgars	324,000

[1] *Ezhegodnik Bolshoi Sovetskoi Entsiklopediia* (*Moscow:* 1960), p. 7.

Koreans		314,000
Greeks		309,000
Buriats		253,000
Yakuts		237,000
Kabardians		204,000
Kara-Kalpaks		173,000
Karelians		167,000
Hungarians		155,000
Gypsies		132,000
Peoples of the North including:		127,000
Evenki	24,500	
Nenets	23,000	
Khanty	19,400	
Chukchi	11,700	
Eveny	9,400	
Nanai	8,000	
Mansi	6,400	
Koriaks	6,300	
Selkup	3,800	
Nivki	3,700	
Ulchi	2,100	
Saam	1,800	
Udege	1,400	
Eskimos	1,100	
Itelmen	1,100	
Ket	1,000	
Orochi	800	
Nganasans	700	
Yukagirs	400	
Aleuts	400	
Gagauz		124,000
Rumanians		106,000
Kalmyks		106,000
Ingush		106,000
Tuvinians		100,000
Uygurs		95,000
Finns		93,000
Karachai		81,000
Adighe		80,000
Abkhaz		65,000
Kurds		59,000
Khakass		57,000
Altaians		45,000
Balkars		42,000
Turks		35,000
Cherkess		30,000
Chinese		26,000
Czechs		25,000

Aissors	22,000
Dungan	22,000
Iranians	21,000
Abaza	20,000
Veps	16,000
Shors	15,000
Slovaks	15,000
Tates	11,000
Arabs	8,000
Beludzhi	7,800
Karaimes	5,700
Yugoslavs	5,000
Albanians	4,800
Udins	3,700
Spaniards	2,400
Afghans	1,900
Mongols	1,800
Italians	1,200
Izhora	1,100
Frenchmen	1,000
Japanese	1,000
Vietnamese	800
Tofalar	600
Other nationalities	17,000
Total	208,826,000

Appendix 2 FULL MEMBERS OF THE POLITBURO, 1919–1952

Andreev, Andrei A.	1932–1952	
Beria, Lavrentii P.	1946–1952	
Bukharin, Nikolai I.	1919–1929	Executed in 1938
Bulganin, Nikolai A.	1948–1952	
Chubar, Vlas Ia.	1935–1938	Suicide in 1938
Kaganovich, Lazar M.	1930–1952	
Kalinin, Mikhail I.	1925–1946	Died in 1946
Kamenev, Lev B.	1919–1926	Executed in 1936
Khrushchev, Nikita S.	1939–1952	
Kirov, Sergei M.*	1930–1934	Murdered in 1934
Kosior, Stanislav V.	1930–1938	Disappeared in 1938
Kosygin, Aleksei N.	1949–1952	
Krestinsky, Nikolai N.	1919–1921	Executed in 1938
Kuibyshev, Valerian V.*	1927–1935	Died in 1935
Lenin, Vladimir I.	1919–1924	Died in 1924
Malenkov, Georgi M.	1946–1952	
Mikoyan, Anastas I.	1935–1952	
Molotov, Viacheslav M.	1925–1952	
Ordzhonikidze, Gregory K.*	1930–1937	Died in 1937
Rudzutak, Jan E.	1926–1932	Disappeared in 1938
Rykov, Aleksei I.	1922–1930	Executed in 1938
Stalin, Joseph V.	1919–1952	
Sverdlov, Jakob M.	1919–1919	Died in 1919
Tomsky, Mikhail P.	1919–1929	Suicide in 1936
Trotsky, Leon D.*	1919–1926	Murdered in 1940
Voroshilov, Klementii E.	1925–1952	
Voznesensky, Nikolai A.	1947–1949	Executed in 1951
Zhdanov, Andrei A.*	1939–1948	Died in 1948
Zinoviev, Gregory E.	1923–1926	Executed in 1936

* Died under circumstances which strongly implicate Stalin as the instigator.

Appendix 3 FULL MEMBERS OF THE PRESIDIUM, 1952–1964

Andrianov, Vasily M.	1952–1953	
Aristov, Averky B.	1952–1961	
Beliaev, Nikolai I.	1957–1960	
Beria, Lavrentii P.	1952–1953	Executed in 1953
Brezhnev, Leonid I.	1957–	
Bulganin, Nikolai A.	1952–1958	Expelled in 1958
Furtseva, Ekaterina A.	1957–1961	
Ignatev, Semen D.	1952–1953	
Ignatov, Nikolai G.	1957–1961	
Kaganovich, Lazar M.	1952–1957	Expelled in 1957
Kirichenko, Aleksei I.	1955–1960	
Khrushchev, Nikita S.	1952–1964	Expelled in 1964
Korotchenko, Demian S.	1952–1953	
Kosygin, Aleksei N.	1959–	
Kozlov, Frol R.	1957–1963	
Kuusinen, Otto W.	1957–1964	Died in 1964
Kuznetsov, Vasili Y.	1952–1953	
Malenkov, Georgi M.	1952–1957	Expelled in 1957
Malyshev, V. A.	1952–1953	
Melnikov, Leonid G.	1952–1953	
Mikhailov, N. A.	1952–1953	
Mikoyan, Anastas I.	1952–	
Molotov, Viacheslav M.	1952–1957	Expelled in 1957
Mukhitdinov, Nuritdin A.	1958–1961	
Pervukhin, Mikhail G.	1952–1957	
Podgornyi, Nikolai V.	1959–	
Poliansky, Dimitri S.	1959–	
Ponomarenko, P. K.	1952–1953	
Saburov, Maksim Z.	1952–1957	Expelled in 1957
Shkiriatov, M. F.	1952–1953	
Shvernik, Nikolai M.	1957–	
Stalin, Joseph V.	1952–1953	Died in 1953
Suslov, Mikhail A.	1955–	
Ustinov, Dimitri F.	1963–	
Voronov, Genady I.	1961–	
Voroshilov, Klementii E.	1952–1960	Expelled in 1960
Zhukov, Georgi K.	1957–1957	Expelled in 1957

Appendix 4   THE PRESIDIUM OF THE SUPREME
SOVIET OF THE USSR, 1970–1974

Chairman: Podgorny, Nikolai V.

Vice-Chairmen: Iasnov, Mikhail A.
                         Liashko, Alexander P.
                         Pritytskii, Sergei O.
                         Niiazbekov, Sabir B.
                         Dzotsenidze, Georgy S.
                         Khalilov, Kurban A.
                         Sumauskas, Motiejus J.
                         Iliashenko, Kiril F.
                         Rubenis, Vitalijs P.
                         Kulatov, Turabai
                         Kholov, Makhmadula
                         Arutiunian, Nagush Kh.
                         Klychev, Annamukhamed
                         Muurisepp, Aleksei A.

Secretary: Georgadze, Mikhail P.

Members: Bolshukhin, Vasilii I.
                         Brezhnev, Leonid I.
                         Budenny, Semeon M.
                         Grishin, Victor V.
                         Kavun, Vasilii M.
                         Konotop, Vasilii I.
                         Kunaev, Dinmukhamed A.
                         Masherov, Piotr M.
                         Mikoyan, Anastas I.
                         Orlova, Galina S.
                         Petrovskii, Ivan G.
                         Pukhova, Zoia P.
                         Rashidov, Shafar R.
                         Sobolev, Leonid S.
                         Shakirov, Midkhat Z.
                         Shelest, Piotr E.
                         Tabeiev, Fikriat S.
                         Tolstikov, Vasilii S.
                         Tsetsegov, Sergei S.
                         Tynel, Lina G.

354

Appendix 5 PLACES, DATES, AND CHIEF CONCERNS OF PARTY CONGRESSES, 1898–1971

First Congress	Minsk	March 13–15, 1898	Founding of the Party
Second Congress	Brussels-London	July 30–August 23, 1903	Bolshevik-Menshevik Split
Third Congress	London	April 25–May 10, 1905	Struggle with the Mensheviks
Fourth Congress	Stockholm	April 23–May 8, 1906	Reconciliation Attempt with the Mensheviks
Fifth Congress	London	May 13–June 1, 1907	Struggle with the Mensheviks
Sixth Congress	Petrograd	July 26–August 3, 1917	Regrouping and Preparation for a Coup
Seventh Congress	Petrograd	March 6–8, 1918	Peace with Germany
Eighth Congress	Moscow	March 18–23, 1919	New Party Program and the Civil War
Ninth Congress	Moscow	March 29–April 5, 1920	Opposition to Over-centralization
Tenth Congress	Moscow	March 8–16, 1921	NEP and Party Discipline
Eleventh Congress	Moscow	March 27–April 2, 1922	Role of Trade Unions in the NEP
Twelfth Congress	Moscow	April 17–25, 1923	Nationality Problem
Thirteenth Congress	Moscow	May 23–31, 1924	Stalin-Trotsky Struggle
Fourteenth Congress	Moscow	December 18–31, 1925	Stalin-Trotsky Struggle
Fifteenth Congress	Moscow	December 2–19, 1927	Stalin's Victory; Industrialization
Sixteenth Congress	Moscow	June 26–July 13, 1930	Elimination of the "Right" Opposition
Seventeenth Congress	Moscow	January 26–February 10, 1934	"Congress of Victors"
Eighteenth Congress	Moscow	March 10–21, 1939	End of the Purge and Preparation for War
Nineteenth Congress	Moscow	October 5–15, 1952	Reorganization of the Party
Twentieth Congress	Moscow	February 14–26, 1956	De-Stalinization
Twenty-first Congress	Moscow	January 27–February 5, 1959	Seven Year Plan
Twenty second Congress	Moscow	October 17–November 1, 1961	Twenty Year Program and De-Stalinization; Struggle with China
Twenty-third Congress	Moscow	March 29–April 8, 1966	1966–1970 Five Year Plan
Twenty-fourth Congress	Moscow	March 30–April 9, 1971	1970–1974 Five Year Plan

Appendix 6 BIOGRAPHICAL NOTES ON IMPORTANT SOVIET OFFICIALS

BERIA, LAVRENTII PAVLOVICH (1899–1953). The long time chief of Soviet security forces, Beria was born in Georgia. He joined the Bolsheviks in 1917, was a member of the Soviet police in Georgia until 1930, and between 1931 and 1938 held important party positions in Georgia. Beria became a member of the CC in 1934 and in 1938 he succeeded Nikolai I. Yezhov as chief of security forces of the USSR—the position he held until 1953. As head of security forces Beria became a candidate member of the Politburo in 1939 and a Deputy Chairman of the Council of Peoples Commissars responsible for police and ammunition production during World War II. In 1946 Beria was elevated to full membership in the Politburo and until Stalin's death he directed the reign of police terror in the USSR and in the satellite states. Following Stalin's death Beria became a First Deputy Chairman of the Council of Ministers and a member (with Malenkov and Molotov) of the triumvirate. His career came to a sudden end on July 10, 1953, when he was stripped of all power, arrested, accused of treason, expelled from the party, and shot.

BREZHNEV, LEONID IL'ICH (1906–). Former Chairman of the Presidium of the Supreme Soviet, Brezhnev was born in the Ukraine. As a youth he specialized in surveying and land improvement in Kursk and in the Urals and in 1935 he graduated as an engineer from the Metallurgical Institute at Dnieprodzerzhinsk. Brezhnev's career however has been in the party which he joined in 1931. In 1939 he advanced to the position of Secretary of the Dniepropetrovsk Party Regional Committee, and during the war (1941–1945) he served as Deputy Director of Political Administration of the Southern Front, advancing to the rank of Major-General. After the war his steady rise in the party continued. In 1950 Brezhnev became the First Secretary of the CC of the Moldavian Communist party; in 1952 he was made a member of the CC of the CPSU, a Secretary of the CC and a candidate member of the Presidium. From 1953 to 1954 Brezhnev was in charge of political indoctrination of the army and from 1954 to 1956 was Second and then First Secretary of the CC of the Communist Party of Kazakhstan. In 1957 Brezhnev became a full member of the Presidium and a Secretary of the CC of the CPSU, and from May, 1960, to July, 1964, acted as the titular head of the USSR. In July, 1964, Brezhnev was relieved of the latter position in order to devote full time and energy to the Secretariat. After the October 15, 1964 coup, Brezhnev was appointed Khrushchev's successor in the party.

BUKHARIN, NIKOLAI IVANOVICH (1888–1938). A leading Bolshevik theorist, Bukharin was born and educated in Moscow. He joined Lenin in 1906 and prior to the revolution of 1917 promoted the Bolshevik cause as editor of *Pravda* and of *Novyi mir* (in New York). In 1917 Bukharin became a member of the party's CC and from 1918 to 1928 he was the editor of *Pravda* and a member of the Politburo. For his support of Stalin against Trotsky Bukharin was promoted to the Head of the Comintern (1926–1929), but when he tried to oppose Stalin's economic policies he was stripped of all powers in 1929. In 1934 Bukharin was readmitted to the party and until 1937 was the editor of *Izvestiia*. He was arrested in the purge of 1938 and executed on Stalin's orders. In October, 1962 he was "rehabilitated" posthumously.

BULGANIN, NIKOLAI ALEKSANDROVICH (1895–   ). Onetime Chairman of the Council of Ministers of the USSR, Bulganin was born in Nizhnii Novgorod (now Gorky). He joined the Bolsheviks in 1917 and until 1922 served with the CHEKA. From 1922 to 1930 he was engaged in economic construction and during the 1930's worked in the Moscow party apparatus. In 1938 Bulganin became the Chairman of the Council of People's Commissars of the RSFSR and a Deputy Chairman of the Council of People's Commissars of the USSR. His other posts have included: member of the Military Council (1941–1944); Deputy People's Commissar for Defense (1944–1947); Minister of Defense (1947–1949 and 1953–1955); member of the Politburo and of the Presidium (1948–1958); and Chairman of the Council of Ministers (1955–1958). In 1958 Bulganin was identified with "the anti-party group," was stripped of all of his powers and relegated into obscurity.

CHICHERIN, GEORGI VASILEVICH (1872–1936). A Soviet diplomat, the son of a nobleman, Chicherin was born in Tambov and educated in St. Petersburg. He entered the Tsarist foreign service but in 1904 joined the revolutionary movement, and until the downfall of the monarchy lived abroad (France, Germany, and England). He returned to Russia in January, 1918, and in May, 1918, became People's Commissar for Foreign Affairs—the position he was to hold until 1930. Chicherin took part in the negotiations at Brest-Litovsk and was one of the chief architects of Soviet foreign policy during the 1920's. He negotiated treaties with Turkey, Iran, and Afghanistan; took part in the Genoa and Lausanne Conferences (1922–1923); and signed the Rapallo Treaty with Germany (April, 1922). Chicherin retired from public office in 1930 because of poor health.

GROMYKO, ANDREI ANDREEVICH (1909–   ). A Soviet diplomat, Gromyko is a graduate of the Minsk Agricultural Institute and the Moscow Institute of Economics. He entered diplomatic service in 1939, first as the Head of the American Section of the People's Commissariat for Foreign Affairs and later as Counsellor of the Soviet Embassy in Washington. From 1943 to 1946 Gromyko served as Soviet ambassador to the United States and Cuba, and from 1947 to 1958 he acted as Deputy Minister for Foreign Affairs. In March, 1958, he was appointed Foreign Minister of the USSR. Gromyko took part in various international conferences including Teheran, Yalta, Potsdam, San Francisco and Geneva, and from 1946 to 1948 acted as permanent Soviet representative at the Security Council of the United Nations where he became well known for his veto tactics. Gromyko joined the Communist party in 1931 and is currently a member of the CC.

KAGANOVICH, LAZAR MOISEEVICH (1893–   ). For many years one of Stalin's major trouble shooters, Kaganovich was born in the Ukraine. He joined the

Bolshevik movement in 1911, took an active part in the revolution of 1917 in the Ukraine, and in 1920 helped to establish Bolshevik control in Turkestan. In the 1920's Kaganovich threw his support to Stalin and was rewarded with membership in the CC (1924). Other positions of Kaganovich included: Secretary of the CC (1924–1925 and 1928–1939); Secretary of the CC of the Communist party (bolshevik) Ukraine (1925–1928 and 1947); Politburo member (1930–1952); and Presidium member (1952–1957). Kaganovich was also very active in the collectivization and industrialization drive and from 1934 to 1941 was in charge of the fuel industry. Following World War II the influence of Kaganovich declined somewhat (because of Stalin's anti-Semitic views), but revived again after Stalin's death. In 1957, for his participation in the "anti-party group," Kaganovich was divested of all power, and in February, 1964, was expelled from the party.

KALININ, MIKHAIL IVANOVICH (1875–1946). For several years the titular head (President) of the USSR, Kalinin was born in Tver Gubernia of poor peasant parents. A self-educated man he joined the Social Democratic movement in 1898, became a loyal follower of Lenin, and until 1917 spent most of the time in prison or in exile. He took an active part in the revolution of 1917 as a member of the Petrograd City *Duma* and later as mayor of the city of Petrograd. In 1919 Kalinin became a member of the CC and Chairman of the Executive Committee of the Soviet. Following Lenin's death Kalinin threw his support to Stalin, became a member of the Politburo (1925–1946), and from 1938 to 1946 acted as Chairman of the Presidium of the Supreme Soviet—titular head of the USSR.

KAMENEV, LEV BORISOVICH (1883–1936). For many years a close associate of Lenin, Kamenev was born and educated in Moscow. He joined the Social Democratic movement in 1901, sided with Lenin in 1903, and until 1917 spent much time in Siberia or abroad. In 1917 he came back to Russia with Lenin and became a member of the Petrograd Soviet. During the final preparations for the Bolshevik seizure of power Kamenev opposed Lenin's tactics, but following the successful coup he became Chairman of the Moscow Soviet (1918–1922) and a member of the Politburo (1919–1925). In the struggle for power that followed Lenin's death Kamenev first joined Stalin but later threw his support to Trotsky. For this indiscretion Kamenev was expelled from the party in 1927, was readmitted in 1928 and reexpelled in 1932. He was executed on Stalin's orders in 1936.

KHRUSHCHEV, NIKITA SERGEEVICH (1894–). Stalin's successor, Khrushchev, son of a coal miner, was born in Kursk Gubernia. He joined the Bolsheviks in 1918 and took an active part in the Civil War. Following that upheaval he worked and studied in the Ukraine (Workers' School at Kharkov University) and later in Moscow. In 1934 Khrushchev became a member of the CC, and from 1935 to 1938 acted as Secretary of the Moscow party organization. In 1938 Stalin entrusted Khrushchev with the execution of the purge in the Ukraine and rewarded him with membership in the Politburo (1939–1952). Except for the year 1947, Khrushchev was in charge of Ukrainian affairs until

1949, when he became a Secretary of the CC and of the Moscow party organization. Shortly after Stalin's death Khrushchev was selected First Secretary of the CC. Using that position he relegated all his opponents into obscurity and emerged as one of Stalin's most perceptive students. On October 15, 1964, without any advance indication he was stripped of party and government leadership.

KIROV, SERGEI MIRONOVICH (1886–1934). For several years a close associate of Stalin, Kirov was born in Viatka Gubernia. Although orphaned at the age of seven, he completed a mechanical education at Kazan. He joined the Bolsheviks in 1904 and spent most of the years before the revolution either in Siberia or the Northern Caucasus. Following the downfall of the monarchy Kirov helped to establish Soviet power in the Caucasus, and in 1923 he became a member of the CC. After Lenin's death he sided with Stalin, was put in charge of the all powerful Leningrad party organization in 1925, became a member of the Politburo in 1930 and a Secretary of the CC in 1934. Kirov's career was ended abruptly on December 1, 1934 by an assassin. His death precipitated the great purge of the 1930's. There is some evidence that suggests that Stalin was the instigator of Kirov's death.

KONEV, IVAN STEPANOVICH (1897–   ). A Marshal of the Soviet Union, Konev joined the Bolsheviks in 1918 and took an active part in the Civil War. In 1926 he was graduated from the Frunze Military Academy where in 1934 he became a lecturer. From 1939 to 1952 Konev was a candidate member of the CC, and he has been a full member since 1952. During World War II Konev distinguished himself as a military strategist in the campaigns in the Ukraine, Poland, and Czechoslovakia. Following the war he was the Soviet representative on the Allied Control Commission in Vienna, and from 1946 to 1955 was Chief Military Commander of Soviet Land Forces and Deputy Minister of Defense. From 1956 to 1960 Konev was Commander in Chief of the Warsaw Pact forces. In 1960 he was relieved of his command on grounds of ill health.

KOSYGIN, ALEKSEI NIKOLAEVICH (1904–   ). Kosygin, who, on October 15, 1964, replaced Khrushchev as Chairman of the Council of Ministers, was born in St. Petersburg in 1904. He fought in the Civil War, and later graduated from the Leningrad Cooperative Technicum (1924), and the Leningrad Textile Institute (1935). He joined the Communist party in 1927, and became a member of the CC in 1939. Because of his apparent administrative abilities, Kosygin has held a number of important positions within the government and the party. These include: Mayor of Leningrad (1938); People's Commissar of Textile Industries (1939–1940); Deputy Chairman of the Sovnarkom of the USSR (1940–1946), and of the Council of Ministers (1946–1964); Chairman of the Sovnarkom of the RSFSR (1943–1946); Minister of Finance (1948); Minister of Light and Consumer Industry (1948–1956); Chairman of the Gosplan (1956–1960); member of the Politburo (1948–1952), and of the Presidium of the CC (1959–present).

LENIN, VLADIMIR IL'ICH (1870–1924). The founder of Russian Communism and of the Soviet state, Lenin was born in Simbirsk (now Ulianovsk). The son of a school administrator, he was educated at the Universities of Kazan and St. Petersburg. A careful student of Russian revolutionaries and later of Karl Marx, Lenin joined the Russian Social Democratic movement in 1893 and two years later, while abroad, he made contacts with George V. Plekhanov and other Russian and European social democratic leaders. He broke with them in 1903 over the issue of tactics and organization, and proceeded to establish his own revolutionary group, the Bolsheviks. He bitterly fought the Mensheviks in the revolution of 1905 and continued to oppose them even more after the collapse of that revolution. Most of the time between 1906 and 1914 Lenin spent in Austria-Hungary, and following the outbreak of World War I he moved to Switzerland, where in 1915–1916 he laid the foundation for the Comintern. He returned to Russia in April, 1917, with the help of the German military leadership, and immediately declared war on the Provisional Government. On November 7, 1917, he achieved his goal—that of overthrowing the Provisional Government—and became the first Chairman of the Council of People's Commissars, the position he held until his death on January 21, 1924.

LITVINOV, MAKSIM MAKSIMOVICH (1876–1951). A Soviet diplomat, Litvinov was born in Bialystok, joined the Russian Social Democratic movement in 1898, and until the downfall of monarchy took an active part in the revolutionary movement at home and abroad (France and England). Litvinov was arrested by the British in 1918 and exchanged for British subjects arrested by the Bolsheviks. Upon his return to Russia he became Lenin's secretary. From 1918 to 1929 Litvinov served as Deputy People's Commissar for Foreign Affairs, and from 1929 to 1939 as People's Commissar for Foreign Affairs. He was a great exponent of "collective security" during the 1930's, and the failure of that policy relegated him into the background. From 1941 to 1943 Litvinov served as Soviet Ambassador to the United States, and from 1943 to 1946 as Deputy Commissar for Foreign Affairs. Following World War II Litvinov's influence declined still further, in part because of Stalin's anti-Semitism.

MALENKOV, GEORGI MAKSIMILIANOVICH (1902–). For a short while Stalin's successor, Malenkov was born in Orenburg, took part in the Civil War, joined the Communist party in 1920, and participated in the efforts to establish Soviet control in Central Asia. From 1921 to 1925 Malenkov studied in Moscow, and from 1925 to 1939 he worked in the CC and in the Moscow party organization. In 1939 he became a member of the CC, a Secretary of the CC, a member of the Orgburo, and during the war served as a member of the State Committee of Defense. In 1946 Malenkov became a member of the Politburo and emerged as Stalin's personal choice to succeed him. Malenkov's impatience to pose as Stalin's rightful heir cost him his leadership in the party on March 14, 1953. Early in 1955 he was forced to resign as Chairman of the Council of Ministers (1953–1955), and in 1957, because he sided against Khrushchev, Malenkov was stripped of all power and relegated into obscurity. In February, 1964, he was expelled from the party.

MALINOVSKY, RODION IAKOLEVICH (1898–1969). A Marshal of the Soviet Union, Malinovsky was born in the Ukraine. He fought in World War I and the Civil War, and joined the Communist party in 1926. In 1930 he was graduated from the Frunze Military Academy, and during World War II took part in the defense of Stalingrad. Later he led Soviet armies across the Ukraine, Rumania, Hungary, Czechoslovakia, and Austria. In 1945 Malinovsky was appointed Commander of Soviet forces in the Far East where he stayed until 1956. In the latter year he became a member of the CC and a Deputy Minister for Defense in charge of ground forces. In 1957, Malinovsky replaced Zhukov as Minister for Defense, and with Khrushchev attended the abortive Paris Summit conference in May, 1960.

MANUILSKY, DIMITRI ZAKHAROVICH (1883–1959). Soviet politician Manuilsky was born in the Ukraine, joined the revolutionary movement in 1903, and spent time in Siberia as well as abroad. Following his graduation from the Sorbonne (1911), Manuilsky continued active revolutionary work, and after the Bolshevik seizure of power he helped to establish Soviet rule in the Ukraine. From 1920 to 1922 he was People's Commissar for Agriculture in the Ukraine and a Secretary of the CC of the CP(b)U. He was also active in the Comintern, and from 1924 to 1943 was one of the Comintern's secretaries. In 1944 Manuilsky became Commissar for Foreign Affairs of the Ukrainian SSR, led the first Ukrainian delegation to the United Nations, and from 1946 to 1953 acted as Deputy Chairman of the Council of Ministers of the Ukrainian SSR. After 1953 his influence declined, and he died in virtual obscurity.

MIKOYAN, ANASTAS IVANOVICH (1895–   ). Stalin's and Khrushchev's chief trouble shooter, Mikoyan was born in Armenia and educated in an Armenian Theological Seminary. He joined the revolutionary movement in 1915, became active in Baku, took part in the Civil War, and helped to establish Soviet power in the Caucasus. During the 1920's Mikoyan worked as a party organizer in Nizhnii Novgorod, Rostov-on-the-Don, and the Northern Caucasus; became a member of the CC in 1923; and threw his support to Stalin. In return he was given membership in the Politburo (1935–1952) and Presidium (since 1952), and has been in charge of foreign and domestic trade and food procurement. Following Stalin's death Mikoyan supported Khrushchev in his rise to power and became his chief trouble shooter in international affairs, and First Deputy Chairman of the Council of Ministers of the USSR. In July, 1964, Mikoyan replaced Brezhnev as titular head of the USSR.

MOLOTOV, VIACHESLAV MIKHAILOVICH (1890–   ). Soviet diplomat Molotov was born in the Viatka Province and educated at the University of Kazan. He joined the Bolsheviks in 1906, and with Stalin founded the newspaper *Pravda* in 1912. He was active in the revolution of 1917 as a member of the Petrograd Soviet, became a candidate member of the Politburo in 1921, threw his support to Stalin against Trotsky, and became a full member of the Politburo in 1926. From 1930 to 1941 Molotov acted as Chairman of the Council of People's Commissars of the USSR, and from 1939 to 1949 he was also in charge of Soviet foreign policy, negotiating treaties with both Nazi Germany and the Allied Powers. Following Stalin's death Molotov again became Minister for Foreign Affairs of the USSR, but lost his position in 1957 for opposition to Khrushchev. At the Twenty-second Party Congress (1961), Molotov was subjected to bitter criticism and since has lived in obscurity. In February, 1964, he was expelled from the party.

RADEK, KARL BERNARDOVICH (1885–?). A Soviet politician and writer on international affairs, Radek was born in Lvov and educated at Cracow and Berne Universities. He joined the Social Democratic movement in 1904, and became very active in Germany where he worked with the Left Wing Social Democrats. During World War I Radek joined Lenin in Switzerland and travelled with him to Russia in April, 1917. He took part in the negotiations at Brest-Litovsk and later went to Germany to prepare for a Communist seizure of power. He spent a year in a German prison, and upon his release in 1919 he became a high-ranking member of the Comintern. Because he sided with Trotsky against Stalin, Radek was expelled from the party in 1927, but was readmitted in 1930. In 1937 he was rearrested, tried for treason, and sentenced to ten years' imprisonment. His ultimate fate has never been made known.

STALIN, JOSEPH VISARIONOVICH (1879–1953). The Soviet dictator Stalin was born in Georgia. The son of a shoemaker, he studied briefly at a theological seminary, but at the age of seventeen joined the revolutionary movement. He was arrested several times but always managed to escape to freedom. He became a high-ranking party official, and took part in the revolution of 1917 and the ensuing Civil War. An original member of the Politburo, Stalin was given charge of the complex nationality problem, and from 1920 to 1923 he was also People's Commissar for Workers' and Peasants' Inspection. In 1922 Stalin was selected General Secretary of the Party, a position he developed into the dictatorial post that enabled him to eliminate ruthlessly all of his opponents and to rule Russia with an iron hand until his death in March, 1953.

SUSLOV, MIKHAIL ANDREEVICH (1902–). A party theoretician, Suslov was born in the Saratov Gubernia, became a member of the Komsomol in 1918, and a party member in 1919. During the Civil War Suslov worked with the Committee of the Village Poor, and from 1924 to 1928 he attended the Moscow Institute of Agriculture. Since 1930 he has been preoccupied with party matters in different capacities—member of the Central Control Commision (1931); Secretary of the Rostov *oblast* committee (1937–1939); and member of the CC (1941–present). From 1944 to 1946 Suslov was active in establishing Soviet authority in Lithuania; he became Secretary of the CC in 1947, editor of *Pravda* (1947–1949), and a member of the Presidium (1955–present). In 1963 he was selected to negotiate Sino-Soviet differences.

TIMOSHENKO, SEMEON KONSTANTINOVICH (1895–). A Marshal of the Soviet Union, Timoshenko was born in the Ukraine, saw action in World War I as a machinegunner, and following the downfall of the monarchy he joined the revolutionary forces. In 1922 Timoshenko completed military school and in

1930 he graduated from a leadership school at the Military Academy. Between 1933 and 1940 he commanded Soviet forces in Belorussia and the Ukraine, and in 1940 he was promoted to the rank of Marshal of the USSR and Minister of Defense. During the early stages of World War II, Timoshenko defended the Ukraine against Nazi attack (Kharkov), but was later overshadowed by younger commanders.

TROTSKY, LEON DAVIDOVICH (1879–1940). A Marxist theoretician, Trotsky was born in the Ukraine, joined the revolutionary movement in 1898, and became active in Russia and abroad. During the revolution of 1905 Trotsky acted as Chairman of the Petrograd Soviet, and following the collapse of the revolution he journeyed into exile. He returned to Russia in 1917, joined Lenin's forces, and as Chairman of the Executive Committee of the Petrograd Soviet he masterminded the Bolshevik seizure of power. He negotiated the Treaty of Brest-Litovsk, organized the Red Army, and took an active part in the Civil War. Though a skilled writer, orator, and organizer, Trotsky's ambition to succeed Lenin was frustrated by his clash with Stalin. In November, 1927, Trotsky was defeated, stripped of all his powers, and exiled to Central Asia. From there he journeyed to Constantinople (1929), then to Norway, and finally to Mexico City where he was assassinated by a Stalinist on August 20, 1940.

TUKHACHEVSKY, MIKHAIL NIKOLAEVICH (1893–1937). A Marshal of the Soviet Union, Tukhachevsky was born in the Smolensk Gubernia and educated in the Corps of Cadets and the Aleksander Military School. He took part in World War I, and following the downfall of the monarchy he joined the revolutionary forces. In 1918 he was given command of a new Soviet army and distinguished himself as an able strategist against Denikin. Tukhachevsky was also a leading military figure in the ill-fated Soviet invasion of Poland in 1920, and together with Trotsky he suppressed the Kronstadt rebellion in March, 1921. From 1921 to 1924 Tukhachevsky was Chief of the Military Academy, and from 1924 to 1937 he was Assistant Chief of Staff. On June 11, 1937, on Stalin's orders, he was arrested and shot, together with many other officers. He was posthumously "rehabilitated" in 1962.

VOROSHILOV, KLEMENTII EFRIMOVICH (1881–1970). A Marshal of the Soviet Union, Voroshilov was born in the Ukraine. He joined the revolutionary movement in 1898, and the Bolsheviks in 1903. In 1917 he was a member of the Petrograd Soviet, took an active part in the Civil War, helped Dzerzhynski to organize the CHEKA, and became a member of the CC in 1921. From 1921 to 1924 Voroshilov was Commandant of the North Caucasus Military District, and from 1925 to 1934 he was People's Commissar for Military and Naval Affairs. For his support of Stalin against Trotsky, Voroshilov was given membership in the Politburo (1926–1952). His other posts included: People's Commissar for Defense (1934–1941); Marshal of the Soviet Union (1935); member of the State Committee for Defense (1941–1945); and participation in a number of conferences during World War II. From 1953 to 1960 Voroshilov was Chairman of the Presidium of the Supreme Soviet, and after 1961 he was forced into obscurity for his opposition in 1957 to Khrushchev.

VYSHINSKY, ANDREI IANUAREVICH (1883–1954). A Soviet jurist and diplomat, Vyshinsky was born in Odessa and educated at the University of Kiev. Originally a Menshevik, Vyshinsky joined the Communist party in 1920 and for the next several years was active in education as a lecturer and later as president of the University of Moscow. From 1931 to 1933 he served as Procurator of the RSFSR, and from 1935 to 1939 as Procurator of the USSR. In 1940 Vyshinsky shifted his attention to foreign affairs and held such posts as First Deputy People's Commissar for Foreign Affairs (1940–1946), Deputy Minister for Foreign Affairs (1946–1949), and Minister for Foreign Affairs (1949–1952). Vyshinsky took part in many wartime conferences (Teheran, Yalta, and Potsdam), and for a time acted as Soviet spokesman at the United Nations.

ZHDANOV, ANDREI ALEKSANDROVICH (1896–1948). One of Stalin's close associates, Zhdanov was born in Mariupol (now Zhdanov), joined the Bolsheviks in 1915, and from 1919 to 1934 worked in party organizations in Tver, the Urals, and Nizhnii Novgorod. He became a member of the CC in 1930, a Secretary of the CC in 1934, and a member of the Politburo in 1939. From 1934 to 1944 Zhdanov was in charge of the Leningrad party organization, and from 1944 until his death he worked in the all-powerful Moscow party apparatus. After World War II Zhdanov became Stalin's chief lieutenant, organized the Cominform in 1947, and masterminded the postwar ideological "rehabilitation" of Soviet citizens. He died under mysterious circumstances on August 31, 1948.

ZHUKOV, GEORGI KONSTANTINOVICH (1896–   ). A Marshal of the Soviet Union, Zhukov was born in Kaluga Province. He joined the Communist party in 1919, took part in the Civil War, graduated from the Frunze Military Academy in 1931, and in 1938–1939 directed Soviet defenses in the Far East. During World War II he served as Chief of Staff of Soviet Forces, organized the defenses of Moscow in 1941 and of Stalingrad in 1942, and in 1943–1945 masterminded the Soviet military strategy that led the Russian forces from Stalingrad to Berlin. Following World War II Stalin relegated Zhukov into the background, but he reemerged after the dictator's death. From 1953 to 1957 Zhukov served as Minister of Defense and allegedly sided with Khrushchev against the "anti-party" group. In October, 1957, however, Zhukov was stripped of his powers and again pushed into obscurity.

ZINOVIEV, GREGORY EVSEEVICH (1883–1936). The onetime head of the Comintern, Zinoviev was born in Elisavetgrad and educated in Berne. He joined Lenin in 1903, collaborated with him on a number of publications, and made the journey with him back to Russia in 1917. He was skeptical of Bolshevik chances to seize power in Russia, but after the coup he became coeditor of *Pravda,* and Chairman of the Comintern. Following Lenin's death Zinoviev became a member of the triumvirate, then sided with Stalin against Trotsky, and subsequently joined Trotsky against Stalin. For this vacillation Zinoviev was stripped af all his posts in 1927 and expelled from the party. Later he was readmitted, but was arrested and shot on Stalin's orders on August 25, 1936.

Appendix 7 [1]   ORDER NO. I, MARCH 14, 1917 [2]

To the garrison of the Petrograd District, to all the soldiers of the guard, army, artillery, and navy, for immediate and strict execution, and to the workers of Petrograd for their information:—

The Soviet of Workers' and Soldiers' Deputies has resolved:

1. In all companies, battalions, regiments, parks, batteries, squadrons, in the special services of the various military administrations, and on the vessels of the navy, committees from the elected representatives of the lower ranks of the above-mentioned military units shall be chosen immediately.

2. In all those military units which have not yet chosen their representatives to the Soviet of Workers' Deputies, one representative from each company shall be selected, to report with written credentials at the building of the State Duma by ten o'clock on the morning of the fifteenth of this March.

3. In all its political actions, the military branch is subordinated to the Soviet of Workers' and Soldiers' Deputies and to its own committees.

4. The orders of the military commission of the State Duma shall be executed only in such cases as do not conflict with the orders and resolutions of the Soviet of Workers' and Soldiers' Deputies.

5. All kinds of arms, such as rifles, machine guns, armored automobiles, and others, must be kept at the disposal and under the control of the company and battalion committees, and in no case be turned over to officers, even at their demand.

6. In the ranks and during their performance of the duties of the service, soldiers must observe the strictest military discipline, but outside the service and the ranks, in their political, general civic, and private life, soldiers cannot in any way be deprived of those rights which all citizens enjoy. In particular, standing at attention and compulsory saluting, when not on duty, is abolished.

7. Also, the addressing of the officers with the title, "Your Excellency," "Your Honor," etc., is abolished, and these titles are replaced by the address of "Mister General," "Mister Colonel," etc. Rudeness towards soldiers of any rank, and, especially, addressing them as "Thou," is prohibited, and soldiers are required to bring to the attention of the company committees every infraction of this rule, as well as all misunderstandings occurring between officers and privates.

The present order is to be read to all companies, battalions, regiments, ships' crews, batteries, and other combatant and non-combatant commands.

[1] The documents appearing in the Appendices have been carefully followed in translation and reprinting. Consequently no effort has been made to regularize spelling, capitalization, or punctuation.

[2] Frank Alfred Golder, ed. *Documents of Russian History, 1914–1917*. Translated by Emanuel Aronsberg. (New York: The Century Co., 1927), pp. 386–387.

Appendix 8 THE PROVISIONAL GOVERNMENT AND WAR AIMS, APRIL, 1917 [1]

Citizens: The Provisional Government, having considered the military situation of the Russian State, and being conscious of its duty to the country, has resolved to tell the people directly and openly the whole truth.

The overthrown government has left the defense of the country in an utterly disorganized condition. By its criminal inactivity and inefficient methods, it disorganized our finances, food supply, transportation, and the supply of the army. It has undermined our economic organization.

The Provisional Government, with the active and vigorous assistance of the whole nation, will make every effort to remove the dire consequences of the old regime. But time does not wait. The blood of large numbers of the sons of our fatherland has been flowing without limit during these two and a half years of war, and still the country remains exposed to the blows of a powerful enemy, who has seized entire provinces of our country, and is now, in the days of the birth of Russian freedom, menacing us with a new, determined assault.

The defense of our own inheritance by every means, and the liberation of our country from the invading enemy, constitute the foremost and most urgent task of our fighters, defending the nation's liberty.

Leaving to the will of the people, in close union with our Allies, the final solution of all problems connected with the World War and its conclusion, the Provisional Government considers it to be its right and its duty to declare at this time that the purpose of free Russia is not domination over other nations, or seizure of their national possessions, or forcible occupation of foreign territories, but the establishment of stable peace on the basis of the self-determination of peoples. The Russian people does not intend to increase its world power at the expense of other nations. It has no desire to enslave or degrade any one. In the name of the loftiest principles of justice, it has removed the shackles from the Polish people. But the Russian people will not permit their fatherland to emerge from this great struggle humiliated and sapped in its vital forces.

These principles will be made the basis of the foreign policy of the Provisional Government, which is unswervingly executing the will of the people and defending the rights of our fatherland, fully observing at the same time all obligations assumed towards our Allies.

The Provisional Government of free Russia has no right to withhold the truth from the people. The State is in danger. Every effort must be made for its salvation. Let the answer of the nation to the truth here revealed

[1] Frank A. Golder, ed. *Documents of Russian History, 1914–1917*. Translated by Emanuel Aronsberg. (New York: The Century Co., 1927), pp. 329–331.

be, not fruitless despair, not discouragement, but a concerted effort to create a single national will. This will give us fresh strength to carry on the fight, and will lead us to salvation.

In this hour of severe trial, let the whole nation find within itself the strength to consolidate the freedom it has won, and work tirelessly for the welfare of free Russia. The Provisional Government, which has taken a solemn oath to serve the people, firmly believes that, with the general and unanimous support of each and every one, it will be enabled to do its duty to the nation to the end.

Prime Minister, PRINCE G. E. LVOV

April 9, 1917

Appendix 9   LENIN'S APRIL THESES, 1917 [1]

1. In our attitude towards the war, which under the new government of Lvov and Co. unquestionably remains on Russia's part a predatory imperialist war owing to the capitalist nature of that government, not the slightest concession to "revolutionary defencism" is permissible.

The class-conscious proletariat can give its consent to a revolutionary war, which would really justify revolutionary defencism, only on condition: (a) that the power pass to the proletariat and the poorest sections of the peasants aligned with the proletariat; (b) that all annexations be renounced in deed and not in word; (c) that a complete break be effected in actual fact with all capitalist interests.

In view of the undoubted honesty of those broad sections of the mass believers in revolutionary defencism who accept the war only as a necessity, and not as a means of conquest, in view of the fact that they are being deceived by the bourgeoisie, it is necessary with particular thoroughness, persistence and patience to explain their error to them, to explain the inseparable connection existing between capital and the imperialist war, and to prove that without overthrowing capital it is *impossible* to end the war by a truly democratic peace, a peace not imposed by violence.

The most widespread campaign for this view must be organised in the army at the front.

Fraternisation.

2. The specific feature of the present situation in Russia is that the country is *passing* from the first stage of the revolution—which, owing to the insufficient class-consciousness and organisation of the proletariat, placed power in the hands of the bourgeoisie—to its *second* stage, which must place power in the hands of the proletariat and the poorest sections of the peasants.

This transition is characterised, on the one hand, by a maximum of legally recognised rights (Russia is *now* the freest of all the belligerent countries in the world); on the other, by the absence of violence towards the masses, and, finally, by their unreasoning trust in the government of capitalists, those worst enemies of peace and socialism.

This peculiar situation demands of us an ability to adapt ourselves to the *special* conditions of Party work among unprecedentedly large masses of proletarians who have just awakened to political life.

3. No support for the Provisional Government; the utter falsity of all its promises should be made clear, particularly of those relating to the renunciation of annexations. Exposure in place of the impermissible, illusion-breed-

[1] V. I. Lenin. *Collected Works,* 4th ed. (Moscow: Progress, 1964) XXIV, pp. 21–24.

ing "demand" that *this* government, a government of capitalists, should *cease* to be an imperialist government.

4. Recognition of the fact that in most of the Soviets of Workers' Deputies our Party is in a minority, so far a small minority, as against a bloc of *all* the petty-bourgeois opportunist elements, from the Popular Socialists and the Socialist-Revolutionaries down to the Organising Committee (Chkheidze, Tsereteli, etc.), Steklov, etc., etc., who have yielded to the influence of the bourgeoisie and spread that influence among the proletariat.

The masses must be made to see that the Soviets of Workers' Deputies are the *only possible* form of revolutionary government, and that therefore our task is, as long as *this* government yields to the influence of the bourgeoisie, to present a patient, systematic and persistent explanation of the errors of their tactics, an explanation especially adapted to the practical needs of the masses.

As long as we are in the minority we carry on the work of criticising and exposing errors and at the same time we preach the necessity of transferring the entire state power to the Soviets of Workers' Deputies, so that the people may overcome their mistakes by experience.

5. Not a parliamentary republic—to return to a parliamentary republic from the Soviets of Workers' Deputies would be a retrograde step—but a republic of Soviets of Workers', Agricultural Labourers' and Peasants' Deputies throughout the country, from top to bottom.

Abolition of the police, the army and the bureaucracy. (The standing army to be replaced by the arming of the whole people.)

The salaries of all officials, all of whom are elective and displaceable at any time, not to exceed the average wage of a competent worker.

6. The weight of emphasis in the agrarian programme to be shifted to the Soviets of Agricultural Labourers' Deputies.

Confiscation of all landed estates.

Nationalisation of *all* lands in the country, the land to be disposed of by the local Soviets of Agricultural Labourers' and Peasants' Deputies. The organisation of separate Soviets of Deputies of Poor Peasants. The setting up of a model farm on each of the large estates (ranging in size from 100 to 300 dessiatines, according to local and other conditions, and to the decisions of the local bodies) under the control of the Soviets of Agricultural Labourers' Deputies and for the public account.

7. The immediate amalgamation of all banks in the country into a single national bank, and the institution of control over it by the Soviet of Workers' Deputies.

8. It is not our *immediate* task to "introduce" socialism, but only to bring social production and the distribution of products at once under the *control* of the Soviets of Workers' Deputies.

9. Party tasks:

    a) Immediate convocation of a Party congress;

    b) Alteration of the Party Programme, mainly:

        1) On the question of imperialism and the imperialist war;

        2) On our attitude towards the state and *our* demand for a "commune state";

3) Amendment of our out-of-date minimum programme.

c) Change of the party's name. Instead of "Social Democracy," whose official leaders *throughout* the world have betrayed socialism and deserted to the bourgeoisie (the "defencists" and the vacillating "Kautskyites"), we must call ourselves the *Communist Party*

10. A new International.

We must take the initiative in creating a revolutionary International, an International against the *social-chauvinists* and against the "Centre."

Appendix 10 THE SOVIET AND WAR AIMS [1]

I. ON THE WAR

RESOLUTION OF THE ALL-RUSSIAN CONFERENCE OF THE SOVIET OF
WORKERS' AND SOLDIERS' DEPUTIES

In the call to the people of the world on March 27, the Soviet of Workers'
and Soldiers' Deputies declared in clear words that in the sphere of foreign
policy the Russian democracy intended to bring about the same ideas of
freedom and right that it had adopted for domestic life.

Numerous meetings of workers, soldiers, and citizens throughout Russia
have approved this stand and have expressed the will of the people, that
while defending its personal freedom it would not allow the revolutionary
enthusiasm of the nation to be used to oppress other peoples, in the form
of either open or concealed seizures of territory, or indemnities.

The Executive Committee of the Soviet of Workers' and Soldiers' Deputies took up the question with the Provisional Government and pointed out
that it was necessary for free Russia to make a public statement renouncing
the plans of conquest of the tsarist government. On April 10, the Provisional
Government published a declaration to the citizens of Russia. It said, "that
the purpose of free Russia is not domination over other nations, or seizure
of their national possessions, or forcible occupation of foreign territories, but
the establishment of stable peace on the basis of self-determination of peoples.
The Russian people does not intend to increase its world power at the
expense of other nations. It has no desire to enslave or degrade any one."

The Russian democracy attaches tremendous importance to this act of
the Provisional Government, and sees in it a step in the direction of the
realization of democratic principles in foreign policy. The Soviet of Workers'
and Soldiers' Deputies will support with energy all the efforts of the Provisional Government along this line. They [Soviets] call on all the peoples both
Allied and enemy, to bring pressure to bear on their Governments to give
up their plans of conquests. In addition to this, each nation, in both coalitions, should insist that its Government persuade its allies to make a general
renunciation of annexation and indemnity. On its part, the Executive Committee emphasizes the necessity for the Provisional Government to enter
into discussion with the Allies for the purpose of working out a general agreement along the line indicated.

Russia's revolutionary people will continue to do its best to bring about,

[1] Frank A. Golder, ed. *Documents of Russian History, 1914–1917*. Translated by
Emanuel Aronsberg. (New York: The Century Co., 1927), pp. 331–333.

as soon as possible, peace on the basis of the brotherhood and equality of free nations. An official renunciation of all ideas of conquest by all the governments would be a most powerful means to bring the war to an end on these terms.

As long as these conditions do not exist, as long as the war continues, the Russian democracy realizes that the weakening of the army and a decline in its fighting efficiency would be a most serious blow to the cause of freedom and to the life interests of the country. For the purpose of most energetically protecting revolutionary Russia from all outside attacks and forcefully defending her against all attempts to interrupt the progress of the revolution [on the inside], the Conference of All-Russian Soviets of Workers' and Soldiers' Deputies calls on the democracy of Russia to mobilize all the living force of the country in all branches of the national life in order to strengthen the rear and front. This is the imperative demand of Russia of the moment; this is necessary for the sake of the success of the revolution.

The Conference of All-Russian Soviets of Workers' and Soldiers' Deputies calls on all laborers in factories, mills, railways, mines, post and telegraph, and all other enterprises for the army and the rear, to work with the greatest zeal. The economic conquest by the working classes and the hope for additional reforms require that the workers' efforts should not be lowered, but that production should increase, so as to provide the civilian population and the army with its necessaries.

The Conference of Soviets of Workers' and Soldiers' Deputies calls the attention of all citizens, especially those engaged in agriculture and transportation, to the danger of a food crisis, an inheritance of the old regime, and appeals to them to exert all their energies to ward it off.

The Conference of Soviets of Workers' and Soldiers' Deputies sends its greetings to the revolutionary soldiers and officers who are defending free Russia from its foes at the front and at home.

Appendix 11   DECLARATION OF THE PROVISIONAL GOVERNMENT, JULY, 1917 [1]

CITIZENS:

The terrible hour is here. The forces of the German Emperor have broken through the front of the Russian national revolutionary army. In this they were helped by the light-mindedness and blind fanaticism of some, the treachery and betrayal of others. The former, as well as the latter, have been threatening the very foundations of newly freed Russia with ruin and disintegration. At this critical moment, when the counter-revolutionary forces that have been in hiding are in a position to take advantage of the general turmoil, the reorganized Provisional Government fully realizes the responsibility with all its heavy burden which falls upon its shoulders. But the Government has firm faith in the might of the great Russian people; it believes in the rapid recovery of the political life of the country, now that the contagious disease which has undermined the people's constitution has come to the surface and has ended in an acute crisis. The Provisional Government believes that this crisis will lead to life and not to death.

Believing strongly in this, the Provisional Government is ready to act and will act with all the energy and determination that the extraordinary times require. Its first and fundamental task is to concentrate its forces against the external foe and against the anarchists and counter-revolutionists in their attempts to upset the internal order. The Provisional Government will stop at nothing to bring this about. In regard to its foreign policy, the Government wishes to repeat what it has said again and again: that the revolutionary army can go into the battle with the fullest assurance that not a drop of Russian blood will be shed for aims that are against the ideals of the Russian democracy, as openly expressed before the world in its peace formula.

With these objects in mind, and on the basis of the declaration of its foreign policy made on May 19, the Provisional Government plans to propose to the Allies that they have a conference some time in August to discuss their foreign policies, in the light of the principles put forward by the Russian revolution. At this conference, Russia's spokesmen will be not only the diplomats but the representatives of the Russian democracy.

In other fields of State activity, the Provisional Government will likewise be guided by the declaration of May 19.

The Provisional Government will see to it that the elections for the Constituent Assembly take place on time, September 30, and that the prepara-

---

[1] Frank A. Golder, ed. *Documents of Russian History, 1914–1917*. Translated by Emanuel Aronsberg. (New York: The Century Co., 1927), pp. 467–469.

tory measures be finished in good season, so as to make it possible to have orderly and free elections.

One of the most important internal undertakings of the Government is to work out and put into force as quickly as possible a system of local self-government on the basis of universal, direct, equal, and secret suffrage. The Provisional Government attaches great importance to the idea that the local self-government bodies should have the confidence of all the population. For that reason it is now inviting public organizations to form local governments by means of uniting the guberniias into larger units, administered by collegiate organs of government.

In its striving to carry out consistently the principles of civic equality, the Provisional Government will abolish in the near future all class distinction, all ranks, orders of merit, except those earned on the field of battle.

For the purpose of fighting the economic disorganization and taking measures for further protection of labor, it is necessary to form, under the Provisional Government, an economic council and main economic committee to proceed at once to work out a general plan for organizing the national economy and labor, to draw up laws for regulating the economic life and industry, and to work out practical plans for carrying out these laws. There is already worked out, and soon will be published, a number of labor laws dealing with the freedom of labor unions, employment bureaus, and arbitration boards. There are being prepared measures on an eight-hour day, all kinds of labor safeguards, all kinds of social insurance for all kinds of hired labor.

The agrarian measures of the Provisional Government are now, as formerly, based on the conviction that the principle underlying land reform should be to hand it over to the toilers, which is in accordance with the fundamental needs of our economic life, the often repeated wishes of the peasants, and the programs of all democratic parties. It is with this in mind that a land reform law is being prepared for the consideration of the Constituent Assembly.

The Provisional Government will in the near future proceed with the following measures:

1. Put a complete stop to the former land policy which disorganized and ruined the villages.

2. Enact measures which will give the Constituent Assembly full freedom in disposing of the land-fund of the country.

3. Regulate the land relations with an eye to the national defense and the food question of the country. This can be done by widening the scope of and strengthening the land committees formed by the State. Their power to settle land questions should be defined by law. They should not touch upon the problem of private land ownership, which the Constituent Assembly alone can solve.

4. To remove by this legal land regulation all serious danger to the State, to land reform, and to the principles of the future State plan of land reform, which reform and plan are threatened by illegal seizures and other lawless acts, to satisfy local needs.

In stating its plans the Provisional Government hopes that all live forces will come to its aid in carrying out its heavy and responsible task. The Government demands a readiness to sacrifice all strength, riches, and even life for the great cause of saving the country, which is no longer a stepmother to the nationalities, but is trying to unite them all on the basis of complete equality and freedom.

Appendix 12   LAWLESS LAND SEIZURES [1]

A. REPORT OF LANDOWNERS

Delegates, representing landowners in the guberniias of Simbirsk, Nizhni-Novgorod, Samara, Saratov, Tver, Kharkov, Poltava, Kursk, Kherson and Ekaterinoslav, submitted the following report to the Provisional Government and the Soviet of Workers' and Soldiers' Deputies:

In the full consciousness of the great moral responsibility before the country, imposed upon us by the Provisional Government, namely, the duty to produce food and fodder for the army and the population, we proceeded to carry out the obligation imposed upon us, totally oblivious to our own interests. However, at the very first steps in this direction, we met with the strongest opposition from village committees and commissars, who are acting illegally and carrying out undisguised propaganda for the abolition by every possible means of private landownership in these guberniias. A situation has thus been created which will compel the above named guberniias, which serve the needs of the largest sugar factories and are for this reason engaged in intensive farming, to cease producing cereals, vegetables, and sugar. The general situation in these guberniias at the present time is as follows:

1. Public organizations and their representatives, contrary to the law, fix the rent on land so low that it does not even cover the necessary payments due on the land.

2. Land is forcibly taken from its owners and handed over to the peasants. In some cases, the land thus seized either remained fallow or was speculated with by being leased to a third party at a higher rate.

3. Wages for labor are arbitrarily set, interfering with freedom of labor and freedom of contract.

4. The sanctity of the home is being violated by searches and by confiscation of movable property. Landowners and their managers are deprived of liberty, without due process of law, for refusing to obey the unlawful demands of the committees and commissars.

5. The committees and their agents usurp the functions of courts, and, contrary to the express provisions of Article I of the Civil Statutes, examine conflicts relating to land and labor.

If the above situation continues, Russia, notwithstanding its rich black earth, will in the very near future become a wilderness covered with weeds, a country with a population poverty-stricken, both morally and materially, with an insignificant amount of low-grade grain, insufficient even for the needs of its cultivators. Her highly efficient agriculture will be ruined, and

[1] Frank A. Golder, ed. *Documents of Russian History, 1914–1917.* Translated by Emanuel Aronsberg. (New York: The Century Co., 1927), pp. 380–381.

there will be a total destruction of the starch, syrup, and sugar-beet production, and pure-bred stock.

Russia's economic ruin is unavoidable. We, the representatives of the guberniias named above, consider it our moral obligation to call this condition to the attention of the Provisional Government and the Soviet of Soldiers' and Workers' Deputies.

Landowners: Lieutenant B. A. Iust, Colonel K. V. Molostov, V. N. Kukol-Iasnopolski.

Appendix 13   DECREE ON PEACE, NOVEMBER, 1917 [1]

The workers' and peasants' government, created by the Revolution of October 24–25 and basing itself on the Soviets of Workers', Soldiers' and Peasants' Deputies, calls upon all the belligerent peoples and their governments to start immediate negotiations for a just, democratic peace.

By a just or democratic peace, for which the overwhelming majority of the working class and other working people of all the belligerent countries, exhausted, tormented and racked by the war, are craving—a peace that has been most definitely and insistently demanded by the Russian workers and peasants ever since the overthrow of the tsarist monarchy—by such a peace the government means an immediate peace without annexations (i.e., without the seizure of foreign lands, without the forcible incorporation of foreign nations) and without indemnities.

The Government of Russia proposes that this kind of peace be immediately concluded by all the belligerent nations, and expresses its readiness to take all the resolute measures now, without the least delay, pending the final ratification of all the terms of such a peace by authoritative assemblies of the people's representatives of all countries and all nations.

In accordance with the sense of justice of democrats in general, and of the working classes in particular, the government conceives the annexation or seizure of foreign lands to mean every incorporation of a small or weak nation into a large or powerful state without the precisely, clearly and voluntarily expressed consent and wish of that nation, irrespective of the time when such forcible incorporation took place, irrespective also of the degree of development or backwardness of the nation forcibly annexed to the given state, or forcibly retained within its borders, and irrespective, finally, of whether this nation is in Europe or in distant, overseas countries.

If any nation whatsoever is forcibly retained within the borders of a given state, if, in spite of its expressed desire—no matter whether expressed in the press, at public meetings, in the decisions of parties, or in protests and uprisings against national oppression—it is not accorded the right to decide the forms of its state existence by a free vote, taken after the complete evacuation of the troops of the incorporating or, generally, of the stronger nation and without the least pressure being brought to bear, such incorporation is annexation, i.e., seizure and violence.

The government considers it the greatest of crimes against humanity to continue this war over the issue of how to divide among the strong and rich nations the weak nationalities they have conquered, and solemnly announces its determination to sign immediately terms of peace to stop this war

[1] V. I. Lenin, *Collected Works,* 4th ed. (Moscow: Progress, 1964), XXVI, pp. 249–253.

on the terms indicated, which are equally just for all nationalities without exception.

At the same time the government declares that it does not regard the above-mentioned peace terms as an ultimatum; in other words, it is prepared to consider any other peace terms, and insists only that they be advanced by any of the belligerent countries as speedily as possible, and that in the peace proposals there should be absolute clarity and the complete absence of all ambiguity and secrecy.

The government abolishes secret diplomacy, and, for its part, announces its firm intention to conduct all negotiations quite openly in full view of the whole people. It will proceed immediately with the full publication of the secret treaties endorsed or concluded by the government of landowners and capitalists from February to October 25, 1917. The government proclaims the unconditional and immediate annulment of everything contained in these secret treaties insofar as it is aimed, as is mostly the case, at securing advantages and privileges for the Russian landowners and capitalists and at the retention, or extension, of the annexations made by the Great Russians.

Proposing to the governments and peoples of all countries immediately to begin open negotiations for peace, the government, for its part, expresses its readiness to conduct these negotiations in writing, by telegraph, and by negotiations between representatives of the various countries, or at a conference of such representatives. In order to facilitate such negotiations, the government is appointing its plenipotentiary representative to neutral countries.

The government proposes an immediate armistice to the governments and peoples of all the belligerent countries, and, for its part, considers it desirable that this armistice should be concluded for a period of not less than three months, i.e., a period long enough to permit the completion of negotiations for peace with the participation of the representatives of all peoples or nations, without exception, involved in or compelled to take part in the war, and the summoning of authoritative assemblies of the representatives of the peoples of all countries for the final ratification of the peace terms.

While addressing this proposal for peace to the governments and peoples of all the belligerent countries, the Provisional Workers' and Peasants' Government of Russia appeals in particular also to the class-conscious workers of the three most advanced nations of mankind and the largest states participating in the present war, namely, Great Britain, France and Germany. The workers of these countries have made the greatest contributions to the cause of progress and socialism; they have furnished the great examples of the Chartist movement in England, a number of revolutions of historic importance effected by the French proletariat, and, finally, the heroic struggle against the Anti-Socialist Law in Germany and the prolonged, persistent and disciplined work of creating mass proletarian organisations in Germany, a work which serves as a model to the workers of the whole world. All these examples of proletarian heroism and historical creative work are a pledge that the workers of the countries mentioned will understand the duty that now faces them of saving mankind from the horrors of war and its consequences, that these workers, by comprehensive, determined, and supremely vigorous action, will help us to conclude peace successfully, and at the same time emancipate the labouring and exploited masses of our population from all forms of slavery and all forms of exploitation.

The workers' and peasants' government, created by the Revolution of October 24–25 and basing itself on the support of the Soviets of Workers', Soldiers' and Peasants' Deputies, must start immediate negotiations for peace. Our appeal must be addressed both to the governments and to the peoples. We cannot ignore the governments, for that would delay the possibility of concluding peace, and the people's government dare not do that; but we have no right not to appeal to the peoples at the same time. Everywhere there are differences between the governments and the peoples, and we must therefore help the peoples to intervene in questions of war and peace. We will, of course, insist upon the whole of our programme for a peace without annexations and indemnities. We shall not retreat from it; but we must not give our enemies an opportunity to say that their conditions are different from ours and that therefore it is useless to start negotiations with us. No, we must deprive them of that advantageous position and not present our terms in the form of an ultimatum. Therefore the point is included that we are willing to consider any peace terms and all proposals. We shall consider them, but that does not necessarily mean that we shall accept them. We shall submit them for consideration to the Constituent Assembly which will have the power to decide what concessions can and what cannot be made. We are combating the deception practised by governments which pay lip-service to peace and justice, but in fact wage annexationist and predatory wars. No government will say all it thinks. We, however, are opposed to secret diplomacy and will act openly in full view of the whole people. We do not close our eyes to difficulties and never have done. War cannot be ended by refusal, it cannot be ended by one side. We are proposing an armistice for three months, but shall not reject a shorter period, so that the exhausted army may breathe freely, even if only for a little while; moreover, in all the civilised countries national assemblies must be summoned for the discussion of the terms.

In proposing an immediate armistice, we appeal to the class-conscious workers of the countries that have done so much for the development of the proletarian movement. We appeal to the workers of Britain, where there was the Chartist movement, to the workers of France, who have in repeated uprisings displayed the strength of their class-consciousness, and to the workers of Germany, who waged the fight against the Anti-Socialist Law and have created powerful organisations.

In the Manifesto of March 14, we called for the overthrow of the bankers, but, far from overthrowing our own bankers, we entered into an alliance with them. Now we have overthrown the government of the bankers.

The governments and the bourgeoisie will make every effort to unite their forces and drown the workers' and peasants' revolution in blood. But the three years of war have been a good lesson to the masses—the Soviet movement in other countries and the mutiny in the German navy, which was crushed by the officer cadets of Wilhelm the hangman. Finally, we must remember that we are not living in the depths of Africa, but in Europe, where news can spread quickly.

The workers' movement will triumph and will pave the way to peace and socialism.

Appendix 14 DECREE ON LAND, NOVEMBER, 1917 [1]

1. Landed proprietorship is abolished forthwith without any compensation.

2. The landed estates, as also all crown, monastery, and church lands, with all their livestock, implements, buildings and everything pertaining thereto, shall be placed at the disposal of the volost land committees and the uyezd Soviets of Peasants' Deputies pending the convocation of the Constituent Assembly.

3. All damage to confiscated property, which henceforth belongs to the whole people, is proclaimed a grave crime to be punished by the revolutionary courts. The uyezd Soviets of Peasants' Deputies shall take all necessary measures to assure the observance of the strictest order during the confiscation of the landed estates, to determine the size of estates, and the particular estates subject to confiscation, to draw up exact inventories of all property confiscated and to protect in the strictest revolutionary way all agricultural enterprises transferred to the people, with all buildings, implements, livestock, stocks of produce, etc.

4. The following peasant Mandate, compiled by the newspaper *Izvestia Vserossiiskogo Soveta Krestyanskikh Deputatov* from 242 local peasant mandates and published in No. 88 of that paper (Petrograd, No. 88, August 19, 1917), shall serve everywhere to guide the implementation of the great land reforms until a final decision on the latter is taken by the Constituent Assembly.

PEASANT MANDATE ON THE LAND

"The land question in its full scope can be settled only by the popular Constituent Assembly.

"The most equitable settlement of the land question is to be as follows:

"(1) *Private ownership of land shall be abolished forever;* land shall not be sold, purchased, leased, mortgaged, or otherwise alienated.

"All land, whether *state, crown, monastery, church, factory, entailed, private, public, peasant, etc., shall be confiscated without compensation* and become the property of the whole people, and pass into the use of all those who cultivate it.

"Persons who suffer by this property revolution shall be deemed to be entitled to public support only for the period necessary for adaptation to the new conditions of life.

[1] V. I. Lenin, *Collected Works,* 4th ed. (Moscow: Progress, 1964), XXVI, pp. 258–260.

382

"(2) All mineral wealth—ore, oil, coal, salt, etc., and also all forests and waters of state importance, shall pass into the exclusive use of the state. All the small streams, lakes, woods, etc., shall pass into the use of the communes, to be administered by the local self-government bodies.

"(3) Lands on which *high-level scientific* farming is practised—orchards, plantations, seed plots, nurseries, hothouses, etc.—*shall not be divided up, but shall be converted into model farms,* to be turned over for exclusive use *to the state or to the communes,* depending on the size and importance of such lands.

"Household land in towns and villages, with orchards and vegetable gardens, shall be reserved for the use of their present owners, the size of the holdings, and the size of tax levied for the use thereof, to be determined by law.

"(4) Stud farms, government and private pedigree stock and poultry farms, etc., shall be confiscated and become the property of the whole people, and pass into the exclusive use of the state or a commune, depending on the size and importance of such farms.

"The question of compensation shall be examined by the Constituent Assembly.

"(5) All livestock and farm implements of the confiscated estates shall pass into the exclusive use of the state or a commune, depending on their size and importance, and no compensation shall be paid for this.

"The farm implements of peasants with little land shall not be subject to confiscation.

"(6) The right to use the land shall be accorded to all citizens of the Russian state (without distinction of sex) desiring to cultivate it by their own labour, with the help of their families, or in partnership, but only as long as they are able to cultivate it. The employment of hired labour is not permitted.

"In the event of the temporary physical disability of any member of a village commune for a period of up to two years, the village commune shall be obliged to assist him for this period by collectively cultivating his land until he is again able to work.

"Peasants who, owing to old age or ill-health, are permanently disabled and unable to cultivate the land personally, shall lose their right to the use of it but, in return, shall receive a pension from the state.

"(7) Land tenure shall be on an equality basis, i.e., the land shall be distributed among the working people in conformity with a labour standard or a subsistence standard, depending on local conditions.

"There shall be absolutely no restriction on the forms of land tenure—household, farm, communal, or co-operative, as shall be decided in each individual village and settlement.

"(8) All land, when alienated, shall become part of the national land fund. Its distribution among the peasants shall be in charge of the local and central self-government bodies, from democratically organised village and city communes, in which there are no distinctions of social rank, to central regional government bodies.

"The land fund shall be subject to periodical redistribution, depending on the growth of population and the increase in the productivity and the scientific level of farming.

"When the boundaries of allotments are altered, the original nucleus of the allotment shall be left intact.

"The land of the members who leave the commune shall revert to the land fund; preferential right to such land shall be given to the near relatives of the members who have left, or to persons designated by the latter.

"The cost of fertilisers and improvements put into the land, to the extent that they have not been fully used up at the time the allotment is returned to the land fund, shall be compensated.

"Should the available land fund in a particular district prove inadequate for the needs of the local population, the surplus population shall be settled elsewhere.

"The state shall take upon itself the organisation of resettlement and shall bear the cost thereof, as well as the cost of supplying implements, etc.

"Resettlement shall be effected in the following order: landless peasants desiring to resettle, then members of the commune who are of vicious habits, deserters, and so on, and, finally, by lot or by agreement."

The entire contents of this Mandate, as expressing the absolute will of the vast majority of the class-conscious peasants of all Russia, is proclaimed a provisional law, which, pending the convocation of the Constituent Assembly, shall be carried into effect as far as possible immediately, and as to certain of its provisions with due gradualness, as shall be determined by the uyezd Soviets of Peasants' Deputies.

5. The land of ordinary peasants and ordinary Cossacks shall not be confiscated.

Appendix 15   DECLARATION OF THE RIGHTS OF THE PEOPLES OF RUSSIA, NOVEMBER, 1917 [1]

The October revolution of the workmen and peasants began under the common banner of emancipation.

The peasants are being emancipated from the power of the landowners, for there is no longer the landowner's property right in the land—it has been abolished. The soldiers and sailors are being emancipated from the power of autocratic generals, for generals will henceforth be elective and subject to recall. The workingmen are being emancipated from the whims and arbitrary will of the capitalists, for henceforth there will be established the control of the workers over mills and factories. Everything living and capable of life is being emancipated from the hateful shackles.

There remain only the peoples of Russia, who have suffered and are suffering oppression and arbitrariness, and whose emancipation must immediately be begun, whose liberation must be effected resolutely and definitely.

During the period of czarism the peoples of Russia were systematically incited against one another. The results of such a policy are known: massacres and pogroms on the one hand, slavery of peoples on the other.

There can be and there must be no return to this disgraceful policy of instigation. Henceforth the policy of a voluntary and honest union of the peoples of Russia must be substituted.

In the period of imperialism, after the February revolution, when the power was transferred to the hands of the Cadet bourgeoisie, the naked policy of instigation gave way to one of cowardly distrust of the peoples of Russia, to a policy of fault-finding and provocation, of "freedom" and "equality" of peoples. The results of such a policy are known: the growth of national enmity, the impairment of mutual trust.

An end must be put to this unworthy policy of falsehood and distrust, of fault-finding and provocation. Henceforth it must be replaced by an open and honest policy which leads to complete mutual trust of the peoples of Russia. Only as the result of such a trust can there be formed an honest and lasting union of the peoples of Russia. Only as the result of such a union can the workmen and peasants of the peoples of Russia be cemented into one revolutionary force able to resist all attempts on the part of the imperialist-annexationist bourgeoisie.

Starting with these assumptions, the first Congress of Soviets, in June of this year, proclaimed the right of the peoples of Russia to free self-determination.

The second Congress of Soviets, in October of this year, reaffirmed this inalienable right of the peoples of Russia more decisively and definitely.

[1] *The Nation*, Vol. 107, No. 2791 (Dec. 28, 1918), p. 81.

The united will of these Congresses, the Council of the People's Commissaries, resolved to base their activity upon the question of the nationalities of Russia, as expressed in the following principles:

1. The equality and sovereignty of the peoples of Russia.
2. The right of the peoples of Russia to free self-determination, even to the point of separation and the formation of an independent state.
3. The abolition of any and all national and national-religious privileges and disabilities.
4. The free development of national minorities and ethnographic groups inhabiting the territory of Russia.

The concrete decrees which follow will be framed immediately upon the formation of a commission for the affairs of nationalities.

Appendix 16 DRAFT DECREE ON THE DISSOLUTION
OF THE CONSTITUENT ASSEMBLY,
JANUARY, 1918 [1]

At its very inception, the Russian revolution produced the Soviets of Workers',
Soldiers' and Peasants' Deputies as the only mass organisation of all the
working and exploited classes capable of leading the struggle of these classes
for their complete political and economic emancipation.

During the whole of the initial period of the Russian revolution the
Soviets multiplied in number, grew and gained strength and were taught by
their own experience to discard the illusions of compromise with the bourgeoisie and to realise the deceptive nature of the forms of the bourgeois-
democratic parliamentary system; they arrived by practical experience at the
conclusion that the emancipation of the oppressed classes was impossible
unless they broke with these forms and with every kind of compromise. The
break came with the October Revolution, which transferred the entire power
to the Soviets.

The Constituent Assembly, elected on the basis of electoral lists drawn
up prior to the October Revolution, was an expression of the old relation of
political forces which existed when power was held by the compromisers and
the Cadets. When the people at that time voted for the candidates of the
Socialist-Revolutionary Party, they were not in a position to choose between
the Right Socialist-Revolutionaries, the supporters of the bourgeoisie, and
the Left Socialist-Revolutionaries, the supporters of socialism. The Constituent
Assembly, therefore, which was to have crowned the bourgeois parliamentary
republic, was bound to become an obstacle in the path of the October Revolution and Soviet power.

The October Revolution, by giving power to the Soviets, and through the
Soviets to the working and exploited classes, aroused the desperate resistance
of the exploiters, and in the crushing of this resistance it fully revealed itself
as the beginning of the socialist revolution. The working classes learned by
experience that the old bourgeois parliamentary system had outlived its purpose and was absolutely incompatible with the aim of achieving socialism,
and that not national institutions, but only class institutions (such as the
Soviets) were capable of overcoming the resistance of the propertied classes
and of laying the foundations of socialist society. To relinquish the sovereign
power of the Soviets, to relinquish the Soviet Republic won by the people,
for the sake of the bourgeois parliamentary system and the Constituent
Assembly, would now be a step backwards and would cause the collapse of
the October workers' and peasants' revolution.

[1] V. I. Lenin, *Collected Works*, 4th ed. (Moscow: Progress, 1964), XXVI,
pp. 434–436.

Owing to the above-mentioned circumstances, the Party of Right Social-ist-Revolutionaries, the party of Kerensky, Avksentyev and Chernov, obtained the majority in the Constituent Assembly which met on January 5. Naturally, this party refused to discuss the absolutely clear, precise and unambiguous proposal of the supreme organ of Soviet power, the Central Executive Committee of the Soviets, to recognise the programme of Soviet power, to recognise the Declaration of Rights of the Working and Exploited People, to recognise the October Revolution and Soviet power. By this action the Constituent Assembly severed all ties with the Soviet Republic of Russia. It was inevitable that the Bolshevik group and the Left Socialist-Revolutionary group, who now patently constitute the overwhelming majority in the Soviets and enjoy the confidence of the workers and the majority of the peasants, should withdraw from such a Constituent Assembly.

The Right Socialist-Revolutionary and Menshevik parties are in fact carrying on outside the Constituent Assembly a most desperate struggle against Soviet power, calling openly in their press for its overthrow and describing as arbitrary and unlawful the crushing of the resistance of the exploiters by the forces of the working classes, which is essential in the interests of emancipation from exploitation. They are defending the saboteurs, the servants of capital, and are going as far as undisguised calls to terrorism, which certain "unidentified groups" have already begun. It is obvious that under such circumstances the remaining part of the Constituent Assembly could only serve as a screen for the struggle of the counter-revolutionaries to overthrow Soviet power.

Accordingly, the Central Executive Committee resolves that the Constituent Assembly is hereby dissolved.

Appendix 17   THESES ON THE QUESTION OF THE
IMMEDIATE CONCLUSION OF A SEPARATE
AND ANNEXATIONIST PEACE, JANUARY
20, 1918 [1]

1. The position of the Russian Revolution at the present moment is such that nearly all the workers and the vast majority of the peasants undoubtedly side with Soviet power and the socialist revolution which it has started. To that extent the socialist revolution in Russia is assured.

2. At the same time, the civil war, provoked by the frantic resistance of the wealthy classes, who realise full well that they are faced with the last and decisive fight for the preservation of private ownership of the land and means of production, has not yet reached its climax. The victory of Soviet power in this war is assured, but some time must inevitably elapse, no little exertion of effort will inevitably be required, a certain period of acute economic dislocation and chaos, which accompany all wars, and civil war in particular, is inevitable, before the resistance of the bourgeoisie is crushed.

3. Furthermore, this resistance, in its less active and nonmilitary forms —sabotage, the hire of declassed elements and agents of the bourgeoisie, who worm their way into the ranks of the socialists in order to ruin their cause, and so on and so forth—has proved so stubborn and capable of assuming such diversified forms, that the fight against it will inevitably require some more time, and, in its main forms, is hardly likely to end until several months have passed. And unless this passive and covert resistance of the bourgeoisie and its supporters is definitely crushed the socialist revolution cannot succeed.

4. Lastly, the organisational problems of the socialist transformation of Russia are so immense and difficult that their solution—in view of the numerous petty-bourgeois fellow-travellers of the socialist proletariat, and of the latter's low cultural level—will also require a fairly long time.

5. All these circumstances taken together are such as to make it perfectly clear that for the success of socialism in Russia a certain amount of time, several months at least, will be necessary, during which the hands of the socialist government must be absolutely free to achieve victory over the bourgeoisie first in our own country and to launch far-reaching mass organisational work on a wide scale.

6. The position of the socialist revolution in Russia must form the basis of any definition of the international tasks of our Soviet power, for the international situation in the fourth year of the war is such that it is quite impossible to predict the probable moment of outbreak of revolution and

[1] V. I. Lenin, *Collected Works*, 4th ed. (Moscow: Progress, 1964), XXVI, pp. 442–450.

overthrow of any of the European imperialist governments (including the German). That the socialist revolution in Europe must come, and will come, is beyond doubt. All our hopes for the *final* victory of socialism are founded on this certainty and on this scientific prognosis. Our propaganda activities in general, and the organisation of fraternisation in particular, must be intensified and extended. It would be a mistake, however, to base the tactics of the Russian socialist government on attempts to determine whether or not the European, and especially the German, Socialist revolution will take place in the next six months (or some such brief period). Inasmuch as it is quite impossible to determine this, all such attempts, objectively speaking, would be nothing but a blind gamble.

7. The peace negotiations in Brest-Litovsk have by now—January 7, 1918—made it perfectly clear that the war party has undoubtedly gained the upper hand in the German Government (which has the other governments of the Quadruple Alliance at its beck and call) and has virtually already presented Russia with an ultimatum (and it is to be expected, most certainly to be expected, that any day now it will be presented formally). The ultimatum is as follows: either the continuation of the war, or a peace with annexations, i.e., peace on condition that we surrender all the territory we have occupied, while the Germans retain *all* the territory they have occupied and impose upon us an indemnity (outwardly disguised as payment for the maintenance of prisoners)—an indemnity of about three thousand million *rubles,* payable over a number of years.

8. The socialist government of Russia is faced with the question—a question whose solution brooks no delay—of whether to accept this peace with annexations now, or to immediately wage a revolutionary war. In fact, no middle course is possible. No further postponement can now be achieved, for we have *already* done everything possible and impossible to deliberately protract the negotiations.

9. On examining the arguments in favour of an immediate revolutionary war, the first argument we encounter is that a separate peace at this juncture would, objectively speaking, be an agreement with the German imperialists, an "imperialistic deal" and so forth, and that, consequently, such a peace would mean a complete break with the fundamental principles of proletarian internationalism.

This argument, however, is obviously incorrect. Workers who lose a strike and sign terms for the resumption of work which are unfavourable to them and favourable to the capitalists, do not betray socialism. The only people who betray socialism are those who secure advantages for a section of the workers in exchange for profit to the capitalists; only such agreements are impermissible in principle.

He betrays socialism who calls the war with German imperialism a defensive and just war, but actually receives support from the Anglo-French imperialists, and conceals secret treaties concluded with them from the people. He does not in the least betray socialism who, without concealing anything from the people, and without concluding any secret treaties with the imperialists, agrees to sign terms of peace which are unfavourable to the weak nation and favourable to the imperialists of one group, if at that moment there is no strength to continue the war.

10. Another argument in favour of immediate war is that, by concluding peace, we objectively become agents of German imperialism, for we afford it the opportunity to release troops from our front, we surrender to it millions of prisoners of war, and so on. But this argument too is manifestly incorrect, for a revolutionary war at the present juncture would, objectively speaking, make us agents of Anglo-French imperialism, by providing it with forces which would promote its aims. The British bluntly offered our Commander-in-Chief, Krylenko, one hundred rubles per month for every one of our soldiers provided we continued the war. Even if we did not take a single kopck from the Anglo-French, we nevertheless would be helping them, objectively speaking, by diverting part of the German army.

From that point of view, in neither case would we be entirely escaping some sort of imperialist bond, and it is obvious that it is impossible to escape it completely without overthrowing world imperialism. The correct conclusion from this is that the moment a socialist government triumphed in any one country, questions must be decided, not from the point of view of whether this or that imperialism is preferable, but exclusively from the point of view of the conditions which best make for the development and consolidation of the socialist revolution which has already begun.

In other words, the underlying principle of our tactics must not be, which of the two imperialisms it is more profitable to aid at this juncture, but rather, how the socialist revolution can be most firmly and reliably ensured the possibility of consolidating itself, or, at least, of maintaining itself in one country until it is joined by other countries.

11. It is said that the German Social-Democratic opponents of the war have now become "defeatists" and are requesting us not to yield to German imperialism. But we recognised defeatism only in respect of one's own imperialist bourgeoisie, and we always discountenanced victory over an alien imperialism, victory attained in formal or actual alliance with a "friendly" imperialism, as a method impermissible in principle and generally wrong.

This argument is therefore only a modification of the previous one. If the German Left Social-Democrats were proposing that we delay concluding a separate peace for a *definite* period, and guaranteed revolutionary action in Germany within this period, the question *might* assume a different aspect for us. Far from saying this, however, the German Lefts formally declare: "Hold out as long as you can, but decide the question from the point of view of the state of affairs in the *Russian* socialist revolution, for we cannot promise you anything positive regarding the German revolution."

12. It is said that in a number of Party statements we actually "promised" a revolutionary war, and that by concluding a separate peace we would be going back on our word.

That is not true. We said that in the era of imperialism a socialist government *had* to "*prepare for and wage*" a revolutionary war; we said this in order to combat abstract pacifism and the theory that "defence of the fatherland" must be completely rejected in the era of imperialism, and, lastly to combat the purely selfish instincts of a part of the soldiers, but we never gave any pledge to start a revolutionary war without considering whether it is possible to wage it at a given moment.

Unquestionably, even at this juncture we must *prepare for* a revolutionary war. We are carrying out this promise, as we have, in general, carried out all our promises that could be carried out at once: we annulled the secret treaties, offered all peoples a fair peace, and several times did our best to drag out peace negotiations so as to give other peoples a chance to join us.

But the question whether it is possible to carry on a revolutionary war *now, immediately,* must be decided exclusively from the point of view of whether material conditions permit it, and of the interests of the socialist revolution which has already begun.

13. Summing up the arguments in favour of an immediate revolutionary war, we have to conclude that such a policy might perhaps answer the human yearning for the beautiful, dramatic and striking, but that it would totally disregard the objective balance of class forces and material factors at the present stage of the socialist revolution now under way.

14. There can be no doubt that our army is absolutely in no condition at the present moment, and will not be for the next few weeks (and probably for the next few months), to beat back a German offensive successfully; firstly, owing to the extreme fatigue and exhaustion of the majority of the soldiers, coupled with the incredible chaos in the matter of food supply, replacement of the overfatigued, etc.; secondly, owing to the utter unfitness of the horses and the consequent inevitable ruin of our artillery; and, thirdly, owing to the absolute impossibility of defending the coastline from Riga to Revel, which affords the enemy a very certain chance of seizing the rest of Lifland, and then Estland, and of outflanking a large part of our forces, and finally, of capturing Petrograd.

15. Further, there is not the slightest doubt that the peasant majority of our army would at the present juncture unreservedly declare in favour of a peace with annexations and not in favour of an immediate revolutionary war; the socialist reorganisation of the army, the merging of the Red Guard detachments with it, and so on, have only just begun.

With the army completely democratised, to carry on war in defiance of the wishes of the majority of the soldiers would be a reckless gamble, while to create a really staunch and ideologically stable socialist workers' and peasants' army will, at the very least, require months and months.

16. The poor peasants in Russia are capable of supporting the socialist revolution led by the working class, but they are not capable of agreeing to fight a serious revolutionary war immediately, at the present juncture. To ignore the objective balance of class forces on this issue would be a fatal error.

17. Consequently, the situation at present with regard to a revolutionary war is as follows:

If the German revolution were to break out and triumph in the coming three or four months, the tactics of an immediate revolutionary war might perhaps not ruin our socialist revolution.

If, however, the German revolution does not occur in the next few months, the course of events, if the war is continued, will inevitably be such that grave defeats will compel Russia to conclude an even more disadvantageous separate peace, a peace, moreover, which would be concluded, not by a socialist government, but by some other (for example, a bloc of the bourgeois Rada and Chernov's followers, or something similar). For the peasant army, which is exhausted to the limit by the war, will after the very first defeats—and very likely within a matter of weeks, and not of months—overthrow the socialist workers' government.

18. This being the state of affairs, it would be absolutely impermissible tactics to stake the fate of the socialist revolution, which has already begun in Russia, merely on the chance that the German revolution may begin in the immediate future, within a matter of weeks. Such tactics would be a reckless gamble. We have no right to take such risks.

19. The German revolution will by no means be made more difficult of accomplishment as far as its objective premises are concerned, if we conclude a separate peace. Probably chauvinist intoxication will weaken it for a time, but Germany's position will remain extremely grave, the war with Britain and America will be a protracted one, and aggressive imperialism will be fully and completely exposed on both sides. A socialist Soviet Republic in Russia will stand as a living example to the peoples of all countries, and the propaganda and revolutionising effect of this example will be immense. There—the bourgeois system and a fully exposed predatory war between two groups of marauders. Here—peace and a socialist Soviet Republic.

20. In concluding a separate peace we free ourselves *as much as is possible at the present moment* from both hostile imperialist groups, we take advantage of their mutual enmity and warfare which hamper concerted action on their part against us, and for a certain period have our hands free to advance and to consolidate the socialist revolution. The reorganisation of Russia on the basis of the dictatorship of the proletariat, and the nationalisation of the banks and large-scale industry, coupled with *exchange of products* in kind between the towns and the small-peasant consumers' societies, is quite feasible economically, provided we are assured a few months in which to work in peace. And such a reorganisation will render socialism invincible both in Russia and all over the world, and at the same time will create a solid economic basis for a mighty workers' and peasants' Red Army.

21. A really revolutionary war at this juncture would be a war waged by a socialist republic against the bourgeois countries, with the aim—an aim clearly defined and fully approved by the socialist army—of overthrowing the bourgeoisie in other countries. However, we *obviously* cannot set ourselves this aim at the *present* moment. Objectively, we would be fighting now for the liberation of Poland, Lifland and Courland. But no Marxist, without renouncing the principles of Marxism and of socialism generally, can deny that the interests of socialism are higher than the interests of the right of nations to self-determination. Our socialist republic has done all it could, and continues to do all it can to give effect to the right to self-determination of Finland, the Ukraine, etc. But if the concrete situation is such that the existence of the socialist republic is being imperilled at the present moment

on account of the violation of the right to self-determination of several nations (Poland, Lifland, Courland, etc.), naturally the preservation of the socialist republic has the higher claim.

Consequently, whoever says, "We cannot sign a humiliating, atrocious, etc., peace, betray Poland, and so forth," does not realise that by concluding peace on the condition that Poland is liberated, he would only be strengthening German imperialism against Britain, Belgium, Serbia and other countries *still further*. Peace on the condition of the liberation of Poland, Lifland and Courland would be a "patriotic" peace *from the point of view of Russia,* but would by no means cease to be a peace *with the annexationists,* with the German imperialists.

January 21, 1918. The following should be added to the above theses:

22. The mass strikes in Austria and Germany, and, subsequently, the formation of the Soviets of Workers' Deputies in Berlin and Vienna, and, lastly, beginning from January 18–20, armed clashes and street fighting in Berlin—all this should be regarded as evidence of the fact that the revolution in Germany has begun.

This fact offers us the opportunity, for the time being, of further delaying and dragging out the peace negotiations.

Appendix 18 AN APPEAL OF THE GOVERNMENT OF THE RSFSR TO THE CHINESE PEOPLE AND TO THE GOVERNMENTS OF SOUTH AND NORTH CHINA, JULY 25, 1919 [1]

At a time when the Soviet forces, having defeated the army of the counter-revolutionary despot Kolchak, supported by foreign bayonets and foreign gold, have triumphantly entered Siberia and are marching to join with the revolutionary people of Siberia, the Council of People's Commissars addresses the following brotherly words to all the peoples of China:

After two years of struggle and incredible efforts, Soviet Russia and the Soviet Red Army are marching across the Urals to the East, not to coerce, not to enslave, not to conquer. Every Siberian peasant and every Siberian worker already knows this. We bring to the peoples liberation from the yoke of foreign bayonet and the yoke of foreign gold, which are stifling the enslaved peoples of the East, including, and particularly, the Chinese people. We bring help not only to our own working classes, but to the Chinese people too, and we once more remind them of what they have been told ever since the Great October Revolution of 1917, but which was perhaps concealed from them by the corrupt press of America, Europe, and Japan.

As soon as the Workers' and Peasants' Government took power into its own hands in October, 1917, it addressed all the peoples of the world, in the name of the Russian people, with the proposal to establish a firm and lasting peace. The foundation on which this peace was to be established was the renunciation of any seizure of foreign territory, the renunciation of any coercive annexation of foreign nationalities, and of any indemnities. Every people, whether great or small, wherever it dwelt, whether up to then it had lived an independent life or was included against its will as a constituent part of another state, should be free in its internal life, and no government was to keep it by force within its frontiers.

Immediately after this the Workers' and Peasants' Government proclaimed that all the secret treaties concluded with Japan, China, and the former Allies were annulled; these were treaties by which the Tsarist Government, jointly with its Allies, by force and bribery enslaved the peoples of the East, and in the first place the people of China, in order to provide profits for Russian capitalists, Russian landlords, and Russian generals. The Soviet Government then proposed to the Chinese Government that they start negotiations to annul the treaty of 1896, the Peking protocol of 1901, and all agreements concluded with Japan between 1907 and 1916; that is,

[1] USSR Ministry for Foreign Affairs. *Dokumenty vneshnei politiki SSSR.* (Moscow: Gospolitizdat, 1958), II, pp. 221–222. Translation by Basil Dmytryshyn.

to return to the Chinese people everything that was taken from them by the Tsarist Government independently, or jointly with the Japanese and the Allies. Negotiations on this question were continued up to March, 1918. Suddenly, the Allies seized the Peking Government by the throat, showered gold on the Peking mandarins and the Chinese press, and forced the Chinese Government to refuse to have any relations with the Russian Workers' and Peasants' Government. Anticipating the return to the Chinese people of the Manchurian Railway, Japan and its allies seized it themselves, invaded Siberia, and even forced Chinese forces to help them in this criminal and unparalleled robbery. And the Chinese people, the Chinese workers and peasants, could not even learn the truth, could not find out the reason for the invasion of Manchuria and Siberia by the American, European, and Japanese robbers.

Now we again address the Chinese people, in order to open their eyes.

The Soviet Government has renounced the conquests made by the Tsarist Government, which deprived China of Manchuria and other areas. Let the peoples living in those areas themselves decide within the frontiers of which state they wish to dwell, and what form of government they wish to establish in their own countries.

The Soviet Government renounces the receipt from China of the 1900 Boxer Rebellion indemnity, and it is obliged to repeat this a third time because, according to the information reaching us, this indemnity, despite our renunciation, is being exacted by the Allies to pay the salaries and to satisfy the whims of the former Tsarist ambassador to Peking and the former Tsarist consuls in China. All these Tsarist slaves have long been deprived of their powers, but they continue at their posts and deceive the Chinese people with the help of Japan and the Allies. The Chinese people should know of this and should expel them from their country as imposters and rogues.

The Soviet Government abolishes all special privileges and gives up all factories owned by Russian merchants on Chinese soil. Not one Russian official, priest, or missionary shall be able to interfere in Chinese affairs, and if he commits a crime, he should be subject to the justice of the local court. In China there should be no authority and no court except the authority and court of the Chinese people. In addition to these principal points, the Soviet Government is ready to discuss all other questions with the Chinese people represented by their plenipotentiaries, and to remove once and for all the acts of coercion and injustice committed in regard to China by former Russian Governments jointly with Japan and the Allies.

The Soviet Government is well aware that the Allies and Japan will again do everything possible to prevent the voice of the Russian workers and peasants from reaching the Chinese people, that the return to the Chinese people of what was taken from them requires first of all putting an end to the robber invasion of Manchuria and Siberia. Therefore it is now sending the news to the Chinese people, together with its Red Army, which is marching across the Urals to the East to help the Siberian peasants and workers, to liberate them from the bandit Kolchak and his ally, Japan.

If the Chinese people wish, like the Russian people, to become free and to avoid the fate which the Allies prepared for them at Versailles, a fate designed to turn China into a second Korea or a second India, they must understand that their only ally and brother in the struggle for freedom is the Russian worker and peasant and their Red Army.

The Soviet Government proposes to the Chinese people, in the person of their government, that they enter now into official relations with us and send their representatives to meet our army.

Deputy People's Commissar for Foreign Affairs [L. Karakhan]

Appendix 19 CONDITIONS FOR ADMISSION TO THE COMMUNIST INTERNATIONAL, 1920 [1]

The first congress of the Communist International did not draw up any precise conditions for the admission of parties to the Third International. When the first congress was convened there were in the majority of countries only communist *trends* and *groups*.

The second congress of the Communist International is meeting in different circumstances. At the present time there are in most countries not only communist trends and tendencies, but communist *parties* and *organizations*.

Application for admission to the Communist International is now frequently made by parties and groups which up to a short time ago still belonged to the Second International, but which have not in fact become communist. The Second International has finally broken down. The inbetween parties and the centrist groups, seeing the utter hopelessness of the Second International, are trying to find a support in the Communist International, which is growing steadily stronger. But in doing so they hope to retain enough "autonomy" to enable them to continue their former opportunist or "centrist" policy. The Communist International is becoming, to some extent, fashionable.

The desire of some leading "centrist" groups to join the Communist International indirectly confirms that it has won the sympathies of the overwhelming majority of the class-conscious workers of the entire world and that with every day it is becoming a more powerful force.

The Communist International is threatened by the danger of dilution by unstable and irresolute elements which have not yet completely discarded the ideology of the Second International.

Moreover, in some of the larger parties (Italy, Sweden, Norway, Yugoslavia, etc.) where the majority adhere to the communist standpoint, there still remains even today a reformist and social-pacifist wing which is only waiting a favourable moment to raise its head again and start active sabotage of the proletarian revolution and so help the bourgeoisie and the Second International.

No communist should forget the lessons of the Hungarian revolution. The Hungarian proletariat paid a high price for the fusion of the Hungarian communists with the so-called "left" social-democrats.

Consequently the second congress of the Communist International thinks

[1] From *The Communist International, 1919–1943. Documents.* Edited by Jane Degras and published by Oxford University Press under the auspices of the Royal Institute of International Affairs. (London: Oxford University Press, 1956), I, pp. 168–172.

it necessary to lay down quite precisely the conditions of admission of new parties, and to point out to those parties which have already joined, the duties imposed on them.

The second congress of the Communist International puts forward the following conditions of adherence to the Communist International:

1. *All propaganda and agitation* must be of a genuinely communist character and in conformity with the programme and decisions of the Communist International. The entire party press must be run by reliable communists who have proved their devotion to the cause of the proletariat. The dictatorship of the proletariat is to be treated not simply as a current formula learnt by rote; it must be advocated in a way which makes its necessity comprehensible to every ordinary working man and woman, every soldier and peasant, from the facts of their daily life, which must be systematically noted in our press and made use of every day.

The periodical press and other publications, and all party publishing houses, must be completely subordinated to the party presidium, regardless of whether the party as a whole is at the given moment legal or illegal. Publishing houses must not be allowed to abuse their independence and pursue a policy which is not wholly in accordance with the policy of the party.

In the columns of the press, at popular meetings, in the trade unions and co-operatives, wherever the adherents of the Communist International have an entry, it is necessary to denounce, systematically and unrelentingly, not only the bourgeoisie, but also their assistants, the reformists of all shades.

2. Every organization which wishes to join the Communist International must, in an orderly and planned fashion, remove reformists and centrists from all responsible positions in the workers' movement (party organizations, editorial boards, trade unions, parliamentary fractions, co-operatives, local government bodies) and replace them by tried communists, even if, particularly at the beginning, "experienced" opportunists have to be replaced by ordinary rank and file workers.

3. In practically every country of Europe and America the class struggle is entering the phase of civil war. In these circumstances communists can have no confidence in bourgeois legality. They are obliged everywhere to create a parallel illegal organization which at the decisive moment will help the party to do its duty to the revolution. In all those countries where, because of a state of siege or of emergency laws, communists are unable to do all their work legally, it is absolutely essential to combine legal and illegal work.

4. The obligation to spread communist ideas includes the special obligation to carry on systematic and energetic propaganda in the army. Where such agitation is prevented by emergency laws, it must be carried on illegally. Refusal to undertake such work would be tantamount to a dereliction of revolutionary duty and is incompatible with membership of the Communist International.

5. Systematic and well-planned agitation must be carried on in the countryside. The working class cannot consolidate its victory if it has not by its policy assured itself of the support of at least part of the rural pro-

letariat and the poorest peasants, and of the neutrality of part of the rest of the rural population. At the present time communist work in rural areas is acquiring first-rate importance. It should be conducted primarily with the help of revolutionary communist urban and rural workers who have close connexions with the countryside. To neglect this work or to leave it in unreliable semi-reformist hands, is tantamount to renouncing the proletarian revolution.

6. Every party which wishes to join the Communist International is obliged to expose not only avowed social-patriotism, but also the insincerity and hypocrisy of social-pacifism; to bring home to the workers systematically that without the revolutionary overthrow of capitalism no international court of arbitration, no agreement to limit armaments, no "democratic" reorganization of the League of Nations, will be able to prevent new imperialist wars.

7. Parties which wish to join the Communist International are obliged to recognize the necessity for a complete and absolute break with reformism and with the policy of the "centre," and to advocate this break as widely as possible among their members. Without that no consistent communist policy is possible.

The Communist International demands unconditionally and categorically that this break be effected as quickly as possible. The Communist International is unable to agree that notorious opportunists, such as Turati, Modigliani, Kautsky, Hilferding, Hilquit, Longuet, MacDonald, etc., shall have the right to appear as members of the Communist International. That could only lead to the Communist International becoming in many respects similar to the Second International, which has gone to pieces.

8. A particularly explicit and clear attitude on the question of the colonies and the oppressed peoples is necessary for the parties in those countries where the bourgeoisie possess colonies and oppress other nations. Every party which wishes to join the Communist International is obliged to expose the tricks and dodges of "its" imperialists in the colonies, to support every colonial liberation movement not merely in words but in deeds, to demand the expulsion of their own imperialists from these colonies, to inculcate among the workers of their country a genuinely fraternal attitude to the working people of the colonies and the oppressed nations, and to carry on systematic agitation among the troops of their country against any oppression of the colonial peoples.

9. Every party which wishes to join the Communist International must carry on systematic and persistent communist activity inside the trade unions, the workers' councils and factory committees, the co-operatives, and other mass workers' organizations. Within these organizations communist cells must be organized which shall by persistent and unflagging work win the trade unions, etc., for the communist cause. In their daily work the cells must everywhere expose the treachery of the social-patriots and the instability of the "centre." The communist cells must be completely subordinate to the party as a whole.

10. Every party belonging to the Communist International is obliged to wage an unyielding struggle against the Amsterdam "International" of the yellow trade unions. It must conduct the most vigorous propaganda

among trade unionists for the necessity of a break with the yellow Amsterdam International. It must do all it can to support the international association of red trade unions, adhering to the Communist International, which is being formed.

11. Parties which wish to join the Communist International are obliged to review the personnel of their parliamentary fractions and remove all unreliable elements, to make these fractions not only verbally but in fact subordinate to the party presidium, requiring of each individual communist member of parliament that he subordinate his entire activity to the interests of genuinely revolutionary propaganda and agitation.

12. Parties belonging to the Communist International must be based on the principle of *democratic centralism*. In the present epoch of acute civil war the communist party will be able to fulfil its duty only if its organization is as centralized as possible, if iron discipline prevails, and if the party centre, upheld by the confidence of the party membership, has strength and authority and is equipped with the most comprehensive powers.

13. Communist parties in those countries where communists carry on their work legally must from time to time undertake cleansing (re-registration) of the membership of the party in order to get rid of any petty-bourgeois elements which have crept in.

14. Every party which wishes to join the Communist International is obliged to give unconditional support to any Soviet republic in its struggle against counter-revolutionary forces. Communist parties must carry on unambiguous propaganda to prevent the dispatch of munitions transports to the enemies of the Soviet republics; they must also carry on propaganda by every means, legal or illegal, among the troops sent to strangle workers' republics.

15. Parties which still retain their old social-democratic programmes are obliged to revise them as quickly as possible, and to draw up, in accordance with the special conditions of their country, a new communist programme in conformity with the decisions of the Communist International. As a rule the programme of every party belonging to the Communist International must be ratified by the regular congress of the Communist International or by the Executive Committee. Should the programme of a party not be ratified by the ECCI, the party concerned has the right to appeal to the Congress of the Communist International.

16. All the decisions of the congresses of the Communist International, as well as the decisions of its Executive Committee, are binding on all parties belonging to the Communist International. The Communist International, working in conditions of acute civil war, must be far more centralized in its structure than was the Second International. Consideration must of course be given by the Communist International and its Executive Committee in all their activities to the varying conditions in which the individual parties have to fight and work, and they must take decisions of general validity only when such decisions are possible.

17. In this connexion, all parties which wish to join the Communist International must change their names. Every party which wishes to join the Communist International must be called: *Communist* party of such and such

a country (section of the Communist International). This question of name is not merely a formal matter, but essentially a political question of great importance. The Communist International has declared war on the entire bourgeois world and on all yellow social-democratic parties. The difference between the communist parties and the old official "social-democratic" or "socialist" parties, which have betrayed the banner of the working class, must be brought home to every ordinary worker.

18. All leading party press organs in all countries are obliged to publish all important official documents of the Executive Committee of the Communist International.

19. All parties belonging to the Communist International and those which have applied for admission, are obliged to convene an extraordinary congress as soon as possible, and in any case not later than four months after the second congress of the Communist International, to examine all these conditions of admission. In this connexion all party centres must see that the decisions of the second congress of the Communist International are made known to all local organizations.

20. Those parties which now wish to join the Communist International, but which have not radically changed their former tactics, must see to it that, before entering the Communist International, not less than two-thirds of the members of their central committee and of all their leading central bodies consist of comrades who publicly and unambiguously advocated the entry of their party into the Communist International before its second congress. Exceptions can be made with the consent of the Executive Committee of the Communist International. The ECCI also has the right to make exceptions in the case of representatives of the centre mentioned in paragraph 7.

21. Those members of the party who reject in principle the conditions and theses put forward by the Communist International are to be expelled from the party.

The same applies in particular to delegates to the extraordinary congresses.

Appendix 20 PRELIMINARY DRAFT RESOLUTION OF THE TENTH CONGRESS OF THE R.C.P. ON PARTY UNITY, MARCH, 1921 [1]

1. The Congress calls the attention of all members of the Party to the fact that the unity and cohesion of the ranks of the Party, the guarantee of complete mutual confidence among Party members and genuine team-work that really embodies the unanimity of will of the vanguard of the proletariat, are particularly essential at the present time, when a number of circumstances are increasing the vacillation among the petty-bourgeois population of the country.

2. Notwithstanding this, even before the general Party discussion on the trade unions, certain signs of factionalism had been apparent in the Party—the formation of groups with separate platforms, striving to a certain degree to segregate and create their own group discipline. Such symptoms of factionalism were manifested, for example, at a Party conference in Moscow (November, 1920) and at a Party conference in Kharkov, by the so-called Workers' Opposition group, and partly by the so-called Democratic Centralism group.

All class-conscious workers must clearly realise that factionalism of any kind is harmful and impermissible, for no matter how members of individual groups may desire to safeguard Party unity, factionalism in practice inevitably leads to the weakening of team-work and to intensified and repeated attempts by the enemies of the governing Party, who have wormed their way into it, to widen the cleavage and to use it for counter-revolutionary purposes.

The way the enemies of the proletariat take advantage of every deviation from a thoroughly consistent communist line was perhaps most strikingly shown in the case of the Kronstadt mutiny, when the bourgeois counter-revolutionaries and whiteguards in all countries of the world immediately expressed their readiness to accept the slogans of the Soviet system, if only they might thereby secure the overthrow of the dictatorship of the proletariat in Russia, and when the Socialist-Revolutionaries and the bourgeois counter-revolutionaries in general resorted in Kronstadt to slogans calling for an insurrection against the Soviet Government of Russia ostensibly in the interest of the Soviet power. These facts fully prove that the whiteguards strive, and are able, to disguise themselves as Communists, and even as the most Left-wing Communists, solely for the purpose of weakening and destroying the bulwark of the proletarian revolution in Russia. Menshevik

[1] V. I. Lenin. *Collected Works*, 4th ed. (Moscow: Progress, 1965), XXXII, pp. 241–244.

leaflets distributed in Petrograd on the eve of the Kronstadt mutiny likewise show how the Mensheviks took advantage of the disagreements and certain rudiments of factionalism in the Russian Communist Party actually in order to egg on and support the Kronstadt mutineers, the Socialist-Revolutionaries and the whiteguards, while claiming to be opponents of mutiny and supporters of the Soviet power, only with supposedly slight modifications.

3. In this question, propaganda should consist, on the one hand, in a comprehensive explanation of the harmfulness and danger of factionalism from the standpoint of Party unity and of achieving unanimity of will among the vanguard of the proletariat as the fundamental condition for the success of the dictatorship of the proletariat; and, on the other hand, in an explanation of the peculiar features of the latest tactical devices of the enemies of the Soviet power. These enemies, having realised the hopelessness of counter-revolution under an openly whiteguard flag, are now doing their utmost to utilise the disagreements within the Russian Communist Party and to further the counter-revolution in one way or another by transferring power to a political group which is outwardly closest to recognition of the Soviet power.

Propaganda must also teach the lessons of preceding revolutions, in which the counter-revolution made a point of supporting the opposition to the extreme revolutionary party which stood closest to the latter, in order to undermine and overthrow the revolutionary dictatorship and thus pave the way for the subsequent complete victory of the counter-revolution, of the capitalists and landowners.

4. In the practical struggle against factionalism, every organisation of the Party must take strict measures to prevent all factional actions. Criticism of the Party's shortcomings, which is absolutely necessary, must be conducted in such a way that every practical proposal shall be submitted immediately, without any delay, in the most precise form possible, for consideration and decision to the leading local and central bodies of the Party. Moreover, every critic must see to it that the form of his criticism takes account of the position of the Party, surrounded as it is by a ring of enemies, and that the content of his criticism is such that, by directly participating in Soviet and Party work, he can test the rectification of the errors of the Party or of individual Party members in practice. Analyses of the Party's general line, estimates of its practical experience, check-ups of the fulfilment of its decisions, studies of methods of rectifying errors, etc., must under no circumstances be submitted for preliminary discussion to groups formed on the basis of "platforms," etc., but must in all cases be submitted for discussion directly to all the members of the Party. For this purpose, the Congress orders a more regular publication of *Diskussionny Listok* and special symposiums to promote unceasing efforts to ensure that criticism shall be concentrated on essentials and shall not assume a form capable of assisting the class enemies of the proletariat.

5. Rejecting in principle the deviation towards syndicalism and anarchism, which is examined in a special resolution, and instructing the Central Committee to secure the complete elimination of all factionalism, the Congress at the same time declares that every practical proposal concerning

questions to which the so-called Workers' Opposition group, for example, has devoted special attention, such as purging the Party of non-proletarian and unreliable elements, combating bureaucratic practices, developing democracy and workers' initiative, etc., must be examined with the greatest care and tested in practice. The Party must know that we have not taken all the necessary measures in regard to these questions because of various obstacles, but that, while ruthlessly rejecting impractical and factional pseudo-criticism, the Party will unceasingly continue—trying out new methods—to fight with all the means at its disposal against the evils of bureaucracy, for the extension of democracy and initiative, for detecting, exposing and expelling from the Party elements that have wormed their way into its ranks, etc.

6. The Congress, therefore, hereby declares dissolved and orders the immediate dissolution of all groups without exception formed on the basis of one platform or another (such as the Workers' Opposition group, the Democratic Centralism group, etc.). Non-observance of this decision of the Congress shall entail unconditional and instant expulsion from the Party.

7. In order to ensure strict discipline within the Party and in all Soviet work and to secure the maximum unanimity in eliminating all factionalism, the Congress authorises the Central Committee, in cases of breach of discipline or of a revival or toleration of factionalism, to apply all Party penalties, including expulsion, and in regard to members of the Central Committee, reduction to the status of alternate members and, as an extreme measure, expulsion from the Party. A necessary condition for the application of such an extreme measure to members of the Central Committee, alternate members of the Central Committee and members of the Control Commission is the convocation of a Plenary Meeting of the Central Committee, to which all alternate members of the Central Committee and all members of the Control Commission shall be invited. If such a general assembly of the most responsible leaders of the Party deems it necessary by a two-thirds majority to reduce a member of the Central Committee to the status of alternate member, or to expel him from the Party, this measure shall be put into effect immediately.

Appendix 21 APPEAL OF THE EXECUTIVE
COMMITTEE OF THE COMMUNIST
INTERNATIONAL FOR HELP FOR THE
FAMINE-STRICKEN AREAS OF RUSSIA,
DECEMBER 4, 1921 [1]

PROLETARIANS OF ALL COUNTRIES! TO THE AID OF THE RUSSIAN
PROLETARIAT

Workers! Over the whole world capitalism is moving towards the attack. The more the capitalist world decays, the higher the wave of unemployment and crisis rises, rolling like an avalanche from country to country, the more impudently capital attacks your organizations, the louder it boasts of its strength and its power. But its foremost heralds and trumpeters, ministers and presidents, bankers and kings, are preparing new wars for humanity and are working out new armament programmes, pushing all the countries of the world into a war which will be more destructive, inhuman, and horrible than its predecessor. It will leave nothing standing and will kill and cripple millions of human beings—workers and peasants, the productive population of city and country.

Comrades! All of you, without distinction of party, must realize this. You must all understand that the only guarantee for your victory is your own strength, your own proletarian power. Who at the present time holds in check the insane plans of the capitalists? Who fills them with terror and fear?

Your Soviet Russia! For every capitalist government fears the armed Russian workers. For every capitalist government understands that Soviet Russia is to-day the chief instrument, *the main weapon in the hands of the world proletariat.*

Imagine that Soviet Russia has fallen. Then the wave of bloody reaction would overwhelm the entire world. Capitalism would then stride in a triumphal march over the skulls of the working-class. It would consolidate its position for long, long years.

[1] From *The Communist International, 1919–1943. Documents.* Edited by Jane Degras and published by Oxford University Press under the auspices of the Royal Institute of International Affairs. (London: Oxford University Press, 1956), I, pp. 301–303.

THEREFORE HELP SOVIET RUSSIA!

Help its workers who have borne the brunt of the first combined blows of the capitalist governments.

IN YOUR OWN INTERESTS HASTEN TO
THE ASSISTANCE OF THE FIRST SOVIET STATE

The Russian workers have only now won the possibility of building up their economy. Only now is production beginning to rise, are the chimneys of its factories beginning to smoke.

But the drought is clipping the wings of the Russian proletariat. In the rich Volga region the grain has completely withered. Millions of human beings are dying in horrible agony. Sickness and starvation are mowing down old and young, and little children are dying with a cry for help on their lips. The situation is serious. The misfortune is great.

PROLETARIANS, HURRY TO THE AID OF SOVIET RUSSIA!

A number of workers' organizations have already given their mite for the Russian workers and peasants. The communists have collected 100,000,000 marks. Other workers' organizations have also given much help. This enables us to feed about 50,000 persons.

BUT THAT IS NOT ENOUGH! HASTEN, FRIENDS OF THE WORKING CLASS

Especially you, workers of North and South America, Australia, and South Africa. You have not yet gone through the bloody battle with capital. You have not yet been drawn into the final conflict. But the capitalist monster is already grasping you by the throat. It is already throwing millions of workers into the streets. It is ready to deal you too the final blow.

HURRY TO THE ASSISTANCE OF YOUR CHIEF FORTRESS, SOVIET RUSSIA!

Help it to grow strong and to consolidate. You will be repaid a hundred-fold. Together, in serried battle ranks, enter the struggle against the famine in Russia.

Long live the solidarity of the workers who will not let down their brothers in distress and misery!

Appendix 22　TREATY OF RAPALLO, APRIL 16, 1922 [1]

The German Government, represented by Reichsminister Dr. Walther Rathenau, and the Government of the Russian Socialist Federal Soviet Republic, represented by People's Commissary Tchitcherin, have agreed upon the following provisions:

ARTICLE I

The two governments agree that all questions resulting from the state of war between Germany and Russia shall be settled in the following manner:

A. Both governments mutually renounce repayment for their war expenses and for damages arising out of the war, that is to say, damages caused to them and their nationals in the zone of war operations by military measures, including all requisitions effected in a hostile country. They renounce in the same way repayment for civil damages inflicted on civilians, that is to say, damages caused to the nationals of the two countries by exceptional war legislation or by violent measures taken by any authority of the state of either side.

B. All legal relations concerning questions of public or private law resulting from the state of war, including the question of the treatment of merchant ships which fell into the hands of the one side or the other during the war, shall be settled on the basis of reciprocity.

C. Germany and Russia mutually renounce repayment of expenses incurred for prisoners of war. The German Government also renounces repayment of expenses for soldiers of the Red Army interned in Germany. The Russian Government, for its part, renounces repayment of the sums Germany has derived from the sale of Russian Army material brought into Germany by these interned troops.

ARTICLE II

Germany renounces all claims resulting from the enforcement of the laws and measures of the Soviet Republic as it has affected German nationals or their private rights or the rights of the German State itself, as well as claims resulting from measures taken by the Soviet Republic or its authorities in any other way against subjects of the German State or their

[1] *The American Journal of International Law.* Supplement XX (1926), pp. 116–117.

private rights, provided that the Soviet Republic shall not satisfy similar claims made by any third state.

ARTICLE III

Consular and diplomatic relations between Germany and the Federal Soviet Republic shall be resumed immediately. The admission of consuls to both countries shall be arranged by special agreement.

ARTICLE IV

Both governments agree, further, that the rights of the nationals of either of the two parties on the other's territory as well as the regulation of commercial relations shall be based on the most-favored-nation principle. This principle does not include rights and facilities granted by the Soviet Government to another Soviet State or to any State that formerly formed part of the Russian Empire.

ARTICLE V

The two governments undertake to give each other mutual assistance for the alleviation of their economic difficulties in the most benevolent spirit. In the event of a general settlement of this question on an international basis, they undertake to have a preliminary exchange of views. The German Government declares itself ready to facilitate, as far as possible, the conclusion and the execution of economic contracts between private enterprises in the two countries.

ARTICLE VI

Article I, paragraph B, and Article IV of this agreement will come into force after the ratification of this document. The other articles will come into force immediately.

Done in duplicate at Rapallo, April 16, 1922.

(Signed) Rathenau   (Signed) Tchitcherin

Appendix 23 LENIN'S "TESTAMENT," DECEMBER 24, 1922 [1]

By stability of the Central Committee, of which I spoke above, I mean measures against a split, as far as such measures can at all be taken. For, of course, the whiteguard in *Russkaya Mysl* (it seems to have been S. S. Oldenburg) was right when, first, in the whiteguards' game against Soviet Russia he banked on a split in our Party, and when, secondly, he banked on grave differences in our Party to cause that split.

Our Party relies on two classes and therefore its instability would be possible and its downfall inevitable if there were no agreement between those two classes. In that event this or that measure, and generally all talk about the stability of our C.C., would be futile. No measures of any kind could prevent a split in such a case. But I hope that this is too remote a future and too improbable an event to talk about.

I have in mind stability as a guarantee against a split in the immediate future, and I intend to deal here with a few ideas concerning personal qualities.

I think that from this standpoint the prime factors in the question of stability are such members of the C.C. as Stalin and Trotsky. I think relations between them make up the greater part of the danger of a split, which could be avoided, and this purpose, in my opinion, would be served, among other things, by increasing the number of C.C. members to 50 or 100.

Comrade Stalin, having become Secretary-General, has unlimited authority concentrated in his hands, and I am not sure whether he will always be capable of using that authority with sufficient caution. Comrade Trotsky, on the other hand, as his struggle against the C.C. on the question of the People's Commissariat for Communications has already proved, is distinguished not only by outstanding ability. He is personally perhaps the most capable man in the present C.C., but he has displayed excessive self-assurance and shown excessive preoccupation with the purely administrative side of the work.

These two qualities of the two outstanding leaders of the present C.C. can inadvertently lead to a split, and if our Party does not take steps to avert this, the split may come unexpectedly.

I shall not give any further appraisals of the personal qualities of other members of the C.C. I shall just recall that the October episode with Zinoviev and Kamenev was, of course, no accident, but neither can the blame for it be laid upon them personally, any more than non-Bolshevism can upon Trotsky.

[1] V. I. Lenin. *Collected Works.* (Moscow: Progress, 1966), XXXVI, pp. 594–596.

Speaking of the young C.C. members, I wish to say a few words about Bukharin and Pyatakov. They are, in my opinion, the most outstanding figures (among the youngest ones), and the following must be borne in mind about them: Bukharin is not only a most valuable and major theorist of the Party; he is also rightly considered the favourite of the whole Party, but his theoretical views can be classified as fully Marxist only with great reserve, for there is something scholastic about him (he has never made a study of dialectics, and, I think, never fully understood it).

December 25. As for Pyatakov, he is unquestionably a man of outstanding will and outstanding ability, but shows too much zeal for administrating and the administrative side of the work to be relied upon in a serious political matter.

Both of these remarks, of course, are made only for the present, on the assumption that both these outstanding and devoted Party workers fail to find an occasion to enhance their knowledge and amend their one-sidedness.

Lenin

December 25, 1922
Taken down by M. V.

ADDITION TO THE LETTER OF DECEMBER 24, 1922

Stalin is too rude and this defect, although quite tolerable in our midst and in dealings among us Communists, becomes intolerable in a Secretary-General. That is why I suggest that the comrades think about a way of removing Stalin from that post and appointing another man in his stead who in all other respects differs from Comrade Stalin in having only one advantage, namely, that of being more tolerant, more loyal, more polite and more considerate to the comrades, less capricious, etc. This circumstance may appear to be a negligible detail. But I think that from the standpoint of safeguards against a split and from the standpoint of what I wrote above about the relationship between Stalin and Trotsky it is not a detail, or it is a detail which can assume decisive importance.

Lenin

January 4, 1923
Taken down by L. F.

Appendix 24 CONSTITUTION AND RULES OF THE COMMUNIST INTERNATIONAL [1]

I. NAME AND OBJECTS

1. The Communist International—the International Worker's Association —is a union of Communist Parties in various countries; it is a World Communist Party. As the leader and organizer of the world revolutionary movement of the proletariat and the bearer of the principles and aims of Communism, the Communist International strives to win over the majority of the working class and the broad strata of the property-less peasantry, fights for the establishment of the world dictatorship of the proletariat, for the establishment of a World Union of Socialist Soviet Republics, for the complete abolition of classes and for the achievement of Socialism—the first stage of Communist society.

2. The various Parties affiliated to the Communist International are called the Communist Party of, . . . name of country (Section of the Communist International). In any given country there can be only one Communist Party affiliated to the Communist International and representing its Section in that country.

3. Membership of the Communist Party and of the Communist International is open to all those who accept the programme and rules of the given Communist party and of the Communist International, who join one of the basic units of a Party, actively work in it, abide by all the decisions of the Party and of the Communist International, and regularly pay Party dues.

4. The basic unit of the Communist Party organisation is the nucleus in the place of employment (factory, workshop, mine, office, store, farm, etc.) which unites all the Party members employed in the given enterprise.

5. The Communist International and its Sections are built up on the basis of democratic centralism, the fundamental principles of which are: (a) election of all the leading committees of the Party, subordinate and superior, (by general meetings of Party members, conferences, congresses and international congresses); (b) periodical reports by leading Party committees to their constituents; (c) decisions of superior Party committees to be obligatory for subordinate committees, strict Party discipline and prompt execution of the decisions of the Communist International, of its leading committees and of the leading Party organs.

Party questions may be discussed by the members of the Party and by Party organisations until such time as a decision is taken upon them by the competent Party committees. After a decision has been taken by the Congress of the Communist International, by the Congress of the respective Sections, or by leading committees of the Comintern, and of its various Sections, these deci-

---

[1] *International Press Correspondence*, No. 84 (1928), pp. 1600–1601.

sions must be unreservedly carried out even if a Section of the Party membership or of the local Party organisations are in disagreement with it.

In cases where a Party exists illegally, the superior Party committees may appoint the subordinate committees and coopt members on their own committees, subject to subsequent endorsement by the competent superior Party committees.

6. In all non-Party, workers' and peasants' mass organisations and in their leading committees (trade unions, co-operative societies, sport organisations, ex-service men's organisations, [and at their congresses and conferences] and also on) municipal bodies and in parliament, even if there are only two Party members in such organisations and bodies, Communist fractions must be formed for the purpose of strengthening the Party's influence and for carrying out its policy in these organisations and bodies.

7. The Communist fractions are subordinated to the competent Party bodies.

Note:

1. Communist fractions in international organisations (Red International of Labour Unions, International Class War Prisoners Aid Society, International Workers Relief, etc.) are subordinate to the Executive Committee of the Communist International.

2. The organisational structure of the Communist fractions and the manner in which their work is guided are determined by special instructions from the Executive Committee of the Communist International and from the Central Committees of the given Sections of the Comintern.

II. THE WORLD CONGRESS OF THE COMMUNIST INTERNATIONAL

8. The supreme body of the Communist International is the World Congress of representatives of all Parties (Sections) and organisations affiliated to the Communist International.

The World Congress discusses and decides programme, tactical and organisational questions connected with the activities of the Communist International and of its various sections. Power to alter the programme and rules of the Communist International lies exclusively with the World Congress of the Communist International.

The World Congress shall be convened once every two years. The date of the Congress and the number of representatives from the various Sections to the Congress to be determined by the Executive Committee of the Communist International.

The number of decisive votes to be allocated to each Section at the World Congress shall be determined by a special decision of the Congress itself, in accordance with the membership of the given Party and the political importance of the given country. Delegates to the Congress must have a free mandate; no imperative mandate can be recognised.

9. Special Congresses of the Communist International shall be convened on the demand of Parties which, at the preceding World Congress had an aggregate of not less than one half of the decisive votes.

10. The World Congress elects the Executive Committee of the Communist International (E.C.C.I.) and the International Control Commission (I.C.C.).

11. The headquarters of the Executive Committee is decided on by the World Congress.

III. THE EXECUTIVE COMMITTEE OF THE COMMUNIST INTERNATIONAL AND ITS SUBSIDIARY BODIES

12. The leading body of the Communist International in the period between Congresses is the Executive Committee, which gives instructions to all the Sections of the Communist International and controls their activity.

The E.C.C.I. publishes the Central Organ of the Communist International, in not less than four languages.

13. The decisions of the E.C.C.I. are obligatory for all the Sections of the Communist International and must be promptly carried out. The Sections have the right to appeal against decisions of the E.C.C.I. to the World Congress, but must continue to carry out such decisions pending the decision of the World Congress.

14. The Central Committees of the various Sections of the Communist International are responsible to their respective Party Congress and to the E.C.C.I. The latter has the right to annul or amend decisions of Party Congresses and of Central Committees of Parties and also to make decisions which are obligatory for them. (Cf. Par. 13).

15. The E.C.C.I. has the right to expel from the Communist International, entire Sections, groups and individual members who violate the programme and rules of the Communist International or the decisions of the World Congress and of the E.C.C.I. Persons and bodies expelled have the right of appeal to the World Congress.

16. The programmes of the various Sections of the Communist International must be endorsed by the E.C.C.I. In the event of the E.C.C.I. refusing to endorse a programme, the Section concerned has the right to appeal to the World Congress of the Communist International.

17. The leading organs of the press of the various Sections of the Communist International must publish all the decisions and official documents of the E.C.C.I. These decisions must, as far as possible, be published also in the other organs of the Party press.

18. The E.C.C.I. has the right to accept affiliation to the Communist International of organisations and Parties sympathetic to Communism, such organisations to have an advisory vote.

19. The E.C.C.I. elects a Presidium responsible to the E.C.C.I., which acts as the permanent body carrying out all the business of the E.C.C.I. in the interval between the meetings of the latter.

20. The E.C.C.I. and its Presidium has the right to establish Permanent Bureaus (Western European, South American, Eastern and other Bureaus of

the E.C.C.I.) for the purpose of establishing closer contact with the various Sections of the Communist International and in order to be better able to guide their work.

Note:

The scope of the activities of the permanent bureaus of the E.C.C.I. shall be determined by the E.C.C.I. or by its Presidium. The Sections of the Communist International which come within the scope of activities of the permanent bureaus of the E.C.C.I. must be informed by the powers conferred on these bureaus.

21. The Sections must carry out instructions of the permanent bureaus of the E.C.C.I. Sections may appeal against the instructions of the permanent bureaus to the E.C.C.I. or to its Presidium, but must continue to carry out such instructions pending the decision of E.C.C.I. or of its Presidium.

22. The E.C.C.I. and its Presidium have the right to send their representatives to the various Sections of the Communist International. Such representatives receive their instructions from the E.C.C.I. or from its Presidium, and are responsible to them for their activities. Representatives of the E.C.C.I. have the right to participate in meetings of the central Party bodies as well as of the local organisations of the sections to which they are sent. Representatives of the E.C.C.I. must carry out their commission in close contact with the Central Committee of the Section to which they are sent. They may, however, speak in opposition to the Central Committee of the given Section, at Congresses and Conferences of that Section, if the line of the Central Committee in question diverges from the instructions of the E.C.C.I. Respresentatives of the E.C.C.I. are especially obliged to supervise the carrying out of the decisions of the World Congresses and of the Executive Committee of the Communist International.

The E.C.C.I. and its Presidium also have the right to send instructors to the various Sections of the Communist International. The powers and duties of instructors are determined by the E.C.C.I., to whom the instructors are responsible in their work.

23. Meetings of the E.C.C.I. must take place not less than once every six months. A quorum must consist of not less than one half of the membership of the E.C.C.I.

24. Meetings of the Presidium of the E.C.C.I. must take place not less than once a fortnight. A quorum must consist of not less than one half of the membership of the Presidium.

25. The Presidium elects the Political Secretariat, which is empowered to take decisions, and which also prepares questions for the meetings of the E.C.C.I. and of its Presidium, and acts as their executive body.

26. The Presidium appoints the editorial committees of the periodical and other publications of the Communist International.

27. The Presidium of the E.C.C.I. sets up a Department for Work Among Women Toilers, permanent committees for guiding the work of definite groups of Sections of the Communist International (Lander Secretariats) and other departments necessary for its work.

IV. THE INTERNATIONAL CONTROL COMMISSION

28. The International Control Commission investigates matters concerning the unity of the Sections affiliated to the Communist International and also matters connected with the Communist conduct of individual members of the various Sections.

For this purpose the I.C.C.:

(a) Examines complaints against the actions of Central Committees of Communist Parties lodged by Party members who have been subjected to disciplinary measures for political differences;

(b) Examines such analogous matters concerning members of central bodies of Communist Parties and of individual Party members as it deems necessary, or which are submitted to it by the deciding bodies of the E.C.C.I.;

(c) Audits the accounts of the Communist International.

The International Control Commission must not intervene in the political differences or in organisational and administrative conflicts in the Communist Parties.

The headquarters of the I.C.C. are fixed by the I.C.C., in agreement with the E.C.C.I.

V. THE RELATIONSHIPS BETWEEN THE SECTIONS OF THE COMMUNIST INTERNATIONAL AND THE E.C.C.I.

29. The Central Committees of Sections affiliated to the Communist International and the Central Committees of affiliated sympathising organisations must send to the E.C.C.I. the Minutes of their meetings and reports of their work.

30. Resignation from office by individual members or groups of members of Central Committees of the various Sections are regarded as disruption of the Communist movement. Leading posts in the Party do not belong to the occupant of that post, but to the Communist International as a whole. Elected members of the Central leading bodies of the various Sections may resign before their time of office expires, only with the consent of the E.C.C.I. Resignations accepted by Central Committees of Sections without the consent of the E.C.C.I. are invalid.

31. The Sections affiliated to the Communist International must maintain close organisational and informational contact with each other, arrange for mutual representation at each others conferences and congresses, and, with the consent of the E.C.C.I., exchange leading comrades. This applies particularly to the Sections in imperial countries and their colonies, and to the Sections in countries adjacent to each other.

32. Two or more Sections of the Communist International which, (like the Sections in the Scandinavian countries and in the Balkans) are politically connected with each other by common conditions of struggle, may, with the consent of the E.C.C.I., form federations for the purpose of co-ordinating their

activities, such federations to work under the guidance and control of the E.C.C.I.

33. The Sections of the Comintern must regularly pay affiliation dues to the E.C.C.I.; the amount of such dues to be determined by the E.C.C.I.

34. Congresses of the various Sections, ordinary and special, can be convened only with the consent of the E.C.C.I.

In the event of a Section failing to convene a Party Congress prior to the convening of a World Congress, that Section, before electing delegates to the World Congress, must convene a Party conference, or Plenum of its Central Committee, for the purpose of preparing the questions for the World Congress.

35. The Young Communist International is a Section of the Communist International with full rights and is subordinate to the E.C.C.I.

36. The Communist Parties must be prepared for transition to illegal conditions. The E.C.C.I. must render the Parties concerned assistance in their preparations for transition to illegal conditions.

37. Individual members of Sections of the Communist International may pass from one country to another only with the consent of the Central Committee of the Section of which they are members.

Communists changing their domicile must join the Section in the country of their new domicile. Communists leaving their country without the consent of the Central Committee of their Section, must not be accepted into other Sections of the Communist International.

Appendix 25 STALIN'S "DIZZY WITH SUCCESS" ARTICLE, MARCH 2, 1930 [1]

The Soviet government's successes in the sphere of the collective-farm movement are now being spoken of by everyone. Even our enemies are forced to admit that the successes are substantial. And they really are very great.

It is a fact that by February 20 of this year 50 per cent of the peasant farms throughout the U.S.S.R. had been collectivised. That means that by February 20, 1930, we had *overfulfilled* the five-year plan of collectivisation by more than 100 per cent.

It is a fact that on February 28 of this year the collective farms had *already succeeded* in stocking upwards of 36,000,000 centners, i.e., about 220,000,000 poods, of seed for the spring sowing, which is more than 90 per cent of the plan. It must be admitted that the accumulation of 220,000,000 poods of seed by the collective farms alone—after the successful fulfilment of the grain-procurement plan—is a tremendous achievement.

What does all this show?

That a *radical turn of the countryside towards socialism may be considered as already achieved.*

There is no need to prove that these successes are of supreme importance for the fate of our country, for the whole working class, which is the directing force of our country, and, lastly, for the Party itself. To say nothing of the direct practical results, these successes are of immense value for the internal life of the Party itself, for the education of our Party. They imbue our Party with a spirit of cheerfulness and confidence in its strength. They arm the working class with confidence in the victory of our cause. They bring forward additional millions of reserves for our Party.

Hence the Party's task is: to *consolidate* the successes achieved and to *utilise* them systematically for our further advancement.

But successes have their seamy side, especially when they are attained with comparative "ease"—"unexpectedly," so to speak. Such successes sometimes induce a spirit of vanity and conceit: "We can achieve anything!" "There's nothing we can't do!" People not infrequently become intoxicated by such successes; they become dizzy with success, lose all sense of proportion and the capacity to understand realities; they show a tendency to overrate their own strength and to underrate the strength of the enemy; adventurist attempts are made to solve all questions of socialist construc-

---

[1] J. V. Stalin. *Works.* (Moscow: Foreign Languages Publishing House, 1955), XII, pp. 197–205.

tion "in a trice." In such a case, there is no room for concern to *consolidate* the successes achieved and to *utilise* them systematically for further advancement. Why should we consolidate the successes achieved when, as it is, we can dash to the full victory of socialism "in a trice": "We can achieve anything!" "There's nothing we can't do!"

Hence the Party's task is: to wage a determined struggle against these sentiments, which are dangerous and harmful to our cause, and to drive them out of the Party.

It cannot be said that these dangerous and harmful sentiments are at all widespread in the ranks of our Party. But they do exist in our Party, and there are no grounds for asserting that they will not become stronger. And if they should be allowed free scope, then there can be no doubt that the collective-farm movement will be considerably weakened and the danger of its breaking down may become a reality.

Hence the task of our press is: systematically to denounce these and similar anti-Leninist sentiments.

A few facts.

1. The successes of our collective-farm policy are due, among other things, to the fact that it rests on the *voluntary character* of the collective-farm movement and on *taking into account the diversity of conditions* in the various regions of the U.S.S.R. Collective farms must not be established by force. That would be foolish and reactionary. The collective-farm movement must rest on the active support of the main mass of the peasantry. Examples of the formation of collective farms in the developed areas must not be mechanically transplanted to underdeveloped areas. That would be foolish and reactionary. Such a "policy" would discredit the collectivisation idea at one stroke. In determining the speed and methods of collective-farm development, careful consideration must be given to the diversity of conditions in the various regions of the U.S.S.R.

Our grain-growing areas are ahead of all others in the collective-farm movement. Why is this?

Firstly, because in these areas we have the largest number of already firmly-established state farms and collective farms, thanks to which the peasants have had the opportunity to convince themselves of the power and importance of the new technical equipment, of the power and importance of the new, collective organisation of farming.

Secondly, because these areas have had a two-years' schooling in the fight against the kulaks during the grain-procurement campaigns, and this could not but facilitate the development of the collective-farm movement.

Lastly, because these areas in recent years have been extensively supplied with the best cadres from the industrial centres.

Can it be said that these especially favourable conditions also exist in other areas, the consuming areas, for example, such as our northern regions, or in areas where there are still backward nationalities, such as Turkestan, say?

No, it cannot be said.

Clearly, the principle of taking into account the diversity of conditions in the various regions of the U.S.S.R. is, together with the voluntary principle, one of the most important prerequisites for a sound collective-farm movement.

But what actually happens sometimes? Can it be said that the voluntary principle and the principle of taking local peculiarities into account are not violated in a number of areas? No, that cannot be said, unfortunately. We know, for example, that in a number of the northern areas of the consuming zone, where conditions for the immediate organisation of collective farms are comparatively less favourable than in the grain-growing areas, attempts are not infrequently made to *replace* preparatory work for the organisation of collective farms by bureaucratic decreeing of the collective-farm movement, paper resolutions on the growth of collective farms, organisation of collective farms on paper—collective farms which have as yet no reality, but whose "existence" is proclaimed in a heap of boastful resolutions.

Or take certain areas of Turkestan, where conditions for the immediate organisation of collective farms are even less favourable than in the northern regions of the consuming zone. We know that in a number of areas of Turkestan there have already been attempts to "overtake and outstrip" the advanced areas of the U.S.S.R. by threatening to use armed force, by threatening that peasants who are not yet ready to join the collective farms will be deprived of irrigation water and manufactured goods.

What can there be in common between this Sergeant Prishibeyev "policy" and the Party's policy of relying on the voluntary principle and of taking local peculiarities into account in collective-farm development? Clearly, there is not and cannot be anything in common between them.

Who benefits by these distortions, this bureaucratic decreeing of the collective-farm movement, these unworthy threats against the peasants? Nobody, except our enemies!

What may these distortions lead to? To strengthening our enemies and to discrediting the idea of the collective-farm movement.

Is it not clear that the authors of these distortions, who imagine themselves to be "Lefts," are in reality bringing grist to the mill of Right opportunism?

2. One of the greatest merits of our Party's political strategy is that it is able at any given moment to pick out the *main link* in the movement, by grasping which the Party draws the whole chain towards one common goal in order to achieve the solution of the problem. Can it be said that the Party has already picked out the main link of the collective-farm movement in the system of collective-farm development? Yes, this can and should be said.

What is this chief link?

Is it, perhaps, *association for joint cultivation* of the land? No, it is not that. Associations for joint cultivation of the land, in which the means of production are not yet socialised, are already a past stage of the collective-farm movement.

Is it, perhaps, the *agricultural commune?* No, it is not that. Communes are still of isolated occurrence in the collective-farm movement. The conditions are not yet ripe for agricultural communes—in which not only production, but also distribution is socialised—to be the *predominant* form.

The main link of the collective-farm movement, its *predominant* form at the present moment, the link which has to be grasped now, is the *agricultural artel.*

In the *agricultural artel,* the basic means of production, primarily for grain-farming—labour, use of the land, machines and other implements, draught animals and farm buildings—are socialised. In the artel, the household plots (small vegetable gardens, small orchards), the dwelling houses, a part of the dairy cattle, small livestock, poultry, etc., are *not socialised.*

The artel is the *main link of the collective-farm movement* because it is the form best adapted for solving the grain problem. And the grain problem is the *main link in the whole system of agriculture* because, if it is not solved, it will be impossible to solve either the problem of stock-breeding (small and large), or the problem of the industrial and special crops that provide the principal raw materials for industry. That is why the agricultural artel is the main link in the system of the collective-farm movement at the present moment.

That is the point of departure of the "Model Rules" for collective farms, the final text of which is published today.[1]

And that should be the point of departure of our Party and Soviet workers, one of whose duties it is to make a thorough study of these Rules and to carry them out down to the last detail.

Such is the line of the Party at the present moment.

Can it be said that this line of the Party is being carried out without violation or distortion? No, it cannot, unfortunately. We know that in a number of areas of the U.S.S.R., where the struggle for the existence of the collective farms is still far from over, and where artels are not yet consolidated, attempts are being made to skip the artel framework and to leap straight away into the agricultural commune. The artel is still not consolidated, but they are already "socialising" dwelling houses, small livestock and poultry; moreover, this "socialisation" is degenerating into bureaucratic decreeing on paper, because the conditions which would make such socialisation necessary do not yet exist. One might think that the grain problem has already been solved in the collective farms, that it is already a past stage, that the principal task at the present moment is not solution of the grain problem, but solution of the problem of livestock- and poultry-breeding. Who, we may ask, benefits from this blockheaded "work" of lumping together different forms of the collective-farm movement? Who benefits from this running too far ahead, which is stupid and harmful to our cause? Irritating the collective-farm peasant by "socialising" dwelling houses, all dairy cattle, all small livestock and poultry, when the grain problem is still *unsolved,* when the artel form of collective farming is *not yet consolidated*— is it not obvious that such a "policy" can be to the satisfaction and advantage only of our sworn enemies?

One such overzealous "socialiser" even goes so far as to issue an order to an artel containing the following instructions: "within three days, register all the poultry of every household," establish posts of special "commanders" for registration and supervision; "occupy the key positions in the artel";

[1] *Pravda,* March 2, 1930.

"command the socialist battle without quitting your posts" and—of course—get a tight grip on the whole life of the artel.

What is this—a policy of directing the collective farms, or a policy of *disrupting* and *discrediting* them?

I say nothing of those "revolutionaries"—save the mark!—who *begin* the work of organising artels by removing the bells from the churches. Just imagine, removing the church bells—how r-r-revolutionary!

How could there have arisen in our midst such blockheaded exercises in "socialisation," such ludicrous attempts to overleap oneself, attempts which aim at bypassing classes and the class struggle, and which in fact bring grist to the mill of our class enemies?

They could have arisen only in the atmosphere of our "easy" and "unexpected" successes on the front of collective-farm development.

They could have arisen only as a result of the blockheaded belief of a section of our Party: "We can achieve anything!" "There's nothing we can't do!"

They could have arisen only because some of our comrades have become dizzy with success and for the moment have lost clearness of mind and sobriety of vision.

To correct the line of our work in the sphere of collective-farm development, *we must put an end to these sentiments.*

That is now one of the immediate tasks of the Party.

The art of leadership is a serious matter. One must not lag behind the movement, because to do so is to lose contact with the masses. But neither must one run too far ahead, because to run too far ahead is to lose the masses and to isolate oneself. He who wants to lead a movement and at the same time keep in touch with the vast masses must wage a fight on two fronts—against those who lag behind and against those who run too far ahead.

Our Party is strong and invincible because, when leading a movement, it is able to preserve and multiply its contacts with the vast masses of the workers and peasants.

Appendix 26 CONSTITUTION OF THE UNION OF SOVIET SOCIALIST REPUBLICS [1]

CHAPTER I. THE SOCIAL STRUCTURE

Article 1. The Union of Soviet Socialist Republics is a socialist state of workers and peasants.

Article 2. The political foundation of the USSR is the Soviets of Working People's Deputies, which grew and became strong as a result of the overthrow of the power of the landlords and capitalists and the conquest of the dictatorship of the proletariat.

Article 3. All power in the USSR belongs to the working people of town and country as represented by the Soviets of Working People's Deputies.

Article 4. The economic foundation of the USSR is the socialist system of economy and the socialist ownership of the instruments and means of production, firmly established as a result of the liquidation of the capitalist system of economy, the abolition of private ownership of the instruments and means of production, and the elimination of the exploitation of man by man.

Article 5. Socialist property in the USSR exists either in the form of state property (belonging to the whole people) or in the form of cooperative and collective-farm property (property of collective farms, property of cooperative societies).

Article 6. The land, its mineral wealth, waters, forests, mills, factories, mines, rail, water and air transport, banks, communications, large state-organized agricultural enterprises (state farms, machine and tractor stations and the like), as well as municipal enterprises and the bulk of the dwelling houses in the cities and industrial localities, are state property, that is, belong to the whole people.

Article 7. The common enterprises of collective farms and cooperative organizations, with their livestock and implements, the products of the collective farms and cooperative organizations, as well as their common buildings, constitute the common, socialist property of the collective farms and cooperative organizations.

Every household in a collective farm, in addition to its basic income from the common collective-farm enterprise, has for its personal use a small plot of household land and, as its personal property, a subsidiary husbandry on the plot, a dwelling house, livestock, poultry and minor agricultural implements—in accordance with the rules of the agricultural artel.

Article 8. The land occupied by collective farms is secured to them for their use free of charge and for an unlimited time, that is, in perpetuity.

Article 9. Alongside the socialist system of economy, which is the predominant form of economy in the USSR, the law permits the small private economy of individual peasants and handicraftsmen based on their own labor and precluding the exploitation of the labor of others.

[1] *Konstitutsiia (osnovnyi zakon) soiuza sovetskikh sotsialistchekikh respublik.* (Moscow: Izvestiia Sov. Deputatov Trud. SSSR, 1960.)

Article 10. The personal property right of citizens in their incomes and savings from work, in their dwelling houses and subsidiary husbandries, in articles of domestic economy and use and articles of personal use and convenience, as well as the right of citizens to inherit personal property, is protected by law.

Article 11. The economic life of the USSR is determined and directed by the state national-economic plan, with the aim of increasing the public wealth, of steadily raising the material and cultural standards of the working people, of consolidating the independence of the USSR and strengthening its defensive capacity.

Article 12. Work in the USSR is a duty and a matter of honor for every able-bodied citizen, in accordance with the principle "He who does not work, neither shall he eat."

The principle applied in the USSR is that of socialism: "From each according to his ability, to each according to his work."

CHAPTER II. THE STATE STRUCTURE

Article 13. The Union of Soviet Socialist Republics is a federal state, formed on the basis of a voluntary union of equal Soviet Socialist Republics, namely:

The Russian Soviet Federated Socialist Republic
The Ukrainian Soviet Socialist Republic
The Belorussian Soviet Socialist Republic
The Uzbek Soviet Socialist Republic
The Kazakh Soviet Socialist Republic
The Georgian Soviet Socialist Republic
The Azerbaidzhan Soviet Socialist Republic
The Lithuanian Soviet Socialist Republic
The Moldavian Soviet Socialist Republic
The Latvian Soviet Socialist Republic
The Kirghiz Soviet Socialist Republic
The Tadzhik Soviet Socialist Republic
The Armenian Soviet Socialist Republic
The Turkmen Soviet Socialist Republic
The Estonian Soviet Socialist Republic

Article 14. The jurisdiction of the Union of Soviet Socialist Republics, as represented by its higher organs of state power and organs of state administration, embraces:

a. Representation of the USSR in international relations; conclusion, ratification and denunciation of treaties of the USSR with other states; establishment of general procedure governing the relations of Union Republics with foreign states;

b. Questions of war and peace;

c. Admission of new republics into the USSR;

d. Control over the observance of the Constitution of the USSR, and insuring conformity of the Constitutions of the Union Republics with the Constitution of the USSR;

e. Confirmation of alterations of boundaries between Union Republics;

f. Confirmation of the formation of new Autonomous Republics and Autonomous Regions within Union Republics;

g. Organization of the defense of the USSR, direction of all the Armed Forces of the USSR, determination of directing principles governing the organization of the military formations of the Union Republics;

h. Foreign trade on the basis of state monopoly;

i. Safeguarding the security of the state;

j. Determination of the national-economic plans of the USSR;

k. Approval of the consolidated state budget of the USSR and of the report on its fulfillment; determination of the taxes and revenues which go to the Union, the Republican and the local budgets;

l. Administration of the banks, industrial and agricultural institutions and enterprises and trading enterprises of All-Union jurisdiction; general guidance of industry and construction under Union-Republican jurisdiction;

m. Administration of transport and communications of All-Union importance;

n. Direction of the monetary and credit system;

o. Organization of state insurance;

p. Contracting and granting of loans;

q. Determination of the basic principles of land tenure and of the use of mineral wealth, forests and waters;

r. Determination of the basic principles in the spheres of education and public health;

s. Organization of a uniform system of national-economic statistics;

t. Determination of the principles of labor legislation;

u. Determination of the principles of legislation concerning the judicial system and judicial procedure and of the principles of criminal and civil codes;

v. Legislation concerning Union citizenship; legislation concerning rights of foreigners;

w. Determination of the principles of legislation concerning marriage and the family.

Article 15. The sovereignty of the Union Republics is limited only in the spheres defined in Article 14 of the Constitution of the USSR. Outside of these spheres each Union Republic exercises state authority independently. The USSR protects the sovereign rights of the Union Republics.

Article 16. Each Union Republic has its own Constitution, which takes account of the specific features of the Republic and is drawn up in full conformity with the Constitution of the USSR.

Article 17. The right freely to secede from the USSR is reserved to every Union Republic.

Article 18. The territory of a Union Republic may not be altered without its consent.

Article 18-a. Each Union Republic has the right to enter into direct relations with foreign states and to conclude agreements and exchange diplomatic and consular representatives with them.

Article 18-b. Each Union Republic has its own Republican military formations.

Article 19. The laws of the USSR have the same force within the territory of every Union Republic.

Article 20. In the event of divergence between a law of a Union Republic and a law of the Union, the Union law prevails.

Article 21. Uniform Union citizenship is established for citizens of the USSR.

Article 22. The Russian Soviet Federated Socialist Republic includes the Bashkir, Buriat-Mongol, Daghestan, Kabardin-Balkar, Kalmyk, Karelian, Komi, Mari, Mordovian, North Ossetian, Tartar, Udmurt, Chechen-Ingush, Chuvash and Yakut Autonomous Soviet Socialist Republics; and the Adighe, Gorny Altai, Jewish, Karachaevo-Cherkess, Tuva and Khakass Autonomous Regions.

Article 23. Repealed.

Article 24. The Azerbaidzhan Soviet Socialist Republic includes the Nakhichevan Autonomous Soviet Socialist Republic and the Nagorny Karabakh Autonomous Region.

Article 25. The Georgian Soviet Socialist Republic includes the Abkhaz and Adzhar Autonomous Soviet Socialist Republics and the South Ossetian Autonomous Region.

Article 26. The Uzbek Soviet Socialist Republic includes the Kara-Kalpak Autonomous Soviet Socialist Republic.

Article 27. The Tadzhik Soviet Socialist Republic includes the Gorny Badakhshan Autonomous Region.

Article 28. The solution of problems pertaining to the administrative-territorial structure of the regions and territories of the Union Republics comes within the jurisdiction of the Union Republics.

Article 29. Repealed.

CHAPTER III. THE HIGHER ORGANS OF STATE POWER IN THE UNION OF SOVIET SOCIALIST REPUBLICS

Article 30. The highest organ of state power in the USSR is the Supreme Soviet of the USSR.

Article 31. The Supreme Soviet of the USSR exercises all rights vested in the Union of Soviet Socialist Republics in accordance with Article 14 of the Constitution, insofar as they do not, by virtue of the Constitution, come within the jurisdiction of organs of the USSR that are accountable to the Supreme Soviet of the USSR, that is, the Presidium of the Supreme Soviet of the USSR, the Council of Ministers of the USSR, and the Ministries of the USSR.

Article 32. The legislative power of the USSR is exercised exclusively by the Supreme Soviet of the USSR.

Article 33. The Supreme Soviet of the USSR consists of two Chambers: The Soviet of the Union and the Soviet of Nationalities.

Article 34. The Soviet of the Union is elected by the citizens of the USSR voting by election districts on the basis of one deputy for every 300,000 of the population.

Article 35. The Soviet of Nationalities is elected by the citizens of the USSR voting by Union Republics, Autonomous Republics, Autonomous Regions, and National Areas on the basis of 25 deputies from each Union Republic, 11 deputies from each Autonomous Republic, 5 deputies from each Autonomous Region and one deputy from each National Area.

Article 36. The Supreme Soviet of the USSR is elected for a term of four years.

Article 37. The two Chambers of the Supreme Soviet of the USSR, the Soviet of the Union and the Soviet of Nationalities, have equal rights.

Article 38. The Soviet of the Union and the Soviet of Nationalities have equal powers to initiate legislation.

Article 39. A law is considered adopted if passed by both Chambers of the Supreme Soviet of the USSR by a simple majority vote in each.

Article 40. Laws passed by the Supreme Soviet of the USSR are published in the languages of the Union Republics over the signatures of the Chairman and Secretary of the Presidium of the Supreme Soviet of the USSR.

Article 41. Sessions of the Soviet of the Union and of the Soviet of Nationalities begin and terminate simultaneously.

Article 42. The Soviet of the Union elects a Chairman of the Soviet of the Union and four Deputy Chairmen.

Article 43. The Soviet of Nationalities elects a Chairman of the Soviet of Nationalities and four Deputy Chairmen.

Article 44. The Chairmen of the Soviet of the Union and the Soviet of Nationalities preside at the meetings of the respective Chambers and have charge of the conduct of their business and proceedings.

Article 45. Joint meetings of the two Chambers of the Supreme Soviet of the USSR are presided over alternately by the Chairman of the Soviet of the Union and the Chairman of the Soviet of Nationalities.

Article 46. Sessions of the Supreme Soviet of the USSR are convened by the Presidium of the Supreme Soviet of the USSR twice a year.

Extraordinary sessions are convened by the Presidium of the Supreme Soviet of the USSR at its discretion or on the demand of one of the Union Republics.

Article 47. In the event of disagreement between the Soviet of the Union and the Soviet of Nationalities, the question is referred for settlement to a conciliation commission formed by the Chambers on a parity basis. If the conciliation commission fails to arrive at an agreement or if its decision fails to satisfy one of the Chambers, the question is considered for a second time by the Chambers. Failing agreement between the two Chambers, the Presidium of the Supreme Soviet of the USSR dissolves the Supreme Soviet of the USSR and orders new elections.

Article 48. The Supreme Soviet of the USSR at a joint meeting of the two Chambers elects the Presidium of the Supreme Soviet of the USSR, consisting of the Chairman of the Presidium of the Supreme Soviet of the USSR, fifteen Deputy Chairmen, a Secretary of the Presidium and sixteen members of the Presidium of the Supreme Soviet of the USSR.

The Presidium of the Supreme Soviet of the USSR is accountable to the Supreme Soviet of the USSR for all its activities.

Article 49. The Presidium of the Supreme Soviet of the USSR:

a. Convenes the sessions of the Supreme Soviet of the USSR;

b. Issues decrees;

c. Gives interpretations of the laws of the USSR in operation;

d. Dissolves the Supreme Soviet of the USSR in conformity with Article 47 of the Constitution of the USSR and orders new elections;

e. Conducts nationwide polls (referendums) on its own initiative or on the demand of one of the Union Republics;

f. Annuls decisions and orders of the Council of Ministers of the USSR and of the Councils of Ministers of the Union Republics if they do not conform to law;

g. In the intervals between sessions of the Supreme Soviet of the USSR, releases and appoints Ministers of the USSR on the recommendation of the Chairman of the Council of Ministers of the USSR, subject to subsequent confirmation by the Supreme Soviet of the USSR;

h. Institutes decorations (Orders and Medals) and titles of honor of the USSR;

i. Awards Orders and Medals and confers titles of honor of the USSR;

j. Exercises the right of pardon;

k. Institutes military titles, diplomatic ranks and other special titles;

l. Appoints and removes the high command of the Armed Forces of the USSR;

m. In the intervals between sessions of the Supreme Soviet of the USSR, proclaims a state of war in the event of military attack on the USSR, or when neccessary to fulfill international treaty obligations concerning mutual defense against aggression;

n. Orders general or partial mobilization;

o. Ratifies and denounces international treaties of the USSR;

p. Appoints and recalls plenipotentiary representatives of the USSR to foreign states;

q. Receives the letters of credence and recall of diplomatic representatives accredited to it by foreign states;

r. Proclaims martial law in separate localities or throughout the USSR in the interests of the defense of the USSR or of the maintenance of public order and the security of the state.

Article 50. The Soviet of the Union and the Soviet of the Nationalities elect Credentials Commissions to verify the credentials of the members of the respective Chambers.

On the report of the Credentials Commissions, the Chambers decide whether to recognize the credentials of deputies or to annul their election.

Article 51. The Supreme Soviet of the USSR, when it deems necessary, appoints commissions of investigation and audit on any matter.

It is the duty of all institutions and officials to comply with the demands of such commissions and to submit to them all necessary materials and documents.

Article 52. A member of the Supreme Soviet of the USSR may not be prosecuted or arrested without the consent of the Supreme Soviet of the USSR, or, when the Supreme Soviet of the USSR is not in session, without the consent of the Presidium of the Supreme Soviet of the USSR.

Article 53. On the expiration of the term of office of the Supreme Soviet of the USSR, or on its dissolution prior to the expiration of its term of office, the

Presidium of the Supreme Soviet of the USSR retains its powers until the newly-elected Supreme Soviet of the USSR shall have formed a new Presidium of the Supreme Soviet of the USSR.

Article 54. On the expiration of the term of office of the Supreme Soviet of the USSR, or in the event of its dissolution prior to the expiration of its term of office, the Presidium of the Supreme Soviet of the USSR orders new elections to be held within a period not exceeding two months from the date of expiration of the term of office or dissolution of the Supreme Soviet of the USSR.

Article 55. The newly-elected Supreme Soviet of the USSR is convened by the outgoing Presidium of the Supreme Soviet of the USSR not later than three months after the elections.

Article 56. The Supreme Soviet of the USSR, at a joint meeting of the two Chambers, appoints the Government of the USSR, namely, the Council of Ministers of the USSR.

CHAPTER IV. THE HIGHER ORGANS OF STATE POWER IN THE UNION REPUBLICS

Article 57. The highest organ of state power in a Union republic is the Supreme Soviet of the Union Republic.

Article 58. The Supreme Soviet of a Union Republic is elected by the citizens of the Republic for a term of four years.

The basis of representation is established by the Constitution of the Union Republic.

Article 59. The Supreme Soviet of a Union Republic is the sole legislative organ of the Republic.

Article 60. The Supreme Soviet of a Union Republic:

a. Adopts the Constitution of the Republic and amends it in conformity with Article 16 of the Constitution of the USSR;

b. Confirms the Constitutions of the Autonomous Republics forming part of it and defines the boundaries of their territories;

c. Approves the national-economic plan and the budget of the Republic and forms economic administration areas;

d. Exercises the right of amnesty and pardon of citizens sentenced by the judicial organs of the Union Republic;

e. Decides questions of representation of the Union Republic in its international relations;

f. Determines the manner of organizing the Republic's military formations.

Article 61. The Supreme Soviet of a Union Republic elects the Presidium of the Supreme Soviet of the Union Republic, consisting of a chairman of the Presidium and the Supreme Soviet of the Union Republic, Deputy Chairmen, a Secretary of the Presidium and members of the Presidium of the Supreme Soviet of the Union Republic.

The powers of the Presidium of the Supreme Soviet of a Union Republic are defined by the Constitution of the Union Republic.

Article 62. The Supreme Soviet of a Union Republic elects a Chairman and Deputy Chairman to conduct its meetings.

Article 63. The Supreme Soviet of a Union Republic appoints the Government of the Union Republic, namely, the Council of Ministers of the Union Republic.

CHAPTER V. THE ORGANS OF STATE ADMINISTRATION OF THE UNION OF SOVIET SOCIALIST REPUBLICS

Article 64. The highest executive and administrative organ of the state power of the Union of Soviet Socialist Republics is the Council of Ministers of the USSR.

Article 65. The Council of Ministers of the USSR is responsible and accountable to the Supreme Soviet of the USSR, or, in the intervals between sessions of the Supreme Soviet, to the Presidium of the Supreme Soviet of the USSR.

Article 66. The Council of Ministers of the USSR issues decisions and orders on the basis and in pursuance of the laws in operation, and verifies their execution.

Article 67. Decisions and orders of the Council of Ministers of the USSR are binding throughout the territory of the USSR.

Article 68. The Council of Ministers of the USSR:

a. Coordinates and directs the work of the All-Union and Union-Republican Ministries of the USSR and of other institutions under its jurisdiction, exercises guidance of the Economic Councils of the economic adminstration areas through the Councils of Ministers of the Union Republics;

b. Adopts measures to carry out the national-economic plan and the state budget, and to strengthen the credit and monetary system;

c. Adopts measures for the maintenance of public order, for the protection of the interests of the state, and for the safeguarding of the rights of citizens;

d. Exercises general guidance in the sphere of relations with foreign states;

e. Fixes the annual contingent of citizens to be called up for military service and directs the general organization of the Armed Forces of the country;

f. Sets up, whenever necessary, special committees and central administrations under the Council of Ministers of the USSR for economic and cultural affairs and defense.

Article 69. The Council of Ministers of the USSR has the right, in respect to those branches of administration and economy which come within the jurisdiction of the USSR, to suspend decisions and orders of the Councils of Ministers of the Union Republics and of the Economic Councils of the economic administration areas and to annul orders and instructions of Ministers of the USSR.

Article 70. The Council of Ministers of the USSR is appointed by the Supreme Soviet of the USSR and consists of:

The Chairman of the Council of Ministers of the USSR;

The First Deputy Chairmen of the Council of Ministers of the USSR;

The Deputy Chairmen of the Council of Ministers of the USSR;

The Ministers of the USSR;

The Chairman of the State Committee of the Council of Ministers of the USSR on Planning;

The Chairman of the Commission of the Council of Ministers of the USSR on Soviet Control;

The Chairman of the State Committee of the Council of Ministers of the USSR on Labor and Wages;

The Chairman of the State Committee of the Council of Ministers of the USSR on Science and Technology;

The Chairman of the State Committee of the Council of Ministers of the USSR on Aircraft Technology;

The Chairman of the State Committee of the Council of Ministers of the USSR on Defense Technology;

The Chairman of the State Committee of the Council of Ministers of the USSR on Radioelectronics;

The Chairman of the State Committee of the Council of Ministers of the USSR on Shipbuilding;

The Chairman of the State Committee of the Council of Ministers of the USSR on Construction;

The Chairman of the State Committee of the Council of Ministers on Chemistry;

The Chairman of the State Committee of the Council of Ministers on Grain Products;

The Chairman of the State Committee of the Council of Ministers of the USSR on Foreign Economic Relations;

The Chairman of the Committee on the Security of the State under the Council of Ministers of the USSR;

The Chairman of the Administrative Board of the State Bank of the USSR;

The Chief of the Central Statistical Board under the Council of Ministers of the USSR.

The Council of Ministers of the USSR includes the Chairmen of the Councils of Ministers of the Union Republics by virtue of their office.

Article 71. The Government of the USSR or a Minister of the USSR, to whom a question of a member of the Supreme Soviet of the USSR is addressed, must give a verbal or written reply in the respective Chamber within a period not exceeding three days.

Article 72. The Ministers of the USSR direct the branches of state administration which come within the jurisdiction of the USSR.

Article 73. The Ministers of the USSR, within the limits of the jurisdiction of their respective Ministries, issue orders and instructions on the basis and in pursuance of the laws in operation, and also of decisions and orders of the Council of Ministers of the USSR, and verify their execution.

Article 74. The Ministries of the USSR are either All-Union or Union-Republican Ministries.

Article 75. Each All-Union Ministry directs the branch of state administration entrusted to it throughout the territory of the USSR either directly or through bodies appointed by it.

Article 76. The Union-Republican Ministries, as a rule, direct the branches of state administration entrusted to them through corresponding Ministries of the Union Republics; they administer directly only a definite and limited number of enterprises according to a list confirmed by the Presidium of the Supreme Soviet of the USSR.

Article 77. The following Ministries are All-Union Ministries:

The Ministry of Foreign Trade;
The Ministry of Merchant Marine;
The Ministry of Transportation;
The Ministry of the Medium Machine-Building Industry;
The Ministry of Transport Construction;
The Ministry of the Chemical Industry;
The Ministry of Power Plant Construction.

Article 78. The following Ministries are Union-Republican Ministries:

The Ministry of Internal Affairs;
The Ministry of Higher and Specialized Secondary Education;
The Ministry of Geological Survey and Conservation of Mineral Resources;
The Ministry of Public Health;
The Ministry of Foreign Affairs;
The Ministry of Culture;
The Ministry of Defense;
The Ministry of Communications;
The Ministry of Agriculture;
The Ministry of Finance.

CHAPTER VI. THE ORGANS OF STATE ADMINISTRATION OF THE UNION REPUBLICS

Article 79. The highest executive and administrative organ of the state power of a Union Republic is the Council of Ministers of the Union Republic.

Article 80. The Council of Ministers of a Union Republic is responsible and accountable to the Supreme Soviet of the Union Republic, or, in the intervals between sessions of the Supreme Soviet of the Union Republic, to the Presidium of the Supreme Soviet of the Union Republic.

Article 81. The Council of Ministers of a Union Republic issues decisions and orders on the basis and in pursuance of the laws in operation of the USSR and of the Union Republic, and of the decisions and orders of the Council of Ministers of the USSR, and verifies their execution.

Article 82. The Council of Ministers of a Union Republic has the right to suspend decisions and orders of the Councils of Ministers of its Autonomous Republics, and to annul decisions and orders of the Executive Committees of the Soviets of Working People's Deputies of its Territories, Regions and Autonomous Regions, as well as decisions and orders of the Economic Councils of the economic administration areas.

Article 83. The Council of Ministers of a Union Republic is appointed by the Supreme Soviet of the Union Republic and consists of:

The Chairman of the Council of Ministers of the Union Republic;

The First Deputy Chairmen of the Council of Ministers;

The Deputy Chairmen of the Council of Ministers;

The Ministers;

The Chairman of the State Commission on Planning;

The Chairman of the State Committee of the Council of Ministers of the Union Republic on Construction and Architecture;

The Chairman of the Committee on the Security of the State under the Council of Ministers of the Union Republic.

Article 84. The Ministers of a Union Republic direct the branches of state administration which come within the jurisdiction of the Union Republic.

Article 85. The Ministers of a Union Republic, within the limits of the jurisdiction of their respective Ministries, issue orders and instructions on the basis and in pursuance of the laws of the USSR and of the Union Republic, of the decisions and orders of the Council of Ministers of the USSR and the Council of Ministers of the Union Republic, and of the orders and instructions of the Union-Republican Ministries of the USSR.

Article 86. The Ministries of a Union Republic are either Union-Republican or Republican Ministries.

Article 87. Each Union-Republican Ministry directs the branch of state administration entrusted to it, and is subordinate both to the Council of Ministers of the Union Republic and to the corresponding Union-Republican Ministry of the USSR.

Article 88. Each Republican Ministry directs the branch of state administration entrusted to it and is directly subordinate to the Council of Ministers of the Union Republic.

Article 88-a. The Economic Councils of the economic administration areas direct the branches of economic activity entrusted to them, and are directly subordinate to the Council of Ministers of the Union Republic.

The Economic Councils of the economic administration areas issue within their jurisdiction decisions and orders on the basis and in pursuance of the laws of the USSR and the Union Republic and decisions and orders of the Council of Ministers of the USSR and the Council of Ministers of the Union Republic.

CHAPTER VII. THE HIGHER ORGANS OF STATE POWER IN THE AUTONOMOUS SOVIET SOCIALIST REPUBLICS

Article 89. The highest organ of state power in an Autonomous Republic is the Supreme Soviet of the Autonomous Republic.

Article 90. The Supreme Soviet of an Autonomous Republic is elected by the citizens of the Republic for a term of four years on a basis of representation established by the Constitution of the Autonomous Republic.

Article 91. The Supreme Soviet of an Autonomous Republic is the sole legislative organ of the Autonomous Republic.

Article 92. Each Autonomous Republic has its own Constitution, which takes account of the specific features of the Autonomous Republic and is drawn up in full conformity with the Constitution of the Union Republic.

Article 93. The Supreme Soviet of an Autonomous Republic elects the Presidium of the Supreme Soviet of the Autonomous Republic and appoints the Council of Ministers of the Autonomous Republic, in accordance with its Constitution.

CHAPTER VIII. THE LOCAL ORGANS OF STATE POWER

Article 94. The organs of state power in Territories, Regions, Autonomous Regions, Areas, Districts, cities and rural localities (*stanitsas,* villages, hamlets, *kishlaks, auls*) are the Soviets of Working People's Deputies.

Article 95. The Soviets of Working People's Deputies of Territories, Regions, Autonomous Regions, Areas, Districts, cities, and rural localities (*stanitsas,* villages, hamlets, *kishlaks, auls*) are elected by the working people of the respective Territories, Regions, Autonomous Regions, Areas, Districts, cities, and rural localities for a term of two years.

Article 96. The basis of representation for Soviets of Working People's Deputies is determined by the Constitutions of the Union Republics.

Article 97. The Soviets of Working People's Deputies direct the work of the organs of administration subordinate to them, insure the maintenance of public order, the observance of the laws and the protection of the rights of citizens, direct local economic and cultural affairs, and draw up the local budgets.

Article 98. The Soviets of Working People's Deputies adopt decisions and issue orders within the limits of the powers vested in them by the laws of the USSR and of the Union Republic.

Article 99. The executive and administrative organ of the Soviet of Working People's Deputies of a Territory, Region, Autonomous Region, Area, District, city or rural locality is the Executive Committee elected by it, consisting of a Chairman, Deputy Chairmen, a Secretary and members.

Article 100. The executive and administrative organ of the Soviet of Working People's Deputies in a small locality, in accordance with the Constitution of the Union Republic, is the Chairman, the Deputy Chairman and the Secretary elected by the Soviet of Working People's Deputies.

Article 101. The executive organs of the Soviets of Working People's Deputies are directly accountable both to the Soviets of Working People's Deputies which elected them and to the executive organ of the superior Soviet of Working People's Deputies.

CHAPTER IX. THE COURTS AND THE PROCURATOR'S OFFICE

Article 102. In the USSR justice is administered by the Supreme Court of the USSR, the Supreme Courts of the Union Republics, the Courts of the

Territories, Regions, Autonomous Republics, Autonomous Regions and Areas, the Special Courts of the USSR established by decision of the Supreme Soviet of the USSR, and the People's Courts.

Article 103. In all Courts cases are tried with the participation of people's assessors, except in cases specially provided for by law.

Article 104. The Supreme Court of the USSR is the highest judicial organ. The Supreme Court of the USSR is charged with the supervision of the judicial activities of all the judicial organs of the USSR and of the Union Republics within the limits established by law.

Article 105. The Supreme Court of the USSR is elected by the Supreme Soviet of the USSR for a term of five years.

The Supreme Court of the USSR includes the Chairmen of the Supreme Courts of the Union Republics by virtue of their office.

Article 106. The Supreme Courts of the Union Republics are elected by the Supreme Soviets of the Union Republics for a term of five years.

Article 107. The Supreme Courts of the Autonomous Republics are elected by the Supreme Soviets of the Autonomous Republics for a term of five years.

Article 108. The Courts of Territories, Regions, Autonomous Regions and Areas are elected by the Soviets of Working People's Deputies of the respective Territories, Regions, Autonomous Regions or Areas for a term of five years.

Article 109. People's Courts are elected by the citizens of the districts on the basis of universal, direct and equal suffrage by secret ballot for a term of five years.

Article 110. Judicial proceedings are conducted in the language of the Union Republic, Autonomous Republic or Autonomous Region, persons not knowing this language being guaranteed the opportunity of fully acquainting themselves with the material of the case through an interpreter and likewise the right to use their own language in court.

Article 111. In all Courts of the USSR cases are heard in public, unless otherwise provided for by law, and the accused is guaranteed the right to defense.

Article 112. Judges are independent and subject only to the law.

Article 113. Supreme supervisory power to insure the strict observance of the law by all Ministries and institutions subordinated to them, as well as by officials and citizens of the USSR generally, is vested in the Procurator-General of the USSR.

Article 114. The Procurator-General of the USSR is appointed by the Supreme Soviet of the USSR for a term of seven years.

Article 115. Procurators of Republics, Territories, Regions, Autonomous Republics and Autonomous Regions are appointed by the Procurator-General of the USSR for a term of five years.

Article 116. Area, district and city procurators are appointed by the Procurators of the Union Republics, subject to the approval of the Procurator-General of the USSR, for a term of five years.

Article 117. The organs of the Procurator's Office perform their functions independently of any local organs whatsoever, being subordinate solely to the Procurator-General of the USSR.

CHAPTER X. FUNDAMENTAL RIGHTS AND DUTIES OF CITIZENS

Article 118. Citizens of the USSR have the right to work, that is, the right to guaranteed employment and payment for their work in accordance with its quantity and quality.

The right to work is insured by the socialist organization of the national economy, the steady growth of the productive forces of Soviet society, the elimination of the possibility of economic crises, and the abolition of unemployment.

Article 119. Citizens of the USSR have the right to rest and leisure.

The right to rest and leisure is insured by the establishment of an eight-hour day for industrial, office, and professional workers, and reduction of the working day to seven or six hours for arduous trades and to four hours in shops where conditions of work are particularly arduous; by the institution of annual vacations with full pay for industrial, office, and professional workers, and by the provision of a wide network of sanatoria, holiday homes, and clubs for the accommodation of the working people.

Article 120. Citizens of the USSR have the right to maintenance in old age and also in case of sickness or disability.

This right is insured by the extensive development of social insurance of industrial, office, and professional workers at state expense, free medical service for the working people, and the provision of a wide network of health resorts for the use of the working people.

Article 121. Citizens of the USSR have the right to education.

This right is insured by universal compulsory seven-year education; by extensive development of secondary education; by free education in all schools of higher education for those who excel in their studies; by instruction in schools being conducted in the native language; and by the organization in the factories, state farms, machine and tractor stations, and collective farms of free vocational, technical and agronomic training for the working people.

Article 122. Women in the USSR are accorded equal rights with men in all spheres of economic, government, cultural, political and other public activity.

The possibility of exercising these rights is insured by women being accorded an equal right with men to work, payment for work, rest and leisure, social insurance and education, and by state protection of the interests of mother and child, state aid to mothers of large families and unmarried mothers, maternity leave with full pay, and the provision of a wide network of maternity homes, nurseries and kindergartens.

Article 123. Equality of rights of citizens of the USSR, irrespective of their nationality or race, in all spheres of economic, government, cultural, political and other public activity, is an indefeasible law.

Any direct or indirect restriction of the rights of, or, conversely, the establishment of any direct or indirect privileges for, citizens on account of their race or nationality, as well as any advocacy of racial or national exclusiveness or hatred and contempt, are punishable by law.

Article 124. In order to insure to citizens freedom of conscience, the church in the USSR is separated from the state, and the school from the church. Freedom of religious worship and freedom of antireligious propaganda is recognized for all citizens.

Article 125. In conformity with the interests of the working people, and in order to strengthen the socialist system, the citizens of the USSR are guaranteed by law:

    a. freedom of speech;

    b. freedom of the press;

    c. freedom of assembly, including the holding of mass meetings;

    d. freedom of street processions and demonstrations.

These civil rights are insured by placing at the disposal of the working people and their organizations printing presses, stocks of paper, public buildings, the streets, communications facilities and other material requisites for the exercise of these rights.

Article 126. In conformity with the interests of the working people, and in order to develop the organizational initiative and political activity of the masses of the people, citizens of the USSR are guaranteed the right to unite in public organizations: trade unions, cooperative societies, youth organizations, sport and defense organizations, cultural, technical and scientific societies; and the most active and politically-conscious citizens in the ranks of the working class, working peasants and working intelligentsia voluntarily unite in the Communist Party of the Soviet Union, which is the vanguard of the working people in their struggle to build a communist society and is the leading core of all organizations of the working people, both public and state.

Article 127. Citizens of the USSR are guaranteed inviolability of the person.

No person may be placed under arrest except by decision of a court or with the sanction of a procurator.

Article 128. The inviolability of the homes of citizens and privacy of correspondence are protected by law.

Article 129. The USSR affords the right of asylum to foreign citizens persecuted for defending the interests of the working people, or for scientific activities, or for struggling for national liberation.

Article 130. It is the duty of every citizen of the USSR to abide by the Constitution of the Union of Soviet Socialist Republics, to observe the laws, to maintain labor discipline, honestly to perform public duties, and to respect the rules of socialist intercourse.

Article 131. It is the duty of every citizen of the USSR to safeguard and fortify public, socialist property as the sacred and inviolable foundation of the Soviet system, as the source of the wealth and might of the country, as the source of the prosperity and culture of all the working people.

Persons committing offenses against public, socialist property are enemies of the people.

Article 132. Universal military service is the law.

Military service in the Armed Forces of the USSR is an honorable duty of the citizens of the USSR.

Article 133. To defend the country is the sacred duty of every citizen of the USSR. Treason to the Motherland—violation of the oath of allegiance, desertion to the enemy, impairing the military power of the state, espionage—is punishable with all the severity of the law as the most heinous of crimes.

CHAPTER XI. THE ELECTORAL SYSTEM

Article 134. Members of all Soviets of Working People's Deputies—of the Supreme Soviet of the USSR, the Supreme Soviets of the Union Republics, the Soviets of Working People's Deputies of the Territories and Regions, the Supreme Soviets of the Autonomous Republics, the Soviets of Working People's Deputies of the Autonomous Regions, and the Area, District, city and rural (*stanitsa,* village, hamlet, *kishlak, aul*) Soviets of Working People's Deputies— are chosen by the electors on the basis of universal, equal and direct suffrage by secret ballot.

Article 135. Elections of deputies are universal: all citizens of the USSR who have reached the age of eighteen, irrespective of race or nationality, sex, religion, education, domicile, social origin, property status or past activities, have the right to vote in the election of deputies, with the exception of insane persons and persons who have been convicted by a court of law and whose sentences include deprivation of electoral rights.

Every citizen of the USSR who has reached the age of twenty-three is eligible for election to the Supreme Soviet of the USSR, irrespective of race or nationality, sex, religion, education, domicile, social origin, property status or past activities.

Article 136. Elections of deputies are equal: each citizen has one vote; all citizens participate in elections on an equal footing.

Article 137. Women have the right to elect and be elected on equal terms with men.

Article 138. Citizens serving in the Armed Forces of the USSR have the right to elect and be elected on equal terms with all other citizens.

Article 139. Elections of deputies are direct: all Soviets of Working People's Deputies, from rural and city Soviets of Working People's Deputies to the Supreme Soviet of the USSR, are elected by the citizens by direct vote.

Article 140. Voting at elections of deputies is secret.

Article 141. Candidates are nominated by election districts.

The right to nominate candidates is secured to public organizations and societies of the working people: Communist Party organizations, trade unions, cooperatives, youth organizations and cultural societies.

Article 142. It is the duty of every deputy to report to his electors on his work and on the work of his Soviet of Working People's Deputies, and he may be recalled at any time upon decision of a majority of the electors in the manner established by law.

CHAPTER XII. ARMS, FLAG, CAPITAL

Article 143. The arms of the Union of Soviet Socialist Republics are a sickle and hammer against a globe depicted in the rays of the sun and surrounded by ears of grain, with the inscription "Workers of All Countries,

Unite!" in the languages of the Union Republics. At the top of the arms is a five-pointed star.

Article 144. The state flag of the Union of Soviet Socialist Republics is of red cloth with the sickle and hammer depicted in gold in the upper corner near the staff and above them a five-pointed red star bordered in gold. The ratio of the width to the length is 1:2.

Article 145. The Capital of the Union of Soviet Socialist Republics is the City of Moscow.

CHAPTER XIII. PROCEDURE FOR AMENDING THE CONSTITUTION

Article 146. The Constitution of the USSR may be amended only by decision of the Supreme Soviet of the USSR adopted by a majority of not less than two thirds of the votes in each of its Chambers.

Appendix 27   OFFICIAL VERDICT AGAINST Y. L. PYATAKOV AND ASSOCIATES IN THE PURGE TRIAL, JANUARY 30, 1937 [1]

[The Military Collegium of the Supreme Court of the U.S.S.R.] in an open Court session, in the city of Moscow, on January 23–30, 1937, heard the case against:

1. *Pyatakov*, Yuri (Georgi) Leonidovich, born 1890, employee;
2. *Sokolnikov*, Grigori Yakovlevich, born 1888, employee;
3. *Radek*, Karl Berngardovich, born 1885, journalist;
4. *Serebryakov*, Leonid Petrovich, born 1888, employee;
5. *Livshitz*, Yakov Abramovich, born 1896, employee;
6. *Muralov*, Nikolai Ivanovich, born 1877, employee;
7. *Drobnis*, Yakov Naumovich, born 1891, employee;
8. *Boguslavsky*, Mikhail Solomonovich, born 1886, employee;
9. *Knyazev*, Ivan Alexandrovich, born 1893, employee;
10. *Rataichak*, Stanislav Antonovich, born 1894, employee;
11. *Norkin*, Boris Osipovich, born 1895, employee;
12. *Shestov*, Alexei Alexandrovich, born 1896, employee;
13. *Stroilov*, Mikhail Stepanovich, born 1899, employee;
14. *Turok*, Yosif Dmitrievich, born 1900, employee;
15. *Hrasche*, Ivan Yosifovich, born 1886, employee;
16. *Pushin*, Gavriil Yefremovich, born 1896, employee;
17. *Arnold*, Valentin Volfridovich, alias Vasilyev Valentin Vasilyevich, born 1894, employee;

all being charged with having committed crimes covered by Articles 58[1a], 58[8], 58[9] and 58[11] of the Criminal Code of the R.S.F.S.R.

The preliminary and Court investigations have established that:

In 1933, in accordance with direct instructions given by the enemy of the people, L. Trotsky, who was deported from the U.S.S.R. in 1929, there was formed in Moscow, apart from the so-called "united Trotskyite-Zinovievite terrorist centre," consisting of Zinoviev, Kamenev, Smirnov and others, an underground parallel anti-Soviet, Trotskyite centre, members of which were the accused in the present case, Y. L. Pyatakov, K. B. Radek, G. Y. Sokolnikov and L. P. Serebryakov.

In accordance with instructions received from the enemy of the people, L. Trotsky, the principal aim of the parallel anti-Soviet Trotskyite centre was to overthrow the Soviet power in the U.S.S.R. and to restore capitalism and the power of the bourgeoisie by means of wrecking, diversive, espionage

[1] U.S.S.R. Peoples Commissariat of Justice. *Report of Court Proceedings in the Case of the Anti-Soviet Trotskyite Centre* . . . (Moscow: 1937), pp. 574–580.

and terrorist activities designed to undermine the economic and military power of the Soviet Union, to expedite the armed attack on the U.S.S.R., to assist foreign aggressors and to bring about the defeat of the U.S.S.R.

In full conformity with this principal aim, the enemy of the people L. Trotsky, abroad, and the parallel anti-Soviet Trotskyite centre, represented by Radek and Sokolnikov, in Moscow, entered into negotiations with certain representatives of Germany and Japan. During the course of negotiation with one of the leaders of the National-Socialist Party of Germany, Rudolph Hess, the enemy of the people, L. Trotsky, promised in the event of a Trotskyite government coming to power as a result of the defeat of the Soviet Union, to make a number of political, economic and territorial concessions to Germany and Japan at the expense of the U.S.S.R., including the cession of the Ukraine to Germany and of the Maritime Provinces and the Amur region to Japan. At the same time, the enemy of the people, L. Trotsky, undertook in the event of seizing power to liquidate the state farms, to dissolve the collective farms, to renounce the policy of industrialization of the country and to restore on the territory of the Soviet Union social relations of capitalist society. Furthermore, the enemy of the people L. Trotsky undertook to render all possible help to aggressors by developing defeatist propaganda and wrecking, diversive and espionage activities, both in time of peace and, in particular, in time of an armed attack on the Soviet Union.

In fulfilment of the instructions of the enemy of the people L. Trotsky, several times received by Radek, and also personally by Pyatakov during a meeting with the enemy of the people L. Trotsky, in December 1935 in the neighbourhood of the city of Oslo, members of the anti-Soviet Trotskyite parallel centre, Pyatakov, Radek, Sokolnikov and Serebryakov developed wrecking, diversive, espionage and terrorist activities.

Local Trotskyite centres were set up in certain large cities in the Soviet Union to exercise direct guidance of anti-Soviet activities in the provinces. In particular, a West-Siberian anti-Soviet Trotskyite centre consisting of N. I. Muralov, M. S. Boguslavsky and Y. N. Drobnis, accused in the present case, was set up in Novosibirsk on the direct instructions of Pyatakov.

Diversive and wrecking work in industry, chiefly in enterprises of importance for defence purposes, and also on the railways, was performed by the accused in the present case at the behest of the enemy of the people Trotsky, and on the instructions and with the direct participation of agents of the German and Japanese intelligence services, and consisted in disrupting plans of production, lowering the quality of product, organizing fires and explosions at factories or factory departments and mines, organizing train wrecks and damaging rolling stock and railway track.

In organizing diversive activities, the accused were guided by the instructions of the enemy of the people Trotsky "to strike palpable blows at the most sensitive places," supplemented by directions from Pyatakov, Livshitz and Drobnis not to shrink before loss of human life, because, "the more victims, the better, since this will rouse the anger of the workers."

In the chemical industry, the accused Rataichak and Pushin, on the instructions of Pyatakov, performed wrecking work with the object of disrupting the State production plan, delaying the construction of new factories and enterprises and spoiling the quality of the construction work on new enterprises.

In addition, in 1934–1935, the accused Rataichak and Pushin organized three diversive acts at the Gorlovka Nitrogen Fertilizer Works, and two of them were accompanied by explosions which caused the death of workers and heavy material loss.

Diversive acts were also organized at the instigation of the accused Rataichak at the Voskressensk Combined Chemical Works and the Nevsky Plant.

In the coal and chemical industries of the Kuznetsk Basin, the accused Drobnis, Norkin, Shestov and Stroilov, on the instructions of Pyatakov and Muralov, carried on wrecking and diversive works with the object of disrupting the output of coal, delaying the building and development of new mines and chemical works, to create conditions of work harmful and dangerous to the workers by allowing gas to accumulate in the galleries and pits, while on September 23, 1936, on the instructions of Drobnis, members of the local Trotskyite organization caused an explosion at the Tsentralnaya Pit in the Kemerovo mine, as a result of which ten workers lost their lives and 14 workers received grave injuries.

On the railways, the diversive and wrecking activities carried on by the accused Serebryakov, Boguslavsky, Livshitz, Knyazev and Turok in accordance with the stand of the anti-Soviet Trotskyite centre, aimed to disrupt the State plan of freight loading, especially for the most important freight (coal, ore, grain), to damage the rolling stock (cars and locomotives) and the railway track, and to organize the wrecking of trains, especially of troop trains.

At the instructions of Livshitz, and being commissioned therefore by an agent of the Japanese intelligence service, Mr. H———, the accused Knyazev in 1935–1936 organized and brought about the wrecking of a number of freight trains, passenger trains and troop trains involving loss of life; as a result of the wreck of a troop train at the Shumikha Station on October 27, 1935, 29 Red Army men were killed and 29 Red Army men injured.

On the direct instructions of the enemy of the people Trotsky, Pyatakov and Serebryakov, members of the anti-Soviet Trotskyite centre, made preparations, in the event of an armed attack on the U.S.S.R., to carry out a number of diversive acts in industries of importance for defense purposes and also on important railway trunk lines.

On the instructions of Pyatakov, the accused Norkin made preparations to set fire to the Kemerovo Chemical Works upon the outbreak of war.

On the instructions of Livshitz, the accused Knyazev proceeded to carry out the commission given him by Mr. H———, an agent of the Japanese intelligence service, to organize during war time the blowing up of railway structures, the burning of military stores and army provision bases, the wreck of troop trains, and also the deliberate infection of trains designed for the transportation of troops, provision supply depots and sanitary centres of the Workers' and Peasants' Red Army with highly virulent bacilli.

In addition to diversive and wrecking activities, the accused Livshitz, Knyazev, Turok, Stroilov, Shestov, Rataichak, Pushin and Hrasche, at the orders of the Trotskyite anti-Soviet centre, engaged in securing and handing over secret information of utmost State importance to agents of the German and Japanese intelligence services.

The accused Rataichak, Pushin and Hrasche were connected with agents of the German intelligence service, Meyerowitz and Lenz, to whom, in 1935–1936, they handed over strictly secret material relating to the condition and operation of chemical plants; Pushin in 1935 handed over to Lenz, agent of the German intelligence service, secret information on the output of products by all the chemical plants of the Soviet Union in 1934, the program of work of all the chemical plants in 1935 and the plan for the construction of nitrogen works, while the accused Rataichak handed over to the same Lenz absolutely secret material on the output in 1934 and the program of the work of chemical enterprises supplying the army for 1935.

The accused Shestov and Stroilov were connected with agents of the German intelligence service Schebesto, Flessa, Floren, Sommeregger and others, and handed over to them secret information about the coal and chemical industries of the Kuznetsk Basin.

The accused Livshitz, Knyazev and Turok regularly transmitted to Mr. H———, agent of the Japanese intelligence service, strictly secret information regarding the technical condition and mobilization capacity of the railways of the U.S.S.R., and also regarding transportation of troops.

At the direct behest of the enemy of the people L. Trotsky, the anti-Soviet Trotskyite centre formed several terrorist groups in Moscow, Leningrad, Kiev, Rostov, Novosibirsk, Sochi and other cities of the U.S.S.R., which engaged in making preparations for terrorist acts against the leaders of the Communist Party of the Soviet Union and the Soviet government, Comrades Stalin, Molotov, Kaganovich, Voroshilov, Orjonikidze, Yezhov, Zhdanov, Kossior, Eiche, Postyshev and Beria; certain terrorist groups (in Moscow, Novosibirsk, in the Ukraine and in Transcaucasia) were under the personal direction of the accused Pyatakov and Serebryakov, members of the anti-Soviet Trotskyite centre.

In organizing terrorist acts, the anti-Soviet Trotskyite centre endeavoured to take advantage of visits paid to the provinces by leaders of the Communist Party of the Soviet Union and the Soviet government.

Thus in the autumn of 1934, Shestov, at the behest of Muralov, endeavoured to carry out a terrorist act against V. M. Molotov, Chairman of the Council of People's Commissars of the U.S.S.R., during his visit to the Kuznetsk Basin, for which purpose a member of the local Trotskyite terrorist group, the accused Arnold, attempted to cause an accident to the automobile in which Comrade V. M. Molotov rode.

Furthermore, on the instructions of Pyatakov and Muralov, the accused Shestov made preparations for a terrorist act against R. I. Eiche, Secretary af the West-Siberian Territory Committee of the C.P.S.U., while the accused Arnold at the instigation of Shestov made preparations for a terrorist act against G. K. Orjonikidze.

Thus the Military Collegium of the Supreme Court of the U.S.S.R. has established that:

I. Pyatakov, Serebryakov, Radek and Sokolnikov were members of the anti-Soviet Trotskyite centre and, at the direct behest of the enemy of the people L. Trotsky, now abroad, with the object of expediting an armed attack on the Soviet Union, assisting foreign aggressors in seizing territory of the Soviet Union, overthrowing the Soviet power and restoring capitalism and the power of the bourgeoisie, directed the treacherous, diversive, wrecking, espionage and terrorist activities of the anti-Soviet Trotskyite organization in the Soviet Union—*i.e.*, have committed crimes covered by Articles 58^{1a}, 58^8, 58^9 and 58^{11} of the Criminal Code of the R.S.F.S.R.

II. Pyatakov and Serebryakov, mentioned in clause I, as well as Muralov, Drobnis, Livshitz and Boguslavsky, members of an anti-Soviet Trotskyite organization, organized and personally directed the treasonable, espionage, diversive and terrorist activities of the members of the anti-Soviet Trotskyite organization—*i.e.*, have committed crimes covered by Articles 58^{1a}, 58^8, 58^9 and 58^{11} of the Criminal Code of the R.S.F.S.R.

III. Knyazev, Rataichak, Norkin, Shestov, Turok, Pushin and Hrasche, while members of an anti-Soviet Trotskyite organization, carried out the instructions of the anti-Soviet Trotskyite centre concerning treasonable, espionage, undermining, wrecking and terrorist activities—*i.e.*, have committed crimes covered by Articles 58^{1a}, 58^8, 58^9 and 58^{11} of the Criminal Code of the R.S.F.S.R.

IV. Arnold, while a member of an anti-Soviet Trotskyite organization, at the instigation of the accused Muralov and Shestov, attempted to carry out terrorist acts against Comrades Molotov and Orjonikidze—*i.e.*, has committed crimes covered by Articles 19, 58^8 and 58^{11} of the Criminal Code of the R.S.F.S.R.

V. Stroilov partially carried out certain individual commissions for espionage and wrecking work—*i.e.*, has committed crimes covered by Articles 58^6 and 58^7 of the Criminal Code of the R.S.F.S.R.

On the basis of the above, and guided by Articles 319 and 320 of the Code of Criminal Procedure of the R.S.F.S.R., *The Military Collegium of the Supreme Court of the U.S.S.R.*

SENTENCES:

1. *Pyatakov,* Yuri (Georgi) Leonidovich, and
2. *Serebryakov,* Leonid Petrovich,

as members of the anti-Soviet Trotskyite centre who organized and directly guided treasonable, espionage, undermining, wrecking and terrorist activities, to the supreme penalty—to be shot.

3. *Muralov,* Nikolai Ivanovich,
4. *Drobnis,* Yakov Naumovich,
5. *Livshitz,* Yakov Abramovich,
6. *Boguslavsky,* Mikhail Solomonovich,
7. *Knyazev,* Ivan Alexandrovich,
8. *Rataichak,* Stanislav Antonovich,
9. *Norkin,* Boris Osipovich,
10. *Shestov,* Alexei Alexandrovich,

11. *Turok,* Yosif Dmitrievich,
12. *Pushin,* Gavriil Yefremovich, and
13. *Hrasche,* Ivan Yosifovich,

as organizers and direct executors of the above-mentioned crimes, to the supreme penalty—to be shot.

14. *Sokolnikov,* Grigori Yakovlevich, and
15. *Radek,* Karl Berngardovich,

as members of the anti-Soviet Trotskyite centre, responsible for its criminal activities, but not directly participating in the organization and execution of acts of a diversive, wrecking, espionage and terrorist nature each to imprisonment for a term of ten years.

16. *Arnold,* Valentin Volfridovich, alias Vasilyev, Valentin Vasilyevich, to imprisonment for a term of ten years.

17. *Stroilov,* Mikhail Stepanovich,

in view of the facts mentioned in point V of the defining section of the present verdict—to imprisonment for a term of eight years.

Sokolnikov, Radek, Arnold and *Stroilov,* who are condemned to imprisonment, shall be deprived of political rights for a period of five years each.

The personal property of all the condemned shall be confiscated.

Enemies of the people, Lev Davidovich Trotsky, and his son, Lev Lvovich Sedov, who were in 1929 deported from the U.S.S.R. and by the decision of the Central Executive Committee of the U.S.S.R. of February 20, 1932, were deprived of citizenship of the U.S.S.R., having been convicted by the testimony of the accused Y. L. Pyatakov, K. B. Radek, A. A. Shestov and N. I. Muralov, and by the evidence of V. G. Romm and D. P. Bukhartsev, who were examined as witnesses at the trial, as well as by the materials in the present case, of personally directing the treacherous activities of the Trotskyite anti-Soviet centre, in the event of their being discovered on the territory of the U.S.S.R., are liable to immediate arrest and trial by the Military Collegium of the Supreme Court of the U.S.S.R.

Appendix 28 TREATY OF NON-AGGRESSION BETWEEN GERMANY AND THE UNION OF SOVIET SOCIALIST REPUBLICS, AUGUST 23, 1939 [1]

The Government of the German Reich and the Government of the Union of Soviet Socialist Republics, desirous of strengthening the cause of peace between Germany and the U.S.S.R., and proceeding from the fundamental provisions of the Treaty of Neutrality, which was concluded between Germany and the U.S.S.R. in April 1926, have reached the following agreement:

ARTICLE I

The two Contracting Parties undertake to refrain from any act of violence, any aggressive action and any attack on each other either severally or jointly with other Powers.

ARTICLE II

Should one of the Contracting Parties become the object of belligerent action by a third Power, the other Contracting Party shall in no manner lend its support to this third Power.

ARTICLE III

The Governments of the two Contracting Parties will in future maintain continual contact with one another for the purpose of consultation in order to exchange information on problems affecting their common interests.

ARTICLE IV

Neither of the two Contracting Parties will join any grouping of Powers whatsoever which is aimed directly or indirectly at the other Party.

ARTICLE V

Should disputes or conflicts arise between the Contracting Parties over questions of one kind or another, both parties will settle these disputes or

[1] U.S. Department of State. *Documents on German Foreign Policy, 1918–1945.* Series D (1937–1945). (Washington: Government Printing Office, 1956), VII, 245–7.

conflicts exclusively by means of a friendly exchange of views or if necessary by the appointment of arbitration commissions.

ARTICLE VI

The present Treaty shall be concluded for a period of ten years with the proviso that, in so far as one of the Contracting Parties does not denounce it one year before the expiry of this period, the validity of this Treaty shall be deemed to be automatically prolonged for another five years.

ARTICLE VII

The present Treaty shall be ratified within the shortest possible time. The instruments of ratification will be exchanged in Berlin. The Treaty shall enter into force immediately upon signature.

Done in duplicate in the German and Russian languages.

Moscow, August 23, 1939.

For the Government
of the German Reich:
v. Ribbentrop

With full power of the
Government of the U.S.S.R.:
V. Molotov

Secret Additional Protocol

On the occasion of the signature of the Non-Aggression Treaty between the German Reich and the Union of Soviet Socialist Republics, the undersigned plenipotentiaries of the two Parties discussed in strictly confidential conversations the question of the delimitation of their respective spheres of interest in Eastern Europe. These conversations led to the following result:

1. In the event of a territorial and political transformation in the territories belonging to the Baltic States (Finland, Estonia, Latvia, Lithuania), the northern frontier of Lithuania shall represent the frontier of the spheres of interest both of Germany and the U.S.S.R. In this connection the interest of Lithuania in the Vilna territory is recognized by both Parties.

2. In the event of a territorial and political transformation of the territories belonging to the Polish State, the spheres of interest of both Germany and the U.S.S.R. shall be bounded approximately by the line of the rivers Narev, Vistula, and San.

The question whether the interests of both Parties make the maintenance of an independent Polish State appear desirable and how the frontiers of this State should be drawn can be definitely determined only in the course of further political developments.

In any case both Governments will resolve this question by means of a friendly understanding.

3. With regard to South-Eastern Europe, the Soviet side emphasizes its interest in Bessarabia. The German side declares complete political *désintéressement* in these territories.

4. This Protocol will be treated by both parties as strictly secret.

Moscow, August 23, 1939.

For the Government of
the German Reich:
v. Ribbentrop

With full power of the
Government of the U.S.S.R.:
V. Molotov

Appendix 29 YALTA CONFERENCE, 1945: ENTRY OF SOVIETS INTO WAR AGAINST JAPAN [1]

The leaders of the three Great Powers—the Soviet Union, the United States of America and Great Britain—have agreed that in two or three months after Germany has surrendered and the war in Europe has terminated the Soviet Union shall enter into the war against Japan on the side of the Allies on condition that:

1. The status quo in Outer-Mongolia (The Mongolian People's Republic) shall be preserved;

2. The former rights of Russia violated by the treacherous attack of Japan in 1904 shall be restored, viz.:

(a) the southern part of Sakhalin as well as all the islands adjacent to it shall be returned to the Soviet Union,

(b) the commercial port of Dairen shall be internationalized, the pre-eminent interests of the Soviet Union in this port being safe-guarded and the lease of Port Arthur as a naval base of the U.S.S.R. restored,

(c) the Chinese-Eastern Railroad and the South-Manchurian Railroad which provides an outlet to Dairen shall be jointly operated by the establishment of a joint Soviet-Chinese Company, it being understood that the preeminent interests of the Soviet Union shall be safeguarded and that China shall retain full sovereignty in Manchuria;

3. The Kuril islands shall be handed over to the Soviet Union.

It is understood, that the agreement concerning Outer-Mongolia and the ports and railroads referred to above will require concurrence of Generalissimo Chiang Kai-Shek. The President will take measures in order to obtain this concurrence on advice from Marshal Stalin.

The Heads of the three Great Powers have agreed that these claims of the Soviet Union shall be unquestionably fulfilled after Japan has been defeated.

For its part the Soviet Union expresses its readiness to conclude with the National Government of China a pact of friendship and alliance between the U.S.S.R. and China in order to render assistance to China with its armed forces for the purpose of liberating China from the Japanese yoke.

J. Stalin
Franklin D. Roosevelt
Winston S. Churchill

February 11, 1945

[1] U.S. Department of State. *Treaties and Other International Agreements of the United States of America 1776–1949*. Compiled under the direction of Charles I. Bevans. (Washington, D.C.: Government Printing Office, 1969), pp. 1022–1023.

Appendix 30 STALIN'S "ELECTION" SPEECH, FEBRUARY 9, 1946[1]

COMRADES!

Eight years have elapsed since the last election to the Supreme Soviet. This was a period abounding in events of decisive moment. The first four years passed in intensive effort on the part of Soviet people to fulfill the Third Five-Year Plan. The second four years embrace the events of the war against the German and Japanese aggressors, the events of the Second World War. There is no doubt that the war was the principal event in the past period.

It would be wrong to think that the Second World War was a casual occurrence or the result of mistakes of any particular statesmen, though mistakes undoubtedly were made. Actually, the war was the inevitable result of the devlopment of world economic and political forces on the basis of modern monopoly capitalism. Marxists have declared more than once that the capitalist system of world economy harbours elements of general crises and armed conflicts and that, hence, the development of world capitalism in our time proceeds not in the form of smooth and balanced progress but through crises and military catastrophes.

The fact is, that the unevenness of development of the capitalist countries usually leads in time to violent disturbance of equilibrium in the world system of capitalism. Moreover that group of capitalist countries which considers itself less adequately provided than others with raw materials and markets usually makes attempts to alter the situation and repartition the "spheres of influences" in its favor by armed force. The result is a splitting of the capitalist world into two hostile camps and war between them.

Perhaps military catastrophes could be avoided if it were possible for raw materials and markets to be periodically redistributed among the various countries in accordance with their economic importance, by agreement and peaceable settlement. But that is impossible to do under present capitalist conditions of the development of world economy.

Thus the First World War was the result of the first crisis of the capitalist system of world economy, and the Second World War was the result of the second crisis.

That does not mean of course that the Second World War is a copy of the First. On the contrary, the Second World War differs essentially from the First in its nature. It must be borne in mind that before attacking the Allied countries the principal fascist states—Germany, Japan and Italy—destroyed the last vestiges of bourgeois democratic liberties at home, established a brutal terrorist regime in their own countries, rode roughshod over the

[1] *Bolshevik*, No. 3 (March, 1946), pp. 1–11. Translation by Basil Dmytryshyn.

450

principles of sovereignty and free development of small countries, proclaimed a policy of seizure of foreign territories as their own policy and declared for all to hear that they were striving for world domination and the establishment of a fascist regime throughout the world.

Moreover, by the seizure of Czechoslovakia and of the central regions of China, the Axis states showed that they were prepared to carry out their threat of enslaving all freedom-loving nations. In view of this, unlike the First World War, the Second World War against the Axis states from the very outset assumed the character of an anti-fascist war, a war of liberation, one the aim of which was also the restoration of democratic liberties. The entry of the Soviet Union into the war against the Axis states could only enhance, and indeed did enhance, the anti-fascist and liberation character of the Second World War.

Thus was organized the anti-fascist coalition consisting of the Soviet Union, the United States of America, Great Britain, and other freedom loving states which played the decisive role in destroying the armed forces of the Axis powers.

That is how matters stand as regards the origin and character of the Second World War.

By now I should think everyone admits that the war really was not and could not have been an accident in the life of nations, that actually this war became the war of nations for their existence, and that for this reason it could not be a quick lightning affair.

As regards our country, for it this war was the most bitter and arduous of all wars in the history of our Motherland.

But the war was not only a curse. It was at the same time a great school that tried and tested all the forces of the people. The war laid bare all facts and events in the rear and at the front; it pitilessly tore off all veils and coverings which had concealed the true faces of the states, governments, and parties and exposed them to view without a mask or embellishment, with all their shortcomings and merits.

The war was something like an examination for our Soviet system, for our state, for our government, for our Communist Party. It summed up the results of their work, saying to us as it were: "Here they are, your people and organizations, their deeds and their days. Look at them well and reward them according to their deeds."

This was one of the positive aspects of the war.

For us, for the voters, this circumstance is of great importance, for it helps us to make a speedy and objective appraisal of the work of the Party and its members and to draw correct conclusions. At another time we would need to study the speeches and reports of representatives of the Party, analyze them, compare their words with their deeds, sum up, and so forth. This involves complex and difficult work and there is no guarantee that mistakes will not be made. It is a different matter now when the war is over and when the war itself has tested the work of our organizations and leaders and summarized its results. Today, it is much easier for us to see how things stand and to arrive at correct conclusions.

And so, what are the results of the war?

There is one basic result in which all other results have their source. This result is that in the upshot of the war our enemies were defeated and we, together with our Allies, emerged the victors. We concluded the war with complete victory over the enemies. That is the basic result of war. But that result is too general and we cannot stop at that. Of course, to crush an enemy in a war like the Second World War, for which the history of mankind knew no parallel, meant to achieve a world historic victory. All that is true. But still, it is only a general result and we cannot rest content with that. In order to grasp the great historic importance of our victory we must examine the thing more concretely.

And so, how is our victory over our enemies to be understood? What is the significance of this victory as regards the development of the internal forces of our country?

Our victory means, first of all, that our Soviet *social* system has triumphed, that the Soviet social system has successfully passed the ordeal in the fire of war and has proved its unquestionable vitality.

As you know, it was claimed more than once in the foreign press that the Soviet social system was a "risky experiment" doomed to failure, that the Soviet system was a "house of cards" which has no roots in real life and had been imposed upon the people by the Cheka, and that a slight push from without was enough for the "house of cards" to collapse.

Now we can say that the war refuted all these assertions of the foreign press as groundless. The war showed that the Soviet social system is a truly popular system springing from the depths of the people and enjoying their mighty support, that the Soviet social system is a form of organization of society which is perfectly stable and capable of enduring.

More than that. There is no longer any question today whether the Soviet social system is or is not capable of enduring, for after the object lessons of war none of the skeptics ventures any longer to voice doubts as to the vitality of the Soviet social system. The point now is that the Soviet social system has shown itself more stable and capable of enduring than a non-Soviet social system, that the Soviet social system is a form of organization, a society superior to any non-Soviet social system.

Second, our victory means that our Soviet *state* system has triumphed, that our multinational Soviet state has stood all the trials of war and has proved its vitality.

As you know, prominent foreign press men have more than once gone on record to the effect that the Soviet multinational state was an "artificial, non-viable structure," that in event of any complications, the disintegration of the Soviet Union would be inevitable, and that the fate of Austria-Hungary awaited the Soviet Union.

Today we can say that the war refuted these assertions of the foreign press as totally unfounded. The war showed that the Soviet multinational state system passed the test successfully, that it grew even stronger during the war and proved itself as the state system perfectly capable of enduring. These gentlemen did not understand that the parallel with Austria-Hungary did not apply, for our multinational state has not grown up on a bourgeois foundation which stimulates sentiments of national distrust and national animosity, but on the Soviet foundation which on the contrary cultivates the sentiments of friendship and fraternal collaboration among the peoples of our state.

As a matter of fact, after the lessons of the war, these gentlemen no longer venture to deny that the Soviet state system is capable of enduring. Today it is no longer a question of the vitality of the Soviet state system, for that vitality can no longer be doubted. The point now is that the Soviet state system has proved itself a model for a multinational state, has proved that the Soviet state system is a system of state organization in which the national question and the problem of collaboration among nations has been settled better than in any other multinational state.

Third, our victory means that the Soviet armed forces have triumphed, that our Red Army has triumphed, that the Red Army bore up heroically under all the trials of war, utterly routed the armies of our enemies and came out of the war as a victor. [Voice from floor: "Under the leadership of Comrade Stalin!" All rise—stormy, prolonged applause, rising to an ovation.]

Now everyone, friend as well as foe, admits that the Red Army proved equal to its great tasks. But this was not the case some six years ago during the prewar period. As you know, prominent men from the foreign press and many recognized military authorities abroad declared more than once that the condition of the Red Army gave rise to grave doubts, that the Red Army was poorly armed and had no proper commanding personnel, that its morale was beneath all criticism, that while it might be of some use in defense, it was useless for an offensive, and that if the German forces should strike the Red Army was bound to crumble like a "colossus with feet of clay." Statements like these were made not only in Germany, but in France, Great Britain and in America as well.

Today we can say that the war has refuted all such statements as unfounded and absurd. The war showed that the Red Army is not a "colossus with feet of clay," but a first-class contemporary army with fully modern armaments, highly experienced commanding personnel and high morale and fighting qualities. It must not be forgotten that the Red Army is the army that utterly routed the German army which but yesterday was striking terror into the armies of the European states.

It should be noted that the "critics" of the Red Army are growing fewer and fewer. What is more, the foreign press now more and more frequently contains items which note the fine qualities of the Red Army, the skill of its fighting men and commanders and the flawlessness of its strategy and tactics. That is but natural. After the brilliant Red Army victories at Moscow and Stalingrad, at Kursk and at Belgorod, at Kiev and Kirovograd, at Minsk and Bobruisk, at Leningrad and Tallinn, at Jassy and Lvov, on the Vistula and the Niemen, on the Danube and the Oder, at Vienna and Berlin, it cannot be but admitted that the Red Army is a first-class army from which much could be learned. [Stormy applause.]

Such is our concrete understanding of our country's victory over its enemies.

Such in the main are the results of the war.

It would be a mistake to think that such a historic victory could have been won if the whole country had not prepared beforehand for active defense. It would be no less mistaken to imagine that such preparations could be carried through in a short time—in the space of some three or four years. It would be a still greater mistake to say that we won only owing to the gallantry of our troops. Of course, victory cannot be achieved without gallantry. But gallantry alone is not enough to vanquish an enemy who has a large army, first-class armaments, well-trained officer cadres, and a fairly good organization of supplies. To meet the blow of such an enemy, to repulse him and then to inflict utter defeat upon him required, in addition to the matchless gallantry of our troops, fully up-to-date armaments and adequate quantities of them as well as well-organized supplies in sufficient quantities. But that, in turn, necessitated having—and in adequate amounts—such elementary things as *metal* for the manufacture of armaments, equipment and machinery for factories, *fuel* to keep the factories and transport going, *cotton* for the manufacture of uniforms and *grain* for supplying the Army.

Can it be claimed that before entering the Second World War our country already commanded the necessary minimum material potentialities for satisfying all these requirements in the main? I think it can. In order to prepare for this tremendous job we had to carry out three Five-Year Plans of national economic development. It was precisely these three Five-Year Plans that helped us to create these material potentialities. At any rate, our country's position in this respect before the Second World War, in 1940, was several times better than it was before the First World War, in 1913.

What material potentialities did our country command before the Second World War?

To help you examine this point, I shall have to report briefly on the work of the Communist Party in preparing our country for active defense.

If we take the figures of 1940, the eve of the Second World War, and compare them with the figures for 1913—the eve of the First World War—we get the following picture.

In 1913 our country produced 4,220,000 tons of *pig iron,* 4,230,000 tons of *steel,* 29,000,000 tons of *coal,* 9,000,000 tons of *oil,* 21,600,000 tons of *marketable grain* and 740,000 tons of *raw cotton.*

Those were the material potentialities with which our country entered the First World War.

Such was the economic base of old Russia which could be drawn upon for prosecution of the war.

Now as regards 1940. In the course of that year our country produced 15,000,000 tons of *pig iron,* or nearly four times as much as in 1913; 18,300,000 tons of *steel,* or nearly four and one-half times as much as in 1913; 166,000,000 tons of *coal,* or more than five and one-half times as much as in 1913; 31,000,000 tons of *oil,* or nearly three and one-half times as much as in 1913; 38,300,000 tons of *marketable grain,* or nearly 17,000,000 tons more than in 1913; 2,700,000 tons of *raw cotton,* or more than three and one-half times as much as in 1913.

Those were the material potentialities with which our country entered the Second World War.

Such was the economic base of the Soviet Union which could be drawn upon for prosecution of the war.

The difference as you see is tremendous.

Such an unprecedented increase in production cannot be regarded as the simple and usual development of a country from backwardness to progress. It was a leap by which our Motherland was transformed from a backward into an advanced country, from an agrarian into an industrial country.

This historic transformation was accomplished in the course of three Five-Year Plan periods, beginning with 1928, the first year of the First Five-Year Plan. Up to that time we had to concern ourselves with rehabilitating our ravaged industry and healing the wounds received in the First World War and the Civil War. Moreover, if we bear in mind that the First Five-Year Plan was fulfilled in four years, and that the fulfillment of the Third Five-Year Plan was interrupted by war in its fourth year, we find that it took only about 13 years to transform our country from an agrarian into an industrial one.

It cannot but be admitted that 13 years is an incredibly short period for the accomplishment of such an immense task.

This fact also explains the storm of conflicting comment which the publication of these figures produced at the time in the foreign press. Our friends decided that a "miracle" took place. Our ill-wishers declared that the Five-Year Plans were "Bolshevik propaganda" and "the tricks of the Cheka." But since miracles do not happen, and the Cheka is not so powerful as to abolish the laws of social development, "public opinion" abroad had to accept facts.

By what policy did the Communist Party succeed in providing material potentialities in the country in such a short time?

First of all, by the Soviet policy of industrializing the country.

The Soviet method of industrializing the country differs radically from the capitalist method of industrialization. In capitalist countries industrialization usually begins with light industry. Since in light industry smaller investments are required and there is more rapid turnover of capital and since, furthermore, it is easier to make a profit there than in heavy industry, light industry serves as the first object of industrialization in these countries. Only after a lapse of much time, in the course of which light industry accumulates profits and concentrates them in banks, does the turn of heavy industry arrive and accumulated capital begins to be transferred gradually to heavy industry in order to create conditions for its development. But that is a lengthy process requiring an extensive period of several decades, in the course of which these countries have to wait until light industry has developed and must make shift without heavy industry. Naturally, the Communist Party could not take this course. The Party knew that war was looming, that the country could not be defended without heavy industry, that the development of heavy industry must be undertaken as soon as possible, that to be behind with this would mean to lose out. The Party remembered Lenin's words to the effect that without heavy industry it would be impossible to uphold the country's independence, that without it the Soviet system might perish. Accordingly, the Communist Party of our country rejected the "usual" course of industrialization and began the work of industrializing the country by developing heavy industry. It was very difficult, but not impossible. A valuable aid in this work was the nationalization of industry, and banking, which made possible the rapid accumulation and transfer of funds to heavy industry.

There can be no doubt that without this it would have been impossible to secure our country's transformation into an industrial country in such a short time.

Second, by a policy of collectivization of agriculture.

In order to do away with our backwardness in agriculture and to provide the country with greater quantities of marketable grain, cotton, and so forth, it was essential to pass from small-scale peasant farming to large-scale farming, for only large-scale farming can make use of new technology, apply all the achievements of agronomical science and yield greater quantities of marketable produce. There are, however, two kinds of large farms—capitalist and collective. The Communist Party could not adopt the capitalist path of development of agriculture, and not as a matter of principle alone but also because it implies too prolonged a development and involves preliminary ruin of the peasants and their transformation into farm hands. Therefore, the Communist Party took the path of the collectivization of agriculture, the path of creating large-scale farming by uniting peasant farms into collective farms. The method of collectivization proved a highly progressive method not only because it did not cause the ruin of the peasants but especially because it permitted, within a few years, to cover the entire country with large collective farms which are able to use new technology, take advantage of all the achievements of agronomic science and give the country greater quantities of marketable produce.

There is no doubt that without a collectivization policy we could not in such a short time have done away with the age-old backwardness of our agriculture.

It cannot be said that the Party's policy encountered no resistance. Not only backward people, who always decry everything new, but many prominent members of the Party as well, systematically dragged the Party backward and tried by every possible means to divert it on the "usual" capitalist path of development. All the anti-Party machinations of the Trotskyites and the Rightists, all their "activities" in sabotaging the measures of our government, had one single aim: to frustrate the Party's policy and to obstruct the work of industralization and collectivization. But the Party did not yield either to the threats from one side or the wails from the other and advanced forward confidently regardless of everything. It is to the Party's credit that it did not pander to the backward, was not afraid to go against the tide and always retained its position as the leading force. There can be no doubt that without such firmness and tenacity the Communist Party could not have upheld the policy of industrializing the country and collectivizing agriculture.

Was the Communist Party able to make proper use of the material potentialities thus created in order to develop war production and provide the Red Army with the weapons it needed?

I think that it was able to do so and with maximum success.

If we leave out of account the first year of war, when the evacuation of industry to the East held up the development of war production, we see that in the remaining three years of the war the Party scored such successes that allowed it not only to furnish the front with sufficient quantities of artillery, machine guns, rifles, aircraft, tanks and ammunition, but to accumulate reserves. Moreover, it is known that the quality of our weapons was not only not inferior to the German but, taken on the whole, was actually superior to them.

It is known that during the last three years of war our tank industry produced an annual average of more than 30,000 tanks, self-propelled guns and armored cars. [Storm of applause.]

Further, it is known that our aircraft industry produced during the same period up to 40,000 planes per year. [Storm of applause.]

It is also known that our ordnance industry, during this period, produced annually up to 120,000 guns of all calibers [stormy applause], up to 450,000 light and heavy machine guns [stormy applause], over 3,000,000 rifles [applause], about 2,000,000 submachine guns [applause]. It is known, finally, that between 1942–1944 our mortar industry produced annually on the average 100,000 mortars [stormy applause].

It must be remembered that at the same time we produced a corresponding quantity of artillery shells, all kinds of mines, aircraft bombs and rifle and machine gun ammunition.

It is known, that over 240,000,000 shells, bombs and mortar shells, and 7,400,000,000 rounds of small arms ammunition were manufactured in 1944 alone. [Thunderous applause.]

Such, in general, is the picture of the supply of arms and ammunition to the Red Army.

As you see, it does not resemble the picture which our army supplies presented during the First World War when the front experienced a chronic shortage of artillery and shells, when the army was fighting without tanks and aircraft, and only one rifle was issued to every three men.

As regards the supply of the Red Army with provisions and uniforms, it is known to all that far from experiencing any shortage in this respect, the front actually had surplus.

That is how matters stand with regard to the work of the Communist Party of our country in the period up to the outbreak of war and during the war itself.

Now a few words about the Communist Party's plans of work for the immediate future. As is known these plans are set forth in the new Five-Year Plan which is shortly to be approved. The principal aims of the new Five-Year Plan are to rehabilitate the ravaged areas of the country, to restore the prewar level in industry and agriculture, and then to surpass this level in more or less substantial measure. To say nothing of the fact that the rationing system will shortly be abolished [stormy, prolonged applause], special attention will be devoted to extending the production of consumer goods, to raising the living standard of the working people by steadily lowering the prices of all goods [stormy, prolonged applause], and to the widespread construction of all manner of scientific research institutions [applause] that can give science the opportunity to develop its potentialities. [Stormy applause.]

I have no doubt that if we give our scientists proper assistance they will be able in the near future not only to overtake but to surpass the achievements of science beyond the boundaries of our country. [Prolonged applause.]

As regards the plans for a longer period ahead, the Party intends to organize a new mighty upsurge in the national economy, which would allow us to increase our industrial production, for example, three times over as compared with the prewar period. We must achieve a situation where our industry can produce annually up to 50,000,000 tons of pig iron [prolonged applause], up to 60,000,000 tons of steel [prolonged applause], up to 500,000,000 tons of coal [prolonged applause], and up to 60,000,000 tons of oil [prolonged applause]. Only under such conditions can we consider that our Motherland will be safeguarded against all possible eventualities. [Stormy applause.] That will take three Five-Year Plans, I should think, if not more. But it can be done and we must do it. [Stormy applause.]

Such is my brief report on the Communist Party's work in the recent past and its plans of work for the future.

It is for you to judge how correctly the Party has been working and whether it could not have worked better. [Laughter, applause].

There is a saying that victors are not judged [laughter, applause], that they should not be criticized and checked upon. That is incorrect. Victors should and must be judged [laughter, applause]; they should and must be criticized and checked upon. This is essential not only for the process but for the victors themselves. [Laughter, applause.] There will be less conceitedness and more modesty. [Laughter, applause.] I consider that in the election campaign the electors are sitting in judgment on the Communist Party as the ruling party. And the election returns will constitute the electors' verdict. [Laughter, applause.] The Communist Party of our country would not be worth much if it feared to be criticized and checked upon. The Communist Party is prepared to accept the electors' verdict. [Stormy applause.]

The Communist Party is not alone in the election struggle. It goes to the polls in a bloc with non-Party people. In by-gone days the Communists treated non-Party people and non-Party status with some mistrust. This was due to the fact that the non-Party flag was not infrequently used as a camouflage by various bourgeois groups for whom it was not advantageous to face the electorate without a mask. That was the case in the past. But now we have different times. Our non-Party people are now divided from the bourgeoisie by a barrier known as the Soviet social system. This same barrier unites non-Party people with the Communists in a single community of Soviet people. Living in this single community they struggled together to build up the might of our country, fought and shed their blood together on the battle fronts for the sake of freedom and greatness of our Motherland and together they forged and hammered out a victory over the enemies of our country. The only difference between them is that some belong to the Party, while others do not. But that is a formal difference. The important thing is that both are furthering the same common cause. Therefore, the block of Communists and non-Party people is a natural and living thing. [Stormy, prolonged applause.]

In conclusion, allow me to thank you for the confidence you have shown me [prolonged, unabating applause. Shout from the audience: "Hurrah for the great leader of all victories, Comrade Stalin!"] in nominating me to the Supreme Soviet. You need not doubt that I shall do my best to justify your trust. [All rise. Prolonged, unabating applause turning into an ovation. From all parts of the hall come cheers: "Long live our great Stalin!" "Hurrah!" "Hurrah for the great leader of the peoples!" "Glory to the great Stalin!" "Long live Comrade Stalin, the candidate of the entire nation! Glory to Comrade Stalin, the Creator of all victories!"]

Appendix 31   A RESOLUTION OF THE INFORMATION
BUREAU ON EXPULSION OF TITO FROM
THE COMINFORM, JUNE 28, 1948 [1]

The Information Bureau, composed of the representatives of the Bulgarian Workers' Party (communists), Rumanian Workers' Party, Hungarian Workers' Party, Polish Workers' Party, All-Union Communist Party (bolshevik), Communist Party of France, Communist Party of Czechoslovakia, and Communist Party of Italy, having considered the problem of the situation within the Communist Party of Yugoslavia and having taken note of the fact that the representatives of the Communist Party of Yugoslavia had refused to attend the meeting of the Information Bureau, unanimously reached the following conclusions:

1. The Information Bureau notes that the leadership of the Communist Party of Yugoslavia has in the recent past pursued an incorrect line on the main questions of domestic and foreign policy, [a line] which represents a departure from Marxism-Leninism. The Information Bureau, in this connection, approves the actions of the CC of the VKP (b), [All-Union Communist Party (bolshevik)], which assumed the initiative in exposing the incorrect policy of the CC of the Communist Party of Yugoslavia, and especially the incorrect policies of Comrades Tito, Kardelj, Djilas, [and] Rankovic.

2. The Information Bureau declares that the leadership of the Yugoslav Communist Party is pursuing an unfriendly policy towards the Soviet Union and the VKP(b). There has developed in Yugoslavia an undignified policy aimed at defaming Soviet military specialists and discrediting the Soviet Army. A special regime was established in Yugoslavia for Soviet civilian specialists, who were placed under the surveillance of the Yugoslav state security organs and were followed constantly. Comrade Yudin, the representative of the VKP(b) in the Information Bureau, and a number of official representatives of the USSR in Yugoslavia, were followed and kept under observation by Yugoslav state security organs.

All these and similar facts reveal that the leaders of the Communist Party of Yugoslavia have assumed a position unworthy of communists, have compared foreign policy of the USSR with the foreign policy of the imperialist powers, and have conducted themselves in their relations to the USSR similarly as in their relations with bourgeois states. Because of this anti-Soviet stand, there developed within the CC of the Communist Party of Yugoslavia slanderous propaganda about the "degeneration" of the VKP(b), "degeneration" of the USSR, etc., borrowed from the arsenal of counterrevolutionary Trotskyism.

The Information Bureau denounces these anti-Soviet attitudes of the leaders of the CPY [Communist Party of Yugoslavia] as being incompatible with Marxism-Leninism and appropriate only to nationalists.

3. In their domestic policy the leaders of the CPY are departing from the positions of the working class, and breaking with the Marxist theory of classes

[1] *Pravda*, June 29, 1948, p. 2.

and of the class struggle. They deny the existence of the growth of capitalist elements in their country, and the accompanied increase of the class struggle in the Yugoslav village. This denial stems from the opportunist tenet, which maintains that in the period of transition from capitalism to socialism the class struggle is not intensified, as Marxism-Leninism teaches, but dies down, as was maintained by opportunists of the Bukharin type, who propagated the theory of peaceful incorporation of capitalism into socialism.

The Yugoslav leaders are pursuing an incorrect policy in the village by ignoring the class differentiation in the village and considering the individual peasantry as a single entity, contrary to Marxist-Leninist teaching about classes and the class struggle, and contrary to the well known thesis of Lenin that small individual farming gives birth to capitalism and the bourgeoisie constantly, daily, hourly, spontaneously and on a mass scale. Moreover, the political situation in the Yugoslav village provides no basis for self-satisfaction and complacency. As long as conditions in Yugoslavia permit individual peasant farming, prevent nationalization of land, allow private property in land to exist, and [as long as Yugoslavia is a place] where much of the land is concentrated in the hands of *kulaks,* where hired labor is employed, etc., so long it is inappropriate to educate the party in the spirit of glossing over the class struggle and of reconciling class contradictions, without at the same time disarming the party itself in the face of the difficulties connected with the construction of socialism.

Leaders of the Yugoslav Communist Party, by maintaining that peasants are "the very foundation of the Yugoslav state," are deviating from the Marxist-Leninist path and are taking the path of the populist *kulak* party regarding the leading role of the working class. Lenin teaches that the proletariat "as the only revolutionary-to-the-end class of contemporary society . . . must be the leader and the master in the struggle of the entire people for a thorough democratic transformation in the struggle of all the working and exploited people against the oppressors and exploiters."

The Yugoslav leaders are violating this thesis of Marxism-Leninism.

As far as the peasantry is concerned, its majority, *i.e.,* poor and medium peasants, can be or already is allied with the working class, with the working class possessing the leading role in that alliance.

The attitude of the Yugoslav leaders mentioned above violates these theses of Marxism-Leninism.

As is evident, this attitude reflects such views as are appropriate for petty-bourgeois nationalists, but not for Marxists-Leninists.

4. The Information Bureau believes that the leadership of the YCP is revising the Marxist-Leninist teaching on the party. According to the Marxist-Leninist theory, the party is the chief leading and guiding force in the country, has its own specific programme, and does not dissolve itself within the non-party masses. The party is the highest form of organization and the most important weapon of the working class. In Yugoslavia, however, the chief leading force in the country is not the communist party, but the People's Front. The Yugoslav leaders have belittled the role of the communist party, and actually have dissolved the party in the non-party People's Front, which includes very diverse class elements (workers, toiling peasantry, individual peasants, *kulaks,*

merchants, small manufacturers, bourgeois intelligentsia, etc.) as well as diverse political groups, including some bourgeois parties. The Yugoslav leaders stubbornly refuse to acknowledge the error of their premise that the Communist Party of Yugoslavia allegedly cannot have its own programme and must be satisfied with the programme of the People's Front.

The very fact that the People's Front alone figures in the political arena in Yugoslavia, while the party and its organizations do not appear openly before the people in their own right, lowers the role of the party in the political life of the country, and undermines the party as an independent political force called upon to win the increasing confidence of the people and to influence the great masses of toilers through open political activity, and open propagation of its views and of its programme. The leaders of the Yugoslav Communist Party are repeating the errors of the Russian Mensheviks regarding the dissolution of the Marxist party into a non-party mass organization. All this testifies to the presence of liquidation tendencies within the Communist Party of Yugoslavia.

The Information Bureau believes that such a policy of the CC of the CPY threatens the very existence of the communist party, and, in the final analysis, carries with it a danger of the degeneration of the Yugoslav People's Republic.

5. The Information Bureau believes that the bureaucratic regime established within the party by the Yugoslav leaders is disastrous for the life and development of the Yugoslav Communist Party. The party has neither intra-party democracy, nor elections, nor criticism and self-criticism. The CC of the CPY, contrary to the unfounded assurances of Comrades Tito and Kardelj, consists not of elected but of co-opted members. The communist party actually is in a semilegal situation. Party meetings are either not held at all or are held in secret, a fact which undermines the influence of the party among the masses. This type of organization of the Yugoslav Communist Party cannot be described as anything but a sectarian-bureaucratic organization. Such [organization] leads to the liquidation of the party as an active, creative organism and cultivates in the party military methods of leadership, similar to the methods which Trotsky advocated in his day.

It is absolutely nonpermissible when the most elementary rights of party members are violated in the Yugoslav Communist Party, and when the slightest criticism of incorrect measures in the party is brutally repressed.

The Information Bureau considers as disgraceful such acts as the expulsion from the party and arrest of members of the CC of the CPY, Comrades Zhuyovic and Hebrang, because they dared to criticize the anti-Soviet attitudes of the leaders of the Yugoslav Communist Party and because they called for friendship between Yugoslavia and the USSR.

The Information Bureau believes that such a disgraceful, purely Turkish, terrorist regime cannot be tolerated within the communist party. The interests and the very existence and development of the Yugoslav Communist Party demand that an end be put to such a regime.

6. The Information Bureau believes that the criticism of the errors of the CC of the CPY by the CC of the VKP(b) and by the CC's of other communist parties, being brotherly help for the Yugoslav Communist Party, should have created for the leadership of the CPY the necessary prerequisites for the speedy

correction of their errors. However, instead of accepting this criticism honestly and adopting the Bolshevik path of correcting their errors, leaders of the YCP, who suffer from boundless ambition, arrogance, and conceit, met this criticism with belligerence and hostility, adopted an anti-party path of indiscriminate denial of their errors, of their violation of the Marxist-Leninist teaching on the attitude of a political party to its mistakes, and thereby they have aggravated their anti-party errors.

Unable to face the criticism of the CC of the VKP(b) and of other CC's of other fraternal parties, Yugoslav leaders assumed a path of direct deceit of their party and of the people, by concealing from the Yugoslav Communist Party the criticism of the erroneous policy of the CC of the YCP, and by concealing also from the party and the people the real cause for the mistreatment of Comrades Zhuyovic and Hebrang.

During the recent past, already after the criticism by the CC of the VKP(b) and by the fraternal parties of the errors of the Yugoslav leaders, the latter tried to introduce a number of new leftist laws. The Yugoslav leaders hastily decreed the nationalization of small industry and trade. The complete unpreparedness for such action, in view of the haste, will only hamper the supply of goods for the Yugoslav population. They also hurriedly promulgated a new law on peasant grain tax, which, because of unpreparedness, will only dislocate grain supplies to the urban population. Finally, the Yugoslav leaders recently announced in loud but unexpected declarations their love of and devotion to the Soviet Union, even though it is well known that in practice they are pursuing to the very present an unfriendly policy towards the USSR.

But this is not all. Leaders of the CPY have lately announced with great fanfare the liquidation of capitalist elements in Yugoslavia. In a letter to the CC of the VKP(b) dated April 13, 1948, Tito and Kardelj wrote that "the plenum of the CC approved the measures proposed by the Politbureau of the CC to liquidate the remnants of capitalism in the country." In accordance with this line, speaking in the Skupshchina on April 25, Kardelj declared: "The days of the last remnants of the exploitation of man by man are numbered in our country." Such a proposal by the leaders of the YCP to liquidate capitalist elements under the prevailing conditions in Yugoslavia, and accordingly of the *kulaks* as a class, cannot be called other than adventurous and un-Marxist. It is impossible to resolve this problem as long as individual peasant farming, which inevitably gives rise to capitalism, prevails in the country, as long as conditions have not been prepared for the massive collectivization of agriculture, and as long as the majority of the toiling peasantry is not convinced of the advantages of collective methods of farming. The experience of the VKP(b) testifies that the liquidation of the last and the most numerous exploiting class—the *kulak* class—is possible only through a mass collectivization of agriculture, and that the liquidation of the *kulaks* as a class is an organic and integral part of the collectivization of agriculture.

To carry out successfully the liquidation of the *kulaks* as a class, and accordingly to liquidate capitalist elements in the village, the party must prepare a detailed plan aimed at restricting capitalist elements in the village, must strengthen the alliance between the working class and the peasantry under the leadership of the working class, and must develop socialist industry capable of producing machinery for the collective administration of agriculture. Haste in this matter can only lead to irreparable harm.

Only on the basis of such measures, carefully prepared and consistently carried out, is it possible to move from the restriction of capitalist elements in the village to their liquidation.

All attempts of Yugoslav leaders to solve this task hastily or by means of bureaucratic decrees signify either that the venture is foredoomed to failure or that it is a boastful and empty demagogic declaration.

The Information Bureau believes that the Yugoslav leaders are trying to demonstrate, by means of such false and demagogic tactics, that they not only firmly support the class struggle, but that they go even further beyond those demands which, in view of the real possibilities, the Yugoslav Communist Party could have used in limiting capitalist elements.

The Information Bureau believes that since these leftist decrees and declarations of the Yugoslav leadership are demagogic and impracticable in the present conditions, they can but compromise the socialist construction in Yugoslavia.

Therefore the Information Bureau considers such adventurist tactics as an undignified maneuver and a nonpermissible political gamble.

As is evident, these leftist demagogic measures and declarations of the Yugoslav leaders are designed to cover up their refusal to recognize and to correct their own errors.

7. Taking into account the situation in the YCP, and seeking to give the leaders of the Yugoslav Communist Party an opportunity to get out of this situation, the CC of the VKP(b) and the CC's of other fraternal parties sought to examine the situation in the Yugoslav Communist Party at a meeting of the Information Bureau on a similar party basis as that on which the Information Bureau examined the activities of other parties at its first meeting. However, the Yugoslav leaders rejected the repeated proposals of fraternal parties to discuss the situation in the Yugoslav Communist Party at a meeting of the Information Bureau.

To avoid the just criticism of the fraternal parties in the Information Bureau, the Yugoslav leaders invented the fable of their allegedly "unequal position." This story contains not a grain of truth. Everyone knows that when the Information Bureau was organized the communist parties agreed that every party should account for its activity before the Information Bureau and that every party has the right to criticize other parties. The Yugoslav Communist Party took full advantage of this right at the first meeting of the nine communist parties. The refusal of the Yugoslavs to report on their activities to the Information Bureau and to listen to criticism of other communist parties represents a violation of the equality of communist parties and is tantamount to a demand for a privileged position for the YCP in the Information Bureau.

8. In view of the above arguments, the Information Bureau expresses its complete accord with the estimation of the situation in the Yugoslav Communist Party, and with the criticism of the errors of the CC of the CPY and the political analysis of these errors, contained in letters from the CC of the VKP(b) to the CC of the CPY between March and May, 1948.

The Information Bureau unanimously concludes that by their anti-party and anti-Soviet views, incompatible with Marxism-Leninism, by their whole conduct, and by their refusal to attend the meeting of the Information Bureau, the leaders of the CPY have placed themselves in opposition to the communist parties affiliated with the Information Bureau, have assumed a path of secession from the united socialist front against imperialism, have assumed a path of betrayal of the cause of the international solidarity of the workers, and have assumed a position of nationalism.

The Information Bureau condemns this anti-party policy and conduct of the CC of the CPY.

The Information Bureau believes that because of all this the CC of the CPY has placed itself and the Yugoslav Communist Party outside the united communist front, and, consequently, outside the ranks of the Information Bureau.

The Information Bureau believes that the basis of all the errors of the leadership of the CPY centers in the undoubted fact that the nationalist elements, which previously existed in a disguised form, have, during the past five or six months, triumphed in the leadership of the CPY, and that the leadership of the CPY has broken with the internationalist traditions of the Yugoslav Communist Party and has taken the path of nationalism.

The Yugoslav leaders strongly overestimate the internal national forces and possibilities, and think that they can preserve the independence of Yugoslavia and build socialism without the support of communist parties of other countries, without the support of the countries of people's democracies, without the support of the USSR. They think that the new Yugoslavia can do without the aid of these revolutionary forces.

Yugoslav leaders, who reveal their poor understanding of the international situation and who are afraid of the blackmailing threats of imperialists, believe that by making concessions to imperialist states they will gain the favor of these states, will be able to reach an agreement with them on Yugoslavia's independence, and will gradually impose on the Yugoslav people orientation on these states, i.e., orientation on capitalism. In this they proceed tacitly from a well-known bourgeois-nationalist thesis that "capitalist states are a lesser danger to the independence of Yugoslavia than is the USSR."

The Yugoslav leaders evidently do not understand, or perhaps pretend they do not understand, that such a nationalist attitude can only lead to the transformation of Yugoslavia into an ordinary bourgeois republic, to the loss of Yugoslav independence, and to the transformation of Yugoslavia into a colony of the imperialist countries.

The Information Bureau does not doubt that within the Communist Party of Yugoslavia there are many healthy elements loyal to Marxism-Leninism, loyal to the internationalist traditions of the Yugoslav Communist Party, and loyal to the united socialist front.

The task of these healthy elements in the CPY is to force their present leaders to recognize openly their errors and to correct them; to break with nationalism; to return to internationalism; and to strengthen in every possible way the united socialist front against imperialism. Should the present leaders of the CPY be incapable of doing this, they should be replaced and new internationalist leadership in the CPY be chosen.

The Information Bureau does not doubt that the Communist Party of Yugoslavia will be able to fulfill this honorable task.

Appendix 32   OFFICIAL GLORIFICATION OF STALIN ON HIS SEVENTIETH BIRTHDAY, DECEMBER 21, 1949 [1]

Dear friend, fighting comrade, teacher and leader:

On your 70th birthday, the Central Committee of the Communist Party of the Soviet Union (Bolsheviks), and the Council of Ministers of the U.S.S.R. warmly salute you, the great companion-in-arms and friend of Lenin, the brilliant continuator of his immortal cause, the indefatigable builder of Communism, our wise teacher and leader.

Together with Lenin, you, Comrade Stalin, built the Bolshevik Party, in close co-operation with Lenin, elaborated the ideological, organisational, tactical and theoretical principles of Bolshevism; tempered the Party in severe battles for the liberation of the working people, and transformed it into the most powerful revolutionary Party in the world.

A fearless revolutionary, brilliant theoretician and splendid organiser, you, together with Lenin, confidently, boldly, firmly and carefully led the Party, the working class to armed uprising, to the Socialist Revolution.

Together with Lenin, you, Comrade Stalin, were the inspirer and leader of the Great October Socialist Revolution, the founder of the first Soviet Socialist State of workers and peasants in the world.

During the years of Civil War and foreign intervention, your genius as organiser and commander led the Soviet people and its heroic Red Army to victory over the enemies of the Fatherland.

Under your direct leadership, Comrade Stalin, vast work was accomplished in establishing the national Soviet Republics, in uniting them into one union—the U.S.S.R.

When death cut short the life of the great Lenin, you, Comrade Stalin, raised aloft the glorious banner of Lenin, and once again boldly and resolutely led our Party along the Lenin path.

The Bolshevik Party, strong in its loyalty to Leninism, blazed the path of Socialist construction, hitherto unknown in history, in a country encircled by capitalist States.

Of the greatest significance for the victory of Socialism was the Lenin theory about the possibility of the victory of Socialism in our country; a theory further developed and enriched by you.

The enemies of Socialism, the enemies of the Soviet people and of the Communist Party tried in vain to divert our Party from the Lenin-Stalin path, to split it from within, to deprive the working class of confidence in their strength, in the possibility of building socialism.

[1] *For a Lasting Peace, for a People's Democracy*, No. 32 (59), December 21, 1949, p. 1.

You ruthlessly exposed the dastardly, criminal attempts of the enemies of the people to disarm the Party ideologically, to smash its unity, to destroy Soviet power and the Socialist Revolution.

In the bitter struggle against the traitors to the cause of Socialism—against the trotskyites, bukharinites, bourgeois nationalists and other enemies—there was welded around you, Comrade Stalin, the leading core of our Party, which upheld the invincible banner of Lenin, consolidated the Communist Party and led the Soviet people on to the high road of Socialist construction.

Carrying out the gigantic programme of Socialist industrialisation of our country elaborated by you, the Soviet people, in an historically short space of time, transformed Russia from a technically and economically backward country into an advanced industrial power.

Your name is associated with the mighty Socialist construction of the Five-Year Plans, with the giants of industry, with new branches of industry, all of which have played a decisive role in strengthening the defence capacity of the State.

Under your wise leadership, Comrade Stalin, an historic turning point was effected in the countryside in 1929, the consequences of which are equal only to the revolutionary upheaval of October 1917.

The Communist Party carried out the complete collectivisation of agriculture, and, on this basis, the liquidation of the kulaks as a class.

As a result of the victories of the collective-farm system and the mechanisation of agriculture, the new Socialist life took root in the Soviet countryside, delivering the working peasantry from bondage, ruin and impoverishment.

Under the leadership of our Party, headed by the beloved Stalin, the Soviet Union became a mighty industrial and collective-farm power; a country of victorious Socialism.

Having built Socialism, the Soviet people once and for all destroyed the exploitation of man by man, created a new social and State order, free of crises and unemployment and ensured a steady rise in the material and cultural level of the working people.

The Constitution of the U.S.S.R., justly called by the people the Stalin Constitution, consolidated the magnificent victories of Socialism, became a magnetic force, a beacon light for the whole of working mankind.

On the basis of the rich experience of the land of Soviets, you, Comrade Stalin, elaborated a complete and all-round teaching on the Socialist State.

In further developing Leninism you reached the brilliant conclusion regarding the possibility of building Communism in our country, and the need to preserve the State under Communism should capitalist encirclement remain.

This conclusion gave the Party and the people a clear perspective of the struggle for the victory of Communism.

The solution of one of the most important questions of the Revolution—the National Question—is linked with your name, Comrade Stalin.

In the fraternal family of Soviet peoples, the formerly oppressed nations have attained unprecedented political, economic, and cultural flowering.

Inspired by you, the friendship between the peoples of the U.S.S.R. was a great gain of the Revolution, one of the sources of the might of our Socialist Fatherland.

With the victory of Socialism, the moral-political unity of the Soviet people, closely consolidated around the Party of Lenin-Stalin, has become invincible.

Our People are imbued with warm and creative Soviet patriotism. Under your leadership, the Bolshevik Party carried out a real cultural revolution in the U.S.S.R.

Your wisdom, indomitable energy and iron will are to be found in every change effected, large or small; changes that are raising our country to ever higher levels.

It is our happiness, the happiness of our people, that the Great Stalin, as leader of the Party and the State, guides and inspires the creative, constructive work of the Soviet people for the flowering of our glorious Fatherland.

Under your leadership, Comrade Stalin, the Soviet Union has become a mighty and invincible force.

When Hitler's Germany forced war on the Soviet Union and mortal danger threatened our Fatherland, you, Comrade Stalin, headed the armed struggle of the Soviet people against fascism—the worst enemy of mankind; rallied all Soviet peoples in the Great Patriotic War; inspired the Soviet people and its Armed Forces to legendary deeds and exploits.

The Party of Lenin and Stalin united the efforts of the front and rear.

Your military and organisational genius brought us victory over fascist Germany and imperialist Japan.

Great commander and organiser of victory, you, Comrade Stalin, created an advanced Soviet military science. The battles directed by you are outstanding examples of military, operational and strategic art.

The first-class military cadres, trained and educated by you carried out with honour the Stalin plans to rout the enemy.

All honest people in the world, and future generations will sing the glory of the Soviet Union, of your name, Comrade Stalin, as the saviour of world civilisation from the fascist pogrom-makers.

In post-war conditions, the whole Soviet people, guided by your counsels, devoted their creative initiative to heal rapidly the aftermath of the war; to carry out the gigantic plans for the further development of national economy and culture in the land of Socialism; to improve the welfare of the working people.

The Lenin-Stalin idea of Socialist emulation, inspiring Soviet patriots to new labour exploits, released the powerful energy of millions of Soviet people to realise the great aim—the victory of Communism.

You, Comrade Stalin, are guiding the foreign policy of the Soviet Union with great firmness and foresight, fighting for peace and security of large and small nations.

The international prestige of the U.S.S.R. as the bulwark of peace and democracy has grown immeasurably.

The working people of the capitalist and colonial countries see in you a true and staunch champion of peace and defender of the vital interests of the people of all countries.

You have kindled in the hearts of all ordinary people of the world an unshakable confidence in the just cause of the struggle for world peace, for the national independence of peoples, for friendship between peoples.

Under your leadership, Comrade Stalin, the Soviet Union played a decisive role in liberating the working people of the New Democracies from the fascist enslavers, from the yoke of capitalists and landlords.

The peoples of these countries are filled with gratitude to you for the disinterested fraternal aid the Soviet Union is rendering them in their economic and cultural development.

Great coryphaeus of science! Your classical works, which developed Marxist-Leninist theory in accordance with the new epoch, the epoch of imperialism and proletarian revolutions, the epoch of the victory of Socialism in our country, are the greatest achievement of mankind, an encyclopaedia of revolutionary Marxism.

Soviet people and the progressive representatives of the working people of all countries draw from these works knowledge, confidence, new strength in the struggle for the victory of the working class and find there the answers to the most burning problems of present-day struggle for Communism.

Like a bright torch your works on the National and Colonial Questions illuminate the path of the national-liberation movement of the peoples of the colonial and dependent countries.

The colossal successes of the forces of peace, democracy and Socialism are illumined by Lenin-Stalin revolutionary thought.

Great architect of Communism! You teach all Bolsheviks to be most exacting towards themselves and others, to criticise shortcomings boldly, and you warn them not to rest on their laurels, not to get bloated with success. You teach us that criticism and self-criticism is an effective weapon in the struggle for Communism, that the integral qualities of Party and Soviet cadres must be Bolshevik modesty, a solicitous and attentive approach to the needs of the people, to be steadfast and principled in the struggle against all manifestations of bourgeois ideology.

Dear Comrade Stalin. You always taught us and still teach us Bolsheviks, to be as the great Lenin was; not to spare our efforts in the service of our people, in every way to contribute to the further blossoming of our beloved Fatherland, to do everything for the victory of Communism.

The Bolshevik Party and Soviet people, all progressive mankind, see in you a teacher and leader, the brilliant continuator of Lenin's immortal work.

The name of Stalin is the name dearest to our people, to the ordinary people of the world. The name of Stalin is the symbol of the coming victory of Communism.

The hearts of Soviet people and millions of working people throughout the world are filled with warm love for you, the Great Stalin.

It is a great happiness to live and create in our Soviet land, to belong to the Party of Lenin-Stalin, to the heroic generation of Soviet people who are fighting in the Stalin epoch for the triumph of Communism under the leadership of Stalin.

Teacher and leader, best friend and fighting comrade, accept our heart-felt wishes to you for many years of health and creative work for the good of the Bolshevik Party, Soviet people and for the happiness of the working people of the world.

Long live our own Stalin!

Central Committee, Communist Party   Council of Ministers
of the Soviet Union (Bolsheviks)   of the U.S.S.R.

Appendix 33 STALIN'S LAST SPEECH, OCTOBER 17, 1952 [1]

[Comrade Stalin's appearance on the rostrum is greeted by the delegates with tumultuous prolonged applause developing into ovation. All rise. Cheers: "Hurrah for Comrade Stalin!" "Long live Comrade Stalin!" "Glory to the great Stalin!"]

Comrades,

Allow me on behalf of our Congress to express thanks to all the fraternal Parties and groups, whose representatives honoured our Congress with their presence or who sent messages of greetings to the Congress,—for their friendly greetings, wishes of success and for their trust. [Tumultuous, prolonged applause growing into ovation.]

Of special value for us is this trust which signifies readiness to support our Party in the struggle for the radiant future for the peoples, in its struggle against war, in its struggle for the preservation of peace. [Tumultuous, prolonged applause.]

It would be a mistake to think that our Party, having become a powerful force, no longer needs support. This is not correct. Our Party and our country have always needed and shall need the trust, sympathy and support of the fraternal peoples abroad.

A peculiarity of this support is that all support for the peace-loving aspirations of our Party on the part of any fraternal Party signifies at the same time support of its own people in their struggle for the preservation of peace. When the British workers in 1918–19, at the time of the armed attack of the British bourgeoisie on the Soviet Union, organised the struggle against war under the slogan "Hands off Russia," this was support, first of all support of the struggle of their people for peace, and then support of the Soviet Union. When Comrade Thorez or Comrade Togliatti declare that their peoples will not fight against the peoples of the Soviet Union [tumultuous applause] this is support, first of all support of the workers and peasants of France and Italy fighting for peace, and then support of the peace-loving strivings of the Soviet Union. This peculiarity of the mutual support is explained by the fact that the interests of our Party not only do not contradict, but, on the contrary, merge with the interests of the peace-loving peoples. [Tumultuous applause.] As for the Soviet Union its interests in general are inseparable from the cause of world peace.

Naturally, our Party cannot remain in debt to the fraternal parties and it must in turn support them and also their people in their struggle for liberation, in their struggle for the preservation of peace. As is known, that is

[1] *For a Lasting Peace, for a People's Democracy*, No. 42 (206), October 17, 1952, p. 1.

precisely what it does. [Tumultuous applause.] After our Party took power in 1917 and after the Party took real measures to do away with capitalist and landlord oppression, representatives of the fraternal Parties, admiring the valour and successes of our Party, named it the "Shock-brigade" of the world revolutionary and working-class movement. In this way they expressed the hope that the successes of the "Shock-brigade" would facilitate the position of the peoples groaning under the yoke of capitalism. I think that our party justified these hopes, especially in the period of the second world war when the Soviet Union, by smashing German and Japanese fascist tyranny, delivered the peoples of Europe and Asia from the menace of fascist slavery. [Tumultuous applause.]

Of course, it was very difficult to fulfill this honourable role, so long as the "Shock-brigade" was all alone and had to carry out this leading role practically single-handed. But this belongs to the past. Now things are altogether different. Now, when from China and Korea to Czechoslovakia and Hungary new "Shock-brigades" have appeared in the shape of the people's democratic countries,—now it has become easier for our Party to fight, and indeed work is going with a swing. [Tumultuous, prolonged applause.]

Those Communist, democratic or worker-peasant Parties which have not yet come to power and which are still working under the heel of the draconic laws of the bourgeoisie, deserve special attention. For them, of course, the work is more difficult. But it is not as difficult for them as it was for us, the Russian Communists, at the time of tsarism, when the slightest forward movement was proclaimed a heinous crime. However, the Russian Communists stood firm, were not afraid of the difficulties and won victory. The same thing will take place with these Parties.

Why, then, will it be less difficult for these Parties to work than was the case with the Russian Communists at the time of tsarism?

Firstly, because they have before their eyes examples of struggle and successes such as we have in the Soviet Union and in the people's democratic countries. Consequently, they can learn from the mistakes and successes of these countries and in this way make their work easier.

Secondly, because the bourgeoisie itself—the main enemy of the liberation movement—has changed, changed substantially, has become more reactionary, has lost contact with the people and by so doing has weakened itself. Obviously, this circumstance too, is bound to make the work of the revolutionary and democratic Parties easier. [Tumultuous applause.]

Formerly the bourgeoisie permitted itself to be liberal, championed bourgeois-democratic freedoms and in doing so created for itself popularity among the people. Now, not even a trace of liberalism remains. Gone is the so-called "freedom of the individual,"—the rights of the individual now are recognised only in the case of those who have capital while all other citizens are regarded as human raw material fit only for exploitation. The principle of equality of people and nations has been trampled underfoot; it has been replaced by the principle of full rights for the exploiting minority and no rights for the exploited majority of citizens. The banner of the bourgeois-democratic freedoms has been thrown overboard. I think that you, representatives of the Communist and democratic Parties, will have to pick up this banner and carry it forward if you wish to rally around yourselves the majority of the people. There is no one else to pick it up. [Tumultuous applause.]

Formerly the bourgeoisie was considered the head of the nation, it championed the rights and independence of the nation, placing them "above everything." Now, not a trace remains of the "national principle." Now the bourgeoisie sells the rights and independence of the nation for dollars. The banner of national independence and national sovereignty has been thrown overboard. There is no doubt that you, representatives of the Communist and democratic Parties, will have to pick up this banner and carry it forward if you wish to be patriots of your country, if you wish to become the leading force of the nation. There is no one else to pick it up. [Tumultuous applause.]

That is how matters stand at present.

Clearly all these circumstances are bound to facilitate the work of the Communist and democratic Parties which have not yet come to power.

Consequently, there is every reason to count on success and victory for the fraternal parties in the countries dominated by capital. [Tumultuous applause.]

Long live our fraternal Parties! [Prolonged applause.]

Long life and good health to the leaders of the fraternal Parties! [Prolonged applause.]

Long live peace among the nations! [Prolonged applause.]

Down with the warmongers! [All rise. Tumultuous, prolonged applause growing into ovations. Cries: "Long live Comrade Stalin!" "Hurrah for Comrade Stalin!" "Long live Comrade Stalin, great leader of the working people of the world!" "Hurrah for the great Stalin!" "Long live peace among the nations!" Cries: "Hurrah!"]

Appendix 34 OFFICIAL CHARGES AGAINST L. P. BERIA AND HIS ASSOCIATES, DECEMBER, 1953 [1]

The Presidium of the Supreme Soviet of the USSR, having reviewed the report of the Council of Ministers of the USSR on the criminal activities of L. P. Beria, as an agent of foreign capital, directed toward the subversion of the Soviet state, decreed on June 26, 1953: to remove L. P. Beria from the post of First Deputy Chairman of the Council of Ministers of the USSR and from the post of Minister of Internal Affairs of the USSR, and to bring Beria to trial. On August 8, 1953, the Supreme Soviet of the USSR confirmed the June 26 decree of the Presidium of the Supreme Soviet of the USSR.

The Office of Procurator of the USSR has now completed the investigation in the case of the traitor to the Motherland, L. P. Beria.

The investigation has established that Beria, using his position, organized a treacherous group of conspirators hostile to the Soviet state, which made it its criminal aim to use organs of the Ministry of Internal Affairs, both centrally and locally, against the Communist Party and the government of the USSR in the interests of foreign capital, striving in their treacherous intents to place the Ministry of Internal Affairs above the Party and government, to seize power and to liquidate the Soviet worker-peasant system, with a view to restoring capitalism and securing the revival of the domination of the bourgeoisie.

Active participants in the treacherous group of conspirators connected with Beria for a period of many years by joint criminal activity in the organs of the NKVD and MVD were: the former Minister of State Security of the USSR and lately Minister of State Control of the USSR, V. N. Merkulov; the former head of one of the administrations of the NKVD of the USSR and lately Minister of Internal Affairs of the Georgian SSR, V. G. Dekanozov; the former Deputy People's Commissar of Internal Affairs of the Georgian SSR, later Deputy Minister of State Security of the USSR, and more recently Deputy Minister of Internal Affairs of the USSR, B. Z. Kobulov; the former People's Commissar of Internal Affairs of the Georgian SSR and lately head of one of the administrations of the MVD of the USSR, S. A. Goglidze; the former head of one of the administrations of the NKVD of the USSR and lately Minister of Internal Affairs of the Ukrainian SSR, P. Ia. Meshik; and the former head of the Investigation Department, for particularly important matters, of the MVD of the USSR, L. E. Vlodzimirskii.

For a period of many years Beria and his accomplices carefully camouflaged and concealed their hostile treacherous activity. After the demise of J. V. Stalin, when imperialist reactionary forces increased their subversive activities against the Soviet state, Beria intensified his actions in order to

[1] *Izvestiia,* December 17, 1953. Translation by Basil Dmytryshyn.

attain his criminal aims, primarily by utilizing organs of the MVD to seize power, which made it possible in a short period of time to lay bare the true face of the traitor of the Motherland and to take decisive measures to put an end to his hostile activity.

Having become Minister of Internal Affairs of the USSR in March, 1953, Beria began more intensively to elevate members of the conspirators' group into a number of leading posts in the Ministry of Internal Affairs. The conspirators subjected to persecution and victimization honest workers of the MVD who had refused to carry out Beria's criminal instructions.

In order to subvert the collective farm system and to create food difficulties in our country, Beria sabotaged and interfered in every possible way with the implementation of most important measures of the Party and the government which were directed toward an upsurge of the economy of collective and state farms and toward steady improvement of the well-being of the Soviet people.

It has also been established that Beria and his accomplices carried out criminal measures aimed at reviving remnants of bourgeois nationalist elements in the Union Republics, sowing hatred and discord between the peoples of the USSR, and primarily at undermining the friendship of the peoples of the USSR with the Great Russian people.

Deprived of any social support whatsoever within the USSR, Beria and his accomplices sought to build their criminal activity on support for their conspiracy from reactionary imperialist forces from abroad.

As has now been established by the investigation, Beria had established links with foreign intelligence services as far back as the Civil War. In 1919, when he was in Baku, Beria committed a betrayal, having become a secret agent in the intelligence service of the counter-revolutionary Mussavat Government in Azerbaidzhan, which operated under the control of British intelligence organs. In 1920 Beria, then in Georgia, again committed an act of betrayal, having established secret contact with the Georgian Menshevik secret police, which was a branch of British intelligence.

The investigation has established that during subsequent years as well Beria maintained and extended his secret criminal contacts with foreign intelligence services through planted spies, whom he was sometimes able to protect from exposure and the punishment they deserved.

Acting as a traitor and a spy to the Motherland, who had sold himself to foreign intelligence services, Beria, throughout the entire length of his criminal activities, with the aid of his accomplices also maintained secret contacts with counter-revolutionary Georgian Menshevik emigrants and with the agents of a number of foreign intelligence services.

Diligently concealing his criminal past and inimical contacts with intelligence services of foreign states, Beria selected as his basic method slander, intrigues, and various provocations against honest Party and Soviet workers, who stood in the path of his hostile intentions toward the Soviet state, and who interfered with his efforts to gain power.

Having managed, with the aid of these criminal methods, to get responsible posts in Trans-Caucasia and Georgia, and then in the MVD of the USSR, and having conceived treacherous aims and plans for seizing power, Beria and his accomplices dealt arbitrarily with people who did not suit them, not shrinking from acts of arbitrariness and lawlessness, basely deceiving the Party and the state.

The investigation has established a number of Beria's criminal machinations directed toward the attaining of careerist aims and designed to prevent the exposure of his hostile nature. The investigation has established that, in order to attain his treacherous aims, Beria—with the aid of his accomplices —waged a campaign of criminal intrigue over a period of years against the outstanding leader of the Communist Party and the Soviet state, Sergo Ordzhonikidze, seeing in him a man who was an obstacle to his further ambition and the fulfillment of his hostile intentions. As has now been established Sergo Ordzhonikidze felt that Beria could not be trusted politically. After the demise of Sergo Ordzhonikidze, the conspirators continued to wreak severe vengeance on members of his family.

The investigation has also established that the conspirators committed terrorist murders of persons from whom they feared exposure. Thus Beria and his accomplices put to death M. S. Kedrov—a member of the Communist Party from 1902, a former member of the Presidium of the All-Russian CHEKA and the Collegium of the OGPU under F. E. Dzerzhinskii. The conspirators had reasons to suspect Kedrov of having at his disposal evidence of the criminal past of Beria. Other facts have also been established relating to terrorist murders committed by the conspirators, with the criminal intent of exterminating honest cadres devoted to the cause of the Communist Party and the Soviet regime.

As established by the investigation, Beria and his accomplices committed a number of treacherous acts, designed to weaken the defense capability of the Soviet Union.

Material brought to light by the investigation has established that members of the conspiratorial group—the accused Merkulov, Dekanozov, Kobulov, Goglidze, Meshik, and Vlodzimirskii—who were linked to Beria through joint criminal activity over many years, carried out criminal assignments set by Beria, helped him to conceal his treasonous past, and committed a number of grave state crimes which have been referred to above.

Thus it has been established that the accused Beria, Merkulov, Dekanozov, Kobulov, Goglidze, Meshik, and Vlodzimirskii, having betrayed the Motherland, acted as agents of international imperialism, as the worst enemies of the Soviet people.

The investigation has also established other evidence regarding crimes committed by Beria, that testify to his deep moral depravity and also evidence regarding his criminal, mercenary activity and his abuse of power.

Having been exposed during the investigation by testimonies of numerous witnesses and indisputable documentary evidence, the accused admitted their guilt of committing a number of grave crimes against the state.

Beria has been committed for trial on the charge of high treason to the Motherland, of organizing an anti-Soviet conspiracy, of committing acts of terrorism, of active struggle against the working class and the revolutionary workers' movement, of acting as a secret agent in the intelligence services of the counter-revolutionary Mussavat Government during the Civil

War period; that is, crimes provided for by Articles 58-1 (b), 58-8, 58-13, 58-11 of the Criminal Code of the RSFSR.

Merkulov, Dekanozov, Kobulov, Goglidze, Meshik, and Vlodzimirskii have been committed for trial on a charge of high treason against the Motherland, of committing acts of terrorism, and of participating in a counter-revolutionary treasonous group of conspirators; that is, crimes provided for by Articles 58-1 (b), 58-8, 58-11 of the Criminal Code of the RSFSR.

In accordance with the decree of the Presidium of the Supreme Soviet of the USSR, the case against Beria, Merkulov, Dekanozov, Kobulov, Goglidze, Meshik, and Vlodzimirskii is subject to a special review of the Supreme Court of the USSR, in accordance with the procedure established by the law of December 1, 1934.

To the Chairman of the Joint Session of the Soviet of the Union and the Soviet of Nationalities:

I ask you to bring to the attention of the Supreme Soviet of the USSR my request to be relieved from the post of Chairman of the Council of Ministers of the USSR.

My request is motivated by practical considerations on the necessity of strengthening the leadership of the Council of Ministers and by the need to have at the post of Chairman of the Council of Ministers another comrade with greater experience in state work. I clearly see that the carrying out of the complex and responsible duties of Chairman of the Council of Ministers is being negatively affected by my insufficient experience in local work, and the fact that I did not have occasion, in a ministry or some economic organ, to direct guidance of individual branches of national economy.

I also consider myself bound to say in the present statement that now, when the Communist Party of the Soviet Union and the workers of our country are concentrating special efforts for the most rapid development of agriculture, I see particularly clearly my guilt and responsibility for the unsatisfactory state of affairs that has arisen in agriculture, because for several years past I have been entrusted with the duty of controlling and guiding the work of central agricultural organs and the work of local party and administrative organizations in the sphere of agriculture. The Communist Party, on the initiative and under the guidance of the Central Committee of the Communist Party of the Soviet Union, has already worked out and is implementing a series of broad measures for overcoming the lagging in agriculture. Among such important measures is, undoubtedly, the reform of agricultural taxation, regarding which I think it opportune to say that it was carried out on the initiative of and in accordance with the proposals of the Central Committee of the Communist Party of the Soviet Union. It is now evident what important role this reform played in the task of developing agriculture. Now, as is known, on the initiative and under the guidance of the Central Committee of the Communist Party of the Soviet Union, a general program has been worked out to overcome the lagging in agriculture and for its most rapid development. This program is based on the only correct foundation: The further development by every means of heavy industry, and only its implementation will create the necessary conditions for a real upsurge in the production of all essential commodities for popular consumption.

It is to be expected that various bourgeois hysterical viragos will busy

[1] *Izvestiia*, February 9, 1955, p. 1. Translation by Basil Dmytryshyn.

themselves with slanderous inventions in connection with my present statement, and the fact itself of my release from the post of Chairman of the USSR Council of Ministers, but we, Communists and Soviet people, will ignore this lying and slander. For every one of us the interests of the motherland, the people, and of the Communist Party stand above everything else.

Expressing the request for my release from the post of Chairman of the Council of Ministers of the USSR, I wish to assure the Supreme Soviet of the USSR that, in the new sphere entrusted to me, under the guidance of the Central Committee of the Communist Party of the Soviet Union and the Soviet Government, monolithic in its unity and solidarity, I will perform in the most conscientious manner my duty and the functions which will be entrusted to me.

G. MALENKOV
Chairman of the Council of
Ministers of the USSR

Appendix 36 THE WARSAW SECURITY PACT,
MAY 14, 1955 [1]

The Contracting Parties,

reaffirming their desire for the establishment of a system of European collective security based on the participation of all European states irrespective of their social and political systems, which would make it possible to unite their efforts in safeguarding the peace of Europe;

mindful, at the same time, of the situation created in Europe by the ratification of the Paris agreements, which envisage the formation of a new military alignment in the shape of "Western European Union," with the participation of a remilitarized Western Germany and the integration of the latter in the North-Atlantic bloc, which increased the danger of another war and constitutes a threat to the national security of the peaceable states;

being persuaded that in these circumstances the peaceable European states must take the necessary measures to safeguard their security and in the interests of preserving peace in Europe;

guided by the objects and principles of the Charter of the United Nations Organization;

being desirous of further promoting and developing friendship, cooperation and mutual assistance in accordance with the principles of respect for the independence and sovereignty of states and of noninterference in their internal affairs,

have decided to conclude the present Treaty of Friendship, Cooperation and Mutual Assistance and have for that purpose appointed as their pleni potentiaries:

[names follow]

who, having presented their full powers, found in good and due form, have agreed as follows:

ARTICLE I

The Contracting Parties undertake, in accordance with the Charter of the United Nations Organization, to refrain in their international relations from the threat or use of force, and to settle their international disputes peacefully and in such manner as will not jeopardize international peace and security.

[1] U.S. Department of State, *American Foreign Policy 1950–1955.* (Washington: Government Printing Office, 1957), I, pp. 1239–1242.

ARTICLE II

The Contracting Parties declare their readiness to participate in a spirit of sincere cooperation in all international actions designed to safeguard international peace and security, and will fully devote their energies to the attainment of this end.

The Contracting Parties will furthermore strive for the adoption, in agreement with other states which may desire to cooperate in this, of effective measures for universal reduction of armaments and prohibition of atomic, hydrogen and other weapons of mass destruction.

ARTICLE III

The Contracting Parties shall consult with one another on all important international issues affecting their common interests, guided by the desire to strengthen international peace and security.

They shall immediately consult with one another whenever, in the opinion of any one of them, a threat of armed attack on one or more of the Parties to the Treaty has arisen, in order to ensure joint defence and the maintenance of peace and security.

ARTICLE IV

In the event of armed attack in Europe on one or more of the Parties to the Treaty by any state or group of states, each of the Parties to the Treaty, in the exercise of its right to individual or collective self-defence in accordance with Article 51 of the Charter of the United Nations Organization, shall immediately, either individually or in agreement with other Parties to the Treaty, come to the assistance of the state or states attacked with all such means as it deems necessary, including armed force. The Parties to the Treaty shall immediately consult concerning the necessary measures to be taken by them jointly in order to restore and maintain international peace and security.

Measures taken on the basis of this Article shall be reported to the Security Council in conformity with the provisions of the Charter of the United Nations Organization. These measures shall be discontinued immediately the Security Council adopts the necessary measures to restore and maintain international peace and security.

ARTICLE V

The Contracting Parties have agreed to establish a Joint Command of the armed forces that by agreement among the Parties shall be assigned to the Command, which shall function on the basis of jointly established principles. They shall likewise adopt other agreed measures necessary to strengthen their defensive power, in order to protect the peaceful labours of their peoples, guarantee the inviolability of their frontiers and territories, and provide defence against possible aggression.

ARTICLE VI

For the purpose of the consultations among the Parties envisaged in the present Treaty, and also for the purpose of examining questions which may arise in the operation of the Treaty, a Political Consultative Committee shall be set up, in which each of the Parties to the Treaty shall be represented by a member of its Government or by another specifically appointed representative.

The Committee may set up such auxiliary bodies as may prove necessary.

ARTICLE VII

The Contracting Parties undertake not to participate in any coalitions or alliances and not to conclude any agreements whose objects conflict with the objects of the present Treaty.

ARTICLE VIII

The Contracting Parties declare that they will act in a spirit of friendship and cooperation with a view to further developing and fostering economic and cultural intercourse with one another, each adhering to the principle of respect for the independence and sovereignty of the others and noninterference in their internal affairs.

ARTICLE IX

The present Treaty is open to the accession of other states, irrespective of their social and political systems, which express their readiness by participation in the present Treaty to assist in uniting the efforts of the peaceable states in safeguarding the peace and security of the peoples. Such accession shall enter into force with the agreement of the Parties to the Treaty after the declaration of accession has been deposited with the Government of the Polish People's Republic.

ARTICLE X

The present Treaty is subject to ratification, and the instruments of ratification shall be deposited with the Government of the Polish People's Republic.

The Treaty shall enter into force on the day the last instrument of ratification has been deposited. The Government of the Polish People's Republic shall notify the other Parties to the Treaty as each instrument of ratification is deposited.

ARTICLE XI

The present Treaty shall remain in force for twenty years. For such Contracting Parties as do not at least one year before the expiration of this period present to the Government of the Polish People's Republic a statement of denunciation of the Treaty, it shall remain in force for the next ten years.

Should a system of collective security be established in Europe, and a General European Treaty of Collective Security concluded for this purpose, for which the Contracting Parties will unswervingly strive, the present Treaty shall cease to be operative from the day the General European Treaty enters into force.

Done in Warsaw on May 14, 1955, in one copy each in the Russian, Polish, Czech and German languages, all texts being equally authentic. Certified copies of the present Treaty shall be sent by the Government of the Polish People's Republic to all the Parties to the Treaty.

In witness whereof the plenipotentiaries have signed the present Treaty and affixed their seals.

Mehmet Shehu	Jozef Cyrankiewicz
Vylko Chervenkov	Gheorghe Gheorghiu-Dej
Andras Hegedus	Nikolai A. Bulganin
Otto Grotewohl	Viliam Siroky

Appendix 37 KHRUSHCHEV'S DE-STALINIZATION SPEECH, FEBRUARY 24–25, 1956 [1]

Comrades, in the report of the Central Committee of the party at the 20th Congress, in a number of speeches by delegates to the Congress, as also formerly during the plenary CC/CPSU [Central Committee of the Communist Party of the Soviet Union] sessions, quite a lot has been said about the cult of the individual and about its harmful consequences.

After Stalin's death the Central Committee of the party began to implement a policy of explaining concisely and consistently that it is impermissible and foreign to the spirit of Marxism-Leninism to elevate one person, to transform him into superman possessing supernatural characteristics akin to those of a god. Such a man supposedly knows everything, sees everything, thinks for everyone, can do anything, is infallible in his behavior.

Such a belief about a man, and specifically about Stalin, was cultivated among us for many years.

The objective of the present report is not a thorough evaluation of Stalin's life and activity. Concerning Stalin's merits, an entirely sufficient number of books, pamphlets and studies had already been written in his lifetime. The role of Stalin in the preparation and execution of the Socialist revolution, in the civil war, and in the fight for the construction of socialism in our country, is universally known. Everyone knows this well. At present, we are concerned with a question which has immense importance for the party now and for the future —(we are concerned) with how the cult of the person of Stalin has been gradually growing, the cult which became at a certain specific stage the source of a whole series of exceedingly serious and grave perversions of party principles, of party democracy, of revolutionary legality.

Because of the fact that not all as yet realize fully the practical consequences resulting from the cult of the individual, the great harm caused by the violation of the principle of collective direction of the party and because of the accumulation of immense and limitless power in the hands of one person—the Central Committee of the party considers it absolutely necessary to make the material pertaining to this matter available to the 20th Congress of the Communist Party of the Soviet Union.

Allow me first of all to remind you how severely the classics of Marxism-Leninism denounced every manifestation of the cult of the individual. In a letter to the German political worker, Wilhelm Bloss, Marx stated: "From my antipathy to any cult of the individual, I never made public during the existence of the International the numerous addresses from various countries which recognized my merits and which annoyed me. I did not even reply to them, except sometimes to rebuke their authors. Engels and I first joined the secret society of Communists on the condition that everything making for supersti-

[1] U.S. Congress. *Congressional Record,* 84th Congress, 2nd Session, vol. 102, part 7, pp. 9389–9402.

tious worship of authority would be deleted from its statute. Lassalle subsequently did quite the opposite."

Sometime later Engels wrote: "Both Marx and I have always been against any public manifestation with regard to individuals, with the exception of cases when it had an important purpose; and we most strongly opposed such manifestations which during our lifetime concerned us personally."

The great modesty of the genius of the Revolution, Vladimir Ilyich Lenin, is known. Lenin had always stressed the role of the people as the creator of history, the directing and organizational role of the party as a living and creative organism, and also the role of the Central Committee.

Marxism does not negate the role of the leaders of the workers' class in directing the revolutionary liberation movement.

While ascribing great importance to the role of the leaders and organizers of the masses, Lenin at the same time mercilessly stigmatized every manifestation of the cult of the individual, inexorably combated the foreign-to-Marxism views about a "hero" and a "crowd," and countered all efforts to oppose a "hero" to the masses and to the people.

Lenin taught that the party's strength depends on its indissoluble unity with the masses, on the fact that behind the party follow the people—workers, peasants and intelligentsia. "Only he will win and retain the power," said Lenin, "who believes in the people, who submerges himself in the fountain of the living creativeness of the people."

Lenin spoke with pride about the Bolshevik Communist Party as the leader and teacher of the people; he called for the presentation of all the most important questions before the opinion of knowledgeable workers, before the opinion of their party; he said: "We believe in it, we see in it the wisdom, the honor, and the conscience of our epoch."

Lenin resolutely stood against every attempt aimed at belittling or weakening the directing role of the party in the structure of the Soviet state. He worked out Bolshevik principles of party direction and norms of party life, stressing that the guiding principle of party leadership is its collegiality. Already during the prerevolutionary years, Lenin called the central committee of the party a collective of leaders and the guardian and interpreter of party principles. "During the period between congresses," pointed out Lenin, "the central committee guards and interprets the principles of the party."

Underlining the role of the central committee of the party and its authority, Vladimir Ilyich pointed out: "Our central committee constituted itself as a closely centralized and highly authoritative group."

During Lenin's life the central committee of the party was a real expression of collective leadership of the party and of the nation. Being a militant Marxist-revolutionist, always unyielding in matters of principle, Lenin never imposed by force his views upon his co-workers. He tried to convince; he patiently explained his opinions to others. Lenin always diligently observed that the norms of party life were realized, that the party statute was enforced, that the party congresses and the plenary sessions of the central committee took place at the proper intervals.

In addition to the great accomplishments of V. I. Lenin for the victory of the working class and of the working peasants, for the victory of our party and for the application of the ideas of scientific communism to life, his acute mind expressed itself also in this that he detected in Stalin in time those negative characteristics which resulted later in grave consequences. Fearing the future fate of the party and of the Soviet nation, V. I. Lenin made a completely correct characterization of Stalin, pointing out that it was necessary to consider the question of transferring Stalin from the position of Secretary General because of the fact that Stalin is excessively rude, that he does not have a proper attitude toward his comrades, that he is capricious and abuses his power.

In December 1922, in a letter to the party congress, Vladimir Ilyich wrote: "After taking over the position of Secretary General, Comrade Stalin accumulated in his hands immeasurable power and I am not certain whether he will be always able to use this power with the required care."

This letter—a political document of tremendous importance, known in the party history as Lenin's testament—was distributed among the delegates to the Twentieth Party Congress. You have read it and will undoubtedly read it again more than once. You might reflect on Lenin's plain words, in which expression is given to Vladimir Ilyich's anxiety concerning the party, the people, the state, and the future direction of party policy.

Vladimir Ilyich said: "Stalin is excessively rude, and this defect, which can be freely tolerated in our midst and in contacts among us Communists, becomes a defect which cannot be tolerated in one holding the position of the Secretary General. Because of this, I propose that the comrades consider the method by which Stalin would be removed from this position and by which another man would be selected for it, a man, who above all, would differ from Stalin in only one quality, namely, greater tolerance, greater loyalty, greater kindness, and more considerate attitude toward the comrades, a less capricious temper, etc."

This document of Lenin's was made known to the delegates at the 13th Party Congress, who discussed the question of transferring Stalin from the position of Secretary General. The delegates declared themselves in favor of retaining Stalin in this post, hoping that he would heed the critical remarks of Vladimir Ilyich and would be able to overcome the defects which caused Lenin serious anxiety.

Comrades, the party congress should become acquainted with two new documents, which confirm Stalin's character as already outlined by Vladimir Ilyich Lenin in his testament. These documents are a letter from Nadezhda Konstantinovna Krupskaya to [Lev B.] Kamenev, who was at that time head of the Political Bureau, and a personal letter from Vladimir Ilyich Lenin to Stalin.

1. I will now read these documents:
"*Lev Borisovich:*
"Because of a short letter which I had written in words dictated to me by Vladimir Ilyich by permission of the doctors, Stalin allowed himself yesterday an unusually rude outburst directed at me. This is not my first day in the party. During all these 30 years I have never heard from any comrade one word of rudeness. The business of the party and of Ilyich are not less dear to me than to Stalin. I need at present the maximum of self-control. What one can and what one cannot discuss with Ilyich—I know better than any doctor, because I know

what makes him nervous and what does not, in any case I know better than Stalin. I am turning to you and to Grigory [E. Zinoviev] as much closer comrades of V. I. and I beg you to protect me from rude interference with my private life and from vile invectives and threats. I have no doubt as to what will be the unanimous decision of the Control Commission, with which Stalin sees fit to threaten me; however, I have neither the strength nor the time to waste on this foolish quarrel. And I am a living person and my nerves are strained to the utmost.

N. Krupskaya"

Nadezhda Konstantinovna wrote this letter on December 23, 1922. After two and a half months, in March 1923, Vladimir Ilyich Lenin sent Stalin the following letter:

2. The Letter of V. I. Lenin
"To Comrade Stalin:
(*Copies For: Kamenev and Zinoviev.*)
"Dear Comrade Stalin:
You permitted yourself a rude summons of my wife to the telephone and a rude reprimand of her. Despite the fact that she told you that she agreed to forget what was said, nevertheless Zinoviev and Kamenev heard about it from her. I have no intention to forget so easily that which is being done against me, and I need not stress here that I consider as directed against me that which is being done against my wife. I ask you, therefore, that you weigh carefully whether you are agreeable to retracting your words and apologizing or whether you prefer the severance of relations between us. [Commotion in the hall]

Sincerely, Lenin

March 5, 1923
Comrades, I will not comment on these documents. They speak eloquently for themselves. Since Stalin could behave in this manner during Lenin's life, could thus behave toward Nadezhda Konstantinovna Krupskaya, whom the party knows well and values highly as a loyal friend of Lenin and as an active fighter for the cause of the party since its creation—we can easily imagine how Stalin treated other people. These negative characteristics of his developed steadily and during the last years acquired an absolutely insufferable character.

As later events have proven, Lenin's anxiety was justified; in the first period after Lenin's death Stalin still paid attention to his (i.e. Lenin's) advice, but, later he began to disregard the serious admonitions of Vladimir Ilyich.

When we analyze the practice of Stalin in regard to the direction of the party and of the country, when we pause to consider everything which Stalin perpetrated, we must be convinced that Lenin's fears were justified. The negative characteristics of Stalin, which, in Lenin's time, were only incipient, transformed themselves during the last years into a grave abuse of power by Stalin, which caused untold harm to our party.

We have to consider seriously and analyze correctly this matter in order that we may preclude any possibility of a repetition in any form whatever of what took place during the life of Stalin, who absolutely did not tolerate collegiality in leadership and in work, and who practiced brutal violence, not only toward everything which opposed him, but also toward that which seemed, to his capricious and despotic character, contrary to his concepts.

Stalin acted not through persuasion, explanation, and patient cooperation with people, but by imposing his concepts and demanding absolute submission to his opinion. Whoever opposed this concept or tried to prove his viewpoint, and the correctness of his position-was doomed to removal from the leading collective and to subsequent moral and physical annihilation. This was especially true during the period following the 17th party congress, when many prominent party leaders and rank-and-file party workers, honest and dedicated to the cause of communism, fell victim to Stalin's despotism.

We must affirm that the party had fought a serious fight against the Trotskyites, rightists and bourgeois nationalists, and that it disarmed ideologically all the enemies of Leninism. This ideological fight was carried on successfully as a result of which the party became strengthened and tempered. Here Stalin played a positive role.

The party led a great political-ideological struggle against those in its own ranks who proposed anti-Leninist theses, who represented a political line hostile to the party and to the cause of socialism. This was a stubborn and a difficult fight but a necessary one, because the political line of both the Trotskyite-Zinovievite bloc and of the Bukharinites led actually toward the restoration of capitalism and capitulation to the world bourgeoisie. Let us consider for a moment what would have happened if in 1928–1929 the political line of right deviation had prevailed among us, or orientation toward "cotton-dress industrialization," or toward the kulak, etc. We would not now have a powerful heavy industry, we would not have the Kolkhozes, we would find ourselves disarmed and weak in a capitalist encirclement.

It was for this reason that the party led an inexorable ideological fight and explained to all party members and to the non-party masses the harm and the danger of the anti-Leninist proposals of the Trotskyite opposition and the rightist opportunists. And this great work of explaining the party line bore fruit; both Trotskyites and the rightist opportunists were politically isolated; the overwhelming party majority supported the Leninist line and the party was able to awaken and organize the working masses to apply the Leninist party line and to build socialism.

Worth noting is the fact that even during the progress of the furious ideological fight against the Trotskyites, the Zinovievites, the Bukharinites and others, extreme repressive measures were not used against them. The fight was on ideological grounds. But some years later when socialism in our country was fundamentally constructed, when the exploiting classes were generally liquidated, when the Soviet social structure had radically changed, when the social basis for political movements and groups hostile to the party had violently contracted, when the ideological opponents of the party were long since defeated politically—then the repression directed against them began.

It was precisely during this period (1935, 1937, and 1938) that the practice of mass repression through the government apparatus was born, first against the enemies of Leninism—Trotskyites, Zinovievites, Bukharinites, long since politically defeated by the party, and subsequently also against many honest Communists, against those party cadres who had borne the heavy load of the Civil War and the first and most difficult years of industrialization and collectivization, who actively fought against the Trotskyites and the rightists for the Leninist party line.

Stalin originated the concept enemy of the people. This term automatically rendered it unnecessary that the ideological errors of a man or men engaged in a controversy be proven; this term made possible the usage of the most cruel repression, violating all norms of revolutionary legality, against anyone who in any way disagreed with Stalin, against those who were only suspected of hostile intent, against those who had bad reputations. This concept, enemy of the people, actually eliminated the possibility of any kind of ideological fight or the making of one's views known on this or that issue even those of a practical character. In the main, and in actuality, the only proof of guilt used, against all norms of current legal science, was the confession of the accused himself, and, as subsequent probing proved, confessions were acquired through physical pressures against the accused.

This led to glaring violations of revolutionary legality, and to the fact that many entirely innocent persons, who in the past had defended the party line, became victims.

We must assert that in regard to those persons who in their time had opposed the party line, there were often no sufficiently serious reasons for their physical annihilation. The formula "enemy of the people" was specifically introduced for the purpose of physically annihilating such individuals.

It is a fact that many persons who were later annihilated as enemies of the party and people had worked with Lenin during his life. Some of these persons had made errors during Lenin's life, but, despite this, Lenin benefited by their work, he corrected them, and he did everything possible to retain them in the ranks of the party; he induced them to follow him.

In this connection the delegates to the party congress should familiarize themselves with an unpublished note by V. I. Lenin directed to the central committee's political bureau in October 1920. Outlining the duties of the control commission, Lenin wrote that the commission should be transformed into a real organ of party and proletarian conscience.

"As a special duty of the control commission there is recommended a deep, individualized relationship with, and sometimes even a type of therapy for, the representatives of the so-called opposition—those who have experienced a psychological crisis because of failure in their soviet or party career. An effort should be made to quiet them, to explain the matter to them in a way used among comrades, to find for them (avoiding the method of issuing orders) a task for which they are psychologically fitted. Advice and rules relating to this matter are to be formulated by the central committee's organizational bureau, etc."

Everyone knows how irreconcilable Lenin was with the ideological enemies of Marxism, with those who deviated from the correct party line. At the same time, however, Lenin, as is evident from the given document, in his practice of directing the party demanded the most intimate party contact with people who have shown indecision or temporary nonconformity with the party line, but whom it was possible to return to the party path. Lenin advised that such people should be patiently educated without the application of extreme methods.

Lenin's wisdom in dealing with people was evident in his work with cadres.

An entirely different relationship with people characterized Stalin. Lenin's traits—patient work with people, stubborn and painstaking education of them; the ability to induce people to follow him without using compulsion, but rather through the ideological influence on them of the whole collective—were entirely foreign to Stalin. He (Stalin) discarded the Leninist method of convincing and educating; he abandoned the method of ideological struggle for that of administrative violence, mass repressions, and terror. He acted on an increasingly larger scale and more stubbornly through punitive organs, at the same time often violating all existing norms of morality and of Soviet laws.

Arbitrary behavior by one person encouraged and permitted arbitrariness in others. Mass arrests and deportations of many thousands of people, execution without trial and without normal investigation created conditions of insecurity, fear, and even desperation.

This, of course, did not contribute toward unity of the party ranks and of all strata of working people, but on the contrary brought about annihilation and the expulsion from the party of workers who were loyal but inconvenient to Stalin.

Our party fought for the implementation of Lenin's plans for the construction of socialism. This was an ideological fight. Had Leninist principles been observed during the course of this fight, had the party's devotion to principles been skillfully combined with a keen and solicitous concern for people, had they not been repelled and wasted but rather drawn to our side—we certainly would not have had such a brutal violation of revolutionary legality and many thousands of people would not have fallen victim of the method of terror. Extraordinary methods would then have been resorted to only against those people who had in fact committed criminal acts against the Soviet system.

Let us recall some historical facts.

In the days before the October Revolution, two members of the central committee of the Bolshevik Party—Kamenev and Zinoviev—declared themselves against Lenin's plan for an armed uprising. In addition, on October 18 they published in the Menshevik newspaper, *Novaya Zhizn*, a statement declaring that the Bolsheviks were making preparations for an uprising and that they considered it adventuristic. Kamenev and Zinoviev thus disclosed to the enemy the decision of the central committee to stage the uprising, and that the uprising had been organized to take place within the very near future.

This was treason against the party and against the revolution. In this connection, V. I. Lenin wrote: "Kamenev and Zinoviev revealed the decision of the central committee of their party on the armed uprising to Rodzyanko and Kerensky . . ." He put before the central committee the question of Zinoviev's and Kamenev's expulsion from the party.

However, after the great Socialist October revolution, as is known, Zinoviev and Kamenev were given leading positions. Lenin put them in positions in which they carried out most responsible party tasks and participated actively in the work of the leading party and Soviet organs. It is known that

Zinoviev and Kamenev committed a number of other serious errors during Lenin's life. In his testament Lenin warned that "Zinoviev's and Kamenev's October episode was of course not an accident." But Lenin did not pose the question of their arrest and certainly not of their shooting.

Or, let us take the example of the Trotskyites. At present, after a sufficiently long historical period, we can speak about the fight with the Trotskyites with complete calm and can analyze this matter with sufficient objectivity. After all, around Trotsky were people whose origin cannot by any means be traced to bourgeois society. Part of them belonged to the party intelligentsia and a certain part were recruited from among the workers. We can name many individuals who in their time joined the Trotskyites; however, these same individuals took an active part in the workers' movement before the Revolution, during the Socialist October revolution itself, and also in the consolidation of the victory of this greatest of revolutions. Many of them broke with Trotskyism and returned to Leninist positions. Was it necessary to annihilate such people? We are deeply convinced that had Lenin lived such an extreme method would not have been used against many of them.

Such are only a few historical facts. But can it be said that Lenin did not decide to use even the most severe means against enemies of the revolution when this was actually necessary? No, no one can say this. Vladimir Ilyich demanded uncompromising dealings with the enemies of the revolution and of the working class and when necessary resorted ruthlessly to such methods. You will recall only V. I. Lenin's fight with the Socialist Revolutionary organizers of the anti-Soviet uprising, with the counterrevolutionary kulaks in 1918 and with others, when Lenin without hesitation used the most extreme methods against the enemies. Lenin used such methods, however, only against actual class enemies and not against those who blunder, who err, and whom it was possible to lead through ideological influence and even retain in the leadership. Lenin used severe methods only in the most necessary cases, when the exploiting classes were still in existence and were vigorously opposing the revolution, when the struggle for survival was decidedly assuming the sharpest forms, even including a civil war.

Stalin, on the other hand, used extreme methods and mass repressions at a time when the revolution was already victorious, when the Soviet state was strengthened, when the exploiting classes were already liquidated, and socialist relations were rooted solidly in all phases of national economy, when our party was politically consolidated and had strengthened itself both numerically and ideologically. It is clear that here Stalin showed in a whole series of cases his intolerance, his brutality and his abuse of power. Instead of proving his political correctness and mobilizing the masses, he often chose the path of repression and physical annihilation, not only against actual enemies, but also against individuals who had not committed any crimes against the party and the Soviet Government. Here we see no wisdom but only a demonstration of the brutal force which had once so alarmed V. I. Lenin.

Lately, especially after the unmasking of the Beria gang, the Central Committee looked into a series of matters fabricated by this gang. This revealed a very ugly picture of brutal willfulness connected with the incorrect behavior of Stalin. As facts prove, Stalin, using his unlimited power, allowed himself many abuses, acting in the name of the Central Committee, not asking for the opinion of the Committee members nor even of the members of the Central Committee's Political Bureau; often he did not inform them about his personal decisions concerning very important party and government matters.

Considering the question of the cult of an individual, we must first of all show everyone what harm this caused to the interests of our party.

Vladimir Ilyich Lenin had always stressed the party's role and significance in the direction of the Socialist government of workers and peasants; he saw in this the chief precondition for a successful building of socialism in our country. Pointing to the great responsibility of the Bolshevik Party, as ruling party of the Soviet state, Lenin called for the most meticulous observance of all norms of party life; he called for the realization of the principles of collegiality in the direction of the party and the state.

Collegiality of leadership flows from the very nature of our party, a party built on the principles of democratic centralism. "This means," said Lenin, "that all party matters are accomplished by all party members—directly or through representatives—who without any exceptions are subject to the same rules; in addition, all administrative members, all directing collegia, all holders of party positions are elective, they must account for their activities and are recallable."

It is known that Lenin himself offered an example of the most careful observance of these principles. There was no matter so important that Lenin himself decided it without asking for advice and approval of the majority of the Central Committee members or of the members of the Central Committee's Political Bureau. In the most difficult period for our party and our country, Lenin considered it necessary regularly to convoke congresses, party conferences, and plenary sessions of the Central Committee at which all the most important questions were discussed and where resolutions, carefully worked out by the collective of leaders, were approved.

We can recall, for example, the year 1918 when the country was threatened by the attack of the imperialistic interventionists. In this situation the 7th party congress was convened in order to discuss a vitally important matter which could not be postponed—the matter of peace. In 1919, while the civil war was raging, the 8th party congress convened which adopted a new party program, decided such important matters as the relationship with the peasant masses, the organization of the Red Army, the leading role of the party in the work of the Soviets, the correction of the social composition of the party, and other matters. In 1920 the 9th party congress was convened which laid down guiding principles pertaining to the party's work in the sphere of economic construction. In 1921 the 10th party congress accepted Lenin's New Economic Policy and the historical resolution called "About Party Unity."

During Lenin's life, party congresses were convened regularly; always when a radical turn in the development of the party and the country took place, Lenin considered it absolutely necessary that the party discuss at length all the basic matters pertaining to internal and foreign policy and to questions bearing on the development of party and government.

It is very characteristic that Lenin addressed to the party congress as the highest party organ his last articles, letters and remarks. During the period between congresses, the central committee of the party, acting as the most authoritative leading collective, meticulously observed the principles of the party and carried out its policy.

So it was during Lenin's life. Were our party's holy Leninist principles observed after the death of Vladimir Ilyich?

Whereas, during the first few years after Lenin's death, party congresses and central committee plenums took place more or less regularly; later, when Stalin began increasingly to abuse his power, these principles were brutally violated. This was especially evident during the last 15 years of his life. Was it a normal situation when 13 years elapsed between the 18th and 19th party congresses, years during which our party and our country had experienced so many important events? These events demanded categorically that the party should have passed resolutions pertaining to the country's defense during the Patriotic War [World War II] and to peacetime construction after the war. Even after the end of the war a congress was not convened for over seven years. Central committee plenums were hardly ever called. It should be sufficient to mention that during all the years of the Patriotic War not a single central committee plenum took place. It is true that there was an attempt to call a central committee plenum in October 1941, when central committee members from the whole country were called to Moscow. They waited two days for the opening of the plenum, but in vain. Stalin did not even want to meet and talk to the Central Committee members. This fact shows how demoralized Stalin was in the first months of the war and how haughtily and disdainfully he treated the Central Committee members.

In practice, Stalin ignored the norms of party life and trampled on the Leninist principle of collective party leadership.

Stalin's willfulness vis-à-vis the party and its central committee became fully evident after the 17th party congress which took place in 1934.

Having at its disposal numerous data showing brutal willfulness toward party cadres, the central committee has created a party commission under the control of the central committee presidium; it was charged with investigating what made possible the mass repressions against the majority of the central committee members and candidates elected at the 17th Congress of the All-Union Communist Party (Bolsheviks).

The commission has become acquainted with a large quantity of materials in the NKVD archives and with other documents and has established many facts pertaining to the fabrication of cases against Communists, to false accusations, to glaring abuses of socialist legality, which resulted in the death of innocent people. It became apparent that many party, Soviet and economic activists, who were branded in 1937–1938 as "enemies," were actually never enemies, spies, wreckers, etc., but were always honest Communists; they were only so stigmatized and, often, no longer able to bear barbaric tortures, they charged themselves (at the order of the investigative judges—falsifiers) with all kinds of grave and unlikely crimes. The commission has presented to the central committee presidium lengthy and documented materials pertaining to mass repressions against the delegates to the 17th party congress and against members of the central committee elected at that congress. These materials have been studied by the presidium of the central committee.

It was determined that of the 139 members and candidates of the party's Central Committee who were elected at the 17th congress, 98 persons, i.e., 70 per cent, were arrested and shot (mostly in 1937–1938). [Indignation in the Hall.] What was the composition of the delegates to the 17th Congress? It is known that 80 per cent of the voting participants of the 17th Congress joined the party during the years of conspiracy before the revolution and during the civil war; this means before 1921. By social origin the basic mass of the delegates to the congress were workers (60 per cent of the voting members).

For this reason, it was inconceivable that a congress so composed would have elected a central committee a majority of whom would prove to be enemies of the party. The only reason why 70 per cent of central committee members and candidates elected at the 17th Congress were branded as enemies of the party and of the people was because honest Communists were slandered, accusations against them were fabricated, and revolutionary legality was gravely undermined.

The same fate met not only the central committee members but also the majority of the delegates to the 17th party congress. Of 1,966 delegates with either voting or advisory rights, 1,108 persons were arrested on charges of antirevolutionary crimes, *i.e.*, decidedly more than a majority. This very fact shows how absurd, wild and contrary to common sense were the charges of counterrevolutionary crimes made out, as we now see, against a majority of participants at the 17th party congress. [Indignation in the hall.]

We should recall that the 17th party congress is historically known as the Congress of Victors. Delegates to the congress were active participants in the building of our socialist state; many of them suffered and fought for party interests during the pre-Revolutionary years in the conspiracy and at the civil-war fronts; they fought their enemies valiantly and often nervelessly looked into the face of death. How then can we believe that such people could prove to be "two-faced" and had joined the camps of the enemies of socialism during the era after the political liquidation of Zinovievites, Trotskyites and rightists and after the great accomplishments of socialist construction? This was the result of the abuse of power by Stalin, who began to use mass terror against the party cadres.

What is the reason that mass repressions against activists increased more and more after the 17th party congress? It was because at that time Stalin had so elevated himself above the party and above the nation that he ceased to consider either the central committee or the party. While he still reckoned with the opinion of the collective before the 17th congress, after the complete political liquidation of the Trotskyites, Zinovievites and Bukharinites, when as a result of that fight and socialist victories the party achieved unity, Stalin ceased to an ever greater degree to consider the members of the party's central committee and even the members of the Political Bureau. Stalin thought that now he could decide all things alone and all he needed were statisticians; he treated all others in such a way that they could only listen to and praise him.

After the criminal murder of S[ergei] M. Kirov, mass repressions and brutal acts of violation of socialist legality began. On the evening of December 1, 1934, on Stalin's initiative (without the approval of the Political Bureau— which was passed two days later, casually), the Secretary of the Presidium of the Central Executive Committee, Yenukidze, signed the following directive:

"1. Investigative agencies are directed to speed up the cases of those accused of the preparation or execution of acts of terror.

"2. Judicial organs are directed not to hold up the execution of death sentences pertaining to crimes of this category in order to consider the possibility of pardon, because the Presidium of the Central Executive Committee [of the] U.S.S.R. does not consider as possible the receiving of petitions of this sort.

"3. The organs of the Commissariat of Internal Affairs are directed to execute the death sentences against criminals of the above-mentioned category immediately after the passage of sentences."

This directive became the basis for mass acts of abuse against socialist legality. During many of the fabricated court cases the accused were charged with "the preparation" of terroristic acts; this deprived them of any possibility that their cases might be re-examined, even when they stated before the court that their confessions were secured by force, and when, in a convincing manner, they disproved the accusations against them.

It must be asserted that to this day the circumstances surrounding Kirov's murder hide many things which are inexplicable and mysterious and demand a most careful examination. There are reasons for the suspicion that the killer of Kirov, Nikolayev, was assisted by someone from among the people whose duty it was to protect the person of Kirov.

A month and a half before the killing, Nikolayev was arrested on the grounds of suspicious behavior but he was released and not even searched. It is an unusually suspicious circumstance that when the Chekist assigned to protect Kirov was being brought for an interrogation, on December 2, 1934, he was killed in a car accident in which no other occupants of the car were harmed. After the murder of Kirov, top functionaries of the Leningrad NKVD were given very light sentences, but in 1937 they were shot. We can assume that they were shot in order to cover the traces of the organizers of Kirov's killing. [Movement in the hall.]

Mass repressions grew tremendously from the end of 1936 after a telegram from Stalin and [Andrei] Zhdanov, dated from Sochi on September 25, 1936, was addressed to Kaganovich, Molotov and other members of the Political Bureau. The content of the telegram was as follows:

"We deem it absolutely necessary and urgent that Comrade Yezhov be nominated to the post of People's Commissar for Internal Affairs. Yagoda has definitely proved himself to be incapable of unmasking the Trotskyite-Zinovievite bloc. The OGPU is four years behind in this matter. This is noted by all party workers and by the majority of the representatives of the NKVD."

Strictly speaking we should stress that Stalin did not meet with and, therefore, could not know the opinion of party workers.

This Stalinist formulation that the "NKVD is four years behind" in applying mass repression and that there is a necessity for catching up with the neglected work directly pushed the NKVD workers on the path of mass arrests and executions.

We should state that this formulation was also forced on the February-March plenary session of the central committee of the All-Union Communist Party (Bolsheviks) in 1937. The plenary resolution approved it on the basis of

Yezhov's report, "Lessons flowing from the harmful activity, diversion and espionage of the Japanese-German-Trotskyite agents," stating: "The plenum of the central committee of the All-Union Communist Party (Bolsheviks) considers that all facts revealed during the investigation into the matter of an anti-Soviet Trotskyite center and of its followers in the provinces show that the People's Commissariat of Internal Affairs has fallen behind at least four years in the attempt to unmask these most inexorable enemies of the people."

The mass repressions at this time were made under the slogan of a fight against the Trotskyites. Did the Trotskyites at this time actually constitute such a danger to our party and to the Soviet state? We should recall that in 1927, on the eve of the 15th party congress, only some 4,000 votes were cast for the Trotskyite-Zinovievite opposition while there were 724,000 for the party line. During the 10 years which passed between the 15th party congress and the February-March central committee plenum, Trotskyism was completely disarmed; many former Trotskyites had changed their former views and worked in the various sectors building socialism. It is clear that in the situation of socialist victory there was no basis for mass terror in the country.

Stalin's report at the February-March central committee plenum in 1937, "Deficiencies of party work and methods for the liquidation of the Trotskyites and of other two-facers," contained an attempt at theoretical justification of the mass terror policy under the pretext that as we march forward toward socialism class war must allegedly sharpen. Stalin asserted that both history and Lenin taught him this.

Actually Lenin taught that the application of revolutionary violence is necessitated by the resistance of the exploiting classes, and this referred to the era when the exploiting classes existed and were powerful. As soon as the nation's political situation had improved, when in January 1920 the Red Army took Rostov and thus won a most important victory over [White General Anton] Denikin, Lenin instructed [Cheka chief Felix] Dzerzhinsky to stop mass terror and to abolish the death penalty. Lenin justified this important political move of the Soviet state in the following manner in his report at the session of the All-Union Central Executive Committee on February 2, 1920:

"We were forced to use terror because of the terror practiced by the Entente, when strong world powers threw their hordes against us, not avoiding any type of conduct. We would not have lasted two days had we not answered these attempts of officers and White Guardists in a merciless fashion; this meant the use of terror, but this was forced upon us by the terrorist methods of the Entente.

"But as soon as we attained a decisive victory, even before the end of the war, immediately after taking Rostov, we gave up the use of the death penalty and thus proved that we intend to execute our own program in the manner that we promised. We say that the application of violence flows out of the decision to smother the exploiters, the big landowners and the capitalists; as soon as this was accomplished we gave up the use of all extraordinary methods. We have proved this in practice."

Stalin deviated from these clear and plain precepts of Lenin. Stalin put the party and the NKVD up to the use of mass terror when the exploiting classes had been liquidated in our country and when there were no serious reasons for the use of extraordinary mass terror.

This terror was actually directed not at the remnants of the defeated exploiting classes but against the honest workers of the party and of the Soviet state; against them were made lying, slanderous and absurd accusations concerning "two-facedness," "espionage," "sabotage," preparation of fictitious "plots," etc.

At the February-March central committee plenum in 1937 many members actually questioned the rightness of the established course regarding mass repressions under the pretext of combating "two-facedness."

Comrade Postyshev most ably expressed these doubts. He said:

"I have philosophized that the severe years have passed, party members who have lost their backbones have broken down or have joined the camp of the enemy; healthy elements have fought for the party. These were the years of industrialization and collectivization. I never thought it possible that after this severe era had passed Karpov and people like him would find themselves in the camp of the enemy. (Karpov was a worker in the Ukrainian Central Committee whom Postyshev knew well.) And now, according to the testimony, it appears that Karpov was recruited in 1934 by the Trotskyites. I personally do not believe that in 1934 an honest party member who had trod the long road of unrelenting fight against enemies for the party and for socialism would now be in the camp of the enemies. I do not believe it. . . . I cannot imagine how it would be possible to travel with the party during the difficult years and then, in 1934, join the Trotskyites. It is an odd thing. . . ." [Movement in the hall.]

Using Stalin's formulation, namely, that the closer we are to socialism the more enemies we will have, and using the resolution of the February-March Central Committee plenum passed on the basis of Yezhov's report—the *provocateurs* who had infiltrated the state-security organs together with conscienceless careerists began to protect with the party name the mass terror against party cadres, cadres of the Soviet state and the ordinary Soviet citizens. It should suffice to say that the number of arrests based on charges of counterrevolutionary crimes had grown ten times between 1936 and 1937.

It is known that brutal willfulness was practiced against leading party workers. The party statute, approved at the 17th party congress, was based on Leninist principles expressed at the 10th party congress. It stated that, in order to apply an extreme method such as exclusion from the party against a central committee member, against a central committee candidate and against a member of the party control commission, "it is necessary to call a Central Committee plenum and to invite to the plenum all Central Committee candidate members and all members of the Party Control Commission"; only if two-thirds of the members of such a general assembly of responsible party leaders find it necessary, only then can a central committee member or candidate be expelled.

The majority of the Central Committee members and candidates elected at the 17th congress and arrested in 1937–1938 were expelled from the party illegally through the brutal abuse of the party statute, because the question of their expulsion was never studied at the Central Committee plenum.

Now when the cases of some of these so-called "spies" and "saboteurs" were examined it was found that all their cases were fabricated. Confessions of guilt of many arrested and charged with enemy activity were gained with the help of cruel and inhuman tortures.

At the same time Stalin, as we have been informed by members of the Political Bureau of that time, did not show them the statements of many accused political activists when they retracted their confessions before the military tribunal and asked for an objective examination of their cases. There were many such declarations, and Stalin doubtless knew of them.

The central committee considers it absolutely necessary to inform the congress of many such fabricated "cases" against the members of the party's central committee elected at the 17th party congress.

An example of the vile provocation, of odious falsification and of criminal violation of revolutionary legality is the case of the former candidate for the Central Committee Political Bureau, one of the most eminent workers of the party and of the Soviet Government, Comrade Eikhe, who was a party member since 1905. [Commotion in the hall.]

Comrade Eikhe was arrested on April 29, 1938 on the basis of slanderous materials, without the sanction of the Prosecutor of the USSR, which was finally received 15 months after the arrest.

Investigation of Eikhe's case was made in a manner which most brutally violated Soviet legality and was accompanied by willfulness and falsification.

Eikhe was forced under torture to sign ahead of time a protocol of his confession prepared by the investigative judges, in which he and several other eminent party workers were accused of anti-Soviet activity.

On October 1, 1939 Eikhe sent his declaration to Stalin in which he categorically denied his guilt and asked for an examination of his case. In the declaration he wrote: "There is no more bitter misery than to sit in the jail of a government for which I have always fought."

A second declaration of Eikhe has been preserved which he sent to Stalin on October 27, 1939; in it he cited facts very convincingly and countered the slanderous accusations made against him, arguing that this provocatory accusation was on the one hand the work of real Trotskyites whose arrests he had sanctioned as First Secretary of the West Siberian Krai [Territory] Party Committee and who conspired in order to take revenge on him, and, on the other hand, the result of the base falsification of materials by the investigative judges.

Eikhe wrote in his declaration: ". . . On October 25 of this year I was informed that the investigation in my case has been concluded and I was given access to the materials of this investigation. Had I been guilty of only one hundredth of the crimes with which I am charged, I would not have dared to send you this pre-execution declaration; however, I have not been guilty of even one of the things with which I am charged and my heart is clean of even the shadow of baseness. I have never in my life told you a word of falsehood, and now, finding my two feet in the grave, I am also not lying. My whole case is a typical example of provocation, slander and violation of the elementary basis of revolutionary legality. . . .

". . . The confessions which were made part of my file are not only absurd but contain some slander toward the Central Committee of the All-Union Communist Party (Bolsheviks) and toward the Council of People's

Commissars, because correct resolutions of the Central Committee of the All-Union Communist Party (Bolsheviks) and of the Council of People's Commissars which were not made on my initiative and without my participation are presented as hostile acts of counterrevolutionary organizations made at my suggestion. . . .

"I am now alluding to the most disgraceful part of my life and to my really grave guilt against the party and against you. This is my confession of counterrevolutionary activity. . . . The case is as follows: Not being able to suffer the tortures to which I was submitted by Ushakov and Nikolayev—and especially by the first one—who utilized the knowledge that my broken ribs have not properly mended and have caused me great pain—I have been forced to accuse myself and others.

"The majority of my confession has been suggested or dictated by Ushakov, and the remainder is my reconstruction of NKVD materials from Western Siberia for which I assumed all responsibility. If some part of the story which Ushakov fabricated and which I signed did not properly hang together, I was forced to sign another variation. The same thing was done to Rukhimovich, who was at first designated as a member of the reserve net and whose name later was removed without telling me anything about it; the same was also done with the leader of the reserve net, supposedly created by Bukharin in 1935. At first I wrote my name in, and then I was instructed to insert Mezhlauk. There were other similar incidents.

"I am asking and begging you that you again examine my case, and this not for the purpose of sparing me but in order to unmask the vile provocation which, like a snake, wound itself around many persons in a great degree due to my meanness and criminal slander. I have never betrayed you or the party. I know that I perish because of vile and mean work of the enemies of the party and of the people, who fabricated the provocation against me."

It would appear that such an important declaration was worth an examination by the Central Committee. This, however, was not done, and the declaration was transmitted to Beria while the terrible maltreatment of the Political Bureau candidate, Comrade Eikhe, continued.

On February 2, 1940 Eikhe was brought before the court. Here he did not confess any guilt and said as follows:

"In all the so-called confessions of mine there is not one letter written by me with the exception of my signatures under the protocols, which were forced from me. I have made my confession under pressure from the investigative judge, who from the time of my arrest tormented me. After that I began to write all this nonsense. The most important thing for me is to tell the court, the party and Stalin that I am not guilty. I have never been guilty of any conspiracy. I will die believing in the truth of party policy as I have believed in it during my whole life."

On February 4 Eikhe was shot. [Indignation in the hall.]

It has been definitely established now that Eikhe's case was fabricated; he has been posthumously rehabilitated.

Comrade Rudzutak, candidate-member of the Political Bureau, member of the party since 1905, who spent 10 years in a Tsarist hard-labor camp, completely retracted in court the confession which was forced from him. The protocol of the session of the Collegium of the Supreme Military Court contains the following statement by Rudzutak:

"The only plea which he places before the court is that the Central Committee of the All-Union Communist Party (Bolsheviks) be informed that there is in the NKVD an as yet not liquidated center which is craftily manufacturing cases, which forces innocent persons to confess; there is no opportunity to prove one's non-participation in crimes to which the confessions of various persons testify. The investigative methods are such that they force people to lie and to slander entirely innocent persons in addition to those who already stand accused. He asks the Court that he be allowed to inform the Central Committee of the All-Union Communist Party (Bolsheviks) about all this in writing. He assures the Court that he personally never had any evil designs in regard to the policy of our party because he had always agreed with the party policy pertaining to all spheres of economic and cultural activity."

This declaration of Rudzutak was ignored, despite the fact that Rudzutak was in his time the chief of the Central Control Commission, which was called into being in accordance with Lenin's concept for the purpose of fighting for party unity. In this manner fell the chief of this highly authoritative party organ, a victim of brutal willfulness; he was not even called before the Central Committee's Political Bureau because Stalin did not want to talk to him. Sentence was pronounced on him in 20 minutes and he was shot. [Indignation in the hall.]

After careful examination of the case in 1955, it was established that the accusation against Rudzutak was false and that it was based on slanderous materials. Rudzutak has been rehabilitated posthumously.

The way in which the former NKVD workers manufactured various fictitious "anti-Soviet centers" and "blocs" with the help of provocatory methods is seen from the confession of Comrade Rozenblum, party member since 1906, who was arrested in 1937 by the Leningrad NKVD.

During the examination in 1955 of the Komarov case Rozenblum revealed the following fact: When Rozenblum was arrested in 1937, he was subjected to terrible torture during which he was ordered to confess false information concerning himself and other persons. He was then brought to the office of Zakovsky, who offered him freedom on condition that he make before the court a false confession fabricated in 1937 by the NKVD concerning "sabotage, espionage and diversion in a terroristic center in Leningrad." [Movement in the hall.] With unbelievable cynicism, Zakovsky told about the vile "mechanism" for the crafty creation of fabricated "anti-Soviet plots."

"In order to illustrate it to me," stated Rozenblum, "Zakovsky gave me several possible variants of the organization of this center and of its branches. After he detailed the organization to me, Zakovsky told me that the NKVD would prepare the case of this center, remarking that the trial would be public. Before the court were to be brought 4 or 5 members of this center: Chudov, Ugarov, Smorodin, Pozern, Shaposhnikova (Chudov's wife) and others together with 2 or 3 members from the branches of this center. . . .

". . . The case of the Leningrad center has to be built solidly, and for this reason witnesses are needed. Social origin (of course, in the past) and the party standing of the witness will play more than a small role.

" 'You, yourself,' said Zakovsky, 'will not need to invent anything. The NKVD will prepare for you a ready outline for every branch of the center; you will have to study it carefully and to remember well all questions and answers which the Court might ask. This case will be ready in four-five months, or perhaps a half year. During all this time you will be preparing yourself so that you will not compromise the investigation and yourself. Your future will depend on how the trial goes and on its results. If you begin to lie and to testify falsely, blame yourself. If you manage to endure it, you will save your head and we will feed and clothe you at the Government's cost until your death.' "

This is the kind of vile things which were then practiced. [Movement in the hall.]

Even more widely was the falsification of cases practiced in the provinces. The NKVD headquarters of the Sverdlov Oblast discovered the so-called Ural uprising staff—and organ of the bloc of rightists, Trotskyites, Socialist Revolutionaries, church leaders—whose chief supposedly was the Secretary of the Sverdlov Oblast Party Committee and a member of the Central Committee, All-Union Communist Party (Bolsheviks), Kabakov, who had been a party member since 1914. The investigative materials of that time show that in almost all *krais, oblasts* [provinces] and republics there supposedly existed rightist Trotskyite, espionage-terror and diversionary-sabotage organizations and centers and that the heads of such organizations as a rule—for no known reason—were first secretaries of *oblast* or republic Communist party committees or central committees. [Movement in the hall.]

Many thousands of honest and innocent Communists have died as a result of this monstrous falsification of such "cases," as a result of the fact that all kinds of slanderous "confessions" were accepted, and as a result of the practice of forcing accusations against oneself and others. In the same manner were fabricated the "cases" against eminent party and state workers—Kossior, Chubar, Postyshev, Kosarev and others.

In those years repressions on a mass scale were applied which were based on nothing tangible and which resulted in heavy cadre losses to the party.

The vicious practice was condoned of having the NKVD prepare lists of persons whose cases were under the jurisdiction of the Military Collegium and whose sentences were prepared in advance. Yezhov would send these lists to Stalin personally for his approval of the proposed punishment. In 1937–1938, 383 such lists containing the names of many thousands of party, Soviet, Komsomol, army and economic workers were sent to Stalin. He approved these lists.

A large part of these cases are being reviewed now and a great part of them are being voided because they were baseless and falsified. Suffice it to say that from 1954 to the present time the Military Collegium of the Supreme Court has rehabilitated 7,679 persons, many of whom were rehabilitated posthumously.

Mass arrests of party, Soviet, economic and military workers caused tremendous harm to our country and to the cause of socialist advancement.

Mass repressions had a negative influence on the moral-political condition of the party, created a situation of uncertainty, contributed to the spreading of unhealthy suspicion, and sowed distrust among Communists. All sorts of slanderers and careerists were active.

Resolutions of the January plenum of the Central Committee, All-Union Communist Party (Bolsheviks), in 1938 had brought some measure of improvement to the party organizations. However, widespread repression also existed in 1938.

Only because our party has at its disposal such great moral-political strength was it possible for it to survive the difficult events in 1937–1938 and to educate new cadres. There is, however, no doubt that our march forward toward socialism and toward the preparation of the country's defense would have been much more successful were it not for the tremendous loss in the cadres suffered as a result of the baseless and false mass repressions in 1937 –1938.

We are justly accusing Yezhov for the degenerate practices of 1937. But we have to answer these questions: Could Yezhov have arrested Kossior, for instance, without the knowledge of Stalin? Was there an exchange of opinions or a Political Bureau decision concerning this? No, there was not, as there was none regarding other cases of this type. Could Yezhov have decided such important matters as the fate of such eminent party figures? No, it would be a display of naivete to consider this the work of Yezhov alone. It is clear that these matters were decided by Stalin, and that without his orders and his sanction Yezhov could not have done this.

We have examined the cases and have rehabilitated Kossior, Rudzutak, Postyshev, Kosarev and others. For what causes were they arrested and sentenced? The review of evidence shows that there was no reason for this. They, like many others, were arrested without the prosecutor's knowledge.

In such a situation, there is no need for any sanction, for what sort of a sanction could there be when Stalin decided everything? He was the chief prosecutor in these cases. Stalin not only agreed to, but on his own initiative issued, arrest orders. We must say this so that the delegates to the congress can clearly undertake and themselves assess this and draw the proper conclusions.

Facts prove that many abuses were made on Stalin's orders without reckoning with any norms of party and Soviet legality. Stalin was a very distrustful man, sickly suspicious; we knew this from our work with him. He could look at a man and say: "Why are your eyes so shifty today?" or "Why are you turning so much today and avoiding to look me directly in the eyes?" The sickly suspicion created in him a general distrust even toward eminent party workers whom he had known for years. Everywhere and in everything he saw "enemies," "two-facers" and "spies." Possessing unlimited power he indulged in great willfulness and choked a person morally and physically. A situation was created where one could not express one's own will.

When Stalin said that one or another should be arrested, it was necessary to accept on faith that he was an "enemy of the people." Meanwhile, Beria's gang, which ran the organs of state security, outdid itself in proving the guilt of the arrested and the truth of materials which it falsified. And what proofs were offered? The confessions of the arrested, and the investigative judges accepted these "confessions." And how is it possible that a person confesses to crimes which he has not committed? Only in one way—because of application of physical methods of pressuring him, tortures bringing him to a state of unconsciousness, deprivation of his judgment, taking away of his human dignity. In this manner were "confessions" acquired.

When the wave of mass arrests began to recede in 1939, and the leaders of territorial party organizations began to accuse the NKVD workers of using methods of physical pressure on the arrested. Stalin dispatched a coded telegram on January 20, 1939 to the committee secretaries of *oblasts* and *krais,* to the central committees of republic Communist parties, to the People's Commissars of Internal Affairs and to the heads of NKVD organizations. This telegram stated:

"The Central Committee of the All-Union Communist Party (Bolsheviks) explains that the application of methods of physical pressure in NKVD practice is permissible from 1937 on in accordance with permission of the Central Committee of the All-Union Communist Party (Bolsheviks) . . . It is known that all bourgeois intelligence services use methods of physical influence against the representatives of the socialist proletariat and that they use them in their most scandalous forms. The question arises as to why the socialist intelligence service should be more humanitarian against the mad agents of the bourgeoisie, against the deadly enemies of the working class and of the *kolkhoz* workers. The Central Committee of the All-Union Communist Party (Bolsheviks) considers that physical pressure should still be used obligatorily, as an exception applicable to known and obstinate enemies of the people, as a method both justifiable and appropriate."

Thus, Stalin had sanctioned in the name of the Central Committee of the All-Union Communist Party (Bolsheviks) the most brutal violation of socialist legality, torture and oppression, which led as we have seen to the slandering and self-accusation of innocent people.

Not long ago—only several days before the present Congress—we called to the Central Committee Presidium session and interrogated the investigative judge Rodos, who in his time investigated and interrogated Kossior, Chubar and Kosarev. He is a vile person, with the brain of a bird, and morally completely degenerate. And it was this man who was deciding the fate of prominent party workers; he was making judgments also concerning the politics in these matters, because having established their "crime," he provided therewith materials from which important political implications could be drawn.

The question arises whether a man with such an intellect could alone make the investigation in a manner to prove the guilt of people such as Kossior and others. No; he could not have done it without proper directives. At the Central Committee Presidium session he told us: "I was told that Kossior and Chubar were people's enemies and for this reason I, as an investigative judge, had to make them confess that they are enemies." [Indignation in the hall.]

He could do this only through long tortures, which he did, receiving detailed instructions from Beria. We must say that at the Central Committee Presidium session he cynically declared: "I thought that I was executing the orders of the party." In this manner, Stalin's orders concerning the use of methods of physical pressure against the arrested were in practice executed.

These and many other facts show that all norms of correct party solution of problems were invalidated and everything was dependent upon the willfulness of one man.

The power accumulated in the hands of one person, Stalin, led to serious consequences during the Great Patriotic War.

When we look at many of our novels, films and historical "scientific studies," the role of Stalin in the Patriotic War appears to be entirely improbable. Stalin had foreseen everything. The Soviet Army, on the basis of a strategic plan prepared by Stalin long before, used the tactics of so-called "active defense," i.e., tactics which, as we know, allowed the Germans to come up to Moscow and Stalingrad. Using such tactics, the Soviet Army, supposedly thanks only to Stalin's genius, turned to the offensive and subdued the enemy. The epic victory gained through the armed might of the land of the Soviets, through our heroic people, is ascribed in this type of novel, film and "scientific study" as being completely due to the strategic genius of Stalin.

We have to analyze this matter carefully because it has a tremendous significance not only from the historical, but especially from the political, educational and practical point of view. What are the facts of this matter?

Before the war, our press and all our political-educational work was characterized by its bragging tone: When an enemy violates the holy Soviet soil, then for every blow of the enemy we will answer with three blows, and we will battle the enemy on his soil and we will win without much harm to ourselves. But these positive statements were not based in all areas on concrete facts, which would actually guarantee the immunity of our borders.

During the war and after the war, Stalin put forward the thesis that the tragedy which our nation experienced in the first part of the war was the result of the "unexpected" attack of the Germans against the Soviet Union. But, comrades, this is completely untrue. As soon as Hitler came to power in Germany he assigned to himself the task of liquidating Communism. The fascists were saying this openly; they did not hide their plans. In order to attain this aggressive end, all sorts of pacts and blocs were created, such as the famous Berlin-Rome-Tokyo Axis. Many facts from the prewar period clearly showed that Hitler was going all out to begin a war against the Soviet state, and that he had concentrated large armed units, together with armored units, near the Soviet borders.

Documents which have now been published show that by April 3, 1941 Churchill, through his ambassador to the USSR, Cripps, personally warned Stalin that the Germans had begun regrouping their armed units with the intent of attacking the Soviet Union. It is self-evident that Churchill did not do this at all because of his friendly feeling toward the Soviet nation. He had in this his own imperialistic goals—to bring Germany and the USSR into a bloody war and thereby to strengthen the position of the British Empire. Just the same, Churchill affirmed in his writings that he sought to warn Stalin and call his attention to the danger which threatened him. Churchill stressed this repeatedly in his dispatches of April 18 and in the following days. However, Stalin took no heed of these warnings. What is more, Stalin ordered that no credence be given to information of this sort, in order not to provoke the initiation of military operations.

We must assert that information of this sort concerning the threat of

German armed invasion of Soviet territory was coming in also from our own military and diplomatic sources; however, because the leadership was conditioned against such information, such data was dispatched with fear and assessed with reservation.

Thus, for instance, information sent from Berlin on May 6, 1941 by the Soviet military attache, Captain Vorontsov, stated: "Soviet citizen Bozer . . . communicated to the deputy naval attache that, according to a statement of a certain German officer from Hitler's headquarters, Germany is preparing to invade the USSR on May 14 through Finland, the Baltic countries and Latvia. At the same time Moscow and Leningrad will be heavily raided and paratroopers landed in border cities . . ."

In his report of May 22, 1941, the deputy military attache in Berlin, Khlopov, communicated that ". . . the attack of the German Army is reportedly scheduled for June 15, but it is possible that it may begin in the first days of June . . ."

A cable from our London Embassy dated June 18, 1941 stated: "As of now Cripps is deeply convinced of the inevitability of armed conflict between Germany and the USSR, which will begin not later than the middle of June. According to Cripps, the Germans have presently concentrated 147 divisions (including air force and service units) along the Soviet borders."

Despite these particularly grave warnings, the necessary steps were not taken to prepare the country properly for defense and to prevent it from being caught unaware.

Did we have time and the capabilities for such preparations? Yes; we had the time and capabilities. Our industry was already so developed that it was capable of supplying fully the Soviet Army with everything that it needed. This is proven by the fact that, although during the war we lost almost half of our industry and important industrial and food-production areas as the result of enemy occupation of the Ukraine, Northern Caucasus and other western parts of the country, the Soviet nation was still able to organize the production of military equipment in the eastern parts of the country, install there equipment taken from the western industrial areas, and to supply our armed forces with everything which was necessary to destroy the enemy.

Had our industry been mobilized properly and in time to supply the Army with the necessary materiel, our wartime losses would have been decidedly smaller. Such mobilization had not been, however, started in time. And already in the first days of the war it became evident that our Army was badly armed, that we did not have enough artillery, tanks and planes to throw the enemy back.

Soviet science and technology produced excellent models of tanks and artillery pieces before the war. But mass production of all this was not organized, and, as a matter of fact, we started to modernize our military equipment only on the eve of the war. As a result, at the time of the enemy's invasion of the Soviet land we did not have sufficient quantities either of old machinery which was no longer used for armament production or of new machinery which we had planned to introduce into armament production. The situation with anti-aircraft artillery was especially bad; we did not organize the production of anti-tank ammunition. Many fortified regions had proven to be indefensible as soon as they were attacked, because the old arms had been withdrawn and new ones were not yet available there.

This pertained, alas, not only to tanks, artillery and planes. At the outbreak of the war we did not even have sufficient numbers of rifles to arm the mobilized manpower. I recall that in those days I telephoned Comrade Malenkov from Kiev and told him, "People have volunteered for the new Army and demand arms. You must send us arms."

Malenkov answered me, "We cannot send you arms. We are sending all our rifles to Leningrad and you have to arm yourselves." [Movement in the hall.]

Such was the armament situation.

In this connection we cannot forget, for instance, the following fact. Shortly before the invasion of the Soviet Union by the Hitlerite army, Korponos, who was chief of the Kiev Special Military District (he was later killed at the front), wrote to Stalin that the German armies were at the Bug River, were preparing for an attack and in the very near future would probably start their offensive. In this connection, Korponos proposed that a strong defense be organized, that 300,000 people be evacuated from the border areas and that several strong points be organized there: anti-tank ditches, trenches for the soldiers, etc.

Moscow answered this proposition with the assertion that this would be a provocation, that no preparatory defensive work should be undertaken at the borders, that the Germans were not to be given any pretext for the initiation of military action against us. Thus, our borders were insufficiently prepared to repel the enemy.

When the fascist armies had actually invaded Soviet territory and military operations began, Moscow issued the order that the German fire was not to be returned. Why? It was because Stalin, despite evident facts, thought that the war had not yet started, that this was only a provocative action, on the part of several undisciplined sections of the German Army, and that our reaction might serve as a reason for the Germans to begin the war.

The following fact is also known. On the eve of the invasion of the territory of the Soviet Union by the Hitlerite army, a certain German citizen crossed our border and stated that the German armies had received orders to start the offensive against the Soviet Union on the night of June 22 at 3 o'clock. Stalin was informed about this immediately, but even this warning was ignored.

As you see, everything was ignored; warnings of certain Army commanders, declarations of deserters from the enemy army, and even the open hostility of the enemy. Is this an example of the alertness of the chief of the party and of the state at this particularly significant historical moment?

And what were the results of this carefree attitude, this disregard of clear facts? The result was that already in the first hours and days the enemy had destroyed in our border regions a large part of our Air Force, artillery and other military equipment; he annihilated large numbers of our military cadres and disorganized our military leadership; consequently we could not prevent the enemy from marching deep into the country.

Very grievous consequences, especially in reference to the beginning of the war, followed Stalin's annihilation of many military commanders and political workers during 1937–1941 because of his suspiciousness and through slanderous accusations. During these years repressions were instituted against certain parts of military cadres beginning literally at the company and battalion commander level and extending to the higher military centers; during this time the cadre of leaders who had gained military experience in Spain and in the Far East was almost completely liquidated.

The policy of large-scale repression against the military cadres led also to undermined military discipline, because for several years officers of all ranks and even soldiers in the party and Komsomol cells were taught to unmask their superiors as hidden enemies. [Movement in the hall.] It is natural that this caused a negative influence on the state of military discipline in the first war period.

And, as you know, we had before the war excellent military cadres which were unquestionably loyal to the party and to the fatherland. Suffice it to say that those of them who managed to survive, despite severe tortures to which they were subjected in the prisons, have from the first war days shown themselves real patriots and heroically fought for the glory of the fatherland; I have here in mind such comrades as Rokossovsky (who, as you know, had been jailed), Gorbatov, Maretskov (who is a delegate at the present Congress), Podlas (he was an excellent commander who perished at the front), and many, many others. However, many such commanders perished in camps and jails and the Army saw them no more.

All this brought about the situation which existed at the beginning of the war and which was the great threat to our Fatherland.

It would be incorrect to forget that, after the first severe disaster and defeats at the front, Stalin thought that this was the end. In one of his speeches in those days he said: "All that which Lenin created we have lost forever."

After this Stalin for a long time actually did not direct the military operations and ceased to do anything whatever. He returned to active leadership only when some members of the Political Bureau visited him and told him that it was necessary to take certain steps immediately in order to improve the situation at the front.

Therefore, the threatening danger which hung over our fatherland in the first period of the war was largely due to the faulty methods of directing the nation and the party by Stalin himself.

However, we speak not only about the moment when the war began, which led to serious disorganization of our Army and brought us severe losses. Even after the war began, the nervousness and hysteria which Stalin demonstrated, interfering with actual military operation, caused our Army serious damage.

Stalin was very far from an understanding of the real situation which was developing at the front. This was natural because, during the whole Patriotic War, he never visited any section of the front or any liberated city except for one short ride on the Mozhaisk highway during a stabilized situation at the front. To this incident were dedicated many literary works full of fantasies of all sorts and so many paintings. Simultaneously, Stalin was interfering with operations and issuing orders which did not take into consideration the real situation at a given section of the front and which could not help but result in huge personnel losses.

I will allow myself in this connection to bring out one characteristic fact which illustrates how Stalin directed operations at the fronts. There is present at this Congress Marshal Bagramian, who was once the chief of operations in the headquarters of the southwestern front and who can corroborate what I will tell you.

When there developed an exceptionally serious situation for our Army in 1942 in the Kharkov region, we had correctly decided to drop an operation whose objective was to encircle Kharkov, because the real situation at that time would have threatened our Army with fatal consequences if this operation were continued.

We communicated this to Stalin, stating that the situation demanded changes in operational plans so that the enemy would be prevented from liquidating a sizable concentration of our Army.

Contrary to common sense, Stalin rejected our suggestion and issued the order to continue the operation aimed at the encirclement of Kharkov, despite the fact that at this time many Army concentrations were themselves actually threatened with encirclement and liquidation.

I telephoned to Vasilevsky and begged him—"Alexander Mikhailovich, take a map (Vasilevsky is present here) and show Comrade Stalin the situation which has developed." We should note that Stalin planned operations on a globe. [Animation in the hall.] Yes, comrades, he used to take the globe and trace the front line on it. I said to Comrade Vasilevsky: "Show him the situation on a map; in the present situation we cannot continue the operation which was planned. The old decision must be changed for the good of the cause."

Vasilevsky replied, saying that Stalin had already studied this problem and that he, Vasilevsky, would not see Stalin further concerning this matter, because the latter didn't want to hear any arguments on the subject of this operation.

After my talk with Vasilevsky, I telephoned to Stalin at his villa. But Stalin did not answer the telephone and Malenkov was at the receiver. I told Comrade Malenkov that I was calling from the front and that I wanted to speak personally to Stalin. Stalin informed me through Malenkov that I should speak with Malenkov. I stated for the second time that I wished to inform Stalin personally about the grave situation which had arisen for us at the front. But Stalin did not consider it convenient to raise the phone and again stated that I should speak to him through Malenkov, although he was only a few steps from the telephone.

After "listening" in this manner to our plea, Stalin said: "Let everything remain as it is!"

And what was the result of this? The worst that we had expected. The Germans surrounded our Army concentrations and consequently we lost hundreds of thousands of our soldiers. This is Stalin's military "genius"; this is what it cost us. [Movement in the hall.]

On one occasion after the war, during a meeting of Stalin with members of the Political Bureau, Anastas Ivanovich Mikoyan mentioned that Khrushchev must have been right when he telephoned concerning the Kharkov operation and that it was unfortunate that his suggestion had not been accepted.

You should have seen Stalin's fury. How could it be admitted that he, Stalin, had not been right. He is after all a "genius," and a genius cannot help but be right! Everyone can err, but Stalin considered that he never erred, that he was always right. He never acknowledged to anyone that he made any mistake, large or small, despite the fact that he made not a few mistakes in the matter of theory and in his practical activity. After the Party Congress we shall probably have to re-evaluate many wartime military operations and to present them in their true light.

The tactics on which Stalin insisted without knowing the essence of the conduct of battle operations cost us much blood until we succeeded in stopping the opponent and going over to the offensive.

The military know that already by the end of 1941, instead of great operational maneuvers flanking the opponent and penetrating behind his back, Stalin demanded incessant frontal attacks and the capture of one village after another. Because of this, we paid with great losses until our generals, on whose shoulders rested the whole weight of conducting the war, succeeded in changing the situation and shifting to flexible-maneuver operations, which immediately brought serious changes at the front favorable to us.

All the more shameful was the fact that, after our great victory over the enemy which cost us so much, Stalin began to downgrade many of the commanders who contributed so much to the victory over the enemy, because Stalin excluded every possibility that services rendered at the front should be credited to anyone but himself.

Stalin was very much interested in the assessment of Comrade Zhukov as a military leader. He asked me often for my opinion of Zhukov. I told him then, "I have known Zhukov for a long time; he is a good general and a good military leader."

After the war Stalin began to tell all kinds of nonsense about Zhukov, among others the following, "You praised Zhukov, but he does not deserve it. It is said that before each operation at the front Zhukov used to behave as follows: He used to take a handful of earth, smell it and say, 'We can begin the attack,' or the opposite, 'The planned operation cannot be carried out.'" I stated at that time, "Comrade Stalin, I do not know who invented this, but it is not true."

It is possible that Stalin himself invented these things for the purpose of minimizing the role and military talents of Marshal Zhukov.

In this connection, Stalin very energetically popularized himself as a great leader; in various ways he tried to inculcate in the people the version that all victories gained by the Soviet nation during the Great Patriotic War were due to the courage, daring and genius of Stalin and of no one else. Exactly like Kuzma Kryuchkov he put one dress on seven people at the same time. [Animation in the hall.]

In the same vein, let us take, for instance, our historical and military films and some literary creations; they make us feel sick. Their true objective is the propagation of the theme of praising Stalin as a military genius. Let us recall the film, *The Fall of Berlin*. Here only Stalin acts; he issues orders in the hall in which there are many empty chairs and only one man approached him and reports something to him—that is Poskrebyshev, his loyal shield-bearer. [Laughter in the hall.]

And where is the military command? Where is the Political Bureau? Where is the Government? What are they doing and with what are they engaged? There is nothing about them in the film. Stalin acts for everybody; he does not reckon with anyone; he asks no one for advice. Everything is shown to the nation in this false light. Why? In order to surround Stalin with glory, contrary to the facts and contrary to historical truth.

The question arises: And where are the military, on whose shoulders rested the burden of the war? They are not in the film; with Stalin in, no room was left for them.

Not Stalin, but the party as a whole, the Soviet Government, our heroic Army, its talented leaders and brave soldiers, the whole Soviet nation—these are the ones who assured the victory in the Great Patriotic War. [Tempestuous and prolonged applause.]

The Central Committee members, ministers, our economic leaders, leaders of Soviet culture, directors of territorial-party and Soviet organizations, engineers, and technicians—every one of them in his own place of work generously gave of his strength and knowledge toward ensuring victory over the enemy.

Exceptional heroism was shown by our hard core—surrounded by glory is our whole working class, our *kolkhoz* peasantry, the Soviet intelligentsia, who under the leadership of party organizations overcame untold hardships, and, bearing the hardships of war, devoted all their strength to the cause of the defense of the fatherland.

Great and brave deeds during the war were accomplished by our Soviet women who bore on their backs the heavy load of production work in the factories, on the *kolkhozes,* and in various economic and cultural sectors; many women participated directly in the Great Patriotic War at the fronts; our brave youth contributed immeasurably at the front and at home to the defense of the Soviet fatherland and to the annihilation of the enemy.

Immortal are the services of the Soviet soldiers, of our commanders and political workers of all ranks; after the loss of a considerable part of the Army in the first war months they did not lose their heads and were able to reorganize during the progress of combat; they created and toughened during the progress of the war a strong and heroic Army and not only stood off pressure of the strong and cunning enemy but also smashed him.

The magnificent and heroic deeds of hundreds of millions of people of the East and of the West during the fight against the threat of fascist subjugation which loomed before us will live centuries and millennia in the memory of thankful humanity. [Thunderous applause.]

The main role and the main credit for the victorious ending of the war belongs to our Communist Party, to the armed forces of the Soviet Union, and to the tens of millions of Soviet people raised by the party. [Thunderous and prolonged applause.]

Comrades, let us reach for some other facts. The Soviet Union is justly considered as a model of a multinational state because we have in practice assured the equality and friendship of all nations which live in our great fatherland.

All the more monstrous are the acts whose initiator was Stalin and which are rude violations of the basic Leninist principles of the nationality policy of the Soviet state. We refer to the mass deportations from their native places of whole nations, together with all Communists and Komsomols without any exception; this deportation action was not dictated by any military considerations.

Thus, already at the end of 1943, when there occurred a permanent breakthrough at the fronts of the Great Patriotic War benefiting the Soviet Union, a decision was taken and executed concerning the deportation of all the Karachai from the lands on which they lived.

In the same period, at the end of December 1943, the same lot befell the whole population of the Autonomous Kalmyk Republic. In March 1944, all the Chechen and Ingush peoples were deported and the Chechen-Ingush Autonomous Republic was liquidated. In April 1944, all Balkars were deported to faraway places from the territory of the Kabardino-Balkar Autonomous Republic and the Republic itself was renamed the Autonomous Kabardian Republic.

The Ukrainians avoided meeting this fate only because there were too many of them and there was no place to which to deport them. Otherwise, he would have deported them also. [Laughter and animation in the hall.]

Not only a Marxist-Leninist but also no man of common sense can grasp how it is possible to make whole nations responsible for inimical activity, including women, children, old people, Communists and Komsosols, to use mass repression against them, and to expose them to misery and suffering for the hostile acts of individual persons or groups of persons.

After the conclusion of the Patriotic War, the Soviet nation stressed with pride the magnificent victories gained through great sacrifices and tremendous efforts. The country experienced a period of political enthusiasm. The party came out of the war even more united; in the fire of the war, party cadres were tempered and hardened. Under such conditions nobody could have even thought of the possibility of some plot in the party.

And it was precisely at this time that the so-called "Leningrad affair" was born. As we have now proven, this case was fabricated. Those who innocently lost their lives included Comrades Voznesensky, Kuznetsov, Rodionov, Popkov, and others.

As is known, Voznesensky and Kuznetsov were talented and eminent leaders. Once they stood very close to Stalin. It is sufficient to mention that Stalin made Voznesensky first deputy to the chairman of the Council of Ministers and Kuznetsov was elected Secretary of the Central Committee. The very fact that Stalin entrusted Kuznetsov with the supervision of the state-security organs shows the trust which he enjoyed.

How did it happen that these persons were branded as enemies of the people and liquidated?

Facts prove that the "Leningrad affair" is also the result of willfulness which Stalin exercised against party cadres. Had a normal situation existed in the party's Central Committee and in the Central Committee Political Bureau, affairs of this nature would have been examined there in accordance with party practice, and all pertinent facts assessed; as a result, such an affair as well as others would not have happened.

We must state that, after the war, the situation became even more complicated. Stalin became even more capricious, irritable and brutal; in particular his suspicion grew. His persecution mania reached unbelievable dimensions. Many workers were becoming enemies before his very eyes. After the war, Stalin separated himself from the collective even more. Everything was decided by him alone without any consideration for anyone or anything.

This unbelievable suspicion was cleverly taken advantage of by the abject *provocateur* and vile enemy, Beria, who had murdered thousands of Communists and loyal Soviet people. The elevation of Voznesensky and Kuznetsov alarmed Beria. As we have now proven, it had been precisely Beria who had "suggested" to Stalin the fabrication by him and by his confidants of materials in the form of declarations and anonymous letters, and in the form of various rumors and talks.

The party's central committee has examined this so-called "Leningrad affair"; persons who innocently suffered are now rehabilitated and honor has been restored to the glorious Leningrad party organization. Abakumov and others who had fabricated this affair were brought before a court; their trial took place in Leningrad and they received what they deserved.

The question arises: Why is it that we see the truth of this affair only now, and why did we not do something earlier, during Stalin's life, in order to prevent the loss of innocent lives? It was because Stalin personally supervised the "Leningrad affair," and the majority of the Political Bureau members did not, at that time, know all of the circumstances in these matters and could not therefore intervene.

When Stalin received certain material from Beria and Abakumov, without examining these slanderous materials he ordered an investigation of the "affair" of Voznesensky and Kuznetsov. With this, their fate was sealed.

Instructive in the same way is the case of the Mingrelian nationalist organization which supposedly existed in Georgia. As is known, resolutions by the Central Committee, Communist Party of the Soviet Union, were made concerning this case in November 1951 and in March 1952. These resolutions were made without prior discussion with the Political Bureau. Stalin had personally dictated them. They made serious accusations against many loyal Communists. On the basis of falsified documents, it was proven that there existed in Georgia a supposedly nationalistic organization whose objective was the liquidation of the Soviet power in that republic with the help of imperialist powers.

In this connection, a number of responsible party and Soviet workers were arrested in Georgia. As was later proven, this was a slander directed against the Georgian party organization.

We know that there have been at times manifestations of local bourgeois nationalism in Georgia as in several other republics. The question arises: Could it be possible that, in the period during which the resolutions referred to above were made, nationalist tendencies grew so much that there was a danger of Georgia's leaving the Soviet Union and joining Turkey? [Animation in the hall, laughter.]

This is, of course, nonsense. It is impossible to imagine how such assumptions could enter anyone's mind. Everyone knows how Georgia has developed economically and culturally under Soviet rule.

Industrial production of the Georgia Republic is 27 times greater than it was before the revolution. Many new industries have arisen in Georgia which did not exist there before the revolution: iron smelting, an oil industry, a machine-construction industry, etc. Illiteracy has long since been liquidated, which, in pre-Revolutionary Georgia, included 78 per cent of the population.

Could the Georgians, comparing the situation in their republic with the hard situation of the working masses in Turkey, be aspiring to join Turkey? In 1955, Georgia produced 18 times as much steel per person as Turkey. Georgia produces 9 times as much electrical energy per person as Turkey. According to the available 1950 census, 65 per cent of Turkey's total population are illiterate, and, of the women, 80 per cent are illiterate. Georgia has 19 institutions of higher learning which have about 39,000 students; this is 8 times more than in Turkey (for each 1,000 inhabitants). The prosperity of the working people has grown tremendously in Georgia under Soviet rule.

It is clear that, as the economy and culture develop, and as the socialist consciousness of the working masses in Georgia grows, the source from which bourgeois nationalism draws its strength evaporates.

As it developed, there was no nationalistic organization in Georgia. Thousands of innocent people fell victim of willfulness and lawlessness. All of this happened under the "genial" leadership of Stalin, "the great son of the Georgian nation," as Georgians like to refer to Stalin. [Animation in the hall.]

The willfulness of Stalin showed itself not only in decisions concerning the internal life of the country but also in the international relations of the Soviet Union.

The July plenum of the Central Committee studied in detail the reasons for the development of conflict with Yugoslavia. It was a shameful role which Stalin played here. The "Yugoslav affair" contained no problems which could not have been solved through party discussions among comrades. There was no significant basis for the development of this "affair"; it was completely possible to have prevented the rupture of relations with that country. This does not mean, however, that the Yugoslav leaders did not make mistakes or did not have shortcomings. But these mistakes and shortcomings were magnified in a monstrous manner by Stalin, which resulted in a break of relations with a friendly country.

I recall the first days when the conflict between the Soviet Union and Yugoslavia began artificially to be blown up. Once, when I came from Kiev to Moscow, I was invited to visit Stalin, who, pointing to the copy of a letter lately sent to Tito, asked me, "Have you read this?"

Not waiting for my reply, he answered, "I will shake my little finger and there will be no more Tito. He will fall."

We have dearly paid for this "shaking of the little finger." This statement reflected Stalin's mania for greatness, but he acted just that way: "I will shake my little finger—and there will be no Kossior"; "I will shake my little finger once more and Postyshev and Chubar will be no more"; "I will shake my little finger again—and Voznesensky, Kuznetsov and many others will disappear."

But this did not happen to Tito. No matter how much or how little Stalin shook, not only his little finger but everything else that he could shake, Tito did not fall. Why? The reason was that, in this case of disagreement with the Yugoslav comrades, Tito had behind him a state and a people who had gone through a severe school of fighting for liberty and independence, a people which gave support to its leaders.

You see to what Stalin's mania for greatness led. He had completely lost consciousness of reality; he demonstrated his suspicion and haughtiness not only in relation to individuals in the USSR, but in relation to whole parties and nations.

We have carefully examined the case of Yugoslavia and have found a proper solution which is approved by the peoples of the Soviet Union and of Yugoslavia as well as by the working masses of all the people's democracies and by all progressive humanity. The liquidation of the abnormal relationship with Yugoslavia was done in the interest of the whole camp of socialism, in the interest of strengthening peace in the whole world.

Let us also recall the affair of the doctor-plotters. [Animation in the hall.] Actually there was no affair outside of the declaration of the woman doctor Timashuk, who was probably influenced or ordered by someone (after all, she was an unofficial collaborator of the organs of state security) to write Stalin a letter in which she declared that doctors were applying supposedly improper methods of medical treatment.

Such a letter was sufficient for Stalin to reach an immediate conclusion that there are doctor-plotters in the Soviet Union. He issued orders to arrest a group of eminent Soviet medical specialists. He personally issued advice on the conduct of the investigation and the method of interrogation of the arrested persons. He said that the academician Vinogradov should be put in chains, another one should be beaten. Present at this Congress as a delegate is the former Minister of State Security, Comrade Ignatiev. Stalin told him curtly, "If you do not obtain confessions from the doctors we will shorten you by a head." [Tumult in the hall.]

Stalin personally called the investigative judge, gave him instructions, advised him on which investigative methods should be used; these methods were simple—beat, beat and, once again, beat.

Shortly after the doctors were arrested, we members of the Political Bureau received protocols with the doctors' confessions of guilt. After distributing these protocols, Stalin told us, "You are blind like young kittens; what will happen without me? The country will perish because you do not know how to recognize enemies."

The case was so presented that no one could verify the facts on which the investigation was based. There was no possibility of trying to verify facts by contacting those who had made the confessions of guilt.

We felt, however, that the case of the arrested doctors was questionable. We knew some of these people personally because they had once treated us. When we examined this case after Stalin's death, we found it to be fabricated from beginning to end.

This ignominious case was set up by Stalin; he did not, however, have the time in which to bring it to an end (as he conceived that end), and for this reason the doctors are still alive. Now all have been rehabilitated; they are working in the same places they were working before; they treat top individuals, not excluding members of the Government; they have our full confidence; and they execute their duties honestly, as they did before.

In organizing the various dirty and shameful cases, a very base role was played by the rabid enemy of our party, an agent of a foreign intelligence service—Beria, who had stolen into Stalin's confidence. In what way could this *provocateur* gain such a position in the party and in the state, so as to become the First Deputy Chairman of the Council of Ministers of the Soviet Union and a member of the Central Committee Political Bureau? It has now been established that this villain had climbed up the Government ladder over an untold number of corpses.

Were there any signs that Beria was an enemy of the party? Yes, there were. Already in 1937, at a Central Committee plenum, former People's Commissar of Health Protection Kaminsky said that Beria worked for the Mussavat intelligence service. But the Central Committee plenum had barely concluded when Kaminsky was arrested and then shot. Had Stalin examined Kaminsky's statement? No, because Stalin believed in Beria, and that was enough for him. And when Stalin believed in anyone or anything, then no one could say anything which was contrary to his opinion; anyone who would dare to express opposition would have met the same fate as Kaminsky.

There were other signs, also. The declaration which Comrade Snegov made at the party's Central Committee is interesting. (Parenthetically speaking, he was also rehabilitated not long ago, after 17 years in prison camps.) In this declaration, Snegov writes:

"In connection with the proposed rehabilitation of the former Central Committee member, Kartvelishvili-Lavrentiev, I have entrusted to the hands of the representative of the Committee of State Security a detailed deposition concerning Beria's role in the disposition of the Kartvelishvili case and concerning the criminal motives by which Beria was guided."

In my opinion, it is indispensable to recall an important fact pertaining to this case and to communicate it to the Central Committee, because I did not consider it as proper to include in the investigation documents.

On October 30, 1931, at the session of the Organizational Bureau of the Central Committee, All-Union Communist Party (Bolsheviks), Kartvelishvili, secretary of the Transcaucasian Krai Committee, made a report. All members of the executive of the Krai Committee were present; of them I alone am alive.

During this session, J. V. Stalin made a motion at the end of his speech concerning the organization of the secretariat of the Transcaucasian Krai Committee composed of the following: first secretary, Kartvelishvili; second secretary, Beria (it was then, for the first time in the party's history, that Beria's name was mentioned as a candidate for a party position). Kartvelishvili answered that he knew Beria well and for that reason refused categorically to work together with him. Stalin proposed then that this matter be left open and that it be solved in the process of the work itself. Two days later a decision was arrived at that Beria would receive the party post and that Kartvelishvili would be deported from the Transcaucasus.

This fact can be confirmed by Comrades Mikoyan and Kaganovich, who were present at that session.

The long, unfriendly relations between Kartvelishvili and Beria were widely known; they date back to the time when Comrade Sergo [Ordzhonikidze] was active in the Transcaucasus: Kartvelishvili was the closest assistant of Sergo. The unfriendly relationship impelled Beria to fabricate a case against Kartvelishvili.

It is a characteristic thing that in this case Kartvelishvili was charged with a terroristic act against Beria.

The indictment in the Beria case contains a discussion of his crimes. Some things should, however, be recalled, especially since it is possible that not all delegates to the Congress have read this document. I wish to recall Beria's bestial disposition of the cases of Kedrov, Golubev, and Golubev's adopted mother, Baturina—persons who wished to inform the Central Committee concerning Beria's treacherous activity. They were shot without any trial and the sentence was passed *ex post facto,* after the execution.

Here is what the old Communist, Comrade Kedrov, wrote to the Central Committee through Comrade Andreyev (Comrade Andreyev was then a Central Committee secretary):

"I am calling to you for help from a gloomy cell of the Lefortovsky prison. Let my cry of horror reach your ears; do not remain deaf; take me under your protection; please, help remove the nightmare of interrogations and show that this is all a mistake.

"I suffer innocently. Please believe me. Time will testify to the truth. I am not an *agent provocateur* of the Tsarist Okhrana; I am not a spy; I am not a member of an anti-Soviet organization of which I am being accused on the basis of denunciations. I am also not guilty of any other crimes against the party and the Government. I am an old Bolshevik, free of any stain; I have honestly fought for almost 40 years in the ranks of the party for the good and prosperity of the nation. . . .

"Today I, a 62-year-old man, am being threatened by the investigative judges with more severe, cruel and degrading methods of physical pressure. They (the judges) are no longer capable of becoming aware of their error and of recognizing that their handling of my case is illegal and impermissible. They try to justify their actions by picturing me as a hardened and raving enemy and are demanding increased repressions. But let the party know that I am innocent and that there is nothing which can turn a loyal son of the party into an enemy, even right up to his last dying breath.

"But I have no way out. I cannot divert from myself the hastily approaching new and powerful blows.

"Everything, however, has its limits. My torture has reached the extreme. My health is broken, my strength and my energy are waning, the end is drawing near. To die in a Soviet prison, branded as a vile traitor to the fatherland—what can be more monstrous for an honest man? And how monstrous all this is! Unsurpassed bitterness and pain grips my heart. No! No! This will not happen; this cannot be, I cry. Neither the party, nor the Soviet Government, nor the People's Commissar, L. P. Beria, will permit this cruel, irreparable injustice. I am firmly certain that, given a quiet, objective examination, without any foul rantings, without any anger and without the fearful tortures, it would be easy to prove the baselessness of the charges. I believe deeply that truth and justice will triumph. I believe. I believe."

The old Bolshevik, Comrade Kedrov, was found innocent by the Military Collegium. But despite this, he was shot at Beria's order. [Indignation in the hall.]

Beria also handled cruelly the family of Comrade Ordzhonikidze. Why? Because Ordzhonikidze had tried to prevent Beria from realizing his shameful plans. Beria had cleared from his way all persons who could possibly interfere with him. Ordzhonikidze was always an opponent of Beria, which he told to Stalin. Instead of examining this affair and taking appropriate steps, Stalin allowed the liquidation of Ordzhonikidze's brother and brought Ordzhonikidze himself to such a state that he was forced to shoot himself. [Indignation in the hall.] Such was Beria.

Beria was unmasked by the party's Central Committee shortly after Stalin's death. As a result of the particularly detailed legal proceedings, it was established that Beria had committed monstrous crimes and Beria was shot.

The question arises why Beria, who had liquidated tens of thousands of the party and Soviet workers, was not unmasked during Stalin's life. He was not unmasked earlier because he had utilized very skillfully Stalin's weaknesses; feeding him with suspicions, he assisted Stalin in everything and acted with his support.

Comrades, the cult of the individual acquired such monstrous size chiefly because Stalin himself, using all conceivable methods, supported the glorification of his own person. This is supported by numerous facts. One of the most characteristic examples of Stalin's self-glorification and of his lack of even elementary modesty is the edition of his *Short Biography*, which was published in 1948.

This book is an expression of the most dissolute flattery, an example of making a man into a godhead, of transforming him into an infallible sage, "the greatest leader, sublime strategist of all times and nations." Finally, no other words could be found with which to lift Stalin up to the heavens.

We need not give here examples of the loathsome adulation filling this book. All we need to add is that they all were approved and edited by Stalin personally and some of them were added in his own handwriting to the draft text of the book.

What did Stalin consider essential to write into this book? Did he want to cool the ardor of his flatterers who were composing his *Short Biography?* No! He marked the very places where he thought that the praise of his services was insufficient. Here are some examples characterizing Stalin's activity, added in Stalin's own hand:

"In this fight against the skeptics and capitulators, the Trotskyites, Zinovievites, Bukharinites and Kamenevites, there was definitely welded together, after Lenin's death, that leading core of the party . . . that upheld the great banner of Lenin, rallied the party behind Lenin's behests, and brought the Soviet people into the broad road of industrializing the country and collectivizing the rural economy. The leader of this core and the guiding force of the party and the state was Comrade Stalin."

Thus writes Stalin himself! Then he adds:

"Although he performed his task as leader of the party and the people with consummate skill and enjoyed the unreserved support of the entire Soviet people, Stalin never allowed his work to be marred by the slightest hint of vanity, conceit or self-adulation."

Where and when could a leader so praise himself? Is this worthy of a leader of the Marxist-Leninist type? No. Precisely against this did Marx and Engels take such a strong position. This also was always sharply condemned by Vladimir Ilyich Lenin.

In the draft text of his book appeared the following sentence: "Stalin is the Lenin of today." This sentence appeared to Stalin to be too weak, so, in his own handwriting, he changed it to read: "Stalin is the worthy continuer of Lenin's work, or, as it is said in our party, Stalin is the Lenin of today." You see how well it is said, not by the nation but by Stalin himself.

It is possible to give many such self-praising appraisals written into the draft text of that book in Stalin's hand. Especially generously does he endow himself with praises pertaining to his military genius, to his talent for strategy.

I will cite one more insertion made by Stalin concerning the theme of the Stalinist military genius. "The advanced Soviet science of war received further development," he writes, "at Comrade Stalin's hands. Comrade Stalin elaborated the theory of the permanently operating factors that decide the issue of wars, of active defense and the laws of counteroffensive and offensive, of the cooperation of all services and arms in modern warfare, of the role of big tank masses and air forces in modern war, and of the artillery as the most formidable of the armed services. At the various stages of the war Stalin's genius found the correct solutions that took account of all the circumstances of the situation." [Movement in the hall.]

And, further, writes Stalin: "Stalin's military mastership was displayed both in defense and offense. Comrade Stalin's genius enabled him to divine the enemy's plans and defeat them. The battles in which Comrade Stalin directed the Soviet armies are brilliant examples of operational military skill."

In this manner was Stalin praised as a strategist. Who did this? Stalin himself, not in his role as a strategist but in the role of an author-editor, one of the main creators of his self-adulatory biography. Such, comrades, are the facts. We should rather say shameful facts.

And one additional fact from the same *Short Biography* of Stalin. As is known, *The Short Course of the History of the All-Union Communist Party (Bolsheviks)* was written by a commission of the party Central Committee.

This book, parenthetically, was also permeated with the cult of the individual and was written by a designated group of authors. This fact was reflected in the following formulation on the proof copy of the *Short Biography* of Stalin: "A commission of the Central Committee, All-Union Communist Party (Bolsheviks), under the direction of Comrade Stalin and with his most active personal participation, has prepared a *Short Course of the History of the All-Union Communist Party (Bolsheviks)*."

But even this phrase did not satisfy Stalin: The following sentence replaced it in the final version of the *Short Biography:* "In 1938 appeared the book, *History of the All-Union Communist Party (Bolsheviks), Short Course,* written by Comrade Stalin and approved by a commission of the Central Committee, All-Union Communist Party (Bolsheviks)." Can one add anything more? [Animation in the hall.]

As you see, a surprising metamorphosis changed the work created by a group into a book written by Stalin. It is not necessary to state how and why this metamorphosis took place.

A pertinent question comes to our mind: If Stalin is the author of this book, why did he need to praise the person of Stalin so much and to transform the whole post-October historical period of our glorious Communist party solely into an action of "the Stalin genuis"?

Did this book properly reflect the efforts of the party in the socialist transformation of the country, in the construction of socialist society, in the industrialization and collectivization of the country, and also other steps taken by the party which undeviatingly traveled the path outlined by Lenin? This book speaks principally about Stalin, about his speeches, about his reports. Everything without the smallest exception is tied to his name.

And when Stalin himself asserts that he himself wrote the *Short Course of the History of the All-Union Communist Party (Bolsheviks),* this calls at least for amazement. Can a Marxist-Leninist thus write about himself, praising his own person to the heavens?

Or let us take the matter of the Stalin Prizes. [Movement in the hall.] Not even the Tsars created prizes which they named after themselves.

Stalin recognized as the best a text of the national anthem of the Soviet Union which contains not a word about the Communist party; it contains, however, the following unprecedented praise of Stalin: "Stalin brought us up in loyalty to the people. He inspired us to great toil and acts."

In these lines of the anthem is the whole educational, directional and inspirational activity of the great Leninist party ascribed to Stalin. This is, of course, a clear deviation from Marxism-Leninism, a clear debasing and belittling of the role of the party. We should add for your information that the Presidium of the Central Committee has already passed a resolution concerning the composition of a new text of the anthem, which will reflect the role of the people and the role of the party. [Loud, prolonged applause.]

And was it without Stalin's knowledge that many of the largest enterprises and towns were named after him? Was it without his knowledge that Stalin monuments were erected in the whole country—these memorials to the living? It is a fact that Stalin himself had signed on July 2, 1951 a resolution of the USSR Council of Ministers concerning the erection on the Volga-Don Canal of an impressive monument to Stalin; on September 4 of the same year he issued an order making 33 tons of copper available for the construction of this impressive monument.

Anyone who has visited the Stalingrad area must have seen the huge statue which is being built there, and that on a site which hardly any people frequent. Huge sums were spent to build it at a time when people of this area had lived since the war in huts. Consider, yourself, was Stalin right when he wrote in his biography that ". . . he did not allow in himself . . . even a shadow of conceit, pride, or self-adoration"?

At the same time Stalin gave proofs of his lack of respect for Lenin's memory. It is not a coincidence that, despite the decision taken over 30 years ago to build a Palace of Soviets as a monument to Vladimir Ilyich, this palace was not built, its construction was always postponed and the project allowed to lapse.

We cannot forget to recall the Soviet Government resolution of August 14, 1925 concerning "the founding of Lenin prizes for educational work." This resolution was published in the press, but until this day there are no Lenin prizes. This, too, should be corrected. [Tumultuous, prolonged applause.]

During Stalin's life—thanks to known methods which I have mentioned, and quoting facts, for instance, from the *Short Biography of Stalin*—all events were explained as if Lenin played only a secondary role, even during the October Socialist Revolution. In many films and in many literary works the figure of Lenin was incorrectly presented and inadmissibly depreciated.

Stalin loved to see the film, *The Unforgettable Year of 1919*, in which he was shown on the steps of an armored train and where he was practically vanquishing the foe with his own saber. Let Kliment Yefremovich [Voroshilov], our dear friend, find the necessary courage and write the truth about Stalin; after all, he knows how Stalin had fought. It will be difficult for Comrade Voroshilov to undertake this, but it would be good if he did it. Everyone will approve of it, both the people and the party. Even his grandsons will thank him. [Prolonged applause.]

In speaking about the events of the October Revolution and about the Civil War, the impression was created that Stalin always played the main role, as if everywhere and always Stalin had suggested to Lenin what to do and how to do it. However, this is slander of Lenin. [Prolonged applause.]

I will probably not sin against the truth when I say that 99 per cent of the persons present here heard and knew very little about Stalin before the year 1924, while Lenin was known to all; he was known to the whole party, to the whole nation, from the children up to the graybeards. [Tumultuous, prolonged applause.]

All this has to be thoroughly revised so that history, literature and the fine arts properly reflect V. I. Lenin's role and the great deeds of our Communist party and of the Soviet people—the creative people. [Applause.]

Comrades, the cult of the individual has caused the employment of faulty principles in party work and in economic activity; it brought about rude violation of internal party and Soviet democracy, sterile administration, deviations of all sorts, covering up the shortcomings and varnishing of reality. Our nation gave birth to many flatterers and specialists in false optimism and deceit.

We should also not forget that, due to the numerous arrests of party, Soviet and economic leaders, many workers began to work uncertainly, showed overcautiousness, feared all which was new, feared their own shadows and began to show less initiative in their work.

Take, for instance, party and Soviet resolutions. They were prepared in a routine manner, often without considering the concrete situation. This went so far that party workers, even during the smallest sessions, read their speeches. All this produced the danger of formalizing the party and Soviet work and of bureaucratizing the whole apparatus.

Stalin's reluctance to consider life's realities and the fact that he was not aware of the real state of affairs in the provinces can be illustrated by his direction of agriculture.

All those who interested themselves even a little in the national situation saw the difficult situation in agriculture, but Stalin never even noted it. Did we tell Stalin about this? Yes, we told him, but he did not support us. Why? Because Stalin never traveled anywhere, did not meet city and *kolkhoz* workers; he did not know the actual situation in the provinces.

He knew the country and agriculture only from films. And these films had dressed up and beautified the existing situation in agriculture. Many films so pictured *kolkhoz* life that the tables were bending from the weight of turkeys and geese. Evidently, Stalin thought that it was actually so.

Vladimir Ilyich Lenin looked at life differently; he was always close to the people; he used to receive peasant delegates and often spoke at factory gatherings; he used to visit villages and talk with the peasants.

Stalin separated himself from the people and never went anywhere. This lasted ten years. The last time he visited a village was in January 1928, when he visited Siberia in connection with grain deliveries. How then could he have known the situation in the provinces?

And when he was once told during a discussion that our situation on the land was a difficult one and that the situation of cattle breeding and meat production was especially bad, a commission was formed which was charged with the preparation of a resolution called "Means toward further development of animal breeding in *kolkhozes* and *sovkhozes*." We worked out this project.

Of course, our propositions of that time did not contain all possibilities but we did chart ways in which animal breeding on *kolkhozes* and *sovkhozes* would be raised. We had proposed then to raise the prices of such products in order to create material incentives for the *kolkhoz*, MTS [Machine-Tractor Station] and *sovkhoz* workers in the development of cattle breeding. But our project was not accepted and in February 1953 was laid aside entirely.

What is more, while reviewing this project Stalin proposed that the taxes paid by the *kolkhozes* and by the *kolkhoz* workers should be raised by 40 billion rubles; according to him the peasants are well off and the *kolkhoz* worker would need to sell only one more chicken to pay his tax in full.

Imagine what this meant. Certainly, 40 billion rubles is a sum which the *kolkhoz* workers did not realize for all the products which they sold to the Government. In 1952, for instance, the *kolkhozes* and the *kolkhoz* workers received 26,280,000,000 rubles for all their products delivered and sold to the Government.

Did Stalin's position, then, rest on data of any sort whatever? Of course not. In such cases facts and figures did not interest him. If Stalin said anything, it meant it was so—after all, he was a "genius," and a genius does not need to count, he only needs to look and can immediately tell how it should be. When he expresses his opinion, everyone has to repeat it and to admire his wisdom.

But how much wisdom was contained in the proposal to raise the agricultural tax by 40 billion rubles? None, absolutely none, because the proposal was not based on an actual assessment of the situation but on the fantastic ideas of a person divorced from reality.

We are currently beginning slowly to work our way out of a difficult agricultural situation. The speeches of the delegates to the Twentieth Congress please us all; we are glad that many delegates deliver speeches, that there are conditions for the fulfillment of the sixth Five-Year Plan for animal husbandry, not during the period of five years, but within two to three years. We are certain that the commitments of the new Five-Year Plan will be accomplished successfully. [Prolonged applause.]

Comrades, if we sharply criticize today the cult of the individual which was so widespread during Stalin's life and if we speak about the many negative phenomena generated by this cult which is so alien to the spirit of Marxism-Leninism, various persons may ask: How could it be? Stalin headed the party and the country for 30 years and many victories were gained during his lifetime. Can we deny this? In my opinion, the question can be asked in this manner only by those who are blinded and hopelessly hypnotized by the cult of the individual, only by those who do not understand the essence of the revolution and of the Soviet state, only by those who do not understand, in a Leninist manner, the role of the party and of the nation in the development of the Soviet society.

The Socialist Revolution was attained by the working class and by the poor peasantry with the partial support of middle-class peasants. It was attained by the people under the leadership of the Bolshevik Party. Lenin's great service consisted of the fact that he created a militant party of the working class, but he was armed with Marxist understanding of the laws of social development and with the science of proletarian victory in the fight with capitalism, and he steeled this party in the crucible of revolutionary struggle of the masses of the people.

During this fight the party consistently defended the interests of the people, became its experienced leader, and led the working masses to power, to the creation of the first socialist state. You remember well the wise words of Lenin that the Soviet state is strong because of the awareness of the masses that history is created by the millions and tens of millions of people.

Our historical victories were attained thanks to the organizational work of the party, to the many provincial organizations, and to the self-sacrificing work of our great nation. These victories are the result of the great drive and activity of the nation and of the party as a whole; they are not at all the fruit of the leadership of Stalin, as the situation was pictured during the period of the cult of the individual.

If we are to consider this matter as Marxists and as Leninists, then we have to state unequivocally that the leadership practice which came into being during the last years of Stalin's life became a serious obstacle in the path of Soviet social development. Stalin often failed for months to take up some unusually important problems, concerning the life of the party and of the state, whose solution could not be postponed. During Stalin's leadership our peaceful relations with other nations were often threatened, because one-man decisions could cause, and often did cause, great complications.

In the last years, when we managed to free ourselves of the harmful practice of the cult of the individual and took several proper steps in the sphere of internal and external policies, everyone saw how activity grew before their very eyes, how the creative activity of the broad working masses developed, how favorably all this acted upon the development of economy and of culture. [Applause.]

Some comrades may ask us: Where were the members of the Political Bureau of the Central Committee? Why did they not assert themselves against the cult of the individual in time? And why is this being done only now?

First of all, we have to consider the fact that the members of the Political Bureau viewed these matters in a different way at different times. Initially, many of them backed Stalin actively because Stalin was one of the strongest Marxists and his logic, his strength and his will greatly influenced the cadres and party work.

It is known that Stalin, after Lenin's death, especially during the first years, actively fought for Leninism against the enemies of Leninist theory and against those who deviated. Beginning with Leninist theory, the party, with its Central Committee at the head, started on a great scale the work of socialist industrialization of the country, agricultural collectivization and the cultural revolution.

At that time Stalin gained great popularity, sympathy and support. The party had to fight those who attempted to lead the country away from the correct Leninist path; it had to fight Trotskyites, Zinovievites and rightists, and the bourgeois nationalists. This fight was indispensable.

Later, however, [Stalin,] abusing his power more and more, began to fight eminent party and Government leaders and to use terroristic methods against honest Soviet people. As we have already shown, Stalin thus handled such eminent party and Government leaders as Kossior, Rudzutak, Eikhe, Postyshev and many others.

Attempts to oppose groundless suspicions and charges resulted in the opponent falling victim of the repression. This characterized the fall of Comrade Postyshev.

In one of his speeches Stalin expressed his dissatisfaction with Postyshev and asked him, "What are you actually?"

Postyshev answered clearly, "I am a Bolshevik, Comrade Stalin, a Bolshevik."

This assertion was at first considered to show a lack of respect for Stalin; later it was considered a harmful act and consequently resulted in Postyshev's annihilation and branding without any reason as a "people's enemy."

In the situation which then prevailed I have talked often with Nikolai Alexandrovich Bulganin; once when we two were traveling in a car, he said, "It has happened sometimes that a man goes to Stalin on his invitation as a friend. And, when he sits with Stalin, he does not know where he will be sent next—home or to jail."

It is clear that such conditions put every member of the Political Bureau in a very difficult situation. And, when we also consider the fact that in the last years the Central Committee plenary sessions were not convened and that the sessions of the Political Bureau occurred only occasionally, from time to time,

then we will understand how difficult it was for any member of the Political Bureau to take a stand against one or another unjust or improper procedure, against serious errors and shortcomings in the practices of leadership.

As we have already shown, many decisions were taken either by one person or in a roundabout way, without collective discussion. The sad fate of Political Bureau member Comrade Voznesensky, who fell victim to Stalin's repressions, is known to all. It is a characteristic thing that the decision to remove him from the Political Bureau was never discussed but was reached in a devious fashion. In the same way came the decision concerning the removal of Kuznetsov and Rodionov from their posts.

The importance of the Central Committee's Political Bureau was reduced and its work was disorganized by the creation within the Political Bureau of various commissions—the so-called "quintets," "sextets," "septets" and "novenaries." Here is, for instance, a resolution of the Political Bureau of October 3, 1946:

"Stalin's Proposal:

"1. The Political Bureau Commission for Foreign Affairs ("Sextet") is to concern itself in the future, in addition to foreign affairs, also with matters of internal construction and domestic policy.

"2. The Sextet is to add to its roster the Chairman of the State Commission of Economic Planning of the USSR, Comrade Voznesensky, and is to be known as a Septet.

"Signed: Secretary of the Central Committee, J. Stalin."

What a terminology of a card player! [Laughter in the hall.] It is clear that the creation within the Political Bureau of this type of commissions—"quintets," "sextets," "septets" and "novenaries"—was against the principle of collective leadership. The result of this was that some members of the Political Bureau were in this way kept away from participation in reaching the most important state matters.

One of the oldest members of our party, Kliment Yefremovich Voroshilov, found himself in an almost impossible situation. For several years he was actually deprived of the right of participation in Political Bureau sessions. Stalin forbade him to attend the Political Bureau sessions and to receive documents. When the Political Bureau was in session and Comrade Voroshilov heard about it, he telephoned each time and asked whether he would be allowed to attend. Sometimes Stalin permitted it, but always showed his dissatisfaction.

Because of his extreme suspicion, Stalin toyed also with the absurd and ridiculous suspicion that Voroshilov was an English agent. [Laughter in the hall.] It's true—an English agent. A special tapping device was installed in his home to listen to what was said there. [Indignation in the hall.]

By unilateral decision, Stalin had also separated one other man from the work of the Political Bureau—Andrei Andreyevich Andreyev. This was one of the most unbridled acts of willfulness.

Let us consider the first Central Committee plenum after the 19th Party Congress when Stalin, in his talk at the plenum, characterized Vyacheslav Mikhailovich Molotov and Anastas Ivanovich Mikoyan and suggested that these old workers of our party were guilty of some baseless charges. It is not

excluded that had Stalin remained at the helm for another several months, Comrades Molotov and Mikoyan would probably have not delivered any speeches at this Congress.

Stalin evidently had plans to finish off the old members of the Political Bureau. He often stated that Political Bureau members should be replaced by new ones.

His proposal, after the 19th Congress, concerning the election of 25 persons to the Central Committee Presidium, was aimed at the removal of the old Political Bureau members and the bringing in of less experienced persons so that these would extol him in all sorts of ways.

We can assume that this was also a design for the future annihilation of the old Political Bureau members and, in this way, a cover for all shameful acts of Stalin, acts which we are now considering.

Comrades, in order not to repeat errors of the past, the Central Committee has declared itself resolutely against the cult of the individual. We consider that Stalin was excessively extolled. However, in the past Stalin doubtless performed great services to the party, to the working class and to the international workers' movement.

This question is complicated by the fact that all this which we have just discussed was done during Stalin's life under his leadership and with his concurrence; here Stalin was convinced that this was necessary for the defense of the interests of the working classes against the plotting of enemies and against the attack of the imperialist camp. He saw this from the position of the interest of the working class, of the interest of the laboring people, of the interest of the victory of socialism and communism. We cannot say that these were the deeds of a giddy despot. He considered that this should be done in the interest of the party, of the working masses, in the name of the defense of the revolution's gains. In this lies the whole tragedy!

Comrades, Lenin had often stressed that modesty is an absolutely integral part of a real Bolshevik. Lenin himself was the living personification of the greatest modesty. We cannot say that we have been following this Leninist example in all respects. It is enough to point out that many towns, factories and industrial enterprises, *kolkhozes* and *sovkhozes*, Soviet institutions and cultural institutions have been referred to by us with a title—if I may express it so—of private property of the names of these or those Government or party leaders who were still active and in good health. Many of us participated in the action of assigning our names to various towns, *rayons*, undertakings and *kolkhozes*. We must correct this. [Applause.]

But this should be done calmly and slowly. The Central Committee will discuss this matter and consider it carefully in order to prevent errors and excesses. I can remember how the Ukraine learned about Kossior's arrest. The Kiev radio used to start its programs thus: "This is Radio (in the name of) Kossior." When one day the programs began without naming Kossior, everyone was quite certain that something had happened to Kossior, that he probably had been arrested.

Thus, if today we begin to remove the signs everywhere and to change names, people will think that these comrades in whose honor the given enter-

prises, *kolkhozes* or cities are named also met some bad fate and that they have also been arrested. [Animation in the hall.]

How is the authority and the importance of this or that leader judged? On the basis of how many towns, industrial enterprises and factories, *kolkhozes* and *sovkhozes* carry his name. Is it not about time that we eliminate this "private property" and "nationalize" the factories, the industrial enterprises, the *kolkhozes* and the *sovkhozes*? [Laughter, applause, voices: "That is right."] This will benefit our cause. After all, the cult of the individual is manifested also in this way.

We should, in all seriousness, consider the question of the cult of the individual. We cannot let this matter get out of the party, especially not to the press. It is for this reason that we are considering it here at a closed Congress session. We should know the limits; we should not give ammunition to the enemy; we should not wash our dirty linen before their eyes. I think that the delegates to the Congress will understand and assess properly all these proposals. [Tumultuous applause.]

Comrades, we must abolish the cult of the individual decisively, once and for all; we must draw the proper conclusions concerning both ideological-theoretical and practical work. It is necessary for this purpose:

First, in a Bolshevik manner to condemn and to eradicate the cult of the individual as alien to Marxism-Leninism and not consonant with the principles of party leadership and the norms of party life, and to fight inexorably all attempts at bringing back this practice in one form or another.

To return to and actually practice in all our ideological work the most important theses of Marxist-Leninist science about the people as the creator of history and as the creator of all material and spiritual good of humanity, about the decisive role of the Marxist party in the revolutionary fight for the transformation of society, about the victory of communism.

In this connection we will be forced to do much work in order to examine critically from the Marxist-Leninist viewpoint and to correct the widely spread erroneous views connected with the cult of the individual in the sphere of history, philosophy, economy and of other sciences, as well as in literature and the fine arts. It is especially necessary that in the immediate future we compile a serious textbook of the history of our party which will be edited in accordance with scientific Marxist objectivism, a textbook of the history of Soviet society, a book pertaining to the events of the Civil War and the Great Patriotic War.

Secondly, to continue systematically and consistently the work done by the party's Central Committee during the last years, a work characterized by minute observation in all party organizations, from the bottom to the top, of the Leninist principles of party leadership, characterized, above all, by the main principle of collective leadership, characterized by the observation of the norms of party life described in the statutes of our party, and, finally, characterized by the wide practice of criticism and self-criticism.

Thirdly, to restore completely the Leninist principles of Soviet socialist democracy, expressed in the Constitution of the Soviet Union, to fight willfulness of individuals abusing their power. The evil caused by acts violating revolutionary socialist legality which have accumulated during a long time as a result of the negative influence of the cult of the individual has to be completely corrected.

Comrades, the 20th Congress of the Communist Party of the Soviet Union has manifested with a new strength the unshakable unity of our party, its cohesiveness around the Central Committee, its resolute will to accomplish the great task of building communism. [Tumultuous applause.] And the fact that we present in all their ramifications the basic problems of overcoming the cult of the individual which is alien to Marxism-Leninism, as well as the problem of liquidating its burdensome consequences, is an evidence of the great moral and political strength of our party. [Prolonged applause.]

We are absolutely certain that our party, armed with the historical resolutions of the 20th Congress, will lead the Soviet people along the Leninist path to new successes, to new victories. [Tumultuous, prolonged applause.]

Long live the victorious banner of our party—Leninism! [Tumultuous, prolonged applause ending in ovation. All rise.]

Appendix 38   STATUTE OF THE COMMUNIST PARTY
OF THE SOVIET UNION ADOPTED BY
THE TWENTY-SECOND PARTY CONGRESS,
OCTOBER, 1961 [1]

The Communist Party of the Soviet Union (CPSU) is the tried and tested militant vanguard of the Soviet people, which unites, on a voluntary basis, the more advanced, the politically more conscious section of the working class, collective-farm peasantry and intelligentsia of the USSR.

Founded by V. I. Lenin as the vanguard of the working class, the Communist party has travelled a glorious road of struggle, and has brought the working class and the working peasantry to the victory of the Great October Socialist Revolution and to the establishment of the dictatorship of the proletariat in the USSR. Under the leadership of the Communist party, the exploiting classes were abolished in the Soviet Union, and the moral and political unity of Soviet society has taken shape and grown in strength. Socialism has triumphed completely and finally. The Communist party, the party of the working class, has now become the party of the Soviet people as a whole.

The party exists for, and serves, the people. It is the highest form of sociopolitical organization, and is the leading and guiding force of Soviet society. It directs the great creative activity of the Soviet people, and imparts an organized, planned and scientifically-based character to their struggle to achieve the ultimate goal, the victory of communism.

The CPSU bases its work on the unswerving adherence to the Leninist standards of party life—the principle of collective leadership, the comprehensive development of inner-party democracy, the activity and initiative of the communists, criticism and self-criticism.

Ideological and organizational unity, monolithic cohesion of its ranks, and a high degree of conscious discipline on the part of all communists are an inviolable law of the CPSU. All manifestations of factionalism and clique activity are incompatible with Marxist-Leninist party principles, and with party membership.

In all its activities, the CPSU is guided by Marxist-Leninist theory and the Program based on it, which defines the fundamental tasks of the party for the period of the construction of communist society.

In creatively developing Marxism-Leninism, the CPSU vigorously combats all manifestations of revisionism and dogmatism, which are profoundly alien to revolutionary theory.

The CPSU is an integral part of the international communist and working-class movement. It firmly adheres to the tried and tested Marxist-Leninist principles of proletarian internationalism; it actively promotes the unity of the entire international communist and workers' movement, and of the fraternal ties with the great army of communists of all countries.

[1] *Pravda*, November 3, 1961, pp. 1–3.

I. PARTY MEMBERS, THEIR DUTIES AND RIGHTS

1. Membership in the CPSU is open to any citizen of the Soviet Union who accepts the Program and Statute of the Party, takes an active part in communist construction, works in one of the party organizations, carries out all party decisions, and pays membership dues.

2. It is the duty of a party member:

A. to work for the creation of the material and technical base of communism; to serve as an example of the communist attitude toward labor; to raise labor productivity; to take the initiative in all that is new and progressive; to support and propagate advanced methods; to master techniques; to improve his skills; to protect and increase socialist property, the mainstay of the might and prosperity of the Soviet country;

B. to put party decisions firmly and steadfastly into effect; to explain the policy of the party to the masses; to help strengthen and broaden the party's ties with the people; to be considerate and attentive to people; to respond promptly to the needs and requirements of the working people;

C. to take an active part in the political affairs of the country, in the administration of state affairs, and in economic and cultural development; to set an example in the fulfillment of his public duty; to assist in developing and strengthening communist social relations;

D. to master Marxist-Leninist theory, to improve his ideological knowledge, and to contribute to the molding and education of the man of communist society; to combat decisively all manifestations of bourgeois ideology, remnants of a private-property psychology, religious prejudices, and other survivals of the past; to observe the rules of communist morality, and to give public interest precedence over his own;

E. to be an active proponent of the ideas of socialist internationalism and Soviet patriotism among the masses of the working people; to combat survivals of nationalism and chauvinism; to contribute by word and by deed to the consolidation of the friendship of the peoples of the USSR and the fraternal bonds linking the Soviet people with the peoples of the socialist countries, with the proletarians and other working people in all countries;

F. to strengthen vigorously the ideological and organizational unity of the party; to safeguard the party against the infiltration of people unworthy of the lofty name of communist; to be truthful and honest with the party and people; to display vigilance, to guard party and state secrets;

G. to develop criticism and self-criticism, boldly to lay bare shortcomings and strive for their removal; to combat ostentation, conceit, complacency and parochial tendencies; firmly to rebuff all attempts at suppressing criticism; to resist all actions injurious to the party and the state, and to give information about them to party bodies, up to and including the Central Committee of the Communist Party of the Soviet Union (CC CPSU);

H. to implement undeviatingly the party's policy with regard to the proper selection of personnel according to their political and professional qualifications; to be uncompromising whenever the Leninist principles of the selection and education of personnel are infringed on;

I. to observe party and state discipline, which is equally binding on all party members. The party has one discipline, one law, for all communists, irrespective of their past services or the positions they occupy;

J. to assist vigorously in the strengthening of the defensive might of the USSR in order that the USSR may lead the tireless struggle for peace and friendship among nations.

3. A party member has the right:

A. to elect and be elected to party bodies;

B. to discuss freely questions of the party's policies and practical activities at party meetings, conferences and congresses, at the meetings of party committees and in the party press; to table motions; openly to express and uphold his opinion as long as the organization concerned has not adopted a decision;

C. to criticize any communist, irrespective of the position he holds, at party meetings, conferences, and congresses, and at the plenary meetings of party committees. Those who commit the offense of suppressing criticism or victimizing anyone for criticism are responsible to and will be penalized by the party, to the point of expulsion from the CPSU;

D. to attend in person all party meetings and all bureau and committee meetings that discuss his activities or conduct;

E. to address any question, statement or proposal to any party body, up to and including the CC CPSU, and to demand an answer on the substance of his address.

4. Applicants are admitted to party membership only individually. Membership in the party is open to politically conscious and active workers, peasants, and members of the intelligentsia devoted to the communist cause. New members are admitted from among the candidate members who have passed through the established probationary period. Persons may join the party on attaining the age of eighteen. Young people up to the age of twenty may join the party only through the Young Communist League (YCL).

The procedure for the admission of candidate members to full party membership is as follows:

A. applicants for party membership must submit recommendations from three party members who have a party standing of not less than three years and who know the applicants from having worked with them, professionally and socially, for not less than one year.

Note 1. In the case of members of the YCL applying for membership in the party, the recommendation of a district or city committee of the YCL is equivalent to the recommendation of one party member.

Note 2. Members and alternate members of the CC CPSU shall refrain from giving recommendations.

B. Applications for party membership are discussed and a decision is taken by the general meeting of the primary party organization; the decision of the latter takes effect after endorsement by the district party committee, or by the city party committee in cities with no district divisions.

The presence of those who have recommended an applicant for party membership at the discussion of the application concerned is optional.

C. Citizens of the USSR who formerly belonged to the Communist or Workers' Party of another country are admitted to membership of the CPSU in conformity with the rules established by the CC CPSU.

Former members of other parties are admitted to membership of the CPSU in conformity with the regular procedure, except that their admission must be endorsed by a regional or territorial committee or the CC of the Communist party of a union republic.

5. Communists recommending applicants for party membership are responsible to party organizations for the impartiality of their description of the political, professional, and moral qualifications of those they recommend.

6. The party standing of those admitted to membership dates from the day when the general meeting of the primary party organization decides to accept them as full members.

7. The procedure of registering members and candidate members of the party, and their transfer from one organization to another is determined by the appropriate instructions of the CC CPSU.

8. If a party member or candidate member fails to pay membership dues for three months in succession without sufficient reason, the matter shall be discussed by the primary party organization. If it is established, as a result, that the party member or candidate member in question has virtually lost contact with the party organization, he shall be regarded as having ceased to be a member of the party; the primary party organization shall pass a decision thereon and submit it to the district or city committee of the party for endorsement.

9. A party member who fails to fulfill his duties as laid down in the Statute or commits other offenses, shall be called to account, and may be subjected to the penalty of admonition, reprimand (or severe reprimand), with entry in the registration card. The highest party penalty is expulsion from the party.

Should the necessity arise, a party organization may, as a party penalty, reduce a party member to the status of candidate member for a period of up to one year. The decision of the primary party organization reducing a party member to candidate membership is subject to endorsement by the district or city party committee. On the expiration of his period of reduction to candidate membership, his readmission to full membership of the party will follow the regular procedure, with retention of his former party standing.

In the case of insignificant offenses, measures of party education and influence should be applied—in the form of comradely criticism, party censure, warning, or reproof.

When the question of expelling a communist member from the party is discussed, the maximum prudence and attention must be shown, and the grounds for the charges preferred against him must be thoroughly investigated.

10. The decision to expel a communist from the party is made by the general meeting of a primary party organization. The decision of the primary party organization expelling a member is regarded as adopted if not less than two-thirds of the party members attending the meeting have voted for it, and is endorsed by a district or city party committee. The decision of the district or city party committee expelling a member from the party takes effect after

endorsement by a regional or territorial committee or the CC of the Communist party of a union republic.

Until such time as the decision to expel him is endorsed by a regional or territorial party committee or the CC of the Communist Party of a union republic, the party member retains his membership or candidate membership card and is entitled to attend closed party meetings.

An expelled party member retains the right to appeal, within the period of two months, to the higher party bodies, up to and including the CC CPSU.

11. The question of calling a member or alternate member of the CC of the Communist party of a union republic, of a territorial, regional, area, city or district party committee, or of an inspection commission, to account before the party is discussed by primary party organizations.

Party organizations pass decisions imposing penalties on members or alternate members of the said party committees, or on members of inspection commissions, in conformity with the regular procedure.

A party organization which proposes expelling a communist from the CPSU communicates its proposal to the party committee of which he is a member. A decision to expel from the party a member or alternate member of the CC of the Communist party of a union republic or a territorial, regional, area, city or district party committee, or a member of an inspection commission, is taken at the plenary meeting of the committee concerned by a majority of two-thirds of the membership.

The decision to expel from the party a member or alternate member of the CC CPSU, or a member of the Central Inspection Commission (CIC), is made by the party congress, and in the interval between two congresses, by a plenary meeting of the CC, by a majority of two thirds of the membership.

12. Should a party member commit an indictable offense, he shall be expelled from the party and prosecuted in conformity with the law.

13. Appeals against expulsion from the party or against the imposition of a penalty, as well as the decisions of party organizations on expulsion from the party shall be examined by the appropriate party bodies within not more than one month from the date of their receipt.

II. CANDIDATE MEMBERS

14. Those joining the party must pass through a probationary period as candidate members in order to familiarize themselves with the Program and Statute of the CPSU and prepare for admission to full membership of the party. Party organizations must assist candidates to prepare for admission to full membership of the party, and test their personal qualities. Probationary membership shall be one year.

15. The procedure for the admission of candidate members (individual admission, submission of recommendations, decision of the primary organization as to admission, and its endorsement) is identical with the procedure for the admission of party members.

16. On the expiration of a candidate member's probationary period the

primary party organization discusses and passes a decision on his application for admission to full membership. Should a candidate member fail, in the course of his probationary period, to show his worthiness, and should he prove, by his personal qualities, that he cannot be admitted to membership in the CPSU, the party organization shall pass a decision rejecting his admission to membership in the party; after endorsement of that decision by the district or city party committee, he shall cease to be considered a candidate member of the CPSU.

17. Candidate members of the party must participate in all the activities of their party organizations; they shall have a consultative voice at party meetings. They may not be elected to any leading party body, nor may they be elected delegates to a party conference or congress.

18. Candidate members of the CPSU pay membership dues at the same rate as full members.

III. ORGANIZATIONAL STRUCTURE OF THE PARTY. INNER-PARTY DEMOCRACY

19. The guiding principle of the organizational structure of the party is democratic centralism, which signifies:

A. election of all leading party bodies, from the lowest to the highest;

B. periodic reports of party bodies to their party organizations and to higher bodies;

C. strict party discipline and subordination of the minority to the majority;

D. the unconditionally binding nature of the decisions of the higher bodies upon lower ones.

20. The party is built on the territorial-industrial principle: Primary organizations are established wherever communists are employed, and are associated territorially in district, city, etc., organizations. An organization serving a given area is higher than any party organization serving part of that area.

21. All party organizations are autonomous in the decisions of local questions, unless their decisions conflict with party policy.

22. The highest leading body of a party organization is the general meeting (in the case of primary organizations); the conference (in the case of district, city, area, regional or territorial organizations); or the congress (in the case of the Communist Parties of union republics and the CPSU).

23. The general meeting, conference or congress elects a bureau or committee which acts as its executive body and directs all the current work of the party organization.

24. The election of party bodies shall be effected by secret ballot. In an election, all party members have the unlimited right to challenge candidates and to criticize them. Each candidate shall be voted upon separately. A candidate is considered elected if more than one-half of those attending the meeting, conference, or congress has voted for him.

25. The principle of systematic renewal of the composition of party bodies and of continuity of leadership shall be observed in the election of those bodies.

At each regular election, not less than one-quarter of the composition of the CC CPSU and its Presidium shall be renewed. Members of the Presidium shall not, as a rule, be elected for more than three successive terms. Particular party officials may, by virtue of their generally recognized prestige and high political, organizational and other qualities, be successively elected to leading bodies for a longer period. In that case, a candidate is considered elected if not less than three-quarters of the votes are cast for him by secret ballot.

The composition of the CC of the Communist parties of the union republics, and of the territorial and regional party committees shall be renewed by not less than one-third at each regular election; the composition of the area, city and district party committees and of the committees or bureaus of primary party organizations, by one-half. Furthermore, members of these leading party bodies may be elected successively for not more than three terms, and the secretaries of primary party organizations, for not more than two terms.

A meeting, conference, or congress may, in consideration of the political and professional qualities of a person, elect him to a leading body for a longer period. In such cases a candidate is considered elected if not less than three-quarters of the communists attending vote for him.

Party members not re-elected to a leading party body on the expiration of their term may be re-elected at subsequent elections.

26. A member or alternate member of the CC CPSU must by his entire activity justify the great trust placed in him by the party. A member or alternate member of the CC CPSU who does not uphold his honor and dignity may not remain a member of the CC. The question of the removal of a member or alternate member of the CC CPSU from that body shall be decided by a plenary meeting of the CC by secret ballot. The decision is regarded as adopted if not less than two-thirds of the membership of the CC CPSU vote for it.

The question of the removal of a member or alternate member of the CC of the Communist party of a union republic, or of a territorial, regional, area, city or district party committee from the party body concerned is decided by a plenary meeting of that body. The decision is regarded as adopted if not less than two-thirds of the membership of the committee in question vote for it by secret ballot.

A member of the CIC who does not justify the great trust placed in him by the party shall be removed from the Commission. This question shall be decided by a meeting of the CIC. The decision is regarded as adopted if not less than two-thirds of the membership of the CIC have voted by a secret ballot for the removal from that body of the member or alternate member concerned.

The question of the removal of a member from the inspection commission of a republican, territorial, regional, area, city or district party organization shall be decided by a meeting of the appropriate commission according to the procedure established for members and alternate members of party committees.

27. The free and business-like discussion of questions of party policy in individual party organizations or in the party as a whole is the inalienable right of every party member and is an important principle of inner-party democracy. Only on the basis of inner-party democracy is it possible to develop criticism

and self-criticism and to strengthen party discipline, which must be conscious and not mechanical.

Discussion of controversial or insufficiently clear issues may be held within the framework of individual organizations or the party as a whole.

Party-wide discussion is necessary:

A. if the necessity is recognized by several party organizations at regional or republican level;

B. if there is not a sufficiently solid majority in the CC on major questions of party policy;

C. if the CC CPSU considers it necessary to consult the party as a whole on any particular questions of policy.

Wide discussion, especially discussion on a countrywide scale, of questions of party policy must be held so as to insure for party members the free expression of their views and preclude attempts to form factional groupings destroying party unity, attempts to split the party.

28. The highest principle of party leadership is collectivism, which is an absolute requisite for the normal functioning of party organizations, the proper education of personnel, and the promotion of the activity and initiative of communists. The cult of the individual and the violations of inner-party democracy resulting from it must not be tolerated in the party; they are incompatible with the Leninist principles of party life.

Collective leadership does not exempt persons in office from their responsibility for the job entrusted to them.

29. The CC of the Communist Parties of union republics, and territorial, regional, area, city and district party committees shall in the period between congresses and conferences, systematically inform party organizations of their work.

30. Meetings of the most active members of districts, city, area, regional and territorial party organizations and of the Communist Parties of union republics shall be held to discuss major decisions of the party and to work out practical measures for their execution, as well as to examine questions of local significance.

IV. HIGHER PARTY ORGANS

31. The supreme organ of the CPSU is the party congress. Congresses are convened at least once in four years. The convocation of a party congress shall be announced at least six weeks before the congress. Extraordinary congresses are convened by the CC of the party on its own initiative or on the demand of not less than one-third of the total membership represented at the preceding party congress. Extraordinary congresses shall be convened within two months. A congress is considered properly constituted if not less than one-half of the total party membership is represented at it.

The norms of representation at a party congress are determined by the CC.

32. Should the CC of the party fail to convene an extraordinary congress within the period specified in article 31, the organizations which demanded it

have the right to form an organizing committee which shall enjoy the powers of the CC of the party with respect to the convocation of the extraordinary congress.

33. The congress:

A. hears and approves the reports of the CC, of the CIC, and of the other central organizations;

B. reviews, amends and endorses the Program and the Statute of the party;

C. determines the line of the party in matters of domestic and foreign policy, and examines and decides the most important questions of communist construction;

D. elects the CC and the CIC.

34. The number of members to be elected to the CC and to the CIC is determined by the congress. In the event of vacancies occurring in the CC, they are filled from among the alternate members of the CC CPSU elected by the congress.

35. Between congresses the CC CPSU directs the activities of the party and the local party bodies; selects and appoints leading functionaries; directs the work of central government bodies and social organizations of working poeple through the party groups in them; sets up various party organs, institutions, and enterprises and directs their activities; appoints the editors of the central newspapers and journals operating under its control; and distributes the funds of the party budget and controls its execution.

The CC represents the CPSU in its relations with other parties.

36. The CC CPSU shall keep the party organizations regularly informed of its work.

37. The CIC supervises the expeditious and proper handling of business by the central bodies of the party, and audits the accounts of the treasury, and the enterprises of the CC CPSU.

38. The CC CPSU shall hold not less than one plenary meeting every six months. Alternate members of the CC shall attend its plenary meetings with consultative voice.

39. The CC CPSU elects a Presidium to direct the work of the CC between plenary meetings and a Secretariat to direct current work, chiefly the selection of personnel and the verification of the fulfillment of party decisions, and sets up a Bureau of the CC CPSU for the Russian Soviet Federated Socialist Republic (RSFSR).

40. The CC CPSU organizes the Party Control Committee of the CC.

The Party Control Committee of the CC of the CPSU:

A. verifies the observance of party discipline by members and candidate members of the CPSU, and takes action against communists who violate the Program and the Statute of the Party, and party or state discipline, and against violators of party ethics;

B. considers appeals against decisions of CC's of the Communist Parties of union republics or of territorial and regional Party committees to expel members from the party or impose party penalties upon them.

V. REPUBLICAN, TERRITORIAL, REGIONAL, AREA, CITY AND DISTRICT ORGANIZATIONS OF THE PARTY

41. The republican, territorial, regional, area, city and district party organizations and their committees take guidance in their activities from the Program and the Statute of the CPSU, conduct all work for the implementation of party policy, and organize the fulfillment of the directives of the CC CPSU within the republics, territories, regions, areas, cities and districts concerned.

42. The basic duties of republican, territorial, regional, area, city and district party organizations, and of their leading bodies, are:

A. political and organizational work among the masses; mobilization of the masses for the fulfillment of the tasks of communist construction, for the maximum development of industrial and agricultural production, for the fulfillment and over-fulfillment of state plans; solicitude for the steady improvement of the material and cultural standards of the working people;

B. organization of ideological work; propaganda of Marxism-Leninism; promotion of the communist awareness of the working people, guidance of the local press, radio and television; and control over the activities of cultural and educational institutions;

C. guidance of Soviets, trade unions, the YCL, the cooperatives and other public organizations through the party groups in them, and increasingly broader enlistment of working people in the activities of these organizations; development of the initiative and activity of the masses as an essential condition for the gradual transition from socialist statehood to public self-government under communism.

Party organizations must not act in place of government, trade union, cooperative or other public organizations of the working people; they must not allow either the merging of the functions of party and other bodies or undue parallelism in work;

D. selection and appointment of leading personnel, their education in the spirit of communist ideas, honesty and truthfulness, and a high sense of responsibility to the party and the people for the work entrusted to them;

E. large-scale enlistment of communists in the conduct of party activities as non-staff workers, as a form of social work;

F. organization of various institutions and enterprises of the party within the bounds of the respective republic, territory, region, area, city or district, and guidance of their activities; distribution of party funds within the given organization; systematic information of the higher party body and accountability to it for their work.

LEADING BODIES OF REPUBLICAN, TERRITORIAL AND REGIONAL PARTY ORGANIZATIONS

43. The highest body of regional, territorial and republican party organizations is the respective regional or territorial party conference or the congress of the communist party of the union republic, and in the interim between their

meetings the regional committee, territorial committee, or the CC of the communist party of the union republic.

44. Regional and territorial party conferences, and congresses of the communist parties of union republics, are convened by the respective regional or territorial committees or the CC of the communist parties of union republics once every two years, and extraordinary conferences and congresses are convened by decision of regional or territorial committees, or the CC of the Communist Parties of union republics, or on the demand of one-third of the total membership of the organizations belonging to the regional, territorial or republican party organization. Congresses of communist parties of those union republics divided into regions (the Ukraine, Belorussia, Kazakhstan and Uzbekistan) may be convened once in four years.

The norms of representation at regional and territorial conferences and at congresses of communist parties of union republics are determined by the respective party committees.

Regional and territorial conferences and congresses of the communist parties of union republics hear and act upon the reports of the respective regional or territorial committee, or the CC of the Communist Party of the union republic, and of the Inspection Commission; discuss at their own discretion other matters of party, economic and cultural development, and elect the regional or territorial committee, the CC of the union republic, the Inspection Commission and the delegates to the congress of the CPSU.

45. The regional and territorial committees, and the CC of the Communist Parties of union republics elect bureaus, which also include secretaries of the committees. The secretaries must have a party standing of not less than five years. The plenary meetings of the committees also confirm the chairmen of party commissions, heads of departments of these committees, editors of party newspapers and journals.

Regional and territorial committees and the CC of the Communist Parties of union republics may set up secretariats to examine current business and verify the execution of decisions.

46. The plenary meetings of regional and territorial committees and the CC of the Communist Parties of union republics shall be convened at least once every four months.

47. The regional and territorial committees and the CC of the Communist Parties of union republics direct the activities of area, city and district party organizations, inspect their work, and regularly hear reports of area, city and district party committees.

Party organizations in autonomous republics, and in autonomous and other regions forming part of a territory or union republic, function under the guidance of the respective territorial committees or CC of the Communist Parties of union republics.

LEADING BODIES OF AREA, CITY AND DISTRICT (URBAN AND RURAL) PARTY ORGANIZATIONS

48. The highest body of an area, city or district party organization is the area, city and district party conference or the general meeting of communists

convened by the area, city or district committee at least once in two years, and the extraordinary conference convened by decision of the respective committee or on the demand of one-third of the total membership of the party organization concerned.

The area, city or district conference (general meeting) hears reports of the committee and inspection commission, discusses at its own discretion other questions of party, economic and cultural development, and elects the area, city and district committee, the inspection commission and delegates to the regional and territorial conference or the congress of the communist party of the union republic.

The norms of representation at area, city and district conferences are determined by the respective party committees.

49. The area, city or district committee elects a bureau, which includes the secretaries of the committee, and confirms the appointment of heads of committee departments and newspaper editors. The secretaries of the area, city and district committees must have a party standing of at least three years. The committee secretaries are confirmed by the respective regional or territorial committee, or the CC of the Communist Party of the union republic.

50. The area, city and district committee organizes and confirms the primary party organizations, directs their work, regularly hears reports concerning the work of party organizations, and keeps a register of communists.

51. The plenary meeting of the area, city and district committee is convened at least once in three months.

52. The area, city and district committee has non-staff instructors, sets up permanent or *ad hoc* commissions on various aspects of party work and uses other ways to draw communists into the activities of the party committee on social lines.

VI. PRIMARY PARTY ORGANIZATIONS

53. The primary party organizations are the basis of the party.

Primary party organizations are formed at the places of work of party members—in factories, on state farms and at other enterprises, collective farms, units of the Soviet Army, offices, educational establishments, etc., wherever there are not less than three party members. Primary party organizations may also be organized on the residential principle in villages·and at house administrations.

54. Shop, sectional, farm, team, departmental, etc., party organizations may be formed at units of the general primary party organization, with the sanction of the area, city or district committee, at enterprises, collective farms and institutions with over 50 Party members and candidate members.

Within shop, sectional, etc., organizations, and also within primary party organizations having less than 50 members and candidate members, party groups may be formed in the teams and other production units.

55. The highest organ of the primary party organization is the party meeting, which is convened at least once a month.

In large party organizations with a membership of more than 300 Communists a general party meeting is convened when necessary at times fixed by the party committee or on the demand of a number of shop or departmental party organizations.

56. For the conduct of current business the primary, shop or departmental party organization elects a bureau for the term of one year.

The number of its members is fixed by the party meeting. Primary, shop and departmental party organizations with less than 15 party members do not elect a bureau. Instead, they elect a secretary and deputy secretary of the party organization.

Secretaries of primary, shop and departmental party organizations must have a party standing of at least one year.

Primary party organizations with less than 150 party members shall have, as a rule, no salaried functionaries released from their regular work.

57. In large factories and offices with more than 300 members and candidate members of the party, and in exceptional cases in factories and offices with over 100 communists by virtue of special production conditions and territorial dispersion, subject to the approval of the regional committee, territorial committee or CC of the Communist Party of the union republic, party committees may be formed, the shop and departmental party organizations at these factories and offices being granted the status of primary party organizations.

The party organizations of collective farms may set up party committees if they have a minimum of 50 communists.

The party committees are elected for the term of one year. Their numerical composition is determined by the general party meeting or conference.

58. In its activities the primary party organization takes guidance from the Program and the Statute of the CPSU. It conducts its work directly among the working people, rallies them around the CPSU, organizes the masses to carry out the party policy and to work for the building of communism.

The primary party organization:

A. enrolls new members to the CPSU;

B. educates communists in a spirit of loyalty to the party cause, ideological staunchness and communist ethics;

C. organizes the study by communists of Marxist-Leninist theory in close connection with the practice of communist construction and opposes all attempts to introduce revisionist distortions into Marxism-Leninism and its dogmatic interpretation;

D. insures the vanguard role of communists in the sphere of labor and in the socio-political and economic activities of enterprises, collective farms, institutions, educational establishments, etc.;

E. acts as the organizer of the working people for the performance of the current tasks of communist construction; heads the socialist emulation movement for the fulfillment of state plans and undertakings of the working people; rallies the masses to disclose and make the best use of untapped resources at enterprises and collective farms, and on a broad scale to apply in production the achievements of science, engineering and the experience of front-rankers; works for the strengthening of labor discipline, the steady increase of labor productivity and improvement of the quality of production, and shows concern for the protection and increase of social wealth at enterprises, state farms and collective farms;

F. conducts agitational and propaganda work among the masses, educates them in the communist spirit, helps the working people to acquire proficiency in administering state and social affairs;

G. on the basis of extensive criticism and self-criticism, combats cases of bureaucracy, parochialism, and violations of state discipline, thwarts attempts to deceive the state, acts against negligence, waste and extravagance at enterprises, collective farms and offices;

H. assists the area, city and district committees in their activities and is accountable to them for its work.

The party organization must see to it that every communist observes in his own life and cultivates among working people the moral principles set forth in the Program of the CPSU—the moral code of a builder of communism:

—loyalty to the communist cause, love of his own socialist country, and of other socialist countries;

—conscientious labor for the benefit of society: He who does not work, neither shall he eat;

—concern on everyone's part for the protection and increase of social wealth;

—a lofty sense of public duty, intolerance of violations of public interests;

—collectivism and comradely mutual assistance: one for all, and all for one;

—humane relations and mutual respect among people: Man is to man a friend, comrade and brother;

—honesty and truthfulness, moral purity, unpretentiousness and modesty in public and personal life;

—mutual respect in the family circle and concern for the upbringing of children;

—intolerance of injustice, parasitism, dishonesty, careerism, and profiteering;

—friendship and fraternity among all peoples of the USSR, intolerance of national and racial hostility;

—intolerance of the enemies of communism, the enemies of peace and those who oppose the freedom of the peoples;

—fraternal solidarity with the working people of all countries, with all peoples.

59. Primary party organizations of industrial enterprises and trading establishments; state farms, collective farms; and design organizations, drafting offices and research institutes directly related to production enjoy the right to control the work of the administration.

The party organizations at ministries, state committees, economic councils and other central and local government or economic agencies and departments, whose function is not that of controlling the administration, must actively promote the improvement of the apparatus, cultivate among the personnel a high sense of responsibility for work entrusted to them, work for the strengthening of state discipline and for the better servicing of the population, firmly combat bureaucracy and red tape, inform the appropriate party bodies in good time of shortcomings in the work of the respective offices and individuals, regardless of what posts the latter may occupy.

VII. THE PARTY AND THE YCL

60. The Leninist YCL of the Soviet Union is a voluntary social organization of young people, an active helper and reserve of the party. The YCL helps the party educate the youth in the communist spirit, draws it into the work of building a new society, trains a rising generation of harmoniously developed people who will live and work and administer public affairs under communism.

61. YCL organizations enjoy the right of broad initiative in discussing and submitting to the appropriate party organizations questions related to the work of enterprises, collective farms and offices. They must be really active in the implementation of party directives in all spheres of communist construction, especially where there are no primary party organizations.

62. The YCL conducts its activities under the guidance of the CPSU. The work of the local YCL organizations is directed and controlled by the appropriate republican, territorial, regional, area, city and district party organizations.

63. Members of the YCL, admitted to the CPSU, cease to belong to the YCL the moment they join the party, provided they do not hold leading posts in YCL organizations.

VIII. PARTY ORGANIZATIONS IN THE SOVIET ARMY

64. Party organizations in the Soviet Army take guidance in their work from the Program and the Statute of the CPSU and operate on the basis of instructions issued by the CC.

The party organizations of the Soviet Army carry out the policy of the party in the Armed Forces; rally servicemen around the Communist party; educate them in the spirit of Marxism-Leninism and boundless loyalty to the socialist homeland; actively further the unity of the army and the people; work for the strengthening of discipline; rally servicemen to carry out the tasks of military and political training and acquire skill in the use of new techniques and weapons, and irreproachably to perform their military duty and the orders and instructions of the command.

65. The guidance of party work in the Armed Forces is exercised by the CC of the CPSU through the Chief Political Administration of the Soviet Army and Navy, which functions as a department of the CC CPSU.

The chiefs of the political administrations of military areas and fleets, and chiefs of the political administrations of armies must be party members of five-years' standing, and the chiefs of political departments of military formations must be party members of three years' standing.

66. The party organizations and political bodies of the Soviet Army maintain close contact with local party committees, and keep them informed about

political work in the military units. The secretaries of military party organizations and chiefs of political bodies participate in the work of local party committees.

IX. PARTY GROUPS IN NON-PARTY ORGANIZATIONS

67. At congresses, conferences and meetings and in the elective bodies of Soviets, trade unions, cooperatives and other mass organizations of the working people, having at least three party members, party groups are formed for the purpose of strengthening the influence of the party in every way and carrying out party policy among non-party people, strengthening party and state discipline, combatting bureaucracy and verifying the fulfillment of party and government.

68. The party groups are subordinate to the appropriate party bodies: CC CPSU, the CC of the Communist parties of union republics, territorial, regional, area, city or district party committees.

In all matters the groups must strictly and unswervingly abide by decisions of the leading party bodies.

X. PARTY FUNDS

69. The funds of the party and its organizations are derived from membership dues, income from party enterprises and other revenue.

70. The monthly membership dues for party members and candidate members are as follows:

Monthly Earnings	Dues	
up to 50 rubles	10 kopeks	
from 51 to 100 rubles	0.5 per cent	
from 101 to 150 rubles	1.0 per cent	
from 151 to 200 rubles	1.5 per cent	of the
from 201 to 250 rubles	2.0 per cent	monthly
from 251 to 300 rubles	2.5 per cent	earnings
over 300 rubles	3.0 per cent	

71. An entrance fee of 2 per cent of monthly earnings is paid on acceptance into the party as a candidate member.

Appendix 39 SOVIET WARNING TO CZECHOSLOVAKIA, JULY 15, 1968 [1]

TO THE CENTRAL COMMITTEE
OF THE COMMUNIST PARTY
OF CZECHOSLOVAKIA

Dear comrades!

On behalf of the Central Committees of the Communist and Workers' Parties of Bulgaria, Hungary, the German Democratic Republic, Poland and the Soviet Union, we address ourselves to you with this letter, prompted by a feeling of sincere friendship based on the principles of Marxism-Leninism and proletarian internationalism and by the concern for our common affairs, for strengthening the positions of socialism and the security of the socialist community of nations.

The development of events in your country evokes in us deep anxiety. It is our firm conviction that the offensive of the reactionary forces, backed by imperialism, against your Party and the foundations of the social system in the Czechoslovak Socialist Republic, threatens to push your country off the road of socialism and that consequently it jeopardises the interests of the entire socialist system.

We expressed these apprehensions at the meeting in Dresden, during repeated bilateral meetings, as well as in letters which our Parties sent in the recent period to the Presidium of the Central Committee of the Communist Party of Czechoslovakia.

Recently we offered the Presidium of the Central Committee of the Communist Party of Czechoslovakia to hold a new joint meeting on July 14th this year so as to exchange information and opinions on the state of affairs in our countries, including the development of events in Czechoslovakia. Unfortunately, the CPC Central Committee Presidium did not take part in this meeting and did not use the opportunity for a collective comradely discussion of the situation that has developed. That is why we thought it necessary to state for you in this letter, with complete sincerity and frankness, our common opinion. We want you to understand us well and assess our intentions correctly.

We neither had nor have any intention of interfering in such affairs as are strictly the internal business of your Party and your state, nor of violating the principles of respect, independence and equality in the relations among the Communist Parties and socialist countries.

We are not coming before you as representatives of the past, who would like to interfere in the correction of mistakes and shortcomings, including the violations of socialist law which have taken place.

[1] *Moscow News*, Supplement to No. 30 (917), 1968, pp. 3–6.

We are not interfering in the methods of planning and management of the socialist national economy of Czechoslovakia, and in your actions aimed at improving the structure of the economy and developing socialist democracy.

We shall hail the settlement of relations between Czechs and Slovaks on healthy foundations of friendly cooperation within the framework of the Czechoslovak Socialist Republic.

At the same time we cannot agree to have hostile forces push your country from the road of socialism and create a threat of severing Czechoslovakia from the socialist community. This is no longer only your cause. It is the common cause of all the Communist and Workers' Parties and states united by alliance, cooperation and friendship. This is the common cause of our countries, which have joined in the Warsaw Treaty to ensure independence, peace and security in Europe, and to set up an insurmountable barrier against the intrigues of the imperialist forces, against aggression and revenge.

At the price of tremendous losses the peoples of our countries gained the victory over hitlerite fascism, won freedom and independence and an opportunity to follow the road of progress and socialism. The frontiers of the socialist world have moved to the centre of Europe, to the Elbe and Sumava mountains. And we shall never agree to have these historical gains of socialism, independence and security of all our peoples being put to threat. We shall never agree to have imperialism, using peaceful or non-peaceful methods, making a gap from the inside or from the outside in the socialist system, and changing in imperialism's favour the correlation of forces in Europe.

The might and firmness of our alliances depend on the inner strength of the socialist system in each of our brother countries, on the Marxist-Leninist policy of our Parties who discharge the leading role in the political and social life of their respective nations and states. Hamstringing of the leading role of the Communist Party leads to the liquidation of socialist democracy and the socialist system. That in itself constitutes a threat to the foundations of our alliance and the safety of the community of our countries.

You are aware of the understanding with which the fraternal Parties treated the decisions of the January Plenary Meeting of the Central Committee of the Communist Party of Czechoslovakia, as they believed that your Party, firmly controlling the levers of power, would direct the entire process in the interests of socialism, and not let anti-communist reaction exploit it to its own ends. We shared the conviction that you would protect the Leninist principle of democratic centralism as the apple of your eye. For the flouting of any aspect of this principle, democracy or centralism, inevitably serves to weaken the Party and its guiding role, by transforming the Party into either a bureaucratic organisation or a debating club. We discussed all these matters time and again at the meetings we had, and received from you assurances that you are aware of all the dangers and are fully resolved to repulse them.

Unfortunately events have taken another course.

Capitalising on the weakening of Party leadership of the country, and demagogically abusing the slogan of "democratisation," the forces of reaction unleashed a campaign against the Communist Party of Czechoslovakia and its honest and devoted cadres, clearly seeking to abolish the Party's leading role, subvert the socialist system, and place Czechoslovakia in opposition to the other socialist countries.

The political organisations and clubs that have emerged of late outside the framework of the National Front have become, in effect, headquarters of the forces of reaction. The Social Democrats are doggedly striving to establish their own party, are organising underground committees, and are seeking to split the working class movement in Czechoslovakia, and to take over the leadership of the country in order to effect a bourgeois restoration. Anti-socialist and revisionist forces have laid hand on the press, radio and television, making of them a rostrum for attacking the Communist Party, disorientating the working class and all working folk, for unbridled anti-socialist demagogy, and for undermining the friendly relations between the Czechoslovak Socialist Republic and the other socialist countries. Some mass communication media are carrying on a systematic campaign of real moral terror against people opposing the forces of reaction or voicing anxiety over the trend of developments.

Despite the decisions of the May Plenary Meeting of the Central Committee of the Communist Party of Czechoslovakia, which indicated the threat emanating from right-wing and anti-communist forces as the main danger, the increasing attacks that reaction has mounted have not met with any rebuff. This is precisely why reaction has been able to publicly address the entire country and to print its political platform under the title of "The 2,000 Words" which contain an outright call for struggle against the Communist Party and constitutional authority, for strikes and disorders. This call represents a serious danger to the Party, the National Front and the socialist state and is an attempt to introduce anarchy. In essence this statement is the organisational and political platform of counter-revolution. The claims made by its writers that they do not seek to overthrow the socialist system, operate without the Communists or rupture alliances with the socialist countries, should kid nobody. This is empty talk, the purpose of which is to legalise the platform of counter-revolution and hoodwink the vigilance of the Party, the working class and all the working folk.

Far from being repudiated, this platform, being so extensively circulated at a responsible moment, on the eve of the extraordinary Congress of the Communist Party of Czechoslovakia, has, on the contrary, also found obvious advocates in the Party rank-and-file and leadership, who support the anti-socialist calls.

Anti-socialist and revisionist forces smear all the activities of the Communist Party, wage a slander campaign against its cadres, and discredit Communists honest and loyal to the Party.

A situation has thus arisen which is absolutely unacceptable for a socialist country.

It is in this atmosphere that attacks are also being made on the CSSR socialist foreign policy, attacks are being undertaken on the alliance and friendship with socialist countries. Voices are heard demanding a revision of our common coordinated policy as regards the FRG, despite the fact that the West German Government invariably pursues a policy hostile to the interests of the security of our countries. The attempts at flirtation of the FRG authorities and revenge-seekers meet with a response among leading circles of your country.

The entire course of events in your country in recent months shows that the forces of counter-revolution, supported by imperialist centres, have developed a broad offensive on the socialist system without meeting due resistance on the part of the Party and the people's power. There is no doubt that the centres of international imperialist reaction are also involved in these events in Czechoslovakia, and are doing everything to inflame and aggravate the situation, and inspiring anti-socialist forces to act in this direction. The bourgeois press under the pretext of praising "democratisation" and "liberalisation" in the CSSR is waging an instigative campaign against the fraternal socialist countries. FRG ruling quarters are especially active, attempting to use the events in Czechoslovakia to sow discord between the socialist countries, to isolate the GDR and carry out their revenge-seeking designs.

Don't you, comrades, see these dangers? Is it possible under such conditions to remain passive, to limit oneself to mere declarations and assurances of loyalty to the cause of socialism and allied obligations? Don't you see that counter-revolution is wresting from you one position after another, that the Party is losing control over the course of events and is further retreating under the pressure of anti-communist forces?

Is it not for the purpose of sowing distrust and enmity towards the Soviet Union and other socialist countries that the press, radio and television of your country unleashed a campaign in connection with the staff exercises of the Armed Forces of the Warsaw Treaty Organisation? Matters went as far as this, that the joint staff exercises of our troops with the participation of several units of the Soviet Army, customary for military cooperation, are being used for groundless accusations of violating the sovereignty of the CSSR. And this is taking place in Czechoslovakia, whose people sacredly honour the memory of Soviet servicemen who gave their lives for the freedom and sovereignty of that country. At the same time near the western borders of your country exercises of military forces of the NATO aggressive bloc are being conducted with the participation of the army of revenge-seeking Western Germany. But not a single word is mentioned about this.

The inspirers of this unfriendly campaign apparently wish to confuse the minds of the Czechoslovak people, disorient them and undermine this truth that Czechoslovakia can retain her independence and sovereignty only as a socialist country, as a member of the socialist community. And only the enemies of socialism can today speculate on the slogan of "defending the sovereignty" of the CSSR from the socialist countries, from those countries with whom alliance and fraternal cooperation create a most reliable foundation of the independence and free development of each of our peoples.

It is our conviction that a situation has arisen, in which the threat to the foundations of socialism in Czechoslovakia jeopardises the common vital interests of other socialist countries. The peoples of our states would never forgive us for being indifferent and careless in the face of such a danger.

We are living in such a time when peace, security and the freedom of peoples more than ever demand the unity of the forces of socialism. The international tension is not relaxing. American imperialism has not rejected its policy of force and open intervention against the peoples fighting for freedom. It continues its criminal war in Vietnam, supports Israeli aggressors in the Near East, and hampers a peaceful settlement of the conflict. The arms race has not been slowed down. The Federal Republic of Germany, in which the neo-fascist forces are growing, is attacking the status quo, demanding the revision of the borders, does not want to give up its aspirations either for seizing the GDR or for getting access to nuclear weapons, and opposes the disarmament proposals. In Europe, where tremendous means of mass destruction have been accumulated, the peace and security of peoples are maintained first of all thanks to the power, unity and peace-loving policy of the socialist states. All of us are responsible for this power and unity of the socialist countries, and for the destiny of peace.

Our countries are linked with one another by treaties and agreements. These important mutual obligations of states and peoples are based on the general aspiration to defend socialism and ensure collective security of the socialist countries. Historic responsibility rests on our parties and peoples, that the revolutionary gains should not be lost.

Each of our Parties is responsible not only to its working class and its people, but also to the international working class, and the world communist movement, and cannot evade the obligations following from this. Therefore, we must be solid and united in defending the gains of socialism, our security and the international positions of the whole of the socialist community.

That is why we believe that a decisive rebuff to the anti-communist forces, and decisive efforts for the preservation of the socialist system in Czechoslovakia are not only your task but ours as well

The cause of defending the power of the working class and all working people, of the socialist gains in Czechoslovakia demands a decisive and bold offensive against the right-wing and anti-socialist forces, and the mobilisation of all means of defence created by the socialist state; the stopping of the activity of all political organisations coming out against socialism; the mastery by the Party of the means of mass information—press, radio, television—and the use of them in the interests of the working class, all working people and socialism; the closing of the ranks of the Party itself on the principled basis of Marxism-Leninism, undeviating observation of the principle of democratic centralism, and the struggle against those who help the inimical forces by their activity.

We are aware that forces exist in Czechoslovakia which are capable of defending the socialist system and inflicting defeat on the anti-socialist elements. The working class, the toiling peasantry, the front-rank intelligentsia —the overwhelming majority of the working people of the Republic are ready to do everything necessary for the sake of the further development of the socialist society. The task today is to provide these healthy forces with a clear-cut perspective, to stir them to action, to mobilise their energy for the struggle against the forces of counter-revolution in order to safeguard and consolidate socialism in Czechoslovakia.

In the face of the danger of counter-revolution and in response to the appeal of the Communist Party, the voice of the working class should ring out in full might. The working class, together with the toiling peasantry, exerted the greatest effort for the sake of the triumph of the socialist revolution. It is precisely they who cherish most of all the safeguarding of the gains of socialism.

We express the conviction that the Communist Party of Czechoslovakia, conscious of its responsibility, will take the necessary steps to block the path of reaction. In this struggle you can count on the solidarity and all-round assistance of the fraternal socialist countries.

Signed by:	Todor Zhivkov	Wladyslaw Gomulka
	Stanko Todorov	Marian Spychalski
	Boris Velchev	Jozef Cyrankiewicz
	Pencho Kubadinsky	Zenon Kliszko
	Janos Kadar	L. I. Brezhnev
	Jenö Fock	N. V. Podgorny
	Walter Ulbricht	A. N. Kosygin
	Willi Stoph	P. E. Shelest
	Herman Axen	K. F. Katushev

Warsaw, July 15, 1968

Appendix 40   PETITION ON CZECHOSLOVAKIA BY
P. G. GRIGORENKO AND I. YAKHIMOVICH,
FEBRUARY, 1969 [1]

To the Citizens of the Soviet Union:

The campaign of self-immolation started by Prague student Jan Palach on January 16, 1969, as a protest against interference in the internal affairs of the CzSSR is not abating. One more live torch, the latest so far, burned in St. Wenceslas Square in Prague on February 21.

This protest, which has taken so horrible a form, is addressed primarily to us, the Soviet people. It is the unsolicited and completely unjustified presence of our troops that brings forth such anger and despair among the Czechoslovak people. Not in vain has Jan Palach's death aroused the entire working people of Czechoslovakia.

We all bear some part of the guilt for his death and for the deaths of other Czechoslovak brothers who have committed suicide. By approving the armed forces' intervention, by justifying it, or by simply remaining silent, we contribute to the continued burning of live torches in the squares of Prague and other cities. The Czechs and the Slovaks have always considered us their brothers. How, then, can we permit the word "Soviet" to become for them synonymous with the word "enemy"?

Citizens of our great country!

The greatness of a country lies not in the might of its armed forces brought down upon a numerically small, freedom-loving nation, but in its moral strength.

Shall we then continue to look on in silence while our brothers perish?

It is now clear to all that the presence of our troops on the territory of the CzSSR is based neither on the defense of our fatherland nor on the interests of the countries of the socialist community.

Is it possible that we lack the courage to admit that a tragic mistake has been made and to do everything in our power to correct it?! It is our right and our duty!

We call on all the Soviet people to use every legal means, without taking hasty and ill-considered action, to bring about the withdrawal of Soviet troops from Czechoslovakia and the renunciation of interference in her internal affairs! Only thus can the friendship between our peoples be restored.

[1] U.S. Congress. 91st Congress, 1st Session. Committee on Government Operations. *Czechoslovakia and the Brezhnev Doctrine.* (Washington: Government Printing Office, 1969), pp. 58–59.

Long live the heroic Czechoslovak people!
Long live Soviet-Czechoslovak friendship!

Piotr Grigorenko
Ivan Yakhimovich

Moscow
February, 1969

Appendix 41 CHINESE PROTEST NOTES AGAINST SOVIET VIOLATIONS OF CHINESE TERRITORIES AND ABUSE OF CHINESE OFFICIALS [1]

A. NOTE OF THE MINISTRY OF FOREIGN AFFAIRS OF THE PEOPLE'S REPUBLIC OF CHINA TO THE SOVIET EMBASSY IN CHINA, MARCH 2, 1969

On the morning of March 2, 1969, Soviet frontier guards intruded into the area of Chenpao Island, Heilunkiang Province, China, and killed and wounded many Chinese frontier guards by opening fire on them, thus creating an extremely grave border armed conflict. Against this, the Ministry of Foreign Affairs of the People's Republic of China is instructed to lodge the strongest protest with the Soviet Government.

At 09:17 hours on March 2, large numbers of fully armed soldiers, together with four armoured vehicles and cars, sent out by the Soviet frontier authorities, flagrantly intruded into the area of Chenpao Island which is indisputable Chinese territory, carried out blatant provocations against the Chinese frontier guards on normal patrol duty and were first to open cannon and gun fire, killing and wounding many Chinese frontier guards. The Chinese frontier guards were compelled to fight back in self-defence when they reached the end of their forbearance after their repeated warnings to the Soviet frontier guards had produced no effect. This grave incident of bloodshed was entirely and solely created by the Soviet authorities. It is another grave new crime perpetrated by the Soviet authorities which have long been deliberately encroaching upon China's territory, carrying out armed provocations and creating ceaseless incidents of bloodshed.

The Chinese Government firmly demands that the Soviet Government punish the culprits of this incident and immediately stop its encroachment upon China's territory and its armed provocations, and reserves the right to demand compensation from the Soviet side for all the losses suffered by the Chinese side. The Chinese Government once again sternly warns the Soviet Government: China's sacred territory brooks no violation; if you should wilfully cling to your reckless course and continue to provoke armed conflicts along the Sino-Soviet border, you will certainly receive resolute counter-blows from the Chinese people; and it is the Soviet Government that must bear full responsibility for all the grave consequences arising therefrom.

[1] *Peking Review*, No. 10, March 7, 1969, pp. 5–7; No. 11, March 14, 1969, p. 5; and No. 33, August 15, 1969, p. 3.

B. TO: THE MINISTRY OF FOREIGN AFFAIRS OF THE U.S.S.R.

After creating the grave incident of armed provocation on Chinese territory of Chenpao Island, the Soviet authorities went still farther and organized a despicable anti-China demonstration before the Embassy of the People's Republic of China at 13:30 hours on March 7. The Soviet authorities collected a group of ruffians who grossly insulted and abused the great leader of the Chinese people Chairman Mao Tse-tung and the Chinese people, barbarously damaged the buildings of the Chinese Embassy, wrecked its newsphoto display cases and threw iron objects and fired air-guns at embassy personnel, thus seriously hampering the normal functioning of the Embassy and seriously menacing the personal safety of its personnel. The Embassy of the People's Republic of China hereby lodges a strong protest against the new anti-China provocation made by the Soviet authorities before the Chinese Embassy and demands that they immediately stop this anti-China farce solely stage-managed by them and compensate for all the losses of the Chinese Embassy caused by the ruffians' sabotaging activities.

It must be pointed out that the above grave new anti-China provocation engineered by the Soviet authorities is a continuation of the armed provocation against China on the Sino-Soviet border which they plotted single-handedly. The Soviet authorities must be held fully responsible for their anti-China crime which has further worsened Sino-Soviet relations.

> The Embassy of the People's Republic of China
> in the Soviet Union

Moscow
March 7, 1969

C. TO: EMBASSY OF THE U.S.S.R. IN CHINA

On the morning of August 13, 1969, the Soviet side sent two helicopters, dozens of tanks and armoured vehicles and several hundred armed troops to intrude into the Tiehliekti area in Yumin County of the Sinkiang Uighur Autonomous Region, China, who penetrated a depth of two kilometers, unwarrantedly fired at the Chinese frontier guards on normal patrol duty, killing and wounding many of them on the spot, and closed in on them. Driven beyond the limits of forbearance, the Chinese frontier guards were compelled to fight back in self-defence. At present, the Soviet side is continuing to amass large numbers of troops and tanks in an attempt to provoke still larger armed conflicts; the situation is developing.

The Chinese Government hereby lodges a strong protest with the Soviet Government against its deliberate intrusion into Chinese territory and provocation of a fresh incident of bloodshed, and demands that the Soviet Government immediately withdraw all its intruding troops from Chinese territory and immediately stop its firing. Otherwise, the Soviet Government must be held fully responsible for all the grave consequences arising therefrom.

Ministry of Foreign Affairs of the
People's Republic of China

Peking
August 13, 1969

A Note on Dates

Between January 1, 1700, and February 14, 1918, Russia officially followed the Julian Calendar. In the eighteenth century that calendar was eleven days behind the Gregorian Calendar used in the West; in the nineteenth century the lag was twelve days; and in the twentieth it was thirteen days. According to the Julian Calendar the serfs were emancipated on February 19, 1861 (March 3, 1861, by the Gregorian Calendar), the government of Imperial Russia collapsed on February 27, 1917 (March 12, 1917 by the Gregorian Calendar), and the Bolsheviks seized power on October 25, 1917 (November 7, 1917 by the Gregorian Calendar). To avoid chronological confusion, all dates are given here by the Gregorian Calendar.

A Note on Old Russian Measures and Weights

Officially, since September 14, 1918, the USSR has used the metric system. Occasionally, however, the following old units are employed:

Linear Measures

arshin = 71.12 cm. = 28 inches
sazhen = 3 *arshins* = 7 feet = 2.13 meters
verst = 500 *sazhens* = 0.66 mile = 1.0668 km.

Square Measures

desiatina = 2.7 acres = 2,400 square *sazhens*
hectare = 2.471 acres

Weights

funt = 0.41 kg. = 0.903 lb.
pud = 16.38 kg. = 36.113 lbs.
ton = 2,204.6 lbs.

BIBLIOGRAPHY

The wealth of documentary, monographic, and periodical literature on the USSR makes selection a difficult task. Items listed below are representative of the vast amount of existing literature. They have been selected not because I necessarily agree with their views, but because they might provide the reader with valuable keys to a fair and accurate understanding of problems treated in this volume. All items included below have been selected for English-speaking students. It also happens, however, that the best works on Soviet history are in English. Those students of Soviet affairs who are multilingual are advised to consult the annotated bibliography edited by Thomas T. Hammond, *Soviet Foreign Relations and World Communism: A Selected Annotated Bibliography* (Princeton: Princeton University Press, 1965).

ADAMS, ARTHUR E. *Bolsheviks in the Ukraine: The Second Campaign, 1918–1919.* New Haven: Yale University Press, 1963.
———, ed. *Readings in Soviet Foreign Policy: Theory and Practice.* Boston: Heath, 1961.
ALLEN, ROBERT L. *Soviet Economic Warfare.* Washington: Public Affairs Press, 1960.
ALLILUYEVA, SVETLANA. *Only One Year.* New York: Harper & Row, 1970.
———. *Twenty Letters to a Friend.* New York: Harper & Row, 1967.

ARMSTRONG, JOHN A. *The Politics of Totalitarianism.* New York: Random House, 1961.

——. *The Soviet Bureaucratic Elite.* New York: Praeger, 1959.

——. *Ukrainian Nationalism, 1939–1945.* New York: Columbia University Press, 1956.

ASPATURIAN, VERNON V. *The Union Republics in Soviet Diplomacy.* Geneva: Librairie E. Drozd, 1960.

AVRICH, PAUL. *Kronstadt 1921.* Princeton: Princeton University Press, 1970.

——. *The Russian Anarchists.* Princeton: Princeton University Press, 1967.

BABITSKY, PAUL, and JOHN RIMBERG. *The Soviet Film Industry.* New York: Praeger, 1955.

BACON, ELIZABETH E. *Central Asians Under Russian Rule: A Study in Culture Change.* Ithaca, N.Y.: Cornell University Press, 1966.

BARGHOORN, FREDERICK C. *Politics in the USSR.* Boston: Little, Brown, 1966.

——. *Soviet Russian Nationalism.* New York: Oxford University Press, 1956.

——. *The Soviet Cultural Offensive.* Princeton: Princeton University Press, 1960.

BASS, ROBERT H., and ELISABETH MARBURY, eds. *The Soviet-Yugoslav Controversy: A Documentary Record, 1948–1958.* New York: Prospect Books, 1958.

BATSELL, WALTER R. *Soviet Rule in Russia.* New York: Macmillan, 1929.

BAUER, RAYMOND A., ALEX INKELES, and CLYDE KLUCKHOHN. *How the Soviet System Works.* Cambridge, Mass.: Harvard University Press, 1956.

BAYKOV, ALEXANDER. *The Development of the Soviet Economic System.* Cambridge: Cambridge University Press, 1946.

BECK, F., and W. GODIN. *Russian Purge and the Extraction of Confession.* New York: Viking, 1951.

BELOFF, MAX. *The Foreign Policy of Soviet Russia, 1929–1941.* 2 vols. New York: Oxford University Press, 1947–1949.

——. *Soviet Foreign Policy in the Far East, 1944–1951.* New York: Oxford University Press, 1953.

BERMAN, HAROLD J. *Justice in the U.S.S.R.* New York: Knopf, 1963.

BIALER, SEWERYN, ed. *Stalin and His Generals: Soviet Military Memoirs of World War II.* New York: Pegasus, 1969.

BLACK, CYRIL E., and THOMAS P. THORNTON, eds. *Communism and Revolution.* Princeton: Princeton University Press, 1964.

BOORMAN, HOWARD L., *et al. Moscow-Peking Axis.* New York: Harper & Row, 1957.

BORKENAU, FRANZ. *The Communist International.* London: Faber, 1938.

BORYS, JURIJ. *The Russian Communist Party and the Sovietization of the Ukraine.* Stockholm: Norstedt and Söner, 1960.

BOURDEAX, MICHAEL. *Religious Ferment in Russia.* New York: St. Martin's Press, 1968.

BRANT, STEFAN. *The East German Rising.* New York: Praeger, 1957.

BRINKLEY, GEORGE A. *The Volunteer Army and Allied Intervention in South Russia, 1917–1921.* South Bend, Ind.: University of Notre Dame Press, 1966.

BRODERSEN, ARVID. *The Soviet Worker.* New York: Random House, 1966.

BROMKE, ADAM, ed. *The Communist States at the Crossroads Between Moscow and Peking.* New York: Praeger, 1965.

BROWDER, ROBERT P. *Origins of Soviet American Diplomacy.* Princeton: Princeton University Press, 1953.

——, and ALEXANDER F. KERENSKY, eds. *The Russian Provisional Government. Documents.* 3 vols. Stanford, Calif.: Stanford University Press, 1961.

BROWN, J. F. *The New Eastern Europe: The Khrushchev Era and After.* New York: Praeger, 1966.

BRUMBERG, ABRAHAM, ed. *Russia Under Khrushchev.* New York: Praeger, 1962.

BRZEZINSKI, ZBIGNIEW K., ed. *Dilemmas of Change in Soviet Politics.* New York: Columbia University Press, 1969.
————. *Africa and the Communist World.* Stanford: Stanford University Press, 1963.
————. *Ideology and Power in Soviet Politics.* New York: Praeger, 1967.
————. *The Soviet Bloc: Unity and Conflict.* Cambridge, Mass.: Harvard University Press, 1960.
BUDUROWYCZ, BOHDAN B. *Polish-Soviet Relations, 1932–1939.* New York: Columbia University Press, 1963.
BUNYAN, JAMES. *Intervention, Civil War, and War Communism in Russia, April–December, 1918. Documents and Materials.* Baltimore: The Johns Hopkins Press, 1936.
————. *The Origin of Forced Labor in the Soviet State, 1917–1921.* Baltimore: The Johns Hopkins Press, 1967.
————, and H. H. FISHER. *The Bolshevik Revolution, 1917–1918. Documents and Materials.* Stanford, Calif.: Stanford University Press, 1934.
CARR, EDWARD H. *The Bolshevik Revolution.* 3 vols. New York: Macmillan, 1951–1953.
————. *German Soviet Relations Between the Two World Wars, 1919–1939.* Baltimore: The Johns Hopkins Press, 1951.
————. *The Interregnum, 1923–1924.* New York: Macmillan, 1954.
————. *Socialism in One Country, 1924–1926.* New York: Macmillan, 1958.
CARSON, GEORGE BARR, JR. *Electoral Practices in the U.S.S.R.* New York: Praeger, 1955.
CATTELL, DAVID T. *Communism and the Spanish Civil War.* Berkeley: University of California Press, 1956.
CHAMBERLIN, WILLIAM H., ed. *Blueprint for World Conquest.* Washington, D.C.: Human Events, 1946.
————. *Russia's Iron Age.* London: Duckworth, 1935.
————. *The Russian Revolution, 1917–1921.* 2 vols. New York: Macmillan, 1935.
————. *Soviet Russia: A Living Record and a History.* Boston: Little, Brown, 1930.
CHERNOV, VICTOR M. *The Great Russian Revolution.* New Haven: Yale University Press, 1936.
CHORNOVIL, VYACHESLAV. *The Chornovil Papers.* New York: McGraw-Hill, 1968.
CHUIKOV, MARSHAL VASILI I. *The Fall of Berlin.* New York: Holt, Rinehart and Winston, 1967.
CIECHANOWSKI, JAN. *Defeat in Victory.* New York: Doubleday, 1947.
CLEMENS, DIANE SHAVER. *Yalta.* Cambridge, Mass.: M.I.T. Press, 1970.
CLEMENS, WALTER C., JR. *The Arms Race and Sino-Soviet Relations.* Stanford, Calif.: Hoover Institution, 1968.
CONQUEST, ROBERT, ed. *Agricultural Workers in the USSR.* New York: Praeger, 1969.
————. *The Great Terror: Stalin's Purge of the Thirties.* New York: Macmillan, 1968.
————. *Power and Policy in the USSR: The Study of Soviet Dynasties.* New York: Harper & Row, 1967.
————. *Russia After Khrushchev.* New York: Praeger, 1965.
————. *Soviet Deportation of Nationalities.* New York: St. Martin's Press, 1960.
CRANKSHAW, EDWARD. *Khrushchev: A Career.* New York: Viking, 1966.
————. *The New Cold War: Moscow v. Peking.* Baltimore: Penguin, 1963.
CURTISS, JOHN S. *The Russian Church and the Soviet State, 1917–1950.* Boston: Little, Brown, 1953.
————. *The Russian Revolutions of 1917.* New York: Van Nostrand, 1957.
DALLIN, ALEXANDER, ed. *Diversity in International Communism: A Documentary Record, 1961–1963.* New York: Columbia University Press, 1963.
————. *German Rule in Russia, 1941–1945.* London: Macmillan, 1957.

DALLIN, ALEXANDER, ed. *Soviet Union and the United Nations*. New York: Praeger, 1962.

———, and THOMAS B. LARSEN, eds. *Soviet Politics Since Khrushchev*. Englewood Cliffs, N.J.: Prentice-Hall, 1968.

DALLIN, DAVID J. *The Real Soviet Russia*. London: Hillis & Crater, 1947.

———. *Soviet Russia's Foreign Policy, 1939–1942*. New Haven: Yale University Press, 1942.

———. *Soviet Foreign Policy After Stalin*. Philadelphia: Lippincott, 1961.

———, and BORIS NIKOLAEVSKY. *Forced Labor in Soviet Russia*. New Haven: Yale University Press, 1947.

DANIELS, ROBERT V. *The Conscience of the Revolution: Communist Opposition in Soviet Russia*. Cambridge, Mass.: Harvard University Press, 1960.

———. *A Documentary History of Communism*. New York: Random House, 1960.

———. *The Nature of Communism*. New York: Random House, 1962.

———. *The Red October: The Bolshevik Revolution of 1917*. New York: Scribners, 1967.

DEANE, JOHN R. *The Strange Alliance*. New York: Viking, 1947.

DEGRAS, JANE, ed. *The Communist International, 1919–1943. Documents*. 3 vols. London: Oxford University Press, 1956–1958.

———, ed. *Soviet Documents on Foreign Policy, 1917–1932*. 2 vols. London: Oxford University Press, 1951–1952.

DENIKIN, ANTON I. *The White Army* London: Cape, 1930.

DENNIS, A. L. P. *The Foreign Policy of Soviet Russia*. New York: Dutton, 1924.

DEUTSCHER, ISAAC. *The Prophet Armed. Trotsky: 1879–1921*. New York: Oxford University Press, 1954.

———. *The Prophet Unarmed. Trotsky: 1921–1929*. New York: Oxford University Press, 1959.

———. *The Prophet Outcast. Trotsky: 1929–1940*. New York: Oxford University Press, 1963.

———. *The Unfinished Revolution: Russia, 1917–1967*. New York: Oxford University Press, 1967.

———. *Stalin: A Political Biography*. New York: Oxford University Press, 1949.

DINERSTEIN, HERBERT S. *Fifty Years of Soviet Foreign Policy*. Baltimore: The Johns Hopkins Press, 1968.

DIXON, BRIGADIER C. AUBREY, and OTTO HEILBRUNN. *Communist Guerilla Warfare*. New York: Praeger, 1955.

DJILAS, MILOVAN. *Conversations with Stalin*. New York: Harcourt, Brace and World, 1962.

———. *The New Class*. New York: Praeger, 1957.

———. *The Unperfect Society: Beyond the New Class*. New York: Harcourt, Brace and World, 1969.

DMYTRYSHYN, BASIL, ed. *Imperial Russia: A Source Book, 1700–1917*. New York: Holt, Rinehart and Winston, 1967.

———. *Moscow and the Ukraine, 1918–1953*. New York: Bookman Associates, 1956.

DOBB, MAURICE. *Soviet Economic Development Since 1917*. London: Routledge & Kegan, 1948.

DONNELLY, DRESMOND. *Struggle for the World: The Cold War, 1917–1965*. New York: St. Martin's Press, 1965.

DRACHKOVITCH, MILORAD, and BRANKO LAZITCH, eds. *The Commintern: Historical Highlights, Essays, Recollections, Documents*. New York: Praeger, 1966.

DYCK, HARVEY L. *Weimar Germany and Soviet Russia, 1926–1933*. New York: Columbia University Press, 1966.

DZIUBA, IVAN. *Internationalism or Russification?* London: Weinfeld & Nicolson, 1968.

EHRENBURG, ILYA. *The War, 1941–1945.* Cleveland: World, 1965.

———. *Post-War Years, 1945–1954.* Cleveland: World, 1967.

ERLICH, A. *The Soviet Industrialization Debate.* Cambridge, Mass.: Harvard University Press, 1960.

EUDIN, XENIA J. and ROBERT M. SLUSSER. *Soviet Foreign Policy, 1928–1934: Documents and Materials.* 2 vols. University Park, Pa.: Pennsylvania State University Press, 1966–1967.

———, and H. H. FISHER. *Soviet Russia and the West, 1920–1927. A Documentary Survey.* Stanford, Calif.: Stanford University Press, 1957.

———, and ROBERT C. NORTH. *Soviet Russia and the East, 1920–1927. A Documentary Survey.* Stanford, Calif.: Stanford University Press, 1957.

FAINSOD, MERLE. *How Russia Is Ruled.* 2nd ed. Cambridge, Mass.: Harvard University Press, 1962.

———. *International Socialism and the World War.* New York: Anchor Books, 1969.

———. *Smolensk Under Soviet Rule.* Cambridge, Mass.: Harvard University Press, 1958.

FARNSWORTH, BEATRICE. *William C. Bullitt and the Soviet Union.* Bloomington, Ind.: Indiana University Press, 1967.

FEIFER, GEORGE. *Justice in Moscow.* New York: Simon & Schuster, 1964.

FEIS, HERBERT. *Between War and Peace: The Potsdam Conference.* Princeton: Princeton University Press, 1960.

———. *Churchill-Roosevelt-Stalin.* Princeton: Princeton University Press, 1957.

FILENE, PETER G. *Americans and the Soviet Experiment, 1917–1933.* Cambridge, Mass.: Harvard University Press, 1967.

FISCHER, GEORGE. *Russian Liberalism.* Cambridge, Mass.: Harvard University Press, 1958.

———. *Soviet Opposition to Stalin.* Cambridge, Mass.: Harvard University Press, 1952.

FISCHER, JOHN. *Why They Behave Like Russians.* New York: Harper & Row, 1946.

FISCHER, LOUIS. *The Soviets in World Affairs.* 2nd. ed. 2 vols. Princeton: Princeton University Press, 1951.

FISCHER, RUTH. *Stalin and German Communism.* Cambridge, Mass.: Harvard University Press, 1948.

FISCHER-GALATI, STEPHEN. *The New Rumania: From People's Democracy to Socialist Republic.* Cambridge, Mass.: MIT Press, 1967.

FISHER, HAROLD H. *The Famine in Soviet Russia, 1919–1923.* New York: Macmillan, 1927.

FISHER, RALPH T. *Pattern for Soviet Youth . . . 1918–1954.* New York: Columbia University Press, 1959.

FLORINSKY, MICHAEL T. *The End of the Russian Empire.* New Haven: Yale University Press, 1931.

———. *Russia: A History and An Interpretation.* Vol. 2. New York: Macmillan, 1955.

FLOYD, DAVID. *Mao Against Khrushchev: A Short History of the Sino-Soviet Conflict.* New York: Praeger, 1964.

GANKIN, OLGA H., and H. H. FISHER. *The Bolsheviks and the World War: The Origin of the Third International.* Stanford, Calif.: Stanford University Press, 1940.

GARTHOFF, RAYMOND L. *Soviet Military Policy: A Historical Analysis.* New York: Praeger, 1966.

GEIGER, H. KENT. *The Family in Soviet Russia.* Cambridge, Mass.: Harvard University Press, 1968.

GOLDER, FRANK A., ed. *Documents of Russian History, 1914–1917.* New York: Century, 1927.

GOLOVIN, N. N. *The Russian Army in the World War.* New Haven: Yale University Press, 1931.

GORCHAKOV, NIKOLAI A. *The Theater in Soviet Russia.* New York: Columbia University Press, 1957.

GRAHAM, LOREN R. *The Soviet Academy of Sciences and the Communist Party, 1917–1932.* Princeton: Princeton University Press, 1967.

GRIFFITH, WILLIAM E., ed. *Communism in Europe: Continuity, Change and the Sino-Soviet Dispute.* Cambridge, Mass.: MIT Press, 1966.

GRIPP, RICHARD C. *Patterns of Soviet Politics.* Homewood, Ill.: Dorsey Press, 1967.

GRONSKY, P. P., and N. J. ASTROV. *The War and the Russian Government.* New Haven: Yale University Press, 1929.

GSOVSKY, VLADIMIR. *Soviet Civil Law.* 2 vols. Ann Arbor, Mich.: University of Michigan Press, 1948.

GUINS, GEORGE C. *The Soviet Law and Soviet Society.* The Hague: Nijhoff, 1954.

HAIMSON, LEOPOLD H. *The Russian Marxists and the Origins of Bolshevism.* Cambridge, Mass.: Harvard University Press, 1955.

HARCAVE, SIDNEY. *The Russian Revolution of 1905.* New York: Collier, 1970.

HART, B. H. LIDDELL, ed. *The Red Army.* New York: Harcourt, Brace and World, 1956.

HAYWARD, MAX, ed. *On Trial: The Soviet State Versus "Abram Tertz" and "Nikolai Arzhak."* New York: Harper & Row, 1966.

HAZARD, JOHN N. *The Soviet System of Government.* Chicago: University of Chicago Press, 1957.

———, and ISAAC SHAPIRO. *The Soviet Legal System: Post Stalin Documentation and Historical Commentary.* 3 parts. Dobbs Ferry, N.Y.: Oceana, 1962.

HOLT, ROBERT T., and JOHN E. TURNER, eds. *Soviet Union: Paradox of Change.* New York: Holt, Rinehart and Winston, 1962.

HUDSON, G. F., *et al. The Sino-Soviet Dispute.* New York: Praeger, 1962.

HULICKA, KAREL, and IRENE M. HULICKA. *Soviet Institutions, the Individual and Society.* Boston: Christopher Publishing House, 1967.

HUNT, R. N. CAREW. *The Theory and Practice of Communism.* New York: Macmillan, 1957.

HYLAND, WILLIAM, and RICHARD W. SHRYLOCK. *The Fall of Khrushchev.* New York: Funk & Wagnalls, 1969.

INKELES, ALEX. *Social Change in Soviet Russia.* Cambridge, Mass.: Harvard University Press, 1968.

———, and KENT GEIGER, eds. *Soviet Society.* Boston: Houghton-Mifflin, 1961.

JASNY, NAUM. *Essays on the Soviet Economy.* New York: Praeger, 1962.

———. *Khrushchev's Crop Policy.* Glasgow: Outram & Co., 1965.

JELAVICH, BARBARA. *A Century of Russian Foreign Policy, 1814–1914.* Philadelphia: Lippincott, 1964.

JOHNSON, PRISCILLA, and LEOPOLD LABEDZ, eds. *Khrushchev and the Arts: The Politics of Soviet Culture, 1962–1964.* Cambridge, Mass.: MIT Press, 1965.

JORRE, GEORGES. *The Soviet Union: The Land and Its People.* London: Longmans, 1961.

KARCZ, JERZY F., ed. *Soviet and East European Agriculture.* Berkeley: University of California Press, 1967.

KARPOVICH, MICHAEL T. *Imperial Russia, 1801–1917.* New York: Holt, 1932.

KASER, MICHAEL. *Comecon: Integration Problems of the Planned Economy.* London: Oxford University Press, 1965.

KASSOF, ALLEN, ed. *Prospects for Soviet Society.* New York: Praeger, 1968.

KATKOFF, VLADIMIR. *Soviet Economy, 1940–1965.* Baltimore: Dangary, 1967.

KATKOV, GEORGE. *Russia 1917: The February Revolution.* New York: Harper & Row, 1967.

KAZEMZADEH, FIRUZ. *The Struggle for Transcaucasia, 1917–1921.* New York: Philosophical Library, 1951.

KENNAN, GEORGE F. *Decision to Intervene.* Princeton: Princeton University Press, 1958.

———. *Russia Leaves the War.* Princeton: Princeton University Press, 1956.

———. *Russia and the West Under Lenin and Stalin.* Boston: Little, Brown, 1961.

———. *Soviet Foreign Policy, 1917–1941.* New York: Van Nostrand, 1960.

KENNEDY, ROBERT F. *Thirteen Days: A Memoir of the Cuban Missile Crisis.* New York: Norton, 1969.

KERENSKY, ALEXANDER F. *The Catastrophe.* New York: Appleton-Century-Crofts, 1929.

———. *Russia and History's Turning Point.* New York: Duell, 1965.

KERTESZ, STEPHAN. *The Fate of East Central Europe.* South Bend Ind.: University of Notre Dame Press, 1956.

KHRUSHCHEV, NIKITA S. *For Victory in Peaceful Competition with Capitalism.* New York: Dutton, 1960.

———. *Khrushchev Remembers.* Boston: Little, Brown, 1970.

KOHLER, FOY D. *Understanding the Russians.* New York: Harper & Row, 1970.

KOHN, S., and BARON A. F. MEYENDORFF. *The Cost of the War to Russia.* New Haven: Yale University Press, 1932.

KOLKOWICZ, ROMAN. *The Soviet Military and the Communist Party.* Princeton: Princeton University Press, 1967.

KORNILOV, ALEXANDER. *Modern Russian History.* New York: Knopf, 1952.

KOROL, ALEXANDER. *Soviet Research and Development: Its Organization, Personnel and Funds.* Cambridge, Mass.: MIT Press, 1965.

KULSKI, W. W. *Peaceful Co-existence.* Chicago: Regnery, 1959.

———. *The Soviet Regime: Communism in Practice.* Syracuse, N.Y.: Syracuse University Press, 1956.

LABEDZ, LEOPOLD, ed. *International Communism After Khrushchev.* Cambridge, Mass.: MIT Press, 1965.

———, ed. *Revisionism.* New York: Praeger, 1962.

LANE, ARTHUR BLISS. *I Saw Poland Betrayed.* Indianapolis, Ind.: Bobbs-Merrill, 1948.

LARSON, THOMAS B. *Disarmament and Soviet Policy, 1964–1968.* Englewood Cliffs, N.J.: Prentice-Hall, 1969.

LAQUEUR, WALTER Z. *The Soviet Union and the Middle East.* New York: Praeger, 1959.

———, and LEOPOLD LABEDZ, eds. *Polycentrism.* New York: Praeger, 1962.

LASKY, MELVIN J., ed. *The Hungarian Revolution.* New York: Praeger, 1957.

LEDERER, IVO J., ed. *Russian Foreign Policy.* New Haven: Yale University Press, 1962.

LENIN, V. I. *Collected Works.* 4th ed. 40 vols. Moscow: Progress Publishers, 1964.

LEONARD, WOLFGANG. *The Kremlin Since Stalin.* New York: Praeger, 1962.

LEVIN, ALFRED. *The Second Duma.* New Haven: Yale University Press, 1940.

LEVINE, IRVING R. *Main Street U.S.S.R.* New York: Doubleday, 1959.

LEYDA, J. *Kino: A History of the Russian and Soviet Film.* New York: Macmillan, 1960.

LIBRACH, JAN. *The Rise of the Soviet Empire.* New York: Praeger, 1964.

LINDEN, CARL A. *Khrushchev and the Soviet Leadership, 1957–1964.* Baltimore: The Johns Hopkins Press, 1966.

LOCKHART, R. H. BRUCE. *British Agent.* New York: Putnam, 1933.

LOEWENTHAL, RICHARD. *World Communism: The Disintegration of a Secular Faith.* New York: Oxford University Press, 1966.

LUCKYJ, GEORGE. *Literary Politics in the Soviet Ukraine, 1917–1934.* New York: Columbia University Press, 1956.

LYDOLPH, PAUL E. *Geography of the USSR.* New York: Wiley, 1964.

MACKINTOSH, J. M. *Strategy and Tactics of Soviet Foreign Policy.* London: Oxford University Press, 1962.

MAC VICKER, CHARLES P. *Titoism: Pattern for International Communism*. New York: St. Martin's Press, 1957.

MADISON, BERNICE Q. *Social Welfare in the Soviet Union*. Stanford, Calif.: Stanford University Press, 1968.

MAGER, N. H., and JACQUES KATEL, eds. *Conquest Without War*. New York: Simon & Schuster, 1961.

MAGUIRE, ROBERT A. *Red Virgin Soil: Soviet Literature in the Twenties*. Princeton: Princeton University Press, 1968.

MANNING, CLARENCE A. *Twentieth Century Ukraine*. New York: Bookman Associates, 1951.

———. *Ukraine Under the Soviets*. New York: Bookman Associates, 1953.

MARCHENKO, ANATOLI. *My Testimony*. New York: Dutton, 1969.

MASSIE, ROBERT K. *Nicholas and Alexandra*. New York: Dell, 1967.

MC CLOSKY, HERBERT, and JOHN E. TURNER. *The Soviet Dictatorship*. New York: McGraw-Hill, 1960.

MC LANE, CHARLES B. *Soviet Strategies in Southeast Asia*. Princeton: Princeton University Press, 1966.

MC NEAL, ROBERT H., ed. *Lenin, Stalin, Khrushchev: Voices of Bolshevism*. Englewood Cliffs, N.J.: Prentice-Hall, 1963.

MEDVEDEV, ZHORES A. *The Rise and Fall of T. D. Lysenko*. New York: Columbia University Press, 1969.

MEISEL, JAMES H., and EDWARD S. KOZERA, eds. *Materials for the Study of the Soviet System*. Ann Arbor, Mich.: George Wahr, 1953.

MEYER, ALFRED G. *Communism*. 3rd ed. New York: Random House, 1967.

———. *Leninism*. Cambridge, Mass.: Harvard University Press, 1957.

———. *The Soviet Political System*. New York: Random House, 1965.

MIKOLAJCZYK, STANISLAW. *The Rape of Poland*. New York: Whittlesey House, 1948.

MILIUKOV, PAUL N. *Russia To-Day and To-Morrow*. New York: Macmillan, 1922.

———. *Russia and Its Crisis*. Chicago: University of Chicago Press, 1906.

MILLER, M. S. *The Economic Development of Russia, 1905–1914*. London: King, 1926.

MOORE, BARRINGTON, JR. *Soviet Politics: The Dilemma of Power*. Cambridge, Mass.: Harvard University Press, 1951.

———. *Terror and Progress in the USSR*. New York: Harper & Row, 1966.

MOOREHEAD, ALAN. *The Russian Revolution*. New York: Harper & Row, 1958.

MORISON, DAVID. *The USSR and Africa*. London: Oxford University Press, 1964.

NAGY, FERENC. *The Struggle Behind the Iron Curtain*. New York: Macmillan, 1948.

NEAL, F. W. *Titoism in Action*. Berkeley: University of California Press, 1958.

NETTL, J. P. *The Eastern Zone and Soviet Policy in Germany*. New York: Oxford University Press, 1951.

———. *The Soviet Achievement*. New York: Harcourt, Brace and World, 1967.

NORTH, ROBERT C. *Moscow and Chinese Communists*. Stanford, Calif.: Stanford University Press, 1953.

NOVE, ALEX. *The Soviet Economy*. Rev. ed. New York: Praeger, 1966.

ORLOV, ALEXANDER. *The Secret History of Stalin's Crimes*. New York: Random House, 1953.

OSBORN, ROBERT J. *Soviet Social Policies: Welfare, Equality and Community*. Homewood, Ill.: Dorsey Press, 1970.

PARES, SIR BERNARD. *The Fall of the Russian Monarchy*. New York: Knopf, 1939.

———. *Russia and Reform*. London: Constable, 1907.

PARK, ALEXANDER. *Bolshevism in Turkestan, 1917–1927*. New York: Columbia University Press, 1957.

PARRY, ALBERT. *The New Class Divided: Russian Science and Technology Versus Communism.* New York: Macmillan, 1965.

PASTERNAK, BORIS. *Doctor Zhivago.* New York: Pantheon, 1958.

PAVLOV, DMITRI V. *Leningrad 1941: The Blockade.* Chicago: University of Chicago Press, 1965.

PAVLOVSKY, GEORGE. *Agricultural Russia on the Eve of the Revolution.* London: Routledge, 1930.

PAYNE, ROBERT. *The Life and Death of Lenin.* New York: Simon & Schuster, 1964.

———. *The Rise and Fall of Stalin.* New York: Simon & Schuster, 1965.

PENKOVSKY, OLEG. *The Penkovsky Papers.* New York: Doubleday, 1965.

PETHYBRIDGE, ROGER. *A Key to Soviet Politics.* New York: Praeger, 1962.

PETROV, VLADIMIR. *"June 22, 1941": Soviet Historians and the German Invasion.* New York: Columbia University Press, 1968.

PIDHAINY, OLEH S. *The Formation of the Ukrainian Republic.* Toronto: New Review Books, 1966.

PIPES, RICHARD. *The Formation of the Soviet Union: Communism and Nationalism, 1917–1923.* Cambridge, Mass.: Harvard University Press, 1954.

———, ed. *Revolutionary Russia: A Symposium.* Cambridge, Mass.: Harvard University Press, 1968.

PISTRAK, LAZAR. *The Great Tactician: Khrushchev's Rise to Power.* New York: Praeger, 1961.

PLOSS, SIDNEY. *Conflict and Decision-Making in Soviet Russia.* Princeton: Princeton University Press, 1965.

PUSHKAREV, SERGEI. *The Emergence of Modern Russia, 1801–1917.* New York: Holt, Rinehart and Winston, 1963.

RADKEY, OLIVER H. *Agrarian Foes of Bolshevism.* New York: Columbia University Press, 1958.

———. *The Elections to the Russian Constituent Assembly of 1917.* Cambridge, Mass.: Harvard University Press, 1950.

RAUCH, GEORG VON. *A History of Soviet Russia.* 3rd ed. New York: Praeger, 1962.

REED, JOHN. *Ten Days That Shook the World.* New York: International Publishers, 1919.

RESHETAR, JOHN S., JR. *A Concise History of the Communist Party of the Soviet Union.* Rev. ed. New York: Praeger, 1964.

———. *The Ukrainian Revolution, 1917–1920.* Princeton: Princeton University Press, 1952.

RIGBY, T. H. *Communist Party Membership in the USSR, 1917–1967.* Princeton: Princeton University Press, 1968.

RIHA, THOMAS. *A Russian European: Paul Miliukov in Russian Politics.* South Bend, Ind.: University of Notre Dame Press, 1969.

RIPKA, HERBERT. *Czechoslovakia Enslaved.* London: Golancz, 1950.

ROBERTS, HENRY L. *Eastern Europe: Politics, Revolution and Diplomacy.* New York: Knopf, 1970.

ROBINSON, GEROLD T. *Rural Russia Under the Old Regime.* New York: Longmans, 1949.

ROSSI, ANGELO. *The Russo-German Alliance.* Boston: Beacon, 1951.

ROZEK, EDWARD J. *Allied Wartime Diplomacy: A Pattern in Poland.* New York: Wiley, 1951.

RUBENSTEIN, ALVIN Z., ed. *The Foreign Policy of the Soviet Union.* New York: Random House, 1960.

———. *The Soviets in International Organizations.* Princeton: Princeton University Press, 1964.

RUSH, MYRON. *The Rise of Khrushchev*. Washington: Public Affairs Press, 1957.
————. *Political Succession in the USSR*. New York: Columbia University Press, 1965.
Russian Oppression in the Ukraine: Reports and Documents. London: Ukrainian Publishers, 1962.
SAKHAROV, ANDREI D. *Progress, Coexistence and Intellectual Freedom*. New York: Norton, 1968.
SALISBURY, HARRISON E. *The 900 Days: The Siege of Leningrad*. New York: Harper & Row, 1969.
————. *War Between Russia and China*. New York: Norton, 1969.
SCHAPIRO, LEONARD. *The Communist Party of the Soviet Union*. New York: Random House, 1960.
————. *The Origin of the Communist Autocracy: Political Opposition in the Soviet State, 1917–1922*. Cambridge, Mass.: Harvard University Press, 1955.
————. *The USSR and the Future: An Analysis of the New Program of the CPSU*. New York: Praeger, 1963.
SCHUMAN, FREDERICK L. *Soviet Politics at Home and Abroad*. New York: Knopf, 1946.
————. *Soviet Russia Since 1917*. New York: Knopf, 1957.
————. *Government in the Soviet Union*. New York: Crowell, 1961.
SCHWARTZ, HARRY. *The Red Phoenix: Russia Since World War II*. New York: Praeger, 1961.
————. *Russia's Soviet Economy*. 2nd ed. Englewood Cliffs, N.J.: Prentice-Hall, 1954.
SCOTT, DEREK J. R. *Russian Political Institutions*. 2nd ed. New York: Praeger, 1961.
SETON-WATSON, HUGH. *The Decline of Imperial Russia, 1855–1914*. New York: Praeger, 1960.
————. *The East European Revolution*. 3rd ed. New York: Praeger, 1961.
————. *From Lenin to Khrushchev*. New York: Praeger, 1960.
————. *The Russian Empire, 1801–1917*. Oxford: Clarendon Press, 1967.
SHABAD, THEODORE. *Geography of the USSR*. New York: Columbia University Press, 1951.
SHAPIRO, LEONARD, ed. *Soviet Treaty Series*. Washington, D.C.: Georgetown University Press, 1950.
SHUB, ANATOLE. *The New Russian Tragedy*. New York: Norton, 1969.
SHUB, DAVID. *Lenin*. New York: Doubleday, 1949.
SHULMAN, MARSHALL D. *Stalin's Foreign Policy Reappraised*. Cambridge, Mass.: Harvard University Press, 1963.
SIMIRENKO, ALEX, ed. *Social Thought in the Soviet Union*. Chicago: Quadrangle Books, 1969.
SIMMONS, ERNST J., ed. *Through the Glass of Soviet Literature*. New York: Columbia University Press, 1953.
SLONIM, MARC. *Modern Russian Literature*. New York: Oxford University Press, 1953.
————. *Russian Theater From the Empire to the Soviets*. New York: World, 1961.
SLUSSER, ROBERT, ed. *Soviet Economic Policies in Postwar Germany*. New York: Praeger, 1953.
SMITH, EDWARD E. *The Young Stalin*. New York: Farrar, Straus & Giroux, 1967.
SNELL, JOHN L., ed. *The Meaning of Yalta*. Baton Rouge, La.: Louisiana State University Press, 1956.
————. *Wartime Origin of the East-West Dilemma Over Germany*. New Orleans: Hauser Press, 1959.

SOKOLOVSKY, MARSHAL V. D. *Soviet Military Strategy*. Englewood Cliffs, N.J.: Prentice-Hall, 1963.

SOLZHENITSYN, ALEXANDER I. *The First Circle*. New York: Harper & Row, 1968.

————. *One Day in the Life of Ivan Denisovich*. New York: Praeger, 1963.

SONTAG, RAYMOND J., and JAMES S. BEDDIE, eds. *Nazi-Soviet Relations, 1939–1941*. Washington, D.C.: Government Printing Office, 1948.

SPINKA, MATTHEW. *The Church in Soviet Russia*. New York: Oxford University Press, 1956.

STAAR, RICHARD F. *Poland, 1944–1962: The Sovietization of a Captive People*. Baton Rouge, La.: Louisiana State University Press, 1962.

STALIN, JOSEPH V. *Collected Works*. 13 vols. Moscow: Foreign Languages Publishing House, 1952–1955.

STEINBERG, JULIEN, ed. *Verdict of Three Decades*. New York: Duell, 1950.

STETTINIUS, EDWARD R., JR., *Roosevelt and the Russians: The Yalta Conference*. New York: Doubleday, 1949.

STROYEN, WILLIAM B. *Communist Russia and the Russian Orthodox Church, 1943–1962*. Washington, D.C.: Catholic University Press, 1967.

STRUVE, GLEB. *Soviet Russian Literature, 1917–1950*. Norman, Okla.: University of Oklahoma Press, 1951.

SUKHANOV, N. N. *The Russian Revolution, 1917: A Personal Record*. New York: Oxford University Press, 1955.

SULLIVANT, ROBERT S. *Soviet Politics in the Ukraine, 1917–1957*. New York: Columbia University Press, 1962.

SYROP, KONRAD. *Spring in October: The Polish Revolution of 1956*. New York: Praeger, 1958.

TANNER, VAINO. *The Winter War: Finland Against Russia, 1939–1940*. Stanford, Calif.: Stanford University Press, 1950.

TARACOUZIO, T. A. *War and Peace in Soviet Diplomacy*. New York: Macmillan, 1940.

TATU, MICHEL. *Power in the Kremlin: From Khrushchev to Kosygin*. New York: Viking, 1969.

TERTZ, ABRAM [pseud.]. *The Makepeace Experiment*. New York: Vintage, 1966.

THOMPSON, JOHN M. *Russia, Bolshevism, and the Versailles Peace*. Princeton: Princeton University Press, 1967.

TIMASHEFF, NICHOLAS S. *The Great Retreat*. New York: Dutton, 1946.

————. *Religion in Soviet Russia, 1917–1942*. New York: Sheed & Ward, 1942.

TOMA, PETER A., ed. *The Changing Face of Communism in Eastern Europe*. Tucson, Ariz.: University of Arizona Press, 1970.

TOMPKINS, STUART R. *The Russian Intelligentsia*. Norman, Okla.: University of Oklahoma Press, 1957.

TOSCANO, MARIO. *Designs in Diplomacy*. Baltimore: The Johns Hopkins Press, 1970.

TOWSTER, JULIAN. *Political Power in the USSR, 1917–1947*. New York: Oxford University Press, 1948.

TREADGOLD, DONALD W. *Lenin and His Rivals*. New York: Praeger, 1955.

————. *Twentieth Century Russia*. 2nd ed. Chicago: Rand McNally, 1964.

————, ed. *The Development of the USSR*. Seattle, Wash.: University of Washington Press, 1964.

————, ed. *Soviet and Chinese Communisms: Similarities and Differences*. Seattle, Wash.: University of Washington Press, 1967.

TRISKA, JAN F., and DAVID D. FINLEY. *Soviet Foreign Policy*. New York: Macmillan, 1968.

TROTSKY, LEON. *The History of the Russian Revolution*. 3 vols. New York: Simon & Schuster, 1932.

TROTSKY, LEON. *Stalin.* New York: Harper & Row, 1941.

⸻. *Terrorism and Communism.* Ann Arbor, Mich.: University of Michigan Press, 1961.

TUCKER, ROBERT C. *The Soviet Political Mind: Studies in Stalinism and Post-Stalin Change.* New York: Praeger, 1963.

⸻, and STEPHEN F. COHEN, eds. *The Great Purge Trial.* New York: Grosset & Dunlap, 1965.

TYRKOVA-WILLIAMS, ARIADNA. *From Liberty to Brest-Litovsk.* London: Macmillan, 1919.

ULAM, ADAM B. *The Bolsheviks.* New York: Collier Books, 1965.

⸻. *Expansion and Coexistence: The History of Soviet Foreign Policy, 1917–1967.* New York: Praeger, 1968.

⸻. *The New Face of Soviet Totalitarianism.* Cambridge, Mass.: Harvard University Press, 1963.

⸻. *Titoism and the Cominform.* Cambridge, Mass.: Harvard University Press, 1952.

ULLMAN, RICHARD H. *Britain and the Russian Civil War.* Princeton: Princeton University Press, 1968.

⸻. *Anglo-Soviet Relations, 1917–1921.* Princeton: Princeton University Press, 1961.

UNTERBERGER, BETTY M. *America's Siberian Expedition, 1918–1920.* Durham, N.C.: Duke University Press, 1956.

VARDYS, STANLEY V., ed. *Lithuania Under the Soviets: Portrait of a Nation, 1940–1965.* New York: Praeger, 1965.

VARNECK, ELENA, and H. H. FISHER. *The Testimony of Kolchak and Other Siberian Materials.* Stanford, Calif.: Stanford University Press, 1935.

VENTURI, FRANCO. *Roots of Revolution.* New York: Knopf, 1960.

VUCINICH, ALEXANDER S. *Science in Russian Culture, 1861–1917.* Stanford, Calif.: Stanford University Press, 1970.

⸻. *The Soviet Academy of Sciences.* Stanford, Calif.: Stanford University Press, 1956.

VUCINICH, WAYNE S., ed. *The Peasant in Nineteenth-Century Russia.* Stanford, Calif.: Stanford University Press, 1968.

VYSHINSKY, A. Y. *The Law of the Soviet State.* New York: Macmillan, 1948.

WADE, REX A. *Russian Search for Peace, February–October, 1917.* Stanford, Calif.: Stanford University Press, 1969.

WARTH, ROBERT D. *The Allies and the Russian Revolution.* Durham, N.C.: Duke University Press, 1954.

⸻. *Soviet Russia in World Politics.* New York: Bookman Associates, 1963.

WEEKS, ALBERT L. *The First Bolshevik: A Political Biography of Peter Tkachev.* New York: New York University Press, 1968.

WEI, HENRY. *China and Soviet Russia.* Princeton: Princeton University Press, 1956.

WEISSBERG, ALEXANDER. *The Accused.* New York: Simon & Schuster, 1951.

WESSON, ROBERT G. *Soviet Foreign Policy in Perspective.* Homewood, Ill.: Dorsey Press, 1969.

WHEELER-BENNETT, JOHN W. *The Forgotten Peace: Brest-Litovsk, March, 1918.* New York: Macmillan, 1939.

WHITE, JOHN A. *The Diplomacy of the Russo-Japanese War.* Princeton: Princeton University Press, 1964.

⸻. *The Siberian Intervention.* Princeton: Princeton University Press, 1950.

WHITING, KENNETH R. *The Soviet Union Today.* New York: Praeger, 1962.

WOLFE, BERTRAM D. *Khrushchev and Stalin's Ghost.* New York: Praeger, 1957.

————. *Marxism: One Hundred Years in the Life of a Doctrine.* New York: Dial, 1965.

————. *Three Who Made a Revolution.* New York: Dial, 1948.

WOLFF, ROBERT L. *The Balkans in Our Time.* Cambridge, Mass.: Harvard University Press, 1956.

WOLIN, SIMON, and ROBERT M. SLUSSER, eds. *The Soviet Secret Police.* New York: Praeger, 1956.

WRANGEL, PIOTR N. *The Memoirs of General Wrangel.* London: Williams and Norgate, 1920.

YARMOLINSKY, AVRAHM. *Literature Under Communism.* Bloomington, Ind.: Indiana University Press, 1957.

————. *Road to Revolution.* New York: Collier, 1962.

ZAGORIA, DONALD S. *The Sino-Soviet Conflict, 1956–1961.* Princeton: Princeton University Press, 1962.

————. *Vietnam Triangle: Moscow, Peking, Hanoi.* New York: Pegasus, 1967.

ZAVALANI, T. *How Strong is Russia?* London: Hollis & Carter, 1951.

ZAVALISHIN, VYACHESLAV. *Early Soviet Writers.* New York: Praeger, 1958.

ZAWODNY, J. K. *Death in the Forest: The Story of the Katyn Forest Massacres.* South Bend, Ind.: University of Notre Dame Press, 1962.

ZINNER, PAUL E., ed. *National Communism and Popular Revolt in Eastern Europe.* New York: Columbia University Press, 1956.